Labor Relations

Labor Relations

David A. Dilts
Kansas State University

Clarence R. Deitsch
Ball State University

MACMILLAN PUBLISHING COMPANY
New York
COLLIER MACMILLAN PUBLISHERS
London

Copyright © 1983, Macmillan Publishing Co., Inc.

Printed in the United States of America.

Macmillan Publishing Co., Inc.
866 Third Avenue, New York, New York 10022

Collier Macmillan Canada, Inc.

Library of Congress Cataloging in Publication Data

Dilts, David A.
    Labor relations.

    Includes bibliographical references and index.
    1. Industrial relations—United States.
2. Trade-unions—United States. 3. Collective
bargaining—United States. I. Deitsch, Clarence R.
II. Title.
HD8072.5.D54   658.3'15   82-15304
ISBN 0-02-329650-X   AACR2

Printing: 1 2 3 4 5 6 7 8   Year: 3 4 5 6 7 8 9 0

ISBN   0-02-329650-X

Preface

The American system of collective bargaining is at a crossroads. The system, once held to be the modern system of labor-management decision-making and industrial jurisprudence, has increasingly come under attack. Along with large unions, it has been bitterly assailed as a major factor responsible for the current economic crisis. The blame for everything from declining productivity to rising prices has been squarely laid at the doorstep of organized labor and the system of collective bargaining. Witness the often-made unfavorable comparison of the American system of collective bargaining with the Japanese system of labor-management decision making.[1]

The obvious question is: "What went wrong?". The not-so-obvious answer can be found in the conflict orientation of the American system of collective bargaining. The system was fashioned and molded by a political, social and economic environment marked by conflict. A noted radical, H. Rap Brown, once remarked that: "Violence is as American as cherry pie."[2] As disturbing as this statement may be, it is essentially correct. Conflict characterizes everything from the political system of checks and balances to modern professional sports. Labor-management relations have not escaped the pervasive influence of violence. Indeed, Galbraith attributes the growth of unions to the emergence of a strong capitalist class which created the need for a countervailing force.[3] It should come as no shock then that the American collective bargaining system stresses conflict. What is disconcerting to labor-relations experts and practitioners alike, however, is the fact that the conflict orientation of the American system of collective bargaining is not conducive to the solution of the serious problems confronting labor and management today; increased productivity, product quality, and employment demand cooperation, not confrontation.

The foregoing considerations prompted the authors to write an introductory labor-relations text emphasizing the need for a cooperative labor-management approach to the solution of problems of mutual interest—an approach based upon trust. While current labor-relations texts frequently point

---

[1] "Lessons from Japan, Inc.," *Newsweek*, (September 29, 1980), pp. 110-112.

[2] Alphonso Pinkney, *American Way of Violence*, New York: Random House, 1972.

[3] John Kenneth Galbraith, *American Capitalism*, Cambridge, Massachusetts: The Riverside Press, 1956, pp. 114-117.

to the need for cooperation, they universally emphasize conflict and mistrust. A cursory reading of any of the standard chapters on the negotiating process, for example, immediately reveals the conflict bias of these texts. The imposition of costs as a means to increase bargaining power, gamesmanship, and the need to dupe the opponent to achieve bargaining goals are issues typically stressed by the authors of these textbooks. This volume, on the other hand, reflects the belief of its authors that an approach to collective bargaining and labor relations wherein commonality of interests, cooperation, and trust are emphasized holds the key to the solution of many of the problems currently facing labor and management.

The authors' view of the labor-management relationship as a cooperative effort finds expression not only through a different emphasis in the treatment of traditional industrial-relations topics but also through in-depth analyses of issues typically ignored or glossed over in other labor-relations texts. Significant space is devoted to such non-traditional issues as discipline, absenteeism, appropriate use of arbitration, grievance minimization techniques, human relations, alternative methods of dispute resolution, and philosophy of grievance administration—an understanding of which is critical to successful implementation of cooperative labor-management problem-solving. In the area of contract administration, for example, the self-defeating nature of a legalistic action-reaction philosophy of contract administration is highlighted by underscoring its enormous costs to each party, thereby giving the reader an incentive to evaluate alternative methods of contract-grievance administration that minimize costs to all parties concerned.

Although many texts have been authored by economists, few, if any, incorporate basic economic analysis to evaluate problems, issues, programs, and policies in the field of labor-management relations. Whatever the rationale, the failure to utilize basic economic principles deprives the reader of eminently useful tools for understanding pressing labor-relations issues and problems. To remedy this deficiency without intimidating the reader, the present volume, in a very straight-forward and simplified fashion, makes use of basic economic concepts to analyze such topics as minimum wage legislation, wage-price guidelines, cost-of-living adjustment (COLA) clauses, and absenteeism.

The authors owe a great debt of gratitude to the many individuals who have made this volume possible, to Nik Dhalokia, James Dworkin, Myron Fottler, Philip Kienast, Thomas Kochan, Robert Lynn, James McClimon and the Iowa PERB, Robert Paul, and John Schmidman for reading and making invaluable comments on and suggestions for the manuscript, our thanks. We would also like to thank Ken Scott and David J. Forgione, Macmillan Publishing Company, for their excellent editorial guidance and assistance in the publication of this book.

Special thanks go to Fred Witney and the late John (Jack) Hogan who awakened in the authors an interest in labor-management relations, encouraged and guided us when disheartened, and whose quality instruction made the writing of this book possible.

Heartfelt thanks also go to Mrs. Marjorie Seib, without whose yeoman's service in typing and preparation of the manuscript, the authors' ideas and thoughts would still be in unintelligible longhand and scattered over at least four states.

Finally, we offer special thanks to our wives, Christina and Margaret, for their continued enthusiastic support of and interest in the progress of the manuscript despite suffering through many months of solitude. To our sons, James, Stephen, Mark, Ross, and Jordan for enduring their fathers' irritable and irascible behavior, our guarantee of that often-promised vacation.

The foregoing assistance, support, and guidance notwithstanding, any shortcomings and errors contained in this volume are solely attributable to the authors.

D. A. D.
C. R. D.

Contents

PART III: Administration of the Labor Agreement

Sector; Multinational Corporations and Collective Bargaining; Agricultural Labor Organizations; White Collar Unionization.
Managerial Aggression: A Threat to Peaceful Labor Relations.
A Career in Labor Relations.
Summary and Conclusions.

Cases

Appendices

Index

Part I

Introduction and the Environment of Collective Bargaining

Chapter 1

Collective Bargaining in Perspective:
The Roles of Labor and Management

Although collective bargaining is one of the nation's oldest and most firmly established economic institutions, it also remains one of the most controversial. This chapter presents an overview of the institution of collective bargaining and introduces the actors who shape and mold labor relations in the United States. Divided into three sections, the chapter examines, in order, the purpose of and plan of study adopted by the authors in writing this labor relations textbook, the definition and domain of collective bargaining and labor relations, and the roles and objectives of the parties to collective bargaining.

Purpose and Approach

Business and non-business majors alike will function within working environments affected to a greater or lesser extent by forces within the labor relations arena. Upon graduation, students may find themselves deeply involved in labor relations as management representatives, union representatives, or union members. On the other hand, involvement may be limited to inconvenience brought about by a work stoppage. Whatever the case, it is important that students understand the labor relations forces that impact their work environment. As pervasive as industrial relations forces are, college/university curricula typically allot time but for a single course in this area. Given that the field of industrial relations has expanded and become increasingly complex over the last several decades, it is imperative that the time allotted for its study be utilized as productively as possible. This concern prompted the authors to write a comprehensive yet in-depth text introducing the discipline of labor relations. The purpose of the text is to provide the beginning student with the industrial relations concepts and principles necessary to function effectively as a union official or member, a representative of management, or simply as an informed citizen. Since all economic, legal, and management principles critical to an understanding of industrial relations are internally developed and explained, the text stands on its own; traditional prerequisite courses in economics, law, and management, although helpful, are not required. Thus, the text ideally fits the slot allocated to the study of industrial relations by most college/university curricula. At the same time, the text's comprehensive and in-depth treatment of topics recommends it as an introductory text for students pursuing an industrial relations major or minor.

Topics and material contained in the book are grouped and examined in chronological sequence under four headings, namely: (1) The Environment of Collective Bargaining; (2) Negotiation of the Labor Agreement; (3) Administration of the Labor Agreement; and (4) New Frontiers in Collective Bargaining. A brief description of the concepts treated under each heading follows.

The Environment of Collective Bargaining

Section I of the book examines the American labor movement, the legal environment of collective bargaining, and the organizational structure and behavior of labor unions. More precisely, Chapters 2 and 3 probe the historical development of the American labor movement with primary emphasis upon factors influencing growth, structure, and philosophy. Chapter 4 surveys the development and current status of the rules and regulations governing the labor-management relationship—labor law. Finally, Chapter 5 concludes the section with a description of the structure and operation of modern labor unions and an analysis of union certification procedures.

Negotiation of the Labor Agreement

Section II focuses upon that aspect of labor relations with which the general public is most familiar—contract negotiations. Chapter 6 sets the stage for negotiations by exploring the meaning of good faith bargaining and by reviewing the substantive issues that constitute the subject matter of bargaining. The negotiation process, different models and stages thereof, and the driving mechanism therein comprise a partial list of the topics studied in Chapter 7 under the heading "The Art and Science of Table Bargaining." Chapters 8 and 9 scrutinize the economic components of the labor agreement. Specifically, Chapter 8 examines wage determination under collective bargaining while Chapter 9 concentrates upon negotiated, economic supplements to wages—popularly labeled fringe benefits. Non-economic contract provisions creating and/or protecting employee and employer rights are treated in Chapter 10.

Administration of the Labor Agreement

Section III explores the less publicized (less glamorous?) but equally, if not more, important side of collective bargaining and labor relations—contract administration and enforcement. The latter's importance lies in the fact that it gives meaning to provisions fashioned and agreed to during table bargaining—it, so to speak, fleshes out the bare bones of the labor agreement. Chapter 11 describes the contractually-created mechanism for contract administration and enforcement—the grievance procedure, defines a grievance, investigates the sources of grievances, and analyzes ways of minimizing grievances. Chapter 12 is devoted to the special problems of contract interpretation and application created by the assessment of discipline—the single most important source of employee grievances. Specifically, topics of discussion include the nature and purpose of discipline, characteristics of an effectively functioning disciplinary procedure, and factors important in the arbitration of discipline-related grievances. Pursuing the topic of arbitration, Chapter 13 presents an overview of arbitration as the preferred method for resolving contract interpretation disputes that arise during the life of the labor agreement. The legal status of arbitration, arbitrator selection, and arbitration procedure are but several of the topics studied in this chapter. The final chapter of Section III, Chapter 14, examines dispute settlement methods other than arbitration, focusing upon the resolution of impasses that arise during the negotiation of new contract terms.

New Frontiers in Collective Bargaining

The final section of the book concentrates upon recent developments and new frontiers in the labor relations field. Chapter 15 compares and contrasts the public and private sectors, noting the unique characteristics of the public sector employer and the impact of those characteristics on public sector bargaining. Particularly noteworthy is the discussion of the public employee's right to strike. Chapter 16 is devoted to an analysis of collective bargaining in the health care industry, its characteristics, and special problems. Chapter 17 concludes the section by exploring the likely direction of future change in the field of industrial relations, by examining the role of the labor relations specialist in this constantly changing and rapidly evolving field, and by giving a few words of advice to aspiring labor relations practitioners.

Collective Bargaining: Defined and Explained

Collective bargaining is an industrial relations system under which labor and management mutually determine the terms and conditions of employment. Bargaining consists of two elements, namely: (1) contract negotiation during which the rights of labor and management are fashioned, agreed upon, and set to language; and (2) contract administration and enforcement during which the language of the labor agreement is given specific meaning in its day-to-day application. The conceptual distinction between these two aspects of bargaining, however, oftentimes becomes blurred in practice. Specific application of a given provision, for example, may give it an entirely different meaning than the one intended by its authors during negotiation. To the extent that the latter occurs, either unintentionally or by agreement, contract negotiation (renegotiation) becomes an ongoing process, and the distinction between it and contract administration evaporates.

Given the complex nature of the institution of bargaining, any attempt to define it by way of a single sentence or paragraph is fraught with the danger of misleading those unfamiliar with the bargaining process. The definition of collective bargaining offered above, for example, may lead one to conclude that the West German system of codetermination and the American system of collective bargaining are the same. Yet, as anyone familiar with the two systems understands, the methods through which mutual determination of terms and conditions of employment occurs are significantly different; where West German workers rely upon representation on the boards of directors of firms to achieve bilateral input, American workers rely upon the efforts of elected representatives at the bargaining table.

An often-heard criticism of collective bargaining is that it is an adversary-based system of industrial relations—labor attempting to wrest as many concessions as it can from management and management attempting to concede as little as possible to labor. In this respect, collective bargaining is not unlike any other exchange mechanism in a market economy; the seller of a good or service attempts to extract the highest possible price from the buyer while the buyer attempts to purchase the good or service as cheaply as possible. Just as the parties to any potential market exchange are at liberty to skirt final execution of the transaction, so too are the parties to the labor exchange free to sidestep final agreement—free to strike or lockout. Thus, collective bargaining might best be viewed as a simple extension of the market system where exchange is voluntary and motivated by self-interest. As such, it is no more adversarial in nature than any other exchange that occurs within the framework of free markets. Indeed, it is the pursuit of self-interest by all economic agents within a competitive environment that guarantees efficient resource utilization. Only when the pursuit of self-interest goes on untempered by the recognition of welfare interdependency does it become a threat to the parties of the bargaining relationship. Although slow in developing and not without substantial cost (e.g., a sharply reduced market share for domestic auto producers), that evolutionary stage of the bargaining relationship has now been reached where mutual dependency and welfare interdependency are recognized economic facts of life that temper the pursuit of self-interest.

Another criticism often leveled against collective bargaining as a system of labor relations is that it is a static process incapable of adequately serving the needs of its participants (i.e., labor and management). Thus, according to its critics, collective bargaining defies exact definition because it lacks relevant substantive content. A stronger argument, however, can be made that it is precisely because of its dynamic qualities that collective bargaining is difficult to define. The definitional problem involving collective bargaining, therefore, has been likened to the problem of securing a detailed description of a fast moving boxcar; rapid movement past the point of observation precludes an accurate accounting of specific characteristics other than the fact that what passed was a boxcar. In other words, the institution of collective bargaining is changing, adapting, and evolving at such an intense pace that all but the broadest and most general of definitions quickly become inaccurate and outdated.

Complicating the problem of defining collective bargaining as an industrial relations system is the fact that bargaining relationships vary from one firm to another. Individual bargaining relationships run the gamut of the evolutionary spectrum from open hostility to close cooperation in problem solving. In short, bargaining relationships are what their participants make them. As such, they reflect the virtues, shortcomings, and idiosyncracies—the heterogeneity of mankind. Hence, a more focused definition of collective bargaining could only be purchased at significant cost—the sacrifice of general applicability.

Labor Relations

The topics and issues that constitute the field of labor relations can be broadly classified into one of two categories, namely: (1) issues related to the economics of unionized labor markets or (2) issues related to the systems of industrial jurisprudence. Both types of issues influence the institution of collective bargaining and the behavior of its participants. Each category is examined in some detail in the pages which follow.

The Economics of Unionized Labor Markets

There are a large number of collective bargaining issues which are purely economic in nature. In the jargon of labor relations, these issues comprise the economic package of bargaining. Probably the best known of the items in the economic package is the wage rate. Of greater controversy, if not of equal magnitude, however, are the alternate forms of labor compensation, loosely termed "fringe" benefits. The term "fringe" is misleading because these employee benefits are in no sense inconsequential in nature, amounting in some cases to as much as forty percent of total labor costs. The increased complexity of compensation-related matters is mirrored by the emergence of a subfield of specialization within the field of labor relations entitled compensation administration. As its name suggests, this subfield focuses upon the analysis, development, and administration of the wage and non-wage components of the firm's economic package.

The economics of unionized labor markets transcends traditional compensation-related topics; it includes any bargaining issue (e.g., absenteeism, wage/price controls, racial/sexual discrimination, etc.) that may be meaningfully examined through use of economic paradigms. Economic analysis is employed not for its own sake but for the understanding that it conveys regarding labor relations topics. To limit the economics of unionized labor markets to compensation-related topics to avoid the rigors of economic analysis is equivalent to, in a manner of speaking, "tossing the baby out with the bathwater"—a prohibitive cost in terms of a more informed understanding of the operation of the institution of collective bargaining. Hence, economic analysis will be utilized throughout the text whenever and wherever conducive to a better understanding of the bargaining process.

A convincing argument can be made that labor relations as a distinct discipline owes its very existence to the shortcomings of the economics discipline. Economic theory yields specific information regarding wage and employment determination only under unrealistically limited sets of circumstances. In terms of Figure 1, for example, economic analysis pinpoints the equilibrium wage and employment levels as W_C and L_C (the intersection point between market demand for and supply of labor), respectively, when it is assumed that conditions of perfect competition prevail, namely: a large number of independent buyers and sellers of labor, no barriers to market entry, a homogeneous supply of labor, and perfect knowledge on the part of all economic agents. Replacing the assumption of a large number of buyers of labor with that of a single buyer of labor (i.e., a market structure referred to as monopsony) changes the wage and employment levels to W_M and L_M, respectively, in Figure 1. In similar fashion, replacing the assumption of a large number of independent sellers of labor with that of a single seller of labor (i.e., a market structure referred to as monopoly) shifts the wage and employment levels to W_U and L_U, respectively, in Figure–1. Yet, under conditions of bilateral monopoly where a union monopolist confronts a firm monopsonist—conditions which approximate the real world of unionized labor markets, the model fails to identify a specific wage/employment combination. Instead, the best that economic analysis can do is to identify settlement ranges for wages and employment—$W_M W_U$ and $L_M L_U$, respectively, in Figure 1—wherein agreement will occur.[1] Labor relations evolved expressly to fill the void created by the inability of neo-classical economics to precisely identify the wage/employment settlement point under conditions of bilateral monopoly (i.e., in unionized labor markets). Thus, from an economist's perspective, labor relations may be likened to the mythological phoenix which derived its vitality from its ancestral ashes—in this case, the ashes were those of neo-classical economics.

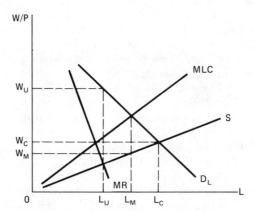

FIGURE 1.1.   Wage and employment under various market structures.

---

[1]A detailed explanation of these economic models may be found in: Edwin Mansfield, *Microeconomics: Theory and Applications*, 2d ed., New York: W.W. Norton and Company, Inc., 1975, Chapters 12–13.

To posit the origin of the discipline of labor relations with the inadequacies of the body of economic thought should not be construed either as a slap in the face to the economics discipline or a denial of the contributions of other disciplines to labor relations. Quite the contrary, the significance of economics for the study of labor relations has already been underscored, and the contributions of other fields (e.g., law, management, political science, psychology, sociology, etc.) to the theoretical and practical understanding of labor relations and collective bargaining will be highlighted as basic concepts and processes are examined. Emphasis was placed upon the origin of labor relations merely to illustrate and stress the importance of the study of labor relations from the conceptual viewpoint of an economist.

Systems of Industrial Jurisprudence

The second broad category of issues within the field of labor relations encompasses topics related either to the externally imposed or internally created legal environments within which the labor management relationship must operate. Both systems of industrial jurisprudence have as their objective the protection of employer and employee rights. Although the body of labor law and its impact upon collective bargaining, as well as the grievance/arbitration procedure and its role in the labor management relationship, are treated in detail elsewhere in this volume, their significance warrants preliminary discussion and comment.

As noted earlier, collective bargaining is another form of voluntary market exchange which is motivated by self-interest. As such, it is an extension of a system of markets wherein the pursuit of self-interest insures efficient utilization of scarce resources. Adam Smith, the Father of Classical Economics, recognized this fact when he wrote:

> It is not from the benevolence of the butcher, the brewer, or the baker, that we expect our dinner, but from their regard to their own interest. We address ourselves, not to their humanity but to their self-love, and never talk to them of our own necessities but of their advantages. Nobody but a beggar chooses to depend chiefly upon the benevolence of his fellow-citizens.[2]

In Smith's view, therefore, social welfare was promoted by the pursuit of individual self-interest. An individual,

> by directing that industry in such a manner as its produce may be of the greatest value, . . . intends only his own gain, and he is in this, as in many other cases, led by an invisible hand to promote an end which was no part of his intention . . . By pursuing his own interest he frequently promotes that of the society more effectually than when he really intends to promote it.[3]

[2]Adam Smith, *The Wealth of Nations*, Cannan Edition, New York: The Modern Library, Inc., 1937, p. 14.
[3]*Ibid.*, p. 423.

The key element for achieving efficient resource usage (i.e., the socially optimum production and distribution of goods and services) through pursuit of self-interest is competition—Smith's "invisible hand." Absent the constructive direction given self-interest by competition and problems develop. Smith recognized the inherent tendency for competition to disintegrate in labor markets as well as the consequences of this disintegration.

> What are the common wages of labour, depends everywhere upon the contract usually made between those two parties, whose interests are by no means the same. The workmen desire to get as much, the masters to give as little as possible. The former are disposed to combine in order to raise, the latter in order to lower the wages of labour.
>
> It is not, however, difficult to foresee which of the two parties must, upon all ordinary occasions, have the advantage in the dispute, and force the other into a compliance with their terms. The masters, being fewer in number, can combine much more easily; and the law, besides, authorizes, or at least does not prohibit their combinations, while it prohibits those of workmen. We have no acts of parliament against combining to lower the price of work; but many against combining to raise it. In all such disputes the masters can hold out much longer. A landlord, a farmer, a master manufacturer, or merchant, though they did not employ a single workman, could generally live a year or two upon the stocks which they have already acquired. Many workmen could not subsist a month, and scarce any a year without employment. In the long-run the workman may be as necessary to his master as his master is to him, but the necessity is not so immediate.
>
> But whether their combinations be offensive or defensive, they are always abundantly heard of. In order to bring the point to a speedy decision, they have always recourse to the loudest clamour, and sometimes the most shocking violence and outrage. They are desperate and act with the folly and extravagance of desperate men, who must either starve, or frighten their masters into an immediate compliance with their demands . . .[4]

The legal environment can fill the role occupied by competition under the classical system of free markets—that of directing individual self-interest toward the public interest. As the above-cited remarks of Adam Smith indicate, society has not been hesitant to use the legal environment as an instrument of economic policy. In the quoted passage, statutory law reinforced the natural advantage enjoyed by the "masters" in the labor exchange. History, however, has also shown the folly of non-neutral use of legal institutions and processes. Congress, for example, recognized the foolishness of legal systems that fail to protect the exercise by all persons of individual and collective rights—that fail to function as an adequate substitute for competition—when it included the following paragraphs, detailing the adverse economic effects of said systems, as an introduction to and justification for the Wagner Act (i.e., the National Labor Relations Act) of 1935.

The Wagner Act went on to establish rules of conduct for the labor-management relationship to prevent either party from exercising undue influence over the labor exchange. When it became apparent that the statute's

[4] Adam Smith, *The Wealth of Nations*, pp. 66–67.

BOX 1–1. The Wagner Act

Findings and Policy. Sec. 1.

The denial by employers of the right of employees to organize and the refusal by employers to accept the procedure of collective bargaining lead to strikes and other forms of industrial strife or unrest, which have the intent or the necessary effect of burdening or obstructing commerce by (a) impairing the efficiency, safety, or operation of the instrumentalities of commerce; (b) occurring in the current of commerce; (c) materially affecting, restraining, or controlling the flow of raw materials or manufactured or processed goods from or into the channels of commerce, or the prices of such materials or goods in commerce; or (d) causing diminution of employment and wages in such volume as substantially to impair or disrupt the market for goods flowing from or into the channels of commerce.

The inequality of bargaining power between employees who do not possess full freedom of association or actual liberty of contract, and employers who are organized in the corporate or other forms of ownership association substantially burdens and affects the flow of commerce, and tends to aggravate recurrent business depressions, by depressing wage rates and the purchasing power of wage earners in industry and by preventing the stabilization of competitive wage rates and working conditions within and between industries.

Experience has proved that protection by law of the right of employees to organize and bargain collectively safeguards commerce from injury, impairment, or interruption, and promotes the flow of commerce by removing certain recognized sources of industrial strife and unrest, by encouraging practices fundamental to the friendly adjustment of industrial disputes arising out of differences as to wages, hours, or other working conditions, and by restoring equality of bargaining power between employers and employees.

It is hereby declared to be the policy of the United States to eliminate the causes of certain substantial obstructions to the free flow of commerce and to mitigate and eliminate these obstructions when they have occurred by encouraging the practice and procedure of collective bargaining and by protecting the exercise by workers of full freedom of association, self-organization, and designation of representatives of their own choosing, for the purpose of negotiating the terms and conditions of their employment or other mutual aid or protection.

---

provisions were no longer effective in maintaining a rough balance in bargaining power, Congress restructured the rules of conduct—amended the legislation—in 1947, 1959, and again in 1974. In short, the rule of law has been substituted for the rule of competition for purposes of channeling individual self-interest toward the public good.

Although the foregoing discussion has been couched in terms of the externally imposed system of industrial jurisprudence, it is equally applicable to the internally created system of industrial jurisprudence—the grievance/arbitration procedure. The latter sets the ground rules for labor/management behavior for the duration of the labor agreement. It prevents the labor/management relationship from degenerating into one governed by the "law of tooth and fang" where economic might makes right. In other words, like its external counterpart, the internal system of industrial jurisprudence serves the interest of all parties concerned—the public good.

The Goals of Unions and Management

Considerable time and effort have been expended in recent years by applied psychologists and organizational behaviorists studying collective bargaining and labor relations. The insights into group behavior provided by these specialists have been significant and will be presented at the appropriate points in the text. Several general observations concerning the behavior of labor and management, however, are worth presently noting.

Unions

Unions are organizations with well-defined goals and objectives—goals and objectives which have been fashioned and molded over time by considerations, for the most part, quite pragmatic in nature. Although unions sometimes engage in rhetoric bordering on the radical, their goals and objectives remain basically conservative, namely: (1) to organize workers, (2) to use the strength derived from numbers (i.e., bargaining power) to negotiate favorable terms and conditions of employment, and (3) to guard and protect the rights of workers won during negotiation as the contract is interpreted and applied in the day-to-day operation of the firm. In the language of organizational behavior, labor's objectives are said to be *micro* oriented rather than *macro* oriented—that is concerned with the welfare of specific (i.e., individual) groups of workers as opposed to the welfare of society as a whole.

Labor's goals and objectives, however, have not always been so narrowly and practically oriented. Prior to the formation of the American Federation of Labor (AFL) in 1886, the American labor movement foundered in search of a guiding philosophy of operation, oftentimes dabbling with reformist schemes alien to the American experience that served only to coalesce the hostility of society (i.e., employers and workers alike) toward unions in general. Indeed, preoccupation with utopian schemes aimed at remaking the socio-economic fabric of society proved to be a major factor contributing to the demise of both the National Labor Union and the Knights of Labor—the immediate predecessors of the American Federation of Labor.

The birth of the AFL in 1886 marked a shift in the goals of the American labor movement—a shift from reformist to "bread and butter" objectives. As the phrase "bread and butter" implies, the sole concern of organized labor, at least of those unions affiliated with the AFL, became that of immediate economic improvement of the conditions of the workplace. According to AFL President Samuel Gompers, the very survival of trade unionism and, hence, any chance for improvement in the standard of living of working people depended upon trade union adoption of "bread and butter" goals—goals which workers understood, were sympathetic with, and would work toward—goals consistent with the American experience.

Gompers also believed that the best methods for achieving "bread and butter" goals were organization and collective bargaining within the framework of American capitalism; political solutions were to be tried only as a last resort.

> "The labor movement, to succeed politically," he (Gompers) declared, "must work for present and tangible results. While keeping in view a lofty ideal, we must advance towards it through practical steps, taken with intelligent regard for pressing needs." Individual workers could and should vote for sympathetic candidates, he believed, but organized labor should keep clear of political parties and neither try to form one of its own nor endorse any existing one. In this way labor would not dissipate its energies in useless causes, but instead could exert continuous pressure for immediate economic improvement in the workplace, thus making more progress than by "dabbling in that cesspool of corruption commonly known as party politics."[5]

Thus, Gompers viewed politics as a quagmire best avoided by organized labor lest it bankrupt itself both morally and financially on issues best handled at the bargaining table or not at all. This contrasts sharply with the *modus operandi* of unions in most other countries where political action is the rule and not the exception (e.g., Solidarity in Poland). In summary, the American labor movement has remained, in all important respects, the labor movement of Samuel Gompers—conservative, "bread and butter" oriented, and non-political.

Management

The term management encompasses three quite distinct managerial groups: managers of private profit-oriented firms, managers of government agencies, and managers of private, nonprofit organizations. Profit maximization (i.e., cost minimization) is assumed to be the overriding concern of the first group of managers. These decision makers establish the conditions necessary for profit maximization, taking into consideration such diverse variables as technology, labor productivity, product differentiation, plant location, government regulations, capital markets, overall economic conditions, and the like. Since public policy affects the firm's ability to earn profits, political issues become an integral part of the manager's planning horizon and political lobbying an accepted tool in the manager's arsenal of weapons for earning a

[5] Harold C. Livesay, *Samuel Gompers and Organized Labor*, New York: Little, Brown and Company, 1978, p. 34.

profit. Managers of private profit-oriented firms have thus become responsive to political signals as well as to product and resource market signals.

Other views of private-sector management behavior do exist. For example, one view holds that managers attempt to maximize firm size. This view of management behavior is premised upon the assumption that managerial success is measured by firm size and the manager's importance within the firm. To the extent that such views simultaneously hold that profit maximization is irrelevant, they are at best unrealistic; to the extent that such views simultaneously presuppose profit maximization as a necessary prerequisite for achievement of secondary goals and objectives by managers, they contribute to the understanding of managerial behavior.

Managers of government agencies are subject to a different type of maximization constraint; these decision makers attempt to maximize the quantity and quality of a particular service from a specified amount of tax revenue. Although somewhat analogous to the maximization problem faced by private profit-oriented managers, important differences exist. As detailed in Chapter 15, the monopoly nature of the public–sector agency and the method of financing most government services subject the public-sector manager to efficiency criteria which are less exacting than those to which his/her private-sector counterpart is subject. In addition, decisions concerning the nature and quantity of the service to be provided are political. Thus, the public-sector manager is more attuned and responsive to political considerations than is the private-sector manager.

Managers of private non-profit organizations operate within an environment which has characteristics of both the private profit and public sectors. As was the case for the public-sector manager, the primary concern is that of providing the maximum amount of a high quality service subject to the constraint of a limited budget. Private non-profit organizations are also like public-sector agencies in that non-market factors determine the nature of the service provided. Unlike the public sector, however, politics play a less important role and private-sector efficiency criteria a more important role in decision–making. The latter is true primarily because the non-profit organization is located in the private sector of the economy.

Common Goals and Objectives

Unions and management share a number of goals and objectives in common. Virtually all labor relations practitioners recognize the benefits of a smoothly functioning system of bilateral decision-making. This applies to both elements of bargaining—contract negotiations and contract administration. Similarly, both parties recognize the high personal stakes in having the organization remain viable—economically competitive and healthy in the case of the private-sector profit–oriented firm, and effective and funded in the case of a private-sector non-profit or public-sector firm.

Few unions would deny management the ultimate responsibility for operating the firm, agency, or organization. Indeed, if the recent economic malaise has done nothing else, it has, as the following quote indicates, brought the primary management function into clear focus for labor unions.

This challenge requires a new level of management expertise. Labor has been and is willing to make reasonable concessions such as increased pay caps, pay reductions, or wage deferrals to assist an airline, but not indefinitely. Eventually, management must do its job effectively.[6]

By the same token, management typically respects the union's rights and obligations in the representation of its membership.

Where differences arise in the labor-management relationship, they involve either the allocation/distribution of profits (revenue)—for example, the union may claim a portion of profits which managers believe is best allocated to research and development—or specific limitations upon management's right to manage and the union's right to represent. The point to be emphasized, however, is that commonality of interests typically prevents any differences that arise between the parties from destroying the bargaining relationship and irreparably injuring the parties thereto.

In the chapters that follow, an effort is made to highlight those areas of the bargaining relationship where the parties' goals are mutually consistent and those where they are not. A warning, however, should be sounded at this point; since each labor/management relationship is unique in some respect, a generalization drawn from a number of relationships may prove inappropriate to another relationship. The student of labor/management relations, therefore, must always be prepared for the case (i.e., bargaining relationship) that proves to be the exception to the rule.

Other Collective Bargaining Participants

In addition to labor and management, other organizations are involved with labor relations and the collective bargaining process. The most notable of the different types of organizations is the administrative law agency. The basic function of such an agency is to implement and enforce the legislation of Congress in specific cases—to administer and apply the statute that specifically created the agency. In the labor relations arena, the most important of these agencies are the National Labor Relations Board (NLRB) and the Equal Employment Opportunity Commission (EEOC) which are charged with enforcement of the Wagner Act and the 1964 Civil Rights Act, respectively. Other institutions and organizations of a non-administrative law type that play an important role in the labor-management relationship include the judicial system, the Federal Mediation and Conciliation Service (FMCS), and public and private dispute settlement groups, to name but a few.

Although the forenamed organizations are a party to the bargaining process, their roles are significantly different than those of labor and management. Their raison d'être is to facilitate joint decision-making. When they have outlived their usefulness to the bargaining parties and the bargaining process, these organizations are either restructured or left to expire. During periods of evolutionary change in bargaining relationships, therefore, one

---

[6]Sally M. Brain, et al., "Special Report: The Productivity Trap," *Air Line Pilot*, (February 1982), pp. 12–62, p. 13.

should expect corresponding change in the institutions that surround the bargaining process. The functions and impact of these outside parties (i.e., agencies and organizations) upon bargaining will be noted as various aspects of the bargaining process are discussed in the following chapters.

Summary and Conclusion

Given the dynamic and complex nature of the institution of bargaining, any attempt to define it by way of a single sentence or paragraph is fraught with the danger of misleading those unfamiliar with the bargaining process. In general, however, collective bargaining may be defined as an industrial relations system under which labor and management mutually determine the terms and conditions of employment. Bargaining consists of two not necessarily distinct activities—contract negotiation and contract administration. The bargaining process, per se, is no more adversarial in nature than any other exchange that occurs within the framework of the market system—the seller of a good or service (union) attempting to extract the highest possible price from the buyer and the buyer (management) attempting to purchase the good or service as cheaply as possible.

The topics and issues that constitute the field of industrial relations can be broadly classified into one of two categories, namely: (1) issues related to the economics of unionized labor markets or (2) issues related to the systems of industrial jurisprudence. The first category transcends purely economic issues that comprise the economic package of bargaining to include any issue (e.g., absenteeism, wage/price controls, racial/sexual discrimination, etc.) that may be meaningfully examined through use of economic paradigms. The second broad category of issues encompasses topics related either to the externally imposed or internally created legal environments. Both systems of industrial jurisprudence have as their objective the protection of employer and employee rights. Both substitute the rule of law for the rule of competition for purposes of channeling individual self-interest toward the public good.

The goals and objectives of American trade unions are conservative, "bread and butter" oriented, and non-political—namely: (1) to organize workers, (2) to use the strength derived from numbers (i.e., bargaining power) to negotiate favorable terms and conditions of employment, and (3) to guard and protect the rights of workers won during negotiation as the contract is interpreted and applied in the day-to-day operation of the firm. Management, on the other hand, focuses upon profit maximization or, in the case of public-sector managers, quantity/quality maximization of a particular service subject to the constraint of a limited amount of tax revenue. Although unions and management share a number of goals and objectives in common (e.g., an economically sound enterprise), differences do develop during bargaining. For the most part, however, the commonality of goals and interests between bargaining parties is sufficiently strong to prevent these differences from destroying the bargaining relationship and irreparably injuring the parties thereto.

DISCUSSION QUESTIONS

1. Why are one or two-sentence definitions of collective bargaining dangerous? Explain.

2. Collective bargaining might best be viewed as a simple extension of the market system where exchange is voluntary and motivated by self-interest. Comment.

3. In what sense does labor relations as a distinct discipline of study owe its very existence to economics? Explain.

4. The system of industrial jurisprudence can fill the role occupied by competition (i.e., Adam Smith's "invisible hand") under the classical system of free markets. In other words, the rule of law can be substituted for the rule of competition. Comment.

5. The American labor movement has remained, in all important respects, the labor movement of Samuel Gompers. Discuss.

6. What prevents differences in goals and objectives between labor and management from developing into open conflict, thereby destroying the bargaining relationship and irreparably injuring the parties thereto? Explain.

7. Arrange the three managerial groups discussed in this chapter in descending order of likely strength of resistance to union demands. Justify your arrangement.

SELECTED REFERENCES

Barbash, Jack, *American Unions: Structure, Government, and Politics*, New York: Random House, Inc., 1967.

Livesay, Harold C., *Samuel Gompers and Organized Labor*, New York: Little, Brown and Company, 1978.

Mansfield, Edwin, *Microeconomics: Theory and Applications*, 2d ed., New York: W.W. Norton & Company, Inc., 1975.

Rees, Albert, *The Economics of Trade Unions*, Chicago, Illinois: University of Chicago Press, 1978.

Smith, Adam, *The Wealth of Nations*, Cannan Edition, New York: The Modern Library, Inc., 1937.

Taylor, Benjamin J. and Fred Witney, *Labor Relations Law*, Englewood Cliffs, New Jersey: Prentice-Hall, Inc., 1975.

Chapter 2

The American Labor Movement:

Growth, Structure and Philosophy—I

Those who ignore the lessons of history are condemned to repeat its mistakes.[1]

The American labor movement is a product of its environment. Economic, social, and political forces constitute that environment. The purpose of this chapter is to examine the historical determinants that have influenced the growth of the American labor movement, fashioned its structure, and shaped its philosophy. From an analytical standpoint, matters would be greatly simplified if various economic, social, and political variables could be neatly classified as exclusively impacting American trade union growth, structure, or philosophy. Unfortunately, simplistic classifications do not accurately reflect the real world. Any given variable may simultaneously affect growth, structure, and philosophy. Further, these latter variables, themselves, interact with one another; changes in labor movement structure and/or philosophy affect trade union growth while changes in the rate of trade union growth, in turn, influence structure and/or philosophy. Rather than presenting another detailed chronicle of historical events in the evolution of the American labor movement—ground which has already been quite extensively traversed by others[2], this chapter will

---

[1] A variant of George Santanyana's statement, "Those who cannot remember the past are condemned to repeat it.", in *The Life of Reason*, rev. ed., New York: Charles Scribner's Sons, 1953, p. 82.

[2] For examples, see: John R. Commons et al., Editors, *A Documentary History of American Industrial Society* Vols. I-IX, Cleveland, Ohio: The Arthur H. Clark Co., 1910; John R. Commons et al., *History of Labour in the United States*, Vols. I–II, New York: The Macmillan Company, 1918; Foster Rhea Dulles, *Labor in America: A History*, 3rd Edition, New York: Thomas Y. Crowell Company, 1966; Joseph G. Rayback, *A History of American Labor*, New York: The Free Press, 1966; Philip Taft, *Organized Labor in American History*, New York: Harper & Row, Publishers, 1964.

focus on American trade union growth, structure, and philosophy, the
economic, social, and political factors responsible therefore; and the
basic relationships there between. As the above quote suggests, a
basic understanding of these historical influences and relationships
better equips an individual to chart and comprehend the course of
future events concerning trade union growth, structure, and
philosophy.

The Framework of Analysis

The seminal work on trade union growth by Ashenfelter and Pencavel, "American Trade Union Growth: 1900–1960",[3] provides an excellent *paradigm* and *point of departure* for identifying and analyzing the various factors responsible for changes in trade union membership, structure, and philosophy. Although the empirical results of the Ashenfelter-Pencavel Model (hereinafter referred to as the A-P Model) are strictly valid only for the period 1900–1960, the single behavioral relationship sheds considerable light upon trade union developments both prior to and following that time period. Use of the A-P Model as a framework of analysis for labor history should not be construed as a deprecation of the contributions of other excellent researchers to the understanding of trade union growth and behavior. Rather, given the authors' training and backgrounds as well as the demonstrated need by students for a concrete analytical structure for understanding and remembering important events in labor history, the authors simply felt most comfortable with the A-P Model as an instructional paradigm. As the following paragraphs clearly demonstrate, if nothing else, the authors do not feel bound (limited) in their analysis of trade union growth to the variables of the A-P Model; they are not wedded to the model as *the* explanation of trade union growth—as used here, it is an aid to understanding—nothing more.

Union Membership: A Rational Employee Decision

The A-P Model incorporates economic, social and political variables to explain the behavior of trade union membership over time. In the case of economic variables, the employee's decision concerning union membership is assumed to be rational and therefore dependent:

> upon his subjective assessment of the expected benefits to be obtained from union membership as against his subjective assessment of expected costs of membership.[4]

Membership Benefits

Expected benefits include higher wages, better working conditions, and job security. The percentage rate of change of prices (ΔP_T) is used to measure

---

[3] Orley Ashenfelter and John H. Pencavel, "American Trade Union Growth: 1900–1960," *Quarterly Journal of Economics*, (August 1969), **83**: 434–48.
[4] *Ibid.*, p. 436.

changes in the benefits associated with union membership. More specifically, the real wage declines at an increasing rate as prices rise at an increasing rate, resulting in an increased desire on the part of the worker to unionize in order to protect the threatened real wage. In short, the perceived benefits of union membership increase as ΔP_T increases.

Membership Costs

Expected costs of union membership include dues and fees, organizing costs, and the possibility of employer retaliation (e.g., rough-shadowing, discrimination, discharge, blacklisting, etc.). Organizing costs and the probability of employer retaliation vary inversely with the strength of the labor demand. When labor is scarce and not easily replaced, the employer is less likely to engage in retaliatory activities. Consequently, employees are more receptive to organizing efforts during periods of expanding employment. Unions capitalize upon greater employee receptivity during periods of expanding employment by undertaking organizational campaigns and membership drives. Such union efforts simultaneously minimize organizing costs both to the union (i.e., more members for a given amount of resources expended) and to the employee (i.e., the trouble and inconvenience of becoming a union member). To capture the costs of union membership, therefore, the A-P Model incorporates the percentage rate of change of employment in the unionized sectors of the economy. (ΔE_T). The costs of union membership decrease as ΔE_T increases. Together, the variables ΔP_T and ΔE_T measure "the movement of the relative benefits and costs of union membership to workers over time."[5]

Trade Unions as Vehicles of Protest

The trade union's role transcends the purely economic one of raising wages. It serves as a forum through which its members, whose horizons for socio-economic advancement are limited to successful labor force participation, share one another's dreams and disappointments, hopes and tribulations, and successes and failures. Not unexpectedly, therefore, trade unions become vehicles of protest—a means of registering discontent and voicing labor's stock of grievances—during and following periods of widespread unemployment. Thus, a major determinant of trade union growth is labor's stock of grievances. The A-P Model utilizes the amount of unemployment in the preceding trough of the business cycle (U_T^p) to measure labor's stock of grievances. Growth in union membership is assumed to vary directly with U_T^p. In other words, increased unemployment during periods of depressed economic activity generates worker discontent culminating in union membership gains.

Once Again the Law of Diminishing Returns

Trade union growth is not immune from one of the more important "engineering" principles of economics, namely, the law of diminishing returns. A.G. Hines observed that: "As membership increases, there is a diminishing

[5] Op. cit., p. 436.

response to a given intensity of recruiting effort."[6] The A-P Model incorporates the ratio of union employment to total employment (T/E_T) in union sectors to capture the impact of this "engineering" principle upon trade union growth.

Climate of Public Opinion: The Legal Environment

The final explanatory variable of the A-P Model is the legal environment. Principles of law reflect prevailing social, cultural, political, and economic beliefs of society. Specifically, labor law embodies society's attitudes toward unions. Whether union organizing drives succeed or fail depends, in large measure, upon whether the body of law governing the employment relationship is sympathetic or hostile toward union goals and activities. In the absence of a legal index reflecting society's attitudes toward unions, the percentage of membership in the House of Representatives affiliated with the National Democratic Party (D_T) is used to gauge the degree of legal support for unions. Use of D_T as a proxy index of legal support for unions can be justified on several grounds: D_T responds fairly rapidly to changes in the climate of public opinion; the Democratic party has proven itself organized labor's "friend", consistently elicited the allegiance of rank-and-file union members, and consequently reaped most of organized labor's rewards;[7] pro-labor legislation has historically been the product of legislative bodies controlled by the Democratic party.

Empirical Results

The A-P Model of American trade union growth is generated by incorporating the above-described relationships into a single behavioral equation as follows:

$$\Delta T_T = \beta_0 + \beta_1 \Delta P_T + \sum_{i=0}^{N} \beta_{2i} \Delta E_{T-i} + \beta_3 g(U_T^p, T - \widehat{m})$$
$$+ \beta_4 \left[\frac{T}{E}\right]_{T-1} + \beta_5 D_T + \epsilon T,$$

where ΔT_T is the annual percentage change in trade union membership at time T, $g(U_T^p, T-\widehat{m})$ is a function of U_T^p and $T - \widehat{m}$, ϵ_T is a disturbance term.... [8]

The empirical results of fitting the A-P Model to the data for the period 1900–1960 substantiate the hypothesized influences of the variables sketched in the preceding paragraphs. Although all variables are significant and together explain approximately 75 percent of the variance in union growth for the period, they differ in their magnitude of impact upon trade union growth. Each of the economic variables ΔP_T and ΔE_T has a relatively strong impact upon union growth (i.e., a one percentage point increase in either ΔP_T or ΔE_T causing, respectively, .65 and .40 percent point changes in union growth)

[6]A.G. Hines, "Trade Unions and Wage Inflation in the United Kingdom, 1893–1961," *Review of Economics Studies*, (October 1964), 31: 229.

[7]V.O. Key, Jr., *Politics, Parties, and Pressure Groups*, New York: Thomas Y. Crowell Company, 1948, pp. 74–78.

[8]Ashenfelter and Pencavel, "American Trade Union Growth: 1900–1960," p. 439.

whereas relatively large changes in U_T^P and D_T are required before labor union growth is noticeably affected. As for the "engineering" variable, "...the significant coefficients on $\frac{T}{E}$...support the hypothesis that further growth of unions is hampered by their own size."[9]

Other Parameters: The Taylor-Witney Prerequisites, Organizational Structure, and Guiding Philosophy

Conspicuous by their absence from the A-P Model are specific variables representing labor markets, union organizational structure, and trade union philosophy. Specific provision for these variables was not necessary because, by 1900, they had achieved, with the notable exception of trade union philosophy embracing the organizational principle of industrial unionism, their present stages of development (i.e., values). Thus, the intercept term (i.e., constant) of the estimated equation of the A-P Model for the time period 1900–1960 captures the combined influence of modern labor markets, union organizational structure, and trade union philosophy.

The eighteenth and nineteenth centuries, however, were vastly different from the period of time examined by Ashenfelter and Pencavel. As regards labor market structure, for example, the Taylor-Witney prerequisites[10] for the development of a permanent union movement *had not* been met: the worker *had not* been forced by economic circumstance to earn a livelihood through the sale of services in the labor market; the worker *did not* perceive labor market participation as a permanent condition—expectations for socio-economic advancement *were not* tied to successful labor-force participation; and labor market conditions *did not* work to the disadvantage of the individual unorganized worker—successful labor-force participation *was not* limited by prevailing market conditions. These prerequisites were not fulfilled on a wide scale until after the Civil War—until the Industrial Revolution had transformed the economic landscape.[11] Similarly, the American labor movement did not settle upon an operational structure and guiding philosophy until the close of the nineteenth century.

If reliable and consistent data were available for the eighteenth and nineteenth centuries, the combined impact upon trade union growth of primitive labor markets (i.e., the absence of the Taylor-Witney prerequisites), an undeveloped union organizational structure, and an unsettled union philosophy could be determined by re-estimating the A-P behavioral relationship and comparing the results with those for the 1900–1960 time period. A smaller intercept term (i.e., constant) for the earlier time period would reflect the expected negative impact upon growth of the previously noted variables. Unfortunately, the data necessary for such an exercise are not available.

Despite the aforementioned problem, the A-P Model provides an effective

---

[9]Ashenfelter and Pencavel, "American Trade Union Growth: 1900–1060," p. 444.

[10]Benjamin J. Taylor and Fred Witney, *Labor Relations Law*, 3rd edition, Englewood Cliffs, New Jersey: Prentice-Hall, Inc., 1979, pp. 5–7.

[11]*Ibid.*, pp. 5–7.

framework for identifying and analyzing the factors responsible for changes in trade union membership, structure, and philosophy. Thus, it is within this framework that the following discussion of the American labor movement is set.

1790–1890: Building the Foundation: A Period of Search and Experimentation

The American Revolution forced the colonies to become self-sufficient. Interruption of trade with England turned demand for industrial products inward, thereby stimulating the growth of domestic industry and, with it, the demand for skilled labor. To meet the demand for skilled labor, apprenticeship standards were relaxed, most often by conscription of child trainees and the reduction in the length of time of the apprenticeship. Skilled tradesmen responded by forming associations to protest the debasement of their trade and the resultant increase in labor supply. As Professor Taft observed: "Complaints against a surplus of learners, runaway apprentices, and 'half-way' journeymen were frequent among the early trade societies."[12] Although spontaneous, unrelated, and ephemeral in nature,[13] these organizations of skilled artisans, shoemakers, building tradesmen, and printers shared a common characteristic with their modern-day counterparts—the goal of protecting the workers' standard of living from various erosive forces. Whereas the source of real wage erosion was a general increase in the price level (ΔP_T in the A-P Model) during the 1900–1960 time period, the source of real wage erosion during the late eighteenth century was a reduction in money wages brought about by an increased supply of poorly trained craftsmen. In both instances, the result was the same—the formation of workers' associations and/or increases in association membership. The foregoing causal relationships lend credence to the hypothesis that trade unions are, at least in part, defensive organizations.[14]

The Nature of Early Bargaining Efforts

The early trade union approach to collective bargaining warrants comment. The natural tendency is to attribute properties characteristic of the modern process to the early attempts to resolve the problems of the workplace. To do so would be the equivalent of crediting the properties and faculties of modern man to the Neanderthal man. Although sharing several properties in common with the modern-day process (e.g., the imposition of costs to force agreement), the early attempts at decision-making could not by any stretch of the imagination be characterized as bilateral in nature—they were in no sense joint problem-solving efforts. Quite the contrary, negotiations were typically

[12] Philip Taft, *Organized Labor In American History*, New York: Harper and Row, Publishers, 1964, p. 7.

[13] The life-span of the first union, a society of shoemakers in Philadelphia, was less than a year.

[14] See: Horace B. Davis, "The Theory of Union Growth," *Quarterly Journal of Economics*, (August 1941), **55**: 611–633; A.A. Blum, "Why Unions Grow," *Labor History*, (Winter 1968), **9**: 39-72.

unilateral in nature. Workers' association viewed their demands as final—not subject to the familiar "give-and-take" of the present-day negotiation process.

> The demands that the body drew up were demands that they expected to have met in full. They were not bargaining proposals, set two or three times higher than the settlement price, but specific bills of wages, sometimes printed and ready to be posted in the shops immediately upon acceptance. Compromise was therefore not intended. The union members had previously sworn among themselves not to work for less than the wages stated in their demands, and they were serious in that oath.[15]

Professor Richardson describes the early actions of employers in a similar vein.

> The employer's approach was equally unilateral. If in a strong position, the employer simply ignored the union demands, or refused them and let the union action run its course. If in a weak position, the employer might accede to the union demands until a better day, when the tables could be turned on the union through a unilateral abolishment of the gains made.[16]

Thus, as Professors Chamberlain and Kuhn have aptly concluded:

> This was not. . .a process of negotiation. It was a procedure for trial of economic strength to determine whose wages decisions would prevail—the union's or the employer's. The spirit of no compromise was further encouraged because certain of the employers, disorganized as they were, frequently conceded to the union at the start of the campaign. This broke the possibility of bringing all the employers into a solid front and also made it difficult for the unions to negotiate for a settlement on any less favorable terms than those already won.[17]

While there were recorded instances of bilateral decision-making (e.g., the negotiations between the Philadelphia Journeymen Cordwainers and their employers in 1799), unilateralism was the norm. Conference rather than confrontation, as the accepted method of union-management dealings, would have to await the establishment of permanent trade unions, more equal distribution of bargaining power, and the demonstration of the mutual advantages of joint decision-making. These conditions were not realized on a wide scale until the late nineteenth century.

Widening Markets: The Emergence of the Factory

Hostilities in Europe and the War of 1812 accelerated the development of American manufacturing. The chief beneficiary was the textile industry. "The shortage of imported cottons increased prices and made the industry attractive

---

[15] Neil W. Chamberlain and James W. Kuhn, *Collective Bargaining*, 2nd Edition, New York: McGraw-Hill Book Company, 1965, p. 6.

[16] Reed C. Richardson, *Collective Bargaining by Objectives: A Positive Approach*, Englewood Cliffs, New Jersey: Prentice-Hall, Inc., 1977, p. 4.

[17] Neil Chamberlain and James W. Kuhn, *Collective Bargaining*, pp. 6–7.

to investors who had heretofore placed their monies in commerce."[18] Although less pronounced in other industries, a familiar pattern began to emerge— household manufacture on a custom-order basis giving way to speculative employment and production (i.e., employment of journeymen and production of goods in advance of demand) by merchant capitalists which, in turn, would give way to the modern factory system of production.

Underlying the expansion of American industry during the first twenty years of the nineteenth century was the widening of markets. Professor Commons identifies "the extension of markets through growth of population and improved transportation"[19] as the single most important factor responsible for the growth of industry and the origin of industrial classes.

> It was the widening of these markets with their lower levels of competition and quality, but without changes in the instruments of production, that destroyed the primitive identity of master and journeymen cordwainers and split their community of interest into the modern alignment of employers' associations and trade union...It was a struggle on the part of the merchant employer to require the same minimum quality of work for each of the markets, but lower rates of wages on the work destined for the wider and lower markets. It was a struggle on the part of the journeymen to require the same minimum wage on work destined for each market, but with the option of a higher wage for a higher market. The conflict came over the wage and quality of work destined for the widest, lowest, and newest market.[20]

To meet the increased competition brought about by extended markets and to minimize the greater risks attendant to production in advance of demand (i.e., risks associated with the factory system of production), employers attempted to lower production costs by cutting both wage rates and working standards. Workers reacted by forming trade unions.

Trade Union Instability

Despite the impetus to trade union growth provided by employer wage cutting undertaken to meet the competition created by widened markets (the equivalent stimulus of an increase of ΔP_T in the A-P Model), by periods of rapid price increase (e.g., 1832–37), and by the steady but slow expansion of industrial employment (ΔE_T in the A-P Model), union membership gains were unspectacular during the first half of the nineteenth century. Indeed, it was not a question of growth for labor organizations but one of their very survival. As Professor Commons succinctly noted, unions had "great difficulty...in staying organized for any purpose." Being highly unstable organizations, they were, in most instances, "mowed down and swept out of existence"[21] during periods of depressed economic activity (e.g., 1810–1820, 1839–1852). Although in-

[18] Philip Taft, *Organized Labor in American History*, p. 3.
[19] John R. Commons et al., *History of Labour in the United States*, pp. 6–7.
[20] *Ibid.*, p. 32.
[21] *Ibid.*, pp. 59–61.

creased membership costs associated with periods of recession and depression (ΔE_T in the A-P Model) certainly contributed to union organizational difficulties during this period, this factor was not the root of the problem—trade unions would later survive and even prosper during periods of high unemployment (e.g., 1873 and the 1930's). Organized labor's instability was primarily the result of a combination of other more fundamental factors.

Politics and Utopian Reform—The Wrong Direction

First, any impulse toward growth in union membership stemming from worker discontent created by extended periods of unemployment (U_T^p in the A-P Model) was quickly dissipated through misdirection to political action and for attempts to remake society to fit the preconceptions of various reformers. Thus, the Mechanics Union of Trade Associations, the first city-wide federation of trade unions formed in 1827 to pool organized labor's resources for the solution of problems of common concern, was transformed, in the course of a little more than a year, into the Working Men's Political Party. Although the era of Jacksonian Democracy provided a fertile environment for political action, the Working Men's Party passed from the scene following the election of 1831. After a brief return to "bread-and-butter" trade unionism occasioned by the rapid increase in the general price level during the period 1832–37 (ΔP_T in the A-P Model), organized labor's attention was again diverted from economic to more esoteric goals—this time by the financial panic of 1837.

> The panic. . . appears to have been caused by speculation induced by an excessive expansion of bank credits, followed by a rapid rise in imports and increases in foreign debts. The demand of English banks for settlement of adverse balance of payments led to fear that it would cause large exports of specie. Banks began to restrict credit, with the consequent decline in economic activity.[22]

An influx of immigrants during the 1840's compounded the already severe unemployment problem. Frustration and hopelessness led workers to question the system itself. labor's stock of grievances (U_T^p in the A-P Model) found expression in a variety of political and utopian ventures rather than in a renewed commitment to business unionism. These alternatives to American capitalism ranged from George Henry Evans' proposal for land reform to Charles Fourier's and Albert Brisbane's scheme for reorganizing society into cooperative colonies called Phalanastries. As Professor Richardson caustically observed: "the labor movement became overshadowed by the preachments of the apostles of utopian reform and an idealized society."[23] In short, organized labor's flirtation with various alternatives to business unionism neutralized worker grievances/discontent (U_T^p in the A-P Model) as a factor contributing to union growth during the first half of the nineteenth century—a factor which would exercise a positive influence upon growth in subsequent periods, once organized labor was firmly committed to a philosophy of "bread-and-butter" trade unionism.

---

[22] Philip Taft, *Organized Labor in American History*, pp. 32–33.
[23] Reed C. Richardson, *Collective Bargaining by Objectives: A Positive Approach*, p. 9.

Socio-Economic Advancement—Obstacle to Organization

Second, although the "engineering" principle of "a diminishing response to a given intensity of recruiting effort"[24] (T/E_T in the A-P Model) did not hinder trade union organizational efforts during the period, recruiting efforts did encounter similar but more serious resistance from another source. For the most part, workers viewed labor market participation as a necessary but temporary rung on the ladder of socio-economic advancement. Once a skill had been learned and/or sufficient capital accumulated, the worker's perception was that of ascending to the top rung of the ladder–self-employment. Failing to achieve this socio-economic pinnacle, the worker could always resort to homesteading and farming. In very few instances, did workers view labor force participation as a permanent station in life. As a result, workers did not see the need for unions or union membership. Hence, worker perception of the process of socio-economic advancement proved to be a formidable and often times impregnable barrier for trade union organizational efforts during the first half of the nineteenth century.

A Hostile Legal Environment

Finally, the climate of public opinion (D_T in the A-P Model) was hostile towards unions and union programs. The animosity of employers and the ill-will of other segments of society were nowhere more clearly evident than in the body of law governing the labor management relationship. The common law doctrine of criminal conspiracy branded unions as criminal in nature and subjected union members to fines and/or imprisonment. Although the stigma of criminality was gradually removed by Shaw's decision in *Commonwealth v. Hunt* in 1842, other legal instruments were devised which effectively impeded labor union growth throughout most of the next ninety years (See Chapter 4).

Need for a Broader Organizational Base

Despite the many obstructions to union growth, some progress was made during the period. Trade unionists came to recognize the need for organization on a broader scale than the local—the local could not effectively cope with the competition generated by regional and national markets. Efforts toward a broader organizational base initially took the form of the city-wide federation (e.g., Mechanics' Union of Trade Association in 1827, General Trades' Union of New York City in 1833, etc.). The first national trades' association, the National Trades' Union, was an outgrowth of a national conference of trades' unions and trade societies convened by the General Trades' Union of New York City in 1834. The National Trades' Union served as an ideal forum and vehicle for exchange of information and discussion of problems confronting locals of the same trade from different geographic regions. As such, it proved to be a needed catalyst to the formation of national unions. Although none survived beyond 1840, five nationals were established during the period immediately following creation of the National Trades' Union.

[24] A.G. Hines, "Trade Unions and Wage Inflation in the United Kingdom, 1893–1961," *Review of Economics Studies,* (October, 1964), **31**: 229.

Working Class Consciousness: Prerequisite for Union Growth

Also evident during this period of time was the growing awareness on the part of an increasing number of workers that their socio-economic advancement depended upon successful labor force participation. A cursory reading of the constitutions of the aforementioned labor organizations reveal an emerging working class consciousness—a prerequisite for the development of a viable and permanent labor movement according to Professors' Taylor and Witney.[25] For example, the preamble of the Mechanics' Union of Trade Associations states:

> The real object of this association is to avert, if possible, the desolating evils which must inevitably arise from a depreciation of the intrinsic value of human labor; to raise the mechanical and productive *classes* to that condition of true independence and equality which their practical skill and ingenuity, their immense utility to the nation and their growing intelligence are beginning imperiously to demand: to...and to assist, in conjunction with such other institutions of this nature as shall hereafter be formed throughout the union in establishing a just balance of power, both mental, moral, political, and scientific, between all the various *classes* and individuals which constitute society at large. [Emphasis added][26]

In a similar vein, the constitution of the National Trades' Union declares one goal of the union to be the recommendation of:

> such measures to the various unions represented herein as may tend to advance the moral and intellectual condition and pecunary interests of the laboring *classes*...[Emphasis added][27]

"Bread-And-Butter Unionism": A Viable Philosophy

Although another forty years would pass before "bread-and-butter trade unionism" would become the widely accepted philosophy underpinning the American labor movement, its proponents grew in number during the first half of the nineteenth century. Trade union disenchantment with political and reformist schemes to remake the economic fabric of society grew as each such experiment met with failure. This disillusionment led many trade union organizations to explicitly ban all such activity. For example, as early as the mid-1830's the Philadelphia General Trades' Union adopted a constitutional provision which stated: "No party, political, or religious questions shall at any time be agitated in, or acted upon by this Union."[28] The more astute among early trade union leaders quickly perceived that societal acceptance of trade unionism, and, hence, its ultimate success, were contingent upon working

---

[25] Benjamin J. Taylor and Fred Witney, *Labor Relations Law*, 3rd Edition, Englewood Cliffs, New Jersey, Prentice-Hall, Inc., 1979, pp. 5–7.

[26] John R. Commons, et al., *A Documentary History of American Industrial Society*, V, Cleveland, Ohio: The Arthur H. Clark Co., 1910, p. 89–90.

[27]*Ibid.*, VI, p. 225.

[28]*Ibid.*, p. 347.

within the framework of the newly emerging market capitalism and avoiding political entanglements. For these farsighted labor officials, adoption of a philosophy of "pure-and-simple business trade unionism" was the key to successful implementation of the programs and goals of organized labor.

Civil War: Catalyst for Growth

The Civil War provided a sharp stimulus to economic activity. The demand that it created for goods and materials had a catalytic impact upon the economic transformation of society begun several decades earlier. Shortly after the close of hostilities in 1865, much of the geographic expanse of the nation had been bridged by various transcontinental railway systems. Greater accessibility by producers to both resource markets and population centers intensified competition. Firm survival depended upon adoption of modern production processes and the latest cost-cutting techniques. Factors which had previously retarded trade union growth crumbled in the wake of the drive for economic efficiency. For example, increased capital requirements necessitated by more intense competition precluded worker entry to the capitalist class, thereby deepening worker awareness that labor force participation was a permanent station in life. Likewise, the widespread substitution of capital for labor in the agricultural sector of economy severely limited self-employment opportunities in farming.

In addition to removing barriers to union growth, the intensity and pace of the economic transformation provided workers direct incentives for organization. Confronted by the need to cut labor costs to remain competitive, employers turned to wage reductions, lengthened workweeks, accelerated production schedules (i.e., intensity of work effort), the breakdown of complex work processes into simple repetitive tasks (i.e., specialization and division of labor), and employment of immigrants, women, and children as cheap forms of labor. So popular did the practice of using immigrants as a cheap source of labor become that it was not uncommon for an employer to send ". . . private agents to Europe to secure help; mines and railroads suffering from want of labor did the same."[29] Regardless of the specific cost-cutting tactic utilized in a given labor-management relationship, the net effect was the same—a reduction in the economic well-being of the employees (the equivalent impact of ΔP in the A-P Model).

Buttressed by wartime inflation, the growth of manufacturing employment, and Lincoln's noninterventionist stance concerning labor disputes (ΔP_T, ΔE_T, and D_T, respectively in the A-P Model), the cost-cutting tactics of employers created an environment conducive to the formation and growth of labor organizations. Twenty–four national unions were established between 1860 and 1869. Not surprisingly, the unions surfaced in the growth sectors of the economy. The more notable of these unions, the dates of organization, and the proximate factors precipitating formation are listed in Table 1.

---

[29] Emerson David Fite, *Social and Industrial Conditions in the North During the Civil War*, New York: The Macmillan Company, 1910, p. 190.

TABLE 2–1.   National Unions Formed in the Wake of The Civil War

Union	Organization Date	Causal Factor
American Miners' Association	January 18, 1861	Wage Cuts
Brotherhood of Locomotive Engineers	May 8, 1863	Wage Cuts
Bricklayers' International Union	October 16, 1865	Wage Cuts/Excess Supply of Labor
The Knights of St. Crispin (Shoemakers)	March, 1867	Technological Displacement/Excess Supply of Labor

Source: Philip Taft, *Organized Labor in American History*, New York: Harper & Row, Publishers, 1964, pp. 53–60.

The National Labor Union: First Labor Federation

As the Industrial Revolution gathered momentum and changed the nation's economic landscape, the need for an organizational framework transcending the national union soon became apparent. Individual, unaffiliated, national unions were not an effective counterveiling force to the rapidly developing corporate power structure. Nor were they proficient in dealing with problems national in scope and character (e.g., immigration, child labor, monetary reform, etc.). "What was required was an effective combining of the strength of organized labor nationwide on matters of common interest."[30] The first postwar effort in this direction was the National Labor Union, founded in 1866. Although formation of a nationwide labor organization was conceptually sound and a practical necessity, the National Labor Union was doomed to failure by its operating philosophy and organizational structure. As Professor Taft pointedly concluded:

> The National Labor Union could never have become the labor federation of the future, because its *basic approach* to the solution of economic problems was *political*. It believed that shorter hours could best be achieved through legislation, and it was suspicious of the efficiency of the strike as a weapon and means of defense. Moreover, *its failure to limit membership to unions* meant that *reformers* and *reform politicians*, usually the more vocal, would *dominate* the proceedings of its conventions and its policies. It offered little beyond friendly sentiments to the trade union local seeking support. Consequently, it could never rally the majority or even a substantial minority of organized workers. Of the more than twenty international unions which functioned through most of the time the National Labor Union was active, not more than four sent delegates to any of the conventions. The number of unions that were represented was never a large proportion of the total active. Inevitably, the National Labor Union became increasingly committed to political activity, with the ultimate result that it finally expired. [Emphasis added][31]

In short, the National Labor Union passed from the scene because of its failure

[30] Reed C. Richardson, *Collective Bargaining by Objectives: A Positive Approach*, p.7.
[31] Philip Taft, *Organized Labor in American History*, p. 65.

to respect individual trade union autonomy in organizational and policy matters and its failure to adopt a business (i.e., "bread-and-butter") trade union philosophy.

Violence Begets Violence: The Molly Maguires

The postwar growth in union membership carried through until the panic of 1873. A precipitous decline in farm prices resulting from an oversupply of agricultural products in the wake of increased efficiency and the conversion of formerly nonproductive public land to agricultural use triggered the depression which lasted until 1878. Sharply falling farm income generated a domino-like reduction in business activity throughout all sectors of the economy. Rising unemployment and sluggish economic activity (the equivalent of ΔE_T and ΔP_T in the A-P Model) abruptly reversed the upward growth trend in trade union membership. Unlike previous depressions, however, the panic of 1873 did not result in the wholesale elimination of national trade unions. Capitalizing on a broader organizational base (i.e., the national union) and drawing upon an experienced leadership hierarchy, many trade unions were able to overcome adversity and survive the severe slump in business conditions—a "first" in the annals of the American labor movement.

The success of organized labor during the decade preceding the panic of 1873 can be gauged by the magnitude and intensity of opposition it generated on the part of employers during the depression years which followed. Emboldened by the depression-weakened labor market (ΔE_T in the A-P Model) and recognizing an excellent opportunity to work off excess inventories (particularly in raw materials industries), employers launched a campaign designed to re-establish the absolute discretionary decision-making authority of management which had been eroded by organized labor during the preceding decade. The use of strikebreakers (i.e., scabs), blacklists, spies, and injunctions to enforce wage cuts spawned violence which, in turn, begot additional violence and destruction of property. For example, the wage cuts initiated by the Baltimore and Ohio Railroad in July of 1877 bred strikes and violence which quickly spread throughout the country.

A number of unions became secret organizations to weather the storm of employer opposition. By far, the most publicized of these secret societies was the Molly Maguires. According to Professor Taft, the Mollies operated in the

> ...anthracite mining area, and much of the violence against persons and property was charged to its members; arson and assault, maiming and murder were its weapons...
> ...Under the rules of the Molly Maguires, any member might make a formal complaint to the bodymaster—the local head. If it were decided that action against a person was required, members from a distant community would be obtained to assault or kill the offender.[32]

Contrary to popular legend, the Molly Maguires was not a labor union but

[32] Philip Taft, *Organized Labor in American History*, p. 73.

rather an ethnic vigilante organization concerned with the prevention and redress of the exploitation of Irish Immigrants. Its reign of terror and violence was only tangentially related to labor relations problems.

> Violence was endemic to the coal fields of the time, and in some instances members of the Molly Maguires were themselves its victims. Hatred between ethnic groups nourished by diverse national origin and religious affiliation were also causes, and robbery and personal vengeance were occasional motives.[33]

Regardless of cause, motive, or source, the blame for the violence was laid squarely at the doorstep of organized labor. Organized labor was lumped with other groups perceived by the public to be hostile to American capitalism—the American way of life. The violence and secrecy-tarnished image of trade unions in the public's eye (D_T in the A-P Model) compounded organizational problems brought on by the depressed level of economic activity and employer opposition.

Detour: The Knights of Labor

One of the secret labor organizations to survive the extended depression of the 1870's was the Nobel Order of the Knights of Labor. Founded in December of 1869 upon the basic principle of cooperation, the organization's stated goal was the elevation of man through the collective efforts of men "who toiled". More specifically, the Knights of Labor hoped to establish an economic system

> which will eventually make every man his own master—every man his own employer, a system which will give the laborer a fair proportion of the products of his toil...[34]

Establishment of the new order was to be effected by means of producers' and consumers' cooperatives, passage of various types of reform legislation (e.g., in banking, land ownership, child labor laws, etc.), and selective use of traditional trade union weapons. Deeply suspicious of organization by specific trade or craft because it neglected the unskilled and focused worker attention upon purely trade concerns (i.e., "bread-and-butter" issues such as higher wages, better working conditions, etc.), the Knights of Labor adopted the organizational structure of "one big union."[35] Only through such a broad-based organizational structure, according to Terrence V. Powderly, Grand Master Workman (i.e., President) of the Knights, could "the errors of the purely trade society"[36] be avoided and the progressive program of the Knights of Labor be implemented.

---

[33] Philip Taft, *Organized Labor in American History*, p. 75.

[34] *Record of Proceeding of the Fourth Regular Session of the General Assembly*, September, 1880, p. 171.

[35] "One big union" refers to an organizational structure where under workers directly achieve membership as individuals without first becoming members of a union organized by craft or occupation. Membership is thus open to skilled and unskilled alike; the only requirement is that the individual "work for a living."

[36] Terrence V. Powderly, *Thirty Years of Labor*, Philadelphia: T.V. Powderly, 1890, p. 81.

Membership in the Knights of Labor increased tenfold from 70,000 in 1884 to 700,000 by 1886. Rather than reflecting the success of the labor organization in meeting the basic needs of its members, increased membership mirrored strong external growth impulses, namely: recovery from the prolonged economic slump of the 1870's and the consequent tightening of labor markets (ΔE_T in the A-P Model); an increased level of worker discontent (i.e., labor's stock of grievances) generated by the severity of the preceding depression (U_T^p in the A-P Model); an improved climate of public opinion regarding union goals and objectives brought about by the public's fear of increased corporate market concentration, regulation of supply, and price fixing (D_T in the A-P Model); and a series of successful strikes carried out against the Union Pacific (1885) and Wabash (1886) Railroads. The last factor— successful strike activity—is classified as an external growth factor on the grounds that the Knights of Labor never totally embraced the strike as an important vehicle for achieving their goals and objectives. Quite the contrary, Terrence Powderly regarded it as "...an ineffectual and harmful weapon."[37] An accurate assessment of the Knights' fortunes during the first six years of the 1880's is that the organization grew in membership in spite of itself.

Rapid membership growth caused internal and external problems for the Knights of Labor. The Order simply was not equipped structurally, philosophically, or managerially to effectively accommodate the large number of workers with widely divergent interests and backgrounds that were added to its membership rolls following the successful strikes of '85 and '86. General disregard of trade union autonomy with respect to internal union affairs and overt rejection of the organizational principle of exclusive jurisdiction[38] bred dissension and created disciplinary problems among rank-and-file members. Tensions were further heightened by the continuing conflict between the "bread-and-butter" concerns of the Order's members and the esoteric concerns of its leadership. Compounding these problems was the lack of any ability on the part of the Order's leadership to manage, direct, and control an organization the size of which the Knights of Labor had become. Lacking a sound organizational structure, an operational philosophy, and basic managerial expertise, the Knights of Labor literally collapsed under its own weight. Although the proximate cause of the organization's demise was a series of poorly timed, planned, and executed strikes in the railroad (1886), meatpacking (1886), and coal industries (1888), the underlying cause was the organization's own inherent weakness. As Professor Taft tersely observed: "The Knights of Labor expired because it could not fulfill any function..."[39]

A Functional Philosophy and Structure: The American Federation of Labor

As noted earlier, astute labor leaders had recognized the need for a national federation of independent trade unions since the time of the Civil War.

---

[37] Philip Taft, *Organized Labor in American History,* p. 90.

[38] Under the principle of exclusive jurisdiction a single union is authorized to organize all workers in a specific occupation or industry—"one union per occupation or industry."

[39] Philip Taft, *Organized Labor in American History,* p. 20.

Discussions concerning the formation of such a federation were initiated in the late 1870's. At the forefront of this movement was the International Typographical Union. Its leadership was convinced that the long-run success of a national federation depended upon its focusing upon "bread-and-butter" issues and not becoming involved with independent political schemes or identified with what were perceived to be radical reformist groups. These and other trade union leaders with similar views ". . . came to realize from observation and experience that dabbling with groups hostile to American capitalism only concentrated all the hostility and force of society against the labor movement."[40] The efforts of the pure trade unionists came to fruition with the formation of the Federation of Organized Trades and Labor Unions of the United States and Canada (FOTLU) in November of 1881.

The pragmatism which would later earmark the American labor movement surfaced shortly after the formation of the FOTLU in 1881. Eschewing direct confrontation with the Knights over basic principles of organization and operation, the pure trade unionists, anxious to realize any benefits that might result from association with the Knights, first worked for change from within as members of the Knights of Labor. Unsuccessful in their efforts to reshape the Knights' basic principles, the goal of the trade unionists became one of peaceful coexistence within the "one big union" framework. Only when their very existence was threatened by the Knights' continued disregard of trade union jurisdiction and autonomy in the wake of the large influx of new members following the successful strikes of '85 and '86 did the pure trade unions take drastic action. On December 8, 1886, forty-two delegates from various trade unions, twelve of which were affiliated with the FOTLU, met in Columbus, Ohio, and formed the American Federation of Labor (AFL).

The new labor federation bore the stamp of its chief architect and first president, Samuel Gompers (1850-1924). Gompers' heretofore unparalleled influence upon the American labor movement was the result of:

> his intelligence and consuming loyalty to the trade union movement; his ability to devote endless hours in its service; his remarkable capacity for work; his knowledge of the needs of labor and his power to express them in writing; his talent for compromise and negotiation; and finally, his acceptance of the limited power which he and the federation could exercise upon affiliates.[41]

Gompers' unionism was an opportunistic, day-to-day, "bread-and-butter" (i.e., wage-centered) business trade unionism founded on acceptance of the American system of capitalism—acceptance of American capitalism because of the possibilities for real wage gains provided thereunder. Given America's economic, social, and political heritage, Gompers felt it imperative that trade unions disavow all radical reformist causes, work through existing political parties, and concentrate upon the short-run, day-to-day problems of the work place. More specifically, trade union activity should properly be limited to increasing labor's share of the fruits of production through the process of

---

[40] Reed C. Richardson, *Collective Bargaining by Objectives: A Positive Approach*, p. 10.
[41] Philip Taft, *Organized Labor in American History*, p. 116.

TABLE 2–2.   Organizational and Operational Principles of the American Federation of Labor (AFL)

I. *Trade Union Autonomy:* Necessary condition to secure national trade union affiliation.

II. *Exclusive Trade Union Jurisdiction*—"One Union per Occupation or Trade": Prerequisite for avoiding internecine warfare between unions resulting in the internal dissipation of scarce resources; the AFL, with a few exceptions, denied affiliation to any union not organized exclusively by craft or trade.

III. *Pure and Simple Business Trade Unionism*—"Bread-and-Butter Trade Unionism": Acceptance and endorsement of American capitalism and a commitment to the solution of the day-to-day problems of the work place which would expand labor's long–run share of output under capitalism; essential for public and rank-and-file support.

IV. *Reliance Upon the Strike and Pressure Politics to Achieve Goals:* Use of the existing political framework and avoidance of independent labor party political action.

collective bargaining—collective bargaining made effective by the strike and pressure politics.

The beliefs of Samuel Gompers became the guiding principles of the American Federation of Labor. These are summarized in Table 2–2. The basic organizational structure and guiding philosophy of the American labor movement were determined with the formation of the American Federation of Labor[42] in 1886. The stage was set for the spectacular gains in union membership experienced over the next fifty-five years.

---

[42] For an in-depth discussion of the advantages of affiliation with the AFL, see Chapter 5.

Chapter 3

The American Labor Movement:

Growth, Structure and Philosophy—II

The emergence of the American Federation of Labor (AFL) constitutes a benchmark in American labor history. Modern labor structure and philosophy date from the formation of the AFL in 1886. This chapter examines the growth of the American labor movement since that date (i.e., the "modern" labor movement) within the framework of the Ashenfelter-Pencavel Model. Thus, it continues and concludes the analysis of American trade union growth begun in Chapter 2.

1890–1940: Take Off

Judged solely by the yardstick of its contribution to the growth of union membership, the American Federation of Labor must be given a poor grade for its performance during the first eight years of the 1890's. Typical of the fate of unions in general was the experience of the United Brotherhood of Carpenters and Joiners; its membership declined from 54,000 in 1893 to 28,000 in 1897— a precipitous decline of almost forty-five percent. One must look beyond absolute numbers, however, to accurately evaluate the performance of the American labor movement during this period. Given the long-run secular decline in prices from 1881 to 1897 which reduced employee benefits union membership (ΔP_T in the A-P Model) and forced labor from an offensive to a defensive position[1]; given the widespread unemployment of the depression years of 1893–1897 which significantly increased the costs of union membership to employees (ΔE_T in the A-P Model); and given the growing power of big business and its increasing hostility toward unionism as manifest during the

---

[1] Alvin H. Hansen, "Cycles of Strikes", *American Economic Review*, (December 1921), **11**: p. 618.

unsuccessful strikes against the Homestead Steel Works of Carnegie Steel Corporation in 1892 and the Pullman Palace Car Company in 1894, trade unions did well simply to survive the period intact.

Triumph of the Organization/Operational Principles of the American Federation of Labor

Ironically, the socio-economic environment which wrecked havoc on union membership rolls during the early 1890's simultaneously set in motion changes which would later contribute to impressive trade union gains. Specifically, the depression of 1893–97 increased labor's stock of grievances (U_T^p in the A-P Model), thereby increasing the attractiveness of unions as vehicles of protest—a means of registering discontent and voicing labor's stock of grievances. In addition, the climate of public opinion (D_T in the A-P Model) became more sympathetic toward unionism.

> Prolonged unemployment, with its accompanying destitution and suffering, tarnished the reputation of business, and the public regarded, at least for a time, the workers' quest for greater security and higher pay as justifiable. Exposures of corporate derelictions made the demands for some countervailing power appear reasonable.[2]

By the end of the decade, seventeen states had passed legislation prohibiting employers from discriminating against workers with regard to hire or tenure of employment because of membership in a labor organization. The state legislation also typically outlawed the yellow-dog contract—prohibited employers from making union non-membership a condition of employment. On the federal level, Congress passed the Erdman Act (1898) banning similar discriminatory behavior on the part of employers in the railroad industry.

With the return of prosperity in 1898, the aforementioned factors combined with a tightening labor market and rising prices (ΔE_T and ΔP_T, respectively, in the A-P Model) to drive union membership dramatically upward. As Table 3–1 indicates, trade union membership increased from 447,000 in 1897 to 2,072,700 in 1904. Of the more than 2 million workers

TABLE 3–1. Total Membership of American Trade Unions, 1897–1911

Year	Membership	Year	Membership	Year	Membership
1897	447,000	1902	1,375,900	1907	2,122,800
1898	500,700	1903	1,913,900	1908	2,130,600
1899	611,000	1904	2,913,700	1909	2,047,400
1900	868,500	1905	2,022,300	1910	2,184,200
1901	1,124,700	1906	1,958,700	1911	2,382,800

Source: Selig Perlman and Philip Taft, *History of Labor in the United States*, Vol. IV, New York: Macmillan Publishing Co., Inc., 1935, p. 13.

[2] Philip Taft, *Organized Labor in American History*, New York: Harper and Row Publishers, 1964, p. 162.

belonging to unions in 1904, four out of every five were members of trade unions affiliated with the American Federation of Labor.[3] The foregoing statistics testify to the efficacy and inherent logic of the organizational/operational principles of the AFL.

Retrenchment

Compared to the growth years of 1898–1904, the following twelve years represented a period of relative stagnation in trade union growth. Organized labor's lackluster performance was the result of several factors.

The Open-Shop Campaign

First, spearheaded by the National Association of Manufacturers (NAM), employers mounted a vigorous anti-union, open-shop campaign. The tenor of the NAM-led campaign against unionism can be gauged from the remarks of its president, David M. Parry, to the New Orleans Convention in 1903, namely:

> Organized labor...does not place its reliance upon reason and justice, but on strikes, boycotts and coercion. It is, in all essential features, a mob knowing no master except its own will. Its history is stained with blood and ruin...It denies to those outside its ranks the individual right to dispose of their labor as they see fit— a right that is one of the most sacred and fundamental of American liberty.[4]

Through direct assistance to employers confronted by union demands for organization and recognition, through spoken and printed propaganda designed to undermine public support of unions; and through lobbying efforts delaying passage of favorable labor legislation, the anti-union campaign effectively impeded extended union organization.

Continued Court Hostility

Second, the United States Supreme Court rendered a series of decisions which severely hampered union organizational efforts. Of crucial importance were the Court's decisions[5] in *Loewe v. Lawlor* (1908) applying the Sherman Act to unions, thereby severely limiting the self-help weapons available to unions for organization; in *Adair v. United States* (1908) invalidating the Erdman Act of 1898; in *Coppage v. Kansas* (1915) striking down protective labor legislation at the state level; and in *Hitchman Coal Co. v. Mitchell* (1917) upholding the enforceability of yellow-dog contracts through use of the injunction.

Industrial Unionism—The Wobblies

Finally, the American Federation of Labor contributed to its own organizational difficulties by ignoring the unskilled and semi-skilled workers in

---

[3] Selig Perlman and Philip Taft, *History of Labor in the United States*, Vol. IV, New York: Macmillan Publishing Co., Inc., 1935, p. 13.

[4] Guilford Taylor, *Labor Policies of the National Association of Manufacturers*, Urbana, Illinois: University of Illinois, 1928, pp. 35–36.

[5] These landmark decisions of the Supreme Court are explored in detail in Chapter 4.

the rapidly expanding mass-production industries. The mass-production factory called for an entirely different approach to organization than by craft. Mass-production workers lacked the critical characteristic which made piecemeal organization by craft possible and, more importantly, effective—an essential identifiable skill or trade. Without this skill or trade, industrial workers were easily replaced. Therefore, to be effective and preclude worker replacement during job actions, organization had to encompass the firm's *entire* workforce, minor differences in skill levels notwithstanding; mass-production required organization on an industrial basis. AFL leaders, with the memories of the problems created by the Knights of Labor's brand of industrial unionism (i.e., "one big union") still indelibly etched upon their minds, stubbornly refused to modify the craft-union organizational principle to accommodate the needs of the industrial worker. Shunned by the AFL, many unskilled and semi-skilled workers turned to radical labor groups for assistance. The most prominent of these was the Industrial Workers of the World (IWW). Founded in 1905 upon the radical premise that "the working class and the employing class have nothing in common,"[6] the Wobblies (IWW) eagerly welcomed industrial workers who were denied the opportunity of AFL membership because they did not possess a skill. Thus, not only did the AFL miss a golden opportunity to directly add new members, it also unwittingly made organization along traditional craft lines more difficult by forcing unskilled and semiskilled workers into the ranks of maverick labor organizations whose violent tactics and radical ideologies undermined public support for unions in general. Despite the severity of the problems encountered during the period, organized labor managed to increase its membership to approximately 3 million by 1917.

Government Support During World War I: The Works' Council

The United States entry into World War I proved a boon to organized labor. Union membership skyrocketed from 3 million in 1917 to over 5 million by 1920. This spurt in union membership was the result of a combination of three factors, namely: an absolute labor shortage brought about by expanded production of war materials, military conscription, and curtailment of immigration (ΔE_T in the A-P Model); a phenomenal rise in prices resulting from excess wartime demand (ΔP_T in the A-P Model); and government protection of the collective bargaining process (D_T in the A-P Model) granted by the Wilson Administration in exchange for a no-strike pledge and cooperation by the AFL for the duration of the war effort.

The Wilson Administration's program to guarantee uninterrupted production through orderly and peaceful labor-management relations during the war years warrants further discussion. Although official recognition and protection of the rights to organize and bargain collectively were conducive to membership gains by established trade unions during World War I, another facet of the program, the "work's council", proved to be important in the spread of unionism to unorganized sectors of the economy after the war. "Work's councils" were established by the National War Labor Board (NWLB) in those

[6] Preamble to the Constitution of the International Workers of the World (IWW).

industries where trade unions had made little or no penetration. Their purpose was the joint resolution of the problems of the work place (i.e., disputes concerning wages, hours, and other terms and conditions of employment) by management representatives and by employee representatives—employee representatives selected on a departmental or shop basis rather than by skill or trade. So successful was the work's-council concept during the war that it became the evolutionary base for the employee representation plans (ERP's) of the 1920's, which, in turn, unfortunately from management's perspective, provided the nuclei for the great industrial unions of the 1930's.

Management Fights Back: Employee Representation Plans and Welfare Capitalism

The American Federation of Labor and organized labor fell upon hard times during the 1920's. The period was one of decline and failure; trade union membership plummeted from 5.1 million in 1920 to 3.4 million by 1929. For those holding a business-cycle theory of trade union growth, the decade presents something of an anomaly; national output grew throughout the period while union membership declined. In light of this perplexing turn of events, proponents of the hypothesis that union membership moves with the business cycle turned to employer open-shop campaigns, employee representation plans (ERP's), welfare capitalism,[7] and unimaginative union leadership as explanations for organized labor's difficulties during this period.

While it cannot be denied that employer programs, designed to convince the worker that unionism was un-American, that meaningful input and representation could be achieved without unions, and that management had the best interests of the worker at heart, were effective in hampering union organizational efforts, a strong argument can be made that their effectiveness was predicated upon the existent politico-economic environment. The same can be said with regard to the negative impact that Samuel Gompers' death in 1924 may have had upon trade union growth. Quite simply, output expanded without the traditional surge in prices or tightening of labor markets. As a result, the benefit/cost ratio ($\Delta P_T/\Delta E_T$ in terms of the A-P Model) of union membership declined, thereby prompting a mass exodus of workers from trade unions. Sumner Slichter comprehended this root cause of labor's difficulties as early as 1929 when he wrote:

> It is undeniable that during recent years the interest of wage earners in unionism has been weak, but this is most plausibly explained by the advance of about 11% in the earnings of factory workers between 1921 and 1926, and by the fact that, during most of the time since 1921, jobs...have not been easy to obtain.[8]

---

[7] Welfare capitalism is a term used to describe a wide variety of employee benefit programs put in place by management during the 1920's. Programs ranged from profit sharing to the provision of recreational facilities.

[8] Sumner Slichter, "The Current Labor Policies of American Industries," *Quarterly Journal of Economics*, (May 1929), **43:** p. 428; for an alternative explanation of labor's difficulties during this period, see: Irving Bernstein, *The Lean Years: A History of the American Worker, 1920–1933*, Boston: Houghton Mifflin, 1960.

Further complicating and burdening organizational efforts during the 1920's was the hostile legal environment (D_T in the A-P Model). Protection of the rights to organize and bargain collectively, free from employer interference, evaporated with the return to a peacetime economy. The Supreme Court continued its assault upon legislation favorable to labor unions. In one year, 1921, the Court proceeded to undo what it had taken the American Federation of Labor dozens of years to accomplish; the Court stripped the Clayton Act of all its protective features with its decisions in *Duplex Printing Press v. Deering* and *American Steel Foundaries v. Tri-City Central Trades Council* and voided state anti-injunction legislation as unconstitutional in *Truax v. Corrigan*.

The Great Depression: Force for Change

Things would get worse for organized labor before they would get better. The collapse of the stock market in October of 1929 signaled the beginning of an economic catastrophe unparalleled in the annals of American history. Output of goods and services was halved, falling from $104 billion in 1929 to approximately $56 billion by 1933. Every third worker in the labor force was either unemployed or seriously underemployed. Construction work, the mainstay of the AFL-affiliated craft unions, was particularly hard hit. Unemployed and unable to pay dues, workers left the fold of organized labor in droves. AFL membership fell from 3 million[9] in 1929 to 2.1 million[10] by mid-1933—a decline of almost 30 percent.

As economic hardship intensified, the prestige of businessmen was quickly transformed to scorn and ridicule. The election of Franklin D. Roosevelt in 1932 represented a resounding no-confidence vote for the conservative business and economic policies which had served the nation so well until the 1920's. The new administration, born of public desperation, immediately embarked upon a series of radical programs designed to stimulate economic recovery. The programs were radical in that they greatly expanded the government's role in domestic economic affairs and recognized the need for and desirability of collective bargaining through autonomous, independent trade unions. The climate of public opinion concerning unionism had come about-face by 1933.

Protection of the Rights to Organize and Bargain Collectively

Under the new administration's leadership, Congress acted quickly and decisively; by mid-1933, the National Industrial Recovery Act (NIRA) had become law. The statute sought to stimulate output and employment by providing for, among other things, the establishment of "codes of fair competition."

Every code of fair competition . . . was required to include a clause recognizing the right of workers to bargain collectively through representatives of their own choosing and to be free of coercion from the employer or his agents in the

[9] American Federation of Labor, *Proceedings*, 1932, p. 49.
[10] Philip Taft, *Organized Labor in American History*, p. 414.

designation of representatives for purposes of collective bargaining. No employee or one seeking employment was to be compelled to join a company union or to refrain from joining a labor union of his choice.[11]

These labor provisions, contained in Section 7(a) of the legislation, sparked a veritable explosion in union membership. The AFL added 800,000 new members in the short span of three months following enactment of the NIRA in June of 1933.[12] The largest gains were registered by the United Mine Workers (UMW), the only dyed-in-the-wool industrial union within the AFL, and by the quasi-industrial Amalgamated Clothing Workers (ACW) and International Ladies Garment Workers Union (ILGWU).[13]

A Broader Organizational Base—The Unskilled and Semi-Skilled

The phenomenal growth of the lone industrial and the two quasi-industrial trade unions only represented the tip of the iceberg. Disillusioned and distraught, factory workers clamoured for representation. With and without the catalytic assist provided by ERP's, industrial unions sprang into existence virtually overnight in most of the mass-production industries. Where spontaneity was inadequate for the establishment of autonomous labor organizations, union adherents "captured" company unions. "At least two of today's mightiest unions, the Steelworkers and the Autoworkers, got their start by capturing the councils management had set up...to give employees representation."[14]

The fact that the NIRA and, later (after the Supreme Court had declared that statute unconstitutional in *A.L. Shecter Poultry v. United States* (1935)), the National Labor Relations Act (NLRA) had their greatest impact upon unskilled and semi-skilled factory workers is easily understood. Earlier attempts by factory workers at organization (i.e., the Knights of Labor and the International Workers of the World) proved futile because they lacked the leverage provided by a nonreplaceable, critical skill. Unlike skilled craftsmen whose threats to withhold labor were effective, in a significant percentage of cases, in bringing employers to terms, the threats of factory workers were empty threats—these workers were easily replaced. The New Deal legislation drastically altered the balance of power between the factory owner and the factory worker by granting the worker "...the leverage of the law in his pursuit of the right to be represented."[15]

A House Divided—Formation of the Congress of Industrial Organizations

In the wake of the influx of factory workers to the AFL, an old problem surfaced: "...the right of workers to organize industrial unions in the mass

---

[11] Philip Taft, *Organized Labor in American History*, p. 418.

[12] *Ibid.*, p. 420.

[13] The ACW and the ILGWU each represented a collection of craft unions bound together for the purpose of solving problems of common concern.

[14] Edwin F. Beal, et al., *The Practice of Collective Bargaining*, 5th Edition, Homewood, Illinois: Richard D. Irwin, Inc., 1979, p. 43.

[15] Reed C. Richardson, *Collective Bargaining by Objectives: A Positive Approach*, Englewood Cliffs, N.J.: Prentice-Hall, Inc., 1977, p. 38.

production industries and retain their affiliation with the AFL."[16] Although the AFL agreed to charter industrial unions at the San Francisco Convention in 1934 and heralded its waiver of "...the old requirement of organization along strictly craft lines..."[17], the Federation never kept its pledges. Instead, mass-production workers were quartered in temporary structures called federal unions for eventual dispersal to traditional craft unions.

Acutely aware that factory workers overwhelmingly favored the industrial form of organization and fearful that any attempt to split the ranks of the factory workers would create disillusionment and result in a missed opportunity for tremendous union growth, the industrial union advocates, led by John L. Lewis (UMW), Sidney Hillman (ACW), and David Dubinsky (ILGWU), bitterly challenged AFL policy at the Atlantic City Convention in 1935. After an emotion-charged debate, the intensity of which was evidenced by the shouting match between John L. Lewis and William L. Hutcheson, President of the Carpenters' Union, the convention voted down, 18,024 to 10,933,[18] a proposal to charter industrial unions in the mass-production industries. The majority of delegates were simply unwilling to discard the time-honored, tradition-steeped craft principle of the Federation and/or, probably more importantly, to relinquish jurisdictional claims to the skilled workers that did exist within the factories. "They wanted them for the job opportunities they represented and to extend their control over the right to learn a trade."[19]

Undaunted and without AFL Executive Council authorization, John L. Lewis and seven other industrial union advocates formed the Committee for Industrial Organization (CIO) less than a month after the Atlantic City Convention. Its purpose was declared:

> to be encouragement and promotion of organization of the unorganized workers in mass production and other industries upon an industrial basis, as outlined in the minority report of the Resolutions Committee submitted to the convention of the American Federation of Labor at Atlantic City; to foster recognition and acceptance of collective bargaining in such industries; to counsel and advise unorganized and newly organized groups of workers; to bring them under the banner and affiliation with the American Federation of Labor.[20]

In August of 1936, the AFL Executive Council ordered the dissolution of the CIO and suspended its unions. Unconcerned, the CIO continued its drive to organize the mass-production industries and began chartering dual unions and central bodies. Although the AFL convention, held in October of 1937, granted the executive council full power to revoke the charters of CIO unions on the grounds of practicing dual unionism, a special joint committee of AFL and CIO representatives was established to set terms for reunification of the two organizations. John L. Lewis, emboldened by recent organizing successes in the automobile, steel, radio, and rubber industries which had increased CIO

[16] Philip Taft, *Organized Labor in American History*, p. 419.

[17] *American Federation of Labor Weekly News Service*, July 22, 1933.

[18] *Report of Proceedings of the Fifty-Fifth Annual Convention* (AFL), 1935, p. 569.

[19] Edwin F. Beal et al., *The Practice of Collective Bargaining*, p. 42.

[20] *Minutes of the Committee for Industrial Organizations*, Washington, D.C., November 9, 1935.

membership to 4 million workers, exceeding AFL membership, rejected the terms. The schism was complete; the Committee for Industrial Organization became an independent federation in 1938—the Congress of Industrial Organizations (CIO).[21]

Organized Labor—Representative Spokesman for the Workingman

Organized labor proved to be an exception to the old adage that "a house divided cannot long endure." The rift between the AFL and the CIO breathed new life into the American labor movement. Its position as spokesman for the workingman seriously threatened by the CIO, the AFL ended it "crafts only" principle, broadened the jurisdictions of affiliated unions, and began chartering industrial unions. By 1941, the AFL had again become America's largest labor federation with a membership of 4.8 million. That same year saw total trade union membership climb to 10.2 million, a fourfold increase from 1933. This meteoric rise in membership, coupled with labor's greatly expanded organizational base, prompted Professors Sloane and Witney to conclude that, by the outbreak of World War II "...the labor movement was not only a major force to be reckoned with but, for the first time, was to a great extent representative of the full spectrum of American workers."[22]

While organized labor's penetration of the labor force was unprecedented in breadth and magnitude, the factors responsible were unique only to the extent of influence exerted by specific variables. The principle engine of past trade union growth, rising prices and expanding employment (ΔP_T and ΔE_T, respectively, in the A-P Model), were only minimally operative. Trade union expansion during the 1930's was primarily driven by an extremely favorable political environment and by a massive inventory of worker grievances generated by widespread unemployment (D_T and U_T^P, respectively, in the A-P Model). The force of this conclusion in no way minimizes the contribution of labor's broadened organizational principle (i.e., organization by craft *and* industry) to membership growth, but rather suggests that the aforementioned political and economic developments were the necessary prerequisites for that contribution.

1940 to Present: Survival in a Mature Economy

Trade union membership continued to increase at a rapid pace during World War II. By war's end, organized labor could count 16.2 million workers as dues–paying members. Union growth, which averaged approximately 15 percent per year during the war, was assured by the same factors responsible for the growth spurt during World War I, namely: price increases, tight labor markets, a favorable political environment (ΔP_T, ΔE_T, and D_T, respectively, in the A-P Model), and increased union security in the form of "maintenance of

---

[21] Philip Taft, *Organized Labor in American History*, pp. 478–522.

[22] Arthur A. Sloane and Fred Witney, *Labor Relations*, 3rd Edition, Englewood Cliffs, New Jersey: Prentice-Hall, Inc., 1977, pp. 83–84.

membership"[23] contract provisions granted by the National War Labor Board in exchange for labor's no-strike pledge for the duration of hostilities. In contrast to World War I, however, a continued stock of worker grievances from the Great Depression (U_T^p in the A-P Model) and substantial penetration of mass-production industries critical to wartime output combined with the previously noted factors to greatly accelerate membership growth.

The Seeds of Postwar Difficulties

Although the overall record of events during the war speaks well of organized labor's commitment to both rank-and-file and public welfare, labor's failure to exercise good judgment in several key areas eroded public support which was an essential ingredient for continued growth and success. First, despite the nation's unswerving resolve to maintain uninterrupted wartime production, not to mention organized labor's no-strike pledge, John L. Lewis capriciously—from the point of view of many observers—called the Mine Workers out on strike in 1942. Second, the intense rivalry between the AFL and CIO which had revitalized the labor movement in the pre-war period now spawned unnecessary and avoidable jurisdictional strikes. Third, some trade unions, with the blessing of the Supreme Court, pursued tactics[24] and goals which the public had historically frowned upon. For example:

> In a suit under the Sherman Act, the Court... even permitted a union to drive an employer completely out of interstate commerce, not because he refused to deal with the union on perfectly satisfactory terms but because the union cherished a long–standing grudge against him. This was the outstanding fact in *Hunt v. Crumboch*, decided in 1945..."[25]

Finally, despite the long-venerated proscription against "dabbling with groups hostile to American capitalism", the neophyte CIO initially welcomed organizational assistance from communist quarters and subsequently refused to expel communist-dominated affiliates.

Organized labor's fall from public grace, begun during World War II, was hastened by the unprecedented level of strike activity which characterized peacetime reconversion in 1946. In that year alone, there occurred 4,630 work stoppages involving 4.9 million workers. The fact that organized labor had, for the most part, abided by its no-strike pledge and had suffered real income losses through wartime wage controls meant very little to the average citizen.

> To a public deprived of many items because of wartime rationing and scarcities, with money in its pocket and a backlog of pent-up demand, this was an affront and an outrage regardless of the right or wrong of the issues involved.[26]

[23] A maintenance-of-membership union security clause requires workers who have elected to become union members to remain members for the duration of the labor agreement.

[24] See the discussion of the Court's decision in *United States v. Hutcheson* (1941) contained in Chapter 4.

[25] Charles O. Gregory, *Labor and the Law*, 2nd Revised Edition, New York: W.W. Norton & Company, Inc., 1961, p. 285.

[26] Reed C. Richardson, *Collective Bargaining by Objectives: A Positive Approach*, p. 47.

The hostile climate of public opinion provided the critical backdrop for the successful enactment of the Labor Management Relations Act[27] (i.e., the Taft-Hartley Act) in 1947. The statute's purpose was the correction of what Congress perceived to be a definite pro-labor bias in the provisions of the Wagner Act.

Passage of the Taft-Hartley Act did not constitute the high water mark of restrictive labor legislation. Revelations of misuse of union funds, corruption, racketeering, and blatant disregard of accepted democratic rules of governance by a few powerful unions, most notably the East Coast Longshoremen and the Teamsters, during the 1957–1959 McClellan Committee Hearings produced additional restrictions upon internal union affairs in the form of the Landrum-Griffin Act of 1959.

Reunification of the AFL and CIO

To stem the rising tide of anti-union sentiment and rekindle interest in union membership through united action, the AFL and CIO merged in December of 1955. Reunification of the two large labor federations was made possible by the elimination of those factors which had precipitated and/or prolonged the division: the AFL had long since abandoned the "crafts-only" organizational principle as had the CIO its "industry-only" principle; the CIO had expelled communist-dominated affiliates whose presence within the federation had enraged conservative AFL leaders; both federation presidents, William Green of the AFL and Philip Murray of the CIO, died in 1952, thereby purging the labor movement of the personal bitterness which these leaders had borne toward one another since formation of the CIO in the late 1930's. As evidenced by the absolute decline in union membership from 18.5 million in 1956 to 17.3 million in 1961, by the decline in the organized proportion of the total civilian labor force from .25 in 1953 to .22 in 1961, and, as noted earlier, by passage of the Landrum-Griffin Act in 1959, AFL-CIO efforts proved to be less than successful.

Economic Growth: A Harsh Taskmaster

The dismal performance of organized labor with regard to membership growth since the merger in 1955 cannot be explained solely in terms of the deteriorating climate of public opinion culminating in restrictive labor legislation (D_T in the A-P Model). Were that the case, there should have occurred a sharp increase in trade union membership during the 1960's and 1970's as a result of federal and state action granting public-sector employees[28] the rights to organize and bargain collectively. Instead, trade union membership increased by less than 5 million between 1961 and 1975, with total civilian labor force penetration barely holding its own at 24 percent through the period before slipping to 20.8 percent in 1980. Thus, while unfavorable public opinion contributed, it in no sense constituted the heart of labor's difficulties.

Strangely enough, the factor primarily responsible for organized labor's

---

[27] See Chapter 4 for a complete discussion of Taft-Hartley and Landrum-Griffin.
[28] Public-sector organization and bargaining are treated in Chapter 15.

problems in recent years is the same factor responsible for the nation's high standard of living—economic growth. A market economy must constantly adjust to changes in consumer wants, technology, and resource availability in order to grow and prosper. Unfortunately, from the perspective of organized labor, many of the recent changes that have recast the nation's economic landscape have also seriously hampered trade union growth.

Of unequaled importance was the change in consumer preferences during the 1950's. As real income levels rose, consumer preferences shifted from goods to services, triggering a transfer of productive resources, human and non-human alike, from goods-producing to service-producing industries—a shift and transfer characteristic of economies in the later stages of economic growth.[29] The shift became vividly apparent in 1956 when white collar employment surpassed blue-collar employment for the first time. The transfer of workers from goods-producing to service-producing industries accelerated during the 1960's, the percentage of non-agricultural jobs located in the service sectors of the economy climbing to 68 percent by 1972.

Standing alone, the structural change in the pattern of employment provides little insight to organized labor's difficulties since the mid-1950's. Coupled with the fact that labor unions have had little success penetrating service industries and white-collar occupations, however, this structural change constitutes the major explanation for labor's organizational problems; it has seriously eroded labor's traditional organizational base of goods-producing employees.

In many ways, organized labor's position today with respect to white-collar employees parallels its position with respect to skilled craftsmen prior to the Industrial Revolution. Where the craftsmen of an earlier age shunned union membership in anticipation of movement up the ladder of socio-economic advancement to self-employment, today's white-collar worker shuns membership out of the belief that socio-economic status has been achieved with white-collar employment. Until organized labor can convince service-sector employees of the need for union membership and simultaneously dispel the belief that union membership diminishes socio-economic status, union penetration of the service-sector will remain limited and overall growth notably unimpressive.

Organized Labor: A Victim of Its Own Success

Technological change during the last quarter century has also worked to labor's disadvantage. The introduction of technologically advanced production techniques accelerated the consumer-driven transfer of workers from goods-producing to service-producing industries by reducing the amount of labor needed per unit of output in the goods-producing sector of the economy. In a real sense, technological displacement of workers is a measure of past trade union success; union-won wage increases have pushed technological change in the direction of labor-saving (as opposed to capital-saving) production tech-

[29]W.W. Rostow, *The Stages of Economic Growth*, Cambridge, England: Cambridge University Press, 1960.

niques. Organized labor's unimaginative attempt to solve the problem through "make-work rules" (i.e., "featherbedding") only succeeded in further tarnishing its image in the public eye.

Besides influencing the direction of technological change in an unfavorable fashion, organized labor fell victim to its past success in two additional ways. First, deep organizational penetration of goods-producing industries has limited the possibility of future membership gains by subjecting organizational efforts to the engineering principle of "a diminishing response to a given intensity of recruiting efforts"[30] (T/E_T in the A-P Model). Second, and more important, wage increases and other improvements in working conditions won by organized labor have spilled over into the unorganized segments of the economy,[31] thereby lessening the need and reducing the motive for organization.

Resource Scarcity and Stagflation: New Challenges

The 1970's placed a new obstacle in the path of trade union growth—a dwindling stock of natural resources. In 1973, the American economy found itself caught in the grips of a severe energy shortage brought about by the OPEC oil boycott. The energy-hungry, goods-producing sector was particularly hard hit. Plagued by declining sales as a result of energy-related price increases in tandem with stiff foreign competition, manufacturing firms sharply curtailed employment, laying off hundreds of thousands of union members. "Stagflation," as the phenomenon of high unemployment coupled with inflation has become popularly known, intensified labor's organizational difficulties by accelerating the decline of the goods-producing sector of the economy begun a quarter century earlier during the ordinary course of economic growth.

No Easy Solutions: "Supply-Side" Economics

After an abortive seven year struggle to eliminate stagflation through traditional economic remedies and prescriptions, the nation turned to more drastic medicine—"supply-side" economics. Under the economic scenario painted by President Ronald Reagan, stagflation was the inevitable consequence of declining productivity produced by government regulations unwarranted on the basis of reasonable cost-benefit analyses and by a level of government taxation that stifled incentives to replace outdated equipment and to add to the nation's stock of productive capital. Elimination of stagflation, therefore, called for a drastic reduction in the size of the public sector. The federal tax and expenditure cuts of mid-1981 were the first steps taken to reduce the size of the public sector.

Although designed for the long-run revitalization of the goods-producing sector which would stem the erosion labor's traditional organizational base, "supply-side" economics has several important short-run implications for organized labor. First, a reduction in the size of the public sector, the one area

---

[30] A.G. Hines, "Trade Unions and Wage Inflation in the United Kingdom, 1893–1961", p. 229.

[31] Arthur A. Sloane and Fred Witney, *Labor Relations*, p. 19.

of the service sector of the economy where labor's organizational efforts have had a certain degree of success, will mean an even slower rate of trade union growth than has occurred recently. Second, expenditure cuts have taken, and are likely to continue to take, the form of drastic reductions in, if not outright elimination of, those social programs which labor fought so long and hard to establish (e.g., Food Stamps, School Lunch, CETA, Social Security, etc.). Third, budget–conscious divisions of government will vehemently oppose public-sector union wage demands unaccompanied by proof of increased productivity—as evidenced by the Reagan Administration's decision to fire striking members of the Professional Air Traffic Controller's Union (PATCO) in August of 1981. Finally, the financially ailing private sector will not only toughen its bargaining opposition to future wage demands in excess of productivity but also condinue to the recent trend of requesting concessions of past wage gains in excess of productivity[32] as well as the elimination of commonplace contract provisions which adversely affect worker motivation and productivity.[33]

Summary and Conclusion

As noted at the outset of Chapter 2, the American labor movement is a product of its environment. Economic, social, and political forces have combined to mold a labor movement unlike any other in the world. Its remarkable staying power and success can be traced to: a business philosophy emphasizing short-term monetary goals as opposed to long-term reformist goals; a flexible approach to problem-solving reflected by an organizational structure under which national and international unions individually set priorities and determine policy; and a staunch commitment to the American model of capitalism. So unique and successful was the American labor movement that the AFL and CIO established their own "state departments" in the 1940's to export the American model of capitalism and unionism abroad.[34]

The magnitude of the problems confronting organized labor at the outset of the 1980's cannot be minimized. The desperate nature of labor's position is reflected by the United Auto Workers' (UAW's) decision to rejoin the AFL-CIO in mid-1981, despite thirteen years of bitter debate and vituperation between the two labor giants concerning the proper direction of the labor movement[35], and by organized labor's decision to sponsor the Solidarity Day Rally held in Washington on September 19, 1981, to protest President Reagan's monetary and fiscal actions. Before taps are sounded for organized labor, however, it should be kept in mind that current problems, while serious, are no

[32] "The Payoff of Wage Moderation," *Business Week*, (January 18, 1982), pp. 22–23.

[33] Clarence R. Deitsch and David A. Dilts, "Getting Absent Workers Back on the Job: The Case of General Motors," *Business Horizons*, (September/October 1981), **24:** pp. 52–58.

[34] Judith E. France, "AFL-CIO Foreign Policy: An Algerian Example, 1954–1962," Unpublished Ph.D. Dissertation, Ball State University, 1981.

[35] The UAW's decision to re-affiliate was facilitated by the death of George Meany, who, as President of the AFL-CIO, was personally involved in the on-going dispute with the UAW; Meany's death removed the personal obstacle to reunification of the UAW and the AFL-CIO.

more life-threatening than those of the past which were successfully overcome. Organized labor will simply have to draw upon those qualities which have given it sustenance and vitality for almost one hundred years. One possible method for improving labor's tarnished image in the eyes of an efficiency-minded public, which deserves greater attention than it has thus far received, is the abandonment of power bargaining (i.e., "economic might makes right") in favor of productivity–related criteria for determining wages and other contract terms during negotiations.

COMMENTARY: Unions Are a Necessary Economic Institution Today by Mr. Arthur W. DeKoster

Mr. DeKoster was born in 1943 and is the newly elected President of his union—International Association of Craftsmen. The I.A.T.C. is a skilled trades union with locals in Michigan, Indiana, Wisconsin, Illinois, Tennessee, and Iowa. Mr. DeKoster has been a member of this union for the last thirteen years and served as the chairman of the bargaining unit at J.I. Case, Bettendorf, Iowa, where he works as a Tool and Die maker. For three years he was Executive Council member from Local #1 located in the Quad-Cities area. During this time he attended union classes at the University of Iowa and the University of Missouri.

Since time began man has struggled to improve his lot. He invented tools to try to improve his livelihood. Unions came into existence for much the same reason, to serve as a tool to solve problems experienced by the worker. A simple fact of life which was true in the beginning and remains so today is that "there is strength in numbers."

The primary objective of any union has always been and remains today to listen to its members and trying to serve their needs.

I believe that unions serve three distinct functions, that of being advisors, instructors and protectors.

As advisors, the union tries to inform members of all their rights under state and federal laws and also their various rights under union and company contract agreements.

As instructors, in our union field of skill trades, we as union officials attempt to help members with apprenticeships and other related training. I believe it is a part of our function as a union to support each other by giving assistance where we can.

The last, and perhaps the most important need of the members remains the same as it was when the first union was formed, that is to protect its membership from abuses by company management. Unfortunately some companies put profit ahead of human rights and needs. This alone would be more than enough justification for a union to exist if there were no other needs fulfilled by union leadership.

True, the problems of union members change with technology and yet they continue to be the same so far as our members are concerned when their livelihood is at stake. A balance between progress and a consideration of human rights should and must be maintained.

I believe we must try to learn from our past experiences, and try to avoid confrontation with company management if and when possible. We must all work toward the best interests of our country. If union members are allowed to produce quality products, this country can continue to set the standards for the rest of the world to pattern themselves after and we can all look forward to a bright future!

DISCUSSION QUESTIONS

1. According to the Ashenfelter-Pencavel Model, upon what major consideration does a worker's decision to join a trade union depend?

2. What factor precludes application of the Ashenfelter-Pencavel Model to trade union growth during the nineteenth century? Assuming that the foregoing factor (i.e., limitation) could be overcome, in what fundamental way would the estimated equation for trade union growth during the nineteenth century differ from the estimated equation for the period 1900–1960? Why?

3. The Industrial Revolution is the historical event most often associated with the birth of the American labor movement. Why?

4. While unlike modern trade unions in many respects, early trade unions shared one thing in common with their modern-day counterparts—their approach to collective bargaining. Comment.

5. The Knights of Labor succeeded in spite of itself. Explain. If the previous statement is an accurate assessment of the Knights rise to ascendancy, what factors—proximate and underlying—were responsible for it demise?

6. The AFL shunned organization of unskilled and semi-skilled workers until the 1930's. Besides its traditional craft-union orientation, what other basic factor explains the AFL's long neglect of factory workers? What developments during the 1930's transformed neglect to concern? Explain.

7. Labor's organization problems during the "Roaring 20's" were the direct result of employer open-shop campaigns, employee representation plans (ERP's) and welfare capitalism. Comment.

8. Although declining public opinion has aggravated labor's organizational problems since World War II, the root of these problems has been economic growth. Explain.

9. The more things change, the more they remain the same. In what way does the previous statement give proper historical perspective to organized labor's current inability to penetrate white-collar occupations?

10. Organized labor has reason to be concerned with the "supply-side" economics of the Reagan Administration. Explain.

SELECTED REFERENCES

Ashenfelter, Orley, and John H. Pencavel, "American Trade Union Growth: 1900–1960", *Quarterly Journal of Economics*, (August 1969), **83**: 434–48.

Beal, Edwin F., et al., *The Practice of Collective Bargaining*, 5th Edition, Homewood, Illinois: Richard D. Irwin, Inc., 1979.

Chamberlain, Neil W., and James W. Kuhn, *Collective Bargaining*, 2nd Edition, New York: McGraw-Hill Book Company, 1965, Chapters 1–2.

Commons, John R., et al., Editors, *A Documentary History of American Industrial Society*, Vols. I-X, Cleveland, Ohio: The Arthur H. Clark Company, 1910.

———, et al., *History of Labour in the United States*, Vols. I–II, New York: The Macmillan Company, 1918.

Dulles, Foster Rhea, *Labor in America: A History*, 3rd Edition, New York: Thomas Y. Crowell Company, 1966.

Galenson, Walter, *The CIO Challenge to the AFL: A History of the American Labor Movement, 1935–41*, Cambridge, Mass.: Harvard University Press, 1960.

Hoffman, Claude E., *Sit-Down in Anderson: UAW Local 663, Anderson, Indiana*, Detroit, Michigan: Wayne State University Press, 1968.

Lester, Richard A., and Joseph Shister, Editors, *Insights into Labor Issues*, New York: The Macmillan Company, 1948.

Perlman, Selig, and Philip Taft, *History of Labour in the United States, 1896–1932*, Vol. IV, New York: The Macmillan Company, 1935.

Perlman, Selig, *A Theory of the Labor Movement*, New York: The Macmillan Company, 1928.

Pierson, Frank C., *Unions in Postwar America*, New York: Random House, Inc., 1967.

Rayback, Joseph G., *A History of American Labor*, New York: The Free Press, 1966.

Richardson, Reed C., *Collective Bargaining by Objectives: A Positive Approach*, Englewood Cliffs, N.J.: Prentice-Hall, Inc., 1977, Chapters 1–3.

Sloane, Arthur A., and Fred Witney, *Labor Relations*, 3rd Edition, Englewood Cliffs, New Jersey: Prentice-Hall, Inc., 1977, Chapter 2.

Taft, Philip, *Organized Labor in American History*, New York: Harper and Row, Publishers, 1964.

Ulman, Lloyd, *American Trade Unionism—Past and Present*, Berkeley, Cal.: Institute of Industrial Relations, University of California, 1961.

Chapter 4

The Legal Environment of the Labor–Management Relationship

Employers and unions are not at liberty to deal with one another in an unencumbered fashion. The labor-management relationship is constrained by a large, growing and increasingly complex body of law. Specifically, the body of labor law consists of the rules governing the behavior of labor and management toward one another as these two groups attempt to divide the fruits of the production process. Many different factors determine the ultimate nature of the rules. Not least in importance are the nation's economic, political and social environments. It is the purpose of this chapter to examine the collection of rules governing the labor-management relationship, the factors that have influenced their development, and their impact on labor relations.

Early Regulation: The Era of Common Law

The bulk of early labor law was common law. Common law consists of accumulated court decisions (i.e., precedents) which have been rendered by the judiciary in the absence of legislatively-authored rules (i.e., statutory law). Kagel explains the concept of common law in Box 4–1. In short, common law is judge-made law.

As is readily apparent, societal values mold and shape the body of common law. A particularly influential force affecting common law is accepted economic dogma. During the period of time extending from the American Revolution well into the 19th Century, the laissez-faire market system, as a mechanism for

---

BOX 4–1. Common Law

When the courts have no written law [constitution or statute] on which to base its decision in a particular controversy, it decides the case on the basis of custom and general principles of right or wrong. These decisions create precedents or rules, which are applied to similar future controversies. The body of law created in this fashion is spoken of as the common law.[1]

---

allocating scarce resources for the satisfaction of human wants, was highly respected. Private property rights stand as the cornerstone of this method of resource allocation. One such property right is the right to manage a business as the owner deems appropriate. Hence, it is not surprising that, as soon as worker's organizations emerged to threaten or challenge traditional management property rights and prerogatives, there also evolved a body of highly restrictive common law to regulate what were then perceived to be revolutionary worker attempts at collective self-help.

Criminal Conspiracy Doctrine

The earliest common law doctrine employed to regulate and control the self-help activities of workers was the criminal conspiracy doctrine. A conspiracy is a combination of two or more persons who band together to prejudice the rights of society or the rights of individuals. Where society's rights are compromised, the conspiracy is criminal in nature. The term civil, on the other hand, is reserved to describe a conspiracy where individual rights are violated. Since associations of working men were viewed as a threat to the basic infrastructure of market capitalism (i.e., private property) as well as an unwarranted interference with the principles governing its operation (i.e., unfettered competition), they were perceived as harmful to the general welfare of society and, therefore, branded criminal conspiracies. Hence, when a group of cordwainers (shoemakers) in Philadelphia banded together and demanded their wages not be reduced in 1806, the Mayor's Court found them guilty of criminal conspiracy (*Commonwealth v. Pullis*).[2]

Illegal Purpose Doctrine

The criminal conspiracy doctrine generated ill will and unrest whenever and wherever it was applied. Growing public opposition prompted the Supreme Judicial Court of Massachusetts, in the case of *Commonwealth v. Hunt* (1842), to reject the concept that unions were illegal "per se" (i.e.,

---

[1] Sam Kagel, *Anatomy of Labor Arbitration*, Washington, D.C.: Bureau of National Affairs, Inc., 1961, p. 139.

[2] John R. Commons and Eugene A. Gilmore, *A Documentary History of American Industrial Society*, III, Cleveland, Ohio: The Arthur H. Clark Company, 1910, p. 69.

criminal conspiracies). Although this decision did not abolish the criminal conspiracy doctrine (since it was binding only in Massachusetts), it substantially decreased its use. Other states rapidly adopted the position of the Massachusetts Court concerning the legal status of workers' associations.

Commonwealth v. Hunt marked a shift from criminal to civil liability as the means for sharply restricting the allowable area of labor union activity. The criminal conspiracy doctrine was supplanted by the *prima facie* tort doctrine. A tort is a civil wrong. Anyone who has sustained injury as a result of a tort is entitled to seek restitution (i.e., compensation) in civil proceedings. According to tort doctrine, economic harm intentionally inflicted upon another is actionable (i.e., subject to civil court proceedings) unless the means are legal and the end is justified. Individual judicial notions of legality and justification governed the disposition of tort cases. Thus, the legality of collective action hinged upon judicial approval of both union means and ends. If either met with judicial disapproval, unionists faced the possibility of civil suit.

During the period in question, 1842–1932, the courts were not disposed to a liberal interpretation of either means or ends as far as the self-help activities of unions were concerned. What constituted lawful means and legitimate purpose was construed in an exceedingly narrow fashion. Other than the traditional strike (i.e., primary labor boycott) for higher wages or improved working conditions, all remaining goals (e.g., closed shop, extended union organization, etc.) as well as the means for achieving these goals were, for the most part, judged to be unlawful.

The judicial view of what constitutes justification for intentional infliction of economic harm warrants further discussion. Under the illegal purpose doctrine, as the *prima facie* tort doctrine became known, economic harm inflicted upon another without recourse to illegal means was permissible if it could be justified as legitimate trade competition. As noted above, legitimate trade competition (i.e., justification) was interpreted quite narrowly. According to the courts, such competition could only exist between individuals or groups of individuals striving against one another on the same socio-economic plane of endeavor. Legitimate trade competition, therefore, did not encompass conflict between workers and property owners. Consequently, the judiciary did not sanction any undertaking that strengthened the position of labor vis-a-vis management. Traditional strikes for higher wages and better working conditions—the only notable deviation from general court proscription of union self-help activities—were sometimes tolerated as a matter of expediency.[3]

The Injunction

If employers had been forced to rely upon trial court litigation as the primary tool for implementation of the illegal purpose doctrine, this common law doctrine would not have been a serious obstacle to the growth of organized labor. Trial court litigation proved to be an ineffectual method for restricting

---

[3] For an excellent in-depth discussion of the illegal purpose doctrine and related topics, see: Charles O. Gregory and Harold A. Katz, *Labor and the Law*, New York: W.W. Norton & Company, Inc., 1979, pp. 31–82.

labor union activities during the latter part of the 19th century. This ineffectiveness was due to three factors. First, the public had become more sympathetic to union problems, programs, and goals as a result of increased product and factor market concentration with its attendant abuses (i.e., ruthless elimination of competitors, price fixing, low wages, poor working conditions, etc.). Hence, employers found it increasingly difficult to procure prosecutors, witnesses, and jury members who shared management's viewpoint of unions and union programs. No longer was a "favorable" decision guaranteed in trial court litigation. Second, the process was time consuming and costly. Finally, trial court litigation was remedial rather than preventative in nature. Injury or damage typically had to have been inflicted before employers could seek redress through trial court litigation.

Commencing about 1880, property owners discovered a more effective anti-union weapon—the injunction. An injunction is a court order directing an individual or group of individuals to refrain from pursuing certain actions; it is a cease-and-desist order. Injunctions are issued by equity courts wherein the judge alone determines all issues of fact and law: whether the order should be granted or denied, whether the directive has been violated (i.e., contempt of court), and, if violated, the nature and extent of penalties to be imposed (i.e., fine and/or imprisonment). As is apparent, equity court proceedings vested significant power in the hands of one person.

Used judiciously and sparingly, the injunction is a valuable judicial tool. Ideally, its use should be restricted to those cases where non-issuance would result in irreparable damage to property, leaving the property owner without legal means of redress or compensation. Justification for issuance of an injunction is that the relative positions of disputing parties (the *status quo*) will remain unchanged in the interim during which the merits of the case are heard and the dispute resolved.

Used capriciously and frequently, as it was until after passage of the Norris-LaGuardia Act in 1932, the injunction became an effective management tool for suppressing unionism. Given the economic and political power structure of the period 1880–1932, employers had little difficulty in persuading local magistrates that the majority of labor self-help activities were enjoinable—that such activities were of dubious legality and threatened irreparable injury to property rights. The abuses which the cease-and-desist order gave rise to in labor disputes are succinctly and emotionally summarized by a statement made by Judge Henry Clay Caldwell[4] written in 1899 (Box 4–2). In other words, the self-help activities of organized labor were judged in accordance with the personal likes and dislikes of judges and employers rather than in accordance with well thought-out, independent, settled standards of law. As a result, most trade union activity came to be viewed as enjoinable "per se" without an accompanying body of opinion (i.e., law) as to why it was such.

Had the injunction maintained the *status quo* in equity court proceedings involving labor unions, the abuses discussed here, although critical from a legal standpoint, would not have constituted the serious obstacle to the growth of organized labor and collective bargaining that they did during the period in

[4]Henry Clay Caldwell, "Trial by Judge," *American Law Review*, **33**: 327–29.

BOX 4–2. Abuse of the Injunction

The modern writ of injunction...has taken the place of the police powers of the State and nation....With it the judge not only restrains and punishes the commission of crimes defined by statute, but he proceeds to frame a criminal code of his own, as extended as he sees proper, by which various acts, innocent in law and morals, are made criminal; such as standing, walking, or marching on the public highway, or talking, speaking, or preaching, and other like acts. In proceedings for contempt for an alleged violation of the injunction the judge is the lawmaker, the injured party, the prosecutor, the judge and the jury. It is not surprising that uniting in himself all these characters he is commonly able to obtain a conviction....

The extent and use of this powerful writ finds its only limitation in that unknown quantity called judicial discretion, touching which Lord Camden, one of England's greatest constitutional lawyers, said: "The discretion of a judge is the law of tyrants; it is always unknown; it is different in different men; it is casual and depends upon constitution, temper, and passion. In the best it is oftentimes caprice; in the worst it is every crime, folly, and passion to which human nature is liable." Mr. Burke pointed out the danger of investing "any sort of men" with jurisdiction limited only by their discretion. He said: "The spirit of any sort of men is not a fit *rule* for deciding on the bounds of their jurisdiction; first because it is different in different men and even different in the same at different times, and can never become the proper directing line of law; and next because it is not reason but feeling, and when it is irritated it is not apt to confine itself within its proper limits."

---

question. The simple fact is that maintenance of the *status quo* as justification for granting injunctions did not exist where labor disputes were concerned. As Felix Frankfurter and Nathaniel Greene[5] pointed out:

> The injunction cannot preserve the so-called *status quo*; the situation does not remain in equilibrium awaiting judgment upon full knowledge. The suspension of activities affects only the strikers; the employer resumes his efforts to defeat the strike, and resumes them free from the interdicted interferences. Moreover, the suspension of strike activities, even temporarily, may defeat the strike for practical purposes and foredoom its resumption, even if the injunction is later lifted.

Equity court proceedings also turned public opinion against workers by branding them as lawbreakers, shifted union resources away from organizational and recognitional efforts to the courts, and dampened worker enthusiasm

---

[5] Felix Frankfurter and Nathaniel Greene, *The Labor Injunction*, New York: The Macmillan Company, 1930, p. 200.

for the programs of organized labor in general. In short, the injunction discriminated against unions:

> Instead of protecting the employer's property against irreparable damage, temporary injunction proceedings could result in irreparable damage to the union's position. This was the usual result regardless of the outcome of future court proceedings.[6]

The effectiveness of the injunction as an anti-union weapon can be gauged by the effort, time, and monetary resources expended by organized labor from 1880 until 1932 in an attempt to secure its statutory regulation at both state and federal levels. Until the Norris LaGuardia Act became law in 1932, the labor injunction remained the most critical and hotly debated issue in the emerging body of law governing labor-management relations.

Yellow-Dog Contract

A rather obscure English common-law doctrine came to play an exceedingly important role in American labor-management relations during the period under discussion, 1880–1932. In *Lumely v. Gye*[7], decided shortly after the middle of the nineteenth century, the English courts established inducement of breach of any contract for personal service as a tort. Persons injured as a result of this tort category were entitled to seek monetary judgments in tort actions against the parties responsible for the harm.

Although not originally intended to control the unpopular activities of labor unions, employers and judges soon discovered that the "Doctrine of *Lumely v. Gye*" provided an excellent theoretical foundation for the issuance of labor injunctions. In the typical scenario the employer exacted from each current or prospective employee a promise, as a condition of continued or initial employment, that he/she would relinquish current union membership and refrain from future membership for the duration of the employment period. When an employer was subsequently confronted with a union organizing campaign, injunctions were routinely sought and granted on the grounds that such activity constituted inducement of breach of contract under the "Doctrine of *Lumely v. Gye.*"

The argument that these anti-union promises were exacted under economic duress (i.e., that the worker had no choice but to agree or lose his/her job) and, therefore, did not enjoy the dignity of a mutually binding, dyed-in-the-wool contract did not impress the courts. Time and time again unions were faced with cease-and-desist orders issued as a result of their organizing efforts where anti-union promises were in effect. Hence, yellow-dog contracts, as these anti-union promises were affectionately termed by trade unionists, became a highly effective device in the arsenal of employer weapons for thwarting extended union organization.

---

[6] Benjamin J. Taylor and Fred Witney, *Labor Relations Law*, 2nd Edition, Englewood Cliffs, N.J.: Prentice-Hall, Inc., 1975, p. 34.

[7] Gregory and Katz, *Labor and the Law*, pp. 93–94.

Statutory Regulation

Given the restrictive nature of the body of common law regarding the proper scope of union activities, organized labor and its supporters turned to political pressure in an attempt to secure legislative relief. Unfortunately from labor's perspective, these efforts were not to come to fruition until 1932.

Sherman Antitrust Act

The Sherman Antitrust Act (1890) was passed in response to public concern over growing business concentration in the manufacture and marketing of goods. Ruthless elimination of competitors resulting in artificial controls over supply, price fixing, and other abuses had convinced the public and their representatives of the need for legislation protecting small businessmen and consumers from the predatory actions of mammoth industrial and commercial enterprises. In an attempt to provide this protection, the Sherman Antitrust Act forbade (and continues to proscribe) contracts and combinations in restraint of trade as well as monopolies and attempts to monopolize trade or commerce.

This legislation should have worked to the advantage of trade unions in their dealings with employers. Reduced product market concentration and power normally translate to a corresponding reduction in factor market influence—a reduction of employer bargaining power in the labor market. Organized labor, however, was prevented from capitalizing on this benefit by the U.S. Supreme Court's decision in *Loewe v. Lawlor*[8] (1908) which brought trade unions under the jurisdiction of the Sherman Act. As a result of this landmark decision, organized labor was forced to redirect its resources to staving off criminal prosecutions, civil damage suits, and injunctions for alleged violations of the Act. For the most part, their efforts proved unsuccessful. In short, instead of bolstering the position of trade unions vis-a-vis employers, the Sherman Act strengthened the arsenal of employer anti-union weapons and employer ability to secure injunctions.

Although the U.S. Supreme Court's determination that Congress intended this statute to encompass the self-help activities of labor remains questionable, particularly in light of the factors (i.e., product market abuses) which prompted passage of the Act and the then-accepted, common-law understanding of restraint of trade as a control over supply and/or price of a *commodity*, a more distressing facet of the Act's implementation was the disparate fashion in which it was applied to labor and business. In the case of business, the Supreme Court distinguished between reasonable and unreasonable restraints of trade in determining Sherman Act violations.[9] In the case of unions, however, a similar "rule-of-reason doctrine" was not applied; the Act was applied literally and uncompromisingly. Thus, a double standard[10] evolved in the judicial application of the Sherman Antitrust Act.

---

[8] *Lowe v. Lawlor*, 208 U.S. 274 (1908)

[9] *Standard Oil Company of New Jersey v. United States*, 221 U.S. 1 (1911). *United States v. American Tobacco Company*, 221 U.S. 106 (1911).

[10] For an in-depth discussion of the double standard, see: Taylor and Witney, *Labor Relations Law*, pp. 52–64.

By the mid-1920's, the only union self-help activity that remained relatively untouched by antitrust litigation was the primary labor boycott (i.e., strike) when undertaken to achieve better wages and working conditions. All the other traditional union pressure tactics—the primary labor boycott undertaken to achieve organization and recognition, the secondary labor boycott, and the consumption boycott—had been found, in one or more cases, to be in violation of the Sherman Act.

The Clayton Act

Organized labor and its supporters were instrumental in securing passage of the Clayton Act in 1914. So enthusiastic and optimistic were labor leaders about the potentially favorable impact of the Clayton Act, they hailed it as the Magna Charta of American labor. Given the normal meaning of the language contained in Sections 6 and 20, labor's euphoria seemed well grounded; Section 6 ostensibly exempted labor unions from the jurisdiction of the Sherman Act, and Section 20 apparently prohibited federal courts from using injunctions in cases stemming from labor disputes, listed traditional union self-help activities which were to be nonenjoinable, and declared that such activities were not to be construed as violations of any law of the United States. Trade unions believed that, at long last, their economic and organizational activities would be free from the debilitating effects of antitrust litigation, yellow-dog contracts, and injunctions.

Since the courts had final say as to the ultimate meaning of the various provisions of the Clayton Act, organized labor's jubilation was short-lived. First, in the *Hitchman* case[11] of 1917, the Supreme Court upheld the enforceability of the yellow-dog contract by means of the injunction—the anti-injunction provisions of the Clayton Act notwithstanding. Then in 1921, the Court destroyed any remaining hope that organized labor may have had for added protection under the Clayton Act by its decision in *Duplex V. Deering*[12] and *American Steel Foundaries v. Tri-City Central Trades Council.*[13]

In the *Duplex* case, the Court, capitalizing upon the loose wording that Congress had used in Sections 6 and 20, held that:

1. Although labor organizations are not in themselves illegal combinations or conspiracies in restraint of trade, nothing in Section 6 exempts ". . . such an organization or its members from accountability where it or they depart from its normal and legitimate objects. . ."
2. The limits placed upon the issuance of injunctions by Section 20 are applicable only where there exists a labor dispute—the latter being narrowly interpreted as a controversy between those in the proximate relationship of employer and employee. Thus, the first paragraph of Section 20 simply ". . . puts into statutory form familiar restrictions upon granting of injunctions already established. . . . It is but declaratory of the law as it stood before."

---

[11] *Hitchman Coal & Coke Company v. Mitchell,* 245 U.S. 229 (1917).

[12] *Duplex Printing Press Company v. Deering,* 254 U.S. 443 (1921).

[13] *American Steel Foundries v. Tri-City Central Trades Council,* 257 U.S. 312 (1921).

3. Since the union self-help economic activities listed and sanctioned by the second paragraph of Section 20 are qualified by such terms as peaceful, lawful, etc., these activities are only lawful if they are in accord with the standards of law established by previous judicial decisions.

The Supreme Court carried its anti-union construction of the Clayton Act a step further in its *American Steel Foundries* decision. Even in those disputes between employers and workers which met the Court's narrow definition of labor dispute, the Court ruled that traditional union self-help activities were not immune from the labor injunction. In the case at point, the Court limited union picketing during an economic strike over wages to one picket per entrance of the factory and declared ". . . that all others be enjoined from congregating or loitering at the plant or in the neighboring street by which access is had to the plant. . . ." The fact that the picketing workers were either the present or laid off employees of the company did not influence the Court's ruling.

In short, as a result of the *Hitchman, Duplex,* and *American Steel Foundries* decisions, organized labor was no better off after passage of the Clayton Act than it was before its passage. As two legal scholars succinctly wrote: "The high court construction of the Clayton Act . . . meant the Act was to leave unchanged the law of industrial relations."[14] Indeed, in one important respect, trade unions were actually worse off; the Sherman Act permitted court issuance of injunctions only upon petition of the Attorney General whereas the Clayton Act permitted court issuance of an injunction upon employer petititon.

Other Attempts at Protective Labor Legislation

Legislative efforts to protect the rights of workers to organize and bargain collectively predated the Clayton Act. By 1900, over a dozen states had enacted statutes prohibiting employers from discriminating against employees in regard to hire and and tenure of employment because of their union activities.[15] These proscriptions encompassed the execution of yellow-dog contracts. Violations were typically punishable by fine and/or imprisonment. The first federal statute directed toward the protection of employee organizing and bargaining rights was the Erdman Act (1898) forbidding discrimination and use of the yellow-dog contract in the railroad industry.

Given the socio-economic tenor of the period, Court response was predictable. In *Adair v. United States* (1908),[16] the Supreme Court struck down Section 10 (i.e., the section prohibiting discrimination and yellow-dog contracts) of the Erdman Act as unconstitutional. A similar fate befell state legislation when the Court ruled the Kansas statute unconstitutional in *Coppage v. Kansas* (1915).[17] The Court's reasoning was essentially the same in

[14]Taylor and Witney, *Labor Relations Law*, p. 74

[15]*Report of the Industrial Commission on Labor Legislation*, V, Washington: U.S. Government Printing Office, 1908, p. 128.

[16]*Adair v. United States*, 208 U.S. 161 (1908).

[17]*Coppage v. Kansas*, 236 U.S. 1 (1915).

both cases. Unwilling to accept the legislative rationale behind either statute, namely, promotion of interstate commerce in the case of the Erdman Act and promotion of citizen welfare in the case of the Kansas statute, the Supreme Court held that the provisions of the Erdman Act and the Kansas statute, prohibiting discrimination and yellow-dog contracts, deprived employers and employees of liberty of contract without due process of law, thereby violating the Fifth and Fourteenth Amendments[18] to the Constitution, respectively.

State statutes aimed at protecting the coercive, economic, self-help activities of organized labor from the equity power of the court were similarly unsuccessful. In 1913, Kansas and Arizona passed legislation remarkably similar to the anti-injunction provisions of the Clayton Act. These state statutes were designed to remove the courts from the labor relations arena. The U.S. Supreme Court's decision in *Truax v. Corrigan*[19] (1921), declaring the Arizona law to be unconstitutional, voided these early state controls on the use of injunctions in labor disputes. According to the Court, the Arizona legislation, by precluding the issuance of injunctions in controversies involving employers and employees growing out of a dispute concerning terms or conditions of employment (i.e., in "labor disputes"), deprived employers of their property (defined here to include their right to operate a business in a profitable manner) without due process of law, and, therefore, violated the Fourteenth Amendment to the Constitution.

The Court's *Truax* decision is particularly interesting in light of its treatment of the Clayton Act. Although the anti-injunction provisions of both pieces of legislation were quite similar, the provisions of the Arizona law were struck down as unconstitutional while the provisions of the Clayton Act, stripped of substantive content through judicial interpretation, were left standing. Reason would appear to dictate consistent court construction of both laws; if the Arizona law violated the Fourteenth Amendment, the Clayton anti-injunction provisions violated the Fifth Amendment. Both should have been ruled unconstitutional. An obvious, though noncomplimentary, explanation for the disparate treatment of these statutes by the Court was expedience; the United States Supreme court did not recognize the need for or the desirability of protective labor legislation and consequently used whatever means at its disposal, however inconsistent, to strike down such legislation. In one respect, the decisions were perfectly consistent; the decisions did not conflict with the social and economic predilections of the judiciary. As Professor Charles O. Gregory observed:

> One must remember that most of the judiciary of that day were men of the old school and that in their economics books, a labor union of any sort was virtual anathema.[20]

---

[18]The Fifth Amendment limits Congressional power to pass legislation abridging constitutionally guaranteed liberties. The Fourteenth Amendment puts a similar limitation upon the power of the states.

[19]*Truax v. Corrigan,* 257 U.S. 312 (1921).

[20]Gregory and Katz, *Labor and the Law,* p. 174.

Modern Labor Law

The Great Depression of the 1930's accomplished what fifty years of union political pressure had failed to bring about: a marked change in the public attitude toward organized labor as reflected by the revolution in labor law. Prior to 1929, the guiding economic philosophy of lawmakers, policy makers, the judiciary, and the general public was laissez-faire capitalism. Free of government and union regulation, the economy had been transformed from subsistent agriculture to manufacturing, had survived numerous recessions, had provided employment opportunities for millions of immigrants, and had increased the general well-being of the populace. This method of resource organization and allocation and its helmsmen (i.e., businessmen) were, in a very real sense, idolized. The Great Depression tarnished these idols. Unemployment approaching 30 percent, under-employment twice the amount of unemployment, a decline in total output of 50 percent, and traditional economic policy prescriptions totally inadequate to the task of solving these problems created a nationwide feeling of helplessness and despair. The market system came increasingly under attack. The former wisdom of businessmen became the unwanted advice of fools. Businessmen were replaced in positions of influence by individuals sympathetic to the goals of organized labor. The willingness of policymakers to try virtually any proposed remedy for the nation's economic ills reflects the desperation of the period. The bulk of modern labor law consists of statutes which were the products of this period of experimentation.

Norris–La Guardia Act

Congress enacted the Norris-La Guardia Act in 1932, and the Supreme Court upheld its constitutionality six years later in *Lauf v. Shinner & Company*[21] (1938). This Act marked a basic shift in the attitude of government toward unionism. For the first time in a federal statute having widespread applicability, Congress recognized that:

1. individual workers were unable ". . . to exercise actual liberty of contract and to protect his freedom of labor, and thereby obtain acceptable terms and conditions of employment. . ." under current economic conditions.
2. the economic structure responsible for the inequality in bargaining power between employer and employee had ". . . developed with the aid of governmental authority for owners of property to organize in the corporate and other forms of ownership association. . ."
3. to insure an opportunity for achieving acceptable terms and conditions of employment (i.e., redressing the imbalance in bargaining power), the individual worker should have ". . . full freedom of association, self-organization, and designation of representatives of his own choosing. . ." for the purpose of bargaining. The worker should also be free from ". . . the interference, restraint, or coercion of employers of labor. . ." in the

[21] *Lauf v. Shinner & Company*, 303 U.S. 323 (1938).

individual or collective exercise of these rights for purpose of bargaining ". . .or other mutual aid or protection.

4. the injunction and enforcement of the yellow-dog contract placed the power of government on the side of management in labor disputes thereby facilitating employer interference with basic employee organizing/bargaining rights with the necessary effect of prolonging the current disparity in bargaining power between employers and employees.

In short, Congress recognized that government was at least partially to blame for prevailing bargaining inequities. To restore a degree of parity in bargaining, Congress moved to sharply limit the equity power of the courts to intervene in labor disputes.

As described earlier, a favorite employer tactic for thwarting extended union organization was the yellow-dog contract. Once executed, employers relied upon the courts to enforce these anti-union promises. Rather than outlaw the yellow-dog contract and run the risk of having the provision overturned as unconstitutional, as had occurred in the case of earlier legislation banning these anti-union promises, Norris-La Guardia simply declared them to be contrary to public policy and unenforceable in any court of the United States. Although employers could still require their execution as a condition of initial hire and continued employment, employees could violate such contracts with court immunity. Thus, Norris-La Guardia effectively destroyed the yellow-dog contract as an obstacle to extended union organization.

The anti-injunction provisions of the Norris-La Guardia Act were an unequivocal, tightly worded, and less radical reformulation of the Clayton Act provisions. It is clear from the language of the Act that Congress did not want the Court to misconstrue its intent of insulating industrial relations from the influence of the courts. Congress wanted to avoid the type of Court construction that had stripped the Clayton Act of its meaning.

In unmistakable language, Norris-La Guardia prohibited the courts from issuing injunctions in cases involving or growing out of labor disputes and specifically listed various union self-help activities which were to be nonenjoinable. Gone from the list were the numerous qualifiers and the loose wording which, in the case of the Clayton Act, had provided the Court the wedge it needed to substitute by way of interpretation its own social and economic predilections for those of Congress. Also absent from the section listing nonenjoinable union self-help activities was the concluding statement that none of the activities were to ". . .be considered or held to be violations of any law of the United States." Congressional omission of this radical and controversial declaration was intended to make the legislation more palatable to the Court, businessmen, and the general public, as well as to underscore the *sole* intent of Congress in passing the Norris-La Guardia Act, namely, to sharply limit the equity power of the courts to interfere in labor disputes.

Norris-La Guardia did not prohibit the issuance of injunctions altogether. Congress was aware that some controversies would develop where injunctive relief was proper. The legislation, however, provided a strict set of standards which were to be observed by the courts before granting injunctive relief in these cases. The standards were designed to prevent the type of abuses (i.e., injunction upon demand, poor quality of evidence, blanket injunctions, time delays, irreparable harm to trade unions, etc.) that were characteristic of labor injunctions prior to 1932.

Critical to the realization of Congressional intent to expand the area wherein unions could function free from court control was the definition of labor dispute. It will be recalled that the Supreme Court, capitalizing upon the obscure terminology used in the Clayton Act to define labor dispute, limited the protective features of that Act, such as they proved to be, to those workers who were the employees of the employer with whom the dispute existed. Such a narrow perception of labor dispute (i.e., a controversy between individuals in the direct relationship of employer and employee) permitted the Supreme Court to severely restrict the area wherein organized labor could operate free from court interference. To preclude the possibility of similar Court behavior in the case of Norris-La Guardia, Congress defined labor dispute broadly to include:

> ...any controversy concerning terms or conditions of employment, or concerning the association or representation of persons negotiating, fixing, maintaining, or seeking to arrange terms or conditions of employment, regardless of whether or not the disputants stand in the proximate relation of employer and employee.

In an earlier discussion of the factors responsible for the deluge of social legislation during the 1930's, it was stated that a large percentage of the statutes were economically motivated (i.e., were attempts to stimulate the level of economic activity). Enactment of Norris-La Guardia was, at least in part, prompted by economic considerations. Although never explicitly stated, a strong argument can be made that the architects of Norris-La Guardia believed that statutory limitation of the equity power of the courts to intervene in labor disputes would eliminate the disparity in bargaining power between employers and employees, thereby leading to higher wages and increased consumer spending—exactly the right prescription for an ailing economy according to the newly emerging Keynesian body of economic thought. This economic scenario is consistent with subsequent Congressional statements of an economic nature justifying passage of the Wagner Act in 1935.

Norris-La Guardia did not commit the federal government to intervention in labor disputes on behalf of labor unions. The official posture of the federal government was laissez–faire. The Act simply placed personal rights on an equal footing with property rights in labor controversies. Employers remained free to fight organized labor by whatever means they could muster, short of relying on yellow-dog contracts and the equity power of the courts. As one recognized legal authority observed, Norris-La Guardia "...belongs to that time bracket in which unions were expected to, and did, depend on their own economic resources to put their programs across."[22]

---

[22] Gregory and Katz, *Labor and the Law*, p. 197.

Wagner Act

The laissez–faire stance of the federal government regarding labor disputes was short lived. The deepening depression, coupled with the growing political power of organized labor, prompted passage of the National Labor Relations Act (NLRA) in 1935. Like the Norris-La Guardia Act and many other statutes passed during the 1930's the Wagner Act (named after its sponsor) was economically motivated and oriented. Unlike the Norris-La Guardia Act, however, the Wagner Act committed the federal government to the direct regulation of labor relations. Specifically, it bound the federal government to aid employees in obtaining organization and collective bargaining. Although amended several times since its passage in 1935, the Wagner Act still stands as the cornerstone of modern labor relations law.

Rationale

Congress meticulously established the need for government regulation of the labor-management relationship in Section 1 of the Wagner Act. According to Congress:

> The denial by employers of the right of employees to organize and the refusal by employers to accept the procedure of collective bargaining lead to strikes and other forms of industrial strife or unrest, which . . .

burdens and obstructs commerce. The resulting inequality in bargaining power between employers and employees who have been denied their organizational rights further burdens and obstructs commerce and " . . . tends to aggravate recurrent business depressions, by depressing wage rates and the purchasing power of wage earners. . . ." The Railway Labor Act of 1926 is then cited, although not by name, as an example of the way in which legislation designed to protect employee organizing and bargaining rights simultaneously safeguards and promotes commerce. Thereupon, Congress declared the policy of the United States to be to:

> eliminate the causes of certain substantial obstructions to the free flow of commerce and to mitigate and eliminate these obstructions when they have occurred by encouraging the practice and procedure of collective bargaining and by protecting the exercise by workers of full freedom of association, self-organization, and designation of representatives of their own choosing, for the purpose of negotiating the terms and conditions of their employment or other mutual aid or protection.

In the above fashion, Congress established its authority under the commerce clause of the Constitution to regulate the labor-management relationship. The Supreme Court was sufficiently impressed by the logic of the Congressional argument to declare the Wagner Act constitutional in *NLRB v. Jones & Laughlin Steel Corporation*[23] in 1937.

---

[23]*NLRB v. Jones & Laughlin Steel Corporation*, 301 U.S. 1 (1937).

Policy Implementation

Section 7 of the Wagner Act delineates basic employee organizing and bargaining rights. Specifically, the provision states that:

> Employees shall have the right to self-organization, to form, join or assist labor organizations, to bargain collectively through representatives of their own choosing, and to engage in concerted activities, for the purpose of collective bargaining or other mutual aid or protection.

Congress adopted a two-pronged approach to guarantee these rights and thereby implement the declared policy of the legislation. First, specified types of employer behavior deemed to be inherently at variance with the stated policy of the legislation were banned. These prohibited *employer* activities, labeled *unfair labor practices (ULP's)*, were:

1. interfering with, restraining, or coercing "...employees in the exercise of the rights guaranteed..." by the Wagner Act;
2. dominating or interfering "...with the formation or administration of any labor organization...";
3. discrimination "...in regard to hire or tenure of employment or any term or condition of employment to encourage or discourage membership in any labor organization...";
4. discharging or discriminating "...against an employee because he has filed charges under..." the Wagner Act; and
5. refusing "...to bargain collectively with the representatives of his employees...."

BOX 4–3.   Strikers Win Steaks on (Westing) House

Abingdon, Va.—Dinner for two. On the House. Westinghouse, that is. That's what some 250 workers at the Westinghouse facility here have won as a result of unfair labor practice charges filed by their union, the International Union of Electrical Workers.

The IUE went to the National Labor Relations Board after the company sent thank-you notes—along with tickets for dinner at a local steak house—to about 50 non-strikers who worked through the union's seven-week walkout at the Westinghouse plant last year.

Since the strikers did not receive dinner tickets, IUE charged the firm with discrimination on the basis of their union activity, and won. The settlement, part of an NLRB order backed up by an appellate court, requires the company to send $20 checks to each of the 250 striking employees to remedy the "oversight."

Next time, maybe, Westinghouse will remember to invite everyone to dinner.

Source: International Union of Electrical Workers Newsletter

Secondly, and more positive in nature, the Wagner Act provided an elaborate procedure for determining the wishes of employees concerning representation for purposes of collective bargaining.

National Labor Relations Board

The National Labor Relations Board (NLRB) was created by Congress to administer, interpret, and enforce the provisions of the Wagner Act. The basic function of such independent, quasi-judicial administration agencies is ". . . the execution of the legislature's general will in a multitude of particular instances, far too numerous for the courts to handle directly."[24] Specifically, the Wagner Act mandated the NLRB to (1) prevent unfair labor practices and (2) resolve questions of representation.

In order to discharge its legally mandated responsibility of preventing unfair labor practices, the NLRB was granted the power, in those cases where it determined that an employer had committed an unfair labor practice, to

> issue and cause to be served on such person an order requiring such person to cease and desist from such unfair labor practice, and to take such affirmative action, including reinstatement of employees with or without back pay, as will effectuate the policies of this Act.

The Supreme Court has given the Board wide latitude in determining the measures it deems necessary to ". . . effectuate the policies. . ." of the Wagner Act. The Court, however, retained the right to review Board orders. Court review could be achieved in either of two ways, namely, (1) direct court appeal of the Board's decision, and (2) employer refusal to obey the Board order resulting in judicial review of the case upon the Board's petition for court enforcement. As the last statement infers, the NLRB does not have the power to enforce its own orders. The Board is required to petition the federal Circuit Court of Appeals having jurisdiction over the matter for enforcement. Congress denied the Board enforcement powers to avoid constitutional problems of due process.

As for its other primary responsibility under the Wagner Act, the resolution of representation questions, the NLRB has utilized three methods to ascertain and safeguard employee wishes concerning representation. Under legally provided and Board-developed procedure, *union recognition can be achieved in* the following *three ways:*

1. Voluntarily—The employer, upon the presentation of evidence that the union represents the majority of employees (i.e., demonstration of union majority status), voluntarily recognizes and begins bargaining with the union;
2. Secret Ballot Election—The employer, confronted by a union demand for recognition, questions the union's majority status or the appropriateness of the bargaining unit. These and any other questions are then resolved by the NLRB as provided for in the legislation. Once the unit appropriate for

---

[24] Gregory and Katz, *Labor and the Law*, p. 233.

bargaining purposes is determined and other representation questions settled, the NLRB conducts a secret ballot election to determine the wishes of the employees concerning representation and bargaining. The union selected by the majority of employees actually voting in the election becomes the exclusive representative of all the employees in the bargaining unit for purposes of collective bargaining; and

3. Mandatory—In rare cases where an employer has engaged in serious unfair labor practices either undermining or preventing the establishment of union majority status, the NLRB will mandate employer recognition without benefit of a secret ballot election (i.e., *Gissel* Bargaining Order).[25]

Bargaining In Good Faith

The most nebulous of the responsibilities required of the employer by the Wagner Act was the duty to bargain in good faith. Greater interpretative difficulties have arisen in connection with the fifth unfair labor practice than with any of the other four. The legislation itself gives virtually no guidance whatsoever to the NLRB in determining what bargaining in good faith entails. Thus, it was left up to the NLRB to determine the meaning of good faith bargaining on a case-by-case basis.

As established through court-approved Board decisions, the duty to bargain in good faith merely requires employers to meet and confer with the representatives of the employees in an honest attempt to resolve differences. While the making of counterproposals is required, the making of concessions is not; a "no" response coupled with its underlying rationale constitutes an acceptable counterproposal. Furthermore, not all subjects are mandatory topics for good faith bargaining. The NLRB has established three categories of bargaining subjects: (1) illegal, (2) voluntary, and (3) mandatory. Only those topics categorized as mandatory (i.e., "wages, hours, and other terms and conditions of employment") must be bargained in good faith.[26] This obligation applies not only at the time of contract negotiation but extends over the life of the contract; an employer may not unilaterally alter any item of the contract which falls into the mandatory bargaining category without committing an unfair labor practice.

Given the complexity of the issue, a reasonable question can be raised as to why Congress felt the need to make good faith bargaining a requirement of the Wagner Act. Quite simply, without this requirement, an employer could superficially abide by the other specific requirements of the legislation yet defeat its overall purpose by refusing to bargain when it came time to negotiate the contract. Recognition and organizational strikes would diminish at the expense of an increase in the number of economic strikes. Although the component mix of strike activity would change, the legislation would not effect a significant reduction in the total number of strikes. To prevent such a metamorphosis and insure a reduction in strike-related obstructions to commerce, Congress mandated employers to bargain in good faith once organization and recognition had been achieved.

---

[25] *NLRB v. Gissel Packing Company*, 395 U.S. 575 (1969).

[26] *NLRB v. Wooster Division of Borg-Warner Corporation*, 356 U.S. 342 (1958).

Wagner Act Impact

That the Wagner Act accomplished its purposes of promoting collective bargaining and reducing strike-related obstructions to the free flow of commerce cannot be denied. The following facts speak for themselves. Union membership ballooned from approximately 4 million in 1935 to 13.8 million in 1944. By 1946, the total number of collective bargaining agreements in force had exceeded 50 thousand. Organizational strikes as a percentage of total strike activity had declined from 50 percent in 1936 to roughly 21 percent in 1945.[27]

Taft–Hartley Act

NLRA provisional weaknesses and oversights (e.g., lack of a mechanism to provide relief to employers caught in the crossfire of two or more unions seeking to represent the same group of employees), liberal Court construction of the Norris-La Guardia Act (e.g., the *Hutcheson*[28] decision of 1941 declaring that the union self-help activities described in Section 4 of the Norris-LaGuardia Act were not only nonenjoinable but legal as well), the wartime coal strikes led by John L. Lewis of the United Mine Workers' Union, the post war spate of work stoppages, union abuses (e.g., expulsion of an employee from the union as a result of internal union politics and subsequently securing his discharge under a union security clause—closed shop, etc.), the inherent pro-union bias of the Wagner Act, and employer political pressure prompted passage of the Taft-Hartley Amendments to the Wagner Act in 1947.

Rationale

During the years following statutory protection of employee bargaining rights under the Wagner Act, Congress became increasingly aware of the need to protect the rights of other groups of individuals. It became painfully apparent that unions were not only capable of, but, indeed, had engaged in behavior violative of the rights of employers and individual employees. In addition, the rights of the general public had oftentimes been compromised by the actions of unions and/or employers. The Taft-Hartley Act (i.e., Labor Management Relations Act—LMRA) was specifically designed to remedy these inequities and restore some balance in bargaining power which was believed to have shifted in the direction of organized labor. Accordingly, in Section 1(b) of the "Short Title and Declaration of Policy" of the Taft-Hartley Act, Congress stated:

> It is the purpose and policy of this Act, in order to promote the full flow of commerce, to prescibe the legitimate *rights of* both employees and *employers* in their relations affecting commerce, to provide orderly and peaceful procedures for preventing the interference by either with the legitimate rights of the other, to protect the *rights of individual employees* in their relations with labor organizations whose activities affect commerce, to define and proscribe practices on the part of labor and management which affect commerce and are inimical to the general

---

[27] See *Monthly Labor Review*, volumes XLIV–LIX.

[28] *United States v. Hutcheson*, 321 U.S. 219 (1941).

welfare, and to protect the *rights of the public* in connection with labor disputes affecting commerce. [Emphasis added]

In short, while the Wagner Act was concerned solely with the bargaining rights of employees, the Taft-Hartley Act was concerned with the rights of a broader spectrum of society.

Policy Implementation

As had been the case under the Wagner Act, the method of policy implementation under Taft-Hartley was two-pronged. *First,* Congress spelled out the rights of specific groups of individuals which were to be considered inviolate. These groups and the more important of their newly guaranteed rights were:

1. *Individual Employees.* Although the bargaining rights of employees were adequately protected under the Wagner Act, their rights as individual workers were not. To correct this weakness, Congress declared that employees "...shall also have the right to refrain from any or all of such activities..." (i.e., bargaining activities). Translated to specific individual employee rights, this general right includes the right to:
   a. Work. In addition to banning the closed shop,[29] Taft-Hartley permits the states to regulate other types of union security clauses. Thus, to the degree permitted by state law, an employee does not have to be a union member to acquire and retain a job.
   b. Individual dues checkoff authorization. Where a union dues checkoff contract provision is legal and a part of the bargaining agreement, Taft-Hartley requires annual authorization by the individual employee prior to actual deduction of dues from the employee's wages.
   c. Present grievances. Where an employee believes that his/her interests would be better served through direct individual presentation of grievances to the employer, the employee can bypass the contractually established grievance procedure.
   d. Protection from internal union abuses. Instances of misuse of union funds and Communist infiltration of certain union leadership hierarchies motivated the Taft-Hartley provisions requiring (A) union officers to file non-Communist affidavits, (B) union financial and constitutional reports to the Secretary of Labor, and (C) unions to cease political contributions in federal elections.
2. *Employers.* Congress recognized the need to protect certain basic employer rights. Among these guaranteed rights were:
   a. Freedom of speech. For a significant period of time following the passage of the Wagner Act (i.e., up until 1941), it was taken for granted that whatever an employer said to his/her employees concerning union organization constituted an unfair labor practice. The 1947 legislation protected an employer's right to express an opinion concerning unionism

---

[29] A closed-shop union security clause requires union membership as a condition of initial hire *and* continued employment.

as long as it did not include a "threat of reprisal or force or promise of benefit."

b. Flexibility to manage. Prior to the 1947 Taft-Hartley Amendments, supervisors were considered employees entitled to the protective features of the Wagner Act; employers were forbidden from discriminating against supervisors for engaging in union activities. Classification of supervisors as employees by the NLRB generated a storm of employer protest. From the employer's point of view, such a classification divided management against itself and severely reduced the ability of an employer to manage effectively. Taft-Hartley specifically excludes supervisors from the definition of "employee".

c. Flexibility to hire. A longstanding criticism of the closed shop union security clause is that it effectively transfers hiring decisions to the union which has successfully bargained such an arrangement. Since the employer is restricted to hiring only union members, the decision as to which worker is hired rests with the union. Taft-Hartley returned this basic management function to the employer by banning the closed shop.

d. The right to petition for a representative election. As noted earlier, the Wagner Act made no provision for employer representation petitions. Consequently, an employer caught in a "tug-of-war" between two unions seeking to represent the same group of employees was forced, often at significant financial cost, to wait for relief until an employee or one of the competing unions petitioned for an election. Under Taft-Hartley, an employer can secure more immediate relief by directly petitioning for a respresentation election *when* confronted by a union demand for exclusive bargaining recognition.

3. *General Public.* Work stoppages not only impose costs upon the immediate parties to the bargaining relationship (i.e., labor and management) but also impose costs upon the general public as well. Although these costs are normally rather insignificant, usually involving no more than the inconvenience of postponing the purchase of, or substituting another good for, the desired good whose production has been interrupted by the work stoppage, they can at times become substantial, threatening the national health and safety. To protect the general public, Taft-Hartley established a detailed procedure for government intervention in labor disputes that imperil national health and safety. *The National Emergency Impasse Procedure*, as these Taft-Hartley provisions have become known, are detailed below.

Second, Congress proscribed certain practices on the part of unions that abridged the newly-guaranteed rights of either employees, employers, or the general public. Specifically, Taft-Hartley made it an *unfair labor practice for a labor organization* to:

1. restrain or coerce employees in the exercise of their collective bargaining rights; or to restrain or coerce an employer in the selection of representatives for contract negotiation and/or administration.

2. cause, or attempt to cause, an employer to discriminate against an employee for nonmembership in a labor organization where a valid union security

clause is in effect except for the failure to tender the dues and initiation fees required for obtaining and retaining membership.
3. refuse to bargain in good faith with an employer.
4. engage in, or influence workers to engage in, a work stoppage, where the objective is:
   a. to force an employer or self-employed person to join a labor organization.
   b. to force an employer or self-employed person to stop using the products of or doing business with any other person or organization.
   c. to force any other employer to recognize and bargain with a particular labor organization unless that labor organization has been certified as the representative.
   d. to force any employer to recognize and bargain with a particular labor organization where another labor organization has been certified.
   e. to force an employer to assign or reassign work to a particular craft or union.
5. require employees, covered by a union security clause, to pay excessive or discriminatory fees or dues.
6. cause or attempt to cause an employer to pay for work not performed or not to be performed (featherbedding).

The stated purpose of the Wagner and Taft-Hartley Acts was the removal and minimization of obstructions to commerce stemming from labor disputes. The legislation was structured to eliminate the causes of organizational strikes and to significantly reduce the number of economic strikes by encouraging the practice and procedure of good faith bargaining. In the vast majority of cases, the provisions of the Wagner and Taft-Hartley Acts guaranteeing employee and employer rights were sufficient to the task of protecting the public interest and serving the common good. By 1947, however, Congress had come to the realization that genuine good faith differences could develop during bargaining which, if left to culminate in a work stoppage, even of minimal duration, might compromise public rights and harm the common good. Therefore, to protect the rights of the general public where an economic strike posed a threat to national health and safety—a problem not addressed by either the Wagner Act nor the other provisions of the Taft-Hartley Act aimed at promoting the public interest, Congress established a *National Emergency Impasse Procedure* consisting of the following steps:

1. Presidential appointment of a board of inquiry to investigate the impasse and submit a written report concerning the facts of the case.
2. Upon submission of the board's report, the President may direct the Attorney General to petition any federal district court for an eighty-day injunction.
3. Upon issuance of an injunction, the parties to the dispute are required to continue bargaining with the assistance of the Federal Mediation and Conciliation Service (FMCS) for the duration of the "eighty-day cooling off period."
4. The board of inquiry is reconvened and required to submit a second report

to the President detailing the current status of the dispute as well as the employer's last offer of settlement at the end of sixty days. The report is then made public.

5. A secret ballot election conducted by the National Labor Relations Board (NLRB) during the fifteen-day period commencing with the sixtieth day of the injunction and ending on the seventy-fifth day to determine whether the employees wish to accept the employer's final offer.

6. NLRB report of election results to the Attorney General during the last five days of the injunction.

7. Dissolution of the injunction at the end of eighty days.

8. Presidential report of the entire proceeding to Congress with possible request for appropriate legislation to terminate the dispute.

9. Work stoppage commences or continues unless resolved by private negotiation or legislative decree.

The basic intent of Congress in establishing the National Emergency Impasse Procedure was to encourage private settlement by means of continued private negotiation efforts conducted with the assistance of a neutral third party (i.e., the federal mediator), by adverse publicity (i.e., bad press) and by the uncertainty created by the possibility of federal legislation to resolve the dispute.

The Viability of Collective Bargaining

The contract stands as the cornerstone of the collective bargaining process. The creation of a workable labor agreement is the ultimate goal of negotiators. It is the *raison d'être* of collective bargaining. Hence, the long-run viability of collective bargaining as the accepted method of joint labor-management decision making depends upon contract integrity and inviolability. Since collective bargaining contracts were typically unenforceable under state statutes and common law[30], and since federal labor legislation never addressed the question of contract enforceability, there had always existed some doubt about the ability of collective bargaining to survive and prosper as a permanent institution. The Taft-Hartley Act dispelled all such doubt by making labor agreements legally enforceable. Specifically, Section 301 granted the parties to collective bargaining the right to bring suits for contract violations in any federal district court. In so doing, Taft-Hartley not only insured the integrity of the labor contract but also the institutional viability of collective bargaining. The latter, quite possibly, was the Taft-Hartley Act's greatest contribution to the development of stable and mature labor-management relationships.

Landrum-Griffin Act

Although the Taft-Hartley Act was generally successful in restoring greater balance in bargaining power which had shifted toward organized labor under the stimuli of the Wagner Act and liberal Supreme Court decisions, the legislation proved inadequate to the task of preventing certain internal union

[30] For an in-depth discussion of early contract enforcement, see: Taylor and Witney, *Labor Relations Law*, pp. 363–374.

practices which threatened the rights of union members. In addition, twelve years' experience under Taft-Hartley revealed structural weaknesses in several of the other provisions defining the NLRB's jurisdiction and regulating secondary pressure activities of labor organizations. Congress reacted to the foregoing Taft-Hartley deficiencies by enacting the Labor-Management Reporting and Disclosure Act (Landrum-Griffin Act) of 1959.

Internal Union Affairs

Public concern with internal union practices pre-dated the era of public support for the institution of collective bargaining which began in 1932. The development of organized labor from a position of relative weakness prior to 1932 to a position of relative strength in the post-World War II period, however, intensified Congressional interest in the internal affairs of unions. Alleged instances of violence, fraud, bribery, extortion, mismanagement of union funds (particularly pension funds), and general racketeering by union officials, managers, and others led to the creation of the Senate Select Committee on Improper Activities in the Labor or Management Field in 1957. The McClellan committee, as the Senate investigating body became popularly known, unearthed:

> a number of instances of breach of trust, corruption, disregard of the rights of individual employees, and other failures to observe high standards of responsibility and ethical conduct...

The first six titles of the Landrum-Griffin Act were the direct product of these revelations. According to the declared policy of the 1959 statute, government regulation of internal union affairs was necessary to eliminate

> or prevent improper practices on the part of labor organizations, employers, labor relations consultants, and their officers and representatives which distort and defeat the policies of the Labor Management Relations Act, 1947...

—in short, the elimination of the types of abuses discovered by the McClellan committee. Specifically, the titles, enforceable by the Secretary of Labor, regulated internal union behavior and certain activities of employers by establishing, respectively:

1. *The Bill of Rights of Members of Labor Organizations.* Union members were guaranteed equal rights and privileges with regard to nomination of candidates, voting in elections, attendance at meetings, participation in union business, freedom of speech, and freedom of assembly. The Bill of Rights also set strict standards and procedures for the determination and assessment of dues. The employee's right to sue the labor organization, protection against arbitrary discipline, and the right to copies of the collective bargaining agreement were also guaranteed under this title.
2. *Specific Union Constitutional/By-law Protection of Employee Rights Established Under Title 1.* Toward this end, this title sets forth annual union and employer reporting and disclosure requirements concerning the constitutional operation and the financial management of the labor organization.

3. *Conditions Under Which a Labor Organization Can Impose a Trusteeship Over a Subordinate Body.* Trusteeships had been utilized by some unions as a means of suppressing rank-and-file dissent with and opposition to political factions currently in power. To correct this and other abuses, Title III permits trusteeships:

> only in accordance with the constitution and by-laws of the organization which has assumed trusteeship...and for the purpose of correcting corruption or financial malpractice, assuring the performance of collective bargaining agreements or other duties of a bargaining representative, restoring democratic procedures, or otherwise carrying out the legitimate object of such labor organizations.

Furthermore, Title III detailed reporting procedures which had to be met within thirty days following imposition of a trusteeship under penalty of fine and/or imprisonment.

4. *Guidelines and Standards for Union Elections.* Procedures and requirements concerning nominations, election frequency, use of union funds, voter eligibility, candidates, type of ballot, role of conventions, and other related election questions were treated in great detail to safeguard the democratic process in internal union administration.

5. *Fiduciary Responsibilities and Eligibility Requirements of Union Officials.* The provision forbids any person:

> who is or has been a member of the Communist Party [Unconstitutional as of 1965] or who has been convicted of or served any part of a prison term resulting from his conviction of robbery, bribery, extortion, embezzlement, grand larceny, burglary, arson, violation of narcotics laws, murder, rape, assault with intent to kill, assault which inflicts grievous bodily injury, or a violation of title II or III of this Act, or conspiracy to commit any such crimes....

from serving in any official capacity with the union. To guarantee the financial integrity of those persons holding office, the law mandates annual reports by officeholders to the Secretary of Labor to contain an extensive accounting of the use of union funds. Personal use of union funds is prohibited. To protect membership funds, all union officers must be bonded. The law also provides stiff penalties for violations of the title and permits court action to recover misused funds from union officials. Title V also prohibits employer expenditures directed at influencing union officers or employee collective bargaining activities.

6. *Miscellaneous Provisions.* The last title, among other things, empowers the Secretary of Labor to investigate alleged violations of the first six titles which fall within the enforcement jurisdiction of that office. This title also prohibits extortionate picketing. The latter is defined as picketing for personal gain as opposed to collective employee gain.

Strengthening Taft-Hartley Provisions

As noted above, a number of structural weaknesses in several Taft-Hartley provisions became apparent as the NLRB administered, interpreted, and enforced the statute. Title VII of Landrum-Griffin contains reworked and/or additional provisions directed toward the elimination of these revealed deficiencies of Taft-Hartley.

One of the more vexing administrative problems that initially arose under the Wagner Act and continued under the Taft-Hartley Act concerned the adjudication of labor disputes that technically occurred within the "current of commerce" but over which the National Labor Relations Board had declined to exercise jurisdiction. Federal preemption precluded the states from exercising their jurisdiction where the federal government had exercised its jurisdiction. Hence, a "no-man's land" had developed without appropriate provision for resolution of such labor disputes. Title VII of Landrum-Griffin addressed the "no-man's land" problem by permitting the states to exercise jurisdiction where the NLRB had refused to do so. While not eliminating the problem (the provision is permissive and not mandatory), Section 14(c)2 of Landrum-Griffin did significantly reduce the incidence of such disputes.

Landrum-Griffin also closed certain loopholes in the *secondary boycott provisions* of Taft-Hartley. Organized labor, supported by the courts, contended that the boycott provisions simply prohibited secondary pressures exerted upon a neutral employer by way of the neutral employer's employees; the same pressure exerted directly upon the neutral by union officials or by contractual arrangement prohibiting employer transactions with "unfair" employers (i.e., the "hot cargo" clause) was permissible under the language of Taft-Hartley. Landrum-Griffin specifically outlawed the "hot cargo" arrangement as well as most types of secondary boycotts regardless of the type of pressure or leverage mechanism utilized.

Toward this same end of more closely controlling the coercive, self-help, economic activities of labor organizations, the 1959 amendments added a *seventh union unfair labor practice* making picketing unlawful under certain circumstances. Prior to Landrum-Griffin, unions were permitted to engage in recognition and organizational picketing for an indefinite period of time. As was true when supervisors were included within the definition of "employee" under the Wagner Act and also in the case of union secondary boycott pressures under the Taft-Hartley Act (picketing typically is the device through which such boycotts are made effective), Congress believed that such extended picketing unduly burdened and limited the employer's right to manage. Consequently, since 1959, it has been an unfair labor practice for a labor organization to engage in recognition and/or organizational picketing:

1. "where the employer has lawfully recognized...any other labor organization and a question concerning representation..."does not exist;
2. "where within the preceeding twelve months a valid election...has been conducted..."; or
3. "where such picketing has been conducted without a petition...being filed within a reasonable period of time not to exceed thirty days from the commencement of such picketing...."

Finally, under the Taft-Hartley Act, *strikers* replaced during the course of an economic strike were denied the *right to vote in any representation election conducted during the labor dispute.* Coupled with the fact that replacements were permitted to vote, these provisions provided employers with a method by which a small union might be broken (i.e., by hiring as many replacements as possible to secure a simple majority vote in a union decertification election). Landrum-Griffin makes it more difficult for employers to destroy a union's majority status in decertification elections conducted during work stoppages by permitting replaced strikers to vote in these elections.

Other Laws Governing Labor Relations

The Taft-Hartley Act, as amended, remains the basic law of the labor–management relationship. Except for several minor changes in coverage and procedure brought about by the 1974 amendments, the provisions of Taft-Hartley, as amended in 1959, have stood the test of time. The durability of the legislation in the face of many serious challenges to labor-management relations over the last two decades testifies to the statute's basic operability and practicability.

Although Taft-Hartley, as amended, has been successful in promoting the peaceful adjudication of labor disputes and eliminating employment discrimination based upon union activity, other employment problems, commanding public attention over the last two decades, fell outside the scope of this statute. As a result, commencing in the early 1960's, Congress enacted a series of statutes aimed at correcting these problems. The more important of these laws which apply to employers and unions and affect labor relations are briefly described below.

The Equal Pay Act of 1963

Enacted as an Amendment to the Fair Labor Standards Act, the Act prohibits employers from discriminating on the basis of sex in the payment of wages (including almost all forms of employee benefits). Unions are prohibited from causing or attempting to cause an employer to discriminate in violation of the legislation. In brief, the goal of the Act is equal pay for equal work. The Equal Pay Act covers all employees. Enforcement and administration of the Act was transferred from the Wage and Hour Division of the Department of Labor to the Equal Employment Opportunity Commission (EEOC) on July 1, 1979.

Title VII of the Civil Rights Act of 1964 as Amended by the Equal Employment Opportunity Act of 1972

Title VII of the Civil Rights Act of 1964, as amended, prohibits discrimination in employment (including hiring, wages, promotion, employee benefits, training, and all other terms and conditions of employment) on the basis of race, color, sex, religion, or national origin. The Act covers private employers with fifteen (15) or more employees, public and private employment agencies, labor unions with fifteen (15) or more members, public and private educational institutions (except with regard to religion in the case of educational institutions with religious affiliation), and state and local governments. Title VII created the Equal Employment Opportunity Commission (EEOC) to administer the Act. Enforcement responsibilities, however, were shared initially by three separate agencies: the EEOC, the Civil Service Commission, and the Justice Department. As a result of ensuing enforcement ambiguities and difficulties, enforcement responsibilities have been centralized under EEOC.

Age Discrimination in Employment Act of 1967

Designed to promote the employment of older workers (i.e., persons between 40 and 70 years of age) based on ability rather than age, the Act as amended in 1978, prohibits discrimination in employment (including hiring, wages, employee benefits and privileges, discharge, and all other terms and conditions of employment) based on age. The legislation covers private employers engaged in interstate commerce who employ twenty (20) or more workers. Also covered are labor organizations and employment agencies. EEOC has administered and enforced the Act since July of 1979.

Occupational Safety and Health Act of 1970

Congress enacted the Occupational Safety and Health Act ". . . to assure so far as possible every working man and woman in the nation safe and healthful working conditions and to preserve our human resources." Unless covered by other federal safety and health laws, the Act applies to every employer operating a business in the current of commerce. The Occupational Safety and Health Administration (OSHA) was established by the Act and given primary responsibility for administering the Act's provisions. More specifically, it is the responsibility of OSHA to secure employer compliance with health and safety standards.

Summary and Conclusion

Unlike the Ten Commandments, the body of labor law was not received from "On-High", chiseled in stone. Influenced and shaped by various social, political, and economic factors, the body of labor law has evolved over the course of two centuries. In essence, labor law is simply the codified value judgments of society regarding the proper socio-economic functions of trade unions and collective bargaining.

If one had to select a single factor of overriding importance in the evolutionary chronicle of the development of labor law, the pragmatic philosophy of the jurisprudence system would be the logical choice. Whenever a change in the law was perceived to serve the common good, it was implemented. Admittedly, the perceptions of various legislative and judicial units sometimes changed slowly. Nevertheless, the changes were eventually made, thereby insuring the development of a living and workable body of labor law. In short, the development of labor law has been guided by the same type of pragmatic philosophy that guaranteed the long-run viability of the labor movement.

Labor relations law will continue to evolve and change as its environment changes. Quite possibly, the immediate future will see some governmental retreat from the labor-relations arena as the recently-elected Administration of President Ronald W. Reagan attempts to implement its apparent public mandate to limit the scope of federal government activity. This public mandate for less government control is supported by a large and growing number of industrial relations scholars who believe that the government's legalistic "fine-tuning" of the labor-management relationship generates more costs than benefits. Whether any changes will materialize remains to be seen. However, if the past is an accurate barometer of the future, one fact is certain: change will take place.

COMMENTARY: Mr. Richard Ringoen Speaks on the Need for Labor Law Reform

Mr. Richard M. Ringoen was elected president and chief executive officer of Ball Corporation in January 1981. Mr. Ringoen joined Ball in 1970 as vice president of the aerospace division in Boulder, Colorado. He later served as vice president and general manager of Ball Brothers Research Corporation, formerly a subsidiary of Ball Corporation, now part of the technical products group. In 1974 he was named corporate vice president, operations, of Ball Corporation and relocated in Muncie. He was elected president and chief operating officer in April 1978.

Prior to joining Ball, Mr. Ringoen served as director of special products of Martin-Marietta, Denver Division, with whom he was employed for 11 years, and had a key role in the development of the Titan ICBM. He was employed by Collins Radio Company of Cedar Rapids, Iowa, from 1948 to 1959, first as a research engineer and later as vice president of engineering for Alpha Corporation, a Collins communication system development subsidiary.

A native of Ridgeway, Iowa, he earned his B.S. and M.S. degrees from the State University of Iowa. His B.S. with highest distinction, was received in the field of electrical engineering in 1947. A year later he received his M.S.; he subsequently completed most of his doctoral requirements, including thesis work on measuring the moon's temperature at various radio frequencies to determine its surface material characteristics.

Mr. Ringoen served for two years in the U.S. Navy. He and his wife Joan have three sons: David, John and Daniel. Mr. Ringoen has been very active in religious and civic affairs. As a member of the Congregational Church, he served as superintendent of Christian education for his church for nine years while residing in Cedar Rapids; he was voted the outstanding layman in Christian education in the state. He was also active in Congregational Churches in Englewood and Boulder, Colorado, while living there. He and his family are members of the High Street United Methodist Church in Muncie. (Mr. Ringoen's name is pronounced as "Ring-in.")

A major mission of management is to utilize human and material resources to compete successfully in the marketplace. The end result of a well-managed enterprise is the creation of products and services for consumers, jobs and the consequent security and opportunity for enrichment for all employees, as well as investment returns for the owners of the enterprise.

One of the most pressing imperatives which must be faced by the management of American business is reform of outmoded labor laws. As a result of a series of federal legislative actions extending back to the Great Depression, the ability of managers to carry out their mission has been severely compromised.

Although there are hundreds of issues in the arena, one which stands out is the effect of government actions on employee compensation. The Davis-Bacon Act (1931) is a prime example of legislation which has created tremendous inflationary pressures on all American industries. This well-intentioned but misdirected legislation inflates costs of federal construction projects. It creates unrealistic wage expectations, adds to federal spending and debt and makes more difficult the task of all businesses to operate profitably. Inflationary labor laws such as the Davis-Bacon Act must be repealed or modified to correct the distorting effect on the economy.

COMMENTARY: Mr. William W. Winpisinger Speaks on the Need for Labor Law Reform

William W. Winpisinger is International President of the International Association of Machinists and Aerospace Workers (IAM). He thus leads one of the oldest, largest and most highly diversified unions in the United States and Canada. Originally an organization of railroad machinists, the IAM now represents workers in some 300 different industries. It is the predominant union in aerospace, air transport and automotive repair.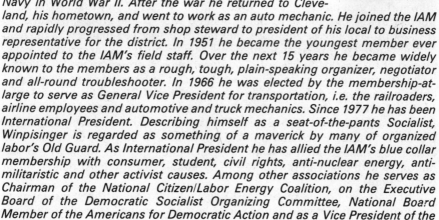
Winpisinger dropped out of high school to join the Navy in World War II. After the war he returned to Cleveland, his hometown, and went to work as an auto mechanic. He joined the IAM and rapidly progressed from shop steward to president of his local to business representative for the district. In 1951 he became the youngest member ever appointed to the IAM's field staff. Over the next 15 years he became widely known to the members as a rough, tough, plain-speaking organizer, negotiator and all-round troubleshooter. In 1966 he was elected by the membership-at-large to serve as General Vice President for transportation, i.e. the railroaders, airline employees and automotive and truck mechanics. Since 1977 he has been International President. Describing himself as a seat-of-the-pants Socialist, Winpisinger is regarded as something of a maverick by many of organized labor's Old Guard. As International President he has allied the IAM's blue collar membership with consumer, student, civil rights, anti-nuclear energy, anti-militaristic and other activist causes. Among other associations he serves as Chairman of the National Citizen/Labor Energy Coalition, on the Executive Board of the Democratic Socialist Organizing Committee, National Board Member of the Americans for Democratic Action and as a Vice President of the AFL-CIO.

In recent years the big business press and other corporate-controlled media have been triumphantly reporting that unions are losing more representation elections than ever before. The lower percentage of union wins is interpreted in a number of ways: i.e. workers no longer want unions, or employers no longer exploit workers, or unions no longer serve the needs of working people. As comforting as these interpretations may be to the business community, they miss what's really happening in America's work places today.

The laws governing relationships between labor and management, even including the anti-union Taft-Hartley and Landrum-Griffin amendments, provide that American workers shall have a *right* to organize and bargain collectively through representatives of their own choosing without interference and coercion from their employers.

Workers are told that is the law of the land. Collective bargaining is supposed to be the policy upon which the industrial relations of the nation are anchored. This policy was adopted almost 50 years ago after a century-and-half of labor management relations mainly characterized by increasingly bitter class struggle, labor relations studded by constant violence and death at places like Homestead and Ludlow and Pullman. These were the kind of labor relations practiced by the infamous Coal and Iron Police in the anthracite fields of Pennsylvania, by Harry Bennett's pluguglies and thugs in the factories of Henry Ford, by the assassins hired by Tom Birdler to terrorize workers in his steel mills.

When Congress passed the Wagner Act in 1935 it intended that the law of the jungle should be supplanted by the rule of law in the work places of America. And once employers accepted free and fair collective bargaining, they were rewarded with the most stable system of industrial relations in the industrialized world.

Unfortunately, however, more and more employers are now trying to subvert the workers' right to bargain collectively through representatives of their own choosing. This is why organized labor made an all out effort a few years ago to secure reforms in federal labor legislation. We went to Congress and we proved by case studies ranging from giant conglomerates like J.P. Stevens to a group of local auto dealerships in West Virginia that the rights of workers under the law were being openly, widely and brutally violated.

We proved, in case after case, how employers are conniving, with the help of a new breed of professional white collar union-busters (who carry briefcases instead of blackjacks) to frustrate and deny union representation. We showed how they do this first by filing endless and time-consuming challenges, objections and appeals back and forth between the NLRB and the courts. In the IAM we have had petitions for union representation elections delayed for years for the most frivolous of reasons. We have had two and three consecutive elections set aside on technicalities. The employer's purpose, of course, is to delay long enough for the work force to either give up voluntarily or be infiltrated with enough brownnosers to eventually defeat the petition for union certification.

Second, we proved by the most poignant and often pathetic testimony of hundreds of ordinary working people, who came from all over the country to testify before both the House and Senate Labor Committees, the extent to which employers openly and illegally retaliate against known union adherents. Thousands upon thousands of workers have been fired and blacklisted on the most frivolous of pretexts in union organizing drives. And though we may eventually be able to get them reinstated to their jobs after long and expensive legal procedures, it is usually after the organizing drive has been destroyed by such techniques. And third, union after union went before Congress and proved, again by actual case examples, that even when representation elections were won despite such delays and intimidation, employers had still another barrier against compliance with both the spirit and the letter of the law. In recent years they have discovered that the law provides no effective or enforceable penalty for violation of their duty to bargain in good faith.

In recent years more and more employers nullify union certification by simply refusing to bargain. They even warn their employees before the representation election that if the union is certified, they don't have to agree to a contract.

These are some of the ways in which employers are denying the rights of working men and women in America today. They are by no means the only ways. They are merely the most conspicuously brazen of the ways in which corporate power has nullified the nation's labor relations policy.

With violations such as these becoming more and more flagrant each year, the labor movement, early in 1977, petitioned Congress for a few modest and long overdue reforms. We asked, for example, that the certification process be speeded up and freed of endless delays based on trivial technicalities. We asked that employers like J.P. Stevens who set out to "chill" organizing drives be subject to more than a light tap on the wrist. We asked that workers fired for exercising legal rights be empowered to sue for punitive as well as compensatory financial and mental damages. And finally we asked that after an employer has had a reasonable time to bargain collectively, and refuses to do so, the workers shall be entitled to compensation for wages lost during periods of such unfair delay.

The need for labor law reform was obvious to a majority in both the House and Senate and especially to members who sat on the respective Labor Committees and heard the testimony of working people first hand. But the corporate establishment, aided and abetted by the big business press and right-wing mass mailing operations (like that of Richard Viguerie) stirred hate and hysteria in the business community from coast-to-coast. For months members of Congress were subjected to enormous and continuous pressures from businessmen back home. Even so the need for labor law reform was so clearly apparent, a bill was passed by the Senate had the majority prevailed. Despite a massive effort by the labor movement we fell two votes short of the 60 needed to break a Republican-Dixiecrat filibuster.

Today the need for labor law reform is greater than ever. Throughout America workers who want union representation are being denied their right to it. As a result grievances are building not merely against individual employers, but against a system that permits and perpetuates such injustice. Corporate America may think that by denying workers their right to organize and bargain collectively, they have won a great victory. But I suggest that in frustrating the process of collective bargaining in America's work places, employers are merely paving the way for a disillusioned and embittered work force. Workers denied the right to bargain collectively may seek to solve their grievances in less peaceful ways. With the defeat of labor law reform the differences between labor and management may once more revert to class struggle in America.

DISCUSSION QUESTIONS

1. Early associations of working men were regarded as *criminal* conspiracies. Why were these organizations considered *criminal* rather than *civil* conspiracies?

2. Why did the injunction replace trial court litigation as the primary employer weapon for controlling labor union activities after 1842?

3. Since the "injunction cannot preserve the so-called status quo" in labor disputes, there exists no proper role for the injunction in labor relations. Comment.

4. Despite the debate over whether the Sherman Antitrust Act (1890) was intended to apply to labor unions, there is general agreement that the courts applied the Act's provisions in a consistent and even-handed fashion to both labor and management. Comment.

5. Reconcile the Supreme Court's treatment of state anti-injunction legislation (particularly the Arizona statute) with its treatment of the Clayton Act.

6. Unlike the Norris-La Guardia Act, where the posture of the federal government was laissez-faire, the Wagner Act committed the federal government to the direct regulation of labor relations. Discuss. In what respects were these two statutes similar?

7. Given the difficulties associated with determining what good faith bargaining entails, why did Congress include this as a requirement of the Wagner Act?

8. The Taft-Hartley Act was a more broadly focused piece of legislation than the Wagner Act. Comment.

9. What was the Taft-Hartley Act's greatest contribution to labor-management relations? Explain.

10. Since the Taft-Hartley Act, as amended in 1959, was successful in coping with employment discrimination based on union activity, the anti-discrimination legislation of the 60's and 70's (e.g., Title VII of the Civil Rights Act of 1964 as amended by the Equal Employment Opportunity Act of 1972) was superfluous and redundant. Discuss.

SELECTED REFERENCES

"Cost of Growing Old: Business Necessity and the Age Discrimination in Employment Act," *Yale Law Journal,* (January 1979), **88:** 565–595.

Brinker, Paul A., and Benjamin J. Taylor, "Secondary Boycott Maze," *Labor Law Journal*, (July 1974) **25**: 418–427.

Feldacker, Bruce, *Labor Guide to Labor Law*, Reston, Virginia: Reston Publishing Co. Inc., 1980.

Frankfurter, Felix, and Nathaniel Green, *The Labor Injunction*, New York: the Macmillan Company, 1930.

Getman, Julius G., *Labor Relations Law, Practice and Policy*, Mineola, N.Y.: The Foundation Press, 1978.

Golub, Ira, "Propriety of Issuing Gissel Bargaining Orders Where the Union Has Never Attained a Majority," *Labor Law Journal*, (October 1978) **29**: 631–642.

Gregory, Charles O., and Harold A. Katz, *Labor and the Law*, New York: W.W. Norton & Company, Inc., 1979.

Hall, Francine S., and Maryann H. Albrecht, *The Management of Affirmative Action*, Santa Monica, Cal.: Goodyear Publishing Company, Inc., 1979.

Labor Relations Expediter (LRX), Washington, D.C.: The Bureau of National Affairs, Inc., Current.

Leslie, Douglas L., *Labor Law*, St. Paul, Minn.: West Publishing Co., 1979.

Meltzer, Bernard D., *Labor Law: Cases, Materials, and Problems*, Boston, Mass.: Little, Brown and Company, 1977.

Player, Mack A., *Employment Discrimination Law: Cases and Materials*, St. Paul, Minn.: West Publishing Company, 1980.

Taylor, Benjamin J., and Fred Witney, *Labor Relations Law*, Englewood Cliffs, N.J.: Prentice-Hall, Inc., 1975.

Wykstra, Ronald A., and Eleanor V. Stevens, *Labor Law and Public Policy*, New York: Odyssey Press (Publishing), 1970.

Chapter 5

Labor Unions:

The Organization and Representation of Labor

Unions have been active in the representation of labor in the United States since before the American Revolution. Yet these institutions are often the subject of controversy and are not well understood by many business and government leaders as well as college students. The purpose of this chapter is to introduce the student to the structure and operation of labor unions as well as to examine how unions become the representatives of employees.

Organized Labor

Organized labor is a term frequently used to collectively describe labor unions. Labor unions have played an important role in American economic and political life by representing the interests of their memberships.

> To most Americans the term "organized labor" means the American Federation of Labor and its associate, the Congress of Industrial Organizations. Though often damned as too weak by its members, or as too strong by business, press, and public, the AFL-CIO enjoys general recognition as a permanent, powerful force. Politicians seek its support and investigate its behavior. Business negotiates with its affiliates, acknowledges its legitimacy, and respects its strength. Presidents consult with its leaders and enlist its participation in government. The American economy, once regarded as the province of unfettered business is now accepted as a partnership among big business, big government, and big labor.[1]

The above quotation suggests the relative importance of organized labor in today's economy. Unions are hated, feared, loved, misunderstood, and relied on by millions of American workers, businessmen and politicians. Therefore, the serious student of labor relations must develop an understanding of what

[1] Harold C. Livesay, *Samuel Gompers and Organized Labor in America*, Boston: Little, Brown and Company, 1978, p. 1.

labor unions are and how they function. In examining labor unions the student must lay aside ideology and rhetoric for rational inquiry and factual analysis if any insight concerning unions and their conduct is to be acquired. Without an understanding of the conduct and goals of organized labor the student will be ill-prepared to contribute to or bargain with a labor union.

Labor unions are not new institutions; their history can be easily traced to the eighteenth century in America and even earlier in Europe. To a large measure the guild system and the early principles of worker representation were brought to the new world by immigrants. However, beyond these early common roots, the interdependence and similarities between European unions and those found in the United States stops. The United States has one of the largest, most heterogeneous and independent labor movements in the world. This is in large measure due to the diverse backgrounds of its leaders and members. In this respect, the American labor movement is the mirror image of the nation and its socio-economic systems. Despite the wide variations in strategies, goals and structures, American labor unions do have some common characteristics as suggested by the following operative definition of a union:

> A labor organization may have fraternal, cultural, or spiritual aims, and it may concern itself with the interests of its members as consumers or as taxpayers, but the activities that make it a "labor organization" (union) are those that have to do directly with the economics of the employment relation. If the latter is outside the scope of its action it is not a labor organization (union) even though all of its members are wage earners. On the other hand, if it serves as the instrument of combined action of its members with respect to the terms of their employment, it must be considered a labor organization,.....[2]

Labor unions are complex organizations. As the definition suggests, they perform many economic as well as social functions. Employees join and form labor unions for several different reasons. Unions are generally organized for the purpose of providing the membership with sufficient bargaining power to be able to influence their terms and conditions of employment. An individual worker, unless he or she is highly skilled or knowledgeable and can be differentiated from all substitute employees, is relatively powerless to influence his/her own terms and conditions of employment. By forming unions and engaging in concerted activities a significant percentage of the employer's work force can successfully influence the terms and conditions of employment by offsetting the individual employee's deficiency in bargaining power.

The definition offered is sufficiently general to include all organizations which are typically associated, by the layman, with the representation of labor for purposes of collective bargaining such as the United Auto Workers (UAW), International Brotherhood of Teamsters (IBT) and the International Brotherhood of Electrical Workers (IBEW), among several others. There are many other organizations and associations that focus substantial efforts on collective bargaining—such as the National Education Association (NEA), American

---

[2] D.A. McCabe and R.A. Lester, *Labor and Social Organization*, Boston: D.C. Heath & Company, 1949, pp. 11–12 (emphasis added).

Nurses Association (ANA) and the American Association of University Professors (AAUP). The definition also fits several other organizations which are typically regarded as purely professional organizations but which are also "the instrument of combined action of its members with respect to the terms of their employment." Organizations engaging in activities designed to control competition within a particular profession or hold, either directly or indirectly, substantial control over entry into a specific profession are practically speaking labor organizations. For example, when the officers of a state affiliate of the American Medical Association (AMA) are on the state's medical certification board and the admissions committees of the medical schools within the state, the AMA may exert almost total control over entry into that profession. The American Bar Association has established a code of ethics which for several years prohibited members from advertising. The ABA argued that it was unprofessional for members of their profession to advertise; but the effect is to reduce competition. Whether such organizations as the AMA or ABA are unions or not is subject to interpretation. However, it is clear that these organizations apply many of the same tactics and have many of the same goals as more traditional craft unions as well as fall within the broad definitions offered here for labor organizations.

The economic, social and legal environments within which unions and firms operate can significantly influence the success and orientation of the labor organization. During the late eighteenth century and early nineteenth century unions were considered by the judiciary to be criminal conspiracies. This made the organization of unions difficult but not impossible. After the passage of the Wagner Act in 1935 the organization of employees was fostered by a favorable legal environment. Besides the legal environment the creation of unions and their success in organizing employees seems to be sensitive to many economic variables. Unions are generally more successful during periods of economic growth while suffering setbacks during recessions. Public opinion also appears to play a significant role in determining the success of union organizing activities (see Chapters 2, 3 and 4).

Employees join unions for a variety of reasons. The real or perceived need for greater job security, compensation and social affiliation are obvious contributors to union growth. There are, however, many other reasons why employees join unions. Probably the single most important reason workers join unions today is the union shop. While it is certainly true that many employees who are required by the labor contract's union security clause to join would have joined the union anyway, there are several other reasons why employees choose to join unions. An employee's bad personal experience with management, such as an unjust disciplinary action or being passed over for a promotion, will often result in the worker joining a union. A general mistrust of management, in cases where foremen are unreliable or show favoritism, will result in workers joining the union. In addition, factors such as peer group pressure, social values, appeals by union organizers, poor working conditions, and low wages will contribute to workers joining unions. In some cases workers even sign up because one or the other of their parents were union members.

Regardless of why workers join or form unions, the continued survival and

BOX 5–1. Preamble of the Constitution of the International Union, United Automobile, Aerospace and Agricultural Implement Workers of America (UAW)

We hold these truths to be self-evident, expressive of the ideals and hopes of the workers who come under the jurisdiction of this International Union, United Automobile, Aerospace and Agricultural Implement Workers of America (UAW); that all men are created equal, that they are endowed by their creator with certain inalienable rights, that among these are life, liberty and the pursuit of happiness. That to secure these rights, governments are instituted among men, deriving their just powers from the consent of the governed. Within the orderly processes of such government lies the hope of the worker.

We hold that the exigencies of the times, the complete subdivision of labor in the development and operation of the industrial mass production system imposes conditions under which the worker is gradually but surely absorbed and controlled by the machine.

We hold these conditions to be utterly at variance with the spirit of justice and the needs of mankind. We believe the right of the workers to organize for mutual protection is the culminating growth of a great industry, which is evidence not only of its increased power but also of an economic and social change in our civilization.

We believe that organized labor and organized management possess the ability and owe the duty to society and maintaining, through cooperative effort, a mutually satisfactory and beneficial employer–employee relationship based upon understanding through the medium of conference.

The worker does not seek to usurp management's functions or ask for a place on the Board of Directors of concerns where organized. The worker through his Union merely asks for his rights. Management invests thousands of dollars in the business. The worker's investment in the business is his sinew, his blood and his life. The organized worker seeks a place at the conference table, together with the management when decisions are made which affect the amount of food he, his wife and family shall consume; the extent of education his children may have, the kind and amount of clothing they may wear; and their very existence. He asks that hours of labor be progressively reduced in proportion as modern machinery increases his productivity. He asks that the savings due to the inauguration of machinery and changes in technical methods shall be equitably divided between management and the worker. The organized worker asks that those who may be discharged be paid adequate dismissal wages to enable him to start afresh in another field; that society undertakes to train him in new skills and that it make provisions through ameliorative social laws for the innocent and residual sufferers from the inevitable industrial shifts which constitute progress.

vitality of organized labor in this country depends on the traditional "bread and butter" issues of the employer-employee relation. However, before proceeding, a few comments are in order concerning the distinction between joining and forming a labor union. In general, unions are formed because management has not provided employees with what they perceive to be reasonable and adequate terms and conditions of employment. Without a peaceful alternative to employer dictation of the terms and conditions of employment (i.e., unions) many economies have been rocked by revolution and instability. Collective bargaining by unions may be looked upon as a substitute for social, economic or political revolution by the working class. The reason for the formation of unions may, therefore, be summarized as purely the need for employee input without the disruptive effects of revolution. Workers join established unions for quite different reasons than why unions are formed. Workers, as was discussed above, often join unions for social reasons, peer pressure, family values, and because of contractual requirements to do so. However, in general, the need to join differs to the extent that workers wish to enjoy the benefits of union representation. Without support, both financial and moral, unions may be severely constrained in their representational efforts and may actually become ineffective. Joining a union may be looked upon as the method by which employees protect the organization and the rights obtained by forming a union.

The primary function of labor unions is to represent their membership for purposes of negotiating and administering a labor contract concerning the terms and conditions of employment. To accomplish this primary function unions engage in both collective bargaining with the employer and political activities designed to protect workers and the institution of collective bargaining through legislative enactments. The collective bargaining and political activities are frequently intertwined in complex strategies aimed at the accomplishment of the same goal. Overall, however, the American labor movement and its component unions are very much less politically oriented than are their counterparts overseas. American unions focus their energies primarily on the collective bargaining determination of private economic issues and engage in political activities only when labor's interests are at stake.

Table 5–1 presents data concerning the size of the unionized labor force for the period 1958–78. As the table indicates union and association membership grew steadily over the period. Yet, the percentages of the work force that was organized declined because the work force grew at a faster rate than union and association membership.

Craft and Industrial Unions

There are two basic types of labor unions. Classified by the nature of the bargaining units they represent, they are commonly called *craft unions* and *industrial unions*. Initially, craft unions organized and represented only specific skilled groups of employees such as electricians, carpenters, plumbers, and machinists, to the general exclusion of all other workers. Industrial unions, on the other hand, organized and represented entire plants or firms including all who were employed within the bargaining unit, skilled and unskilled alike.

TABLE 5–1. National Union and Employee Association Membership as a Proportion of Labor Force and Nonagricultural Employment, 1957–78* (Numbers in thousands)

Year	Membership Excluding Canada	Total Labor Force		Employees in Nonagricultural Establishments	
		Number	Percent Members	Number	Percent Members
Unions and associations:					
1968	20,721	82,272	25.2	67,897	30.5
1969	20,776	84,240	24.7	70,384	29.5
1970	21,248	85,903	24.7	70,880	30.0
1971	21,327	86,929	24.5	71,214	29.9
1972	21,657	88,991	24.3	73,675	29.4
1973	22,276	91,040	24.5	76,790	29.0
1974	22,809	93,240	24.5	78,265	29.1
1975	22,361	94,793	23.6	77,364	28.9
1976	22,662	96,917	23.4	80,048	28.3
1977	22,456	99,534	22.6	82,423	27.2
1978	22,880	102,537	22.3	84,446	27.1
Unions:					
1958	17,029	70,275	24.2	51,324	33.2
1959	17,117	70,921	24.1	53,268	32.1
1960	17,049	72,142	23.6	54,189	31.5
1961	16,303	73,031	22.3	53,999	30.2
1962	16,586	73,442	22.6	55,549	29.9
1963	16,524	74,571	22.2	56,653	29.2
1964	16,841	75,830	22.2	58,283	28.9
1965	17,299	77,178	22.4	60,765	28.5
1966	17,940	78,893	22.7	63,901	28.1
1967	18,367	80,793	22.7	65,803	27.9
1968	18,916	82,272	23.0	67,897	27.9
1969	19,036	84,240	22.6	70,384	27.0
1970	19,381	85,903	22.6	70,880	27.3
1971	19,211	86,929	22.1	71,214	27.0
1972	19,435	88,991	21.8	73,675	26.4
1973	19,851	91,040	21.8	76,790	25.9
1974	20,199	93,240	21.7	78,265	25.8
1975	19,553	94,793	20.6	77,364	25.3
1976	19,634	96,917	20.3	80,048	24.5
1977	19,902	99,534	20.0	82,423	24.1
1978	20,246	102,537	19.7	84,446	24.0

*Totals include reported membership and directly affiliated local union members. Total reported Canadian membership and members of single-firm unions are excluded.

Source: BLS Bulletin 2079 Directory of National Unions and Associations, 1979, Table 6.

Today, however, the lines of distinction between craft and industrial unions are often blurred or nonexistent. Many unions which were traditionally craft unions have organized and now represent industrial units; many industrial unions have sought to represent craft bargaining units. Much of the change in the traditional areas of representation occurred during the closing months of the 1950s and the early 1960s as a result of what was termed "raiding". Unions seeking to expand their own membership would attempt to get members of other unions to change their certified bargaining representative—hence the term raiding. By expanding its membership a union could increase its financial base enabling it to engage in further organizational efforts and better represent its membership. Skeptics, however, have argued that much of this raiding was a reflection of the particular union leader's ego. The union which engaged in raiding, so the argument goes, did so simply to enlarge its ranks for the purpose of gaining status in the labor community and political clout which some rather ruthless union leaders desired. Since those days the AFL-CIO has made considerable progress in curbing this raiding activity by its affiliated unions and locals. Further, unions have found that their efforts are better spent on organizing the unorganized. This, however, has not precluded many unions from seeking membership in industries which they have not traditionally organized. For example, in the late 1970s the UAW became the certified bargaining representative of a non-teaching bargaining unit at Wayne State University.

It is interesting, however, to examine the differences in the traditional views of what constitutes a craft and an industrial union. These distinctions lend valuable insight into the operation of labor organizations. Craft unions are frequently termed exclusive unions, exclusive in the sense that they often restrict their membership to assure a relative scarcity of their skills and hence higher wages. The apprentice program is the *modus operandi* of exclusive unionism. The union, at times, in combination with management administers these apprentice programs which are designed to teach new employees the requisite skills of the occupation. Education, experience and physical standards are often specified and sometimes are varied to meet the economic circumstances facing the union and the firm. If an excessive number of workers apply for apprenticeships standards may be raised; as more jobs become available apprenticeship standards may then be lowered. The essence of this type of unionization is the restriction of the supply of a particular class of labor. This union strategy is analogous to the strategies employed by certain professional organizations discussed earlier in this chapter. The analysis in Box 5–2 applies to both craft unions and many professional organizations.

Industrial unions are termed inclusive because they attempt to bring each craft together with unskilled employees in one group for purposes of collective bargaining. By organizing all of the skill groups of an employer, the union hopes to gain bargaining power through its ability to withhold all of the employer's work force if a strike is undertaken. Additionally, by utilizing such organizational techniques the union hopes to gain universal support from workers and, hence, strength through numbers.

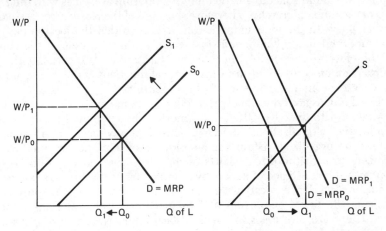

BOX 5-2. Craft and Industrial Union Effects on Wages and Employment (in otherwise competitive labor markets)

Craft Union

Industrial Union

Craft unions attempt to restrict supply hence pushing S_0 to S_1, increasing the wage from W/P_0 to W/P_1 with an associated decrease in employment from Q_0 to Q_1.

Industrial unions do not restrict supply but rather through sheer force of numbers refuse to allow the wage to fall below W/P_0 and permit employers to hire any number of employees at that wage. However, if the demand curve shifts right of MRP_1, a higher wage would have to be paid to attract additional workers.

Structure of Unions

There are three basic formalized components of the American labor movement. These components are the local union, the national (or as some are called the international, denoting locals in Canada and/or Mexico) and the federation. Each of these organizational levels has its own characteristics and performs specific functions. There is some structural variation among unions and as one would expect some overlap in the functions of the various organizational levels. In the following sections each of these organizational levels will be discussed briefly.

The Local Union

Unionized workers are members of the local union rather than the national or international union with which the local is affiliated. The local union is the organizational component which handles the everyday problems which arise in collective bargaining and with which the membership has daily contact. The local membership elects its own local officers who in turn represent the membership in the collective bargaining relationship as well as with the higher levels of the union hierarchy. Therefore, because of the closer association of the membership with the local union it can be argued that the local union is the most important union component in the daily administration of the contract and, therefore, quite possibly, in collective bargaining. It is certainly the most important union component in terms of social functions and is the component with which the membership most often identifies.

Local unions are typically *chartered* by a national union which in turn may be *affiliated* with the AFL-CIO—the American Federation of Labor-Congress of Industrial Organizations. Local unions typically are formed when an employer is organized. Often the employees of a particular employer are organized through the direct efforts of the organizing agency of the national union with the assistance of supportive employees of the firm. However, it is not uncommon for a local association to be formed for the purposes of organizing the firm's employees and then to seek a charter from a national union. There are rare cases in which a local union is formed to organize an employer and then remains independent. Local single firm unions which are not chartered by a national union are becoming relatively scarce because of the advantages in affiliating with larger national unions which have a larger financial base and trained professional assistance. By remaining independent, these single firm locals deny themselves the protective financial and professional service umbrella offered by national unions.

Selection of local union officers is accomplished through direct elections once the local is established. These elections are governed by the by-laws of the local labor organization. The union's by-laws are the rules that govern the organization and are specified, either in part or total, by the constitution of the national union which grants the local its charter. Although by-laws differ from union to union, it is not uncommon for the by-laws to specify several elective offices such as; president, vice president, secretary-treasurer, sargent-at-arms, grievance committeepersons (stewards), and alternate grievance committeepersons. These offices as well as their function differ from organization to organization, with some locals even placing responsibility for operation of the local in the hands of an employed business agent and relegating the top four or five elected officials to observers or figure heads. The business agent is frequently in evidence in large craft union locals particularly in the building trades. The local union also elects delegates to national conventions who represent their locals at these meetings. These delegates are often presented with a wide agenda of issues to be decided in the national convention. Through these delegates the respective locals gain input into the national union's decision making process. More importantly, in most unions, the national convention delegates elect the national union's officers. Thus, the local union is a democratic (direct elections) organization which achieves input at the level of the national union through elected representatives (a republican form of government).

In most cases local union officers receive little or no monetary benefit for holding union office. Generally the only reward for the union officer is the prestige within his union and community associated with holding an office in the local union or the self satisfaction associated with service to a cause in which one believes. The typical union officer is a dedicated unionist who views service to the union as a duty. Union officials such as ex-president of the Teamsters, Jimmy Hoffa, are exceedingly rare in the history of organized labor. When corrupt union officials are discovered they make headlines as did Hoffa, due to the fact that these cases are rare. The more appropriate models of union leaders are respected honest officials such as George Meany or Walter Reuther.

The primary function of the local union, as was alluded to above, is to represent employees in the collective bargaining process. Frequently the bulk of contract negotiations is done on the national level, leaving only those issues which impact specifically upon the local for the affiliated locals to negotiate. This, however, is not the case for unions which are not affiliated with a national union. The unaffiliated union must generally negotiate their own contract without the assistance of a parent organization. Local officers generally represent the membership in the national contract negotiations (in the case of the UAW, the membership is proportionately represented on two levels— skilled trades and general labor). When bargaining is done on the national level, the primary responsibility of the local becomes that of contract administration.

Many national unions provide local unions with various types of technical support—labor lawyers, accountants, industrial engineers, and legislative lobbyists. This support is regionalized geographically to tailor the support to the individual needs of the various locals. This is accomplished by establishing regional or district offices of the national union. For example, UAW Region 3, headquartered in Indianapolis, provides services to all UAW locals in Indiana, Kentucky and Southern Ohio. UAW Region 3 director, Dallas Sells, attends local meetings and serves as advisor to the various locals. If technical assistance is needed Mr. Sells is authorized to request the required assistance from the UAW international union.

The National Union

The national union besides providing technical assistance in negotiating and administering labor contracts provides many other services to locals and their members.[3] The types of services most often provided either directly by the national union or through state or regional offices of the national union include financial assistance to locals and their members during strikes, the administration of pension plans and other fringe benefits, the offering of local officer training programs, the publication of various training and information bulletins and periodicals, and lobbying in state legislatures as well as in Congress.

---

[3] Many unions are termed international unions because they have affiliates in Mexico and Canada.

Probably the most important function of the national union is organizing. Most organizational campaigns are conducted by the national union rather than locals. Although the AFL-CIO provides assistance to its affiliates in organizational campaigns, the Federation does not directly organize workers. The national union has the resources of many local unions from which to draw, making it the natural focal point of organizational activities. Local unions have fewer resources and a smaller base from which to muster resources, making it difficult for locals to engage in long and sometimes expensive organizing drives. Therefore these activities are more effective when left in the hands of the national union. Local unions are also very limited in the geographic range of their activities which suggests that without the national union very little incentive would exist for organizational activities except in states where unions are well established. The AFL-CIO is merely a federation of several unions and is not a union in the sense that it engages in collective bargaining or the organization of workers.

Table 5–2 presents membership data for the largest national unions and associations. The two largest national unions are the Teamsters (IBT) and the UAW. Both of these unions were independents (not affiliated with the AFL-CIO) until 1981 when the UAW reaffiliated with the AFL-CIO. Since the UAW reaffiliated there has been speculation that the Teamsters may also reaffiliate. The reuniting of the Teamsters and the AFL-CIO may come to pass but it is important to remember that the reasons for the IBT and UAW leaving the AFL-CIO were quite different. In the case of the UAW its president, Walter Reuther, and the president of the AFL-CIO George Meany had substantially different styles and the two men reportedly were fierce rivals. The personal rift between these two leaders developed over several years into a major barrier to UAW affiliation with the AFL-CIO. New leadership has gained control of both organizations and the differences between the organizations have been laid aside for the mutual benefits of reaffiliation. In the case of the Teamsters, alleged union corruption in the IBT resulted in its severance from the AFL-CIO. These wounds too may have healed and the IBT may reaffiliate but only time will tell. The next largest 17 national unions are associated with the Federation. The largest unaffiliated association is the National Education Association (NEA), the second largest labor organization and almost ten times as large as the next largest association.

The structure of national unions may vary considerably but most of these organizations have several common characteristics. We will briefly examine two unions, the United Auto Workers and the United Steelworkers, both of which are affiliated with the AFL-CIO.

The United Auto Workers (UAW)

The United Auto Workers, based in Detroit, Michigan, is an industrial union which organizes and represents workers in the automotive, aerospace, and agricultural equipment industries as well as clerical workers outside these industries (Wayne State University is an example). The UAW was affiliated with the CIO until 1955 and became affiliated with the AFL-CIO when the two

TABLE 5-2. National Unions and Employee Associations Reporting 100,000 Members or More, 1978.* (in thousands)

Organization†	Members	Organization†	Members
Unions:		Unions:—Continued	
Teamsters (Ind.)	1,924	Railway Clerks	200
Automobile Workers	1,499	Rubber	200
Steelworkers	1,386	Retail, Wholesale	198
State, County	1,020	Painters	190
Electrical (IBEW)	1,012	Oil, Chemical	180
Machinists	921	Fire Fighters	176
Carpenters	769	Transportation Union	176
Retail Clerks	736	Iron Workers	175
Service Employees	625	Bakery, Confectionery,	
Laborers	610	Tobacco	167
Communications Workers	508	Electrical (UE) (Ind.)	166
Clothing and Textile		Sheet Metal	159
Workers	501	Transit Union	154
Meat Cutters	500	Boilermakers	146
Teachers	500	Transport Workers	130
Operating Engineers	412	Printing and Graphic	120
Hotel	404	Maintenance of Way	119
Ladies' Garment	348	Woodworkers	118
Plumbers	337	Office	195
Musicians	330	Associations:	
Mine Workers (Ind.)	308	National Education	
Paperworkers	284	Association	1,696
Government (AFGE)	266	Nurses Association	187
Electrical (IUE)	255	Classified School	
Postal Workers	246	Employees	150
Letter Carriers	227	Police	140
Government (NAGE) (Ind.)	200	California	105

*Based on reports to the Bureau. All unions not identified as (Ind.) are affiliated with the AFL-CIO.
†For mergers and changes since 1978, see Appendix A.

Source: BLS Bulletin 2079, Directory of National Unions and Employee Associations, 1979, Table 9.

federations merged in 1955. The UAW left the AFL-CIO in 1968 and did not reaffiliate with the Federation until the Spring of 1981.

The UAW is organized, for purposes of negotiating and administering contracts, by Intracorporation Departments (one for each major corporation and a catch-all department for clerical and other workers). In addition there are several staff departments which conduct specialized activities such as education, arbitration services to locals and public relations (See Figure 5-1 for complete listing). The departments of the UAW which are responsible for organizing are called the National Wage and Hour Councils. These twenty councils are responsible for the specific industries with which the UAW bargains. The responsibility of the National Wage and Hour Councils is to assist regional offices and staff departments in organizing unorganized facilities and to assist in the standardization of working conditions and terms of employment within industries.

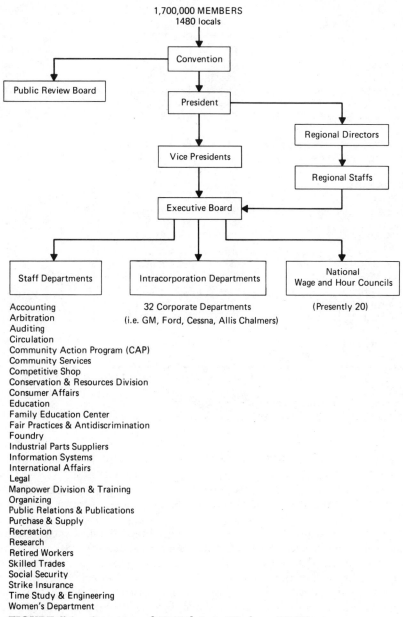

FIGURE 5.1.   Structure of United Auto Workers (UAW).

The United Steelworkers (USW)

The United Steelworkers is an industrial union much the same as the UAW. The Steelworkers have staff departments along the same lines as the UAW with the exception that financial departments fall under the secretary-

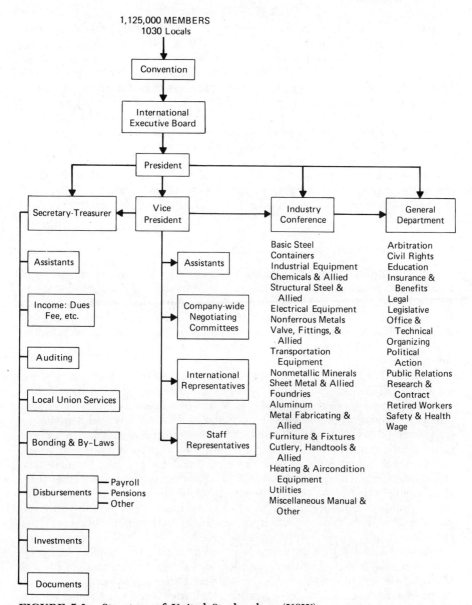

FIGURE 5.2. Structure of United Steelworkers (USW).

treasurer rather than the executive council. The Steelworkers are governed by their executive council, placing the president's office below the council in the chain of command, unlike the UAW. The organizational activities of the USW are conducted by specific staff departments, as are contract negotiations. There are, however, several industry conferences which assist in these activities as is the case with the UAW.

From an examination of the structure of the USW international union, it becomes evident that, while this organization is an industrial union, it is active in a wider range of industries than is the UAW. As one might suppose, many locals of the USW are craft unions, a situation not uncommon in many of the larger industrial unions today. There is considerable similarity between the United Auto Workers and the United Steelworkers even though these unions have developed independently. The similarities are a result of three things. First, both unions have similar demands placed upon them by their affiliated locals. Since both unions are primarily active in the manufacturing sector of the economy, many of the problems faced by the various locals of both unions are very similar. Secondly, many of the activities of any large national union are generic and do not vary substantially from industry to industry. Finally, these two organizations are relatively mature unions with structures which have evolved over time so as to make for the most efficient and effective national union possible.

The Federation

National unions are autonomous organizations which may voluntarily opt for affiliation with the AFL-CIO or remain independent. If dissatisfied with the AFL-CIO an affiliated union may voluntarily withdraw from the Federation as the UAW did in 1968. Voluntarism is an important element of the philosophy of the AFL-CIO. No national union is required to affiliate or withdraw from the Federation except in cases where the national does not abide by the AFL-CIO's constitution.

National unions may also merge, if they so desire, without interference from the AFL-CIO as evidenced by the 1969 creation of the United Transportation Union from the merger of five previously autonomous railway unions. National unions will frequently merge if facing financial hardship or organizational problems. It is likely that as more difficult organizing campaigns in the South and service industries are undertaken more mergers will occur.

National unions affiliate with the Federation for the benefits that such affiliation offers. The primary benefit of affiliation is some protection from membership *raiding*. As was discussed earlier, raiding is the term applied to one union attempting to dislodge an established union to acquire the disputed membership. This type of activity is costly to both unions because those resources could have been expended on the organization of nonunion employers. AFL-CIO constitutionally prohibits such union tactics. Affiliation thus frees resources, otherwise expended for raiding or protection of present units, for the organization of non-union firms. Other advantages of affiliation include facilitating coordinated bargaining and assistance in organizing efforts. The Federation does not negotiate contracts on behalf of its affiliated unions. It

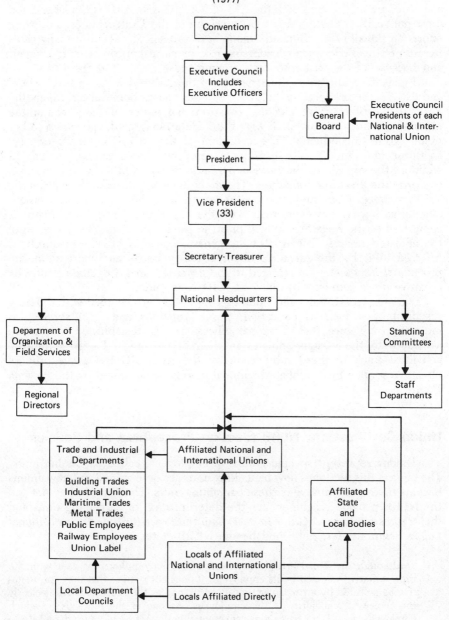

16,000,000 MEMBERS
112 NATIONAL or INTERNATIONAL UNIONS
(1977)

FIGURE 5.3. Structure of AFL-CIO/CLC.

does, however, assist in coordinating union activities thereby making coalition bargaining easier and more effective. There is also prestige and political power associated with affiliation with the AFL-CIO. The AFL-CIO is the largest and most politically influential labor organization in the United States. Lobbying efforts on behalf of its affiliated unions have proven successful in many cases because of the Federation's leadership role in the American labor movement and because of the vast resources it commands.

Figure 5–3 illustrates the structure of the AFL-CIO. As with the UAW and USW, the Federation holds a periodic convention during which the Federation's officers are elected, constitutional issues decided, committee reports rendered, internal policies of the Federation framed, and various other union business conducted. The president of the AFL-CIO, the secretary-treasurer, and the 33 vice-presidents comprise the *executive council*. In addition, the president, the secretary-treasurer and six of the vice presidents comprise the *executive committee*. The executive committee's role is primarily advisory concerning issues affecting the operation of the union. Final decision-making authority, however, rests with the president. The *general board* is comprised of the *executive council* plus the chief executive officers of each of the affiliated unions. The role of the *general board* is to rule on questions referred to it by the *executive council*. Policy issues and more mundane procedural issues may be referred to the *general board* if deemed politically sensitive or as required by the AFL-CIO constitution.

Various departments and standing committees are charged with differing responsibilities such as education, public relations and legal services as indicated in Figure 5–3. Regional offices are also established to provide assistance to the various affiliates in their organizing and representational activities. Each of these subdivisions of the AFL-CIO has as its primary objective service to its affiliated national unions, as indicated by the flows in Figure 5–3.

Union Certification: NLRB Election Procedures and Policies

Unions represent specific groups of employees, called bargaining units. The topic of this section is how bargaining units are determined and how unions become the representative of these bargaining units. The Taft-Hartley Act and the NLRB provide machinery for the determination of bargaining units and their representatives. *A Guide to Basic Law and Procedures under the National Labor Relations Act,* published by the NLRB states in part:

> Although the Taft-Hartley Act requires that an employer bargain with the representative selected by its employees, it does not require that the representative be selected by a particular procedure so long as the representative is clearly the choice of a majority of the employees. As one of the methods by which employees can select a bargaining representative the Act provides for the NLRB to conduct representation elections by secret ballot.
> The NLRB can conduct such an election only when a petition has been filed requesting one. A petition for certification of representatives can be filed by an

employee or a group of employees or any individual or labor organization acting on their behalf, or it can be filed by an employer. If filed by or on behalf of employees, the petition must be supported by a substantial number of employees who wish to be represented for collective bargaining and must state that their employer declines to recognize their representative. If filed by an employer, the petition must allege that one or more individuals or organizations have made a claim for recognition as the exclusive representative of the same group of employees.[4]

The Court and NLRB policy concerning bargaining unit determination and union certification are the topics of this section.

Establishment of Appropriate Bargaining Units

A union may be certified as the representative of a specific group of employees only if that group constitutes an *appropriate* bargaining unit. The appropriateness of a particular bargaining unit has been the subject of considerable controversy since passage of the Wagner Act in 1935. Section 9(b) of Taft-Hartley states, in part:

> The Board shall decide in each case whether, in order to assure to employees the fullest freedom in exercising the rights guaranteed by this Act, the unit appropriate for the purposes of collective bargaining shall be the employer unit, craft unit, plant unit or subdivision thereof. . . .

The NLRB has established standards which it will apply in the case–by–case determination of the appropriateness of bargaining units. It must be remembered that the Act requires *an appropriate* bargaining unit and not necessarily the *most* appropriate unit. These standards are:

> (1) the extent and type of union organization and the history of collective bargaining on behalf of the employees involved or other employees of the same or of other employers in the same industry; (2) the duties, skills, wages, and working conditions of the employees; (3) the relationship between the proposed unit or units and the employer's organization, management and operation of his business, including the geographical location of the various plants involved; and (4) the desires of the employees themselves. . . .[5]

While these standards apply generally, the NLRB has found it necessary to deal with more specific problems individually. Craft workers, managerial employees, and professional employees have each received special attention from the NLRB.

The treatment of craft workers has been a particularly thorny issue for the NLRB ever since the early days under the Wagner Act.[6] NLRB policy for the

---

[4] National Labor Relations Board, Office of the General Counsel, *A Guide to Basic Law and Procedures under the National Labor Relations Act*, Washington, D.C.: Government Printing Office, 1976, pp. 10–11.

[5] National Labor Relations Board, *Fourteenth Annual Report* (1949) pp. 23–33.

[6] See Benjamin Taylor and Fred Witney, *Labor Relations Law*, Englewood Cliffs, N.J.: Prentice-Hall, 1979 pp. 314–320 for detailed discussion.

first thirty-one years was characterized by a trial and error treatment of craft workers. It was not until the *Mallinckrodt*[7] decision in 1966 that the NLRB developed its present standards concerning the placement of craft workers. The *Mallinckrodt* decision involved the NLRB's construction of Section 9(b) (2) of the Taft-Hartley Act which states:

> the Board shall not decide that any craft unit is inappropriate for such purposes (collective bargaining) on a prior Board determination, unless a majority of the employees in the proposed craft unit vote against separate representation. . . .

These craft unit determination cases have involved skilled trades employees petitioning to be separated from industrial bargaining units. Frequently these craft workers constitute a small minority of the membership in industrial unions and often feel they are not adequately represented because of their minority status. These skilled workers, therefore, petition the NLRB for separation from the present bargaining unit or "craft severance." The *Mallinckrodt* case involved such an issue. Factors considered by the NLRB for craft severance include: (1) whether the employees constitute a recognizable craft; (2) whether the employees have a separate and an established identity; (3) the existing conduct and pattern of bargaining and the effect of craft severance on the present bargaining relations; (4) the history of the conduct and pattern of bargaining within the industry; (5) the degree of integration of the craft within the production system; (6) the desires and qualifications of the union seeking to represent these employees; and (7) the desires of the craft workers and their employer concerning craft severance.

The NLRB has applied these criteria on a case-by-case basis. Where the weight of evidence indicates that craft employee severance would impose an undue hardship upon the employer[8] or the present union,[9] the NLRB has generally refused to grant craft severance. When it has been shown that no hardship would be imposed on the existing union or employer[10] or that the existing union has not adequately or fairly represented the craft workers, severance is generally granted.[11]

Managerial employees may form labor unions for purposes of collective bargaining. The NLRB, however, has not asserted jurisdiction over these employees since its *Packard Motor Car Company*[12] decision in 1945. In the *Bell Aerospace* case in 1974 the United States Supreme Court ruled that managerial employees "are excluded from the scope of Taft-Hartley."[13] This laid to rest the controversy concerning unionization of managerial employees.

---

[7] *Mallinckrodt Chemical Works*, 162 NLRB 48 (1966).

[8] *Firestone Tire & Rubber Co.*, 222 NLRB 808 (1967).

[9] *Mobil Oil Corp.*, 169 NLRB 287 (1968).

[10] *Towmotor Corp.*, 187 NLRB 1027 (1971).

[11] *Buddy L. Corp.*, 167 NLRB 808 (1967).

[12] *Packard Motor Car Company*, 61 NLRB 4 (1945); for a more detailed discussion of the development of this law see Taylor and Witney *Labor Relations Law*, pp. 320–332.

[13] *NLRB v. Bell Aerospace Co.*, 416 U.S. 267 (1974).

The Court reasoned that it was not the intent of Congress to protect organizational activities and collective bargaining for supervisory personnel. However, in 1980, this body of law took an interesting turn. The United States Supreme Court ruled in the *Yeshiva University* case[14] that college faculty constituted managerial employees because (the faculty's) "authority in academic matters is absolute." Further, the Court noted that the faculty at Yeshiva exercised "authority (through the committee system) which in any other context unquestionably would be managerial." The managerial classification could thus be applied to other institutions and employees who have some impact upon the formulation of policies and the governance of the institution. Such employees as registered nurses, teachers in private schools, and bus drivers could possibly be reclassified as managerial employees if sufficient influence on the policy of the firm could be shown.

Employees such as lawyers, engineers, and nurses who are classified as professional employees are treated differently from the groups already discussed. Professional employees have been granted the right to form their own union or join rank-and-file production unions. The NLRB has broadened the definition of professional employees for purposes of collective bargaining in order to give highly trained persons a greater opportunity for autonomous representation. The NLRB defined professional positions as those which "require knowledge of an advanced type in a field of learning customarily acquired by a course of specialized intellectual instruction in an institution of higher learning as distinguished from a general academic education."[15] Section 9(b) (1) of Taft-Hartley states:

> That the Board shall not decide that any unit is appropriate for such purposes (collective bargaining) if such unit includes both professional employees and employees who are not professional employees unless a majority of such professional employees vote for inclusion in such unit....

Hence, depending upon their wishes, professional employees may be grouped with the rank and file or establish their own separate bargaining unit. Neither the NLRB nor the rank and file union may impose a particular bargaining unit on professionals. Therefore, professional employees must decide whether to be separately represented or included in a rank and file unit.

Elections

There are basically two ways for a union to gain recognition—the employer's voluntary recognition or NLRB representation election procedures. If the employer voluntarily recognizes the union, there is no need to petition the NLRB for a representation election. If the employer refuses to voluntarily recognize the union, one of two election procedures may be utilized, the *consent election* or the *directed election*. The consent election occurs when the

[14]*NLRB v. Yeshiva University*, 103 LRRM 2526.
[15]*Free Press Company*, 76 NLRB 152 (1948).

employer refuses to voluntarily recognize the union but either petitions for or voluntarily submits to a representation election. The directed election is an NLRB ordered election utilized when the employer refuses to voluntarily cooperate in the election procedure. The major substantive difference between the two procedures is the nature of the employer's participation—voluntary or compulsory.

Once the appropriate bargaining unit has been established either by the NLRB or by mutual agreement of the union and management, the NLRB will schedule and conduct a representation election. However, prior to the election, and frequently prior to the bargaining unit determination, the union and the employer conduct extensive election campaigns. The purpose of these campaigns is to influence the employee's votes in the upcoming representation election. However, the NLRB has established a policy of maintaining, as much as possible, what it has termed *laboratory* conditions for the conduct of representation elections. The purpose for these laboratory conditions is to guarantee the employees their rights under Section 7 of Taft-Hartley. Unions as well as employers are, therefore, restricted somewhat in what they may do prior to and during a representation election campaign. In general, neither the employer nor the union may coerce, threaten, or bribe employees to secure their votes.[16] Limitations are placed on the use of what are termed *captive audience speeches*. A captive audience speech is a speech delivered by the employer to a massed assembly of employees on company time and property where the management's position concerning unionism is spelled out for the workers. The NLRB requires that no captive audience may be utilized within twenty-four hours of a representation election.[17] The employer is also required to provide the union, through the NLRB regional office, a current list of names and addresses of all bargaining unit personnel within seven days after an election is scheduled.[18]

Either party may use distortion, misrepresentation of facts, or lie concerning the issues in a representation election.[19] The NLRB has reasoned that employees are "capable of recognizing campaign propaganda for what it is and discounting it." Whether this statement is correct or not has been the subject of a thirty-year legal controversy, the results of which are not likely to be conclusively settled for some time. However, at this time lies and propaganda are acceptable representation election campaign tools. A word of caution, the NLRB has over the past thirty years changed its position on this issue several times. Not only is honesty the *best* policy, it is likely to become NLRB policy again in the not too distant future.

The final issue to be dealt with concerns the representation election petition. The NLRB requires at least 30 percent of the members of the appropriate bargaining unit to indicate an interest in organization before it will

[16] See for example, *NLRB v. Gissel Packing*, 395 U.S. 575 (1969); *Ohmite Manufacturing Co.*, 217 NLRB 435 (1975); *Western Cartridge Co. v. NLRB*, 134 F., (2d) 240, (1943); *Savaur Manufacturing Co.*, 414 U.S. 270 (1973); and *Lau Industries*, 210 NLRB, 182 (1974).

[17] *Peerless Plywood*, 197 NLRB 427 (1953).

[18] *Excelsior Underwear, Inc.*, 156 NLRB 1236 (1966).

[19] *Shopping Kart Food Market*, 228 NLRB 190 (1977).

conduct an election. Signed union authorization cards constitute one method of indicating the required bargaining unit interest for an election. The NLRB, however, has established standards of reliability for bargaining authorization cards[20] namely: (1) no threats, coercion, or promise of benefits by union organizers; (2) no misrepresentation of what the card authorizes; and (3) if the employee reads and writes English he will be presumed to understand the bargaining authorization card. If the employer resists recognition of the union thereby requiring a petition to the NLRB for a representation election, unions normally will not make such a petition unless at least a majority of the employees have signed authorization cards. The reason for this reluctance is twofold. First, not all employees who sign authorization cards will vote, and, secondly, there is often some doubt as to exactly who is in the bargaining unit and, hence, eligible to vote. The latter consideration is particularly important for craft and professional employees.

Fair Representation

Unions are obligated to fairly and in good faith represent *all members of the bargaining unit.* This includes nonunion bargaining unit personnel in open shops and right-to-work law states. The employer also has an obligation not to interfere in the employee's right to fair representation. For example, if a union refuses to process an employee's grievance, the union subjects itself to a possible unfair labor practice charge and law suit. In the *Miranda* decision, the NLRB in pertinent part stated:

> Section 7...gives employees the right to be free from unfair or irrelevant or invidious treatment by their exclusive bargaining agent in matters affecting their employment. This right of employees is a statutory limitation on...bargaining representatives,...[21]

This, however, does not mean that unions must process all grievances employees file. It does not constitute an unfair labor practice for a union to refuse to process a meritless grievance or a grievance which is of little or no substantive importance.[22] The union, however, must decide which grievances to process on individual case merits and not in a racially, sexually, or other arbitrarily discriminatory manner.

This union obligation has caused considerable controversy in states which have right-to-work laws. Section 14(b) of Taft-Hartley permits states to enact legislation prohibiting the union shop and other types of union security clauses that require employees to join or financially contribute to the union after their 31st day of employment. The controversy arises over the fact that nonunion personnel must be represented by the union as equals with dues-paying

[20] Commonly called the Cumberland Doctrine, these standards were enunciated in the following cases: *Cumberland Shoe Corporation,* 144 NLRB 1268 (1964); *Levi Strauss & Co.,* 172 NLRB 57 (1968); *McEven Manufacturing Co.,* 172 NLRB 990 (1968); and *Gate of Spain Restaurant,* 192 NLRB 1091 (1971).

[21] *Miranda Fuel Company,* 140 NLRB 181 (1963).

[22] *Huges Tool Company,* 147 NLRB 166 (1964).

members, yet cannot be compelled to support the union. This "free-rider" phenomenon associated with right-to-work laws has led many union supporters to criticize Section 7 of Taft-Hartley.

Employers may also subject themselves to law suits, unfair labor practice charges, and adverse arbitration awards by interfering with an employee's right to fair representation. Employees are entitled to union representation in both the grievance and disciplinary procedures; if the employer fails to notify the union or interferes with the union in its representation of employees, management commits an unfair labor practice.[23]

Summary and Conclusions

The primary function of a labor union is to represent bargaining unit members in collective bargaining concerning their terms and conditions of employment. While unions may serve social and fraternal functions as well, the terms and conditions of employment are their major concern. Three distinct structural levels of union organization exist, namely: (1) the local; (2) the national (or international); and (3) the Federation. The responsibilities and functions of each are different-with some degree of overlap.

Unions become the certified bargaining representative of a bargaining unit either through voluntary employer recognition or through NLRB certification procedures. If the NLRB receives an election petition, it will define the appropriate bargaining unit, guarantee employees the opportunity to hear both union and management positions, and conduct a representation election.

The union and the employer are required to observe the employees' right to fair representation. Failure by either party to do so could result in a law suit or an unfair labor practice charge.

DISCUSSION QUESTIONS

1. What might be the disadvantages for a local union if it chooses not to affiliate with a national union? Advantages?

2. What explanation is there for the UAW and the USW to be so similar in their organizational structure?

3. What is the rationale for the NLRB to establish an appropriate bargaining unit? What problems might arise if the NLRB lacked the authority to establish bargaining units?

4. Specifically what is fair representation? What does fair representation have to do with Section 7 of Taft-Hartley?

5. Why might an employer request an NLRB certification election?

---

[23]This is discussed in detail in Chapters 11, 12, and 13.

SELECTED REFERENCES

Ashenfelter, Orley, "Racial Discrimination and Trade Unionism," *Journal of Political Economy,* (May-June 1972) pp. 491–504.

Barbash, J., *Labor's Grass Roots,* New York: Harper & Row, Publishers, 1961.

Bok, D.C. and J.T. Dunlop, *Labor and the American Community,* New York: Simon & Schuster, Inc., 1970.

Chamberlain, N.W., D.E. Cullen, and D. Lewin, *The Labor Sector,* New York: McGraw-Hill Book Company, 1980.

Cohen, Sanford, *Labor in the United States,* Columbus, Ohio: Charles E. Merrill Publishing Company, 1970.

Estey, M.S., *The Unions: Structure, Development and Management.* 2nd Edition, New York: Harcourt Brace Jovanovich, 1976.

Friedman, Milton, "Some Comments on the Significance of Labor Unions for Economic Policy," *The Impact of the Union,* ed., David M. Wright, New York: Harcourt Brace Jovanovich, 1951.

Hall, B.H., ed., *Autocracy and Insurgency in Organized Labor,* New Brunswick, N.J.: Transaction Books, 1972.

Hildebrand, George H., *American Unionism: An Historical and Analytical Survey.* Reading, Mass.: Addison-Wesley Publishing Co., Inc., 1979.

Litwick, Leon, *The American Labor Movement,* Englewood Cliffs, N.J.: Prentice-Hall, Inc., 1962.

McAdams, A.K., *Power and Politics in Labor Legislation,* New York: Columbia University Press, 1964.

Meltzer, B.D., *Labor Law,* 2nd edition, Boston: Little, Brown and Company, 1977.

Perlman, Mark, *Labor Union Theories in America,* Evanston, Ill.: Row, Peterson and Co., 1958.

Perlman, Selig, *A History of Trade Unionism in the United States,* New York: Macmillan, 1929.

Rehmus, C.M., et. al., (eds.) *Labor and American Politics: A Book of Readings, rev. ed.,* Ann Arbor, Mich.: University of Michigan Press, 1978.

Romer, Sam, *The International Brotherhood of Teamsters: Its Government and Structure,* New York: John Wiley & Sons, Inc., 1962.

Taft, Philip, *Organized Labor in American History,* New York: Harper & Row, Publishers, 1964.

Taylor, B.J. and Fred Witney, *Labor Relations Law,* 3rd Edition, Englewood Cliffs, N.J.: Prentice-Hall, 1979.

Ulman, Lloyd, *The Government of the Steel Workers' Union,* New York: John Wiley & Sons, Inc., 1972.

Ulman, Lloyd, "Multinational Unionism: Incentives, Barriers, and Alternatives," *Industrial Relations,* (February 1975), 14(1).

Wright, D.M., ed., *The Impact of the Union,* New York: Kelley and Macmillan, 1956.

Part II

Negotiation of the Labor Agreement

Chapter 6

Setting the Stage for Negotiations:

Bargaining in Good-Faith and the Substantive Issues of Collective Bargaining

This chapter is concerned with the legal requirements to bargain in good-faith and the substantive issues of negotiations. Good-faith bargaining has been specifically defined by the NLRB and the courts. These definitions will be presented here. This discussion is divided into five sections, the first examines the nature and role of a labor contract, the second examines the statutory requirements of good-faith bargaining, the third and fourth outline the obligation to bargain in good-faith during the negotiation and administration of the contract respectively and the final section describes the substantive issues of collective bargaining.

The Nature and Role of the Labor Agreement

The purpose of this section is to introduce the labor contract and its role in the employer-employee relation and to outline the requirements and limitations placed on negotiators. Collective bargaining is conducted in a complex and interrelated economic, legal and social environment. Without an understanding of this environment it is improbable that the student can fully appreciate the nature and operation of contract negotiation and administration which are presented in the following chapters.

Companies and individuals regularly enter into contracts. Contracts may be written, verbal, or even implied but in any form there is typically an offer, an acceptance, and something of value exchanged. When a restaurant enters into a contract to purchase meat from a vendor, the restaurant receives meat in exchange for money paid to the vendor. When a manufacturing company sells its products, it agrees to deliver specified goods for an agreed-upon price. A company may also enter into contracts with individual employees. In these cases the employee will frequently be required to provide services exclusively to the firm in exchange for specified compensation. Contracts between professional athletes and their teams are good examples of such contracts. Union contracts or labor agreements differ substantially from these various types of contracts. The union does not sell anything to the employer directly but simply acts as the agent of the employees in negotiating the terms and conditions of employment.

The basic reason most often proposed for employees forming unions is that as individuals they are easily replaced and therefore relatively powerless in comparison to the employer. It is more difficult for an employer to ignore the demands of the entire workforce. Hence by forming unions, the employees gain bargaining power relative to the employer. The result is that the employer's unilaterally established personnel policies will now be modified through negotiations by the employees' bargaining agent—the union. This is because the employees can achieve through concerted action what could not be achieved through individual action—input into the formulation of the terms and conditions of employment. Therefore, the function of the union contract is

---

BOX 6–1. The Role of Labor Unions—A Portion of a Lecture Presented by George W. Taylor in the University of Pennsylvania, Benjamin Franklin Lecture Series, March 19, 1962

Perhaps it was fortunate that even while the "Wealth of Nations" was still a best seller, economic individualism was giving way to the organization as the dominant institution. A synthetic but powerful "person"—the corporation—was created without benefit of Adam's rib. More and more, the individual had to adjust to the status of a worker for the corporation and, later on, as a member of the union organization. The government might still leave the individual alone, but the organization did not and doubtless could not if its economic function was to be performed. Where was it said: "One trouble about laissez-faire was that nobody ever made clear who was to leave what alone?" At any event, the organizational revolution produced the business corporation and, later as a countervailing power, the labor union. The primary function of these institutions was to serve the self–interests of particular constituencies. Great power, rivaling that of many a governmental agency, came to reside in these private agencies. The general welfare would thereby automatically be enhanced, or so it was assumed, by the freedom of the private institutions to operate subject solely to market constraints. The earlier doctrine of individual laissez-faire was refashioned and asserted as organizational laissez-faire.

simply to set rules and limits on management's prerogatives in offering employment to all individual employees.

The nature and scope of the labor agreement depends substantially on the union, the employer and his employees. The law governing collective bargaining will influence the behavior of the bargaining agents and in large part contribute to the eventual form the contract will take. In general the labor contract defines the specific rights of the union and the employees on any topic which it addresses. The employees' economic compensation, job security, efforts, promotions, and most issues directly concerning the terms and conditions of employment will be discussed in negotiations. What eventually will be included in the contract will be decided by the negotiators. The following sections outline the law which, within broad limits, shapes these negotiations and identifies the issues of collective bargaining.

Good-Faith Bargaining as Defined by Taft-Hartley

The duty to bargain in good-faith has been one of the central principles of labor law since the *new deal* period of the "great depression." Section 7 (a) of the National Industrial Recovery Act of 1933 (NIRA) provided that firms in industries covered by the Act must subscribe to the following conditions:

> (1) That employees shall have the right to organize and bargain collectively through representatives of their own choosing, and shall be free from the interference, restraint, or coercion of employers of labor, or their agents, in the designation of such representatives or in self organization or in other concerted activities for the purpose of collective bargaining or other mutual aid or protection; (2) That no employee and no one seeking employment shall be required as a condition of employment to join any company union or to refrain from joining, organizing or assisting a labor organization of his own choosing.

The National Labor Board (and its successor the first NLRB), the administrative agency for Section 7 (a) of the NIRA, interpreted this section of the Act as implicitly requiring employers and unions to bargain in good-faith.[1] When the NIRA was declared unconstitutional[2] in 1935, the basic tenets of good-faith bargaining espoused in the *Houde* case were written into the National Labor Relations Act (Wagner Act) passed later the same year. The Wagner Act, Section 8 (5) declared it to be an unfair labor practice for an employer: "To refuse to bargain collectively with the representatives of his employees...." However, no such requirement was made of unions; it was assumed by Congress that unions would bargain in good-faith. In 1947 Congress enacted several unfair labor practice provisions which still govern unions today. The relatively conservative, Republican dominated Congress enacted, among other provisions, Section 8 (b) (3) of the Taft-Hartley Act which placed the same obligation to bargain in good-faith on unions as had been imposed on management twelve years earlier.

[1] *Houde Engineering Corp.*, 1 NLRB (old series) 35 (1934).
[2] *Schechter Corporation v. United States*, 295 U.S. 495 (1935).

The Wagner Act authorized the NLRB to formulate remedies which would effectuate the purposes of the Act and allowed the NLRB to petition the courts to enforce their orders through the use of the injunction. These remedies have included back-pay and reinstatement for unlawfully discharged employees as well as the cease–and–desist orders noted above. This topic will be discussed in detail later in this chapter.

Congress also incorporated into the Taft-Hartley Act Section 8 (d) which requires, in part:

> For the purposes of this section, to bargain collectively is the performance of the mutual obligation of the employer and the representative of the employees to meet at reasonable times and confer in good faith with respect to wages, hours, and other terms and conditions of employment, or the negotiation of an agreement, or any question arising thereunder, and the execution of a written contract incorporating any agreement reached if requested by either party, but such obligation does not compel either party to agree to a proposal or require the making of a concession. . . .

The *central* language of Section 8 (d) are the phrases "confer in good faith" and "wages, hours, and other terms and conditions of employment." Section 8 (d) defines what constitutes collective bargaining for purposes of the Act. It has been interpreted by the NLRB and the courts to prohibit specific types of behavior by the bargaining parties. Such things as refusal to meet and confer with the other party for the purpose of collective bargaining, refusal to execute a written contract concerning agreed to terms, and reneging upon agreements while negotiating the contract have been found by the NLRB to be, per se, violations of the duty to bargain in good-faith. The Section 8 (d) requirement to collectively bargain in good-faith is, thus, closely related to Sections 8 (a) (5) and 8 (b) (3) of Taft-Hartley.

Violations of the duty to bargain collectively under Sections 8 (a) (5) and/or 8 (b) (3) can be specific actions or general conduct by an employer or a union. The *totality of conduct* doctrine has been applied by the NLRB and the courts in determining whether a party is collectively bargaining in good-faith. If, through the general conduct of a party, it is apparent that there is intent not to bargain or there is no honest desire to reach an agreement, the totality of the party's behavior may constitute a violation of its obligation to bargain in good-faith. Such violations are often difficult to detect and the entire pattern of conduct of the party or parties must be examined.

There are specific proscriptions placed upon the union and the employer to bargain in good-faith. These include: (1) refusing to respond to a party's request for a bargaining meeting[3]; (2) refusing to execute a written contract governing agreed to terms and conditions of employment[4]; (3) rejecting a party's proposals without offering a counterproposal[5]; (4) attempting to undermine the union or insistence by an employer that any contract exclude

---

[3] *NLRB v. Montgomery Ward & Co.* 133 F. (2d) 676 (1943).

[4] *American Newspaper Publishers Assn. v. NLRB* 193 F. (2d) 782 (1951).

[5] *Globe Cotton Mills v. NLRB.* 103 F. (2d) 91 (1939).

the union as a party to the agreement[6]; (5) refusal to send representatives to negotiations who have the authority to enter into an agreement[7]; (6) reneging on agreed to contractual provisions[8]; (7) deliberately impeding negotiations or lacking intent to enter into a collective bargaining agreement[9]; and (8) an employer granting concessions to employees while negotiating with the union.[10]

Nothing in Taft-Hartley mandates agreement; the Act only requires bargaining in good-faith. Sections 8 (a) (5), 8 (b) (3), and 8 (d) simply require the parties to meet and confer with the intent of negotiating an agreement. The parties to collective bargaining are under no obligation to execute a contract if no agreement can be reached in any given subject area. Labor and management must take a positive approach to negotiations and refrain from the specific actions noted above. Thus, the body of law limits, broadly speaking, the voluntary nature of collective bargaining. The purpose of this limitation is to foster peaceful labor-management relations. The theory behind Congressional interference in free collective bargaining is that, if the parties must bargain over certain basic topics and refrain from behavior which undermines the bargaining process, it is less likely that workstoppages and industrial warfare will occur. It does appear that the theory was correct and that this body of law has contributed to industrial peace.

An interesting question has arisen concerning whether an employer or union must continue to bargain in good-faith when the other party refuses to meet its bargaining obligation. While the NLRB has handled such cases on an individual basis, the body of case law has not produced any clear guiding principles. Under the Wagner Act, the NLRB developed the concept that, if the union refused to bargain in good-faith, the employer's obligation to bargain in good-faith continued but the union's refusal would become a relevant consideration in any union allegation that the employer violated Section 8 (a) (5) requirements. In light of Taft-Hartley 8 (b) (3) and 8 (d) requirements, it appears, at first glace, that the NLRB would require a party to bargain in good-faith regardless of the behavior of the other party. However, a strong argument can be made that this should not be required; if the union or employer refuses to bargain in good-faith, it may not be possible to determine the bargaining intent of the other party and, therefore, there exists no rationale for continuing the mandate to bargain in good-faith.[11]

The Obligation During Contract Negotiations

The United States Supreme Court, in the 1958 *Borg-Warner* case,[12] upheld the National Labor Relations Board's authority to provide operational

---

[6]*American Numbering Machine Co.* 10 NLRB 536 (1938).

[7]*Great Southern Trucking Co. v. NLRB.* 127 F. (2d) 180, (1942).

[8]*NLRB v. Norfolk Shipbuilding & Drydock Coys.* 172 F. (2d) 813 (1949).

[9]*Na Mac Product Corp.* 70 NLRB 298 (1964) and *NLRB v. Griswold Manufacturing Co.* 106 F (2d) 713 (1939).

[10]*Aluminum Ore Co. v. NLRB.* 131 F. (2d) 485 (1942).

[11]*Times Publishing Co.* 72 NLRB 676 (1947).

[12]*NLRB v Wooster Division of Borg-Warner Corp.*, 356 U.S. 342 (1958).

definitions of good-faith bargaining and the "terms and conditions of employment." The issue before the NLRB in the Borg-Warner case was whether certain demands of the employer were indeed "terms and conditions" of employment. The employer refused to execute a labor contract with a local union unless the agreement included (1) a last offer prestrike vote allowing non-union as well as union employees to cast ballots and (2) a union recognition clause excluding the international union with which the local was affiliated and certified by the NLRB as the bargaining representative. The National Labor Relations Board ruled that the employer's insistence upon the inclusion of these types of issues in the contract constituted a refusal to bargain within the meaning of Section 8 (a) (5) of Taft-Hartley. The United States Supreme Court reviewed this case and agreed with the NLRB. The Supreme Court determined that these issues were not within the intended meaning of "terms and conditions of employment" under Section 8 (d) of Taft Hartley and therefore not mandatory issues of collective bargaining.

The court's decision in *Borg-Warner* affirmed the NLRB's authority to determine the scope of collective bargaining. The Court, however, did not give the NLRB carte blanche to dictate the terms of a contract. The NLRB has only the authority to require bargaining in good-faith over mandatory issues, but not their inclusion in any contract. As a result of this decision the NLRB may determine what issues are mandatory and what issues are voluntary for purposes of collective bargaining under the Taft-Hartley Act. The primary criticism of the *Borg-Warner* decision has been that it does not specifically outline how the Board is to determine whether an issue is a mandatory or nonmandatory item of bargaining. Unions have complained that the *Borg-Warner* decision limits, unreasonably, the range of negotiations. Unions also complain that neither the NLRB nor the courts are staffed with people possessing the necessary practical experience and expertise to properly classify bargaining items as mandatory. To an extent this is to be expected. Unions gain rights through the contract and if the employer is not required to negotiate concerning certain issues, the union may find that these issues are difficult, if not impossible, to bring within the "four corners" of the contract. If these issues are not governed by the contract, the union cannot claim any associated rights concerning them. The result has been the camouflaging, to some extent, of union bargaining demands. Frequently unions will append nonmandatory items to mandatory bargaining demands. For example, if the employer refuses to discuss shop disciplinary rules (which are voluntary bargaining topics), the union may append shop disciplinary rules demands to the economic package (which is a mandatory issue). The union may demand a settlement on shop rules as a condition for more favorable settlement of the wage issue. This borders on a failure to bargain in good–faith. If the union demands the inclusion of its version of shop disciplinary rules as a condition for negotiating the economic package or signing the contract and then proceeds to bargain these voluntary issues to an impasse, it has committed an unfair labor practice. If the union has a nonmandatory bargaining demand rejected by the employer, the union may make excesive demands concerning mandatory issues in an attempt to force the employer to reconsider. This again is not an uncommon tactic, paralleling the above cited example, but it is less likely to result in an unfair labor practice charge.

Justice Stewart, in a concurring opinion with the majority, in the *Fibreboard Paper Products*[13] case further explained the *Borg-Warner* Doctrine. In part Justice Stewart stated:

> Nothing the Court holds today should be understood as imposing a duty to bargain collectively regarding such managerial decisions, which lie at the core of entrepreneurial control....

This concurring opinion has been adopted by the NLRB as the operational definition of voluntary bargaining topics. The NLRB has classified topics which are central to the operation of the firm and are normally reserved to managerial discretion as voluntary bargaining issues. Marketing, hiring, product lines and characteristics, financing, and utilization of supervisory personnel are central to managerial prerogatives and are obviously voluntary issues of bargaining. Certainly issues which have no direct effect upon the employer-employee relation and are central to the efficient operation of the firm are classified by the NLRB as voluntary issues of bargaining. However, a classification problem arises when an issue is both at the core of entrepreneurial control and is a term or condition of employment. In these cases, the NLRB has attempted to ascertain in which category the issue most closely fits, weighing the evidence and determining the impact of its decision. An example of such a case is subcontracting. The NLRB has determined that the effects of subcontracting on employees are more directly related to the terms and conditions of employment than to the core of management rights and, therefore, mandatory issues of bargaining. The decision to subcontract, however, is at the core of entrepreneurial control and the NLRB has ruled the decision to subcontract is a voluntary issue of bargaining. However, little consistency, few principles, and even less criteria have emerged from the NLRB's treatment of these borderline cases except the weight of evidence shall govern in each specific case. It is, therefore, impossible to give much insight beyond the fact that the NLRB reviews each of these cases on individual merits. The body of law concerning this topic is currently evolving.

Since the land-mark decision in the *Borg-Warner* case, the NLRB has established three major categories of bargaining items and delineated each category's relation to bargaining in good-faith. These substantive categories are: (1) Mandatory issues—these items must be negotiated if either side so demands and failure to bargain in good-faith over these topics is an unfair labor practice; (2) Voluntary issues—demands concerning these items may be negotiated if mutually agreeable but may not be bargained to an impasse; and (3) Illegal issues—demands concerning these items are, per se, unfair labor practices. The final section of this chapter is devoted to reviewing the demands that fall under each specific category of bargaining items.

---

[13] *Fibreboard Paper Products v. NLRB*, 379 U.S. 203 (1964).

Boulwarism and Bargaining in Good Faith

This method of negotiation, named after its designer, former General Electric Vice President of Public and Employee Relations, Lemuel R. Boulware, consists of an array of tactics, primarily designed, as General Electric insists, to arrive at an "equitable and just settlement based upon the facts." The tactical array deployed by General Electric in its negotiations consisted of five basic elements: (1) company determination of what (what it surmised) was needed by its employees in the agreement; (2) company establishment of the bargaining agenda and assumption of the initiative in negotiations, generally with the union being precluded from specifying issues; (3) the company's presentation of a single offer to the union; (4) company modification of its offer only in the face of newly established facts; and (5) commencement of an extensive public and employee relations campaign to convince employees and the general public that the company was interested in what was best for its employees.

Boulwarism was effective primarily because GE dealt with numerous unions representing its production and skilled employees. The International Union of Electric Workers (IUE), the United Electrical Workers (UE), the International Brotherhood of Electrical Workers (IBEW), the United Auto Workers (UAW), and the Machinists (IAM) all represented groups of General Electric's employees. The factionalization of representation made the unions a much less formidable force than if GE had one structured and powerful union with which to deal. As a result Boulwarism proved to be successful for GE, allowing the firm to virtually dictate the terms and conditions of employment to its employees.

As may have been expected, the unions (specifically the IUE) charged that GE was not bargaining in good-faith as was required by Section 8 (a) (5) of Taft-Hartley and filed an unfair labor practice charge. In examining the totality of General Electric's conduct the NLRB ruled that GE's "take it or leave it" table bargaining together with its public and employee relations campaign amounted to an attempt to undermine collective bargaining—hence, a failure to collectively bargain.[14] The Circuit Court enforced the NLRB decision and the Supreme Court refused to review the matter thus condemning Boulwarism as bad-faith bargaining. These developments did not convince GE to totally abandon this bargaining strategy. GE again employed the strategy in the 1969 negotiations thereby provoking a work stoppage. The unions, realizing that the success of Boulwarism was based upon the axiom "divide and conquer", united and employed coalition bargaining. Consequently, since 1965, this GE bargaining strategy has met with much less success, and, has, since 1973, been largely supplanted by more traditional bargaining strategies.

Good-Faith Bargaining During the Life of the Contract

Section 8 (d) of Taft-Hartley obligates the parties to bargain concerning the "terms and conditions of employment" not only during negotiations but also in

---

[14]*General Electric Co.* 197 NLRB 46 (1968).

good-faith during the life of the contract. This later Section 8 (d) bargaining requirement has been a topic of controversy. Employers, in response to changing economic circumstances and technology, have argued that they should be free to efficiently operate the firm. The dynamic nature of the American economy, employers have argued, makes it "necessary" to on occasion modify or even eliminate a contractual provision in order to reduce costs and improve production methods. However, if employers are granted this freedom, what then is the implication for the *Borg-Warner* Doctrine? The NLRB has provided the answer to this question.

In the *Fibreboard Paper Products* case an employer, to save costs, subcontracted bargaining unit maintenance work during the effective period of the contract. The result of the employer's subcontracting was the loss of several bargaining unit jobs. Consequently, the union filed an unfair labor practice charge alleging that the employer's subcontracting violated the labor agreement and constituted a failure to bargain in good-faith. The union asked that the affected employees be reinstated with back pay. The Supreme Court, in its review of the case, determined that management violated its obligation to bargain in good-faith under Section 8 (d) of Taft-Hartley. The Court reasoned that subcontracting is a mandatory issue of collective bargaining because it directly affects the terms and conditions of employment and is subject to the requirement to bargain in good-faith even during the effective period of the labor agreement, which the management in *Fibreboard Paper Products* did not do. If the proposed change is bargained to an impasse, the employer has discharged its obligation to collectively bargain in good-faith. Upon exhausting the bargaining process, without agreement, the employer may then proceed unilaterally with the desired contract modification. However, if the union believes that the employer, by instituting the change, has violated the labor agreement it may seek a remedy through the grievance-arbitration process.[15]

Employers frequently charged that the *Fibreboard* decision unduly restrained their right to efficiently operate the firm. In subsequent cases[16] the NLRB and the Courts modified the *Fibreboard* doctrine. It was decided that if the contract contained language permitting the employer to make unilateral changes in specific areas, bargaining is not required. Additionally, if the employer had an established history of subcontracting (and like actions) and the union was unsuccessful in negotiating contract language limiting this management prerogative, there is *no* employer obligation to bargain such issues to an impasse prior to modifying the labor agreement. Even in the face of modification of the *Fibreboard* doctrine by the NLRB and the Courts, employers still actively debate the propriety of this decision.

In response to employer desires and the Nixon appointment of a new member to the NLRB, the *Fibreboard* requirement of bargaining proposed contract modifications to an impasse was abnegated in the controversial *Collyer*[17] decision. Since the *Collyer* decision in 1971, the NLRB has not

[15] See Chapter 13 for an examination of labor arbitration.

[16] *Westinghouse Electric Corp.* (Mansfield Plant), 150 NLRB 1574 (1965).

[17] *Collyer Insulated Wire*, 192 NLRB 837 (1971). For other dimensions of this decision see Chapter 13.

required the employer to discharge the obligation to bargain in good-faith prior to modifying an existing contract. Instead the employer may institute whatever changes he deems necessary to the effective operation of the firm. If the union believes that the employer has violated either Sections 8 (d) or 8 (a) (5) of Taft-Hartley, its only recourse is the grievance procedure and arbitration. The second major dimension of the *Collyer* decision is that the NLRB will no longer enforce Sections 8 (d) or 8 (a) (5) of Taft-Hartley, but rather defer its jurisdiction in these cases to arbitration.

As one might expect, the *Collyer* decision has been subject to considerable debate. Unions charge that the NLRB has "run out" on its authority and responsibility to enforce the Taft-Hartley Act, leaving organized labor at a distinct disadvantage in the collective bargaining process. Employers, naturally, are pleased with the decision which they claim allows them the freedom to more efficiently operate their firms. The freedom, in this case, comes from the fact that the NLRB will defer to arbitration matters involving changes in existing contracts, hence, allowing employers to more easily circumvent the requirement of good-faith bargaining during the administration of the contract.

Remedies for Failure to Bargain in Good-Faith

Section 10 (c) of the Taft-Hartley Act empowers the NLRB to formulate remedies for violations of the act. The section states, in part:

> the Board shall state its findings of fact and shall issue and cause to be served on such person an order requiring such person to cease and desist from such unfair labor practice, and to take such affirmative action including reinstatement of employees with or without back pay, as will effectuate the policies of this Act. . . .

The NLRB has, in matters involving Section 8 (d), Section 8 (a) (5), and Section 8 (a) (3) ordered reinstatement of employees with and occasionally without back pay as was deemed appropriate. The NLRB, however, has been hesitant to employ remedies beyond reinstatement and back pay. In the *Ex-Cell-O*[18] case, an administrative law judge ordered the company to "make the union whole" for violating Section 8 (d) of Taft-Hartley. The employer was ordered to render the union back pay in an amount equal to the difference between its wage rates and union rates in the area—as a remedy for the employer's failure to bargain in good-faith after the union had won a representation election. The employer was also ordered to assume litigation costs. The NLRB, upon review, refused to uphold the administrative law judge's remedy, claiming that the judge had no authority to make such an order. In subsequent cases, where blatant bargaining violations have been proven, the NLRB (at the prodding of two different Circuit Courts of Appeal) awarded litigation expenses in addition to back pay.

If the case is deferred to arbitration, remedies are typically limited to reinstatement of contractual rights and back pay. Arbitrators must establish remedies which are consistent with the national labor policy. Otherwise, the NLRB will not defer to the arbitrator's award. Therefore it makes little

---

[18] *Ex-Cell-O*, 185 NLRB, 107 (1970).

difference, in so far as the remedy is concerned, whether the case is decided by the NLRB or is deferred to arbitration. There is, however, one important difference between NLRB adjudication and arbitration—that difference being cost. The cost of arbitration is divided equally between the parties to the dispute (except for advocates fees), while the Office of the General Counsel represents complaining parties in unfair labor practice cases. Arbitrators typically do not award litigation expenses. Therefore arbitration is a more costly procedure to the complaining party than NLRB litigation.

Substantive Issues of Collective Bargaining

The law and the *Borg-Warner* doctrine, to a large extent, shape the nature and the conduct of collective bargaining. Even though an issue is classified as a mandatory topic of bargaining, it does not have to be included in any labor contract. Equally true is the fact that many voluntary issues of collective bargaining are included in labor contracts. The parties to the collective bargaining relation determine what is and is not to be included in their contracts, as long as the issue does not fall into the illegal category. However, the classification of these issues into voluntary or mandatory categories will impact the course of negotiations as well as the substantive content of the labor contract. For example, a party wishing to negotiate a voluntary issue may find it difficult if not impossible to get the issue on the table if their opponent chooses not to bargain the issue. Consequently, it becomes necessary to make concessions on mandatory topics or to agree to discuss voluntary issues the other party wishes to negotiate to get a voluntary issue on the bargaining agenda. The result is that contracts are bargained more as packages today than was true before the *Borg-Warner* decision, thus requiring greater sophistication and care in negotiations.

Mandatory Bargaining Issues

Mandatory issues are topics which both parties are obligated to bargain over in good-faith—if either party so demands. Wages, hours, and other terms and conditions of employment—items specifically listed in Section 8 (d) of Taft-Hartley—have been interpreted by the NLRB and the Courts as mandatory issues for bargaining. These bargaining topics may be negotiated to an impasse; unions may strike concerning these items; employers may lockout; and, either party may refuse to sign the labor agreement unless they are satisfied with the contract language covering these issues.

The following mandatory bargaining topics are arranged by the area of the bargaining relation which they impact. These classifications are intended to be exhaustive. The NLRB and the courts, however, frequently review the classification of bargaining items and it is not uncommon for an item to be reclassified. For example, pensions of retired workers were classified as a mandatory item of bargaining the the *Inland Steel*[19] decision of 1948, but

---

[19] *Inland Steel v. NLRB*, 170 F. (2d) 247 (1948).

reclassified as voluntary bargaining issues in 1971 with the *Pittsburgh Plate Glass*[20] decision. While this observed legal flexibility is necessary because of the dynamic nature of industrial relations, it also serves to make the *Borg-Warner* doctrine classification scheme somewhat unpredictable and confusing.

Economic Issues

Economic issues deal with the compensation of employees and are intricately interrelated. Any economic issue in an economic package contains three characteristics: (1) method of payment; (2) magnitude of payment; and (3) rationale for the payment. Since economic issues are typically negotiated as a whole package these issues are more interrelated than most.

Economic Issues[21]
1. Wages
2. Paid vacations, holidays, and time off.
3. Changes in the basis of payment from hourly to salary, etc.
4. Bonus payments and merit pay.
5. Prices of inplant food services (whether company provided or not).
6. Group insurance: health, dental, optical, life, and accident.
7. Piece rates and incentive plans.
8. Stock purchase plans and profit sharing.
9. Overtime premiums
10. Discounts on company products.
11. Shift differentials.
12. Procedures for income tax withholding.
13. Severance pay.
14. Musician price lists.
15. Changes in insurance carriers or coverage.
16. Company provided houses, utilities, and maintenance.
17. Truck rental prices, for company rented vehicles of employee-operators.
18. Pensions (to include benefits) for presently working employees.

Economic issues are also intertwined with bargaining issues affecting effort, intensity of labor utilization, and many other work standard issues. The result is that frequently the economic package includes many issues that fall under several of the following categories.

Union-Mangement Relation Issues

These items have been construed by the NLRB and the courts to be "terms and conditions of employment." While typically not directly related to

[20] *Local 1 Chemical Workers v. Pittsburgh Plate Glass Co.*, 404 U.S. 157 (1971).

[21] Sources of these items include: R.A. Gorman, *Basic Text on Labor Law—Unionization and Collective Bargaining*, St. Paul: West Publishing Co., 1976, pp. 523–529; B.D. Meltzer, *Labor Law Cases, Materials and Problems*, Second Edition, Boston: Little, Brown, and Company, 1977, pp. 724–758; R. Richardson, "Positive Collective Bargaining," in D. Yoder and H.G. Heneman, Jr. eds., *Employee and Labor Relations*, Vol. 3, of *ASPA Handbook of Personnel and Industrial Relations*, Washington: Bureau of National Affairs, 1976 pp. 7–127; D.L. Leslie, *Labor Law*, St. Paul: West Publishing Co., 1979, pp. 191–225; and the *Industrial Relations Guide Service*, Englewood Cliffs, N.J.: Prentice-Hall, Inc.

the working conditions of employees, these issues involve the union, the negotiation of the contract, or administrative issues related to the representation process whereby employees influence their terms and conditions of employment. Since union representation and negotiation is the accepted method for employees to collectively influence their terms and conditions of employment, these issues constitute mandatory bargaining topics.

Union-Management Relation Issues[22]
1. Duration of the labor agreement.
2. Union security, including: agency shop, union shop, and nondiscriminatory hiring halls (only where legal).
3. Union dues and fees checkoff, when properly authorized by the employee.
4. Grievance procedure, including arbitration.
5. Reinstatement of economic strikers.
6. No-strike clauses.
7. Arrangements for contract negotiations (e.g., time, place, and etc.)
8. Superseniority for union officials.
9. Seniority provisions covering employees who leave and then re-enter the bargaining unit.
10. Management rights clauses.
11. Most favored nation clauses.
12. Union recognition clauses.

Hours and Work Standards

This category of issues, as previously mentioned, is closely related to economic issues and many of these issues are frequently included in the economic package. As is obvious from Section 8 (d) of Taft-Hartley, these issues are, per se, mandatory issues of collective bargaining. Since hours are specifically mentioned in Section 8 (d) it is easy to see that most of the following topics are variations of hours or are concerned with the effort to be expended during hours of employment.

Hours and Work Standards[23]
1. Hours of work, including shift scheduling and the standard work week (as limited by the Fair Labor Standards Act).
2. Break times, clean-up periods, and rest periods.
3. Lunch periods.
4. Work-loads and job rates.
5. Job assignment transfers (when across pay classifications).
6. Production ceilings and floors.
7. Subcontracting.
8. Supervisors and/or nonbargaining unit employees doing bargaining unit work.

[22]See footnote 21.
[23] Ibid.

Changes in Plant Location or Production

This category of mandatory bargaining items may be the subject of more controversy than any other. Employers have argued that most of these topics are within the core of entrepreneurial control and therefore should *not* be mandatory bargaining items. Unions, on the other hand, have argued that these issues impact directly upon the employer-employee relation and should be considered mandatory bargaining topics. The NLRB and courts have, however, ruled that the terms and conditions of employment are actually central to the following issues. It is true that each of these items has some impact on the right of management to operate the firm but, on a case–by–case basis, the NLRB and the courts have determined that the terms and conditions of employment have greater priority.

Changes in Plant Location or Production[24]
1. Changes in employee status, including becoming an independent contractor, reclassification of jobs, automation displacement, and changes in work standards.
2. Seniority rights in relocated plants.
3. Partial and/or total plant closing.
4. Supplemental unemployment benefits and eligibility.
5. Temporary layoffs and recalls due to inventory, plant closing, or production changes.
6. Plant relocation.
7. Plant reopening.
8. Retraining or assistance in obtaining employment for workers displaced by automation, technological change, or plant closing-relocation.

Personnel Administration

This category of mandatory bargaining items constitutes "terms and conditions" of employment. These topics relate almost universally to the employees' work assignments and job security which are conditions of employment. Again, as should be obvious from Section 8 (d) of Taft-Hartley, these issues are mandatory issues of collective bargaining.

Personnel Administration[25]
1. Discipline—shop disciplinary rules are a voluntary bargaining issue but the penalty for a violation of a shop disciplinary rule is a mandatory issue.
2. Layoffs and recalls.
3. Retirement age.
4. Promotions and demotions.
5. Establishment or loss of seniority.
6. Transfers and shift preferences.
7. Sick leave and certain authorized leaves of absence.
8. Job posting procedures.
9. Employee physical exams.

[24]See footnote 21.
[25] Ibid.

10. Lie detector use in discipline procedures.
11. Removing racially discriminatory personnel practices.
12. Prices of items served by restaurants and bars if tips are a portion of the compensation package and the distribution of tips.

Voluntary Bargaining Issues

This category of bargaining issues, according to the courts and the NLRB, does not constitute "terms and conditions of employment" for purposes of Section 8 (d) of Taft-Hartley. From a practical standpoint, if the topic fits neither the mandatory nor the illegal bargaining category, the employer and the union may agree to negotiate the issue, but only if such negotiation is mutually acceptable. Unions may not strike nor may employers lockout as a result of an impasse that arises in the negotiation of a voluntary issue. Neither party may demand negotiation of a voluntary item as a condition for the signing of the labor agreement. If either party demands negotiation of a voluntary item contrary to the wishes of the other party, the National Labor Relations Board will find a per se violation of Section 8 (d)—an unfair labor practice. If the NLRB defers such a case to a private arbitrator, the arbitrator will in general find an unfair labor practice for breach of the Section 8 (d) duty to bargain in good-faith. The NLRB will make no further inquiry into the conduct of negotiations nor the conduct of either party, but simply find a failure to bargain in good-faith over the terms and conditions of employment. Arbitrators, on the other hand, will consider the circumstances surrounding the failure to bargain.[26]

Demands which the NLRB and the courts have classified as voluntary issues of collective bargaining include:

Voluntary Issues[27]

1. Posting of a contract performance bond by the union.
2. Posting of a contract performance bond by the employer.
3. Any issue dealing with the internal administration of the union.
4. Unions fining members for crossing picket lines during a strike.
5. Determination of who may vote in union elections, including strike, contract ratification, or officer elections.
6. Expenditures for or employer participation in promotional campaigns or advertising.
7. Product design, corporate financing, sales, and product lines.
8. Prices the firm charges for its product.
9. Pensions and other rights and benefits for presently retired employees.
10. Compensation of supervisory and other non-bargaining unit employees.
11. Discipline of supervisors.

---

[26] See Chapter 13 for a discussion of the arbitration process. Arbitrators are bound by their ethics, the contract, and in some cases the law to give the parties ample opportunity to present their arguments and evidence.

[27] See R.A. Gorman, *Basic Text on Labor Law—Unionization and Collective Bargaining.* St. Paul: West Publishing Co., 1976, pp. 523–529 for further discussion of these issues.

12. Extension of contract provisions to other facilities not presently certified by the NLRB as a part of the bargaining unit.
13. Extension of an arbitration award to cover the employer's non-bargaining unit employees.
14. Shop disciplinary rules and safety rules.
15. Procurement of equipment, materials, and intermediate products.

Illegal Issues

Illegal issues may not be negotiated nor included in the labor agreement. To do either constitutes an unfair labor practice. It is also an unfair labor practice for either party to demand negotiation of an illegal issue. Illegal issues are bargaining topics that are either expressly prohibited by some provision of the Taft-Hartley Act or some other statute such as the Fair Labor Standards Act or the Civil Rights Act of 1964. These items rarely become an issue of collective bargaining; however, if negotiated, not only does this constitute an unfair labor practice, but the contract provision is not enforceable either through arbitration or the courts.

Different bodies of labor law oftentimes cloud the distinction between illegal and other types of bargaining issues. Virtually all labor laws classify bargaining issues. These categories, however, differ from law to law. Featherbedding is a case in point. Featherbedding involves the negotiation of "make work" rules and in the extreme is an illegal item of collective bargaining under Taft–Hartley. Specifically, Section 8 (b) (6) prohibits a labor union from causing or "attempting to cause an employer to pay or deliver or agree to pay or deliver any money or other thing of value, in the nature of an exaction, for services which are not performed or not to be performed." On the other hand, featherbedding is permissible under the provisions of the Railway Labor Act. Featherbedding, therefore, is an illegal or legal bargaining topic depending on the industry where it occurs. Further complicating the issue is the fact that lesser forms of this activity have been ruled by the United States Supreme Court to be lawful under Taft-Hartley as long as there is work to be performed by the employee.[28] Even if the job assigned to the employee is wasteful or could be easily performed by presently employed workers, this does not constitute illegal featherbedding. The NLRB has ruled that, while make-work rules are lawful, contract provisions covering said rules must specify some duties and require the employee to spend time on the job.

Items which have been banned by Taft-Hartley include:

Illegal Issues[29]
1. Closed shop union security.
2. Compulsory union dues and fees checkoff.
3. Featherbedding.
4. Union shop or Agency shop security agreements in states having laws

---

[28] *American Newspaper Assoc. v. NLRB*, 345 U.S. 110 (1953); See R.D. Leiter *Featherbedding and Job Security*, New York: Twayne Publishers, 1964, for further discussion of this topic.

[29] These items are specifically enumerated in the Taft-Hartley Act.

prohibiting these arrangements under the authority of Taft-Hartley Section 14(b).

5. Discrimination against an employee for union membership or lack thereof except for failure to tender fair and reasonable union dues and fees under a legal union security arrangement.
6. Hot cargo agreements.
7. Right-to-strike concerning union jurisdiction over bargaining unit.
8. Requiring any employee of a health care institution with a bona fide religious objection to the payment of union dues or fees to tender such payment.
9. Right to modify or terminate a contract other than as provided for by Section 8 (d) of Taft-Hartley.

Items which have been banned by other statutes are too numerous to list here.

Summary and Conclusions

The labor contract differs from general business contracts in that a union acts as an agent for all employees of the employer to limit management's authority to establish the terms and conditions of employment. The role of the labor union is to equalize bargaining power between the employer and employees. The nature and role of the labor agreement is influenced by the legal environment but is primarily determined by management and the union in free and voluntary negotiations.

During contract negotiations, the union and employer must bargain in good–faith concerning mandatory issues of collective bargaining; where mutually agreeable the parties may bargain over voluntary issues; the negotiators may not bargain over illegal issues. The National Labor Relations Board and the courts have from time to time reclassified bargaining items. Therefore, the composition of these classifications is constantly changing.

During the life of the contract the employer may modify the labor agreement without consulting the union. Employer modification of the contract, however, is not without risk. Although the NLRB has ruled it will no longer enforce the unfair labor practice provisions of Taft-Hartley concerning the employer's and union's obligation to bargain in good-faith during the administration of the labor contract, it will defer enforcement where possible to private arbitrators. The risk inherent with employer modification of a labor contract is an adverse arbitration award that may involve an unfair labor practice. Aggrieved employees may be reinstated with back pay—at substantial cost to the employer.

DISCUSSION QUESTIONS

1. What are the trade-offs involved with the *Collyer* doctrine as opposed to the *Fibreboard* doctrine?

2. Why have the NLRB and the courts established what issues may not, may, and must be bargained over? Does this classification scheme impose constraints on what form the labor agreement will take? If so how?

3. What problems may arise by deferring Section 8 (d) cases to private arbitration? What are the benefits of such deferral?

4. Boulwarism is a unique approach to collective bargaining. Does this approach lend insight into what good-faith bargaining is? What makes Boulwarism bad-faith bargaining?

5. Do Sections 8 (a) (5), 8 (b) (3) and 8 (d) differ in the requirements placed upon the parties to collective bargaining? If so, how and are these sections necessary to assure good-faith bargaining?

6. What is a labor contract? How does it differ from other contracts? What is the role of labor law in shaping the labor agreement?

SELECTED REFERENCES

Baumback, Clifford M., *Structural Wage Issues in Collective Bargaining*, Lexington, MA: D.C. Heath & Company, 1971.

Chamberlain, Neil W. and Kuhn, James W., *Collective Bargaining*, 2nd Ed., New York: McGraw-Hill Book Company, 1965.

Gorman, R.A., *Basic Text on Labor Law Unionization and Collective Bargaining*. St. Paul: West Publishing Co., 1976.

Healy, James J. Ed., *Creative Collective Bargaining: Meeting Today's Challenge to Labor Management Relations*. Englewood Cliffs, N.J.: Prentice-Hall, Inc., 1965.

Leslie, D.L., *Labor Law*, St. Paul: West Publishing Co., 1979.

McCaffery, Robert M., *Managing the Employee Benefits Program*, New York: American Management Association, 1972.

Taylor, B.J. and Fred Witney, *Labor Relations Law*, Englewood Cliffs, N.J.: Prentice-Hall, Inc., 1979.

Tracy, Lane, "The Influence of Noneconomic Factors on Negotiators," *Industrial and Labor Relations Review*, (January 1974), **27**: 2.

Chapter 7

Negotiating a Contract:
The Art and Science of Table Bargaining

Table bargaining is the component of labor management relations that the average citizen is most familiar with. This awareness is created by constant media reference to major collective bargaining contracts currently being or shortly-to-be negotiated. Yet, despite this wide publicity, the negotiation process remains shrouded in mystery for many people. It is the purpose of this chapter to describe and analyze the bargaining process, its driving mechanism, the behavior and objectives of participants and various techniques/devices that expedite and facilitate agreement.

Traditional Models: Three Different Approaches

Analyses of the negotiation process have historically followed one of three separate, although not necessarily mutually exclusive, approaches. In lieu of better terminology, these may be labeled the deductive, inductive, and institutional approaches.

Deductive Bargaining Model

Deductive models typically proceed from a very restricted set of assumptions concerning human behavior. Deductive reasoning is utilized to develop bargaining principles or laws that are then utilized to predict whether agreement is possible or where agreement will occur. Given the validity of the assumptions made, these models represent a theoretically elegant and concise explanation of the negotiation process and method for identification of the final settlement point—should such a point exist.

The deductive model is the favorite analytical tool of economists.[1] The best

[1] For examples, see: H.C. Cross, "A Theory of the Bargaining Process," *American Economic Review*, (March 1965), **55**: 67–94; John Cross, *The Economics of Bargaining*, New York: Basic Books, Inc., Publishers, 1969; J.C. Harsanyi, "Notes on the Bargaining Problem," *Southern Economic Journal*, (April 1958), **24**: 471–76; J. Pen, *The Wage Rate Under Collective Bargaining*, Cambridge, Mass.: Harvard University Press, 1959.

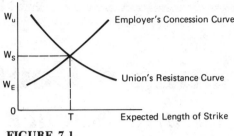

FIGURE 7.1.

known economic model is one developed by J.R. Hicks.[2] Figure 7–1 illustrates this model. OW_E is the wage rate that management would set if it had the unilateral power to do so. On the other hand, if the union possessed all the power, it would set the wage rate at OW_U. Except in rare cases, neither party possesses the power to unilaterally impose these wage rates. Agreement is the result of the costs imposed by a possible work stoppage, the expected length of which is measured along the horizontal axis of the graph of Figure 7–1.

The employer's concession curve depicts the various wage rate-expected strike length combinations that are equally costly to the firm. For example, rather than incur the costs associated with a strike of expected length OT, the employer would agree to any wage rate in the range OW_E to OW_S. The employer will increase its offer along the curve as the length of an expected strike increases. Similarly, the union's resistance curve depicts various combinations of wage rates and expected strike lengths that are equally costly to the labor organization. For example, rather than calling a strike of expected length OT, the union would accept any wage rate in the range OW_S to OW_u. Union wage demands will decrease as the length of an expected strike increases. Both parties' decisions as to resist or concede are made on the basis of cost comparisons—a comparison of strike costs with the costs associated with the wage rate concession. If the former exceed the latter, concession occurs.

Since both parties' willingness to concede or resist depends upon expected strike length, intersection of the employer's concession with the union's resistance curve is inevitable. The negotiator's sole responsibility during negotiations is to identify the other party's concession/resistance curve, thereby pinpointing the contract settlement point—where intersection occurs. Strikes, under the Hicksian framework, are either the result of irrational behavior or the failure by a negotiator to successfully discharge his/her negotiating responsibility—to discover the opponent's concession/resistance curve.

Major contributions of the Hicksian Model include (1) identification of a major factor bringing agreement during negotiations—the strike and its attendant costs, (2) emphasis on the rational aspects of the bargaining process, and (3) focus upon the need for complete information and the importance of learning in any effective negotiation process.

[2] John R. Hicks, *The Theory of Wages*, New York: The Macmillan Company, 1932, Chapter 2.

These contributions, however, are only realized at significant cost. This cost is illustrated by the limitations of the Hicksian and other similar deductive bargaining models. First, these models make unrealistic assumptions concerning both the amount of knowledge a negotiator is capable of achieving and the criteria the negotiator utilizes to make decisions. It is assumed that collective decision making is completely analogous to individual rational decision making.

Second, it is assumed that the employer's concession curve and the union's resistance curve are static—that the positions of these curves do not change during bargaining. The essence of collective bargaining, however, consists of various tactics, strategies, and activities designed to influence and persuade. Hence, collective bargaining is, by nature, dynamic. The dynamics involve attempts to move and shift an opponent's concession/resistance curve in a manner that will insure the most favorable outcome possible. The curves cannot be assumed to be static. Such an assumption is contrary to the basic nature of the bargaining process.

Third, the model seems to imply that a party's willingness to resist or concede depends solely upon its estimate of the length of a possible strike— that the shapes of the resistance/concession curves depend solely upon estimated strike length. However, such estimates of strike length are themselves based upon the behavior and intensity of purpose exhibited by the other party during the negotiation process. Hence, the rate of concession (i.e., the shape of the concession/resistance curve) depends upon a party's perception of what the other party is actually doing during negotiations as compared to the behavior that had been expected before the negotiation process got underway. Consequently, the role of learning is even more important than the model implies, not only for purposes of identifying the settlement point, but, more importantly, as a factor bringing agreement during the negotiation process. In this sense, learning deserves a weight equal in importance to estimated length of strike (i.e., strike costs).

The last shortcoming of the deductive bargaining model stems from the limitations noted above. The limited information at the disposal of negotiators, the extent to which collective decision making differs from individual rational decision making, the behavioral constraints on rational decision making, the tactical and strategic aspects of the negotiation process, and the importance of learning as a factor affecting concession rates reduce the explanatory value and predictive power of the deductive bargaining model. Simply stated, it is difficult, if not impossible, to test empirically. These limitations, however, should not obscure the contributions of the model. As a starting point the model provides valuable insights to the bargaining process.

Inductive Bargaining Models

Where deductive models proceed from a strict set of assumptions to logically reasoned principles or laws to explain the negotiation process, the inductive research approach relies upon observation of real-world phenomena to discover cause and effect relationships. Variables identified as possibly affecting bargaining behavior and bargaining outcomes are tested under controlled laboratory conditions to determine the nature and magnitude of impact. Since the variables focused upon impact bargaining behavior, these models are commonly referred to as behavioral bargaining models.[3]

Behavioral models typically build upon the foundation established by deductive models. By incorporating strategic, interpersonal, psychological, and structural variables, such as bluffing, hard versus soft bargaining, degree of trust, conflict intensity, organizational factionalism, deadline pressures, communication opportunities, and the like, the models help explain deviation from solutions predicted by deductive models.

Although inductive models significantly contribute to an understanding of the negotiation process, they suffer from one of the limitations which afflicts deductive models; it is difficult to empirically test a specific behavioral cause and effect relationship due to the many behavioral variables impacting the bargaining process.

Institutional Bargaining Models

The institutionalists[4] march to the beat of a different drummer. Theoretically elegant and precise models are cast aside in favor of a highly descriptive analysis detailing the influence of environmental variables upon the course of negotiations. The concept of bargaining power is a central feature of institutional analysis; it is the vehicle through which convergence of bargaining positions is achieved under the institutional framework of analysis. Economic, legal, historical, organizational, and structural variables are examined in terms of their impact upon bargaining power and, therefore, upon the bargaining process.

The Negotiation Process: Pragmatic Approach

The following pages examine contract negotiations as an essentially rational process subject to both behavioral and institutional influences. The analysis is eclectic in the sense that it incorporates various elements of the three approaches. Rather than striving to achieve methodological neatness and predictive accuracy, the narrative analysis pursued here is simply intended to impart a basic understanding of the negotiation process, the driving mechanism of the process, and the multitude of factors impacting that process.

The Rational Negotiator

Central to the negotiation process is the assumption that both parties behave in a rational manner. Rationality, in the context used here, simply

---

[3] The best example of the behavioral approach is the work of Richard E. Walton and Robert B. McKersie, *A Behavioral Theory of Labor Negotiations*, New York: McGraw-Hill Book Company, 1965.

[4] The institutional approach is closely associated with the University of Wisconsin, most notably the work of Professors John R. Commons and Selig Perlman. For examples, see: John R. Commons, *Institutional Economics: Its Place in Political Economy*, New York: The Macmillan Company, 1934; and Selig Perlman, *A Theory of Labor Movement*, Reprints of Economic Classics, New York: A.M. Kelly, Publishers, 1966.

requires the negotiator to compare the benefits with the costs of a particular course of action and to undertake that action only when benefits exceed costs—when the benefit-cost ratio exceeds one. Since all decisions are made within the context of uncertainty, the comparison is made in terms of expected (i.e., perceived) benefits and costs. Hence, rationality is dependent upon the perceived benefit-cost ratio: it is relative rather than absolute in nature. Thus, in this sense, the assumption that the parties to the bargaining process are rational is quite realistic.

Driving Mechanism: Bargaining Power

The driving mechanism of the bargaining process is bargaining power. The concept of bargaining power has long held center stage in discussions of the negotiation process. Professor John R. Commons defined bargaining power as "...the proprietary ability to withhold products or production pending the negotiations for transfer of ownership of wealth."[5] For Professor John T. Dunlop, bargaining power was the relative ability of two contracting parties to influence the wage, in light of all prevailing factors.[6] The concept of bargaining power which can be extended to all items on the bargaining agenda and which is used here is that of Chamberlain and Kuhn: bargaining power is "...the ability to secure another's agreement on one's own terms."[7]

A party's bargaining power is dependent on an opponent's willingness to agree on that party's terms. In view of the rationality assumption previously discussed, bargaining power is nothing more than the willingness of an opponent to agree to the party's proposal based on a consideration of the benefit-cost ratio of so doing. Hence, in the industrial relations context, the bargaining power of the union for any proposal it makes is:

$$\text{Union Bargaining Power (UBP)} = \frac{\text{Management's Expected Benefits From Agreement (MEBA)}}{\text{Management's Expected Costs From Agreement (MECA)}};$$

while the bargaining power of management for any proposal it makes is:

$$\text{Management Bargaining Power (MBP)} = \frac{\text{Union's Expected Benefits From Agreement (UEBA)}}{\text{Union's Expected Costs From Agreement (UECA)}}.$$

Since perceived benefits and costs are the critical variables in the decision-

[5]Commons, *Institutional Economics: Its Place in Political Economy*, p. 267

[6]John T. Dunlop, *Wage Determination Under Trade Unions*, New York: The Macmillan Company, 1944, p. 78.

[7]Neil W. Chamberlain and James W. Kuhn, *Collective Bargaining*, 2d. ed., New York: McGraw-Hill Book Company, 1965, p. 170.

making process, expected benefits and costs are used to calculate/measure bargaining power. The heart of the negotiation process is found in each party's attempt, through a variety of devices, to increase the opponent's perceived benefits and to reduce the opponent's perceived costs of each item requested at the bargaining table. Bargaining power is increased to the extent that a negotiator succeeds in raising an opponent's benefit-cost ratio. When the ratio exceeds one, settlement (i.e., agreement) occurs.

Settlement Range

Numerous issues confront the negotiators at contract negotiation time. For each item on the bargaining agenda, a range of possible points of settlement exists. Figure 7–2 illustrates one such "settlement range."[8] Point C represents the current contractual wage rate. It also represents what management would like to achieve in bargaining this item—the management target (M_T). Identification of the current wage rate as the management target in negotiations reflects the old adage that "labor proposes and management disposes": that management benefits from maintenance of the status quo. Although oftentimes the case, management has recently taken a more active role in demanding changes in current contract provisions. This more active role (proposing instead of disposing) could be illustrated by placing the management target (M_T) to the left of Point C. Traditional identification of the two points, however, simplifies the following analysis without limiting its application in any way. Point M_r represents management's resistance point—what management must achieve at minimum during negotiations. Points U_t and U_r are the corresponding points for the union.

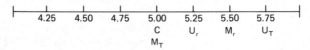

FIGURE 7.2.   Settlement Range Issue: Wage Rate.

Bargaining Duty of the Negotiator

The negotiator's duty during the bargaining process is to discover the opponent's resistance point and move it toward the negotiator's target point. Movement is contingent upon the ability of the negotiator to influence the opponent's perception of the benefit-cost ratio (i.e., MEBA/MECA or UEBA/UECA as the case may be) associated with a particular demand. In terms of Figure 7–2, for example, the union negotiator will attempt to increase management's estimate of the benefits to the company of settling at U_T, while at the same time trying to minimize management's perceived costs of settling at this point. Agreement occurs whenever perceived benefits exceed perceived costs—whenever MEBA/MECA or UEBA/UECA > 1.

---

[8] For an in-depth treatment of the concept, see: Walton & McKersie, *A Behavioral Theory of Labor Negotiations*, pp. 13–45.

Concealment of the resistance point is critical to the negotiator's success in reaching the target. Revelation of the resistance point precludes achievement of the target point. For example, should it become known to management that the union's resistance point (Ur in Figure 7–2)—the lowest wage rate that the union would accept without first calling a strike—is $5.25, management would have little incentive to settle at a higher wage rate closer to the union's target rate of $5.75. Settlement at any wage rate higher than $5.25 would involve greater cost and little in the way of benefits for management. Hence, the union negotiator would not possess the bargaining power necessary to secure management's agreement at the target wage rate.

The major component of management's perceived benefits from agreement on the union's terms is avoidance of strike costs. Consequently, the union negotiator will concentrate efforts upon highlighting the intensity of membership commitment to union demands (i.e., membership willingness to strike), the low cost of a strike to the membership (i.e., the ability of the membership to sustain a long strike), and the substantial cost to management of any work stoppage. Other benefits, such as increased productivity resulting from less worker absenteeism, reduced materials scrappage, and increased worker morale will be stressed. Efforts to de-emphasize out-of-pocket employer expenses associated with agreement on the union's terms will also be undertaken. In short, the union negotiator attempts to convince his/her counterpart that settlement on the union's terms is the only rational thing to do.

Similarly, the management representative will do everything within his/her power to convince the union that the benefits from agreement on management terms far outweigh the costs of such agreement. Potential benefits underscored by the management negotiator include: union/worker avoidance of the costs associated with a work stoppage, the possibility of management concessions in other areas, a generally improved labor-relations climate, a more competitive market position for the employer due to lower labor costs with a resultant increase in employment for currently idle union members, and increased social responsibility as perceived by the public. The costs of agreement to the union will also be minimized. For example, the management negotiator might simply stress that management terms are significantly better than those achieved by other unions in different industries. Again, the general thrust of negotiation efforts is to convince the union that the only rational course of action is agreement—on management terms.

Bargaining Gamesmanship

Collective bargaining gamesmanship (i.e., concealing one's resistance point in order to convince the opponent that it coincides with what is really the target point) is fraught with danger. This practice may not generate sufficient information for the opponent to make an intelligent decision either to accept or reject a proposal. For example, constant exaggeration and bluffing by union negotiators may make it impossible for management to determine when the union is serious about a particular item on the bargaining table. Not believing the issue to be serious, management underestimates the benefits from agreement, overestimates the costs of agreement (thinking the union will back off and eventually settle for something less), and rejects the demand. Not only does the tactic reduce the union's bargaining power, it may also precipitate an unnecessary work stoppage.

Stages of the Negotiation Process: The Four P's of Negotiation

The negotiation process can be broken down into four rather distinct phases: preparation, posturing, prioritizing positions, and pressure bargaining. The behavior of each party and the activities typically taking place during the four "P's" of the negotiation process are discussed in the following paragraphs.

Preparation

Effective negotiations, the attainment of bargaining goals, and the development of a workable contract instrument require more than the instinctive response of the "playing by ear performance"; thorough preparation is an absolute prerequisite.

Complexity of Issues

Collective bargaining contracts have become increasingly complex as labor–management relationships have matured. The days of negotiating a single wage rate and standard workweek for a homogeneous group of workers have gone the way of the dinosaur. Management and labor representatives must address and resolve such wage-related issues as call-in pay, cost-of-living allowance, wage-improvement factors, starting rates, job classifications, rate ranges, labor-grade pay steps, temporary rates and classifications, overtime rates, overtime apportionment, payment for downtime, pay premiums for undesirable shifts, work sharing during periods of declining sales, and layoff procedure. These wage-related issues do not begin to exhaust the list of topics covered by modern contracts. Fringe benefits and administrative issues further complicate the negotiation process. Indeed, the administrative issue of discipline, alone, consumes an inordinate amount of the negotiators' time. It's no wonder that a modern-day collective bargaining agreement often spans more than 300 pages in length![9]

Given the Homeric nature of the negotiation task, experienced negotiators recognize the need for extensive preparations commencing months prior to actual negotiations. In several cases (i.e., steel industry), the parties begin preparations for the next round of negotiations as soon as the present contract has been signed.

Sources of Bargaining Data

Parties seeking to make contract changes bear the burden of justifying these proposed changes. Without data, proof is hard to come by. Bargaining data and information are available through many sources. The federal

[9]*The Agreement Between General Motors Corporation and the UAW*, Effective October 1, 1979, the master agreement alone, covers 400 pages.

government compiles and makes available upon request statistics pertaining to almost every imaginable type of activity. General information relevant to bargaining published by the U.S. Department of Labor, Bureau of Labor Statistics, alone, includes *Employment and Earnings, Consumer Price Index, Labor Turnover, Special Labor Force Reports, Major Collective Bargaining Settlements, Union Wage Rates for Building Trades, Real Earnings, Automation and Technological Change,* and *Family Budgets,* to name but a *few.* The Federal Reserve System is also a prolific publisher of economic data.

In addition to public sources, management and labor can secure data and other information useful for bargaining from various private special interest groups. The National Association of Manufacturers (NAM), for example, collects a wide variety of information which may aid firms preparing for contract negotiations. Many of these employer groups categorize and catalogue contract provisions by type. Close scrutiny of this material permits firms to anticipate union demands in upcoming contract talks. Similar information is available from the AFL-CIO to its national and local affiliates. Most national unions and larger corporations also support research departments specifically for the purpose of providing the specialized data needed for collective bargaining.

A party to the negotiation process is entitled to certain types of information in the possession of the other party. An employer's duty to bargain in good-faith under the Wagner Act, as interpreted and amended, includes the duty to provide the union with the information it needs to engage in informed bargaining. Specifically, a firm is required to furnish to the union representatives, upon request, the information needed to prepare for negotiations, to bargain intelligently, and to effectively enforce and administer the current contract. For example, if the union is contemplating a proposal on overtime, the union can request data on the amount of overtime as well as its distribution. The required information may cover a wide spectrum of topics. Although rare, the employer is also entitled to union data germane to bargaining. Thus, under a hiring-hall contract provision, an employer may request information concerning the union's ability to direct a sufficient number of qualified persons to satisfy the employer's manpower requirements.

Labor and management negotiators represent the rank-and-file and various levels of management. If the contract is to function effectively and be accepted by union members and those charged with its enforcement, negotiators do well to solicit the input of their respective constituencies prior to formulating demands. To paraphrase an old cliché, "hell hath no fury like a constituency scorned." For the union, this input may be obtained by means of:

1. The Suggestion Box.
2. Questionnaires.
3. The Union Meeting.
4. Meetings with Union Stewards.
5. Analyses of the Types of Grievances.
6. Analyses of Arbitration Awards.

Management may detect problem contract areas through consultations with operating subordinates (i.e., superintendents, industrial engineers, and foremen). Foremen are a particularly good source of information vital to management's determination of issues of critical interest to the union.

> Some companies have their foreman conduct informal meetings with employee groups. The purpose of this is to understand the needs and problems faced by the employees. Foremen are in a good position to understand the strength of feeling about these matters and the willingness of the employees to strike.[10]

Foremen are familiar with rank-and-file pressures upon union leadership as well as the sources of these pressures (e.g. political factionalism). Such information is indispensable to anticipating and preparing for upcoming union proposals.

> General Motors reportedly utilizes automatic data processing equipment for this prenegotiating analysis. By tabulating the incidence of each issue persisting in upward movement through the grievance machinery, management is in a position to estimate the importance of most of the union's demands.[11]

Some negotiators have developed their own systems for ferreting out essential bargaining information.

> One negotiator claimed that he could walk through the shop and by some kind of intuitive assessment of the atmosphere tell what was on the minds of the workers. As a negotiator, he knew the ranges of issues, but by walking through the shop, he sought the intensity of feeling behind these issues and whether people were furious enough to force a showdown.[12]

Whatever techniques are utilized, union and management negotiators have become aware, sometimes painfully so, of the value and necessity of securing "grass roots" organizational input for bargaining.

Strikes

Preparation cannot overlook the possibility that an impasse during negotiation might lead to a work stoppage. Consequently, negotiation preparations must include planning for a strike or lockout. To understand the need for preparation, the ramifications of a work stoppage for both labor and management must be understood. The costs of a work stoppage to the union and its membership include:

1. Loss of wages by employees. Drain on financial resources of union.
2. Loss of institutional security. A strike may result in a loss of membership and even threaten the status of the union as bargaining agent. Many employees may find other jobs during the strike and do not return after the strike ends. The employee replacements may not be as likely to join the union or may at least delay joining. Other employees who went through the strike may drop their

---

[10] Walton & McKersie, *A Behavioral Theory of Labor Negotiations*, p. 62.
[11] Ibid.
[12] Ibid.

membership. Rival unions or rival factions within the union may exploit a strike situation and acquire employee support for themselves.
3. Loss of goodwill with management. This leads to antagonisms which may not disappear with termination of strike. Management may be more adamant in the future, retaliating in ways of its own. The deterioration in plant relationships can result in a disadvantage to both parties, since the informal accommodations worked out to the mutual satisfaction of both parties may be contingent upon continuing trust and the elimination of trust threatens these working arrangements.
4. Loss of public image. A strike may give the appearance that the union is acting irresponsibly and ignoring the public's interest in maintaining the flow of goods and services. [13]

Management's costs include:

1. Loss of operating profits (short run) and market position (longer run). Possible damage to plant and equipment through idleness.
2. Loss of management's status with higher management or stockholders. If the strike does not seem necessary or if it appears to have been mishandled, the managers responsible for negotiations may suffer a loss of prestige. Their careers may be adversely affected.
3. Loss of goodwill with labor. Both the union-management realtionship and employee relations can suffer, resulting in low morale, low productivity, and resistance to changes initiated by management, etc.
4. Loss of public image. The strike can have an adverse effect on attitudes of customers, governmental agencies, or legislative bodies. [14]

Strike costs to the union can be minimized to the extent that:

1. The strike is timed to coincide with periods of economic prosperity where alternative employment opportunities for the membership are abundant. Since the union initiates the work stoppage in most cases, it is not mere coincidence that the incidence of strike activity is more pronounced during the upswing of the business cycle; relative costs are lower for the union than during periods of recession.
2. The strike is timed to coincide with membership preferences for leisure time. A strike occurring during hunting/fishing season where the majority of the membership engage in such recreational pursuits may increase worker satisfaction.
3. The union is successful in getting the membership to limit credit commitments prior to upcoming contract talks. The latter reduction in outstanding debt reduces worker dependency on income which will be interrupted should a strike occur.
4. The union is successful in enlarging its strike fund (i.e., "War chest") and making arrangements with other unions for financial assistance should the work stoppage be a prolonged one.

[13] Walton & McKersie, *A Behavioral Theory of Labor Negotiations*, p. 31
[14] Ibid., pp. 31–32.

David Dubinsky reportedly had an imaginative technique for getting the most psychological impact out of the limited funds of the garment workers. He would open an organization campaign in a new area by depositing a substantial sum to the account of the union in a leading local bank. When local garment manufacturers learned of the deposit, they would assume that the union was able to finance a long strike and capitulate. Only later might they learn that the entire sum had been placed locally on the express condition that it be returned intact after serving its psychological purpose.[15]

5. The union solicits rank-and-file input in framing bargaining demands. An agenda of bargaining items drawn up in the foregoing fashion has a greater likelihood of rank-and-file support than unilaterally determined positions. Factionalism is less likely as union leaders cultivate membership solidarity by means of worker input to the bargaining process.
6. The union undertakes an extensive, well-thought-out public relations effort to educate the general public concerning the ultimate fairness and justification of its bargaining proposals.

On the other hand, management strike costs will be reduced to the extent that:

1. Management can replace economic strikers with other workers. The ability to replace is a function of overall and industry-wide economic conditions. High levels of unemployment are conducive to this strike breaking tactic. However, use of strike breakers is rare except for relatively small employers in regions where unions are weak.
2. Management can carry on production utilizing managerial, supervisory, and clerical workers outside their usual job classification. Management's ability to continue operations is dependent upon the nature of the production process itself. Highly capital-intensive, automated processes lend themselves to continued production in the face of work stoppages. Oil and chemical production, not to mention communications, fall within this category.
3. Management or management's customers can stockpile and build inventories in anticipation of a strike. The nature of the good produced determines the ultimate feasibility of this tactic. Durables can be inventoried whereas perishables cannot. Service industries do not have this option.
4. Management can draw upon other revenue sources during the period of interrupted production. Product diversification permits an employer to subsidize the struck product line utilizing revenue generated from operating divisions not covered by the bargaining relationship. Fixed costs can be defrayed in this manner. Where diversification has not been realized, the same result can be achieved by employer mutual assistance agreements. The airlines have long utilized this arrangement.
5. Management undertakes a public relations campaign intended to convince the general public of the fairness and reasonableness of its bargaining

[15]Walton & McKersie, A Behavioral Theory of Labor Negotiations, p. 80.

proposals. Management's claims for greater efficiency and flexibility characterize such public relations efforts.

To the degree that either party is successful in implementing these tactics, its relative bargaining power is increased. Reduced strike costs translate to reduced benefits from agreeing on the opponent's terms; the opponent's bargaining power is decreased accordingly.

Procedural Issues

Preparation for negotiation should extend to such mundane and seemingly trivial matters as the procedural operation of the negotiating sessions. An orderly framework for exchange of information is essential to the successful execution of the bargaining function. Meeting ground rules should ideally be established prior to the first scheduled bargaining session. Without procedural structure, negotiation sessions can easily degenerate to name-calling, counterproductive, shouting matches. Items which must be attended to include:

1. Meeting Place
2. Meeting Time
3. Meeting Frequency
4. Meeting Length
5. Selection of Chairman or Co-Chairman—Necessary if only to preserve order by recognizing speakers.
6. Size and Composition of Negotiation Teams—Bargaining teams should be limited to reasonable numbers. Otherwise, they become unwieldy, difficult to assemble, have a greater propensity to become disorderly, and are more likely to digress to personal problems rather than concentrate upon bargaining issues.
7. Exchange of Proposals Prior to Initial Negotiating Session
8. Bargaining Agenda
9. Maintenance of a Record of the Proceedings and Items of Agreement
10. Caucus/Adjournment Rights
11. Caucus Facilities
12. Role of Neutrals in Impasse Settlement

More than a few bargaining relationships have started off on the wrong foot due to insufficient detail and attention to the procedural issues outlined above. A framework wherein the parties are, at minimum, able to identify points of disagreement, that is, are able "to agree to disagree" increases the likelihood of settlement by focusing resources on problem areas.

Posturing

To the uninitiated, the opening bargaining session may seem carnivalistic and take on airs not unlike those surrounding the premier of a Hollywood extravaganza. Both parties typically invite a wide variety of guests from various levels of their respective organizations. Oftentimes, news reporters and film crews are present to capture the "pomp and circumstance" for the general public. The union presents its long list of demands, unmatched in their unrealism except for the management proposals which soon follow. Both management and union negotiators wax eloquent in their justifications of each item. Encouraged by the presence of their constituents and the general hoopla of the occasion, the negotiators engage in emotional rhetoric during this first bargaining session. Ultimate agreement amid this theatrical and grandstanding environment would be nothing short of a miracle.

The fanfare that accompanies initial negotiations is understandable in view of the importance of the task that lies before the negotiators. Seasoned negotiators are well-versed in the rituals of the bargaining process. They are fully aware that grandstanding emotionalism is intended for the consumption of their respective constituencies present at these early sessions. Such showmanship serves the purpose of convincing colleagues that their interests will be protected when serious bargaining commences.[16] The behavior of negotiators during this phase of the negotiation process might aptly be compared to the mating behavior of peacocks which is intended to attract and maintain a partner. In bargaining, the peacock behavior of the negotiator is intended to guarantee membership solidarity.

The long list of demands ("laundry list") should be listened to carefully, but not taken at face value. Both parties recognize that some of the demands are critical (i.e., must be met), some are important but may be traded away, and others are added as "fillers" with the expectation of being traded away. The long list of exaggerated demands does, however, serve several useful and important functions. First, union and management, having solicited the input of the members of their respective organizations, can put forth the pet proposals of their constituents, take a strong stance on those viewed as meritorious, and allow those of low priority to be deleted by the other party— with political immunity. The opponent becomes the scapegoat and whipping boy for those members whose proposals have been deleted. The negotiators enjoy the best of both worlds; they have demonstrated to constituents that their concerns have been voiced at the bargaining table, at the same time remaining in complete control as to which proposals reach the stage of serious negotiation. This is particularly important for unions where political factionalism has been a problem. Management negotiators perform the screening function for rank-and-file demands thereby insulating union negotiators from potentially damaging political abuse.

Presentation of a long list of inflated demands also serves one of the basic objectives of the negotiation process; it camouflages the negotiator's true priorities and resistance points on key issues. Low priority items and demands which the negotiator does not expect to achieve become fodder for the "horse trading" that will take place during the later stages of the bargaining process. As sports general managers are fond of saying, "You have to give up something to get something in return."

Successful use of an inflated list of demands to camouflage priorities and resistance points underscores the importance of thorough preparation for

---

[16] Given the impact of a large interested audience upon the behavior of negotiators in early private-sector, bargaining sessions, a better argument against so-called "sunshine bargaining laws" in the public sector could not be made.

bargaining. Proposals, the ramification of which are not understood by those putting them forth or which cannot be justified, will immediately be perceived for what they really are—trade bait. A wily opponent will readily isolate priority issues and resistance points through the process of elimination.

Finally, experienced negotiators recognize that novel bargaining demands generate reactionary-like resistance on the part of those hearing the proposals for the first time. Neither party can realistically be expected to agree to such a demand the first time it is presented. Its initial presentation, however, plants the "seed" in the mind of the negotiator. The seed is carefully nurtured by repetition of the proposal at subsequent rounds of contract negotiations. The passage of time permits the other party to become thoroughly familiar with the proposal and its implications. As a result, it begins to appear less novel, radical, and outlandish, and more compatible with organizational goals. Opposition tends to wither away. The seed eventually germinates; what at one time appeared to be a totally unacceptable proposal becomes a part of the signed contract. Hence, presentation of a long list of demands at the outset of the negotiation process is part of a long-run bargaining strategy—introduction of non-traditional bargaining topics which the negotiator seeks to achieve in the future.

The posturing stage of the negotiation process normally does not generate any convergence in bargaining positions, nor should it be expected to. The second phase of the negotiation process is not well suited for compromise, concession, and agreement; it is undertaken for public and constituency consumption. Its primary purpose is to close organizational ranks behind the negotiating teams—what Walton and McKersie described as "intraorganizational bargaining"[17]—thereby preparing the way for the give-and-take of the later stages of the negotiation process that will culminate in settlement.

Prioritizing Positions

The theatrics of the posturing stage of bargaining do not preclude transmittal of information invaluable to the later stages of negotiations. The trained negotiator will listen to opposing proposals in order to determine intent and intensity, to identify points of agreement and possible solutions, to isolate weaknesses, and to discover signals as to possible areas of accommodation. The verbal behavior and body language of the members of a negotiating team provide a wealth of information about their interest in and degree of commitment to proposals on the bargaining table.

Re-evaluation

The third stage of the negotiation process, prioritizing bargaining demands, consists of an in-depth assessment of the information generated during the early stages of bargaining, re-evaluation of target and resistance points based upon the information generated, drafting counterproposals, continued probing of the other negotiating team to produce further information, identification of areas of possible agreement and areas of clear disagreement, and

[17] Walton & McKersie, *A Behavioral Theory of Labor Negotiations*, p. 281.

formulation of a tactical and strategic plan of operation to achieve priority proposals. This stage is marked by a sharp reduction in the number of individuals participating in the bargaining process. The negotiating sessions are closed to all persons except the designated representatives of labor and management. The difficult task of negotiating a workable agreement begins in earnest—a task of impossible proportions if undertaken in context of the audience effect of open negotiations.

Package Bargaining

Since no party can realistically expect to win every issue during bargaining, the negotiator's job becomes one of fashioning a "package" of items which reflects to the greatest extent possible the priorities of the constituency. Package bargaining minimizes the likelihood of an impasse by emphasizing areas of agreement; priority issues on both sides of the bargaining table are included in various packages. Negotiation continues on a positive note, progress is made, areas of disagreement are methodically reduced and eliminated, and settlement is achieved. On the other hand, item-by-item bargaining tends to emphasize the negative. It highlights differences in bargaining proposals, transforms these differences into principled issues, and hinders; if not precludes, movement to areas of agreement. Item-by-item bargaining is not conducive to the establishment of a pattern of agreement.

The key to successful package bargaining is negotiator flexibility— willingness to listen, discuss, and remain fluid on the issues. A negotiator approach to bargaining typified by the presentation of proposals as issues for consideration and discussion rather than as ultimatums "which must be met or else" promotes cooperation rather then conflict. Flexibility on the part of the negotiator is the catalyst for a smoothly functioning negotiation process and for the development of a workable collective bargaining contract.

Counterproposal is a term synonymous with the collective bargaining process. *Webster's Third New International Dictionary*, however, defines the term simply as "a rejoiner to something proposed." In this sense, a counter-proposal has minimal value as a tool in collective bargaining. To be an effective device or technique for bringing parties closer together during negotiations, the usual context in which the term is used, the counterproposal must take the form of a concession or a compromise, it must connote flexibility. Concession (oftentimes referred to as "trading point procedure") involves the trading away of an item or items in exchange for another item or items. If the negotiator is skillful and has done his/her homework, the item(s) traded away will be of low priority (maybe even "filler") while the item(s) received in exchange is (are) of high priority. For example, management may concede dues checkoff for more stringent disciplinary penalties for casual absence. Favorable packages emerge in this manner—the more artful the negotiator and the greater his/her bargaining power, the more favorable the package.

Certain items cannot be traded away to build the package. This occurs where both parties attach a high priority to the item or issue. Resolution of the impasse without recourse to economic force may only be possible through counterproposals that involve compromise. For example, the union may demand a cost-of-living-adjustment (COLA) clause where wage rates are adjusted on a monthly basis. Management, on the other hand, may counter by agreeing to a COLA clause where wage rates are adjusted annually. After several such counterproposals, each involving some compromise, final agreement may be a COLA clause where wages are adjusted biannually.

Techniques of Conflict Avoidance

Seasoned negotiators recognize the necessity of avoiding unnecessary impasses and conflict. Various techniques of conflict avoidance and resolution are employed in the day-to-day negotiation process to direct discussion to productive channels. The most common and effective of these techniques include:

1. *The Bargaining Book.* The book is used to record progress during negotiations. Its chief value is that it provides the negotiating teams with an accurate log of discussions, making areas of agreement and disagreement immediately apparent. The bargaining book typically contains existing contract clauses, desired changes, additions, and/or deletions proposed by the union, management, or both teams. Key arguments accompanying desired changes are also recorded, not to mention the other team's behavior and reactions to various proposals. Thus, the book is not only useful for identifying areas of consensus and disagreement, but it can also become an important instrument for isolating resistance points on specific issues. Both functions are essential to building the package alternatives that will generate overall contract settlement. In a sense, the bargaining book is to the negotiation process what Houston Control is to manned space travel. It charts the course, identifies hazards, and provides information on the basis of which hazards may be overcome. In short, the bargaining book provides direction to the negotiation process. A sample page from a typical book is presented below.

2. *Yes Habit.* Discussions should proceed from areas of common agreement rather than from controversial issues. Once a foundation for agreement has been established, it becomes progressively easier to achieve concurrence where positions initially appeared to be irreconcilable. An atmosphere conducive to settlement is established.

Union Bargaining Book
Sample Page

Present Clause	Change Desired	Reason for Change	Management Reaction	Management Counterproposal	Management Argument

FIGURE 7.3.

3. *Forced Choice.* Decisions are frequently difficult to make. The degree of difficulty increases with the importance of the decision. Aware of this fact, experienced negotiators attempt to ease the burden of decision-making on the part of opponents through the presentation of alternative proposals. The alternatives force a choice between proposals which are often of equal value to the team presenting them but not of equal value to the team expected to accept them. In this situation, the opponent has the opportunity to select the alternative which is least objectionable (i.e., most beneficial). If, on the other hand, a single proposal is presented, it may be one that an opponent, for one reason or another, simply cannot accept. Thus, an impasse develops which could have possibly been avoided had several alternatives been presented.

4. *Problem-Oriented Discussions.* Constructive bargaining sessions are issue-centered rather than personality-centered. The productivity of negotiation sessions is directly related to the degree of objectivity achieved during negotiation sessions. Personality-centered disputes increase tensions, breed mistrust, and divert resources away from the solution of problems of common concern. In short, personality clashes destroy (often for lengthy periods of time) the atmosphere of cooperation necessary for the resolution of bargaining differences. Most experienced negotiators will admit that the majority of bargaining crises stem from mistakes in human relations (i.e., personality-centered discussions). The human-relations "commandments" in Box 7–1 are suggested as one method for preventing bargaining sessions from becoming personality-centered.

5. *Subcommittees.* As noted earlier, the subject matter of collective bargaining is not only extensive, but complex as well (e.g. pensions, insurance, job classifications, incentive rates, etc.) It is unrealistic to expect all negotiating team members to be proficient and learned in all areas of contract negotiation. Recognizing this fact, skilled bargainers make frequent use of

---

BOX 7–1. The Ten Commandments of Human Relations

1. Don't be arrogant and condescending.
2. Admit mistakes and apologize when wrong.
3. Recognize the significance and importance of another's comment or statement.
4. Respect other viewpoints.
5. Be able to distinguish between fact and opinion.
6. Maintain your sense of humor and never lose your temper.
7. Don't equivocate; tell the truth and bargain in good faith.
8. Always allow for face-saving; avoid backing an opponent into a corner from which there is no graceful exit.
9. "Win" an agreement, not a specific argument.
10. Remember that every contract has an expiration date, but the labor-management relationship does not.

subcommittees. Rather than have negotiations disrupted, hindered, or sabotaged by team members unfamiliar with these complex agenda items, negotiators delegate bargaining responsibility for these issues to subcommittees made up of members from both teams skilled and trained in these matters. Subcommittees report their findings and recommendations to both bargaining parties.

6. *Caucus.* The right to caucus in privacy is invaluable to continued progress in bargaining. Specifically, it serves several important functions:

   a. It provides an opportunity to evaluate progress in negotiations, to consider the opponent's counterproposals, to redefine targets on the basis of information gained during bargaining, and to draft counterproposals.

   b. It relieves tensions built up during negotiations and refreshes bargaining team members.

   c. It gives the bargaining team an opportunity to "rein in" specific team members who are leading negotiations astray or are deviating from prearranged tactics.

7. *Drafting Contract Language.* As agreement is reached on each issue or package of issues, consensus should also be secured concerning contract language that accurately reflects the negotiators' intent and meaning. As soon as this consensus is achieved, the provision should be committed to writing and initialed by both parties. Drafting delays increase the likelihood that previously settled issues will again be disputed when the negotiators attempt to commit these issues to writing.

Pressure Bargaining

As bargaining enters its final stages, the great majority of issues will have typically been resolved. If not, at least those issues preventing final contract settlement will have been clearly identified. The approaching strike deadline provides the incentive for negotiators to settle their remaining differences. The benefits from agreement, which the negotiators had previously discounted in view of what seemed to be a far-off contract expiration date, now take a greater significance. Each team re-evaluates its positions on unresolved issues in light of the costs that may result without settlement. Bargaining activity picks up: sessions become longer, caucuses more frequent, and movement from dead center more noticeable. The ingenuity of skilled negotiators when placed under the gun of an approaching deadline seems limitless. For example, intractable issues are often discussed informally in restaurants, bars, and washrooms, thereby removing them from the scrutiny of colleagues who may have an *axe to grind.* Such discussions between key representatives of each side frequently generate breakthroughs, which would otherwise have been impossible with the full complement of members from both bargaining teams present.

Two widely used techniques for bringing agreement during the final stages of negotiation are the long-range, joint-study committee and third-party intervention. Long-range, joint-study committees are typically utilized where one or more issues remain unresolved during "eleventh-hour" negotiations. These committees are given the responsibility for reaching an agreement after the current contract has expired. The hope of negotiators is that resolution of critical issues will take place under more favorable conditions—in a less tension–packed and pressure-laden environment. Joint-study committees do, of course, labor under the spectre of later deadlines.

Neutral, third-party intervention may take several forms. These include arbitration, fact finding, and mediation. In arbitration, a neutral third party, mutually selected by labor and management, decides a dispute which the parties find irresolvable. Fact finding resembles arbitration (indeed, it is often referred to as advisory arbitration) except that the neutral's report is not binding. Both procedures involve hearings during which the disputants have the opportunity to present evidence and arguments supportive of their respective positions. The neutral's decision (i.e., report/recommendations) is based on said evidence and arguments. Arbitration and fact finding of disputes arising during the negotiation and creation of new contract provisions (i.e., interest arbitration and fact finding) are seldom utilized outside the public sector.

Mediation is by far the most common form of third-party intervention used to resolve impasses that develop during contract negotiations. Based on the tenet of voluntary acceptance, successful mediation depends upon the objectivity which the neutral brings to negotiations, the neutral's resourcefulness in identifying and creating solutions, and the neutral's basic power of persuasion. In some disputes, on the other hand, the intervention of the mediator simply provides an opportunity for parties who have maneuvered themselves into a corner (i.e., taken an untenable position) to give ground, in response to the suggestions of the neutral, without appearing to yield to the opponent. Here, mediation serves as a face saving technique; negotiators can abandon difficult positions without loss of prestige.[18]

Bargaining Impasse: The Strike

Notwithstanding both parties' extensive preparations for bargaining, their good-faith desire to reach a mutually satisfactory agreement, and use of various techniques and devices to promote settlement, strikes will invariably take place from time-to-time.

Strike Causes

Work stoppages can be traced to a variety of causes. These include:

1. The genuine inability to agree on some bargaining issue(s).
2. The inability of union negotiators to "sell" the contract to the rank-and-file for ratification purposes. This represents a breakdown in "intraorganizational bargaining."
3. Strategic, tactical, and human relations errors that preclude opportunities for concession, compromise, and, therefore, settlement.

---

[18]The role of neutrals in dispute settlement is discussed in greater detail in Chapters 13 and 14.

Some strikes are deliberately provoked by one or both of the parties. The intentional work stoppage may serve several purposes:

1. The union views the strike as a long-term investment. Although serving no apparent purpose in current negotiations, the union may neverthless engage in a work stoppage to enhance the credibility of the strike threat in future negotiations.
2. The union views the strike as a tool for quelling political factionalism within the organization. Identification of an external threat normally increases organizational solidarity.
3. The strike provides an outlet for membership discontent, frustration, and emotions. As such, it may be a necessary step for eventual membership ratification of the agreement.
4. Management may view the strike as an effective method for reducing excess inventories. Public sector agencies may see the work stoppage as the only realistic method for keeping within their allotted budgets.

It is indeed unfortunate that the only time public attention is focused on labor-management relations is when the process, for one reason or another, temporarily fails to generate an agreement in a peaceful fashion. The adverse publicity that results from strikes obscures the fact that the vast majority of collective bargaining contracts are negotiated or renegotiated without recourse to economic warfare.

The Forces of Settlement

Even in those cases where peaceful settlement does not initially occur, two factors operate in the direction of settlement. First, the rate of subjective strike costs (i.e., subjective strike costs per day) to each disputant increases as the strike continues. This increase occurs regardless of whether the actual dollar per day costs increase or remain unchanged. For the employer, actual dollar costs increase as inventories are depleted, sales drop, and customers turn elsewhere (sometimes permanently), thereby raising the rate of subjective strike costs. For the worker, although actual dollar per day costs typically remain unchanged, the rate of subjective strike costs does increase as forced leisure becomes tedious, as savings evaporate, as creditors become less willing to extend credit, and as the union strike fund is drawn down. In brief, the marginal subjective disutility of each additional strike day increases as the point of bankruptcy approaches. Hence, the expected benefits from agreement increase for both parties. Eventually, said benefits will exceed costs and settlement will occur.

Continued negotiation during the work stoppage is the second factor conducive to eventual settlement. Further meetings lead to the correction of misconceptions based upon misinformation transmitted during pre-strike negotiating sessions. Once true resistance points become known, the disputants are likely to revise the expected benefits from agreement upward with a consequent decrease in their willingness to continue the strike. This second factor once again stresses the importance of preparation, information, and learning in both pre- and post-strike negotiating sessions.

Proofreading the Agreement: Preparing the Way for Effective Contract Administration

The responsibility for serviceable contract provisions rests with management and labor negotiators. Contract provisions should clearly reflect the needs and desires of the parties. Just as an effectively functioning contract mirrors the wisdom, foresight, and hard work of the negotiators, a poorly functioning agreement oftentimes indicates a job poorly done during contract negotiation.

An important part of the negotiator's responsibility is the drafting of the final agreement. If contract provisions are to successfully guide the labor-management relationship, clarity of meaning is an absolute prerequisite. Provisions should be understandable and concise. Terminology foreign to those responsible for contract enforcement/administration and to those covered by the terms of the agreement should be avoided. If illustrations and examples aid understanding, they should be included.

Once contract provisions are committed to paper, a good test of their meaning is to have a wide variety of different individuals, wholly unfamiliar with what has transpired during negotiations, read and interpret each provision of the contract. Particularly appropriate candidates for this "provisional intent test" are those who enforce/administer, police, or are governed by the terms of the agreement—stewards, foremen, department superintendents, shop chairmen, plant managers, grievance committeemen, rank-and-file members, etc. If provisional meaning is misconstrued, revision is in order.

After the contract is negotiated, committed to writing, read for meaning, revised where necessary, reread by the negotiators for typographical errors, the news media and other interested persons should be invited to the signing ceremony. The publicity and recognition for a job well done is warranted upon completion of the difficult task of contract negotiation. It is, indeed, cause for celebration. The execution of the signed contract, however, does not terminate the bargaining responsibilities of management and labor representatives. An equally, and in many respects, a more important job still lies ahead—the task of making the contract work. Careful proofreading of the newly-negotiated contract facilitates subsequent contract administration and enforcement.

Summary and Conclusion

Contract negotiation can be viewed from many perspectives. Each has something of value to contribute to an understanding of the dynamics of the bargaining process. Observers of and participants in the negotiation process should keep in mind three basic characteristics of that process: (1) the welfare interdependency of labor, management, and the public, (2) the rational decision-making of participants, and (3) the paramount importance of good human relations. In addition to a straightforward description of the negotiation process, this chapter has stressed human relations-oriented techniques/devices instrumental to moving the decision-making criteria of negotiators in the direction of peaceful contract settlement—a settlement that promotes the welfare of all parties concerned.

DISCUSSION QUESTIONS

1. The Hicksian bargaining model identifies the point of peaceful contract settlement. Why might *peaceful* settlement occur at a point other than the point of concession curve intersection identified in the Hicksian model?

2. Collective bargaining is described as a process of bilateral problem solving. In what sense is collective bargaining multilateral in nature?

3. Newspapers frequently label strikes as irrational since their "strike cost calculators" indicate that union strike costs far exceed benefits achieved through the work stoppage. For example, calculations might indicate that a $1.00 increase in the wage rate is necessary to offset the costs of a two-day strike whereas the union settles for a $.50 increase. Are the newspapers correct in their assessment of such strikes?

4. What impact would so-called "sunshine" bargaining laws (i.e., laws mandating open negotiations) have upon bargaining in the private sector?

5. The practice of good human relations during bargaining precludes the need for mediation of labor disputes. Comment.

6. Why do a greater number of strikes occur during the upswing of the business cycle than during the downswing?

7. Although "part and parcel" of the negotiation process, bargaining gamesmanship is inherently destructive of the ultimate goal of bargainers—a mutually beneficial agreement. Comment.

SELECTED REFERENCES

Ashenfelter, Orley and George E. Johnson, "Bargaining Theory, Trade Unions, and Industrial Strike Activity," *American Economic Review*, (March 1969), **59:** 35–49.

Cross, H.G., "A Theory of the Bargaining Process," *American Economic Review*, (March 1965), **55:** 67–94.

Heider, Fritz, *The Psychology of Interpersonal Relations*, New York: John Wiley & Sons, Inc., 1958.

Hicks, J.R. *The Theory of Wages*, New York: Macmillan, 1968, Chapter 7.

Nierenberg, Gerald I., *The Art of Negotiating*, New York: Cornerstone Library Publications, 1968.

Pen, Jan, "A General Theory of Bargaining," *American Economic Review*, (March, 1952) **42:** 24–42.

Ruben, Jeffrey A., and Bert R. Brown, *The Social Psychology of Bargaining and Negotiation*, New York: Academic Press, Inc., 1975.

Stevens, Carl M., *Strategy and Collective Bargaining Negotiation*, New York: McGraw-Hill Book Company, 1963.

Walton, R.E., and Robert B. McKersie, *A Behavioral Theory of Labor Negotiations*, New York: McGraw-Hill Book Company, 1965.

Young, Oran R., ed., *Bargaining Theories of Negotiations*. Urbana, Ill.: University of Illinois Press, 1975.

Chapter 8

Wages and Collective Bargaining

This and the following chapter deal with the collective bargaining determination of the economic package or the total compensation of employees. The economic package is comprised of wages, salaries or piece rates which are the subjects of this chapter and economic supplements discussed in the following chapter. The topics to be surveyed in this chapter include (1) bargaining standards for wage determination; (2) methods for wage adjustment during the contract; (3) government intervention in the determination of wages and hours; and (4) job evaluation.

Wages and related economic issues are often the most difficult issues encountered in collective bargaining. The air traffic controllers strike in 1981 is a testimony to the difficulty which may arise due to wage issues. During the early summer FAA and union negotiators had hammered out a settlement which was then placed before the union's membership. The air traffic controllers rejected the settlement by an overwhelming majority of those voting in the ratification election. The reason most often cited by PATCO members for voting against ratification was that the wage settlement was much below what had been expected even though the tentative agreement had called for over a thirty percent increase in the base wage over three years in addition to cost of living adjustments. The wage issue was deemed sufficiently important for PATCO members to strike in violation of law, for which many PATCO officials went to jail and most controllers were fired by President Reagan. It should also be noted that wages, as is the case for other federal employees, were not even to be considered during negotiations; wages are an illegal bargaining topic for federal employees. This case is a dramatic testimony to the importance of wage issues in collective bargaining.

Collective Bargaining Determination of Wages

Before examining the standards utilized by negotiators to determine wages, two constraints upon the wage determination process deserve attention.

Wage determination, even under collective bargaining, is not conducted in a vacuum. Pressure is exerted on the negotiators both from within and from without their respective organizations. These two influences which limit the wage determination process are referred to as internal and external wage structures.

Internal wage structure refers to the ranking of wage classifications within the firm. It is important that management and the union *equitably* and *efficiently* allocate compensatory resources among employees. Equity dictates that employees be paid a "fair day's pay for a fair day's work". In other words, an employee's wage should reflect, relative to other wage classifications, the skills, knowledge, responsibilities, risks, and effort associated with his or her duties. If the wage structure of the firm does not adequately reflect the equity criterion, the employer and the union may find that employees become dissatisfied, creating grievances, high turnover rates, low moral, and political problems.

From the standpoint of economic efficiency, an employee's wage should reflect the relative abundance or scarcity of the skills and knowledge required by the subject work assignment as well as the productivity of the employee. The firm must also assure its viability by, among other things, attracting employees possessing the skills essential to the firm for efficient production. The external wage structure and the firm's position therein is, therefore, important. If the firm's wage structure overcompensates employees, profitability hence viability may be threatened particularly in industries where production is labor intensive and relatively high labor costs place the firm at a competitive disadvantage. Conversely, if the firm's wage structure is relatively low in comparison with firms utilizing employees with similar skills, the firm's position in the external structure of wages may make it difficult for the employer to attract and retain the employees necessary to continue operations. Therefore a delicate balance must be struck between the equity and efficiency requirements imposed by the internal and external structures of wages.[1]

Unfortunately economics has yet to offer us a "scientific" model of wage determination under collective bargaining. The problem arises from the fact that economic circumstances and the goals of bargaining parties differ across bargaining relationships. Three standards reflect most of the economic, legal, and institutional forces that influence labor and management in the negotiation of wages; these are the: (1) *comparative norm;* (2) *ability to pay;* and (3) *standard of living.*

The Comparative Norm

The comparative norm embodies the concept of the external wage structure. Union and company negotiators base their wage demands, at least in part, on the standards which have been established in labor-management contracts in industries and economic environments relatively similar to their

[1] For further discussion of the operation of these wage structures see J.T. Dunlop, "The Task of Contemporary Wage Theory," in G.W. Taylor and F.C. Pierson, eds, *New Concepts in Wage Determination,* New York: McGraw-Hill Book Company, 1957.

BOX 8–1. Hourly Union Wages: Selected Building Trades, 1978, by Region

Trade	United States	New England	Middle Atlantic	Border State	South-east	South-west	Great Lakes	Middle West	Mountain	Pacific
Journeyman										
Bricklayers	$13.14	$12.42	$14.60	$11.47	$10.70	$11.07	$13.69	$12.47	$13.65	$14.45
Carpenters	13.35	11.96	14.28	11.44	10.39	10.52	13.71	12.26	12.25	15.39
Electricians	14.38	13.79	15.09	12.49	11.91	12.11	14.53	14.31	14.02	17.13
Elevator Constructors	14.22	13.19	14.31	13.65	12.25	12.52	15.00	13.73	13.29	16.52
Marble Setters	12.44	12.08	12.85	11.51	10.52	11.00	13.33	12.05	11.41	14.67
Plasterers	12.75	12.06	13.04	10.82	10.09	10.90	12.94	11.58	12.16	15.07
Plumbers	14.13	13.39	14.63	12.51	11.59	11.25	14.50	14.02	13.61	18.03
Tile layers	12.69	12.10	12.41	10.87	10.06	10.24	12.73	12.08	11.66	14.48
Helpers and Laborers										
Bricklayer Tenders	$10.63	$ 9.77	$12.29	$ 6.95	$ 7.24	$ 7.79	$10.81	$10.55	$10.22	$13.07
Building Laborers	10.60	9.43	11.12	8.06	7.00	7.77	11.01	10.21	9.42	12.34
Elevator Constr.										
Helpers	10.42	9.57	10.76	9.83	8.98		10.82	9.99	9.63	11.87
Marble Setter Helpers	10.33	10.41	22.70	10.25	9.39		11.41	10.43	9.81	10.89
Plasterers' Laborers	10.88	9.71	11.20	8.88	7.73		11.35	11.00	10.51	14.32
Plumbers' Laborers	9.14	10.01	11.71	7.62	7.00		11.80	11.89	8.02	11.73
Tile Layer Helpers	10.62	10.32	10.60	7.76	7.66		11.50	10.42	10.12	12.05

Source: BLS, Bulletin 2038, Union Wages and Benefits: Building Trades–July 3, 1978

own. Managment will not normally desire to be at the top of the external wage structure while the union will attempt to ensure that it won't be at the bottom either. The basic idea from management's perspective when utilizing the comparative norm is to establish a wage package that assures an adequate supply of labor at the least cost. The union, on the other hand, will wish to use contracts for comparisons which support the best possible wage package. As should be obvious each side will select a wage settlement for comparison purposes which best supports their position.

The wage settlements used as norms by the negotiators are generally those of unionized firms within the same industry, using essentially the same technology, or of close geographic proximity. There are problems with this type of approach. The profitability of the firm used as a norm may constrain or enhance the wage settlement; variables such as the skill of the negotiators, other difficult issues on the table, and the cost-benefit estimates of a strike may all influence specific negotiations. The optimal wage level for one firm may not be a viable settlement for another, the basic idea being simply to get within the "ball park." Adoption of this wage standard requires that the parties "fine tune" the comparative norm to their individual circumstances. However, where the comparative norm is used, there is often a *pattern* to wage settlements in extensively unionized industries.

The automobile industry may be the best example of how pattern bargaining works.[2] The UAW is the dominate union in the auto industry and has a long established history of picking a "target" firm with which to negotiate (the big three auto agreements expire within close proximity of one another). The "target" firm[3] is the key to the UAW's strategy. Generally the union picks the firm which is most profitable and able to resist union demands to establish settlement patterns for the remaining firms. The rationale is that if the UAW can establish its demands with the dominate firm the rest of the industry will fall into line without much problem.

This bargaining strategy has been unusually successful for the auto workers. However, the 1979 Chrysler negotiations illustrate a very important point about pattern bargaining. Chrysler was on the verge of bankruptcy when the contract was settled with the UAW in the late fall of 1979. When the financial problems of Chrysler reached a crisis the company was forced to seek government assistance. Senator Richard Lugar of Indiana proposed legislation requiring the UAW to agree to a decrease in wages over the previously agreed to levels. This the UAW voluntarily did, but in cases where firms within the industry were financially unable or less suited to the established pattern, the auto workers had an established history of tailoring the wage settlements, within limits, to the need of the firm.[4] This is not a purely unselfish policy on the part of the UAW; it was not that many years ago that Packard and Studebaker became extinct causing the UAW a substantial loss of member-

---

[2] See H.M. Levinson, "Pattern Bargaining: A Case Study of the Automobile Workers." *Quarterly Journal of Economics, (May 1964)*, 74: 296–317.

[3] In 1973, 1976, and 1979 General Motors was selected.

[4] The American Motors settlements of the early 1970s illustrate this point.

ship.[5] The demise of these two firms is still relatively fresh in the minds of top UAW officials as was demonstrated again in early 1982 with the reopening of the Ford and GM contracts and the concessions made by the UAW to help those troubled companies through their financial difficulties.

Besides the possibility of pattern bargaining, the extent that an industry is unionized will in several ways effect specific wage settlements. First, if a relatively large majority of firms in an industry are of approximately equal size and use approximately the same proportion of labor, then settlements that are closer to positions demanded by a labor union would not inflict major damage to any firm's competitive position through increased labor costs. This result is, however, dependent on the profitability of the firm and the elasticity of demand for the firm's products. In general if the firm faces relatively elastic demand it must absorb a greater proportion of increased production costs than if the demand for its products is relatively inelastic. This issue will be addressed in greater detail later in this chapter. On the other hand, if one firm is placed in the position of having to pay the union wage, when none of its competitors are organized and therefore not subject to union wage standards, then this union firm may be placed at a competitive disadvantage. The greater the percentage of total costs accounted for by labor the greater the importance of the extent of union organization to the competitive position of the firm. This phenomenon is a function of the firm's technology and is generally measured by the ratio of labor costs to all other costs or the cost of capital and is termed "labor intensity." The greater the labor intensity of operations the more sensitive management will be to increased wage demands. The second influence concerns the expectations of the union and its membership. The union is in the business of representing its membership; if industry wage standards obtained by the negotiators are not satisfactory to the rank–and–file union members the union will be perceived to be ineffective. Union members will compare their wage settlements with those obtained by other unions for their members. If negotiators do not obtain satisfactory wage settlements vis–a–vis other comparable firms then the membership's dissatisfaction may result in the negotiators not being retained. In other words, the greater the extent of organization in an industry the higher the wage expectation of workers resulting in generally greater incentives for negotiators to obtain as high a wage settlement as possible. This second influence ties back into the first when the management position is considered. If relatively high wages have been granted historically and have become widespread in the industry then management will typically have built this wage structure into their corporate planning which, all other things equal, will result in less management resistance to union wage demands.

Just as financial comparisons of firms must be closely scrutinized, so must other characteristics of the firms before a pattern is set. The technology, products, method of compensation (i.e., piece rate, task rate, or hourly rate), and skills required of employees differ from firm to firm within industries and must be accounted for if the wage settlement is to be viable. For example, to

---

[5] For a further discussion of union behavioral models see Chapter 7.

BOX 8–2. **Percentage Wage and Benefit Settlements in Major Collective Bargaining Units, 1973–1978**

	Annual Average					
Sector and Measure	1973	1974	1975	1976	1977	1978
Wage and benefit settlements, all industries						
First-year settlements	7.1	10.7	11.4	8.5	9.6	8.3
Annual rate over life of contract	6.1	7.8	8.1	6.6	6.2	6.3
Wage rate settlements, all industries						
First-year settlements	5.8	9.8	10.2	8.4	7.8	7.6
Annual rate over life of contract	5.1	7.3	7.8	6.4	5.8	6.4
Manufacturing						
First-year settlements	5.9	8.7	9.8	8.9	8.4	8.3
Annual rate over life of contract	4.9	6.1	8.0	6.0	5.5	6.6
Nonmanufacturing (except construction)						
First-year settlements	6.0	10.2	11.9	8.6	8.9	8.0
Annual rate over life of contract	5.4	7.2	8.0	7.2	5.9	6.5
Construction						
First-year settlements	5.0	11.0	8.0	6.1	6.3	6.5
Annual rate over life of contract	5.1	9.6	7.5	6.2	6.3	6.2

Source: Monthly Labor Review

compare teacher's contracts with those obtained in the steel industry makes little economic sense and may result in expectations which are inconsistent with a negotiated settlement.

Ability to Pay

Profits have traditionally been a signal to unions of a firm's ability to pay wage increases. Union negotiators frequently reason that a firm making high profits should be able to institute generous wage increases while firms making low profits are in a position to grant only relatively modest wage increases. Unfortunately, this is a gross oversimplification and is recognized as such by most seasoned negotiators for both labor and management.

Other factors play an important role in the wage-paying ability of the firm. Among these factors are: (1) the labor intensity of the operations: (2) rate of technological development within the industry: (3) responsiveness of consumers of the firm's products to price changes; (4) ability of the firm to substitute capital for labor; and (5) product market concentration.

You may recall that the concept of labor intensity was introduced earlier in this chapter. Labor intensity and ability of the firm to pay are highly interrelated. Consider the following example. If profits are relatively high, for example twelve percent, the union may believe it has reason to be optimistic concerning a wage settlement. Not necessarily so; if labor costs are a large percentage of total costs, say eighty percent, then a slightly over seventeen percent increase in wages would exhaust the firm's total profits. The profits of a firm must be used for several purposes if the firm is to remain viable: the stockholders expect a dividend; the firm must retain some earnings to guarantee financial solvency during hard times, as well as for research and development of new methods and products. Without profits there would be no incentive for stockholders to continue to own their portion of the company and certainly additional investment would be jeopardized. Without retained earnings the firm may experience difficulty during a recession and have to curtail operations or even close down. Without research and development technological progress slows and the firm may lose out to more technologically advanced operations which offer a better product at a lower price. At the other extreme if a firm is earning a five percent profit and labor costs amount to only one percent of the firm's total cost then a seventeen percent increase in wages would lower the firm's profit insignificantly to slightly over 4.8%. Therefore the firm in the second example is *more* able to pay than the previous firm.

In industries such as electronics, where rapid technological advance is evident, firms need to invest heavily in new technology to remain competitive. For example, if Texas Instruments had spent its profits on wage increases in the late 1960s and early 1970s rather than on new technology and equipment they would not have survived the rapid adoption of stamped circuits and microcircuitry which dramatically improved hand held calculators and reduced the price of these instruments even more dramatically.

Consumers often share the burden of higher labor costs in the form of higher prices. This too is limited by the responsiveness of consumers to price changes. Elasticity of demand is commonly used to measure this responsiveness. Figure 8–1 illustrates the case where producers have raised their prices (shift in supply schedule from S_0 to S_1) due to higher labor costs. In the case of a relatively inelastic demand curve, producers may pass along substantial portions of the increased labor costs through price increases allowing total revenue to increase enough to offset at least a portion of the increase in labor costs. The producer facing the elastic demand curve in Figure 8–2, however, is not that fortunate. By increasing his price to help defray the increased cost of labor he has suffered a reduction in his total revenue because consumers responded to the higher price by purchasing (more than proportionately) less of the commodity. Therefore, market demand plays an important role in determining the ability of a firm to pass along the increased production costs. The factors that determine the degree to which consumers respond to price changes are: (1) availability of substitute products (the more substitutes the greater the elasticity); (2) proportion of income spent (the more the item costs in general the greater the elasticity of demand); and (3) whether the good

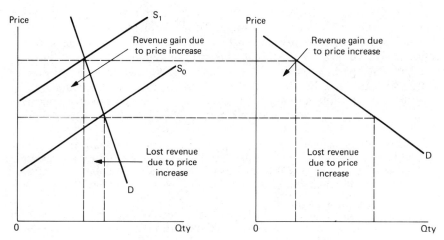

FIGURE 8.1.   Relatively Inelastic Consumer Demand.   **FIGURE 8.2.   Relatively Elastic Consumer Demand.**

is a luxury or necessity (luxuries tend to have elastic demand, necessities-inelastic demand).

Finally, in many cases where labor costs have become high for given levels of production relative to the cost of capital, employers have cut back on the use of labor through automation. If unions consider only the profit levels of the firm and ignore the possibility that machinery can be utilized more intensively and labor less intensively to produce the required levels of output, unions could negotiate their membership out of their jobs. Automation has been a common management response to excessively high wages. However, where substitution of machinery for labor is not a viable alternative, high labor costs may be avoided by plant relocation to areas where there is an abundance of laborers willing to work for significantly lower wages. The relocation of manufacturing facilities by U.S. Steel and General Motors to southern states, and the relocation overseas (primarily the Far East and Mexico) of American garment and textile manufacturers attests to the fact that if labor cost differentials are large enough a firm can build new facilities and pay significant transportation costs (cheaper in some cases) rather than continue to pay excessively high wages in their original locations. In fairness, many multinational firms have cited the above labor cost situations as their reasons for moving while the evidence indicates that tax breaks and subsidization of the firm's operations by the host nation amount to greater savings. Undoubtedly the controversy will continue though it is certain in many cases labor costs do play a significant role in the relocation of operations overseas.

The *Truitt* Decision and the Ability to Pay

In 1956, the United States Supreme Court rendered a landmark decision concerning the firm's claimed inability to pay wage demands in the *Truitt*

Manufacturing Company case.[6] In this case the employer claimed that it was financially unable to meet the wage demands of the union. The union demanded the employer present evidence to support this claim; the company refused. The union claimed that this refusal amounted to a failure, on management's part, to bargain in good–faith and filed an unfair labor practice charge with the NLRB. The NLRB ruled that in this case the employer was obligated, by its duty to bargain in good-faith, to support such claims. The Court reviewed the *Truitt* case and in part stated:

> Good faith bargaining necessarily requires that claims by either bargainer should be honest claims. This is true about an asserted inability to pay an increase in wages. If such an argument is important enough to present in the give and take of bargaining, it is important enough to require some sort of proof of its accuracy.

This decision, which is still law today, does not require either party to concede to wage demands. Neither does the decision establish what constitutes "proof of accuracy." The *Truitt* decision simply states that if an employer claims a financial inability to meet a wage demand he must be able to present adequate proof of such. Otherwise, the NLRB will find a failure to bargain in good-faith. The NLRB will decide, on a case–by–case basis, what constitutes a claim of inability to pay and the appropriate proof. This decision has had important impact on the conduct of collective bargaining. It has become common practice for management to claim that it would rather not pay specific wage demands instead of claiming an inability and thus falling under the *Truitt* decision's obligation to support that claim with evidence. Not only is much of this evidence regarded by management to be sensitive but there is substantial uncertainty as to what constitutes adequate evidence. The 1981 baseball strike presented an interesting variant on the theme established in the *Truitt* decision. Negotiators for the owners had never claimed an inability to meet union demands at the bargaining table. However, during a press conference one of the owners and his representative alluded to possible financial hardships if the union's demands were met. The Player's Association asserted that this constituted a claim of an inability to pay and demanded evidence of such at the bargaining table or else they would file charges with the NLRB. The issue was settled through collective bargaining but it would have been interesting to see how the courts and the NLRB would have viewed such a statement made to the press rather than at the bargaining table.

Standard of Living

Employees and therefore their unions are primarily concerned with the adequacy of their wages to assure themselves and their families an "acceptable standard of living." This "acceptable standard of living" is, of course, a highly subjective criterion. An acceptable standard of living can imply anything from freedom from starvation and exposure, to extreme affluence. In 1883, Samuel Gompers is reported to have responded to a congressional committee's query

---

[6]*NLRB v. Truitt Manufacturing Company*, 351 U.S. 149 (1956).

TABLE 8–1. Urban Budgets for a 4-Person Family (Autumn 1978 Nominal Dollars)

	Lower Budget			Intermediate Budget			Higher Budget		
	Urban U.S.	*Metro Areas*	*Non-Metro Areas*	*Urban U.S.*	*Metro Areas*	*Non-Metro Areas*	*Urban U.S.*	*Metro Areas*	*Non-Metro Areas*
Total Cost	11546	11685	10925	18622	18982	17016	27420	28186	24000
Total Cost of Consumption	9391	9485	8968	14000	14238	12940	19225	19670	17236
Food	3574	3616	3388	4609	4667	4351	5806	5921	5291
Housing	2233	2267	2081	4182	4179	3750	6345	6531	5512
Transportation	856	812	1053	1572	1578	1544	2043	2079	1885
Clothing and Personal Care	1148	1159	1098	1612	1624	1555	2338	2355	2263
Medical Care	1065	1096	927	1070	1100	933	1116	1147	974
Other Family Consumption	515	536	420	956	990	808	1578	1637	1312
Other costs	501	505	489	810	818	773	1365	1388	1266
Social Security and Disability Insurance Payments	719	730	669	1073	1085	1022	1091	1094	1079
Personal Income Taxes	935	965	799	2738	2841	2281	5739	6035	4419

Source: U.S. Bureau of Labor Statistics, Autumn Urban Family Budgets and Comparative Indexes for Selected Urban Areas, 1978 (Supplement to Bulletin 1570-5).

about what unions wanted with four words "more, more, more,—now!" What then might serve as a reasonably objective measure of what constitutes a decent standard of living? The answer to this question depends critically on to whom the question is put. Virtually any standard that negotiators or the present authors might suggest will have some element of subjectivity; to expect labor or management not to be purposefully subjective is naïve.

The bargaining parties have at their disposal some relatively unbiased estimates of what constitutes a decent standard of living. The U.S. Department of Labor's Bureau of Labor Statistics publishes budget statistics for various standards of living. These statistics, however, are based on expenditures typical of a specific type of family and are therefore somewhat subjective and thus may serve only as a general guideline. Inference beyond what the data actually measure is technically incorrect but these data may provide useful guideposts as long as their limitations are recognized.

These data are for three "adequate standards of living": lower, inter-mediate, and higher. The budgets described are for a characteristic family of four: a 38 year old employed husband, a housewife (not employed outside the home), a thirteen year old boy and an eight year old girl. The lower budget category assumes the family rents its home. For the other two categories it is assumed the family is purchasing their dwelling. The "other costs" category includes such items as gifts, charitable contributions, life insurance, and occupational expenses.

These data are also published for most major metropolitan areas in the United States. This allows for union and management comparisons which are in close geographic proximity to their own areas. However, the use of these data are frequently the subject of controversy. Employers, as may be expected, have often argued that these family budgets contain unwarranted items and are therefore biased. This is especially true if the data indicates that a higher wage than management has offered should be paid. Unions naturally argue the higher budgets are more accurate, especially if this supports the union's wage demands. The debate will undoubtedly continue over the accuracy and applicability of these data. However, lacking a uniformly acceptable source of data, these types of information will still be used by the bargaining parties as evidence to support their demands and as a *rough* guide to negotiations.

Wage Adjustment During the Effective Period of the Contract

The typical labor contract is negotiated specifying an effective period of three years. Others are effective for four or more years. A worker's earnings can be significantly eroded by high rates of inflation if no method is provided to adjust wages during a lengthy contract. For example, the Consumer Price Index (CPI) for 1975 was 161.2, three years later the CPI increased by 34.2 points or 21.2 percent. If a contract negotiated in 1975 expired in 1978 without adjusting the employees' wages, they would have lost 21.2 percent of their real income by the end of the contract period. Nominal wages (monetary hourly wage), by remaining constant over a three year inflationary period, reduce the employees' command over goods and services—a reduction in the real wage.

Why then do the parties bargain contracts to be effective for such long periods of time or why don't the parties forecast inflation rates and include annual increases which at least partially offset the effects of inflation, you might ask? The first question has, in part, been answered in some contracts which call for the annual reopening of the contract to renegotiate the wage (to be discussed in the following paragraphs). Forecasting, however, is an extremely unreliable method for wage adjustment. It is doubtful that any forecasting method could be obtained whose accuracy would endear it to both labor and management. To illustrate the point: over the preceding decade this country has consistently suffered inflation but the annual percentage increases in the CPI have fluctuated substantially from a low of 3.3 percent in 1972 to a high in 1974 of 11.0 percent. With such variations in the CPI and the difficulty in accounting for all the factors which contribute to inflation it is little wonder that even the big econometric forecasting models such as Chase or the Wharton models have poor track records.

Aware of these problems, labor and management have adopted two methods of wage adjustment during the life of the contract: (1) wage-reopener clauses and (2) escalator clauses. Each of these methods will be discussed in the sections that follow.

The Wage Reopener

The wage reopener method of compensation adjustment during the life of the contract is a relatively simple vehicle. A clause is negotiated into the contract which allows either or both parties to reopen negotiations for the purpose of adjusting wages or the economic package at specified periods during the life of the agreement. It is not uncommon for the reopener clause to specify the annual anniversary of the signing of the contract as the date for reopening the negotiations. It is also typical of most reopener clauses that negotiations concerning any issue other than the economic package be prohibited.

The wage reopener clause has not been widely adopted; the Bureau of Labor Statistics estimated that only 6.4 percent of all major agreements, covering approximately 5.1 percent of unionized workers, contained wage reopener clauses in 1978.[7] The primary reason this relatively simple contract language is not more readily adopted relates to the problems associated with renegotiating a wage annually. Wages are a highly emotional and complex issue to settle, and frequently result in strikes and lockouts. For example, in calendar 1977 workstoppages resulting from wage issues comprised 59.5 percent of total work cessations in the United States.[8] The risks of strike associated with wage renegotiation are more than most parties are willing to assume. Secondly, both labor and management will frequently demand the negotiation of issues other than the wage rate; this is not the intent of the wage-reopener clause. These

[7] U. S. Department of Labor, Bureau of Labor Statistics, *Characteristics of Major Collective Bargaining Agreements, January 1, 1978,* Bulletin 2065 (April 1980) Washington, D.C.: GPO, p. 51.

[8] U. S. Department of Labor, Bureau of Labor Statistics, *Analysis of Work Stoppages,* Bulletin 2032 (1979) p. 23.

two phenomenon alone are sufficient to ensure that wage-reopeners will not become widely adopted.

Escalator Clauses

Of 1,536 major agreements in the 1978 BLS survey of labor contracts, 706 (or about 47.1 percent) covering 4,277,700 employees contained escalator clauses.[9] The escalator clause circumvents problems associated with the wage-reopener clause because the escalator *automatically* increases or decreases the wage as the price level rises or falls (we have yet to experience substantial deflation while an operable escalator was in place). The escalator was first adopted by General Motors and the UAW in 1948. Many firms and unions soon followed this lead because of anticipated inflation resulting from the Korean War.

Escalator clauses (or Cost of Living Adjustment—COLA clauses) operate according to a negotiated and predetermined formula. Most contracts "tie" the escalator clause to the CPI or some variation of the CPI. In most UAW contracts a weighted average of American and Canadian prices are used (since the UAW represents many employees working in Canadian subsidiaries of American auto firms). The typical escalator clause calls for the COLA adjustment to be superimposed on the employees hourly wage for one year then "rolled–in" to the hourly wage after the first year. Employees typically receive their COLA quarterly, however, UMW contracts generally call for semi-annual payments and UAW contracts require monthly disbursements. The 1979 GM-UAW contract requires an additional 1¢ per hour for every .25 the CPI increases, while other widely adopted versions require 1¢ per hour for every .3 or .4 change in consumer prices.

As is typical with many issues of this nature escalator clauses are the subject of considerable controversy. Employers have displayed tough opposition to COLA clauses because of the unabated inflation this nation has recently experienced. COLA adds to the wage automatically to offset the effects of inflation. The greater the rate of inflation the more is added to labor costs, frequently erroding the firm's profits and in some cases requiring the firm to raise prices. This escalation of wages adds to the uncertainty of future operating costs for management. Fearful of the effect of accelerating inflation on labor costs, but willing to concede an escalator clause to circumvent more troublesome wage issues in future negotiations, some employers have been successful in imposing *ceilings* on these adjustments. A ceiling is an additional contract provision which limits the amount an escalator can increase wages during any specified period. For example, a ceiling may require that the employer add no more than 15¢ per hour in COLA during any calendar year. Some variations on this theme require that COLA be determined incrementally—for the first 5 points of increase in the CPI the employer adds 1¢ per .3 increase in the CPI, for the next 3 points of increase 1¢ per .5, and nothing beyond 8 points per calendar year. Some unions have demanded floors be imposed when the COLA clause specifies that it may reduce the hourly wage

---

[9]*Characteristics of Major Collective Bargaining Agreements*, p. 50.

should deflation occur. Floor clauses generally require two consecutive quarters of deflation before downward adjustments are made and that the total downward ajustment can be no more than was added to the wage by COLA.

To the casual observer, COLA clauses may appear to be an excellent method of protecting the real earnings of employees. This is not totally accurate. COLA is not designed to protect the real wage of the employee but is simply to keep the employee's nominal wage, within certain limits, close to its original purchasing power. With a 1¢ adjustment per .4 increase in the CPI (if no ceiling is present) the base wage which is being protected from the errosive effect of inflation is $2.50 per hour, 1¢ per .3 increase in the CPI protects $3.33 per hour, and 1¢ per .2 increase in the CPI protects $5.00 per hour. This is quite easy to see; since the CPI is an index number computed against some base year (CPI = 100.00 in 1967) and the adjustment factor normally required in escalator clauses is 1¢ per some increase, x, in the CPI, the real wage which is protected by the escalator is the inverse of the CPI requirement or $1/x$.

If the escalator is protecting such a small portion (in most cases) of the employee's wages why do so many require 1¢ per every .25, .3, or .4 increase in the CPI? This is not a difficult question to answer—most labor disputes which result in strikes concern wage issues. Wage issues are most likely to result in work stoppages when the effective period of the expiring contract was marked by high rates of inflation. This high inflation rate will cause the real wage to be erroded over the contractual period. Therefore, to be as monetarily

---

BOX 8–3. Operation of a Typical Cola Clause

Initial hourly wage	$ 8.00
Initial CPI	120.00
Escalator formula	1¢ per .4 increase in CPI
CPI at end of contract	132.00
Percentage increase in CPI	10.0% (12.0 points)
Nominal wage required at end of contract to be worth the initial $8.00	$ 8.80
Actual wage with COLA	8.30
Required catch-up	.50

It is obvious that the escalator fell short of protecting the real wage at the end of the contractual period by 50¢ per hour, but it did add 30¢ per hour over the life of the contract. The catch-up required without the escalator clause has been reduced 37.5 percent with the adoption of COLA. This reduction in the catch-up demands of the union should lessen the probability of an impasse over this portion of the wage settlement. In other words; the purpose of an escalator is really two-fold; naturally the most obvious purpose is to, in part, protect the employees' real wages but maybe an even more important purpose is to reduce union's "catch-up" demands thereby reducing the probability of a strike concerning wages.

well off the union will need the nominal wage to "catch-up" with the real wage rate to make up for buying power lost to inflation which was not offset by the escalator during the effective contractual period. Consider the example contained in Box 8–3.

An interesting variation on the escalator theme has been adopted by some labor-management negotiators—the *annual improvement factor*. These types of clauses operate on much the same principle and with essentially the same goals as an escalator. The annual improvement factor, however, is "tied" to productivity rather than CPI changes. Most frequently these clauses will grant an increase in wages directly proportional to increases in the productivity of the firm (e.g., a two percent increase in productivity will result in a two percent wage increase) and adjustments are typically made annually. These clauses are found in varying combination with CPI escalators and negotiated periodic fixed–sum wage increases. Management, quite naturally, favors this type of arrangement over COLA since wages are directly tied to the firm's output rather than the economic environment which may not directly reflect the firm's ability to pay or viability.

Government Intervention in Wage Determination

Two forms of government intervention in wage determination will be examined here: (1) the Fair Labor Standards Act and (2) Wage-Price Controls. The Fair Labor Standards Act (FLSA) was signed into law June 25, 1938 and has been a continuing influence in the labor market since. Wage and price controls, however, are more alien to the nation's labor market in that they are an "on-again-off–again" form of intervention. These controls have been utilized only twice in recent years, during World War II and the Nixon administration. We will first examine the Fair Labor Standards Act before turning our attention to wage and price controls.

Fair Labor Standards Act

The Fair Labor Standards Act, commonly called the Wage and Hours Act, provides for a standard forty-hour work week, above which overtime premiums must be paid. The FLSA contains provisions for minimum wages applicable to all employees working in interstate commerce except for certain exempt workers.[10] The regulation of the standard work week and the requirement of an overtime premium for hours worked in excess of forty has had the impact of establishing minimum hours standards which have become the starting point for negotiations on these issues. The law requires that all nonexempt employees must be paid at the rate of not less than one and one-half times the regular rate at which they are employed for all hours in excess of forty per week.

The second major provision of the Act provides for minimum wages for

[10]These exemptions are listed in Section 13 of the Act, and include: teachers, managerial and professional employees and workers in retailing, fishing, certain agricultural activities, newspapers, and other like industries.

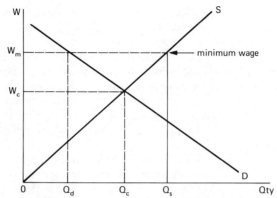

FIGURE 8.3. Minimum wage in an otherwise competitive labor market.

nonexempt workers. Originally established at 25¢ per hour in 1938, the minimum wage has been raised over the years to its present $3.35 per hour. The minimum wage has been subject to controversy since its beginnings. Three positions have emerged from this controversy. The minimum wage is alleged to: (1) create unemployment, hence erroding the standard of living of the poor; (2) increase the standard of living of poor people; and (3) protect organized labor from "cheap" domestic labor.

The logic behind the argument that unemployment results from the imposition of a minimum wage rests on the assumption that the affected workers face a competitive labor market (See Figure 8.3).

In an otherwise competitive labor market, the imposition of a minimum wage will result in unemployment (if enforceable and enforced). The quantity of labor represented by the line segment Qd-Qc is the quantity of previously employed labor now unemployed and line segment Qc-Qs represents the quantity of labor attracted by the higher wage which is unable to secure work and are therefore unemployed. The standard of living of the affected workers (or their total earnings) depends on the price elasticity of demand for labor. With relatively elastic demand, in the relevant range, total labor earnings decline with the imposition of a minimum wage and conversely if demand is relatively inelastic then total earnings will increase. A second major issue concerning the economic analysis employed in examining minimum wages is the assumption of a perfectly competitive labor market. This assumption simplifies the analysis dramatically and leads to the well known results reported previously. If, however, an imperfectly competitive labor market is assumed as the beginning point then these results are not necessarily correct. Depending on the relative magnitude of the controlled and the equilibrium wage we should expect an indeterminant solution at worst and at best an increase in labor earnings without the loss of employment opportunities.[11]

---

[11] See Belton Fleisher, *Labor Economics: Theory and Evidence*, Englewood Cliffs, N.J.: Prentice-Hall, Inc., 1970, Chapter 10 for a detailed examination of imperfect labor markets and the impact of minimum wages in these markets.

Organized labor has historically supported minimum wage legislation. The motivation for this union support is subject to debate. Some economists and employers have charged that this support is evidence of organized labor attempting to defend its wage standards from the competition of "cheap" domestic labor by increasing the price of that competitive labor. Unions and their supporters argue that the conditions and standards imposed on all workers are the legitimate concern of organized labor. Which contention is valid is not readily apparent. The evidence is inconclusive. However, organized labor has a long and consistent history of support for legislation which generally improves the working conditions and terms of employment of all workers. In addition, minimum wages have historically been far below union wage rates; however, the labor markets most affected by the minimum wage are the ones unions have found the most difficult to organize. This suggests the possibility that minimum wages may not facilitate unionization in low wage markets. The conclusions suggested by this fact are consistent with both views presented above; which is correct is open to speculation.

Wage and Price Controls

During World War II and again in August of 1971, wage and price controls were implemented in an attempt to curb inflation. The history of these controls is a matter of record. However, the impact of such controls on collective bargaining is worthy of discussion. Under the Nixon wage-price controls and again under Carter's voluntary wage-price guidelines, employers pointed to the government wage restrictions as their authority for resisting union demands for higher wages. These legal bases provided employers with considerable support and incentive to resist wage demands in excess of the controls as well as ready-made public support for their positions. Union demands for higher wages were publicly viewed as self-serving behavior which asked society in general to bear the burden of higher wages through accelerating rates of inflation. Regardless of the validity of these arguments, unions were placed at a strategic disadvantage in bargaining for increased wages.

The enforcement of wage and price controls has historically been an almost impossible task. Producers will change the characteristics or quality of their commodities, resort to "black-markets", or simply ignore the law. Unions, on the other hand, divert their attention to administrative issues or devise methods to circumvent the restrictions imposed on obtaining the desired wage. Besides the obvious problems associated with the enforcement of wage and price controls these policies are doomed, by their very nature, to be short lived. Organized labor, management, and consumers all perceive themselves to be the victims of inflation rather than contributors to increasing prices. The result is that sacrifices required by such controls are politically unpopular and are perceived to be unjust by all affected.

Shorter Workweek Response to Wage Controls

Several union responses are possible when wage and price controls are imposed. From the principles of labor supply we know that workers will substitute hours of leisure for hours of work above some wage rate, hence offering fewer hours of work as the wage rate increases.[12] What are the motives of organized labor in demanding shorter standard workweeks? The two motives most frequently cited are (1) the desire to share employment more evenly across the union's membership while allowing workers a greater opportunity to enjoy the fruits of their labor and (2) the desire to obtain higher effective wage rates than could otherwise be achieved through the activation of overtime premiums at an earlier point in the workweek.

Figure 8.4 illustrates the logic behind the second union response. The kinked line *OABC* depicts the income opportunities open to a worker under a typical contract where a straight-time hourly wage rate of $10 per hour is in effect for the standard 40-hour workweek and an overtime premium of time-and-a-half for any time worked in excess of 40 hours. The slope of line segment OB represents the straight-time hourly wage rate of $10 per hour. Likewise, the slope of line segment BC represents the wage plus overtime premium totaling $15 per hour. In response to a control on wages, the union could simply bargain the standard workweek back from 40 hours, for example, to 34 hours per week. The overtime premium of time-and-a-half would now activate at 34 hours (Point A) rather than 40 hours (Point B). The income opportunities open to the worker under the new shorter standard workweek are shown by the kinked line *OADE*. The straight-time wage rate that would generate the same income that the worker earns for 40 hours of work under the shorter workweek

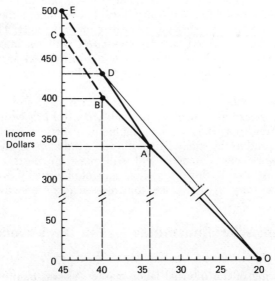

FIGURE 8.4.   Standard Work Week/Higher Effective Wage Rate.

[12] A.M. Carter, *Theory of Wage and Employment*, Homewood, IL: Richard D. Irwin, Inc., 1959, pp. 77–94.

(34 hours at straight-time and 6 hours at time-and-a-half) is represented by the slope of line *ODE*. In the figure, this rate is $10.75 per hour.

Although there has been an increase in the effective hourly wage rate of 7.5 percent ($10.00 to $10.75 per hour) through the bargaining of a shorter work week, there has been no increase in the actual wage rate as far as wage-price controls are concerned. The union, so to speak, "can have its cake and eat it too"; it can bargain an effective wage increase, significantly in excess of the wage control and, at the same time, publicize the union's contribution in the fight against inflation by pointing to its technical non-violation of the guideline. Of course, the degree to which a union can circumvent the wage-price controls in the above manner depends upon the magnitude of the workweek reduction it can successfully bargain.

Unions during the Nixon controls met with some success in bargaining for these hidden pay raises. Union contracts in the auto, steel, and health care industries have generated similar increases in earnings without a higher hourly rate. In the case of the health care industry, the American Nurses Association secured a reduction of the standard workweek from 40 to 37.5 hours in contracts bargained over the period 1971 to 1973 primarily in response to low pattern settlements brought on by wage controls.

The approaches in the basic steel and auto industries have differed somewhat from the nurses. In these manufacturing industries the unions have negotiated more paid holidays and personal paid authorized leave time. Rather than a shorter standard workweek the Steelworkers and Auto Workers have negotiated shorter standard work years. The union's goal was essentially the same as the nurses in that if the same output was to be obtained then employers would either have to offer overtime work or hire more workers. The USW and UAW met with rather limited success compared with the nurses because automation of certain manufacturing jobs could and did pick up some of the slack whereas in registered nursing capital is generally not easily substituted for a nurse.

Producers were able, in many cases, to at least in part, offset the increased labor costs by downsizing, reductions in quality control procedures, substitution of cheaper raw materials, and curtailment of certain warranties. This changing of the product by many firms allowed producers to concede to the union shorter workweek demands and still pass the costs along to the consumer. As illustrated in this discussion, control of virtually every aspect of production is necessary if wage-price controls are to be effective.

Job Evaluation: What Constitutes "A Fair Day's Work for a Fair Day's Pay"

The structuring of the internal labor market, as was pointed out in this chapter's introduction, is of paramount importance to both labor and management. Many different "scientific" methods are employed to objectively analyze each job, rank that job in the internal wage structure, and determine the quantity of output the employer should reasonably expect. The job evaluation system, briefly described here, involves method analysis and time study.

There are four basic standards to any objective job evaluation system: (1) effort; (2) job conditions; (3) responsibility; and (4) skill. For the time study of a task to be meaningful, an accurate and exhaustive method analysis must be conducted. Industrial engineers specifically trained in these methods are utilized to conduct these methods analyses. For each job the most efficient method, involving the least motion, movement, and physical strain which still allows the task to be accomplished must be determined. An employee must then be selected for the timing of the job; the employee selected should be an average or normal employee working at a normal rate (a rate that will not result in undue fatigue after an eight hour shift). The timing of the job is typically done at several periods during a day and for several days. The timing data is then statistically analyzed to ensure its reliability and consistency. If the timing sample proves reliable and reasonably consistent the mean of the sample will be used for production rate setting purposes.

The timing data must then be adjusted to reflect an efficient and equitable hourly production rate. To account for normal and unavoidable job down time and the other three evaluation standards a system of allowances is normally employed. A key job within the "cluster" of technologically or administratively related jobs will be selected as a norm for comparison of the remaining jobs. An allowance will then be added to or deducted from each job's production rate to control for differences in skill, responsibility, and job conditions. The result is that each will have a different required production rate for an equal hourly wage. If the employer, however, requires relatively equal production rates rather than compensation, then the hourly wage or piece rates can be readily found by indexing the job evaluation data and appropriately adjusting the hourly wage or piece rate. For example, consider three jobs with equal responsibility and job conditions but differing effort and skill requirements. On comparable operations the production rates were: Job A-100; Job B-120; Job C-80. Job B requires 10 percent less skill than Job A but Job A requires 10 percent less skill than Job C. The production rates adjusted for the skill allowance are: Job A-90; Job B-120; Job C-88; these are the required production rates for equal pay. If each job is required to produce 100 parts and the hourly wage for the skill adjusted production rates above was $10 per hour the new hourly wages for equal production rates then become: Job A-$11.01; Job B-$8.33; and Job C-$11.36. The same procedures can be applied to obtain the appropriate piece rates or task rates. The objective in any system, regardless of the method of payment, is to assure internal consistency between wages as fairly and objectively as possible.

Summary and Conclusions

Wages are a particularly emotional and thorny issue for labor and management negotiators. Wages and related issues result in more strikes and controversy than any other set of issues in collective bargaining. A delicate balance between the internal and external wage structures must be maintained otherwise equity as well as efficiency may be erroded.

At this point there is no scientific model of wage determination under collective bargaining. There are, however, three basic standards which are commonly employed by negotiators in determining wage rates; these are the: (1) comparative norm; (2) ability of the firm to pay; and (3) standard of living. Each of these standards embodies economic, institutional and legal concepts which make them useful guideposts for the collective bargaining of wages. In addition two basic methods are used to adjust wages during the effective life of the contract; these are the wage reopener clauses and escalator or COLA clauses. The wage reopener allows for the renegotiation of wages at specified periods during the life of the contract which implies a risk of strike activity during these negotiations. The escalator, on the other hand, adjusts wages automatically according to a predetermined formula. The purpose of the escalator is basically two-fold: to reduce the probability of strikes over wage issues and to keep workers' wages close to the real levels originally negotiated.

Government intervention in collective bargaining determination of wages, beyond the Taft-Hartley Act, includes the Fair Labor Standards Act which regulates hours and imposes minimum wages on the majority of firms in the United States. Minimum wages have been subject to considerable debate; the results of and motivation for these laws are somewhat speculative. Wage and price controls have from time to time been imposed on the nation's labor markets but are relatively easy to circumvent and generally politically unpopular which results in such policies being short-lived.

Job evaluation is necessary to ensure internal wage consistency within firms which implies fairness of the structure of compensation. Job evaluation must consider four characteristics of a specific task, fairly and objectively, if it is to be effective in assuring internal wage consistency; these are: (1) effort, (2) job conditions, (3) responsibility, and (4) skill.

COMMENTARY: Mr. Douglas A. Fraser Speaking on the Topic of COLA Clauses

Douglas A. Fraser, the man Reader's Digest *called "the labor leader everyone respects," rose through the ranks to become the UAW's sixth International president.*

He was born in a working class district in Glasgow, Scotland on Dec. 18, 1916, and came to the United States with his parents when he was six years old; the family settled in Detroit. After attending Chadsey High School, he went to work as a metal finisher in the DeSoto plant of Chrysler Corp. at the age of 18.

Mr. Douglas A. Fraser became active in UAW Local 277. He was elected to various local offices, including steward, chief steward, recording secretary and, finally, local president in 1943. He served three terms in that position.

In 1947, Fraser was appointed an International representative, assigned to the union's Chrysler Department. He caught the eye of the UAW president Walter P. Reuther who selected him as an administrative assistant in 1951—a position he held for eight years. While serving in that capacity, he was involved

*in many major negotiations. Mr. Fraser during the next two decades served in
several elective offices of the UAW and was elected President of UAW in 1977.*

*Mr. Fraser is an officer or member of many labor, civic and governmental
bodies.*

*He is married to Dr. Winifred Fraser, an associate professor of psychology
and associate dean of the Graduate School of Wayne State University. They live
in Detroit.*

In these inflationary times, cost-of-living protection is absolutely essential if the
workers' standard of living is not to be eroded. Most UAW members have what
we believe to be the best COLA clause in the country, and yet even that
provision does not totally compensate them for the increases in the cost of
living.

In fact, the purchasing power of millions of American workers has seriously
deteriorated in recent years.

The first cost-of-living escalator clause in the U.S. was negotiated between
the UAW and the General Motors Corporation in 1948. The idea had first been
suggested by GM President Charles E. Wilson, who was heavily criticized for it
by fellow industrialists. Some union leaders criticized UAW President Walter
P. Reuther for accepting the COLA principle. History has shown that Wilson
and Reuther had greater vision than their critics.

In defending the principle behind COLA, Wilson wrote—in an article
published in the September 1952 *Reader's Digest*:

Escalator clauses "are attacked by people who insist upon talking about
'the wage-price spiral.' I contend that we should not say 'the *wage*-price spiral.'
We should say 'the *price*-wage spiral.' For it is not primarily wages that push up
prices. It is primarily prices that *pull* up wages."

I COULD NOT IMPROVE UPON THAT 30-YEAR OLD QUOTE.

COMMENTARY: Mr. Richard Ringoen Discusses
COLA Clauses *

Another pervasive effect of governmental action is the role of the Consumer
Price Index in the establishment of many employee compensation packages.
Since salaries, wages and benefits are the largest element in a company's cost of
doing business, institutionalization of the cost-of-living adjustment (COLA) tied
to the Consumer Price Index is equally detrimental to the health of private
enterprise.

Today, 10% of the nation's workers are covered by COLA. Employers first
agreed to a cost-of-living adjustment because it brought labor peace more
easily. The inflation rate was about two percent when COLA first gained
popularity in the early 1950s. It remained there until the late 1960s, when it
climbed to the 3% to 6% range. Then the price tag rose dramatically in the '70s,
with inflation reaching double-digit proportions. For firms with COLA, it now

---

*For Biography See End of Chapter 4.

accounts for 60% of annual labor-cost boosts. Such increases are becoming increasingly difficult for firms to bear.

What are the answers? Government can play a role in moderating the impact of legislative intrusions into the free enterprise system. The method for calculating the Consumer Price Index, upon which COLA adjustments are based, should be revised to more accurately reflect the real-world environment, eliminating from the calculation those items which are not common to most consumers.

In the final analysis, it is only through a cooperative effort by business and labor that the disruptive effects of inflation and wage increases not linked to improvement in productivity can be brought under control. .

DISCUSSION QUESTIONS

1. Why is internal and external wage structuring important to a firm? To a Union?

2. Is there an interrelationship between the three standards for wage determination? Explain.

3. What incentives are there for management to equitably and objectively evaluate jobs and assign wage rates?

4. What specifically is the firm's ability to pay? What special complications are involved with this wage determination standard?

5. Critically evaluate escalator clauses. Do escalator clauses provide insight into the wage negotiation process?

6. What is the economic rationale for Samuel Gomper's philosophy concerning the unions goals of—"more, more, more—now." Is this an overstatement of union desires (in an economic context)?

SELECTED REFERENCES

Barbash, J., "Union Interests in Apprenticeship and Other Training Forms," *Journal of Human Resources*, (Winter, 1968), **3:** 63–85.

Baumback, C.M., *Structural Wage Issues in Collective Bargaining*, Lexington, Mass.: D.C. Heath & Company, 1971.

Carter, A.M., *Theory of Wages and Employment*, Homewood, ILL.: Richard D. Irwin, Inc., 1959.

Doeringer, P.B. and M.J. Piore, *Internal Labor Markets and Manpower Analysis*, Lexington, Mass.: Heath-Lexington Books, 1971.

Dunlop, John T., *Wage Determination Under Trade Unions*, New York: Augustus M. Kelly, Inc., 1950.

Dunlop, John T., ed., *The Theory of Wage Determination*, New York: St. Martin's Press, Inc., 1952.

Dunn, J.D. and F.M. Rachel, *Wage and Salary Administration: Total Compensation Systems*, New York: McGraw-Hill Book Company, 1971.

Fleisher, B.M. and T.J. Kniesner, *Labor Economics: Theory Evidence, and Policy*, Second edition, Englewood Cliffs, N.J.: Prentice-Hall, Inc. 1980.

Fogel, Walter A., "Job Rate Ranges: A Theoretical and Empirical Analysis," *Industrial and Labor Relations Review*, (July 1964), **18**: 584–97.

Garbarino, J.W., *Wage Policy and Long-Term Contracts*, Washington, D.C.: The Brookings Institution, 1962.

Henderson, Richard, *Performance Appraisal: Theory of Practice.*, Reston, Va.: Reston Publishing Company, Inc., 1980.

Lester, R.A., *Economics of Labor*, New York: Macmillan 1964.

Lewis, H.G., *Unionism and Relative Wages in the United States*, Chicago: University of Chicago Press, 1963.

Miller, R.L. and R.M. Williams, *Unemployment and Inflation*, St. Paul, Minn.: West Publishing Company, 1974.

Myers, C.A. and Paul Pigors, *Personnel Administration: A Point of View and a Method*, 7th ed., New York: McGraw-Hill Book Company, 1973.

Rapping, L.A. "Monopoly Rents, Wage Rents, and Union Wage Effectiveness," *Quarterly Review of Economics and Business*, (Spring 1967), **7**: 31–47.

Reder, Melvin, "The Theory of Occupational Wage Differentials," *American Economic Review*, (December 1955), **45**: 833–52.

Rees, Albert, *The Economics of Trade Unions*, Chicago: University of Chicago Press, 1962.

Rees, Albert, "The Effects of Unions on Resource Allocation," *Journal of Law and Economics*, (October 1963), **6**: 69–70.

Sauer, R.L., "Selecting the Best Job Evaluation Plan," *Industrial Engineering*, (March, 1971), **9**: 16–20.

Weber, A.R., *In Pursuit of Price Stability: The Wage-Price Freeze of 1971*, Washington, D.C.: The Brookings Institution, 1973.

Weintraub, Sidney, *Some Aspects of Wage Theory and Policy*, Philadelphia: Chilton Book Company, 1963.

Weiss, Leonard, "Concentration and Labor Earnings," *American Economic Review*, (March 1966), **56**: 96–117.

Chapter 9

Economic Supplements and Collective Bargaining

The previous chapter dealt with the determination of wages under collective bargaining. Wages are only part of the economic package, the remainder of employee compensation is in the form of economic supplements—fringe benefits. The topics to be examined in this chapter include: (1) paid time off, including vacations, paid holidays, and authorized leaves of absences; (2) pensions; (3) health care plans; (4) supplemental unemployment benefits (SUB), (5) non-competitive seniority; and (6) the economic effect of fringe benefits.

It is not uncommon for labor agreements to specify a variety of economic supplements or as they have come to be commonly called fringe benefits. Various types of insurance plans, pensions, and a wide range of paid days off are typical of most labor contracts today. In fact, one-third of the total compensation of union employees in this country is currently in the form of economic supplements. Many of these economic supplements were introduced by employers before unions organized their firms, some being in place in excess of forty years. More recent developments in this area, due primarily to union negotiations, include supplemental unemployment benefits, dental and optical insurance as well as college tuition assistance for the employee and his immediate family.

The term, fringe benefit, is commonly used to describe economic supplements, however, many employers object to this term. To these employers, fringe benefit carries the connotation of compensation beyond that due the employee for services rendered, a retainer of sorts. This is simply not what most employers have in mind when such supplements are negotiated. These economic supplements are negotiated as compensation for services rendered which take the form of something other than an hourly wage or piece rate. Unions, on the other hand, support the view that many of these economic supplements are negotiated to protect employee rights. Supplemental unemployment benefits are an obvious example of what unions would argue are protective contract provisions. Paid holidays, it is argued, also fit into this category of protection from the loss of income because of the unavailability of work due to a facility being closed for a holiday. This controversy will be further examined in the appropriate sections which follow.

These benefits are frequently negotiated along with the hourly wage as a total economic package and then the package is distributed over the wage and various other forms of compensation. For example, the total economic settlement may be for fifty cents per hour during the first year. The fifty cents per hour may be distributed as 5¢ per hour for medical insurance, 1¢ per hour for life insurance, 6¢ per hour for pensions, and 38¢ per hour for the wage rate. This illustrates an important point concerning fringe benefits and why some employers object to the use of the word *fringe* to describe these methods of compensation—these benefits represent a direct cost of labor to the employer exactly the same as if they were hourly wages. Employers have frequently alleged, in some cases justifiably, that their employees take these benefits for granted and consider only their hourly wage as compensation. The employee may never fully appreciate the cost to the employer nor the value they receive as a result of these benefits. In cases where fringe benefits are not tied to hours worked employers find themselves paying for work they do not receive when an employee absents himself from work. This some employers claim hides the seriousness of absenteeism from employees and results in this industrial offense being taken too lightly by unions and their membership.

Many bargaining relations have differing attitudes, needs, and goals which are frequently reflected in the provisions of their contract. Fringe benefits are no exception to this rule; however, only the major and widely adopted economic supplements will be discussed here for the sake of brevity.

Paid Time Off

Paid time off is included in virtually every collective bargaining agreement currently in force in this country. The form in which paid time off is granted varies considerably across bargaining relationships. There are 72 major collective bargaining agreements which allow employees to take extended paid vacations (sabbatical leaves) by accumulating authorized days off and vacations over some specified period of time, typically five or six years. One United Mine Workers local in the West Virginia-Kentucky area negotiated one paid day off for each of its members during the deer hunting season. The UAW in 1976 negotiated a clause in the General Motors agreement which allowed for seven randomly scheduled days off during the final year of the contract (commonly called "hit" days). Under the 1979 UAW-GM agreement the total number of "hit" days are increased to a maximum of ten during the final year of the contract's effective period.

The basic goal of labor organizations in negotiating paid time off is threefold. First unions wish to increase job security (and possibly membership) by demanding employees be granted time off hence requiring more replacement labor resulting, unions hope, in constant or possibly increasing employment levels. Whether such tactics accomplish this goal is open to considerable debate and the answer critically depends on the magnitude of increased labor costs due to paid days off. The second union goal is to give employees time away from their jobs so that they may enjoy the "fruits" of their labor. Employers have not resisted these demands as vigorously as one might have supposed. Employers are generally concerned with labor productivity; it is frequently reasoned that authorized and scheduled days off reduce casual absenteeism, allowing employers to more effectively plan labor force activities. Employers as well have occasionally reasoned that employee morale is improved if the employee is allowed sufficient time to pursue outside interests. This reasoning is also open to considerable debate. These first two union incentives are associated with the fringe benefit definition of paid time off. The third union incentive to negotiate paid time off is to protect employees' earnings potentials. It is reasoned that employees should not be penalized because the employer does not continue operations during holidays nor should an employee's earnings for any pay period containing a holiday be abnormally low. By demanding that employees be paid for holidays on which no work was available unions claim they are protecting the employee from the employer's decision not to offer work on those days hence guaranteeing the employee's earning potential. This line of union argument places paid holidays in the protection of employees' rights category rather than in the fringe benefit category.

The most widely adopted forms of authorized paid absence are: (1) paid vacations; (2) paid holidays; and (3) authorized leaves of absence. Each of these will be briefly discussed in the following paragraphs.

Paid Vacations

Of the 1,536 major collective bargaining agreements surveyed by the Bureau of Labor Statistics (BLS) in January 1978, paid vacations were specified in 1,394 or 91 percent of these contracts.[1] This wide adoption of paid vacation clauses is a post-World War II phenomenon. Prior to the Second World War employees were granted time off only if they were willing to sacrifice their earnings for the applicable period. Therefore, the inclusion of paid vacations in labor contracts has been a rather dramatic development in the past four decades.

Labor agreements specify a wide range of eligibility requirements and periods of duration for vacations. The maximum time off specified by a vacation clause in the 1978 BLS survey was eight weeks (in three different agreements). The majority of collective bargaining agreements call for graduated vacation plans; only six of 1,536 specified uniform vacation benefits.[2] Uniform vacation benefits were typically two weeks vacation for employees with greater than one year of service regardless of total seniority.

Graduated vacation plans reward employees for length of service. The

---

[1] U.S. Department of Labor, Bureau of Labor Statistics, *Characteristics of Major Collective Bargaining Agreements*, January 1, 1978, Bulletin 2065, Washington, D.C.: GPO, p. 75.
[2] Ibid.

typical graduated vacation plan grants the employee: one week of vacation after one year of service, two weeks after the third year, three weeks after the tenth year, four weeks after twenty years, and a maximum of five weeks after the twenty-fifth year.

The typical method of payment of vacation benefits calls for the employee to receive his normal pay for the period he was on vacation; however, some contracts call for an employee to receive vacation pay on a particular date, to be used whenever (or if) the employee takes his vacation. A problem arises in the first instance, in cases where the employee chooses not to take a vacation, or where the employer requires the employee to work during his vacation—how then is he to receive his vacation entitlement? Normally the contract will specify that at the end of the fiscal or calendar year employees will receive payment for any unused vacation days. This, however, is not universal; some contracts require the employee to utilize his vacation or lose the benefit for that year. In the case of involuntary loss of a scheduled vacation it may be rescheduled *or* the employee may receive an overtime premium for his inconvenience and his vacation rescheduled. Some contracts provide for the loss of the time off and payment of the equivalent of vacation pay.

As should be apparent from the preceeding discussion vacation benefits vary considerably from contract to contract. This is to be expected since the labor requirements of firms differ substantially. Many manufacturing facilities (especially those engaged in assembly work or which utilize assembly line techniques) schedule close down periods for vacations so as to minimize variations in the number of employees available for work. Firms which provide a service or which engage in retailing have a need to remain in continuous operation therefore requiring as even a distribution of vacation periods during the calendar year as possible. Unions, as may be expected, argue that the scheduling of an employee's vacation should be the prerogative of the employee rather than management. The obviously conflicting points of view have produced many compromise solutions to vacation scheduling. The most typical compromise is to allow seniority to govern. The most senior employee is allowed to schedule his vacation, constrained generally by the company's forecasted need for labor, with junior employees allowed to select the remaining available vacation periods.

Paid Holidays

In the previously cited BLS survey, 1,291 of the 1,536 contracts or about 84.1 percent specified paid holidays and another 232 or 15.1 percent made provision for unpaid time off for certain holidays. The same dramatic increase, as was witnessed for vacations, is in evidence for the inclusion of paid holidays since World War II. These contracts normally allot time off for New Year's Day, Memorial Day, Independence Day, Labor Day, Thanksgiving, and Christmas. The mode in the BLS survey for paid holidays was ten, indicating more holidays or multiple days for holidays such as Christmas are commonplace. The mode for unpaid holidays was six indicating that the six major holidays listed above are generally alloted employees.

Most labor contracts require the payment of an "overtime" premium if the

BOX 9–1. Holiday Provisions–Major Labor Agreements in 1976 and 1978

Number of Holidays	1976 Agreements	1978 Agreements
All agreements	1570	1536
Total with paid holiday	1316	1291
Fewer than 6 days	29	25
6 days	26	20
7 days	69	45
8 days	114	91
9 days	252	195
10 days	422	359
11 days	190	275
12 days	68	97
13 days	26	42
14 days	33	34
15 days	17	18
16 days	3	6
17 days	1	0
18 days	0	2
19 days	1	1
20 days	0	4
No reference to paid holidays	254	245

Source: BLS bulletins 2013 and 2065.

employee works during a holiday. For paid holidays the BLS reports a model overtime premium of double time and one-half; for contracts specifying unpaid holidays the mode was double time. Some labor agreements also give the employer the right to require an employee to work on a holiday. The lowest seniority individuals are commonly specified as the first employees who may be required to work holidays.

Paid holidays, as with vacation, reflect the economic needs of the employer as well as the desires of the work force to be home during holidays. Hospital, drug store, police, fire, and public utility employees obviously are required to work during many holidays because of the necessity to provide continuous services. In these industries unions have typically argued that fair and equitable distribution of holiday time off is necessary to ensure high morale and efficiency. Seniority and rotating duty rosters have been the common response to holiday allocation problems in these industries.

Authorized Leaves of Absence

A wide variety of authorized leaves of absence, both paid and unpaid, are frequently specified in labor agreements. Military, educational, and personal absences are generally allowed but without pay. Certain benefits such as medical and life insurance are frequently continued at the employer's expense as well as the employee's seniority accumulating for some limited period. Leaves for which the employee is entitled to full benefits and generally some proportion of their pay include sick leaves and maternity leaves. These contractual provisions are typically negotiated by unions for job security. For example, if a woman becomes pregnant it is unreasonable that she must forego her employment to give birth. Further, if an employee goes to school to obtain skills which will benefit his employer the loss of his employment will be a disincentive to education. Employers are aware of the benefits which they obtain from educational leaves and have not resisted such provisions.

Pensions

The United States Supreme Court ruled that pensions were a mandatory subject for collective bargaining in 1949.[3] Since that time there has been a significant increase in the number of agreements which include pension plans. In 1949 fewer than 40 percent of the labor agreements then in force provided for worker pensions. By 1976 this figure had more than doubled to over 80 percent.[4]

Pensions vary both in their form and their administration among bargaining relations. To qualify for a pension, years of service as well as a minimum age are generally specified. The administration of the pension fund may be through the union, the company, a joint labor-management committee, or through a separate private company. For example, General Motors employees may retire after thirty years of service regardless of age and receive a total pension of $650 per month. The pension fund is administered by a joint UAW-GM committee with the members selecting an impartial chairman who does not count in establishing a quorum and may vote only in ties "involving the processing of individual cases, not on the development of procedures." The funding of the pension is based on years of employee service. The company pays a negotiated sum into the pension trust fund on the annual anniversary of the agreement for each man-year of service. The Teamsters, on the other hand, manage their own fund and their contracts specify a lump sum be paid weekly to the fund for each employee.

The passage in 1974 of the Employee Retirement Income Security Act (ERISA) was a response to infrequent but extensively reported (in the media) mishandling of pension funds by unions and management as well as the widely publicized losses of employees' pension due to employer's moving or closing down operations. ERISA requires that an employee, after ten years of service, in most cases, shall have a vested interest in his or her pension. This provision was aimed, at least in part, at preventing age discrimination and to ensure that an employee's benefits would not be precluded if he had rendered ten years service but did not stay with the firm for a greater period of time or the firm closed or moved prior to the employee acquiring sufficient seniority to retire.

[3]*Inland Steel Co. v. United Steelworkers of America*, 336 U.S. 969 (1949).

[4]This estimate is derived from the U.S. Department of Labor, Bureau of Labor Statistics *Handbook of Labor Statistics, 1978*, Bulletin 2000, Washington, D.C.: GPO, Table 109.

ERISA also requires the pension fund to be reasonably and responsibly administered. Firms and their unions, when administering a pension program, may not make risky loans, low interest nor interest-free loans, nor may they invest in their own company's stock. This is to ensure that there will be no misuse of pension funds nor tying of a pension to the continued viability of the firm.

Pensions have become major issues for collective bargaining primarily for two reasons; first, people are living longer today than they did thirty to forty years ago and secondly, unions have seen pensions as well as early retirement as job security provisions. In the first four decades of this century it was not uncommon for a person to go to work in his pre-teenage years and work until the day he died. This way of life left the worker with nothing much to look forward to. If he should become disabled or too old to perform useful work then he had to be supported by his children rather than having the independence afforded by the various social programs and pension plans of today. To provide this security and independence as well as to improve worker morale many firms (especially railroads and government) provided pension plans. The success of these early plans provided the basis for later union demands for pensions to be included in their contracts. With the development of medical technology from the 1940s to present the life expectancy of the average American worker has increased from just over fifty years to nearly seventy years which has added to the importance of these union demands.

Unions have responded to automation and changing technology with demands for job security provisions. The *attrition principle* is illustrative of this type of union job security demand. The attrition principle, simply stated, is that the employer may not make any long term reduction in force except for natural loss of workers (e.g., voluntary quits, death, and retirement). By providing pension and early retirement incentives low seniority employees are provided with some degree of job security because any loss of jobs will be through not replacing retired employees rather than layoffs. Therefore, from this perspective pensions and early retirement provisions may be viewed as a sort of job security provision.

Health Care Plans

Employers, in many cases, have not shown extreme resistance to the inclusion of health care plans in the contract. Some employers have reasoned that such plans provide them with an indirect benefit—a healthier more reliable work force. It has been argued that if this portion of compensation were paid in the form of an hourly wage employees might choose to spend the money on other goods and services. By directly providing health care insurance to employees, many employers reason that their workers are more apt to take care of physical ailments, avail themselves of preventive medical procedures, and therefore be healthier, more reliable and more productive employees. This is a reasonable argument which unions have found little fault with. Employees benefit in two distinct ways from receiving compensation in this manner: (1) "payments in kind" or receiving goods and services for compensation are *not* taxed and (2) frequently employees could not provide this type of insurance for themselves as cheaply as a large company purchasing the plan on a group basis. This later point is of particular interest. Large corporations such as ITT or Exxon have a large number of employees. These large employment levels give the employer leverage in negotiating group rates with insurance companies. The insurance company saves marketing and administrative costs by dealing with one large customer rather than thousands of individuals. These cost savings can and are frequently passed on, at least in part, to the large group customers.

These health care plans often include hospitalization, major medical coverage, and more recently, dental, optical, and cancer protection. Many contracts provide these benefits to retirees as well as presently employed workers. Two distinct methods of funding are in evidence for health care programs: contributory and noncontributory. Contributory plans require the employee to pay for some portion of the cost of his and his family's coverage, typically half. It is frequently argued that the employee is less likely to abuse this benefit if he has to pay a portion of any increase in premiums. This argument is, of course, open to some criticism. One individual may use the benefit wisely while others abuse it; therefore, the one person acting alone makes no difference in the group outcome. This has been labeled the "free-rider" effect because the inverse is also true; if everyone else utilizes the benefit wisely one individual can often abuse the benefit and not cause a higher rate. The cost of conservation then falls upon most members of the group allowing an individual a free ride.

Approximately 95 percent of the collective bargaining agreements in force in 1978 contained hospitalization, surgical, and medical benefits.[5] Optical, dental, and cancer benefits are relatively new to collective bargaining agreements and no statistics were available concerning the percentage of contracts containing these benefits—it is safe to assume less than 10 percent of all collective bargaining agreements have such provisions.

Supplemental Unemployment Benefits

In the 1978 BLS survey only 14.3 percent of the major agreements contained Supplemental Unemployment Benefit (SUB) clauses.[6] Of the 220 agreements which contained SUB programs 192 or 87.3 percent were in manufacturing industries. This is to be expected, since this class of industries is most susceptible to cyclical economic variations and short-term unemployment.

Supplemental unemployment benefits are designed to maintain worker incomes during periods of *temporary* unemployment. For example, layoffs for inventory or technological changes as well as short term cyclical variations are the types of unemployment for which SUB is designed. The operation of SUB programs varies widely across contracts. The following is typical of SUB plans

[5]*Handbook of Labor Statistics, 1978*, Table 109.

[6]*Characteristics of Major Collective Bargaining Agreements*, January 1, 1978, p. 101.

BOX 9-2.   Health, Insurance, and Retirement Plans for Hotel and Motel Employees in Selected Geographic Regions–1978. (percentage of nonoffice and nonsupervisory workers)

Type of Plan	Boston	New York	Pitts- burgh	Miami	Chi- cago	Las Vegas	Los Angeles
Life insurance	83	99	82	40	97	98	86
noncontributory	68	97	78	20	77	98	77
Accidental death and dismember- ment insurance	83	99	63	37	40	98	17
noncontributory	61	97	44	17	20	98	17
Sickness and accident insur- ance or sick leave or both	84	96	60	11	94	96	12
noncontributory	57	83	25	1	70	95	—
Long-term disa- bility insurance	11	—	7	2	98	—	16
noncontributory	7	—	3	2	77	—	16
Hospitalization insurance	93	99	82	92	98	98	90
noncontributory	71	97	53	76	77	98	77
Surgical insurance	93	99	87	88	98	98	90
noncontributory	71	97	58	72	77	98	77
Medical insurance	93	83	87	88	98	98	90
noncontributory	71	81	58	72	77	98	77
Major medical insurance	45	58	79	37	34	3	90
noncontributory	26	56	50	22	13	3	77
Retirement plans	67	95	41	64	65	97	76
noncontributory	63	95	37	63	64	97	69
No Plans	4	1	12	8	15	2	10

Source: BLS Bulletin 2055 Industry Wage Survey: Hotels and Motels (May 1978)

negotiated in the automobile and steel industries. The employer is obligated to contribute to the SUB trust fund some negotiated amount, generally three or four cents per hour, until the trust fund reaches some negotiated level. It is the intent that this level be sufficient to cover some short period of unemployment for the total work force, generally two or three weeks. When the fund reaches this level the employer's obligation to contribute to the fund ceases until the fund falls below this maximum funding level and then contributions resume. To become eligible to receive SUB benefits the employee must have acquired some minimum amount of seniority, one year is generally required. The employee's maximum SUB entitlement is usually one week for each two years of seniority, limited to no more than fifty-two weeks of total SUB benefits. However, a further universal requirement is that the employee must be eligible for state unemployment benefits which in turn requires that the employee loses his job through no fault of his own. The loss of employment resulting from discipline or voluntary quitting does not qualify an employee for SUB benefits. The benefits provided for in SUB clauses vary significantly from one contract to the next. Some provide for a specified weekly sum such as $50 to $60 while others require the employee's state unemployment benefits plus his SUB equal some percentage of his take-home pay—80 to 95 percent is common.

In moderately prolonged recessions it is not uncommon for SUB funds to become exhausted rather quickly. Many SUB clauses contain provisions to protect higher seniority employees from the possibility of being laid off only to find that the SUB fund has been exhausted by younger employees. Some contracts allow for seniority inversion for purposes of layoff. These clauses allow the most senior employee to apply to be the first worker laid-off. For short layoffs this affords senior employees the opportunity to take time off while drawing the majority of his pay. Employers, however, have resisted such provisions due to the need to have the most experienced employees on the job. Some contracts, especially after the 1974 recession, have included provisions for two SUB funds, one for employees with five years or less seniority and one for senior employees, thus protecting older workers from the loss of income. Another commonly employed method is to reduce the junior workers' eligibility as the SUB fund becomes exhausted. If the level of the trust fund declines to 65 percent of its maximum level then laid-off employees with five years or less seniority will lose an additional one week of eligibility for each week drawn from SUB, at 50 percent an additional two weeks may be lost, and at 35 percent four additional weeks may be deducted from the employee's eligibility. If the SUB fund reaches some critical level, generally three to five percent, all benefits stop.

High seniority employees have frequently objected to unions expending efforts to obtain SUB programs. Senior employees in normal circumstances almost never have the opportunity to draw SUB, therefore, these employees would rather see the employer expenditures for SUB in other benefits or the hourly wage rate. The seniority inversion clause and the dual SUB funds are union responses to the concern of its high seniority membership.

Non-Competitive v. Competitive Seniority

A short discussion of the term seniority is in order to clarify the uses of the word. There are two distinct types of seniority: noncompetitive and competitive. Noncompetitive seniority is the length of service of an employee, used for the purpose of determining the employee's eligibility for various benefits and rights under the contract. For example, if an employee is eligible for one week of vacation after his first year of employment, this is based on noncompetitive seniority. Competitive seniority, on the other hand, involves an employee's rights relative to other employees' rights under the contract. As an example, for purposes of the lay-off provisions of a contract a senior employee is generally afforded greater job security relative to employees with less seniority. Competitive seniority, in this case, means an employee's right to a job relative to other more senior employees, hence competitive seniority. The same principle applies to promotions, transfers, shift preferences, and recalls when they are based upon seniority.

It is interesting to note that competitive seniority is, in a sense, a fringe benefit. Seniority is the basis for differentiating among employees, in varying degrees, in most labor contracts. Therefore, as an employee acquires seniority he is also acquiring greater rights under the contract relative to junior employees. Higher paying jobs, job security, shift preference, and better working conditions are frequently associated with seniority and represent significant benefits to employees.

The Economic Impact of Fringe Benefits: A Case Study of GM's Absenteeism Problems

Frequently fringe benefits are subject to controversy. The analysis[7] which follows is based on the experience of one firm and is intended to illustrate the types of problems which may result from contract administration and fringe benefit programs. The student is cautioned against generalizing the conclusions of this case to all firms, since each firm and union have unique bargaining relations which may or may not produce the same results.

The following jingle, written by the wife of Ira Steward, the leader of the Eight Hour Day Movement summarizes two of the historical goals of organized labor—shorter hours and higher hourly rates of pay:

> Whether you work by the piece
> or work by the day
> Decreasing the hours
> Increases the pay[8]

These goals have been so pervasive that they permeate the current effective hourly wage structures of many firms. Illustrative of this fact is the following table which indicates effective hourly wage rates paid to General Motors'

---

[7] These ideas first appeared in: Clarence R. Deitsch and David A. Dilts, "To Cut Casual Absenteeism: Tie Benefits to Hours Worked," *Compensation Review*, (First Quarter 1981), 13: 41–46; The principles and concepts developed therein were then used to analyze the casual absenteeism problem of General Motors. The results and recommendations of the G.M. study were subsequently published in: Clarence R. Deitsch and David A. Dilts, "Getting Absent Workers Back on the Job: The Case of General Motors," *Business Horizons*, (September/October 1981), 24: pp. 52–58; General Motors and the United Auto Workers apparently adopted and incorporated a number of these recommendations as part of *The Agreement Between General Motors Corporation and The UAW*, executed in March, 1982.

[8] Marcia L. Greenbaum, "The Shorter Workweek," in Bakke, Kerr, and Anrod, eds. *Unions, Management and the Public*, Harcourt Brace Jovanovich, Inc., New York, 1967, pp. 434–441.

employees (in 1979) for different amounts of time spent on the job. Although the nominal hourly wage rate remains constant at $10 per hour throughout the week until overtime is encountered, the effective hourly wage rate declines over the work week until additional hours worked at extremely high overtime premiums again pull the effective hourly wage rate up. This behavior results from the fixed component of compensation—fringe benefits in the amount of $230 per week which are paid regardless of the number of hours worked. Herein lies the rational explanation for excessive absenteeism.

Figure 9–1 graphically illustrates the response of a typical absentee to the wage structure shown in Table 9–1. Curves I_1 and I_2 are two of the employee's indifference curves. All combinations of income and leisure, represented by points along I_1, yield the same level of satisfaction. Again, the employee is indifferent as to which of these points is chosen. However, all points along I_2 are preferred to all points along I_1 because combinations along I_2 include a greater quantity of the goods (i.e., income and leisure) measured along the axes of the graph.

Line AF depicts the total weekly earnings (including the monetary equivalent of fringe benefits) of the employee as provided by the contract

TABLE 9–1.   General Motors Average Effective Hourly Wage Rates Inclusive of Fringe Benefits and Exclusive of Contractually Authorized Paid Absences.[9]

Hours Worked	Total[a] Weekly Earnings	Earnings Per Eight Hours Worked	Average Effective Hourly Wage Rate (2/1)	Marginal Effective Hourly Wage Rate ($\triangle 2/\triangle 1$)
0	$230	—	∞	$10
8	310	$ 80	$38.75	10
16	390	80	24.38	10
24	470	80	19.58	10
32	550	80	17.19	10
40	630	80	15.75[b]	10
48	750[c]	120	15.63	10
56	910[d]	160	16.25	10

[a]These figures inclue the monetary equivalent of fringe benefits—$230 per week.
[b]Although fringe benefits cost General Motors $200 per week per worker, or $5 per hour, pro-rated over a scheduled 40 hour week, the taxable monetary equivalents for the average employee are, respectively, $230 per week and $5.75 per hour. Hence, for 40 hours worked, the average effective wage rate is $15.75 (i.e., $10 per hour plus $5.75 per hour).
[c]This figure is calculated based on 40 hours at the straight time nominal wage of $10 per hour, 8 hours at time and a half ($15 per hour), and fringe benefits of $230.
[d]This figure is calculated based on 40 hours at $10 per hour, 8 hours at time and a half ($15 per hour), 8 hours at double time ($20 per hour), plus fringe benefits of $230.

[9]Compensation figures refer to the 1976–79 contract and were provided by Richard O'Brian, Director of Compensation for General Motors Corporation; nothing herein should be interpreted as the official positions of any representatives of General Motors Corporation or of the UAW but are solely the opinions of the authors.

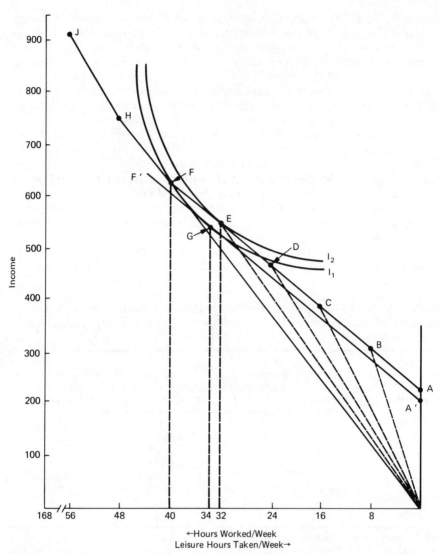

FIGURE 9.1. Leisure/Work Choice of the Typical Absentee.

between General Motors and the UAW for different hours worked per week. The slope of line AF is the marginal effective hourly wage rate (i.e., $10 per hour) under the contract. This wage rate can also be thought of as the price of absenteeism (i.e., leisure) per hour. Distance OA measures the amount of fringe benefits (i.e., $230) authorized by the contract regardless of the number of hours worked or taken as leisure. As Figure 9–1 illustrates, the employee selects point E, working 32 hours, earning $550 in income, and taking 8 hours of leisure. The employee voluntarily chooses to be absent from work 8 hours each week.

Line *OF* illustrates total weekly earnings of the same employee for different hours worked under a wage structure where the value of fringe benefits is tied directly to the number of hours worked; the employee only qualifies for the full value of fringe benefits with the completion of 40 hours of work. The slope of line *OF* is the new marginal effective hourly wage rate of $15.75 per hour ($10 per hours wage plus $5.75 per hour in fringe benefits). This modified wage structure induces the employee to select point *F*, working 40 hours, earning $630 in income, and taking only those hours of leisure which are contractually authorized. Casual absenteeism, in this case, is not a problem.

As is immediately apparent from Figure 9–1, the contractually specified wage structure promotes casual absences. Specifically, payment of fringe benefits in an amount unrelated to the number of hours worked creates the absenteeism problem in three ways.[10] First, fringe benefits reduce the marginal effective hourly wage rate from $15.75 per hour to $10 per hour, as indicated by the slopes of lines *OF* and *AF* respectively. This reduces the price of leisure (i.e., absenteeism) and induces the employee to substitute leisure for income— to "buy" more leisure. The impact of this substitution effect can be illustrated graphically by drawing a line, *A'F'*, parallel to line *AF* and tangent to indifference curve I_1 at point *G*. Confronted with the now lower price of leisure, $10 per hour, represented by the slope of line *A'F'*, and at the same time, limited to the same level of satisfaction generated by the original choice of point *F*, the employee chooses point *G*. The distance between points *F* and *G*, measured horizontally along the Hours Worked—Week Axis, identifies the impact of the lower price of leisure upon the number of hours the employee chooses to work each week (i.e., substitution effect). The lower marginal effective wage rate of $10 per hour induces the employee to choose 6 hours of leisure—to be absent from the job 6 hours each week.

Second, fringe benefits constitute a "windfall" transfer of income to the employee because this portion of compensation is not related to hours worked. As is the case for any other increase in income, employee demand for "normal" goods will increase and the demand for "inferior" goods will decline. Since leisure falls within the former category and work within the latter category, the windfall income transfer created by fringe benefits induces the employee to buy more leisure and work fewer hours. The income transfer is represented graphically by the parallel upward shift of line *A'F'* to line *AF*. As a result of this shift, the employee achieves a greater level of satisfaction by moving from point *G* to point *E*, with hours of work declining from 34 to 32. Hence, the windfall income effect of fringe benefits compounds the absenteeism problem by reinforcing the substitution effect—by inducing the employee to select 2 hours of leisure in addition to the 6 hours noted above.

Finally, to the extent that the average effective hourly wage rate is the key variable in understanding the employee leisure-work decision-making process, a declining average effective hourly wage rate, caused by fringe benefits unrelated to hours worked, will encourage employee absenteeism by reducing

---

[10] Although Figure 9-1 portrays the case of a typical absentee, the factors responsible for the absentee's behavior are operational in the case of workers with good work habits, but to a lesser extent.

the price of leisure (i.e., absenteeism) as the number of hours spent on the job increases.[11] The reduced price of leisure induces the employee to "buy" more of this commodity—to be absent from work.

Given an effective wage structure similar to the one negotiated by General Motors Corporation and the United Automobile Workers, and assuming that an employee knows his/her own tastes and preferences, the employee will choose the combination of work and absenteeism—32 hours of work and 8 hours of absenteeism in the case of the employee of the above graph—that generates the highest level of satisfaction. The employee then selects the specific eight-hour shift(s) to be absent—the one(s) consistent with the employee's highest level of satisfaction.

The employee's ability to select additional leisure beyond the contractually authorized amount has not been limited through contract administration. Contract provisions governing the administration of discipline, particularly those addressing the problem of absenteeism, have not been enforced. Grievance adjudication between General Motors and the UAW has long been characterized by lax enforcement of shop rules governing absenteeism. In recent years, General Motors has shown a propensity to concede to the union's demands concerning discipline cases for a variety of reasons: to establish and promote the image of a reasonable employer, to minimize production delays, to improve the atmosphere of the bargaining relationship, and to secure concessions from the union concerning grievances that have an immediately apparent direct monetary cost. Whatever the rationale, the end result is the same: first-line supervisors, consistently undermined by mid- and upper-level management at the later stages of the grievance procedure, become reluctant to "write-up" disciplinary cases involving absenteeism and eventually ignore the problem altogether. By the same token, employees soon come to realize that there are no sanctions for casual absences. In short, contract administration facilitates the rational employee response to contractually structured incentives for casual absences by removing the attendent personal costs. This combination of factors permits the employee to achieve a higher level of satisfaction than would otherwise be possible under the intended terms and conditions of the contract—an increase in satisfaction represented by the difference between curves I_1 and I_2 in the above graph.

Costs of Absenteeism[12]

General Motors Corporation normally employs approximately 500,000 members of the United Automobile Workers Union. During fiscal year 1979, General Motors suffered a five (5) percent casual absenteeism rate which

---

[11] In terms of Figure 9-1, the average effective hourly wage rate for a specific number of hours worked is represented by the slope of a straight line drawn from point 0 to the point on the earnings line which corresponds to the specified number of hours worked. As is apparent, the slopes of these lines (i.e., *OA, OB, OC, OD, OE,* & *OF*) decline as the number of hours worked increases.

[12] Refer to footnote 9 for source of data for this section; total cost figures were derived from the data provided by GM.

translates into 25,000 employee absences each scheduled workday. Given 250 scheduled workdays annually, absenteeism claims 6,250,000 man-days or 50 million man-hours each year. Each hour of labor during which the worker is absent costs General Motor $20 rather than the normal $15–$5 in contractually guaranteed fringe benefits paid to the absent worker and $15 in compensation paid to the absent worker's replacement. The total annual explicit cost of casual absenteeism, therefore, amounts to one-quarter of a billion dollars or twenty-five percent of the total labor costs for the subject hours of work, a rather incredible sum. However, this one-quarter of a billion dollars in absentee costs does not include the implicit costs such as: grievance administration, loss of production, and poor morale, which could be as much as four times that figure.

Summary and Conclusions

Since the end of the Second World War there has been a rather dramatic increase in the inclusion of economic supplements in labor agreements. The majority of contracts grant employees such benefits as: paid vacations, paid holidays, numerous paid or unpaid leaves of absence, and health care plans. In response to the cyclical nature of the manufacturing sector of this nation's economy about 14.3 percent of all major agreements grant employees supplemental unemployment benefit rights. Non-competitive seniority is frequently used as a standard for eligibility in granting fringe benefits. Competitive seniority differs from noncompetitive seniority in that the former is concerned with the relative rights of employees and not the absolute right of employees under the contract.

As was demonstrated in the case of GM and the UAW, high wages in conjunction with substantial fringe benefit programs and lax enforcement of shop rules prohibiting absenteeism provides incentives for economically rational employees to be absent. The wage and benefit costs to GM, without including indirect costs, amounted to one quarter of a billion dollars in 1979, indicating that fringe benefits can, in certain circumstances, be very costly.

DISCUSSION QUESTIONS

1. Explain why there has been such a dramatic increase in the adoption of fringe benefits in labor agreements.

2. What might GM do to eliminate the excessive costs of casual absenteeism it presently suffers?

3. Why have so few SUB programs been adopted?

4. Why might unions wish to have pay raises in the form of fringe benefits rather than increases in the hourly wage? Why might management resist these demands but be willing to pay the equivalent in wages?

SELECTED REFERENCES

Becker, Gary S., "A Theory of the Allocation of Time," *Economic Journal*, (September 1965) **75:** 493–517.

Dankert, Clyde E., "Shorter Hours in Theory and Practice," *Industrial and Labor Relations Review*, (April 1962), **16:** 307–22.

Deitsch, Clarence R. and David A. Dilts, "To Cut Casual Absenteeism: Tie Benefits to Hours Worked," *Compensation Review*, (First Quarter 1981), **13:** 41–46.

Deitsch, Clarence R. and David A. Dilts, "Getting Absent Workers Back on the Job: The Case of General Motors," *Business Horizons*, (September/October 1981), **24:** 52–58.

Epperson, Lawrence L., "The Dynamics of Factor Comparison/Point Evaluation," *Public Personnel Administration*, (January/February 1975) **4:** 38–48.

Foegen, J.H., "Employee Benefits: Imagination Unlimited," *Labor Law Journal*, (January 1978) **29:** 37–39.

Freeman, Lee A., "Fringe Issues and Their Cost," *Mass Transportation*, (November 1947), pp. 570–74.

Greenough, W.C. and F.P. King, *Pension Plans and Public Policy*, New York: Columbia University Press, 1976.

Henderson, R.I., *Compensation Management: Rewarding Performance*, Second Edition, Reston, Virginia: Reston Publishing Company, Inc. 1979.

Lewis, H.G., "Hours of Work and Hours of Leisure," *Proceedings of the Industrial Relations Research Association*, (December 1956) pp. 196–206.

Mahoney, Thomas A., "Justice and Equity: A Recurring Theme in Compensation," *Personnel*, (September/October 1975) **52:** 60–66.

McKersie, R.B. and L.E. Hunter, *Pay, Productivity, and Collective Bargaining*, London: Macmillan & Company Ltd., 1973.

Patten, Thomas H., *Pay: Employee Compensation and Incentive Plans*, New York: The Free Press, 1977.

Sibson, R.E., *Compensation*, New York: AMACOM, 1974.

Stamas, George D., "Long Hours and Premium Pay," *Monthly Labor Review*, April 1979, pp. 41–45.

Yount, H.H., "Total Compensation-Cost, Comparison, and Control," *Compensation Review*, (4) 1971, pp. 9–19.

Chapter 10

Non-Economic Issues and Collective Bargaining:
Employer and Employee Rights

The purpose of this chapter is to examine the various administrative and institutional issues which may arise during collective bargaining. These issues are typically the most important items in the day to day administration of the labor agreement. The topics to be discussed include management rights, competitive seniority, job security, shift preferences and transfers, promotions, union security issues, and checkoff.

Introduction

Few scholars in their respective fields have spurred major revolutions in academic thought. In 1958 John Dunlop published his book *Industrial Relations Systems* which revolutionized thought in labor relations. Dunlop gave labor relations a central point of analysis which, to that date, the discipline lacked. Dunlop suggested that work rules should be the basis of analysis. Two distinct classes of work rules can be identified; these are: (1) rules governing compensation and (2) rules which specify the respective rights and responsibilities of employees, employers, and unions. The first set of rules are discussed at length elsewhere in this text; the second set are the topics of the present chapter.

A labor contract deals not only with compensatory and hours issues but will also generally outline specific rights granted to the employees and their union. These administrative and institutional issues deal primarily with the interface between management and labor as well as the needs of the respective organizations. These non-economic issues are generally not associated with the glamour of contract negotiations and are therefore frequently ignored by the news media's coverage of contract settlements or work stoppages. It must be remembered, however, that these issues are central to the day to day conduct of contract administration. Union security, management rights and seniority are the types of issues which may result in long and bitter work stoppages.

Managerial Prerogatives

Collective bargaining is a peaceful method whereby employees and their unions may influence their terms and conditions of employment. Management often views the collective bargaining process as infringement on its authority to operate the firm. This management view is in essence correct but often the reasoned logic of this argument is lost in rhetoric. The primary objective of organized labor is the restriction of managerial power concerning the employer–employee relation. Controversy concerning this labor objective has, as one might expect, evolved into debate over the tradeoffs between economic efficiency and equity. Few unions find fault with the notion that a profit making firm must be operated efficiently but they typically will resist any action by management perceived to be harmful to the union as an institution or to its membership. Unions will often focus on the fairness of work rules and compensation while management's central concern is generally on the efficient operation of the firm. Where controversy develops in the proprietary sectors of the American economy it generally concerns equity-efficiency tradeoffs. It must be remembered, however, that equity and efficiency are not necessarily contradictory goals. Often the union and management find large areas over which they are both ideologically and pragmatically in complete agreement. In other words, there is no requirement that collective bargaining must be an adversary process.

Managerial prerogatives take on added meaning in the public and non-profit arenas. In the nonprofit sectors of the economy and especially in government the employer is more apt to view his role not only as a force for economic efficiency but also as protector of the public interest (however perceived by management). Managers may often view their source of authority as being derived from the sovereignty of the state which should not be infringed upon for the good of the citizens. The public manager's counterpart in the private sector will view his/her rights as emanating from the property rights of the owners of the firm. The significant difference is that often the prerogatives of public sector managers are delegated to them by law and may not be restricted successfully by collective bargaining. If collective bargaining is utilized for such purposes public sector managers appeal to public opinion with arguments that the public interest will be harmed if managerial prerogatives are limited. Often these arguments are meritless though in many cases the public interest could be at risk. Regardless, an added dimension of management rights is in evidence in the nonprofit/public sector of the economy.

Two principle views of management rights have thus far emerged; these are the *residual* and *trusteeship* theories. Harold Davey has observed that residualists seem to be "preoccupied with historical primacy."

> They (residualists) espouse what can be termed the Book of Genesis approach (that is, *in the beginning there was management*). In such a context, the union as a "late arrival" can claim only those controls over a previously unlimited management authority that it can negotiate into the contract.[1]

Residualists tend to view their prerogatives in nonunion firms to be virtually absolute (except as limited by law).[2] In other words, residualists will typically claim if management has not given away a particular prerogative in the collective bargaining process then the management right is solely reserved for management to exercise. Those managers who have adopted the residualist view are often ideologically opposed to unionization and collective bargaining because they believe them to be synonymous with the errosion of their freedom to operate the firm. In the extreme, residualists adhere to a strict policy of inflexibility concerning their managerial rights and antiunion activities. In other words, they will refuse to concede any right which they perceive to be within the realm of managerial authority. This extreme residualist view will often produce labor relations difficulties. The collective bargaining process depends on reasoned compromise and if either party refuses to be swayed by sound economic evidence and logic then difficulties are bound to arise. Ideology is a poor basis for negotiations and if allowed to control the bargaining relation will breed mistrust, suspicion and often open hostility. The vast majority of managers in today's economy recognize the problems associated with these types of ideology and successfully avoid allowing ideology a place in collective bargaining. Generally a more enlightened version of the residual theory of management rights is applied and aids in the reduction of the probability that ideological differences would prevent peaceful negotiations. Adherence to managerial prerogatives is, however, a legitimate concern of management. It is management's obligation to the owners of the firm to operate the firm in the best interests of the stockholders. If ineffective in this obligation management bears the responsibility. The result is that management must concern itself with its rights and the efficient operation of the firm. On the other hand, if management is presented with reasonable evidence and convincing arguments that certain prerogatives can be limited without harm to the firm, then ideology should not prevent fair and reasonable settlements.

The trusteeship theory of managerial prerogatives is in some ways the antithesis of the residual theory. Managers envisage themselves to be the employees of the owners of the firm, the same as members of the bargaining unit, but with different responsibilities. Management's authority is viewed more as a set of obligations rather than a set of sovereign rights. The proponent of the trusteeship theory will tend to view the role of management as that of an

---

[1] Harold W. Davey, *Contemporary Collective Bargaining*, third ed., Englewood Cliffs, N.J.: Prentice-Hall, Inc., 1972.

[2] Business ethics play a critical role here. It is not the authors' intent to minimize the importance of business ethics but for sake of brevity they are deemed to be beyond the scope of the present work.

activity coordinator whose functions include the assurance of an efficiently run firm but also with considerations for employee and customer satisfaction.

Ideology is frequently less important to managers who ascribe to this view of managerial prerogatives. These managers will not typically view unionization and collective bargaining as necessarily limiting their managerial prerogatives. Less rigidity in management rights are in evidence with this view and the result is less potential for unnecessary labor–management disputes.

Management Rights Clauses

The effect of most contract provisions is to limit managerial prerogatives. One management response to the contractual errosion of their prerogatives has been to include a management-rights clause in the contract. Over sixty percent of major labor agreements included such provisions in 1978.[3] These provisions

---

BOX 10–1. Management Rights Clause in an Agreement between a Publicly Owned Hospital and a Nurses Association

Article I, Section 1,

a. The County retains all rights respecting decisions and actions affecting the operation and management of its business where not specifically in conflict with this Agreement.

b. It is agreed that the management of the County and the direction of the working forces, including but not limited to, the right to hire, promote, transfer, assign, suspend, demote, to discharge or otherwise discipline employees, to increase or decrease the working force; to determine the methods, means, personnel and schedules by which the efficiency of government operations entrusted to the County is to be maintained; to establish, revise and implement safety and health standards; to contract or subcontract work; to discontinue all or any part of its operations; to transfer all or any part of its operations; to transfer work from the bargaining unit; to determine the need for additional educational courses, training programs, on-the-job training, and cross-training, and to assign employees to such duties for periods to be determined by the county: to establish new jobs, or to eliminate or modify existing job classifications; to adopt and enforce rules, regulations, policies and procedures governing the conduct of its working forces, provided, however, that such rules, regulations, policies and procedures shall be uniformly and equitably enforced; and to take whatever other action is deemed appropriate by the County, is vested exclusively in the County, except when specifically in conflict with this Agreement.

---

[3] U.S. Department of Labor, Bureau of Labor Statistics, *Characteristics of Major Collective Bargaining Agreements*, January 1, 1978, Bulletin 2065, Washington, D.C.: GPO, p. 15–16.

are designed to prevent unions from encroaching on managerial prerogatives which have not been negotiated away. Disputes arise, however, when the union believes that the exercise of some managerial prerogative compromises a right guaranteed in the labor agreement.

The management rights clause illustrated in Box 10–1 is not uncommon; however, the scope and length of such clauses vary considerably. A hospital located in Kansas City, Missouri has a management rights clause which consists of only two sentences while a manufacturing firm located in Detroit, Michigan bargained a management rights clause over twelve pages in length.

Seniority and Related Issues

Competitive seniority is one of the basic tenets of organized labor.[4] The greater the length of the employee's service the greater seniority the employee has acquired, in general. Competitive seniority involves the relative rights of employees under the collective bargaining contract and typically governs job security, promotion and transfer issues. Today virtually every labor agreement contains some provision granting employees rights on the basis of their competitive seniority.

Since the end of the Second World War the use of seniority has gained importance in collective bargaining. Two reasons have been consistently offered for the widespread use of competitive seniority. These reasons are that both management and labor have come to believe that the competitive seniority system is just and more objective (hence less arbitrary) than alternative systems. The justice in the system stems from the notion that an employee who has given long years of faithful service should be treated preferentially relative to employees with less years of service. Of course this argument is somewhat naïve but it does recognize the employee's investment of time with the firm. The second argument is as experience is obtained the employee becomes better qualified for an array of jobs hence more valuable to the firm. Length of service is, however, not necessarily related to the intensity or quality of service but it is difficult if not impossible to measure and account for these factors. Therefore to prevent measurement and interpretation problems from introducing arbitrary biases into the personnel system, seniority has been opted for in most labor agreements.

Seniority can only be gained or lost as specified in the labor agreement. Contracts vary as to how an employee gains or loses seniority. Seniority may be acquired for the entire period that a worker is employed by a firm or only for the period that a worker was a member of the bargaining unit. If an employee is transferred from one plant to another then seniority may continue or be lost during the period of employment at the first location. Seniority may be lost if the employee quits, is disciplined, becomes a member of management or changes skill classifications.

The seniority clause presented in Box 10–2 is a rather common seniority

[4]Noncompetitive seniority governs the eligibility of employees for economic supplements and is discussed in Chapter 9.

BOX 10–2. Article 25, Seniority, of the Agreement between St. Louis County Water Company and Utility Workers Union of America

Article 25

Seniority

Section 1. Seniority is a right accruing to employees through length of service which entitles them to preferences provided for in this Agreement.

Section 2. System Seniority is the total length of employment beginning with the date of last entering the employ of the Company prior to or during the term of this agreement.

Section 3. Job seniority is the total accumulated time between dates during which an employee earns pay in a particular job classification, provided the employee qualifies in such classification.

Section 4. A complete seniority list shall be prepared from the service records of the Company and submitted to the Union. Copies of this list shall be posted on the bulletin boards of the Company. Any exception taken to the seniority as shown on the list shall be reconciled by the Union and the Company within 30 days after the list is posted, after which the list shall be considered accurate as of the date of the posting. The seniority list shall be brought up to date every six months thereafter by such revision as may be necessary to meet the requirements of this section.

Section 5. Regardless of length of service, a complete loss of seniority shall be incurred by an employee who:

a. Voluntarily terminates employment. Absence from work without valid reason shall be considered to be voluntary termination of employment.
b. Is discharged for cause.
c. Fails to report for service within five days after notice has been sent by registered mail to that employee's last known address, when being recalled after a layoff.
d. Is absent for one year on leave of absence without pay.
e. Has been laid off for one year.

Section 6. Employees with the same hiring date shall have system seniority preference in accordance with the reverse alphabetical order of their surnames. Employees with the same job seniority in a classification shall have job seniority preferences in accordance with the alphabetical order of their surnames. For vacation preference selection only, the most senior employee shall be determined in alphabetical order in an odd numbered year and in reverse alphabetical order in an even numbered year.

provision. The student should note the specific definitions of seniority, how seniority may be gained, lost, and how management may differentiate between employees with equal seniority.

Seniority Units

Seniority rights, in general, may be exercised only in the applicable *seniority unit*. A seniority unit may be defined as a group of employees whose seniority rights are relative for all members of the group. For example, if a particular seniority unit contains three members—Jim with 5 years seniority, Tom with 4 years and Steve with 2 years—and the contract specified that all personnel actions shall be based upon seniority, then Jim will be the last laid-off and the first recalled or promoted and Steve will be the first laid-off and the last recalled or promoted. In other words Jim has more seniority rights than Tom and Tom has more seniority rights than Steve. Seniority units fall into three structural categories: (1) company on plantwide seniority; (2) departmental or occupationwide seniority and (3) occupation in combination with departmental, company or plantwide seniority.

Company or plantwide seniority units allow an employee to exercise his/her seniority rights anywhere within the company or plant. In other words, the employee's length of service with the company is synonymous with seniority. For example, if a higher paying job were to become vacated any employee may bid for the job regardless of occupation and department (under a strict plant or company system). The employee with the greatest seniority which bid for the job will be the successful applicant. There are two major problems with structuring seniority units in this manner. First, few plants or companies are structured so as to allow employees to transfer from job to job without incurring considerable training costs. Differing occupations and skill levels are typical of not only manufacturing but most service operations. The second major problem arises from the chain reaction which is often set into motion by the transfer of an employee. In the case of a promotion a senior employee may move from a desired job into a better job followed by numerous changes by less-senior employees. This process may involve dozens of employees moving from job to job and take several weeks. Management will object to this chaotic transferring of employees and will consequently resist such a seniority system. Unions on the other hand, will typically prefer company or plantwide seniority because it allows for greater coverage of seniority rights and affords the greatest protection to higher seniority employees.

Department or occupational seniority systems require the establishment and maintenance of separate seniority lists for several units within a company or plant. Seniority rights, under such systems, may be exercised only within a specific department or occupational group. It is not uncommon for competitive seniority to be accumulated only while in the specific unit. This type of system may result in a worker with thirty years of service to the company having less competitive seniority than a worker with one year of service. This type of situation may result if the thirty year veteran is assigned to another department where much younger employees have worked for several months. Labor and management have recognized this paradox and in many cases allowed employees' length of total service to govern but only within a specific department or occupation. In the case of skilled trades or specific occupational groups it is not uncommon for seniority to accumulate only with the particular trade or occupation. The use of this type of seniority unit eliminates much of the chain reaction bumping phenomenon associated with promotions, transfer or layoffs in broader seniority units. Interdepartmental transfers are discouraged if the adapted version of department seniority allows credit only for time served in a particular department. Unions will often object to these types of seniority units because they limit the scope of seniority rights and grant less protection for higher seniority employees.

As a result of the problems associated with the strict versions of plant, company, departmental, or occupational seniority, compromise solutions have developed. Under these compromise seniority structures employees can apply their seniority in one unit for one purpose and in other units for other purposes. For example, for purposes of promotion or shift transfers department seniority may be required while for layoffs and recall plantwide seniority may be utilized. This type of combination seniority system affords senior employees greater job security while eliminating much of the potential chaos associated with interdepartmental bumping resulting from transfers or promotions.

Exceptions to Seniority

It is rather common for a labor agreement to outline specific exceptions to the exercise of seniority rights. Employers will often reserve the contractual right to retain certain "indispensable," "exceptional" or "specially skilled" employees rather than lay them off in line with their seniority. For example, if an employee is the only one within a specific occupation who possesses a particularly needed skill then the employer may retain that employee rather than lay him/her off. Unions will frequently negotiate exceptions granting union officials *super-seniority* in their particular department, occupation or plant so as to prevent them from being bumped or laid-off. The union's need here is rather obvious because without the official the union's operation may be impaired and during periods of high layoff rates or bumping, grievance committee and other representatives could be lost to their constitutuencies. Allowing officials to be laid-off or transferred would require additional union elections or loss of representation neither of which would be acceptable to most unions.

A second common exception to the seniority system involves the first 30 to 90 days of an employee's career. Newly hired employees are typically subjected to a specified probationary period (generally 30–90 days) during which time they may not accrue any earned seniority. The employer may transfer, demote, promote, layoff, and discharge a probationary employee without consideration of earned seniority.

Finally, many contracts allow employers to temporarily layoff workers without regard to seniority under specified circumstances. Generally these circumstances include such things as the taking of inventory, equipment breakdowns, material shortages, fire, flood, and power failures. One additional constraint is universally imposed on management's right to use the temporary layoff provision: duration of the layoff. Many contracts specify that a temporary layoff cannot exceed five days while others allow for periods as short as 24 hours and as long as 10 working days. Management must be careful to ensure that any temporary layoff does not exceed the allowable time period otherwise seniority must be the basis for layoff if the employer's action is to remain consistent with the requirements imposed by the labor agreement.

Seniority and Civil Rights

Title VII of the 1964 Civil Rights Act was designed to prevent and remedy overt racial discrimination. Seniority systems may appear to be inconsistent with the purpose and intent of the Civil Rights Act for numerous reasons. Primary among these reasons is an established seniority system, which may reflect racial or sexual discrimination in the firm's hiring practices, will preclude an appropriate adjustment of seniority without necessarily compromising seniority rights of nonminorities. The result is that minorities may still bear a disproportionate burden of layoffs and find it relatively difficult to obtain promotions and transfers. Congress was aware of these problems and the central role of seniority when Title VII of the Civil Rights Act was passed. Section 703 (h) of the Act states:

> 703(h) Notwithstanding any other provision of this title, it shall not be an unlawful employment practice for an employer to apply different standards of compensation, or different terms, conditions, or privileges of employment pursuant to a bona fide seniority or merit system, or a system which measures earnings by quantity or quality of production or to employees who work in different locations, provided that such differences are not the result of an intention to discriminate because of race, color, religion, sex, or national origin; nor shall it be an unlawful employment practice for an employer to give and to act upon the results of any professionally developed ability test provided that such test, its administration or action upon the results is not designed, intended or used to discriminate because of race, color, religion, sex, or national origin. It shall not be an unlawful employment practice under this title for any employer to differentiate upon the basis of sex in determining the amount of the wages or compensation paid or to be paid to employees of such employer if such differentiation is authorized by the provisions of Section 6 (d) of the Fair Labor Standards Act of 1938 as amended (29 U.S.C. 206 (d)).

The difficulty arises here as to what extent the Supreme Court will apply Section 703 (h) in the protection of seniority systems. In 1976 the Court handed down its ruling in the celebrated *Franks v. Bowman Transportation* case.[5] In this case the Court found that a number of black applicants had been denied employment on the basis of their race by Bowman Transportation. The Circuit Court of Appeals ruled that the appropriate remedy in this case was backpay for the victims of the racial discrimination and that the granting of seniority retroactive to the date of the discriminatory refusal of employment was

[5] *Franks v. Bowman Transportation Co.*, 424 U.S. 747 (1976).

unnecessary. The Supreme Court disagreed with the Circuit Court's formulation of the remedy and ordered retroactive seniority in addition to backpay. The Supreme Court reasoned that payment for lost earnings did not make the black employees whole for damages suffered as a result of the discrimination. Seniority is the basis for the determination of which employees would be promoted, transferred, laid-off, recalled and so forth. Since these rights are based on the magnitude of an employee's seniority any damage to the employee's seniority position would have to be remedied if the workers were to be made whole. Therefore the Court held that employees who suffered racial discrimination were entitled to seniority in addition to backpay from the date of the discrimination to restore not only their full entitlement to economic supplements but also their competitive position in the seniority unit.

The U.S. Supreme Court handed down a decision in 1977 which somewhat limited its decision in the *Franks* case. In the *T.I.M.E.-D.C.*[6] case the Court ruled that an employee who suffered pre-Title VII discrimination cannot be awarded relief which pre-dates the act. In other words, if an employee was the victim of discrimination in a bona fide seniority system which occurred prior to the effective date of Title VII then retroactive seniority and other forms of relief cannot be awarded to a date earlier than the effective date of Title VII. This decision has had the effect of limiting the amount of backpay and retroactive seniority which may be granted a discrimination victim.

Unions have been extremely critical of these Supreme Court decisions. Unions have argued that employers are the ones responsible for hiring employees and not the unions. If discrimination occurs which results in minorities not being hired or being hired at a later date then the employer should bear, totally, any burden of a Court imposed remedy. Under the *Franks* and *T.I.M.E.-D.C.* decisions unions charge that innocent bystanders (the remainder of the seniority unit members) are forced to bear the burden of the Court's remedy. The granting of retroactive seniority causes the redistribution of seniority rights away from workers who have accumulated seniority through years of service to victims of racial discrimination.[7]

Job Security

As a result of stiff foreign competition, increased automation, movement of operations, and the increased incidence of bankruptcies job security issues have become increasingly important. These economic problems serve to illustrate one of the earliest theories for the rise of the labor movement. In his now classic work,[8] Selig Perlman hypothesizes that workers are most concerned with job security and turn to labor unions for greater employment security.

Unions have employed numerous strategies to increase the job security of

[6]*International Brotherhood of Teamsters v. U.S.*; U.S. Supreme Court No. 75–636, (May 31, 1977), and *TIME-DC v. U.S.* Sup. Crt. No. 75–672 (May 31, 1977).

[7]See UAW arguments reported in *Daily Labor Report*, June 10, 1975, pp. A–4 through A–7.

[8]Selig Perlman, *A Theory of the Labor Movement*, New York: Macmillan, 1928.

the membership. These strategies can be classified into two major groups—noncontractual and contractual. Noncontractual strategies are employed outside of the collective bargaining relationship and involve political and public opinion activities while contractual strategies involve the bargaining of specific job security provisions.

Noncontractual strategies are not necessarily limited to union activities. Often management supports and actively participates in many of these strategies and on occasion management is the prime catalyst. The case of the auto industry illustrates the two basic noncontractual strategies of political action and influencing public opinion.

The automobile industry for the past several years has faced increasingly effective foreign competition. The UAW as well as the auto firms have lobbied extensively for increases in tariffs on Japanese and German built automobiles. By increasing the tariffs the domestic producers and unions hope to raise the price of the imports sufficiently to give American built passenger cars a competitive advantage in the marketplace hence increasing profits and employment opportunities. The second strategy jointly employed by the UAW and the auto firms is a public relations campaign. An extensive advertising campaign by management coupled with a union public relations campaign including public statements by union officials, extensive union literature and bumper stickers calling attention to the auto worker's plight were aimed at influencing the American public's automobile purchasing decisions.

There are numerous contractual strategies which have been applied in an attempt to increase employee job security. These strategies are typically proposed by unions but in a few cases management has not resisted these demands and in some cases management has even proposed job security provisions. In the majority of bargaining relations, however, labor and management have found these issues difficult and often impasses result. In the 1982 contract reopening talks both Ford and GM proposed job security provisions in exchange for wage concessions from the UAW. Union contractual demands have included: (1) shorter workweeks; (2) joint labor-management consultation prior to instituting any changes in technology, layoffs or shutdowns; and (3) severance payments. Three major job security provisions deserve further discussion; these are: (1) the attrition principle; (2) restrictions on subcontracting; and (3) retraining programs.

The *attrition principle* is often adopted in labor agreements as a job security measure. The agreement will state, as previously discussed, that reductions in the work force can occur only through voluntary quits, retirements, permanent disabilities, disciplinary discharges, and deaths—in other words natural attrition. Unions, by negotiating such provisions, extend to present job holders considerable protection but often at the cost of reduction in new hire opportunities hence loss of union membership over time. Managements have not demonstrated substantial resistence to these types of provisions in most cases. In cases where a significant percentage of workers are approaching retirement age, the voluntary quit rates are high or no significant reductions in the labor force are anticipated management will typically find these types of provisions an acceptable compromise solution to the job security problem.

Subcontracting and movement of operations either overseas or elsewhere in the United States often results in substantial losses of bargaining unit jobs. These types of management actions are generally done to save costs, speed delivery or broaden markets. Unions are, for the most part, aware of the economic realities facing the firm and will rarely push for provisions which would endanger the viability of the firm. However, unions almost universally wish to prevent unilateral management actions which adversely affect employment levels. Nearly three-fourths of all labor contracts remain silent on the issue of subcontracting and four-fifths of all agreements remain silent on movement of operations. This reflects the union's basic philosophy of letting management run the firm until employment, wages or other basic needs of the membership are endangered, then demanding bargaining.

Numerous types of contractual provisions have been adopted to control the advent of subcontracting or the movement of the firm's operations. These limiting clauses include such things as: (1) outright prohibition of subcontracting or plant movement if bargaining unit jobs are lost; (2) granting the union veto powers over such changes; (3) joint union-management study committees; (4) allowances for subcontracting only if equipment or personnel are lacking within the bargaining unit; (5) requirements that the company prove to the union that movement of operations or subcontracting is necessary to avoid substantial adverse impact on the cost, quality or availability of the firm's product; and (6) no–layoff guarantees to current bargaining unit personnel if subcontracting is occurring and hiring preference if plant movement is anticipated.

The contract language presented in Box 10–3 is from a Teamsters contract governing local hauling. This subcontracting clause is not uncommon in the trucking industry.

Retraining programs have been a common response to automation. Displacement of bargaining unit jobs because of advancement in technology can occur for two reasons—replacement of workers by machinery and changes in skill needs. If skills are needed by the firm because of a change in technology it is typical for the union to demand that displaced workers be trained (at company expense) to fill the new positions. The obvious question then becomes what if no new positions are available? What good is any retraining? Unions have pressed for retraining, under these circumstances, to prepare the displaced worker for employment by a new employer. The basic union concern, being demonstrated in these cases, is more individual income security or protection of earnings potential than specific job security.

Shift Preferences and Transfers

Employees often have preferences for work during either day or night shifts and may prefer work in different departments. The result of these individual tastes has been that unions negotiate contractual provisions allowing employees, within limits, to obtain preferred departments and hours of work. Management, on the other hand, will wish to maintain control of the work force

BOX 10–3.   Article 32, Subcontracting, National Master Freight Agreement and Central States Area Local Cartage—Supplemental Agreement (Teamsters)

Section 1. For the purpose of preserving work and job opportunities for the employees covered by this Agreement, the Employer agrees that no work or services of the kind, nature or type covered by, presently performed, or hereafter assigned to the collective bargaining unit will be subcontracted, transferred, leased, assigned or conveyed in whole or in part to any other plant, person or nonunit employees, unless otherwise provided in this Agreement.

The Employer may subcontract work when all of his regular employees are working, except that in no event shall road work presently performed or runs established during the life of this Agreement be farmed out. No dock work shall be farmed out except for existing situations established by agreed to past practices. Overflow loads may be delivered by drivers other than the Employer's employees provided that this shall not be used as a subterfuge to violate the provisions of this Agreement. Loads may also be delivered by other agreed to methods or as presently agreed to. Owner-Operators performing subcontracted work which is permitted herein shall receive no less than the wages, hours and general working conditions of this Agreement and the applicable Supplement.

The normal, orderly interlining of freight for peddle on occasional basis, where there are parallel rights, and when not for the purpose of evading this Agreement may be continued as has been permitted by past practice providing it is not being done to defeat the provisions of this contract. The interlining of freight or a division of tariff, for any purpose, including local cartage, dock, hoisting and delivery is included within the term subcontracting as used in this Article and may be continued as has been permitted by past practice providing it is not being done to defeat the provisions of this contract.

In the event that an Employer signatory to this Agreement utilizes personnel on a regular basis which has been supplied by a labor contractor, as such to perform subcontracted work permitted by this Agreement, such personnel shall receive the wages, hours and general working conditions provided herein.

Section 2. Within five (5) working days of filing of grievance claiming violation of this Article, the parties to this Agreement shall proceed to the final step of the grievance procedure, without taking any intermediate steps, any other provision of this Agreement to the contrary notwithstanding.

and prevent wholesale transferring of resources to maintain order in the work place. Therefore, in the majority of labor agreements employees have the right to apply for transfers and shift preferences but these rights are generally limited by seniority. Under company or plantwide seniority systems employees may apply for and receive a transfer from shift to shift or department to department, seniority permitting. Frequently a transfer or shift preference may be obtained once per year; only under rare circumstances will a contract authorize a transfer every six months. If more than one occupation is included in a plant then there are also skill requirements for interdepartmental transfers.

Seniority becomes a thorny issue in contracts which authorize shift preferences and transfers but specify departmental seniority units. If the contract authorizes the exercise of total length of service with the firm in any department seniority unit then it should be expected that the departments offering the least irksome work, most overtime and most pleasant conditions would be populated with the highest seniority personnel—the same result as obtained in plantwide units. The problem arises when seniority is allowed to accumulate only in the department unit. By transferring from one department into another the employee would lose all seniority rights and would essentially have the same competitive rights as a new hire; therefore there is a built-in disincentive for transfers. This would have the effect of assuring greater stability in each department's work force but at the cost of fewer people familiar with a wide range of the firm's operations and at least potentially lower morale.

Transfers to and from various occupational seniority units result in essentially the same types of problems as interdepartmental transfers. An entirely different set of problems is in evidence for those who transfer in and out of the bargaining unit. Employees who leave the bargaining unit to take a managerial, plant protection or professional job are treated in a variety of ways. Some contracts specify that seniority will accrue to any employee who leaves the bargaining unit for some other position with the firm hence retaining competitive seniority rights. Many others allow credit earned to stand but do not allow seniority to accrue for time served outside of the seniority unit. The wide variation in these seniority/transfer provisions reflect the various specific needs of the firm, union and employees. If it is necessary for bargaining unit personnel to be promoted to professional jobs, the union may understandably desire to accommodate any of those employees who later wish to return to the bargaining unit.[9] The case of bargaining unit personnel being assigned to managerial positions, however, meets stiff union resistance on the issue of seniority continuation. Many union leaders and members believe the potential for abuse is too great if seniority is allowed to accrue while an employee is serving in a managerial capacity. Seniority is intended to differentiate between seniority unit personnel and it is therefore often deemed inappropriate to allow seniority to accrue while the employee is elsewhere. It is also possible that during recessions employees could be protected from layoffs by temporary transfer to a management position—the type of favoritism unions have historically objected to.

[9]See Chapter 17 for further discussion of what constitutes professional employment.

Promotions

Promotions are often a controversial issue. Higher wages, better working conditions and more job security are frequently associated with an employee obtaining a promotion. During the pre-Wagner Act days it was not uncommon for managers to show favoritism to friends or relatives in handing out promotions. Unions have, therefore, historically supported the idea that promotions should be based upon some demonstrable merit. Seniority has typically been the criteria suggested by unions because it is a very quantifiable standard which leaves little or no room for subjectivity. Management, on the other hand, will typically argue that seniority and merit are not necessarily synonomous and differences in employee qualifications should be taken into account. In practice there are very few labor agreements which specify that promotions will be granted solely on the basis of seniority or solely on the basis of employee qualifications. Two compromise contract provisions are the most frequently adopted. The controlling phrases in these two types of provisions are "most senior qualified" and "most qualified senior" employee shall be promoted. Well, you might ask, aren't these provisions specifying the same thing? The answer is most certainly, no! In the first phrase the most senior worker or the employee with the greatest seniority who is capable of filling the job will be promoted. In the second phrase the most qualified worker or the employee with the greatest ability to perform the job will be promoted with seniority being used to differentiate between equally qualified employees.

Qualifications pose significant problems in the administration of contract provisions which govern promotions. Such items as tests, previous occupations,

---

BOX 10–4. Promotion List Clerk-Typist I's Applying for Clerk-Typist II

	Seniority Date	Words per Minute (3 errors or less) (average three tests)	50 pts. Filing Exam
Arthur	September 1976	60	31
Jane	November 1976	77	32
Linda	August 1977	67	34
Mary	July 1978	66	31
William	December 1978	77	34

The clerk typist II job consists of approximately 67% typing and 33% filing. Both examinations applied are valid and job related. Under a Clause Requiring the *Senior Most Qualified Employee to be Promoted*—William is Promoted.

Under a Clause Requiring Most Senior Qualified Employee to be Promoted if 60 on the typing test and 30 on the filing test are minimal qualifications, then Arthur is promoted.

If 100 minimum points are required then Jane is promoted.

specialized education, and trial periods are frequently utilized to determine an applicant's qualifications for a particular job. A word of warning is necessary concerning the use of tests and educational requirements—any test or educational standard utilized by an employer must be job related[10] and must be a valid measure of the employee's ability to perform the subject job.[11] If statistical evidence can be shown that minorities do poorly on the test relative to whites then the employer is obligated to show the validity and specific relevance of the test to job requirements or be found in violation of Title VII of the 1964 Civil Rights Act.[12]

Trial periods are also frequently specified in labor agreements as a measure of an applicant's ability to perform a specific job. It is common for the contract to state a specific time for the trial period (typically ten to twenty working days) and criteria for judgment of the applicant's abilities. The employee is entitled to the trial period test if he is the senior employee and the most senior qualified employee is to be promoted unless management can clearly show that the employee does not possess the requisite skills or knowledge to perform the duties associated with the job. Under clauses requiring the most qualified senior employee be promoted then the employee is entitled to the test period if there is doubt as to the applicant's abilities relative to other applicants. Problems arise in the application of a test period in cases where the contract does not specify time periods or criteria for differentiating among employees. If no reasonable past practice has been established governing these issues then management is constrained only to a reasonable, nonarbitrary and consistent application of the trial period.

Union Security Issues

Union security issues are an emotional and highly controversial area of labor relations. A union security clause is a contractual provision which requires employees to join the union or pay the equivalent of union dues and fees after some specified period of time. These provisions involve compulsory union participation—the source of the controversy. Union members typically resent being required to work with nonunion employees. The fact that nonunion workers share in the benefits negotiated by the union without at least financially supporting the union (commonly called the free-rider effect) is the source of this resentment. Those individuals opposed to compulsory union membership generally cite moral reasons such as the freedom of association as the basis for their objections.

There are four basic types of union security arrangements; these are: (1) open shop; (2) agency shop; (3) union shop; and (4) closed shop. Each of these forms differ in the timing and the degree of the union membership requirement and the amount of freedom of choice accorded employees concerning joining the union.

[10] *Griggs v. Duke Power Company*, 401 U.S. 424 (1971).

[11] *U.S. v Masonary Contractors Ass'n of Memphis Inc.*, 497 F. 2d 871, 875 (6th Cir 1974).

[12] *Albemarle Paper Company v. Moodes*, 422 U.S. 405, 955 Ct. 2362, 45L. ed. 2d 280 (1975)

The *open shop* may be viewed as the absence of a union security arrangement. It is estimated that less than twenty percent of all union contracts remain silent on the issue of union security, hence allowing the open shop. Under this form of security arrangement no employee is required to join or financially contribute to the labor organization.

The *agency shop* arrangement does not require an employee to join a labor organization but does require the employee to make a financial contribution to the union which is typically the equivalent of the union fees and dues. In some circumstances unions allow the equivalent of dues and fees to be contributed to a charitable organization if the employee has a bona fide religious objection to joining or contributing to a union. The basic union purpose in negotiating such a security arrangement is to obtain sufficient finances to be an effective bargaining representative of the employees and to minimize the free-rider effect. Employers typically do not resist this form of security clause as fiercely as the union shop because no employee is forced to join the union.

The *union shop* security clause requires that after some specified period of time, generally 31 to 90 days, the employee must join the union. The Taft-Hartley Act requires that under the union shop an employee cannot be required to join the union until after the thirtieth day of employment (as will be discussed later there is an exception to this rule). If a union shop security clause is negotiated in an existing contract then the thirty day requirement applies only to workers who were not members of the union or who are subsequently hired and will not apply to those who were previously union members.[13] In one case the NLRB invalidated a newly bargained union shop clause because it required all workers who had been in the firm's employ for thirty days or more at the effective date of the new agreement to join the union.[14] In other words, all employees must be granted a minimum grace period of thirty days before being required to join a labor organization except those who already are union members in a pre-existing bargaining relation where a new union shop clause is negotiated. The two major advantages to the union under such a security arrangement is that the entire bargaining unit must become union members allowing better bargaining unit control by the union and greater financial resources. With only union members in the bargaining unit both the union and management will experience less interemployee hostility because of the removal of the potential for union-nonunion employee conflict.

During World War II a compromise between the union shop and open shop security arrangements was developed; commonly called the *maintenance-of-membership*, this did not require workers to join the union but did require any worker who joined the union to remain a member during the life of the contract. At the end of the effective period of the contract there was an escape period during which the employee could withdraw from the union; however, if the employee did not avail himself of this escape period opportunity then he had to remain a member during the effective life of the next contract. The typical escape period was about fifteen days; however, there was some variation in the timing as well as the length of the escape period. Maintenance-of-

[13] *Charles Krause Milling Company,* 97 NLRB 336 (1951).
[14] *Continental Carbon, Inc.,* 94 NLRB 1026 (1951).

membership provisions declined rapidly after the Second World War and are very rare today.

The *closed shop* is the most restrictive of all union security arrangements. Under this type of provision an employee must be a member in good standing of the union prior to being employed. The closed shop turns the union into the employment agency for the employer. In 1947 the Taft-Hartley Act prohibited the closed shop in contracts covered by the Act. Allegations of union corruption in the operation of hiring halls[15], primarily concerning bribery and racial discrimination, resulted in the prohibition of the closed shop.

The closed shop served a useful function because of its hiring hall feature for employers in many industries. In trucking, long-shoring and the construction trades, employers who frequently move their operations or who experience differing labor needs over time found the hiring hall an extremely valuable asset. Employers and unions alike urged Congress to reinstitute the closed shop or at least the hiring hall because of its central importance in the trucking, long–shoring and construction industries. In the Landrum-Griffin Act passed into law in 1959 Congress authorized the use of the hiring hall in the construction industry so long as employees were not required to join the union before their seventh day of employment. The NLRB, in addition, has not prohibited the use of the hiring hall in long-shoring provided the hiring hall is operated in a non-discriminatory manner.

Right-to-Work Laws

Section 14(b) of Taft-Hartley authorizes states to enact laws prohibiting the union and/or agency shop forms of union security. Section 14(b) of Taft-Hartley states:

> "nothing in this Act shall be construed as authorizing the execution or application of agreements requiring membership in a labor organization as a condition of employment in any State or Territory in which such execution or application is prohibited by State or Territorial law."

The states which have such statutes are Alabama, Arizona, Arkansas, Florida, Georgia, Iowa, Kansas, Louisiana, Mississippi, Nebraska, Nevada, North Carolina, North Dakota, South Carolina, South Dakota, Tennessee, Texas, Utah, Virginia, and Wyoming. Considerable controversy surrounds these statutes. This controversy centers on the issues of morality and power.

Is it morally right to force an employee to join a union? There is no clearly right or wrong answer to this question. Proponents of right-to-work legislation claim that it is unjust and immoral to require any person to join a union to keep his/her job. Opponents argue that it is immoral and unjust for employees who refuse to join a union to enjoy the benefits and protections of union negotiated contracts without contributing to the labor organization. One curious aspect of the morality issue is that many of the employers who argue so vehemently in

---

[15] Hiring halls were the focal point of the closed shop. An applicant went to the union hiring hall to join the union and to obtain work.

support of right-to-work laws are the ones who required that employees join company dominated unions during the 1930s. While there is some hypocrisy in the morality arguments there is no clear indication of what is morally correct but simply some interesting trade–offs and arguments.

The second major argument is focused on power. It is clear that when the contract contains a union security provision the union has greater control over the bargaining unit and financial resources. These products of union security bestow on the union a comparative advantage in collective bargaining. Equally true is that the employer weakens the union's position if a union security clause can be kept out of the contract; thus, the employer gains relative bargaining power. Often the issue of power is avoided in arguments concerning right-to-work legislation. In other words, the real issue is the relative bargaining power of management and labor and morality is used to divert attention from power.

Checkoff

The checkoff clause is an agreement requiring the employer to deduct the union dues and fees from employees' paychecks and turn these funds over to the union. It is not uncommon for the employer to be permitted to withhold a sufficient amount from payment to the union to cover the expenses of the payroll deduction of employees' dues and fees. Some contracts, however, specify that the employer will provide this service without charge.

The negotiation of checkoff provisions does not typically result in significant labor disputes. These types of provisions are most commonly negotiated in bargaining relations where union security arrangements have been negotiated. Employers rather than having union officials collecting dues on company property will often prefer the checkoff procedure. The checkoff minimizes confusion at the place of work as well as tends to minimize regular contact between union officials and the membership. Unions will typically prefer the checkoff arrangement because it minimizes the time and effort normally required in collecting dues and fees. Secondly, the checkoff is a rather reliable method of collecting payments and contributes to the financial stability of the union. It is not uncommon for labor and management to both desire the checkoff system because of its inherent simplicity and associated benefits.

The Taft-Hartley Act regulates the use of the checkoff. The checkoff authorization must be voluntary. The negotiation of a compulsory checkoff provision is prohibited by the Act. The checkoff is lawful only if the employee authorizes it in writing and has the contractual right to revoke the authorization after the effective life of the contract or one year, whichever is shorter.

Summary

There are basically two theories of management rights; these are the residual theory and the trusteeship theory. Managers who subscribe to the residual theory believe that all prerogatives not modified by law or the contract are theirs to exercise. Trusteeship proponents believe that managers must please not only the customer and stockholder but also the employee even if that means granting rights normally reserved as management prerogatives. Residualists tend to view collective bargaining as inconsistent with managerial goals and responsibilities while trusteeship subscribers do not believe that collective bargaining is necessarily a constraint on management.

Seniority is the basis for the determination of employee rights. Competitive seniority establishes employees relative rights to promotions, transfers and job security. Seniority units differ substantially from contract to contract; however, there are three basic units: (1) company or plantwide; (2) occupational or departmental seniority and (3) combinations of occupational and company, plant or department units.

Job security issues have become increasingly important in those sectors of the economy most affected by foreign competition, inflation and automation. Unions have responded to these issues by demanding the inclusion of such contract provisions as the attrition principle, restrictions on subcontracting and retraining programs. Other union responses to the loss of jobs have been aimed at the political arena and public opinion.

There are four basic forms of union security arrangements: (1) open shop; (2) agency shop; (3) union shop; and (4) closed shop. Union security issues have been the subject of considerable debate and controversy. Section 14(b) of the Taft-Hartley Act allows states to enact right-to-work laws. Twenty states have passed right-to-work laws which prohibit the union and/or agency shop form of union security clause. The checkoff of union dues and fees is generally included in contracts which contain union security clauses. The checkoff must be voluntarily authorized by the employee and the authorization is revokable.

COMMENTARY: Mr. Harold Scott Speaks on the Importance of Seniority in the Collective Bargaining Relation.

Mr. Scott is a University of Michigan graduate with nine years of employee relations experience. His job titles during those nine years include: Employment Supervisor, Gemini Corp.; Job Analyst, Michigan-Wisconsin Pipeline Co.; Salaried Employee Representative, American Motors Corp.; Labor Relations Administrator, Sr., Manager, Employee Relations, and Corporate Manager, Labor Relations, Bendix Corporation.

Seniority is one of the most important provisions of a collective bargaining relationship. In most collective bargaining agreements, it is the sole basis for determining who is laid off and recalled, and is at least a consideration for promotion. In some companies rates of pay, shift preference, vacation, overtime, and fringe benefits are impacted by an employee's length of service. A basic bargaining objective has always been seniority consideration.

The unions' initial purpose of pursuing seniority provisions in collective bargaining agreements was to protect those employees who have contributed the most time to a company from being capriciously terminated or discharged. As a result, his job security is in direct relation to the length of time he has with the company.

In addition, consideration of seniority minimizes the complaints of unfair and discriminatory treatment and aids in decreasing conflict in the adversarial relationship.

COMMENTARY: Mr. James A. Thompson Speaking on the Importance of Seniority Clauses.

Mr. James A. Thompson, General Vice President and Research and Education Director of the Association of Western Pulp and Paper Workers; a Labor Union with its national office located in Portland, Oregon. Mr. Thompson has been involved in the West Coast Pulp and Paper Industry for 28 years, the last 6 in his current position. He came from the rank and file, holding many positions in his local union, including that of Local Union President for a number of years. He currently is a public member of the Board of Governors of the Oregon State Bar Association, and also chairs the Board of Pacific Northwest Labor College.

Why is *seniority* so important to workers covered by collective bargaining agreements? Simply stated, without a meaningful seniority clause for protection in event of layoffs or promotions, workers are afforded little, if any, job protection whatsoever.

Take the case of a worker in a non-union manufacturing plant. Even though a worker may have been a model employee for twenty-plus years of employment, there's nothing that precludes the boss from hiring his rich aunt's son to fill a job opening that the veteran employee had attempted to work into during his entire time with the company. Likewise, without some type of seniority protection, the reverse could hold in the event the company has to lay off; the rich aunt's greener-than-grass son stays on the payroll while our twenty-year person joins the ranks of the unemployed. This kind of move happens, unfortunately, on almost a daily basis in unorganized work places.

Conversely, if this same situation occurred in a shop with a strong labor agreement in effect, our veteran employee would have built-in safeguards protecting him or her from the "favorite son" approach used in many of the non-union places of business.

What is contained in a "strong" labor agreement that provides for seniority protection both upward and downward movement? Let's review some typical clauses found in union shop West Coast pulp and paper mill Labor Agreements.

1. *Promotion.* The parties agree that a job opening on any rung of a ladder above the bottom rung shall be filled by the most senior qualified employee then on the

next rung below the rung that is to be filled. Exceptions to the foregoing may be established by mutual agreement.

2. *Demotion.* In all cases of layoff or curtailment extending longer than forty-eight hours, a senior qualified employee will not continue on layoff as long as a junior employee is working in the mill. Any employee affected by a curtailment not desiring to accept the job his seniority entitles him to, may elect to layoff for the period of the curtailment. Commencing with the most senior employee and continuing in the order of mill seniority, the employees involved in the layoff or curtailment shall be entitled to job selection when considering the jobs available.

These are only two examples of why seniority is so important in the shop. Any number of additional seniority provisions appear in most labor agreements. Is it any wonder that labor organizations fight for, and have many times been forced to call strikes over, job protection language that guarantees the workers some form of seniority protection?

DISCUSSION QUESTIONS

1. Is it possible that some of the job security provisions discussed in this chapter could result in fewer employment opportunities? Explain.

2. Outline the major differences between the residual and the trusteeship theories of management rights.

3. Can a bona fide seniority system be in violation of the 1964 Civil Rights Act? If so how? Who typically is harmed by court remedies and who is helped?

4. Outline and critically evaluate the various forms of union security arrangements?

5. What are right-to-work laws? In detail explain the controversy concerning these statutes.

SELECTED REFERENCES

Brandt, Floyd S., "Unions, Management and Maintenance Subcontracting—An Industry Experience," *Labor Law Journal,* (July 1963) **14:** 601–13.

Chamberlain, Neil W., *The Union Challenge to Management Control,* New York: Harper and Row, Publishers, 1948.

Chandler, M.K., *Management Rights and Union Interests,* New York: McGraw-Hill Book Company, Inc. 1964.

Feldesman, William, "How Issues of Subcontracting and Plant Removal Are Handled by the National Labor Relations Board," *Industrial and Labor Relations Review,* (January 1966), **19:** 253–64.

Freedman, Audrey, *Security Bargains Reconsidered: SUB, Severance Pay, Guaranteed Work.* New York: The Conference Board, 1978.

Hartman, P.T., *Collective Bargaining and Productivity,* Berkeley: University of California Press, 1969.

Koretz, R.F., "How Issues of Subcontracting and Plant Removal Are Handled by the Courts," *Industrial and Labor Relations Review*, (January, 1960), **19:** 239–52.

McDermott, T.J., "Union Security and Right-to-Work Laws," *Labor Law Journal*, November 1965, pp. 667–78.

Meyers, Frederic, *Right-to-Work in Practice*, New York: Fund for the Republic, 1959.

Pulsipher, A.G. "The Union Shop: A Legitimate Form of Coercion in a Free-Market Economy," *Industrial and Labor Relations Review*, (July 1966), **19.**

Shultz, G.P. and A.R. Weber, *Strategies for Displaced Workers*, Wesport, Conn.: Greenwood Press, Inc., 1966.

Slichter, S.H., J.J. Healy and E.R. Livernash, *The Impact of Collective Bargaining upon Management*, Washington, D.C.: The Brookings Institution, 1960.

Smith, Jr., A.B., "The Impact on Collective Bargaining of Equal Employment Opportunity Remedies," *Industrial and Labor Relations Review*, (April 1975), **28.**

Stone, Morris, *Managerial Freedom and Job Security*, New York: Harper and Row, Publishers, 1963.

Torrence, G.W., *Management's Right to Manage*, Washington, D.C.: The Bureau of National Affairs, 1959.

Wallen, Saul, "How Issues of Subcontracting and Plant Removal Are Handled by Arbitrators," *Industrial and Labor Relations Review*, (January 1966), **19:** 265–72.

Part III

Administration of the Labor Agreement

Chapter 11

Grievances:
Their Causes, Settlement and Prevention

The true test of the success of contract negotiations comes when the parties endeavor to administer the labor agreement. Grievance administration comprises the bulk of labor relations activity in the majority of bargaining relations. It is therefore necessary for the student of labor relations to fully understand the causes of grievances, the operation of the grievance procedure and what may be done to minimize the occurrence of grievances and the difficulties associated with their settlement.

This chapter is divided into four major sections: the first deals with the causes of grievances, the second section describes the operation of the grievance procedure, the third outlines the union's duty to fairly represent employees, and the final section suggests programs which may be utilized to minimize grievances.

Grievances

Labor relations authorities often disagree as to the precise meaning of the term *grievance*. Employees may become discontent if they think that they have been treated unfairly by management. The dissatisfied employee may even register a complaint in hopes that the problem may be corrected. In the broadest sense of the term a complaint may be thought of as a grievance. On the other hand, some labor relations authorities would disagree with this definition. It is quite possible, especially in nonunion facilities that a complaint could be readily ignored by those with the authority to correct the employee's perceived difficulty. To these authorities the term grievance implies something much more specific. In the narrow view, a grievance is specifically what the parties to the collective bargaining agreement say it is. Employees depend on the contract to delineate and define their rights in the employer-employee relation. If the employer violates a provision of the contract, compromising an employee's rights, the employee has a grievance. If, on the other hand, the employer's action is not covered by the contract or the action is specifically excluded from the coverage of the grievance procedure, the employee does not have a grievance but merely a complaint. Consider the following contract language and situation.

In a small midwestern manufacturing facility management has retained the right to assign employees to particular departments, jobs and shifts, limited only as follows:

Section 4. **A.** Management shall post any job opening in any skill class, department and shift on the first working day of the week at least one hour before the end of the first shift.

B. Such posting will be made on the union bulletin board in each department.

C. The successful bidder for the position will be the most senior qualified employee bidding for the job before the end of the first shift on Monday of the following week.

D. If no employee bids for the job management will assign the most junior qualified employee to the opening so long as the employee so assigned is not required to take a reduction in his or her hourly wage.

A coil winder job became open on second shift and management posted the job. No employee bid for this semiskilled job within the specified period of time. The personnel records showed that only two employees not presently assigned to the coil winding job had experience on the job, Mr. Jones with one year of seniority and Mr. Smith with ten years of seniority and both were assigned to first shift general production jobs. Mr. Jones was informed that he was being promoted to the coil winding job, which paid 3¢ per hour more than the general rate and that the job was on second shift which paid 10¢ per hour shift differential. Mr. Jones complained that he attended college during the evening and he did not want the promotion. Does Mr. Jones have a grievance? His supervisor showed Mr. Jones Section 4 of the contract and explained that he was the most junior qualified employee and would have to accept the job. Mr. Jones then went to the union steward and registered his complaint. The steward told Mr. Jones that if his supervisor was correct then he would have to take the promotion. The steward said he would check the personnel records but unless there was an employee junior to Mr. Jones who was qualified for the job Mr. Jones didn't have a grievance. The steward found that Mr. White had less seniority than Mr. Jones but was already assigned to the coil winding department on the day shift. The question remains: does Mr. Jones have a grievance? The steward told Mr. Jones that it was a matter of interpretation of Section 4 of the contract. The central issue is whether Mr. Jones or Mr. White is the junior employee for puposes of Section 4 of the contract and therefore Mr. Jones does have a grievance. But whether Mr. Jones has to take the second shift job is an entirely different matter.

Mr. Jones may have a remedy under the contract but that depends on whether the intent of Section 4 was to include employees already in the coil winding classification. Since the contract did not specify how this situation was to be handled and no reference is made to how the union and management had handled past cases it is open to speculation whether Mr. Jones will win in this case or not. Two things are certain, however, Mr. Jones must comply with the directives of management since the responsibility for the efficient operation of the firm rests with management. Secondly, if Mr. Jones disobeys the orders of his supervisor and does not report for work on the second shift coil winding job he may be disciplined for failure to comply with management's orders.

The grievance process, therefore, may be viewed as an action-reaction process. Management's responsibility is to efficiently operate the firm which typically requires that supervisors must make certain decisions. The employee is obligated to comply with these managerial directives and may be disciplined for failure to do so. If the employee then believes that his or her contractual rights have been violated then the employee may seek remedy through the grievance procedure outlined in the labor agreement. The grievance processing procedure may, however, take several weeks or even months and during this period the employee must conform with management's directives.

Without the grievance procedure the employee has no formalized method to appeal management's decisions. The majority of nonunion personnel policies have no formal grievance procedure. Employees in these companies must appeal to management to reconsider its actions and if management is not inclined to do so then the employee is left with no recourse but to accept management's decision or seek employment elsewhere. The grievance procedure is an orderly and peaceful method of contract enforcement and dispute settlement. But maybe even more importantly the grievance procedure may be thought of as a safety valve whereby employees may express dissatisfaction openly and relieve pressures which may lead to serious problems such as high turnover rates, worker alienation, and even strike activity. Further discussion of these issues will be offered in the following sections of this chapter.

Causes of Grievances

Often grievances are, at the same time, both similar and dissimilar. Although unique in terms of personnel, human needs, contractual provisions, past practice (shop common law), economic conditions, and other relevant factors, every grievance is reasonable from some perspective. Self-interest, however perceived, is served or promoted by the filing of a grievance. Whether the grievance is filed as purely an expression of dissatisfaction or is an earnest attempt to protect one's contractual rights the employee is doing what he believes is serving his best interests. Though diverse, grievances can be classified into three categories by cause and the type of self-interest served. These categories are: (1) grievances caused by misunderstanding; (2) grievances caused by intentional contract violations; and (3) grievances that are symptomatic of problems outside the scope of the labor agreement.

Misunderstanding

Grievances which result from misunderstanding are generally the product of disagreement concerning the circumstances surrounding a grievance, a lack of familiarity with the contract, or an inadequate labor agreement. Whatever the source of misunderstanding, self-interest motivates the aggrieved party to use the grievance procedure in an attempt to protect contractual rights or what are perceived to be contractual rights.

Grievances stemming from disputed facts in the administration of specific contract provisions are, for the most part, inevitable even in the most mature and efficient of bargaining relations. For example, there will always be disputes concerning the guilt or innocence of employees who are disciplined for alleged violations of the labor agreement or shop rules. The reasonableness or fairness of the discipline imposed will also be subject to honest disagreement. An analogy may be drawn between the American system of justice and the grievance procedure. The court of original jurisdiction or trial court is mirrored to an extent by the supervisor's original determination of guilt or innocence in a case. If the employee is dissatisfied with the decision of his supervisor or he believes that the procedure utilized in his discipline was unfair then the employee may appeal to the grievance procedure. The appeal process goes through successively higher levels of management and union structure until the court of last resort or arbitration is appealed to for a final and binding decision. Grievances over the facts or procedures utilized in a case are to be expected in the day-to-day administration of the contract.

An unclear contract is a constant source of grievances. Language that is clear and unequivocal to many reasonable and experienced individuals may not have the same meaning to others. Although clear and specific contract language significantly reduces possible areas of misunderstanding, it will not make the meaning of agreed-to contract terms immediately obvious in all cases. On the other hand, an unusually large number of grievances growing out of ambiguous contract language may indicate that the union and management negotiators failed in their collective bargaining responsibilities and as a result produced an inadequate contract. For example, the intent of a contract clause requiring the promotion of the "senior qualified" person to a better paying position could easily have been clarified by posing the following questions at the time the provision was agreed to: Which is the key word for purposes of promotion, "senior" or "qualified"? How are qualifications to be determined? On what basis is seniority measured? Similar questions concerning all contract provisions, raised *and* resolved during the negotiation process, will minimize grievances during the life of the contract. An effectively functioning grievance procedure is dependent upon the foresight and hard work of the negotiators in bargaining the contract.

Regardless of how well the contract is written and understood by the negotiating parties, grievances will still arise if the document goes unread by those persons who are charged with, or affeced by, its application and enforcement. Whether the cause is ignorance of the contract on the part of the employees, union grievance representatives, or supervisors the end product is the same—needless and avoidable grievances.

Although contract ignorance, wherever found, is inexcusable, it is somewhat more understandable in the case of first-line supervisors. Supervisors are typically not rewarded for effective grievance management. Rather, rewards are normally tied to the achievement of production goals. The result of this reward structure is that first line supervisors and often higher level managers become fixed on specific production objectives and often lose sight of closely related areas such as labor relations. Occasionally the link between effective grievance management and the achievement of production goals is not well understood by supervisors. Engineers and other technically trained individuals may have had no formal training in labor related topics and may not understand fully the role of labor or the union in the firm's goal directed activities. Therefore, the contract may be frequently ignored by those who must work within its limitations.

While somewhat more understandable, the production–motivated behavior of supervisors is, at the same time, potentially more harmful to the labor-management relationship than employee ignorance of the same contract. The ineptitude of supervisors in contract administration spawns aggressive employee behavior. Subjected to the pressure of meeting production targets while at the same time besieged by employee grievances, supervisors may accommodate employee demands in whatever fashion necessary to maintain production—thereby providing further incentives for the filing of grievances. The result is a body of precedents (past practices) that undermines the contract.

Union stewards may also be unfamiliar with the contract. Most local union officials are elected, therefore the steward or grievance representative may be selected more on the basis of popularity rather than his or her knowledge of the contract or skills as a negotiator. While unfortunate, this result of union democracy may, at least in part, be remedied if the union conducts steward training programs. AFL-CIO affiliated unions and most of the major unaffiliated national unions or their regional offices conduct grievance processing sessions designed to assist the newly elected union steward to sharpen his or her negotiation tools and better understand the labor agreement. Employees may misunderstand a contract provision or be unaware of the agreed-to interpretation of a specific clause and as a result file grievances. Since most union grievance representatives are elected they may be unwilling to drop a grievance even if they are aware that the grievant has misunderstood the contract. Educational programs for union stewards and even employees (at the local level) will frequently reduce these types of grievances. Many unions will instruct stewards in the handling of such grievants and impress upon the steward his or her obligation to inform employees when they have misunderstood the contract so as to increase the likelihood that the grievance procedure will remain a viable institution.

There are also more mundane sources of misunderstanding which frequently result in grievances. These sources of misunderstanding are often closely related to and may even be indistinguishable from many of the items discussed in the section on symptomatic grievances. Common sources of misunderstanding include breakdowns in communication, mistrust and differences in goals and perceptions.

Breakdowns in communication are not uncommon in any organization. When information is transmitted from any organizational component to another the message sent must be the same as the message received or communications are said to have broken down. If the various levels of management fail to communicate then management may become less effective which could produce employee grievances. Without effective control and coordination of activities employees may not know what is expected of them and find that management's expectations vary significantly from time to time which in turn will result in confusion over work standards and contract interpretation. Grievances will also arise if management fails to communicate with employees and the union. If an employee is kept informed on issues which concern his contractual rights, it is less likely that different interpretations will develop between the employee and the supervisor. It is also likely that the employee will perceive greater involvement in the firm and his or her job, a matter directly related to job satisfaction. A satisfied employee is less likely to take exception with management decisions and look for different possible contractual interpretations.

Communication between management and the union is also an important determinant of the incidence of grievance filing. While various potential interpretations of contract provisions or the implications of certain actions exist, the union and management which effectively communicate with one another are more likely to be able to work out differences than if no channels of communication are open. This issue will be addressed in greater detail in the final section of this chapter.

Mistrust of the management by employees or the union will tend to reduce communication and increase suspicion. In such an environment employees and union representatives are likely to become much more watchful and are more likely to search for interpretations of the contract and events which are favorable to their own position. Unfortunately where mistrust is allowed to develop it is more likely that open hostility between the bargaining agents may also develop. Escalation of such difficulties is possible in any bargaining relation and is to be avoided if at all possible. This issue will be addressed in further detail in the final section of this chapter.

The allocation of rights and resources will at times result in the union and management setting conflicting goals. Often in cases where the contract is not clear and its intent is not specifically spelled out, shades of difference may result in its interpretation. Often subtle differences in the interpretation of the contract may result in the parties taking positions designed to further some specific objective. It is not uncommon for a party to attempt to negotiate changes in the contract during its administration in hopes of acquiring more than they were able to obtain in the negotiation of the contract. The grievance procedure is the vehicle through which the union will attempt such modifications. If management institutes such goal oriented modifications employees will typically appeal to the grievance procedure to prevent the loss of their perceived rights. The end result will be a greater number of grievances being filed. This particular issue is closely related to intentional contract violations which are discussed in the following section.

Intentional Contract Violations

Grievances falling within this category are either the result of a deliberate disregard of contract provisions or efforts to capitalize on ambiguous contract language and/or past practice. Since management is responsible for active contract administration, it has a greater number of opportunities for deliberate contract violations than does labor. The temptation to violate the contract occasionally becomes irresistible. These violations are usually rationalized on the grounds of being economically necessary or of little substantive importance to the employees. Consider the case of a carpentry subcontractor who bids for a job installing doors in an apartment building. Since the architect did not specify whether the doors should be prefitted with the necessary hardware or whether the hardware was to be fitted on the doors at the construction site the subcontractor opted to purchase prefitted doors. The prefitted doors cost the subcontractor one dollar more per door than purchasing the hardware and doors separately. Working at normal rate a journeyman carpenter could install hardware on two doors per hour. A journeyman carpenter earns ten dollars per hour at the union rate; therefore the subcontractor stands to save four dollars per installed door over what he bid the job for. The problem arises over the fact that the union contract contains a work preservation clause which requires the fitting of such hardware be done on the site. In this case the subcontractor was aware that the use of the prefitted doors violated the contract but the cost savings was substantial and since the carpenters were obtaining work the subcontractor hoped that the issue of the hardware installation would be overlooked by the union. Obviously this reasoning is rationalization on the part of the subcontractor and the real issue is the cost savings. The majority of unions which have negotiated work preservation clauses would grieve over such a management action.

On the other hand, inadequate contract language in conjunction with favorably perceived past practice, provides incentives to employees to file grievances. This is often a problem in bargaining relations where management tends to give in to union demands regardless of their merit. Employees may hope to gain through the grievance–arbitration process what they were unable to achieve at the bargaining table. For example, it is relatively common for public school teachers to file grievances concerning the school's evaluation system when the contract remains silent on the issue of evaluation. In cases where the evaluation is unfavorable the fairness of the procedure is attacked but often teachers will file the grievances hoping that the school's management will concede to some limitation on the use of evaluations therefore gaining rights through the grievance procedure which were not obtained in negotiations. In each of the above cases, grievances arise because the parties, in pursuit of self-interest, try to achieve some right or privilege not explicitly conveyed by the contract.

Symptomatic Grievances

Symptomatic grievances make up the final category of grievances. These grievances are the hardest to identify and prevent. As the name implies, the grievance itself is not the real problem. It is simply a way for the employee to show dissatisfaction and frustration with either job or non-job related problems. There are three basic causes of symptomatic grievances: (1) personal problems; (2) union politics; and (3) unfavorable contract language. Often it is difficult to untangle the causes of symptomatic grievances. It is not uncommon for union politics to become involved with unfavorable contract language and/or personal problems. Therefore the following discussion may, in practice, describe grievances with determinants overlapping two or more symptomatic categories.

The human element, (i.e., emotions, personalities, differing goals and incentives) can play havoc with personnel policies, contract administration, and production schedules. However, when labor is utilized in the production of commodities or the providing of services the human element must be accounted for. This category of symptomatic grievances can be subcategorized by the nature of the personal problem involved: (1) medical problems; (2) family problems; (3) self-actualization problems; and (4) social problems. None of these causes are easily diagnosed; however, certain medical problems may be more visable than the other categories. Underemployment or overemployment of an individual employee may result in frustration and dissatisfaction with his work. The result may be that the employee will file trivial grievances or exhibit behavior which results in discipline. It may be that management or the union may be able to identify the source of the employee's problem and correct it; however, many such cases may go undetected. A rather unfortunate example of this type of grievance involved a cook in a major metropolitan hospital located in the midwest. The cook who was recently employed began to become uncooperative, hostile, and frequently filed trivial grievances. Her supervisor and union grievance representative were at a loss to explain her sudden change in behavior and filing of grievances. By accident while processing a grievance for her, the union grievance representative discovered the problem. After the union steward filled out the grievance form he got up from his chair to get a cup of coffee then returned and asked the cook to read the grievance form and sign it if it represented her views. After five minutes of rather close examination the employee stated she was satisfied with the document and signed it. The union representative then started to sign the grievance form and realized the cook had signed a grievance form outlining another employee's grievance. Closer examination of the employee's background revealed that she could not read. In her position as a cook she was required to read instructions of various kinds governing the preparation of food, safety, and equipment maintenance. During her first three months of employment the cook that she was hired to replace was continually with her to assist in her training and therefore the grievant's reading skills were never tested. When the previous cook retired the grievant's only source of information were the written instructions which she could not read. She became fearful for her job and the frustration built up resulting in her hostility and grievance activity.

Serious medical problems, such as cancer or heart problems may be easily hidden by the employee. Yet the emotional distress and physical pain may modify the employee's behavior. Quite frequently these persons become irritable and even openly hostile. Many employers, especially in industries requring hazardous work or physical strength, require routine and periodic physical examinations. In many cases these types of physical problems can be detected and appropriate action taken. But left undetected the employee may become aggressive, resulting in the filing of grievances and causing fellow workers considerable distress. The union grievance representative may often find that these types of cases present particularly difficult political problems. The filing of meritless grievances puts the union grievance representative in the position of having to tell an aggressive or hostile employee that his or her problem is not contractual. Frequently the employee may turn this hostility toward the union steward. The easy way out for the union steward is to file the grievance but not to press the point with management. This, however, may result in the grievance representatives undermining their own positions with their management counterparts. Then add to this complicated set of circumstances the grievant's disgruntled fellow employees and the union representative has a serious problem. The only course of action for the union grievance representative is to be honest with this type of grievant and tell them when their grievances have no merit. If possible it may be wise to offer to assist the employee in finding a solution to his or her real problem or seek the assistance of the firm's human relations department. Great care should obviously be taken in these types of cases.[1]

Drug abuse is another potential cause of symptomatic grievances. Drug abuse may produce grievances from two separate sources: discipline and irrational behavior. Drinking and other forms of drug abuse frequently result in discipline for absenteeism, possession of the drug on company property, and poor workmanship. These offenses are particularly troublesome because they require corrective or progressive discipline which may result in discipline being issued several times, resulting in grievances and arbitration which may be associated with discipline. Many employers have, in cooperation with the union, established drug abuse programs within the human relations section of their personnel departments and many smaller firms have taken parallel actions. These programs have been developed because the discipline-grievance cycle has proven to be of little or no value in eliminating drug abuse problems.

Family problems are also difficult to detect. Divorce, illness in the family, problems with children, and financial problems may all have an adverse effect on an employee's performance. Absences, grievances filed out of hostility, and morale problems are often associated with difficulties at home. Here again, many larger firms have employed counselors within their human relations sections to deal with diagnosed family problems. Union officers, especially in smaller bargaining units may personally know the grievant and often assist in the diagnosis of these types of problems. Firms without the resources to employ a psychologist or industrial sociologist have typically employed the discipline-grievance process or in more enlightened cases directed the employee to seek outside help. The basic solution here has been the same as with medical cases—if at all possible cure the problem rather than treat the symptom.

Self-actualization problems are more directly tied to the firm and the employee's role in the work place. Some employees assigned to routine

---

[1]See T.F.Connors, *Problems in Local Union Collective Bargaining*, Detroit, MI: UAW-Solidarity House, 1975, for a discussion of how the UAW suggested that its grievance representatives handle these and similar problems.

assembly or clerical jobs may become bored, frustrated, or even hostile while others take the assignment in stride. Where possible, many firms have rotated employees between jobs so that no employee is assigned to a particularly boring job for an excessive period of time. This is only possible when the contract allows management to assign employees to specific jobs within a job classification. The majority of labor contracts do not restrict management's ability to assign personnel within a job classification. A word of caution is appropriate—on occasion seniority employees have been known to grieve over such a rotation scheme since they often feel that they are entitled to an easier job because of their length of service. Most contracts, however, do not bestow such rights on employees for length of service.

Employees with college educations or who possess specific skills and high expectations may become a source of grievances. If unable to market their degrees or skills, they are often forced to take jobs for which they may feel overqualified. Frustration is sure to follow, especially if opportunities for advancement are limited. This frustration is quite likely to surface in the form of symptomatic grievances.

Employees who have physical or mental limitations or who are in some manner underqualified for the job to which they are assigned are subject to distress and frustration which may also result in grievances. Most labor agreements require trial periods and/or training for employees promoted to higher paying jobs and if wage increases are involved the potential for grievances is even greater. Where possible efficient screening and testing of employees for job assignments is worthwhile but in many cases simply too costly. Effective supervision and employee observation, therefore, may be the only viable alternative.

The final human relations category is social problems. This category encompasses personality conflicts between employees and their supervisors, emotionally disturbed individuals, racial tensions, sexual harassment and a whole array of similar problems. Few generalizations are possible concerning this category. Employees with emotional problems fit well into the medical category; however, the remainder of these problems typically require fair and firm administration of the contract and personnel policies. Where such problems have reached major magnitudes they are rarely solved without active union cooperation.

Grievances generated by internal union politics represent a no-win situation for managers. What management must understand is that unions are political organizations. Differences are bound to arise between cliques or factions of labor unions. Occasionally, however, a union faction may utilize the grievance procedure for political gain. For example, if one political faction of the union wins the elective office of grievance representative the other faction may attempt to embarrass the representative by filing grievances which the union cannot be reasonably expected to win. Typically issues not covered by the contract or covered by unclear language which generate rank–and–file emotions and support are the targets of such political abuses of the grievance procedure. A strict neutral position by management concerning union politics has proven to be the best prevention of this type of grievance. Special efforts to resolve grievances presented by one political faction of the union typically precipitate grievances in protest from the other political factions. Management, in spite of its good intentions, will inevitably find itself embroiled in internal union affairs resulting in an accelerating use of the grievance procedure for political purposes. The union and its membership must be exceedingly careful about allowing the grievance procedure to be used for political purposes. The union could easily undermine its credibility with management and its membership if politics are allowed to surface in the grievance procedure.

Finally, a symptomatic grievance designed to highlight unfavorable contract provisions should be recognized for what it is, a bargaining tactic to bring about change in contract provisions. For example, if the contract does not limit management's right to temporarily transfer employees the union may file grievances when management exercises this prerogative. Seniority and union recognition clauses are often cited as the contractual basis for such grievances but temporary transfers are the real problem. Studies of the frequency of grievance filing show that the number of grievances filed increases as contract expiration dates draw near. Not only will this tactic be utilized to change specific contract provisions but also to attempt to gain a general advantage in negotiations. This overloading of the grievance procedure has long been recognized as a favorite bargaining tactic of unions. As such, symptomatic grievances of this nature have best been handled at the negotiation table and not during the administration of a soon to expire contract. Unions should be cautious about employing such bargaining tactics. Unsettled meritless grievances do not constitute bargaining power. Sophisticated management negotiators will typically not be moved by the quantity of grievances unless there is merit to the allegations. A real danger of workstoppage is associated with this union tactic. If valuable negotiation time is diverted to the discussion of meritless grievances filed purely to attain bargaining power then less time may be available to discuss substantive issues and the strike deadline may overtake the negotiations before attention is turned to real issues.

The Grievance Procedure

The grievance procedure stands as the cornerstone of the system of industrial relations law.[2] This mechanism performs the same function for the labor contract that the multi-tiered court system performs for the body of federal, state, and local law. The grievance structure is the method through which the collective bargaining agreement is interpreted and given meaning as the contract is applied and administered by management and the union in the day-to-day operation of the firm.[3] Further, just as the court structure provides due process for the protection of the rights of the general citizenry, the grievance structure provides due process for the protection of the contractual rights of employees.

[2]Management is universally precluded from the use of the grievance procedure; however, the disciplinary procedure serves essentially the same purpose.

[3]In those cases where a formal collective bargaining agreement does not exist (i.e., non-union firms), management-determined personnel policies and rules constitute the equivalent of the private contract law.

The specific form that the grievance procedure takes will vary substantially from one employment relationship to the next, depending upon the individual needs, personalities, characteristics, and circumstances of each relationship. In short, there is not one structural form of the grievance procedure appropriate for every employment relationship. Labor and management should adopt the structure that best facilitates the prompt and impartial settlement of grievances within their bargaining relationship.

Typically the formal grievance procedure will consist of from three to five steps, depending on the size of the firm and the degree to which grievance settlement authority is delegated within the firm and the union. The initial step in the grievance settlement process typically is informal discussions between the dissatisfied or aggrieved employee and his or her supervisor. In these preliminary discussions many misunderstandings and differences can be straightened out without resort to the formal grievance procedure. In fact, many firms and unions experience a settlement rate approaching ninety percent at this initial step.[4] The first step in the formal grievance procedure (which is the second step in the overall settlement process in many agreements) is to commit the grievance and the circumstances surrounding it to writing, its signing by the grievant and the union grievance representative and its presentation to the grievant's supervisor for an answer. In general discussions concerning the allegation will occur in an attempt to settle the grievance and management will answer the grievance in writing, either remedying the alleged violation or denying the grievance. If the grievance is denied by the supervisor then it will proceed through the formal grievance procedure. The intermediate steps in the procedure involve progressively higher levels of management and union representation until the grievance reaches the firm's top personnel or labor relations officer and the union's top grievance representative. If no settlement is reached by the time the grievance has reached the highest grievance officers the union may then demand that the dispute be submitted to arbitration, which management is obligated to grant if the contract contains an arbitration clause.

At each step in this procedure there are generally time limits imposed. For example, if an employee believes he or she has been denied rights under the contract then the employee must file the grievance within some specified period of time, generally three to five working days. Management is then required to answer the grievance within a specified period of time, generally three to five working days. If the union is dissatisfied with management's response then the steward must process the grievance to the next step within some specified period of time; five working days is not uncommon. This process continues until all internal remedies have been exhausted, at which time the union may demand arbitration (but must do so within the time limit specified in the contract). Any of these time limits may be extended by mutual consent; however, if one party or the other unilaterally fails to comply with the time requirements they risk an adverse arbitration award.[5]

[4]An employer may not require that the first step in the grievance settlement process exclude the union. See *NLRB* v *Lakeland Bus Lines, Inc.*, 187 F. (2d) 888 (1960) and *Miranda Fuel Company*, 140 NLRB 181 (1963).

[5]See doctrine of laches in Chapter 13.

BOX 11–1. Characteristics of Effective Grievance Procedures

1. Collective bargaining agreements should contain provisions that grievances and disputes involving the interpretation or application of the terms of the agreement are to be settled without resort to strikes, lockouts, or other interruptions to normal operations by an effective grievance procedure with arbitration as its final step.
2. To be effective, the procedure established for the settlement of such grievances and disputes should meet at least the following standards:
   a. The successive steps in the procedure, the method of presenting grievances or disputes, and the method of taking an appeal from one step to another should be so clearly stated in the agreement as to be readily understood by all employees, union officials, and management representatives.
   b. The procedure should be adaptable to the handling of the various types of grievances and disputes which come under the terms of the agreement.
   c. The procedure should be designed to facilitate the settlement of grievances and disputes as soon as possible after they arise. To this end:
      (1) The agreement should provide adequate stated times limits for the presentation of grievances and disputes, the rendering of decisions, and the taking of appeals.
      (2) Issues should be clearly formulated at the earliest possible moment. In all cases which cannot be settled in the first informal discussions, the positions of both sides should be reduced to writing.
      (3) Management and the union should encourage their representatives to settle at the lower steps grievances which do not involve broad questions of policy or of contract interpretation and should delegate sufficient authority to them to accomplish this end.
      (4) The agreement should provide adequate opportunity for both parties to investigate grievances under discussion.
      (5) Provision should be made for priority handling of grievances involving discharge, suspension, or other disciplinary action.
   d. The procedure should be open to the submission of grievances by all parties to the agreement.
3. Managements and unions should inform and train their representatives in the proper functioning of the grievance procedure and in their responsibilities under it. In such a program it should be emphasized:
   a. That the basic objective of the grievance procedure is the achievement of sound and fair settlements and not the 'winning' of cases;
   b. That the filing of grievances should be considered by foremen or supervisors as aids in discovering and removing causes of discontent in their departments;

Box 11–1. (continued)

   c. That any tendency by either party to support the earlier decisions of its representatives when such decisions are wrong should be discouraged.

   d. That the willingness of management and union officials to give adequate time and attention to the handling and disposition of grievances and disputes is necessary to the effective functioning of the procedure;

   e. That for the sound handling of grievances and disputes both management and union representatives should be thoroughly familiar with the entire collective bargaining agreement.

Source: The President's National Labor-Management Conference, No. 5–30, 1945, (U.S. Department of Labor, Division of Labor Standards, Bulletin No. 77, pp. 45–46, 1946).

BOX 11–2. A Steel Worker's Grievance Procedure

Section 1

Should any grievance or differences arise between the Company and its employees, or the Union, as to the meaning and application of the provisions of this Agreement, or should any local trouble of any kind arise in the plant, an earnest effort shall be made to settle the same promptly in the following manner.

Section 2

First: Any employee who believes that he has a justifiable complaint or grievance shall discuss the complaint or grievance with his foreman, with or without the stewart or committeeman of the department being present, as the employee may elect, in an attempt to settle same. However, any such employee may instead report the matter directly to his stewart or zone committeeman and in such event, the stewart or committeeman shall take it up with the foreman. If the grievance is handled by the zone committeeman without a steward, the chairman of the grievance committee or the Union President shall be called promptly if such committeeman considers the grievance of urgent nature.

   a. In the absence of a steward in his department and committeeman in his zone, an employee may notify his foreman who shall call a committeeman from some other zone or the chairman or president.

Box 11–2. (continued)

Section 3

Second: If no settlement is reached, the grievance or difference shall be reduced to writing and presented to the foreman for an answer in writing, which shall be given within three (3) working days. If the Committee decides that the grievance is valid, the same shall be presented by the complaining employee, and/or the Committee to the Company at a regular or special meeting. The Company shall have until the next regular meeting, after such filing to give their decisions, except in discharge cases the Company's decision will be given within three (3) working days. Any grievance not settled in any one meeting shall automatically be carried over to the next meeting. All grievances shall be presented to the Company in writing within thirty (30) working days after knowledge of the cause of such grievances except grievances pertaining to standard hours.

Section 4

Third: If no settlement is reached the matter may then be presented by the Union to a representative of the National organization of the Union and the matter may then be presented at a meeting attended by the complaining employee, the Shop Committee, the representative of the National organization and the Company.

Section 5

Fourth: If the differences shall not have been satisfactorily settled in the manner previously provided, then the matter may be appealed to an impartial arbitrator to be appointed by method mutually agreed upon by the Company and the Union; if such appointment cannot be mutually agreed upon, then an arbitrator shall be selected under the rules of the American Arbitration Association, provided it is the type of case on which an arbitrator is authorized to rule. Cases not appealed to the arbitrator within twenty-one (21) days from the date of decision after third step shall be considered settled on the basis of the decision given. The arbitrator shall hear the facts presented by both parties and the complaining employee, including any written briefs prepared by either party. The expense and salary incident to the services of the arbitrator shall be paid one-half by the Company and one-half by the Union and all other expenses shall be borne by the party incurring them. In the case of grievances resulting from conditions described in Article VIII, VIII(A), VIII(B), VIII(C) and VIII(E), the impartial arbitrator shall be one who is versed in Industrial Engineering and the C.W.S. Job Evaluation Manual.

Box 11–2. (continued)

Section 6

Powers of the arbitrator are to rule in all cases where differences exist as to interpretation of contract.

Section 7

The arbitrator shall have no power to add to or subtract from or modify any of the terms of this Agreement nor to establish or change any wage rate, nor to rule on any dispute arising regarding production standards, except as provided for under Section 5 of this Article. Any case appealed to an arbitrator, on which he has no power to rule shall be referred back to the parties without decision.

Section 8

The arbitrator shall have no power to order back pay in any case of a shutdown, strike or stoppage.

Section 9

Grievance cases resulting from conditions described in Articles VIII, VIII(A), VIII(B), VIII(C) and VIII(E), may, for the purpose of expediting the permanent setting of standards, have the Second and Third Steps of the Grievance procedure combined provided an International Representative of the Union is present. If an agreement is not reached in the Third Step, then immediately the problem will be submitted to a special committee of two (2) members from the Union and two (2) members from Management who will use whatever methods as may consist of all day time studies or of four (4) or eight (8) hour test runs by the regular operator of the job or jobs involved. The committee shall be guided by Articles VIII, VIII(A), VIII(B), VIII(C) and VIII(E), of the contract. Any settlement agreed upon shall be final and shall apply retroactively to date of institution of grievance. If settlement is not reached by the four (4) man committee within a reasonable period of time, the Union may request arbitration as outlined in Section 5 of this Article. The arbitrator selected to resolve the dispute may, at his discretion, make an actual study of the disputed standard and shall determine whether or not the standard is equitable. If the arbitrator finds the standard inequitable to either party, he shall establish a proper standard consistent with the provisions set forth under Article VIII for setting such standards. The findings and decisions of the arbitrator shall be binding on both parties. The Company and the Union shall share equally the cost of his services.

Box 11–2. (continued)

Section 10

International representatives, or any other duly accredited Union representatives, shall have access to the Company's premises at all reasonable times, after reporting to the Company's Personnel Office, for the purpose of conferring with management or with local Union representatives regarding grievances or other matters involving the relations between the parties, provided the Company has received proper notification from the International Union, authorizing such person or persons to act as representatives.

Section 11

When there is a dispute concerning rates, job classifications, or incentive plans the Company shall furnish to the Union such information concerning rates, job classifications, or incentive plans as may be applicable to the dispute, upon request.

Provided by the United Steelworkers of America.

An effectively operating grievance procedure is the basis for a peaceful collective bargaining relation. If the grievance procedure functions properly it will seldom be noticed. Let the grievance procedure fail, however, and it will become the source of major difficulties and maybe even open hostilities.

Fortunately the majority of grievance procedures in this country effectively and peacefully perform the function for which they were designed. There are characteristics common to properly functioning grievance procedures. These characteristics were first described by the President's National Labor-Management Conference in 1945. These observations are as relevant today as they were at the end of World War II.

The grievance procedure presented in Box 11–2 is offered as an example of the typical grievance procedure contained in United Steelworkers of America contracts. The student should compare these provisions with the recommended grievance procedure characteristics outlined in Box 11–1.

The Duty to Fairly Represent

Unions are obligated to fairly represent all members of the bargaining unit for which they were certified as the exclusive bargaining representative. The union may not discriminate against an employee on the basis of race, sex, religion, or lack of union membership. This principle was first announced in a landmark Supreme Court decision concerning the Railway Labor Act[6] and its application was extended to the Taft-Hartley Act eleven years later.[7]

In *Vaca* v. *Sipes*[8], the United States Supreme Court was presented with a case in which an employee filed suit against his union for breach of its duty to fairly represent him. The employee, Mr. Owens, had been on sick leave and when he was discharged from the hospital attempted to return to work. Mr. Owens suffered from high blood pressure and the employer's physician stated that if Mr. Owens returned to work his health would be endangered. When Mr. Owens attempted to return to work his employer discharged him. The union represented Mr. Owens through the grievance procedure but then refused to arbitrate his grievance because a doctor employed by the union examined Mr. Owens and stated that he concurred with the company's physician. Mr. Owens then sued in state court alleging that his union failed to fairly represent him. The state court awarded Mr. Owens damages but the U.S. Supreme Court reversed the lower court. The Supreme Court ruled that the courts as well as the NLRB have jurisdiction in this area. The Court further ruled that the courts were not to substitute their opinion concerning the merits of the case for the union's. If no evidence is presented that the union's refusal to arbitrate was made in bad–faith then the courts may not second-guess the union. The union is not required to take all grievances to arbitration but it must decide whether to take a grievance to arbitration on the merits of the case in an honest, good-faith and nondiscriminatory manner. The Court's reasoning was that if a union was required to demand arbitration in every grievance case the union could become financially unable to properly represent the bargaining unit as well as overloading the nation's private arbitrators.

The *Vaca* v. *Sipes* decision points out an interesting problem with the grievance-arbitration process. Management may have an incentive to force grievances to the arbitration process. Management's actions are appealed in the grievance procedure; therefore an appealed managerial decision will remain in force unless management reverses its own decision or the arbitrator overturns it. Given the nature of the grievance-arbitration process if the union is dissatisfied with management's final answer the union must expend its limited financial resources to obtain an arbitrator's award. However, there is no guarantee that an arbitrator's award will be favorable. If the union is placed in the position of having to take every unsatisfactorily answered grievance to arbitration then management could easily bankrupt the union. Even under the principle established under *Vaca* v. *Sipes*, management still has a strong incentive to force cases to arbitration, tying up union financial resources and possibly erroding the union's bargaining power. This management strategy is especially effective with small bargaining units and bargaining units without union security clauses which have relatively small percentages of union members.

---

[6]*Steele* v. *Louisville & Nashville Railroad*, 323 U.S. 192 (1944).

[7]*Syres* v. *Oil Worker Local 23*, 350 U.S. 892 (1955)

[8]*Vaca* v. *Sipes*, 386 U.S. 171, (1967)

In the *Anchor Motor Freight*[9] case the Supreme Court was presented with a case involving a different aspect of fair representation. In this case eight truck drivers were discharged for allegedly filing false reimbursement vouchers for motel expenses. The union failed to fully investigate the circumstances concerning the allegations. As it turned out the truck drivers were actually charged the amount they claimed and the motel clerk was the thief. This information was not discovered before the arbitration hearing and therefore the arbitrator upheld the discharges. After the arbitrator's award was issued, the additional evidence was obtained, and the employees sued the union and the company. The lower federal courts refused to overturn the arbitrator's award because of the Supreme Court's decision in *Enterprise Wheel & Car Corporation*[10] in which the Court removed judicial review of arbitrator's awards. The Supreme Court reviewed the *Anchor Motor Freight* case and reversed the lower courts. The Supreme Court reasoned that when a union fails to provide fair representation which results in an adverse award then the wrongly discharged employees are entitled to an appropriate remedy. The Court ruled that the union and the employer would be required to bear the burden of the remedy. The employees were ordered to be reinstated with backpay paid jointly and shared equally by the union and the employer. The reasoning for the equal sharing of the backpay was that management wrongly discharged the employees and the union provided inadequate representation in the grievance–arbitration process.[11]

Minimization of Grievances

Grievances are costly to both management and labor. Every grievance diverts resources away from the normal operation of the firm and the union to the dispute settlement process. Grievances which are unresolved in the grievance procedure must be settled in the arbitration process (or worse by strike or law suit) which may cost the parties thousands of dollars per grievance. In addition to these obvious costs, there are long-run costs resulting from the harmful impact that grievances have on the labor-management relationship. At best, grievance resolution is a *negative sum game*. The *winner* of the dispute simply regains whatever it was that was threatened or lost as a result of the other party's action; there is rarely a net gain. *Victory* neither removes the antagonism generated by the grievance and the resulting harm done to the relationship nor does it recover the resources spent by both sides during settlement.

As substantial as the costs of grievance resolution are, these costs are insignificant in comparison to the benefits produced by an efficiently function-ing procedure. Further, these costs can and have been reduced by manage-

[9]*Hines* v. *Anchor Motor Freight*, 424 U.S. 554 (1976).

[10]*Steelworkers* v. *Enterprise Wheel & Car Corp.* 363 U.S. 593 (1960); see Chapter 13 for further discussion.

[11]See Chapter 13 for a detailed discussion of the impact of the *Anchor Motor Freight* decision on the arbitration process.

ment's adoption of an appropriate philosophy of contract administration. In those labor-management relationships where the grievance procedure has become overtaxed (i.e., where the costs of grievance resolution are unacceptably high), this state of affairs can, at least in part, be traced to the philosophy of contract administration.

Minimizing Grievance Costs by an Appropriate Philosophy of Contract Administration

The grievance procedure is only as effective as the philosophy of contract administration that guides its use. The traditional action-reaction philosophy of contract administration by nature breeds mistrust and hostility, generating unnecessary and avoidable grievances. Openly hostile bargaining relations are rare in today's economy but when they are observed it is typically in new bargaining relationships. As the parties become more adept in their roles and the bargaining relation matures the philosophy of contract administration typically evolves through several stages.[12] These stages range in increasing order of maturity (maturity is not necessarily a function of the age of the bargaining relation) from: (1) hostility; (2) armed truce; (3) power bargaining; (4) accommodation; to (5) cooperation. As the bargaining relation matures the parties learn to communicate with one another. Trust and understanding frequently develop, making the job of contract administration easier for both parties. Effective grievance management requires a philosophy of contract administration that not only views the grievance procedure as the most important communications vehicle of the labor-management relationship, but also accepts the systematic elimination of the underlying causes of grievances as the basis for minimizing grievances. Once adopted, what will be called the *developing communication* philosophy of contract administration will make it easier to put into operation the techniques that reduce the number of grievances.

Techniques for Grievance Minimization

"An ounce of prevention is worth a pound of cure" is an old adage applicable to grievance administration. The following methods of grievance minimization have been utilized in a wide cross section of bargaining relations; however, the success of each is dependent upon the nature and circumstances of the individual bargaining relation. Which techniques are employed will also depend upon the maturity of the bargaining relationship. Elaborate grievance minimization techniques normally require a cooperative philosophy of grievance administration. The appropriate philosophy is the product of years of experience and interaction between the parties; it is an unrealistic expectation in newly established relationships that may have experienced long and bitter union organizational drives. Unfortunately where grievance minimization is most typically needed is in newly established bargaining relations. However,

[12] See Benjamin M. Selekman, *Labor Relations and Human Performance*, New York: McGraw-Hill Book Company, 1974, for a further discussion of these stages.

the process of grievance administration can benefit from minimization techniques at even the most matured evolutionary stages. These remarks apply to both management and the union and require the active and honest participation of both parties if they are to be successful.

Table Bargaining

An efficiently functioning grievance–arbitration procedure reflects the wisdom, foresight, and hard work of labor and management during contract negotiations. There is no single technique more important or simple for preventing grievances than clear and adequate contract language. Any and all questions that the contracting parties have in their own minds concerning the phrasing, wording, and meaning of specific clauses should be raised *and* resolved at the time of the table bargaining sessions. If separate *articles of understanding* are necessary to pinpoint the meaning of contract provisions, labor and management are wise to put forth the extra effort required to write such additions to the agreement.[13] Otherwise, grievances will invariably arise in these same areas during contract administration.

A serviceable contract provision not only requires clear meaning but also must meet the needs of the contract parties. A sure way to generate grievances is for labor and management to adopt language simply because that language has been successful elsewhere. Each bargaining relationship is unique; language that has served one relationship well will not necessarily be functional for another. Hence, contractual provisions should be tailored to meet the specific and disparate needs of each labor-management relationship.

Understanding the Contract

Does a serviceable collective bargaining agreement, the provisions of which are clear and specific as to meaning, reduce the number of grievances? The answer to this question is definitely no unless the contract is read and understood by those charged with the responsibility of administering the document. Effective grievance management demands that management and union personnel at all levels be well-educated as to the letter and intent of each contract clause. A particularly effective method of familiarizing supervisory and union personnel with the contract is through the use of joint training sessions, with labor–management negotiators acting as training session group leaders. As the contract is read from beginning to end, supervisors and union representatives should be given the opportunity to raise substantive questions as to the meaning of each contract provision. Where questions do arise, these may be resolved in consensus fashion before moving on to other provisions. For example, if a contract specifies that temporary layoffs shall be of no longer than five days duration, does this mean five working days or five calendar days, and are paid holidays included within this five day limitation? If a contract requires

---

[13] This is a common method employed by management and unions to clarify contract language on personnel policies during the life of the contract or to handle short-run problems. For example, see the GM-UAW contract negotiated in 1979.

that temporary layoffs are to be by seniority, what is the appropriate seniority unit, by plant, department, or job classification? These types of questions will produce answers that clarify the contract and make administration more effective and less likely to produce disagreements. A second round of meetings between union representatives and rank-and-file members is then required to inform employees about the consensus meaning of contract provisions settled upon in the labor-management joint training sessions. In short, the training sessions and meetings are intended to, as far as is possible, weed-out misunderstanding as a potential cause of grievances.

These joint training sessions have proven useful in reducing grievances in four other important ways.

First, negotiators, aware of the fact that the product of their bargaining efforts will be closely examined and that they will be questioned on the meaning of provisions by those groups they represent, will have a greater incentive to *tailor* a clear and adequate contract.

Second, the sessions give upper-echelon management the opportunity to interact with first-line supervisors. Effective contract administration should be stressed in these meetings as the critical factor for the achievement of individual production goals. Since rewards are normally tied to the achievement of production goals, first-line supervisors will develop a greater commitment to effective contract administration.

Three, union leadership and grievance representatives will have an opportunity to interact with the rank–and–file union membership. Employees will become more informed as to what their rights are and union officials will have an opportunity to ascertain the desires and concerns of the union membership. The result should be better understanding between the membership and their officers hence better grievance administration.

Finally, joint training sessions promote an atmosphere of cooperation and understanding characteristic of mature bargaining relationships. This will tend to reduce the number of grievances resulting from intentional contract violations and misunderstanding. Many unions conduct their own training sessions independent of management and a significant number of companies utilize similar techniques. These are positive steps since internal communication is important. However in the authors' view this is a second best solution since union interaction with management is not facilitated.

Contract Administration

Although effective table bargaining plus familiarity with the meaning of contract provisions will eliminate many of the causes of grievances, these techniques need to be supplemented by a philosophy that eliminates the incentives to file grievances.

The *developing communication* philosophy of contract administration discussed earlier reduces misunderstandings and eliminates incentives to file grievances. Indeed, joint training sessions are but the first important aspect of this philosophy. The training sessions demonstrate management concern for the protection of employee contractual rights. If successful, there will be fewer management contract infractions that lead to grievances and as a result of the atmosphere of trust and cooperation created by the training sessions, employees will be less inclined to perceive and file grievances.

The second important component of the *developing communication* philosophy of contract administration (i.e., the component responsible for reduced incentives to file grievances) is the "firm but fair" approach to grievance settlement. Employees often become aggressive simply because they have discovered that aggressive behavior yields results. Self-interest motivates employees to take advantage of any opportunity to achieve rights and privileges not specified by the contract. Union grievance representatives must be especially careful to weed-out meritless grievances to insure that union resources are wisely used and that meritless grievances cannot serve to undermine the union's credibility.

The grievance procedure, not to mention the contract, is undermined whenever management takes a reasonable position on the disputed issue but yields in the face of actual or threatened economic pressure. The "firm but fair"approach to grievance resolution requires management to investigate all relevant facts fully, to analyze applicable contract provisions carefully, to develop a reasonable position on the basis of the information at its disposal, and to adhere firmly to its position when challenged. This approach does not mean that management should not listen to opposing arguments, cannot be swayed by convincing evidence, will not change its position if proven wrong, or will not renegotiate weak or inoperative contract provisions. The "firm but fair" policy, however, does mean that management will not yield to actual or threatened pressure. Consider the case where a member of supervision lays a worker off, as the contract specifies, because of a necessity to reduce the work force and the employee has the lowest seniority in his unit. The union then produces proof that the employee was wrongly laid off because the seniority list was in error. It is an unreasonable position for management to contend that the seniority list, correct or incorrect, must be the basis for its decision and refuse to reinstate the wronged employee with the backpay due him. On the other hand, if the union threatens to strike over an issue on which management has taken the correct action, it is unreasonable for management to change its position purely on the basis of a union's threat to strike. This approach to grievance administration reduces grievances whereas a policy of appeasement or inflexibility encourages them. The union must also demonstrate a responsible use of its economic power. Threats of strike must be reserved for issues that are of sufficient importance for such drastic action; otherwise the union may find itself in the position of having to prove its desire and ability to strike.

The *developing communication* philosophy of contract administration is incompatible with permitting past practices to develop that contravene the language and spirit of the labor agreement. The "firm but fair" approach to contract administration is less likely to produce past practices which are inconsistent with the contract. If such a body of contradictory past practices develop they serve only to increase the incentives for employees to file grievances. On the other hand, past practice that is mutual in nature and that clarifies ambiguous contract language reinforces the recommended philosophy of contract administration by strengthening cooperation.

In many agreements labor and management have incorporated or appended to the contract a statement detailing the role past practice is to play in the bargaining relationship. For example, in the building trades where the hiring hall is used and many different employers work with the same union, a *totality of agreement* clause is frequently adopted. This clause simply states that past practices have *no* contractual status. This type of language is necessary in bargaining relations where there are many different employers each with different needs and personnel requirements; otherwise a confusing mire of contradictory past practices are likely to develop serving only to make the contract more difficult to administer.

Human Relations

A well-structured grievance procedure, based on the *developing communication* philosophy of contract administration, meets employee needs for security, participation, and recognition, thereby eliminating some of the causes of symptomatic grievances. However, it cannot, nor should it try to eliminate the frustration of each employee based on personal inadequacies and failure in job and non-job related areas. In trying to do everything for every employee, the grievance procedure would become overtaxed and less effective in all areas. What is required is a supplement to the grievance procedure and philosophy of contract administration such as a human relations or education program that can attend to and reduce the causes of symptomatic grievances. Unions should play an active role in these efforts. In some cases where management has failed in this responsibility unions have taken steps in this area.[14]

In the wake of growing worker alienation in recent years, many firms have established human relations departments to handle employee problems and complaints, regardless of origin. These departments are designed to reduce symptomatic grievances by helping employees with personal problems that lead either to job-related problems (e.g., drunkenness) that end in disciplinary actions and accompanying grievances or to the filing of trivial grievances because of frustration. Since many human relations departments operate more or less independently of the industrial relations departments, employees typically do not perceive the departments as posing a threat to them through contract administration and enforcement. Human relations department's services have included general employee counseling, referral of employees to private and community organizations for specialized counseling, removal of or additional training for supervisors insensitive to employee needs, promotion or transfer of previously over-qualified personnel, additional training and schooling (at company expense) of under-qualified employees, and the establishment of a system of rewards for cost-minimizing suggestions (e.g., the suggestion box). Similar types of departments have proven worthwhile for many firms where grievance procedures have become burdened by symptomatic grievances.

[14] For example, drug abuse problems have been addressed by a number of unions through education and counseling programs.

Summary and Conclusions

Grievances are based on the contract. The employee attains his rights through the contract and may grieve over the loss of those rights only as specified by the labor agreement. The causes of grievances are many and varied but may be generally categorized as: (1) intentional violations; (2) misunderstandings; and (3) symptomatic grievances.

The grievance procedure employed by the parties to collective bargaining is a multistep procedure. Typically, specific time limits are placed on the filing, answering and appealing of the grievance to the next step in the procedure. The union is required to fairly represent all members of the bargaining unit in good–faith; failure to do so could result in a law suit or unfair labor practice charges. This, however, does not require all grievances to be processed to arbitration so long as the union fairly represents the members of the bargaining unit honestly and without discrimination.

Successful use of techniques to minimize grievances requires establishing an appropriately structured, widely understood, and efficiently functioning grievance procedure. It also calls for the adoption of a clinical approach to contract administration. Such an approach views the grievance procedure as the most important communications vehicle in the labor-management relationship. It accepts the need to systematically eliminate the underlying causes of grievances as the basis of effective contract administration.

Reducing the number of grievances also requires an atmosphere of trust and cooperation. Honesty and credibility are absolute prerequisites for the development of this atmosphere. Dishonesty, more than any other factor, can destroy progress toward grievance minimization. It undermines cooperation, thereby scuttling the possibility of collective problem-solving.

Grievances will always occur, but they need not be numerous, burden the grievance procedure, nor weaken the bargaining relationship if approached with honesty and a spirit of cooperation. In short, effective grievance management requires a strong joint labor-management commitment to eliminate the underlying causes.

COMMENTARY: Mr. C. Neil Norgren Speaks on the Topic of the Grievance Procedure.

Mr. C. Neil Norgren is President of C. A. Norgren Company, a manufacturing firm specializing in the production of pneumatic products based in Littleton, Colorado. Mr. Norgren joined the firm in 1938 and has held several managerial and executive positions prior to becoming President in 1962. In addition he serves as a member of the board of directors of several other firms. Mr. Norgren is a veteran of World War II serving his country as a member of the U.S. Army Air Corps.

Mr. Norgren attended the University of Colorado and has remained a resident of the Denver area since that time. He is very active in civic, service and social affairs in Denver. Among his various activities he is one of the co-founders and a past President of the Denver Executive Club and has served in various capacities in organizations such as University of Colorado Foundation, Arapahoe County Community Chest, Mile High United Way, and the American Cancer Society as well as numerous industry and business organizations.

A grievance procedure in any industrial relations program, if administered fairly and impartially, does provide the worker with unbiased arbitration, eliminates fear of reprisal, and maintains job preservation. A sound grievance procedure also provides the worker with an avenue of recourse to prejudicial supervision. A grievance procedure must be an impartial and speedy review of an individual's complaint, with the capability of being heard in the final step by the officer of the company responsible for whatever location is involved if necessary. However, the legitimacy of the grievance procedure and its extensive use can be blamed on an unenlightened and uncaring management. Every individual, regardless of his or her station in life or his or her job responsibility, is entitled to be treated with human dignity and recognition of his or her human needs and desires.

An enlightened management, who has a sincere and genuine interest in the welfare of his or her fellow workers, will provide not only the working environment for a clean and safe work place, but will provide the leadership for a supervisory staff that is also geared to a "people oriented" responsibility. If supervision is working with the hourly employee for the best interests of the customer and granting the employee the respect of a human being to which he is entitled, then the problems associated with a grievance procedure are greatly diminished and oftentimes can be resolved without the formality of a grievance procedure.

In order to work toward establishing a grievance-procedure-free atmosphere, management must genuinely, sincerely, and honestly want to recognize the needs of his or her employees as individuals and make every effort to satisfy these needs within the economic capability of the company for which he or she is responsible. Management can do this through many avenues, e.g., attitude surveys and their follow-up, comprehensive wage and fringe benefit studies and maintenance of them, personal contact and interest, a clean and safe working environment, development of an atmosphere of mutual trust and respect, helping to create an attitude of pride in one's job and work place, receptiveness to the legitimate suggestions of those people whom he or she supervises, a genuine interest in the welfare of his or her fellow worker. A grievance procedure is a very necessary avenue of job security; but oftentimes an avenue of hostility. I am suggesting that a "caring" management cannot only minimize the number of grievance procedures but can eliminate the hostility in their application.

DISCUSSION QUESTIONS

1. If there is no contract can an employee still have a grievance? Is there a difference between a grievance and a grieveable issue under the contract?

2. Under what circumstances might management wish to intentionally violate a labor contract?.

3. Why is it important to minimize grievances? Under what circumstances might management or the union wish to maximize grievances?

4. What advantages are there in preventing grievances rather than solving them as they arise?

5. What, specifically, are the roles of management and the union in grievance administration? How do they differ? In what ways are they similar?

6. Compare and contrast symptomatic grievances with grievances caused by: (1) intentional violations and (2) misunderstanding. Might there be elements in common across these categories?

7. What is the central role of communication between the parties in grievance administration? Can grievances be effectively resolved without communication? Explain.

SELECTED REFERENCES

Ash, Philip, "The Parties to the Grievance," *Personnel Psychology* (Spring 1970), pp. 13–38.

Baer, Walter E., *Grievance Handling: 101 Guides for Supervisors*. New York: American Management Association, 1970.

Braun, Kurt, *Labor Disputes and Their Settlement*, Baltimore: The Johns Hopkins University Press, 1955.

Bureau of National Affairs, Inc., *Grievance Guide*, Washington, D.C.: BNA, 1978.

Chandler, Margaret K., *Management Rights and Union Interests*. New York: McGraw-Hill Book Company, 1964.

Corzine, James E., "Structure and Utilization of a Grievance Procedure," *Personnel Journal*, (September, 1967) **46:** 484–489.

Cox, Archibald, "Rights Under a Labor Agreement," *Harvard Law Review*, (February 1956) **69:** 601–657.

Helmes, Robert H., ed., *Handling Employee Grievances*, Chicago: Public Personnel Association, 1968.

Kuhn, James W., *Bargaining in Grievance Settlement*, New York: Columbia University Press, 1961.

Lapp, John A., *How to Handle Labor Grievances*, New York: National Foreman's Institute, Inc., 1945.

Somers, Gerald G., *Grievance Settlement in Coal Mining*, Morgantown: West Virginia University, Business and Economic Study, Vol. 4, No. 4, 1956.

Stagner, Ross and Hjalmar Rosen, *Psychology of Union Management Relations*, Delmont, Calif: Wadsworth, 1965.

Stone, Morris, *Labor Grievances and Decisions*, New York: Harper & Row, Publishers, 1965.

Trotta, Maurice S., *Handling Grievances: A Guide for Management and Labor*, Washington, D.C.: Bureau of National Affairs, Inc., 1976.

Whyte, W.F., *Pattern for Industrial Peace*, New York: Harper & Row, Publishers, 1951.

Chapter 12

Discipline and the Disciplinary Procedure

Discipline is of central importance to the efficient and orderly opera-tion of any organization yet it is one concept that is often misunder-stood and misapplied in the labor-management setting. In contract administration, discipline often demands much of the union steward's and manager's time and efforts. It is, therefore, important for the student of labor relations to understand the goals and mechanics of an effective disciplinary procedure. The topics to be discussed in this chapter are: (1) the nature, purpose, goals, and operation of the disciplinary procedure; (2) the nature of disciplinary offenses; (3) the appropriateness of penalties; and (4) the relation between arbitration and the disciplinary procedure.

Nature, Purpose, Goals, and Operation of the Disciplinary Procedure

There are three specific definitions offered by Webster's dictionary for the noun *discipline*. These are: "(1) instruction; training of the mind, or body, or the moral faculties; (2) subjection to authority; and (3) self control." Webster's dictionary defines the verb discipline in two ways "(1) to train, and (2) to improve behavior by judicious penal methods."

As should be obvious, discipline can be thought of in a passive and an active sense. In the passive sense, an employee's self control which is consistent with the firm's goals and needs is passive discipline. An employee who performs his assigned duties in a manner consistent with the expectations of management will need no corrective action applied by supervision. If management finds no disciplinary action necessary then the union will typically not need to take action. In the active sense discipline can be divided into two component parts—positive discipline and negative discipline. Positive disci-pline is the first of Webster's definitions of the noun discipline and the first of the two definitions of the verb. Positive discipline involves the acquisition of skills, knowledge, atitudes, and a general employee conduct which furthers the goals of the firm. Organizational behaviorists have devoted a great deal of effort to examining such concepts as motivation, incentives and communication which are related to the positive disciplining of a work force. More directly related to the idea of positive discipline, however, are training and positive reinforcement of desired behavior (which will be discussed later in this chapter). Negative discipline is the adversive control of behavior. Again negative discipline requires, as does positive discipline, an action on the part of management which may, in turn, require a reaction by the union. Management, once it has identified sources of disorder or inefficiency, must promulgate rules which prohibit such activity and outline penalties that the offender should expect. Once the rules and penalties are in place management must then fairly and firmly administer its policies so as to assure their creditability and effectiveness.

Positive discipline is involved with the union-management relation in several ways. First the incentive system of the firm is typically structured around the economic package and administrative issues such as promotion, transfer, layoffs and training programs. These items are subject to collective bargaining. Since the goals of labor and management frequently differ concerning these issues a positive disciplinary program may be substantially modified by the union's input through bargaining. For example, management may perceive that after so many parts are produced during an eight hour shift a manufacturing employee should be compensated at a higher rate for each additional part produced. The union is likely to object to this incentive program for several reasons. First, such an incentive system may have the effect of putting union members out of work since increased output is likely, at least in the short run. Secondly, employees may rush their work or become unduly fatigued resulting in an increased burden on the disciplinary/grievance procedure through discipline for absenteeism or poor workmanship. Finally, the incentive structure may result in increased competition between union members which could result in political problems for the union.

Negative discipline may be appropriate to modify certain behaviors while positive discipline should be used in other cases. It is important to properly diagnose the causes of unacceptable or marginal behavior and apply the appropriate corrective tools. Frequently management will find it necessary to punish wrong behavior or even rid the firm of useless or counterproductive employees. Often positive incentives can be utilized to elicit favorable responses in particular areas. However, with varying forms of unacceptable behavior, these incentives prove to be an inappropriate modification technique. For example, it is inappropriate to offer a monetary reward to habitual absentees if they improve their attendance. First, this incentive may be perceived by employees who regularly attend work as inequitable and may result in more individual workers becoming absentee problems so that they too may "correct" their problem and share in the benefits. Secondly, compensation to an individual to comply with minimum job requirements is the wage that he earns; therefore additional rewards are inappropriate and are unlikely to elicit the desired response. The "stick" or discipline is the appropriate response in these cases. If an employee fails in his responsibility to come to work the employer must use "corrective" discipline. Corrective discipline, in this sense, means warning the employee he is following the wrong path and that if further penalties are to be avoided he must modify his behavior to be consistent with the requirements of his job. If the employee is allowed to continue being excessively absent, as in the case of no disciplinary procedure, then he will "learn" that there is no possibility of an adverse disciplinary action befalling him or her.

In cases which involve extreme antisocial behavior or cases in which it becomes apparent that the employee cannot render services to the firm which are of value then the employer is left with little recourse but to terminate the employer-employee relation with the individual. The first point is easily illustrated in the case of assaulting a member of supervision. Assault is a crime in society; it is disruptive of production activities, and is an offense which lends considerable doubt as to the predictability of the employee's future behavior. Discharge is an appropriate management response in such serious cases. Not only does it remove an employee whose behavior is inconsistent with the objectives of management but it serves notice upon the remaining work force that such behavior will result in the loss of one's employment. The second point is illustrated in the case of an employee who is convicted of a felony and sentenced to a term in prison. The employee may not have committed the offense on company time or property but as a result of his actions he can no longer offer services to the firm. The employer may terminate the offender's employment on the basis that he will be forced to absent himself from his place of employment without *good reason*. In less serious cases where an employee has been shown to be incapable of continued service to the firm the employer may discharge the employee. For example, if the employee became totally disabled as the result of an automobile accident the employer may terminate the employer-employee relation with the individual; however, this is not generally considered a disciplinary discharge and carries no stigma of wrongdoing.

Throughout the following discussion it must be remembered that management has the right to require an employee to perform whatever tasks are assigned to her or him, except as limited by law, the contract, or obvious danger to personal safety. If an employee fails to comply with the proper directives of management he or she is subject to discipline. Discipline, however, must be issued for just cause (or simply, cause; they are equivalent terms). What constitutes just cause is to be found in the shop disciplinary rules and labor contract. Just cause for discipline is limited to actions which directly impact upon the efficient, safe and orderly operation of the firm. For example, failure to maintain personal appearance standards may be just cause for discipline in the case of a sales clerk (or any other employee which has personal contact with the firm's customers) but for other classes of employees dress codes, hair cuts, or shaving rules may not be just cause for discipline, such as in the case of factory workers or coal miners.

Just cause for discipline is a contractual consideration in the operation of the disciplinary procedure; however, there are behavioral considerations also. Management must ascertain the causes and factors contributing to employee behavior to determine what corrective actions are most likely to assure employee compliance with management standards. To this end, performance analysis is a necessary component of any effective personnel policy and

---

BOX 12–1. The Problem of Discipline—An Excerpt from "Discipline and Discharge in the Unionized Firm" by Orme W. Phelps

Discipline, in one form or another, is an element of all organized activity. Its function is to maintain order by setting limits to individual behavior which may jeopardize the interests of the group. Discipline is essentially negative, operating through penalties for wrong behavior rather than rewards for right action, as in the case of incentives. With human beings, group discipline is not instinctive, as with insects and some animals. It must therefore be enforced. The manner of enforcement—raising questions of how, for what, and by whom—reacts in turn upon the morale of the organization. Justice aside, it is no easy thing to strike the proper balance between severity and leniency. In general, the answer has been cued to the needs of the system, tending toward rigor when times are difficult and toward relaxation when the permanence and prosperity of the group structure seem assured.

---

disciplinary procedure. Performance analysis is a term applied to the study of the factors resulting in employee's performance failures. Examination of these factors will lend insight into the motivations of employees to engage in certain activities or to refrain from others. Often it will be found that certain incentives may be in place in the firm's personnel policy which result in specific employee actions. For example, if packaging inspectors in a bakery are paid on the basis of piece rate but there is no method to document which inspector is responsible for which shipment of bread, then inspectors may ship as much bread as possible even if it means failing to properly inspect the packaging. Piece rate payment is an incentive to ship as large a quantity of bread as possible and the lack of documentation of inspection precludes inspector accountability. The greater the number of inspectors the less likely it will be that a supervisor will be able to detect which inspector's performance was inadequate. One response might be to pick one inspector and arbitrarily impose a penalty or worse yet punish the entire group of inspectors. This type of discipline is counterproductive. Employee morale will be diminished; the authority of management will be undermined because respect for supervision will be lost, and if the case went to arbitration, resources would be wasted since no arbitrator would uphold such a management action. The proper management response would be to institute an inspection documentation procedure, post the company's personnel policy concerning the failure to properly inspect and document bread packaging and to include in the policy the penalty for improper performance. This management action would correct the underlying cause of the inadequate performance and make clear to employees what they could expect if performance did not improve. Probably even more important is that there would now be a method to identify the employee who inadequately performed therefore making the threat of discipline realistic where before it was not. The basic idea with the implementation of performance analysis is to determine what causes or contributes to specific employee actions. In many cases a change in incentives or the work design of a particular job will be appropriate and not discipline. But where it is determined that discipline is necessary then the penalty should be designed to correct the failure in performance and not be simply an arbitrary sanction. In extreme cases, however, discharge may be determined to be appropriate. If the employee action is so contrary to acceptable behavior or the employee has not responded to appropriate corrective action then management is usually left with little recourse but to terminate the worker's employment.

The fairness and reasonableness of the disciplinary procedure will affect employee morale and attitudes. Rules which are unduly restrictive or not based on the needs of the firm may result in employee hostility or alienation because of, at least perceived, infringement on the personal freedom of the individual worker. If rules are not posted or distributed and penalties are assessed for actions for which the employee was unaware that discipline was a possibility, then such discipline is likely to produce fear, alienation, or even open hostility. The fairness of discipline for violation of unpublished rules is easily attacked in arbitration and will in most cases result in the action being set aside. As John F. Mee observed:

> Demotions, layoffs and discharges are problems that most organizations would prefer to avoid. When they are necessary, however, the feeling of the individuals affected may be in part mitigated if the organization is in a position to justify its actions in terms of employee performance. If the employees affected, and others as well, realize that fairness and consideration are the keynotes of personnel policy, rather than favoritism, whim, and expediency, the "climate" of personnel relations may in some measure be improved.[1]

On the other hand, a fair, objective and firmly enforced disciplinary procedure will maintain an orderly work environment based on respect for management's authority and trust in managerial actions. Union and management personnel will then find that the disciplinary procedure will produce fewer grievances and that attention can be directed to other areas of collective bargaining and other responsibilities.

Further, it is worthy to note, unions are concerned with the nature and operation of the disciplinary procedure. While it may be argued that unions have few if any direct goals which may be attained through discipline, unions are deeply concerned about the fairness and reasonableness of the procedure. Virtually all contracts allow employees to file grievances concerning any controversies arising out of the disciplinary procedure. Therefore unions frequently find disciplinary matters are brought to the grievance procedure. Secondly, matters of contractual interpretation and application may arise in the disciplinary procedure. For example, an employee assigned to a specific job may be disciplined for failing to produce an adequate quantity or quality of output. Obviously, work standards and their determination are of paramount

---

[1] John F. Mee, ed., *Personnel Handbook*, New York: The Ronald Press Company, 1951, p. 283.

importance in such controversies. The rights of the union as well as the employees under the contract are often the central issues in these disputes resulting in the union's need to defend its perceived contractual rights.

Finally, unions have a right and an obligation to fairly represent their memberships. The employee has the right to demand and receive union representation during the disciplinary procedure, including investigatory interviews.[2] Employees also have the right to fair and good-faith representation by their union (hence granting the union the right to be present in disciplinary proceedings—for its own protection).[3]

Professors Slichter, Healy, and Livernash have outlined the principle influences unions have exerted on managements' disciplinary procedures and policies; these are:

1. The desirability of a forthright disciplinary policy is now appreciated by management.
2. Management has learned the wisdom of developing reasonable rules and regulations to govern the conduct of employees and of making these standards of behavior known to all employees.
3. In administering its rules and regulations, management has been stimulated to seek more uniformity of application.
4. Greater care in investigating the facts surrounding any given case of employee misbehavior has been a product of union pressures.
5. The union must be credited with the development of more orderly and sophisticated procedures in the administration of discipline.
6. Collective bargaining has been influential in molding management's entire philosophy of discipline.
7. Finally, and perhaps most important, some managements have learned that experiences with employee discipline provide a significant tool for the improvement of management.[4]

As illustrated by these seven influences on the disciplinary procedure unions have an affirmative role to play in discipline. Not only are penalties for violations of shop rules mandatory issues of collective bargaining but the union may be thought of as the "overseer" of the disciplinary procedure. Management must be more sure of its case and its procedure than it would need to be in the absence of unions.

Nonunion firms, it is interesting to note, are often required by the courts to show just cause, fair dealing and good–faith in disciplinary actions.[5] Several test cases have been heard by the courts since 1979 and it appears that many

---

[2] *NLRB v. Weingarten, Inc.*, 461 U.S. 969 (1975); this has been extended to include an employee's right to consult with the union prior to an investigatory interview in *Amax Inc.*, *Climax Molybdenum Co. Div.* 227 NLRB 1189 (1977).

[3] See *Vaca v. Sipes*, 386 U.S. 171 (1967) and *Hines v. Anchor Motor Freight, Inc.*, 424 U.S. 554 (1976).

[4] S.H. Slichter, J.J. Healy, and E.R. Livernash, *The Impact of Collective Bargaining on Management*, Washington, D.C.: The Brookings Institution, 1960, pp. 624–626.

[5] "The Growing Costs of Firing Nonunion Workers," *Business Week*, (April 6, 1981), pp. 95–98.

state courts in California, Michigan, Washington and New Hampshire are developing a common law principle requiring that discipline be for just cause and that the employer must administer a fair and nondiscriminatory procedure. For example, an employee named Olga Monge was discharged by her supervisor because she refused to go on a date with him. Ms. Monge then sued Beebe Rubber Company and the New Hampshire Supreme Court awarded her $1000 in damages ruling that discharges motivated by "bad faith or malice" harm the "public good."[6]

Operation of the Disciplinary Procedure

Most labor agreements do not specify the precise nature of the disciplinary procedure. It is common for the right to discipline employees to be included in the management's rights clause of the contract. Primarily as a result of arbitrators' construction of what's fair and reasonable, managements have typically promulgated specific disciplinary procedures and shop rules. These procedures typically vary according to the nature of the offense committed, the needs of the firm and the influence that the union is able to exert. In general, offenses which may be eliminated by corrective action are subject to a corrective-progressive disciplinary procedure. Most progressive disciplinary procedures call for numerous steps, each more severe than the previous step, to correct an employee's behavior. A common progressive disciplinary procedure may include the following steps: (1) a verbal warning; (2) a written warning; (3) a three day disciplinary lay-off; (4) a thirty day disciplinary lay-off; and finally (5) discharge. These steps vary considerably between bargaining relations as well as across types of offenses. As few as two steps and as many as seven are not uncommon. In general the more serious the offense the fewer procedural steps will be in evidence. For example, absenteeism may be punishable through five or six steps while horseplay may require only a written warning and a thirty day disciplinary lay off prior to discharge.

The Nature of Offenses

There are many types of employee misconduct that may warrant discipline for just cause. These types of offenses may be categorized as follows: (1) conduct away from the plant; (2) conduct on company property by off duty employees; and (3) conduct on company property by on duty employees.

Conduct Away from the Plant

Management has the right to establish, promulgate, and enforce work and safety rules except where specifically modified by the contract or by law. This includes rules prohibiting certain employee conduct away from the plant which

---

[6] The Growing Cost of Firing Nonunion Workers," pp. 95–98.

substantively effects or reflects upon the employer. As Arbitrator D.E. Ferguson has observed:

> While it is true that the employer does not (by virtue of the employee-employer relation) become guardian of the employee's every personal action and does not exercise parental control, it is equally true that in those areas having to do with the employer's business, the employer has the right to terminate the relationship (or discipline the employee) if the employee's wrongful actions injuriously affect the business.[7]

It must be remembered, however, that the employee's misconduct must substantively and adversely effect the operation or reputation of the firm (directly and obviously). The public expression of political views which differ from the employer's, the employee being a defendant in a law suit, or accusations against the employee for criminal activity, while possibly adversely reflecting on the employer, causes him no substantive harm and are not just causes for discipline. If the employee slanders or libels the company or its product, engages in industrial espionage, or holds the company or its product up to public ridicule then the employer may have just cause for discipline. Discipline for these activities will generally be sustained by an arbitrator even if the employer has not promulgated rules prohibiting these actions. Lesser offenses by employees away from the firm generally require specific employer prohibition of such acts for an arbitrator to sustain the discipline.

In cases where some action by the employee, such as child molestation, wife beating or the like, results in the refusal or inability of other employees to work with the individual, the employer may generally terminate his or her employment because the employee can no longer perform services of value. The nature and seriousness of the offense must be considered before ascertaining whether the termination is to be considered discipline. If convicted of a crime resulting from the above activities (even though no work time was lost) just cause for discipline is generally deemed to exist. If the employee precipitated or was shown to have actively participated in a wildcat strike or urged other employees to engage in a wildcat strike, sabotage or a work slow-down, even if the communication was not on company time or property this also constitutes just cause for discipline.

Off Duty Conduct on Company Property

Off duty employees have a responsibility to abide by reasonable safety and applicable work rules while on company property. An employee smoking in a paint booth, participating in an altercation, assaulting a supervisor, or defacing company property is subject to discipline just the same as though he were on duty. If the employer has a properly promulgated rule against loitering on

---

[7] Arbitrator D.E. Ferguson, *Inland Container Corp.* 28 LA 312 (1957): emphasis added; reported in Frank Elkouri and Edna Elkouri, *How Arbitration Works*, Washington, D.C.: Bureau of National Affairs, Inc., 1973, p. 617.

company property for longer than a specified period prior to or after a shift, employees may be disciplined for violation of this rule.

On Duty Conduct on Company Property

Two types of offenses generally occur in an industrial setting: habitual and incidental offenses. Habitual offenses include such things as absenteeism, poor quality workmanship, failure to make production rates, drunkenness, and tardiness which are reoccuring patterns of conduct. The employer, depending upon the nature of the employee's job assignment, the nature of the firm's business, and the history of the employer's policies and procedures concerning discipline, may have an obligation, if not a desire, to use corrective discipline in such cases. With habitual offenses it is possible that the employee's behavior can be modified into more acceptable patterns through the use of penalties. This, as you may recall, is termed the adversive control of behavior. If such modification is successful then recruitment and training costs of new employees can be avoided; therefore corrective discipline may be more cost efficient than simply discharging and replacing offenders. It is also frequently reasoned that the employer and the work may contribute to the habitual offender's conduct (lack of adequate training or lax enforcement of shop rules); in such cases the employer is obligated to use corrective discipline.

Incidental offenses may be broken down into two categories: crimes in society and violations of shop rules. Both of these categories may be subclassified by the seriousness of the offenses. Incidental offenses which are crimes in society include: theft, assault, battery, rape, fraud, criminal negligence and vandalism. Violation of shop rules which have been properly promulgated and which are reasonable also constitute just cause for discipline. Further discussion of shop rules and their appropriate penalties are presented in the following section.

Appropriateness of Penalties

Penalties must be appropriate for the offense which the employee has committed for several reasons. An employee's conduct may be modified into desired channels if the penalty imposed for a particular offense is deemed reasonable and just. If the penalty is perceived by the offender and his fellow employees as being overly harsh then management's judgement, intentions and wisdom become suspect. One outcome is that employees may seek employment elsewhere, resulting in the high costs associated with recruiting and training replacements. Employees may also become fearful, openly hostile and even rebellious which may be even more costly than high turn-over rates. If, on the other hand, employees perceive a penalty for a particular offense as too light then the penalty may not serve as a deterrent to the offensive behavior. For example, if the penalty assigned to unexcused absence is a written warning for ten absences, before any further penalty is assigned, then employees will risk nothing by being absent ten times during the year without authorization. The written warning in this case is ineffective for the first ten occurrences. Besides the behavioral aspects of the appropriateness of penalties there are a couple of legal complications. In general, arbitrators will sustain a penalty imposed by management unless he or she finds the penalty is unreasonable, excessive, arbitrary or capricious. If management assigns a penalty that is unwarranted there is the very real possibility that the arbitrator will either set aside the discipline or mitigate the penalty.

Slichter, Healy, and Livernash offer an example of a well structured statement of shop rules and appropriate penalties for their violations:

A. A violation of any of the following regulations by an employee is considered inexcusable and will result in immediate discharge:
   1. Deliberate damage to Company property or to the property of other employees.
   2. Stealing.
   3. Fighting.
   4. Carrying concealed weapons or any other violation of criminal laws.
   5. Immoral conduct or indecency.
   6. Willful hampering of production or failure to carry out definite instructions or assignments.
   7. Gross insubordination.
   8. Falsification of records.
   9. Hiding, concealing or the misappropriation of Company property or the property of other employees.
   10. Gambling or conducting gambling activities.
   11. Sleeping on the job.
   12. Punching clock card of another employee.
B. The violation of any of the following rules by an employee is considered a serious misconduct. The first violation of any of these rules will be punishable by three days off without pay. The second violation of any of these regulations will result in release.
   1. Careless waste of materials or abuse of tools and equipment.
   2. Possessing intoxicants or drugs in the plant or reporting to work under the influence of intoxicants or drugs.
   3. Insubordination.
   4. Playing of pranks or "horseplay."
   5. Unauthorized selling, soliciting or canvassing.
   6. Disorderly conduct.
   7. Producing or concealing defective work through obvious carelessness or negligence.
   8. Abusive or threatening language.
   9. Excessive absence from work or habitual tardiness.
C. The violation of any of the following regulations by an employee is considered misconduct and is not to be tolerated. The first offense will bring a reprimand. The second offense will be punishable by three days off without pay. Any further offense may result in release.
   1. Absence from work area without permission or satisfactory excuse.
   2. Loitering.
   3. Leaving job or work area before end of shift.
   4. Failure to report personal injury.
   5. Smoking in prohibited areas.
   6. Posting unauthorized notices, defacing walls, or tampering with bulletin boards.

7. Wage attachments.
8. Improper parking or improper operation of cars on company property.
9. Unreported absence or absence without justifiable cause.[8]

As illustrated, each of these classes of offenses is assigned a penalty consistent with the seriousness of the offense. The penalties proscribed for group B and C offenses call for corrective discipline. Often with such penalties provisions are made for management to grant leniency. If the progression from a lesser penalty to a more severe penalty is required (that is no provision for managerial leniency) it is not uncommon for the shop rules to include an amnesty clause. These clauses typically specify that after the issuance of a reprimand or a disciplinary lay-off, if the employee does not violate the shop rules for some period of time (generally one or two years) the employee's record will automatically have the discipline removed. If the penalty provisions of the shop rules use language such as *management may* or *at management's discretion* a specific penalty shall be imposed then management is left with the possibility of granting leniency. Leniency is a prerogative of management and should not be confused with mitigation of a penalty by an arbitrator. The arbitrator has no authority to award leniency; he may, however, mitigate penalties which are inappropriate. Leniency is not concerned with the appropriateness of a penalty but is simply giving the employee a second chance.

Management may unilaterally establish the shop and safety rules. The penalties for the violation of shop rules are, however, mandatory issues of collective bargaining and management must bargain in good-faith with the union concerning these penalties.[9] It is within management's prerogatives to administer discipline or to grant leniency. Once the decision has been made to discipline an employee and a penalty is assigned, management is again obligated to collectively bargain with the union through the grievance procedure. If an impasse is reached concerning the discipline given an employee management must submit to arbitration, if the contract requires arbitration as the final step in the grievance procedure.

Frequently when discipline is challenged in the arbitration process it is because of disputed facts surrounding the offense or the reasonableness or fairness of the penalty. Often it is not management's intent to discriminate against an employee but frequently it is difficult to determine what an appropriate penalty is on a case–by–case basis. Employees with many years of service without prior discipline should be granted leniency, *ceteris paribus*. Other circumstances may also serve to mitigate a penalty, such as extenuating circumstances, nonenforcement or lax enforcement of shop rules, and deficiencies in the handling of the disciplinary procedure. Inconsistent treatment of employees in the disciplinary procedure will frequently result in the arbitrator mitigating the penalty based on lack of fairness. One union, aware of the special circumstances which may affect management in the

---

[8] Slichter, Healy, and Livernash, *The Impact of Collective Bargaining on Management*, pp. 635–636.

[9] *Capital Times Co.*, 223 NLRB 651 (1976).

administration of the disciplinary procedure has included the following in a training manual for union stewards:

> Management handles discipline in the plant in about the same way most of us handle discipline in the home. When things are going well for us we permit the children to stretch the boundries of permissible behavior. When things are going wrong we are liable to be overly severe in our discipline.[10]

This same manual also reflects the fact that in disciplinary cases management does make an effort to keep emotions from playing a role in disciplinary process.

> In many contracts there is a stipulation that a man must be suspended for a number of days before management can proceed with a discharge. This seems a wise provision. It gives the parties sufficient time to think about the problem.
> There are many management representatives who use this same principle in nearly all discipline cases. They think about it overnight before they decide to follow through with the discipline. While some people occasionally will get away with something when this system is used, it avoids the lasting ill-feeling that may result from discipline dispensed in anger.[11]

These statements clearly illustrate two important points concerning discipline. First, as much as possible, management must remain objective in the administration of the disciplinary procedure. Emotions, personalities, and other extraneous factors have no place in the administration of the disciplinary procedure. To allow such factors into the discipline/grievance process will assure problems for both the union and management. Mistrust, suspicion and more instances of disciplinary offenses are all likely results. Secondly, the union may be a valuable institution for management in the administration of the disciplinary procedure. The union, if cooperative and mature, may help to ensure the correctness of the procedure as well as assist in the investigation of alleged violations. But for management to rely upon the union for assistance in such adversary proceedings is clearly inappropriate. Even when the union steward may be in sympathy with management's position his primary obligation is to represent the employee; management cannot expect the union official to neglect his responsibility to the rank–and–file membership.

Finally, where management has failed in its administration of the disciplinary procedure it can generally be attributed to one or more of the following deficiencies. These managerial deficiencies include: (1) failure to conduct an adequate and complete investigation of the facts and circumstances surrounding the alleged misconduct; (2) laxity in enforcement of the disciplinary procedure resulting in inconsistent application of discipline and inappropriate signals concerning labor force behavior; (3) greater concern with uniform rather than consistent application of discipline resulting in unreasonable penalties in individual circumstances; (4) confusion may arise when manage-

---

[10]T.F. Connors, *Problems in Local Union Collective Bargaining*, Detroit, MI.: UAW-Solidarity House, 1975, p. 136.

[11]Ibid, p. 138.

ment has not properly promulgated shop rules and a disciplinary procedure as well as identified the members of supervision having the authority to issue discipline; and (5) the disciplinary procedure cannot properly function if emotions and personalities are not kept out of it.

Arbitration and the Disciplinary Procedure

Discipline and discharge cases comprise a significant proportion of the cases which reach the arbitration stage of the grievance procedure. Three areas of arbitral thought are of particular interest in these cases: (1) the burden and quantum of proof; (2) arbitral standards for review of penalties; and (3) arbitral remedies for improper discharge or inappropriate discipline.

Burden and Quantum of Proof

As will be discussed in the following chapter, management bears the initial burden of proof in disciplinary cases. The nature of the offense will dictate what quantum (quantity and quality) of evidence will be necessary for management to prove its case. In general, arbitrators require a greater quantum (quality and quantity) of proof the more serious the allegation and severe the penalty. In cases which involve violations of shop rules (which are not crimes in society) and a penalty less than discharge, arbitrators require that the preponderance of evidence support the allegation. Cases which involve discharge or allegations of crimes in society have a much greater significance for the employee. There is a social stigma attached to the commission of a criminal act which reflects not only on the individual's character but also on his potential as a productive employee. The loss of one's employment is by itself a serious matter but if the employee is discharged for a criminal offense the employee may find it difficult if not impossible to secure alternative employment. Arbitrators have, therefore, required a greater quantum of evidence in such cases. When discharge has been assessed as a penalty for misconduct an arbitrator will generally require a preponderance of clear and convincing evidence. If the case involves criminal misconduct then arbitrators have most frequently required evidence which supports the allegation to be beyond a reasonable doubt.

There are some interesting complexities concerning required proof in disciplinary matters. In general arbitrators have required evidence to conform more closely to the courtroom rules of evidence. Arbitrators generally allow the admission of evidence such as hearsay and depositions, but if an employee is accused of moral turpitude or criminal activity it is inconsistent with commonly held principles of due process and reasonableness to allow a discharge for these offenses to remain if the quality of the evidence is questionable.

In American industrial relations instances such as altercations, production slow-downs, and wildcat strikes may arise which involve group discipline. Arbitrators rarely sustain discipline, in such matters, unless the guilt of each individual can be shown. One exception to this general rule is where complicity can be shown. Employees are frequently required by shop rules or the contract to fully cooperate in the grievance and disciplinary procedures. Arbitrators, even in the absence of an explicit requirement, frequently argue that employees have an implicit obligation to cooperate with management as well as the union in disciplinary procedures. If an employee involves himself in an offense by refusing to give evidence against a fellow employee or actively participates in a cover–up of misconduct, the employee may subject himself to discipline.

Arbitrators have long held that the penalty must fit the offense. This requires management's action to be reasonable but also consistent. A strictly uniform application of a disciplinary procedure may result in arbitral modification or overturning of penalties. While uniformity assures each offense receives the same penalty, the circumstances and facts surrounding each offense makes the case unique and it must be handled as such. For example, theft is a serious matter regardless of the circumstances. An employee who has a thirty year spotless work record should not receive the same penalty for petty theft as a new hire receives for grand larceny.

In cases involving corrective discipline no general (or for that matter consistent) body of arbitral thought has yet emerged. The Elkouris have summarized the major views of the arbitration profession:

1. There are cases in which management was held obligated to use corrective discipline although there was no indication that management had ever approved its use either by the agreement or by unilaterally instituting corrective discipline in the past.
2. It has been said that the formalization of a corrective discipline program is a matter for negotiations by the parties, not for the arbitrator. It also has been said that it is one thing to determine whether or not a contract permits discharging an employee under given circumstances, but that it is entirely another matter for an arbitrator to conclude that an employee's discharge violated a contract because of the absence of a corrective discipline program where none is specified by the agreement.
3. There are cases in which discharge was upset where the company had a corrective discipline system but failed to abide by it.
4. Where an employer was reluctant to suspend the employee and used counseling and warnings instead (as predischarge measures), this demonstrated a desire to help rather than hurt the employee, an arbitrator said, for which the employer should not be criticized.
5. Where there were "no circumstances to suggest that corrective discipline would rehabilitate the grievant into a satisfactory employee," discharge without corrective discipline was upheld.
6. In adopting a corrective discipline program a company was held not to have surrendered its right to invoke summary discharge for serious offenses warranting such action. Also, the mere fact that an agreement specified the use of corrective discipline for some offenses did not necessarily mean that it must be used for all offenses.
7. In sustaining discharge, arbitrators sometimes have stressed the fact that corrective discipline had been used without avail.[12]

---

[12] Elkouri and Elkouri, *How Arbitration Works*, pp. 631–632.

Arbitral Remedies for Improper or Inappropriate Discipline

Unless clearly and specifically prohibited by the contract an arbitrator may assess a lesser penalty than originally imposed by the employer. Regardless of the penalty, if it is *not shown* that the discipline was for just cause and was properly imposed, the arbitrator, even in the absence of contract language, may order reinstatement of the wrongly disciplined employee with all rights due him to include backpay.

With inappropriate penalties arbitrators have reduced discharges to disciplinary layoffs and even reprimands. In cases where the contract required the arbitrator to sustain or reverse the discipline in total, arbitrators have on occasion sustained discharges (or some other severe penalty) but recommended that management grant leniency if appropriate.

Summary and Conclusions

Discipline is a necessary tool for effective management. Without the fair and firm administration of a reasonable disciplinary procedure management would be left without a method of ensuring an orderly work place. Without an orderly work place and a means to ensure compliance with its directives management would not be able to efficiently operate its production facilities.

Discipline for an alleged offense must be for just cause. There are a wide variety of types of misconduct for which discipline is appropriate. Industrial offenses, crimes, and moral turpitude are general categories which may be further subcategorized as incidental and habitual offenses. Each type of offense may vary in its severity and the penalty must reflect the seriousness of the misconduct. The Taft-Hartley Act and its interpretation by the NLRB and the courts allow employers to unilaterally establish shop rules but management must collectively bargain concerning the penalties to be imposed for their violation.

A great many cases which reach arbitration involve the propriety of discipline and the appropriateness of specific penalties. The result is that the common law and principles of arbitration have a significant impact on the nature and operation of the disciplinary procedure. Management may find its discipline overturned or penalty mitigated if it does not consistently, reasonably, and fairly administer its disciplinary procedure.

COMMENTARY: Mr. Harold Scott* Speaks on Discipline.

My understanding of discipline is that there exists a desire to require by law the establishment of a justifiable reason for discipline before management can legally take disciplinary action against one of its employees.

In an effort to modify the behavior of its employees, management sometimes resorts to discipline. Contrary to popular belief, the purpose is to

---

*For Mr. Scott's Biography, See Chapter 10, Page 214.

correct or modify undesirable behavior. Generally the behavior that warrants modifications is disruptive, unproductive or unsafe. As long as management exercises this prerogative for modification of such behavior, a statute requiring just cause for the administration of discipline is not necessary.

Unless expressed otherwise in the collective bargaining agreement, discipline is the prerogative of management. Management chooses when to correct an employee's behavior through discipline or when not to. If just cause is not established, the grievance procedure can be utilized to resolve the issue in an equitable manner. In fact, employees and their unions are adept at utilizing the grievance procedure even when just cause has been established.

Any company that would discipline without just cause subjects itself to an insecure work force, because discipline as a result of misconduct or a rules violation serves as an indicator of management's expectations of its work force. In a non-union environment, unjust discipline could certainly precipitate an organization attempt.

A statutory requirement for just cause would be to the detriment of the labor-management relationship; the resolution of disputes by use of the grievance procedure is the essence of that relationship. The ability of the parties to work out their differences in an orderly fashion without the interference of outside sources promotes cooperation and interdependence and has been effective for many years. In my judgment, if just cause becomes law, the necessity of grievance procedures would be diminished, thereby diminishing the importance of union representation.

Because of the many remedies offered by courts, the case load for courts and attorneys would be significantly increased, as would the amount of time from the onset of the dispute to its final resolution. By pursuing remedies through the courts rather than the grievance procedure, employees could seek more than just back pay (i.e., mental anguish, defamation of character may be taken into consideration by judges).

DISCUSSION QUESTIONS

1. What is the difference between uniformly and consistently administering the disciplinary procedure? What problems are associated with this difference?

2. Does management have an obligation to impose corrective discipline in habitual offense cases?

3. How have unions affected the administration of disciplinary procedures?

4. What rationale might be proposed for shop rules being voluntary issues of collective bargaining while penalties for their violation being mandatory bargaining topics?

5. What is the impact of arbitration on: (a) the administration of the disciplinary procedure; (b) the types of offenses; and (c) the appropriateness of penalties?

6. What specifically is meant by an appropriate penalty? How might a manager, union steward or arbitrator go about determining whether a penalty is appropriate to a particular offense?

SELECTED REFERENCES

Baer, W.E. *Discipline and Discharge Under the Labor Agreement*, New York: American Management Association, 1972.

Black, J.M., *Positive Discipline*, New York: American Management Association, 1970.

Benewitz, M.C., "Discharge Arbitration and the Quantum of Proof," *Arbitration Journal*, No. 29, June 1973.

Bureau of National Affairs, *Employee Performance: Evaluation and Control*, Personnel Policies Forum Survey No. 108, Washington, D.C.: BNA, Inc. 1975.

Connors, T.F., *Problems in Local Union Collective Bargaining*, Detroit, MI.: UAW-Solidarity House, 1975.

Fisher, R.W., "When Workers are Discharged—An Overview:," *Monthly Labor Review*, (1973) **96**(6): 4–17.

Gersuny, Carl, *Punishment and Redress in A Modern Factory*, Lexington, MA.: D.C. Heath & Company, 1973.

Jones, D.L., *Arbitration and Industrial Discipline*, Ann Arbor, MI.: Bureau of Industrial Relations of the University of Michigan, 1961.

Miner, M.E. and Miner, J.B., *Policy Issues in Contemporary Personnel and Industrial Relations*, New York: Macmillan, 1977.

Phelps, O.W., *Discipline and Discharge in the Unionized Firm*, Berkeley, CA.: University of California Press, 1959.

Rosen, B., and Jerdee, T.H., "Factors Influencing Disciplinary Judgments," *Journal of Applied Psychology*, (1974), 327–331.

Spelfogel, Evan J. "Wildcat Strikes and Minority Concerted Activity-Discipline, Damage Suits and Injunctions," *Labor Law Journal*, (September 1973), **24**(9).

Staudohar, Paul D., "Individual and Collective Rights in Public Employment Appeals Procedures," *Labor Law Journal*, (July 1975) **26**: 435–38.

Steinmetz, Lawrence L. "The Unsatisfactory Performer: Salvage or Discharge," *Personnel*, (May-June 1968), **45**:(3) 46–54.

Stessin, Lawrence, *Employee Discipline*, Washington, D.C.: Bureau of National Affairs, Inc., 1960.

Stessin, Lawrence, *The Practice of Personnel in Industrial Relations: A Case-Book*, New York: Pitman Publishing Corp. 1964.

Stessin, Lawrence, "Management Prerogatives and Plant Rule Violations," *Arbitration Journal*, 1959, **14.**

Van Horne, R.D., "Discipline: Purpose and Effect," *Personnel Journal*, (September 1969), **48**: 728–731.

Wohlking, W. "Effective Discipline in Employee Relations," *Personnel Journal*, (1975), **54**: 489–500.

Yagoda, R., "The Discipline Issue in Arbitration: Employer Rules," *Labor Law Journal*, September 1964, **15.**

Chapter 13

Arbitration of Labor Disputes

Labor relations in this country has a long history of peaceful dispute settlement. Much of the peaceful nature of labor dispute resolution is attributable to the institution of arbitration. The present chapter deals with the process of labor arbitration under collective bargaining and contains three major sections. The introductory section defines arbitration, the second section outlines the development of the statutory basis of labor arbitration in the private sector and the final section describes the practice and procedure of labor arbitration. The discussion of other methods of dispute settlement is presented in Chapter 14.

In our economic system it is quite natural that labor-management disputes arise over the terms and conditions of employment. Wages and hours as well as the definition of the respective rights of the employer, his employees, and their union are central to the collective bargaining relation. Frequently the parties find themselves unable to resolve differences concerning these issues. Controversies which develop over these issues are not confined to the negotiation of the labor contract but also arise over the application and interpretation of the agreement. Such conflict, per se, is not unhealthy but the results of uncontrolled conflict can be very costly to all parties concerned. Disputes which result in court litigation and/or work-stoppages are not only economically expensive but may result in irreparable damage to the employer-employee relation. Aware of the costs of unbridled conflict the parties to the majority of labor contracts have chosen a less costly and more therapeutic alternative to strikes and/or law suits—voluntary labor arbitration.

Voluntary labor arbitration is a procedure in which the parties to a dispute agree to be bound by the decision of an impartial third party. In other words, management and the union voluntarily agree, normally in the labor contract itself, to submit unresolved disputes to an arbitrator for settlement. The decision of the arbitrator is generally agreed to be final and binding. The arbitrator (the impartial third party) is expected to base his decision on the labor agreement (contract) as well as the arguments and evidence presented by the parties. While in this respect arbitration resembles judicial proceedings, arbitration procedures and practices are less formal, more therapeutic, and typically quicker and less expensive. This view of the relation between arbitration and the judicial process is summarized by Clarence Updegraff:

> In all systems of primitive law, three elements of social control invariably seem to make early appearances. In the Roman law, these social controls were designated as *fas, boni mores,* and *lex.* The weakest of these in the beginning of the historical period was *lex,* or law. In all legal systems that truly develop to maturity it comes to be the dominant factor, but *fas,* the ethical or religious teaching, and *boni mores,* public opinion, always remain important factors. The judge comes to deal almost entirely with law. At any rate, it dominates his technique of decision. The arbitrator, however, deals with all three.
>
> This background gives a clue to the reason why arbitration seems to be much preferred to actions in the courts in some areas and in relation to certain types of disputes. As formerly indicated, judges are, in the main, expected to apply and to emphasize legal principles, the element of social control designated by the Romans as *lex.* Arbitrators are expected to apply not only the law, but also ethical concepts and precepts of behavior resting upon custom or public opinion. It should be noted, however, that the authority or jurisdiction of the arbitrator may be sharply limited by the form of submission under which he is acting. If that narrowly restricts him to strict legal interpretation of a contract or a statute, he may not, with any binding effect, proceed into wider fields.[1]

Arbitration, as was mentioned earlier, is a therapeutic dispute settlement process. The parties to a dispute do not have to resort to economic power to settle their differences. In the majority of cases where economic warfare is utilized to settle a dispute there are lasting scars left on the bargaining relation. Mistrust, suspicion and recrimination are common results of industrial warfare. Arbitration allows the parties to circumvent these continuing problems. Further, the arbitrator is a respected neutral expert in labor relations. The arbitrator provides the parties to a dispute an opinion with his or her award. The arbitrator's opinion provides the parties with useful feedback concerning the interpretation of contract language and the conduct of the administration of their contract. This feedback can be used to improve the contract and its administration which should assist in preventing future disputes involving the same or similar issues. For example, in a recent case a dispute arose over the interpretation of a recall provision in the article of the contract concerning seniority. The recall of employees from layoffs rarely occurs in this particular bargaining relationship but since there were several employees on layoff the dispute was of critical importance. The union interpreted the recall provision as requiring management to recall by seniority regardless of skill class; management interpreted the recall provision as allowing skilled employees to be recalled independently of unskilled or semiskilled workers. The arbitrator's award and opinion provided not only a settlement of the dispute at hand but

---

[1] Clarence M. Updegraff, *Arbitration and Labor Relations,* 3rd ed., Washington, D.C.: Bureau of National Affairs, Inc., 1970, pp. 4–6.

provided the parties with guidance for their future recalls hence preventing future disputes over this issue.

Arbitration may be categorized by the types of disputes the arbitrator is asked to resolve. *Rights arbitration,* widely adopted in both the public and private sector, is concerned with disputes over the application and interpretation of an existing contract and its provisions. Rights arbitration is divided into two basic categories by type of dispute: grievances and disciplinary matters. Disputes which concern the meaning or application of specific contractual provisions are the topics of grievances and therefore rights arbitration. Disciplinary matters frequently are settled by arbitrators when questions concerning the fairness of the disciplinary procedure or the facts surrounding an alleged offense cannot be resolved within the collective bargaining process and therefore find their way into the grievance procedure. Grievances concerning a wide range of issues are also subject to arbitration in most contracts. For example, if the contract specifies that the senior qualified employee shall be promoted when higher paid jobs become open then disagreements may arise as to what constitutes a qualified employee and the dispute may be placed before the arbitrator to interpret what is meant by "qualified employee" or "senior employee."

The arbitration of disputes concerned with the creation of new contract provisions is commonly referred to as *interest arbitration.* For example, if during contract negotiations an impasse (an impasse is reached when it becomes clear that no agreement is likely to occur through collective bargaining) is reached concerning a particular issue, such as subcontracting or the economic package, the parties may submit the dispute to a neutral third party. The arbitrator selected will conduct a hearing and gather the available facts concerning the dispute upon which he will base his decision. In many cases a state labor law will require the parties to abide by the arbitrator's decision. However, in some states the arbitrator's decision is simply advisory. Advisory interest arbitration is commonly called "factfinding." Interest arbitration, in either form, is rarely observed outside of the public sector; however, interest arbitration is beginning to be adopted by some private sector employers and their unions but as yet its impact has been relatively unnoticed outside of professional sports.

Arbitrators: Who They Are and How They Become Arbitrators

Arbitrators are selected mutually by management and the union which are the parties to an unsettled dispute. Generally, the parties will select an arbitrator from a panel provided by an administrative agency organized for the purpose of maintaining lists of qualified arbitrators. The Federal Mediation and Conciliation Service (FMCS) and the National Mediation Board (NMB) are two federal agencies, created by Taft-Hartley and the Railway Labor Act respectively, which, among their other functions, maintain panels of professional arbitrators. The American Arbitration Association (AAA) is a private nonprofit organization formed for the purpose of developing and maintaining panels of arbitrators as well as improving the arbitration process and providing information to arbitrators, management, and unions (Further discussion of AAA selection procedures is offered in the final section of this chapter). In addition to these agencies many states maintain panels of arbitrators specifically for disputes in public employment. State Public Employment Relations Boards (PERBs) differ substantially in their jurisdiction and make-up. Many states provide for voluntary submission of disputes for all government agencies and

---

BOX 13–1. Code of Professional Responsibility for Arbitrators of Labor–Management Disputes of the National Academy of Arbitrators, American Arbitration Association, and Federal Mediation and Conciliation Service.

1. Arbitrator's Qualifications and Responsibilities to the Profession

A. General Qualifications

1. Essential personal qualifications of an arbitrator include honesty, integrity, impartiality and general competence in labor relations matters. An arbitrator must demonstrate ability to exercise these personal qualities faithfully and with good judgement, both in procedural matters and in substantive decisions.

   a. Selection by mutual agreement of the parties or direct designation by an administrative agency are the effective methods of appraisal of this combination of an individual's potential and performance, rather than the fact of placement on a roster of an administrative agency or membership in a professional association of arbitrators.

2. An arbitrator must be as ready to rule for one party as for the other on each issue, either in a single case or in a group of cases. Compromise by an arbitrator for the sake of attempting to achieve personal acceptability is unprofessional.

B. Qualifications for Special Cases

1. An arbitrator must decline appointment, withdraw, or request technical assistance when he or she decides that a case is beyond his or her competence.

   a. An arbitrator may be qualified generally but not for specialized assignments. Some types of incentive, work standard, job evaluation, welfare program, pension, or insurance cases may require specialized knowledge, experience or competence. Arbitration of contract terms also may require distinctive background and experience.

   b. Effective appraisal by an administrative agency or by an arbitrator of the need for special qualifications requires that both parties make known the special nature of the case prior to appointment of the arbitrator.

even allow private sector bargaining relations to utilize their services. States, such as Indiana, maintain separate arbitration panels under different agencies for different groups of public employees. The Indiana Division of Labor maintains a panel of professional arbitrators to settle state employee disputes while the Indiana Educational Employment Relations Board handles fact-finding and arbitration under the state's teacher collective bargaining law. While there are variations on the Indiana example many states such as Michigan, New York, New Jersey, Iowa and Kansas, to mention just a few, maintain panels of full and part-time arbitrators and mediators.

There are basically two levels of requirements to become an arbitrator. First, the administrative agencies have requirements to be included on their panels. The FMCS, for example, requires that the applicant be unquestionably impartial (e.g., clergyman, college professor, or attorney in private practice), experienced in labor relations (a minimum of five arbitration cases or equivalent experience), and honest. The NMB and AAA have similar requirements. State agencies, however, vary considerably in their requirements. Some states, such as Iowa and Michigan, maintain essentially the same standards as the FMCS for admission to their panels. Indiana and Kansas, however, do not require evidence of substantial experience in labor relations for admission to their panels. The second level of arbitrator qualification concerns acceptability to labor and management. Once an arbitrator is admitted to an administrative agency's panel this is not a guarantee that he or she will ever hear a case. Management and the union will closely examine the arbitrator's background, previous decisions, honesty, and integrity before selecting him or her to serve as their arbitrator. Substantial experience over a wide range of issues and industries is characteristic of most successful and widely acceptable arbitrators. Failure to remain impartial, the exercise of poor judgement, or dishonesty will typically end an arbitrator's career. Integrity, expertise in labor relations, and honesty are prerequisites to becoming an arbitrator but inexperience is the single biggest obstacle to becoming an acceptable and successful arbitrator.

While many of the following remarks are applicable to the public sector as well as the private sector, and to both rights and interest arbitration, it is the intent of the authors to specifically describe the evolution and operation of rights arbitration in the private sector. The intent is not to neglect interest arbitration nor the public sector but only to limit this chapter to manageable proportions.

The Legal Status of Arbitration

In 1925, Congress passed the United States Arbitration Act.[2] The Congressional intent in passing this Act was to make contracts involving interstate or

[2]9 U.S.C.A. & 1–14. Also commonly called the Federal Arbitration Act. For a detailed discussion of this legislation see Archibald Cox, "Grievance Arbitration in the Federal Courts," *Harvard Law Review* Vol 67 (1954) pp. 591–607.

international commerce enforceable without requiring the aggrieved party to resort to the courts for a remedy. In other words, if a party to a contract believed that he had been harmed in some way, rather than filing suit in the courts he could go to arbitration instead. The U.S. Arbitration Act among its provisions outlined procedures for the selection of an arbitrator, allowed the arbitrator to issue summons compelling witnesses to attend the hearing or the presentation of records and other documents, and provided for suit in the federal courts for enforcement of arbitrators' awards. This legislation, by its passage, lent considerable legal support to the institution of arbitration both in labor and commercial disputes. This legislation, from the date of its enactment, was the subject of controversy. Paragraph 1 of the Act excluded, for purposes of the Act, "contracts of employment." Even with this exclusion many courts were willing to support arbitration clauses in collective bargaining agreements reasoning that contracts between employers and unions were *not* "contracts of employment" within the intent of Congress but rather agreements between unions representing employees and an employer. Therefore no direct employer-employee relation existed making the agreement a "contract of employment."

In 1957, a landmark United States Supreme Court decision was issued in the *Lincoln Mills* case,[3] which made the U.S. Arbitration Act's application to labor contracts a moot issue. In its opinion, the Court cited Section 301 of the Labor-Management Relations Act of 1947 (Taft-Hartley), rather than the U.S. Arbitration Act, as the authority for federal courts to enforce arbitration provisions contained in collective bargaining agreements thus circumventing the controversy caused by the exclusion of "contracts of employment" in the former statute. The majority opinion in the *Lincoln Mills* case, reasoned Justice Frankfurter, was a silent rejection of the applicability of the United States Arbitration Act to labor disputes. As a result of the *Lincoln Mills* decision the Taft-Hartley Act became the statutory authority for the courts to enforce arbitration awards rather than the United States Arbitration Act. This changed little since Section 301 of Taft-Hartley permits either party to a labor contract to bring suit for breach of contract which is essentially the same enforcement procedure required under the United States Arbitration Act. The Supreme Court ruled that since arbitration was voluntarily agreed to by the employer in exchange for a no-strike pledge from the union, Section 301 allowed suit in the Courts for enforcement of the arbitration clause. Taft-Hartley places no requirements, per se, on the procedure utilized in arbitration, which the former Act did to the extent that arbitrator selection procedures were specified and subpeona powers were granted. This clarification in the statutory authority for labor arbitration simply allowed a greater degree of freedom to the parties in determining their own dispute resolution machinery. This is not to say the United States Arbitration Act was without value in labor dispute settlement; quite the contrary, Congress and many federal courts interpreted the Act as confirming arbitration as the preferred method of dispute resolution during the 22 years after 1925 and before the passage of Taft-Hartley.

---

[3] *Textile Workers v. Lincoln Mills of Alabama*, 77 S. CT., 913 (1957).

The Taft-Hartley Act and Arbitration

It is clear from the *Lincoln Mills* decision that the statutory authority for labor arbitration comes from the Taft-Hartley Act. Two specific provisions of Taft-Hartley apply to private sector labor arbitration: Sections 203 and 301. Section 203 declares that the most desirable way to settle disputes arising over the interpretation and application of a labor agreement is a mutually acceptable method, hence voluntary labor arbitration. Not only does Taft–Hartley establish arbitration as the national labor policy but it also provides enforcement machinery. Section 301 of Taft-Hartley allows for suit in federal courts to enforce collective bargaining agreements hence arbitration awards in industries significantly affecting interstate commerce. Taft-Hartley, therefore, places at the disposal of the party which has been wronged and won a favorable arbitration award, the power of the federal courts to enforce the award. To illustrate this point analyses of the following landmark Supreme Court decisions are offered.

The United States Supreme Court, on June 20, 1960, handed down three decisions that not only consolidated arbitration's role in labor relations but defined the court's relation to arbitration. With these decisions, commonly referred to as the "Steelworkers Trilogy," the Supreme Court left little doubt that it fully supports the system of private labor arbitration in the United States.[4]

In the first case, *Warrior & Gulf Navigation Co.*, the employer, faced with a demand by the union to arbitrate over the employer's subcontracting out of certain bargaining unit work, went to court to obtain a ruling that the dispute was nonarbitrable. This was a common tactic employed by management to circumvent the final step in the grievance procedure, especially in cases dealing with subcontracting, plant closures, and changes in production methods. The District Court ruled that it was within management's prerogatives to subcontract work under a broad management rights clause, which in part stated "matters which are strictly a function of management should not be subject to arbitration," hence nonarbitrable. The United States Supreme Court again reversed the lower court, ruling that unless the issue was *clearly and specifically* exempted from the arbitration clause the matter of arbitrability again, was a matter for the arbitrator to decide. The Supreme Court's ruling in this case left the courts in the position of ordering arbitration when the contract specified arbitration without inquiry into the merits of the case. The U.S.S.C. ruled that the merits of the case are for the arbitrator to rule upon and not the courts.

In the second case, *American Manufacturing*, a District Court was asked by the employer to declare a grievance was not arbitrable because the employee's grievance was meritless. The grievance arose concerning the reinstatement of an employee to his job after he had been awarded compensa-

---

[4]*United Steelworkers of America v. American Manufacturing Co.*, 363 U.S. 564 (1960); *United Steelworkers of America v. Warrior & Gulf Navigation Co.*, 363 U.S. 574 (1960); *United Steelworkers of America v. Enterprise Wheel & Car Corp.*, 363 U.S. 593 (1960).

tion for a job–related injury which resulted in the employee becoming permanently and partially disabled. The lower court ruled that the grievance was "a frivolous, patently baseless one, not subject to arbitration under the collective bargaining agreement." The Supreme Court reversed the lower court, ruling that the arbitration clause provided for the resolution of all disputes involving the application and interpretation of the contract and "not merely those that a court may deem to be meritorious." The Supreme Court's decision, in essence, stated that arbitrators are to decide whether a case is arbitrable and not the courts. The arbitrator is the authority in this field of common law and the parties bargained for the arbitrators determination of arbitrability and the Supreme Court ruled that the courts should not interfere.

In the third case, *Enterprise Wheel & Car Corp.*, an arbitrator reinstated discharged employees with backpay for periods during which the contract had expired. The employer then refused to comply with the award and the union consequently sued for its enforcement under Section 301 of Taft-Hartley. The federal District Court refused to order enforcement because the judge was persuaded that since the contract had expired the arbitrator had exceeded his authority to issue an award in this controversy. The Supreme Court reversed the lower court and ordered enforcement of the award. In so doing, the Supreme Court pointed out that in voluntary arbitration the parties bargained for the construction and interpretation of the contract by the arbitrator and *not* by the courts; therefore the courts were not to overrule arbitrators because they disagree with his construction and interpretation of the labor agreement. This extends even to whether or not the parties have a labor contract. In other words, the United States Supreme Court removed the judicial review of an arbitrator's award except in rare and specific cases which are addressed in the following section.

The Trilogy Cases have strengthened the voluntary arbitration process in this country. The U.S. Supreme Court's decisions in these cases have made it perfectly clear to the judiciary that arbitration is a legitimate method of dispute resolution which is *not* inferior to judicial processes. The courts are not to interfere in the adjudication of labor disputes through arbitration. Unless the arbitrator obviously fails to conduct a fair and proper hearing or clearly exceeds his authority, the Trilogy decisions instruct the courts to support this method of dispute settlement. Since 1960 the courts have further defined the scope of this dispute settlement process. The courts have expanded the role arbitration is to play in collective bargaining while at the same time limiting the impact of the Trilogy Cases on judicial review.

Expansion of Arbitration and the *Collyer* Doctrine

The National Labor Relations Board has developed a policy of deferring enforcement of specific sections of the Taft-Hartley Act to private labor arbitrators. This policy, today commonly referred to as the *Collyer* Doctrine,[5] further expands the importance and scope of labor arbitration. In the several cases which comprise the *Collyer* Doctrine the United States Supreme Court

---

[5] *Collyer Insulated Wire*, 192 NLRB 837 (1972).

has favorably recognized the NLRB's policy of deferral to private arbitrators. For example, if a grievance case also involves an unfair labor practice then both the arbitrator and the NLRB may have jurisdiction. To illustrate this point, suppose an employer subcontracts bargaining unit work (in apparent violation of the contract) and refuses to negotiate with the union concerning this issue (an unfair labor practice). In such cases there is overlapping jurisdiction between arbitration and the NLRB but the NLRB will allow the total dispute to be settled in arbitration hence deferring to arbitration its jurisdiction over the unfair labor practice. The Supreme Court has taken the stance that in cases of overlapping jurisdiction neither the NLRB nor the arbitration process should be totally pre-empted.[6] To this end, the NLRB had already established a deferral policy in its decision in the *Spielberg Manufacturing Co.* case.[7] The Board stated that it would accept arbitration awards in cases of overlapping jurisdiction, as a method of encouraging voluntary dispute settlement, provided the arbitration procedure meet the following three standards: (1) the arbitrator conducted a fair hearing; (2) the parties agreed that the award is final and binding; and (3) the arbitrator's award was consistent with and not repugnant to the Taft-Hartley Act and the national labor policy. A further requirement was added six years later in the *Monsanto Chemical Co.* case.[8] This fourth requirement is that the arbitrator must consider the issue that would have been before the NLRB. This policy of deferral was extended to unfair labor practices, representation cases, and employee's Section 7 rights cases. In 1973 the NLRB added a fifth requirement for deferral of its jurisdiction in the *Jacobs Transfer, Inc.* case.[9] The NLRB will not defer its jurisdiction to an existing arbitration award involving the statutory rights of an individual worker unless the employee has been adequately and fairly represented in good–faith by the union. The decision in *Collyer*[10] expanded the method of deferral rather than substantive issues which may be subject to deferral. In this case, the NLRB announced that it would defer to arbitration prior to the issuance of an award, in addition to the previous policy of deferring jurisdiction to an arbitrator after an acceptable award had been rendered. Since the *Collyer* case, however, the NLRB has refused to defer cases which involved violations of employee's rights under Section 7 of Taft-Hartley.[11] At present, therefore, it is unclear how the deferral policy of the NLRB will evolve where the statutory rights of individuals are involved.

Limitations on the Trilogy Decisions

In light of the Trilogy decisions and the deferral policy of the NLRB one might assume that arbitration is untouchable through the judicial process. This

---

[6] *Smith v. Evening News Association*, 371 U.S. 195 (1962); *Carey v. Westinghouse Electric Corp.* 375 U.S. 261 (1964).

[7] *Spielberg Manufacturing Company*, 112 NLRB 1080 (1955).

[8] *Monsanto Chemical Company*, 130 NLRB 1097 (1961).

[9] *Jacobs Transfer, Inc.*, 201 NLRB 210 (1973).

[10] *Ibid.*

[11] *General American Transportation Corp.* 228 NLRB 808 (1977); *Roy Robinson, Inc.*, 228 NLRB 828 (1977).

is *not* the case. Since the Supreme Court issued its Trilogy decisions three major limitations have developed concerning nonreviewability of arbitrators' awards. An arbitrator's award may be reviewed in cases where: (1) arbitrators have exceeded their authority; (2) there are violations of constitutional or statutory rights at controversy; and (3) the union has not discharged its obligation to fairly represent an employee.

The courts in the *Torrington* case[12] overturned an arbitrator's award on the basis that the arbitrator lacked jurisdiction in the case. In this case, the arbitrator upheld a past practice the employer had established of paying his employees one hour's pay on election day. When the employer announced that he was terminating the practice, the union grieved and subsequently won an arbitration award upholding the union's right to the one hour paid absence. The employer refused to comply with the arbitrator's award; consequently the union sued for enforcement under Section 301 of Taft-Hartley. The courts refused to enforce the award claiming the arbitrator had exceeded his authority. The arbitrator, reasoned the Second Circuit Court of Appeals, is bound by the contract and since the agreement specifically prohibited the arbitrator from altering, modifying, or adding to the contract, an award based on past practice concerning an issue on which the contract was silent was beyond the jurisdiction of the arbitrator. Critics of this decision claim that the court was simply substituting its interpretation of the labor agreement for that of the arbitrator, hence eroding the Trilogy decisions.

The second major limitation on the Trilogy decisions involves employees' rights under statutory law. In *Alexander v. Gardner-Denver*[13] the Supreme Court ruled that where a case involved Title VII of the Civil Rights Act of 1964 an arbitrator's award is not final and binding and is subject to judicial review. A court will not enforce an award requiring discriminatory treatment of an employee. If an employer, however, unilaterally changes the terms and conditions of employment (in violation of the contract) to avoid racial or sexual discrimination, the changes may fall under the arbitrator's jurisdiction but the arbitrator is not the appropriate authority to hear civil rights controversies, hence overlapping jurisdiction. Where the "central" issue in a labor dispute involves alleged violations of an employee's civil rights, the arbitrator's jurisdiction is pre-empted by that of the agencies charged with the responsibility of enforcing applicable statutory law and the judiciary.

The third limitation involves the union's duty to fairly represent individuals within its membership. In a case[14] that involved the discharge of eight truck drivers for filing falsified expense accounts the Supreme Court put unions on notice that the courts will upset arbitration awards and require (at least in part) unions to make their members whole for failure to fairly represent. In this case, neither the employer nor the union conducted an adequate investigation. The grievants claimed that the clerk at a motel where they had stayed actually charged them what their expense accounts reflected and that the clerk must be the thief. In reality the clerk had made false entries in the register and

---

[12] *Torrington v. Metal Products Workers Local 645*, 363 F., 2d 677 (1966).

[13] *Alexander v. Gardner—Denver*, 415 U.S. 36 (1974).

[14] *Hines v. Anchor Motor Freight, Inc.*, 424 U.S. 554 (1976).

pocketed the difference; neither the union nor the company had discovered this evidence, resulting in the arbitrator sustaining the discharges. In reviewing the *Anchor Motor Freight* case, the United States Supreme Court reversed the arbitration award on the grounds that the award was arbitrary and in error because the union failed in its obligation to represent the membership "honestly and in good–faith and without invidious discrimination or arbitrary conduct" hence tainting the arbitration process. The Court, however, did make a distinction between errors in processing a grievance and errors in proper discharge of the union's obligation to fairly represent its membership. The Court recognized that there are bound to be minor errors of omission or commission in processing a grievance, over which the courts ought not to set aside an arbitrator's award. Errors in the union's performance of its obligation of good–faith representation of its membership which substantively affect the arbitrator's award cannot be allowed to stand. The arbitration profession has watched the developments since this decision to see if this case will provide the basis for wholesale reversal of arbitrator's awards. To date, there has been no evidence of such reversals.

Quid Pro Quo: Arbitration for No-Strike Pledge

Collective bargaining is a dynamic process of "give and take" involving the mutual resolution of the problems of the work environment. This view is nowhere more clearly evident than in the National Labor Relations Board's and court's *quid pro quo* treatment of arbitration and no-strike clauses. Simply stated, management exchanges its unilateral decision making authority (by conceding an agreement to arbitrate) for a pledge from the union not to strike for the life of the contract. By so doing, the parties are substituting a peaceful voluntary method of dispute settlement for industrial warfare consistent with the provisions of Section 203 of the Taft-Hartley Act.

In the *Shell Oil*[15] case of 1948, the NLRB ruled that no-strike clauses, and therefore, arbitration clauses were mandatory issues of collective bargaining. The *quid pro quo* view is so well entrenched that the United States Supreme Court has held that if a union has agreed to submit a particular dispute to binding arbitration, the union violates the collective bargaining agreement if it later strikes over the dispute—even in the absence of an explicit no–strike clause in the contract.[16]

An agreement to include no-strike and arbitration clauses in a contract does not bar the exclusion of specific disputes from the arbitration process (e.g., the United Auto Workers, for years, refused to arbitrate and maintained the right to strike over certain work standards disputes). The *Borg-Warner* doctrine[17] simply requires that both parties bargain in good–faith concerning arbitration and no-strike clauses. The NLRB does not have the authority to determine substantive contract terms.[18] Therefore the NLRB cannot require

---

[15] *Shell Oil*, 77 NLRB 206 (1948).

[16] *Local 1974 Teamsters v. Lucas Flour Co.*, 82 S. Ct 571 (1962).

[17] See Chapter 6 for further discussion of this doctrine and bargaining in good–faith.

[18] *Local 357 Teamsters v. NLRB*, 365 U.S. 667 (1961).

the inclusion of a no-strike clause nor an arbitration clause but if either is included in the contract the *quid pro quo* exchange of rights will be presumed by the NLRB as well as the courts. The determination of specific issues where management concedes an arbitration clause in exchange for the union's no-strike pledge are the sole responsibility of the parties to the bargaining process.

Enforcement of no-strike clauses, however, has gone through a much more controversial legal development than the enforcement of arbitration clauses. The United States Supreme Court refused to allow the use of the labor injunction to enforce a no-strike provision of a labor contract in the *Sinclair Refining Company* case.[19] The Court reasoned that the Norris-La Guardia Act prohibited the use of an injunction when strike activity was involved. Further, because Taft-Hartley did not make wildcat strikes (strikes in violation of a no-strike clause) an unfair labor practice, the employer's only recourse was suit for breach of contract under Section 301 of Taft-Hartley. Eight years later the Supreme Court changed policy in its decision in the *Boys Markets* case[20] of 1970. In this case the Supreme Court argued that the previous ruling in *Sinclair Refining* was "a significant departure from our otherwise consistent emphasis upon the congressional policy to promote the peaceful settlement of labor disputes through arbitration." Under the *Boys Markets* decision employers could obtain injunctive relief from employee strikes in violation of a contractual prohibition of strikes. In 1976 the Supreme Court modified its decision in the *Boys Market* case. The Court ruled in the *Buffalo Forge* case[21] that for an employer to obtain an injunction ordering strikers back to work the issue causing the strike must be covered by the contract's arbitration clause. If the issue is specifically excluded from the arbitration process or is not covered by the contract then the employer cannot obtain an injunction to enforce the no-strike clause in the labor agreement. These Supreme Court decisions again reflect the *quid pro quo* view of the relation of no-strike and arbitration provisions.[22]

The Arbitration Process

Regardless of the nature of the arbitration clause, the arbitration machinery is normally set into motion only when a settlement has not been reached in the grievance procedure. Just as the United States Supreme Court is the Court of final appeal in the multi-tiered judicial system, arbitration is the Court of last resort in the judicial system of the contract—the grievance procedure. The purpose of submitting a dispute to arbitration is the enforcement of contractual rights. Arbitrators are asked to interpret and apply the language of the negotiated contract; however, arbitrators do not enforce their awards. Upon receiving an award from the arbitrator the successful party may

[19] *Sinclair Refining Co. v. Atkinson*, 370 U.S. 238 (1962).

[20] *Boys Markets v. Retail Clerks*, 398 U.S. 235 (1970).

[21] *Buffalo Forge v. United Steelworkers*, 75 S. Ct. 339 (1976).

[22] See Benjamin Taylor and Fred Witney, *Labor Relations Law* (3rd edition) Englewood Cliffs, N.J.: Prentice-Hall, Inc., 1979, pp. 421–425 for further discussion.

then seek a court order for enforcement if the losing party does not voluntarily comply. Therefore, the appropriate and central question for the student of labor relations is: how do arbitrators decide cases? The answer to this question, naturally, depends on the dispute and the specific contract language. There are, however, some useful general observations which can be made.

Negotiating the Arbitration Clause

Since the arbitration clause of the collective bargaining agreement determines the limits of the arbitrator's jurisdiction, the arbitration clause language is critical to the interpretation and meaning the contract will eventually receive. The arbitration clause defines the issues open to the arbitration process. Two general categories of arbitration clauses are common in the private sector. The *broad arbitration clause* typically permits arbitration of "any difference" or "any dispute" that surfaces over the life of the contract. Although specific issues may be excluded, broad clauses commonly permit arbitration of a wide range of issues, sometimes including interest disputes as well as rights disputes. On the other hand, *narrow arbitration clauses* characteristically limit arbitration to claims that involve rights created by specific contract provisions. The arbitrator is typically confined to the application and interpretation of the collective agreement and is prohibited from "adding to, subtracting from, or modifying" any terms of the agreement. Additionly, the grievance procedure may specifically define a grievance which results in essentially the same sort of limitation on an arbitrator's jurisdiction. A narrow definition will limit a grievance, for purposes of the grievance procedure hence arbitration, to disputes arising over the specific provisions included in the written contract. The broad definition of grievance generally states that any controversy arising between the parties is a grievance. Such grievance definitions are commonly found in conjunction with arbitration clauses.

The parties to collective bargaining must, as with all provisions of the agreement, tailor the contract to their specific needs. The broad arbitration clause allows for an almost unlimited range of issues to be brought to arbitration. While this type of clause may reduce the possibility of industrial warfare in the short-run, the parties may be allowing the arbitrator the authority to rewrite their contract. Unless there are overwhelming reasons for the adoption of a broad arbitration clause the parties to labor contracts have in general opted for the narrow language. By restricting the arbitrator to the application and interpretation of the agreement as well as limiting the arbitrator's jurisdiction the parties find that the arbitration process becomes more predictable. This predictability, however, requires that the parties more carefully tailor the labor agreement to their specific needs; otherwise the contract may impose unwanted restrictions on both parties.

The Procedural Nature of Arbitration

Since arbitration is the final step in the grievance procedure the requirements negotiated into the grievance procedure impact upon the arbitration process. There are three procedural characteristics of labor arbitration directly dependent on the grievance procedure: (1) disputes subject to the grievance-arbitration procedure; (2) employees eligible to utilize the grievance procedure; and (3) propriety of the use of the grievance procedure.

Labor contracts containing narrow arbitration clauses normally exclude certain controversies from arbitration. It is not uncommon for contracts to exclude certain controversies from the grievance procedure as well. The most common topics handled in this manner are voluntary issues of collective bargaining such as pensions for presently retired workers, education programs, suggestion programs, and utilization of nonbargaining personnel. Besides direct exclusion of topics from the grievance-arbitration process, the parties may render an issue nonarbitrable by simply excluding language covering the topic from the contract. It is a well established principle of arbitration that if the contract is silent concerning a particular issue, with the existence of a narrow arbitration clause, the issue is nonarbitrable.

The availability of the grievance-arbitration procedure to different categories of employees is typically outlined by the contracting parties. Probationary employees are generally excluded from the grievance-arbitration process. Practice varies, however, concerning the treatment of part-time employees. These employees are often excluded from the grievance-arbitration procedure. Specific exclusion of certain categories of employees does not preclude the union or its representatives from filing grievances on behalf of these employees, if general contractual rights of the union or its membership are at controversy. For example, if the contract states that "no bargaining unit work will be performed by supervisory personnel" and "probationary employees (those who have been employed less than ninety days) are excluded from the utilization of the grievance procedure" a union may still grieve over contract violations such as supervisory personnel doing bargaining unit work even if the job is normally assigned to a probationary employee.

Proper use of and compliance with the steps of the grievance procedure are exceedingly important. For a grievance to be arbitrable it must be properly filed. Most grievance procedures outline specific time limits for the processing of a grievance at each step. Although time limits may be extended by mutual agreement, arbitrators will rule against any party unilaterally violating the time constraints.[23] Courts, as previously discussed, will review an arbitrator's award if the arbitrator has exceeded his authority or the fairness of the procedure is questionable. Therefore a complete and accurate record of the grievance processing is necessary to ensure the integrity of the grievance procedure and eliminate possible grounds for appeal to the courts.

Selection of the Arbitrator

Contracts vary in the techniques specified for the selection of an arbitrator. Some contracts provide for a permanent umpire for the life of the contract or for

---

[23]This is termed the doctrine of laches. For a more thorough discussion of this principle see Owen Fairweather, *Practice and Procedure in Labor Arbitration.* Washington D.C.; Bureau of National Affairs, Inc. 1973 pp. 18 and 92.

some subperiod thereof. The advantages of using a mutually acceptable permanent arbitrator include: (1) elimination of delays in choosing a neutral after a dispute arises; (2) greater likelihood of selecting an impartial umpire thoroughly familiar with the firm's labor relations; (3) familiarity with contract terminology and shop common law resulting in reduced hearing time and consequent cost savings; and (4) the development of a consistent body of precedents useful in resolving disputes at an earlier step in the grievance procedure. Potential drawbacks include award-splitting by the umpire to insure continued acceptability by the disputants and the locking in of the parties to a potentially unqualified or prejudiced arbitrator for some significant period of time. Permanent umpires are most often characteristic of mature bargaining relationships.

Other contracts specify the use of tripartite arbitration boards consisting of one member selected by management, one member selected by labor, and a neutral third member who normally serves as panel chairman. Because of the partisan makeup of such panels, decisions are rarely unanimous. Where tripartite boards are utilized, contracts most often state that the majority opinion shall prevail as final and binding. In effect, the neutral is the decision-maker of record. Less frequently, contracts will specify that the decision-making authority of the neutral is absolute.

The major advantage of arbitration panels is the advocate members' contribution to the decision-making process of the neutral. Greater familiarity with and a better appreciation of the circumstances, events, and problems of the work environment that gave rise to the dispute can be obtained through the neutral's interaction with partisan panel members. On the other hand, the major disadvantages of arbitration panels stem from the selection of panel members and panel interaction itself: the delays and subsequent increase in costs resulting from appointment of partisan members, hearing and post-hearing reargument of the merits of the case, and the time required for the writing of minority opinions. Because of these delays and associated costs, the use of arbitration panels is rare when compared to other mechanisms for the final adjudication of rights disputes.

By far, ad hoc arbitration is the most common method of disposing of grievance disputes. The temporary arbitrator is selected to hear the case after the dispute has arisen. The contract will spell out how the neutral will be selected from a list of arbitrators provided by a specific agency organized for this purpose. Organizations such as the American Arbitration Association, the Federal Mediation and Conciliation Service, National Mediation Board, and many state agencies (discussed earlier in this chapter), develop and maintain panels of qualified arbitrators. These organizations will provide a list of possible arbitrators either free on request or on payment of a fee.

The actual selection of an ad hoc arbitrator is a relatively similar process under most administrative agencies. Under the AAA rules the parties formally submit their dispute to the AAA, pay an administrative fee and the AAA will send a panel containing an odd number of arbitrators. The parties will then alternately strike the name of an unacceptable arbitrator until one is left to hear the case. If all arbitrators on the first panel are judged to be unacceptable then another panel may be obtained. If the parties are unable to agree upon an arbitrator to hear the case the AAA will appoint an arbitrator to hear the case if requested to do so.

The major advantage of ad hoc arbitration is flexibility in the selection of neutrals. Qualified arbitrators can be selected more than once while unqualified ones need not be. The parties can choose an arbitrator whose area of expertise best suits the dispute requiring resolution. Ad hoc arbitration minimizes favoritism and award-splitting while increasing the likelihood that decisions will be rendered on the merits of the case. Disadvantages include: (1) selection delays; (2) lack of familiarity with contract provisions; (3) ignorance of shop practices; (4) inadequate understanding of the special problems and circumstances of the work environment; and (5) the development of a potentially conflicting body of precedents incapable of providing guidance to the parties in settling disputes without going to arbitration.

How Arbitrators Decide Cases

Even though arbitration is an informal and quasi-judicial process, arbitrators have borrowed certain useful concepts from jurisprudence. Since arbitration involves the interpretation and application of the labor contract, the principles of contract law have been heavily relied upon by practioners. These principles, however, have been somewhat modified to fit the needs of the contracting parties. These principles are: (1) the jurisdictional construction principle; (2) the residual rights construction principle; and (3) the parol rules of evidence.

The *jurisdiction construction principle* holds that the arbitrator derives his authority from and must look to the contract to render his award. The arbitrator cannot exceed nor contradict the language of the contract and the record of evidence developed through the arbitration hearing. The main contribution of this principle is that if a controversy is covered by clear and unequivocal contract language the arbitrator is (as are the parties) bound by that language. Conversely, if an issue is not covered by the contract between the parties the issue is not arbitrable.

However, if the parties by their actions have shown the intent of the contract by establishing a clear past practice, then this past practice may become a portion of the contract between the parties. Oral and *de facto* (by the fact of the parties' own acts) contracts (where not specifically prohibited by clear and unambiguous contract language) are consistent with the jurisdiction construction principle.[24] Assuming custom and past practice to be well-established and mutual in nature, it has served as a distinct and binding condition of employment where the contract is silent, to clarify and implement ambiguous contract language, and to amend clear and unambiguous contract language. Mr. Justice Douglas, writing for the majority in the *Warrior and Gulf Navigation* case, stated that:

> the labor arbitrator's source of law is not confined to the express provisions of the contract, as the industrial common law—the practices of the industry and the

[24] Fairweather, *Practice and Procedure in Labor Arbitration*, p. 179.

shop—is equally a part of the collective bargaining agreement although not expressed in it.[25]

This view of custom and past practice is shared by labor arbitrators. For example, Arthur T. Jacobs has written:

> A union-management contract is far more than words on paper. It is also all the oral understandings, interpretations and mutually acceptable habits of action which have grown up around it over the course of time. Stable and peaceful relations between the parties depend upon the development of a mutually satisfactory super-structure of understanding which gives operating significance and practicality to the purely legal working of the written contract. Peaceful relations depend, further, upon both parties faithfully living up to their mutual commitments as embodied not only in the actual contract but also in the modes of action which have become a part of it.[26]

Problems frequently arise in bargaining relations because the parties do not take special care to ensure that contract language and past practice are mutually consistent and conform to the desires of the parties. Conflicting past practice and contractual language is a major source of grievances hence arbitration cases. Past practice that has attained the status of common law may be altered by means of specific contract language. However, such language must be strong, clear, precise, and unequivocal in meaning.

If no clear and unequivocal contract language nor established past practice can be shown enlightening the arbitrator as to the intent of the contracting parties, then arbitrators generally apply the *residual rights construction principle*. The residual rights construction principle requires any rights inherent in the employee-employer relation not modified by law or expressly vested in a party by the labor contract are the prerogative of management. In other words, employees obtain and lose rights only as specified by the contract or as may be specified by law. Otherwise those rights not placed by the contract reside with management. If the arbitrator exceeds his jurisdiction then he is imposing upon the parties terms and conditions of employment which were not bargained for; this no arbitrator can do.

For issues generally covered by the contract but having unclear or ambiguous language, the arbitrator must rely on the intent of the parties. This intent may be discovered by, in order of their application: (1) the parol rules of evidence; (2) past practice; and (3) evidence of intent outside the agreement.

The *parol rules of evidence* requires the arbitrator to view the contract as a whole and to, if possible, ascertain from that document the intent of the contracting parties. In other words, if the contract governs the disputed issue (even in general terms) and the language is not clear in meaning, the contract must then be viewed as a whole, reading each provision to ascertain the intent of the unclear language before evidence outside the four corners of the contract may be considered.

[25] Op. cit.

[26] Arthur T. Jacobs, Arbitrator, *Coco-Cola Bottling Co. and IBT Local 812* (1947).

Past practice, as was shown, can become a portion of the contract. The party basing its argument on past practice must show that the practice is well established, mutually acceptable, and relied upon. If any of these three requirements remain unfulfilled then there is not a past practice. A word of caution is in order—one or two occurrences do not establish a past practice. For the establishment of a past practice it must be shown that *several* occurrences of this interpretation of the contract have taken place and the practices must demonstrate relatively consistent intent of the parties. Further, both parties must have agreed to the interpretation demonstrated by the past practice. Finally, if the aggrieved party did not rely upon the contract interpretation associated with the past practice then the practice is irrelevant to the case.

Evidence outside the contract is rarely available. Witnesses and documents concerning the negotiation process and the intent of the negotiators are about the only outside evidence ever presented in arbitration procedures. This evidence, however, is frequently contradicted by the opposing party. If the intent is not mutual and understood as such then this evidence is of little or no value. In these situations the arbitrator is typically left with arguments lacking the weight of evidence and, therefore, no basis for an award.

Each of these principles of contract construction is applied by the arbitrator to ascertain the meaning the parties have intended for the contract. Without these standards for arbitral authority, arbitration, as a method of dispute resolution, becomes unpredictable, slipping into a chaotic mire of opinions without reason, and ultimately falling into disuse.

Discovery of Evidence

The arbitration profession has also relied upon judicial thought for its rules of evidence. While the rules of evidence applied in arbitration are basically recognizable to jurists they tend to be less formal and procedurally more liberal than judicial courtroom standards. Hearsay evidence, affidavits, depositions, and electronically gathered evidence are all admissible, within broad limits, in labor arbitration, while in courtroom proceedings these types of evidence are typically inadmissible. Procedurally, advocates may ask leading questions in direct examination, witnesses may or may not be sworn (as the parties desire), and the advocates may wander more freely in their questioning of witnesses (even to some extent pursuing seemingly irrelevant questions). This informality in the discovery of evidence not only reduces the technical nature of courtroom advocate proceedings but enhances the therapeutic value of the arbitration process. The parties are given the opportunity to air all their arguments and evidence; if serving no other purpose, this at least allows the parties to get the entire controversy (problem) "off their chests."[27]

Arbitrators may discover evidence in any number of ways: (1) through the use of submission agreements; (2) pre-hearing briefs; (3) during the arbitration hearing; and (4) post-hearing briefs. The arbitrator is ethically, and in some

---

[27] The one exception to this general rule is the State of Colorado which has a statute requiring that courtroom procedures be utilized in arbitration.

BOX 13–2. American Arbitration Association

Submission to Arbitration

Date:

The named Parties hereby submit the following dispute to arbitration under the VOLUNTARY LABOR ARBITRATION RULES of the American Arbitration Association.

_____

_____

_____

_____

_____

We agree that we shall abide by and perform any Award rendered hereunder and that a judgement may be entered upon the Award.

_____

_____

Employer

Signed by   Title

Address

Union   Local

Signed by   Title

Address

_____

_____

PLEASE SIGN TWO COPIES

cases legally, obligated to give the parties an adequate and fair opportunity to present their arguments and evidence. In keeping with this obligation arbitrators generally allow the parties to present their cases utilizing any or all four evidential introduction methods, requiring only that the other party be provided with the evidence and arguments presented to the arbitrator.

A *submission agreement* may be employed to submit a dispute to arbitration, requesting the arbitrator to decide some specific controversy, most often in cases where the contract either contains no arbitration clause or requires a submission. Submission agreements usually contain *stipulations*. A stipulation is an agreement between the parties to accept certain facts or circumstances as true. By stipulating facts the parties remove the need to introduce evidence to establish these facts.

Pre-hearing and post-hearing briefs are documents utilized to outline arguments and introduce specific types of documentary evidence. Frequently these briefs are utilized instead of opening or closing statements during the hearing and are generally used in cases involving complicated issues.

The hearing itself is conducted much the same as a courtroom proceeding. Both parties are given the opportunity to make opening statements. Following the opening statements, the party requesting the affirmative action (the party bearing the burden of proof) is generally required to present their case first. In grievance cases the union goes first and in disciplinary matters management presents its case first. Both parties have the opportunity to cross-examine witnesses. After both parties have presented their cases they then have the opportunity to present closing statements. In normal arbitration proceedings the hearing is adjourned (pending transcripts and post-hearing briefs); the arbitrator then considers the arguments and evidence presented and prepares a written award. However, there has been some experimentation with an expedited procedure. In this type of procedure transcripts of the hearing and post-hearing briefs are waived and the arbitrator renders a bench award (orally at the end of the hearing or within hours of adjournment) or a summary written award within a few days of adjournment. The basic idea of the expedited procedure is to reduce the time between the hearing adjournment and the receipt of the award as well as reduce costs.

Arbitration Costs

The costs of arbitration are substantial. In addition to the arbitrator's per diem charges, which average approximately $300, other expenses include: (1) the arbitrator's travel, lodging, and meals; (2) the hearing room; (3) the preparation of transcripts if desired; (4) the travel and lost work time of witnesses; and (5) the agency fee for providing the arbitration panel. It is worth noting that the arbitrator's per diem rate applies to travel time, the time required for research and study, the time involved in the preparation of the opinion and award, as well as the time devoted to the actual hearing. The above costs do not include advocate attorneys' fees or other expenses incurred by the disputants in preparation for arbitration. These costs are borne by the parties incurring them.

Specific contractual arrangements are typically made for payment of the arbitrator's fees and expenses. Although some contracts require the losing party to pay the entire amount, common consensus is that such an arrangement has the potential for causing abuse of the arbitration process. The financially weaker member of the bargaining relationship may be discouraged from processing meritorious disputes for fear of exhausting its limited resources. The vast majority of contracts prescribe equal sharing of arbitration costs. When the contract is silent, arbitrators typically divide the costs equally between the parties.

Although arbitration may appear to be a time-consuming and expensive process, it is less so than the alternative methods of resolving rights disputes (e.g., economic warfare and court litigation.) Under certain circumstances, the costs of arbitration may be reduced through expedited arbitration. During a typical arbitration pre-hearing briefs may be submitted, a hearing conducted, post-hearing briefs filed, an opinion prepared, and the award written. This scenario may take as long as three months. On the other hand, expedited arbitration can reduce the time involved to one day, substantially reducing the costs. Given the present one-year average for NLRB enforcement procedures and even longer and more costly courtroom litigation, arbitration appears to be a bargain.

Summary and Conclusions

The United States Supreme Court has looked favorably upon the process of labor arbitration. The Trilogy decisions rendered by the Court have given arbitration, as a process of dispute settlement, considerable judicial support. This support, however, has been limited by rulings that arbitration may be pre-empted by the judiciary in cases involving employees' constitutional and statutory rights. As this law develops a more consistent policy governing the relation between the courts and the arbitration process will undoubtedly emerge.

Arbitration is an informal quasi-judicial process, voluntarily adopted by labor and management to peacefully settle contractual disputes. While much less formal, the arbitration process borrows heavily from contract law and judicial rules of evidence. The informal nature of voluntary labor arbitration speeds the settlement process as well as reduces the cost of dispute resolution relative to the alternative strikes and law suites.

DISCUSSION QUESTIONS

1. Is the Court's decision in the *Enterprise Wheel & Car Corp.* case consistent with the ruling in *Torrington?* If not, which case is more conducive to peaceful dispute settlement? What are the trade-offs between the decisions in these two cases?

2. Why might the courtroom rules of procedure and evidence be desirable in labor arbitration cases? Would the use of such rules defeat any of the purposes of using arbitration to settle labor disputes?

3. If arbitration were a compulsory rather than a voluntary process might the courts have treated arbitration less favorably in the Trilogy decisions? If so, why?

4. Under what circumstances is a dispute nonarbitrable? What is necessary for an arbitrator to determine a dispute is arbitrable?

5. Under rights arbitration clauses how might discipline cases be heard by an arbitrator? Is there any procedural or substantive difference in a contract interpretation case and a disciplinary case? Explain.

6. Compare and contrast the costs and benefits of arbitration with the costs and benefits of other forms of dispute settlement. Which method of dispute settlement would you prefer in general? Why? Can you cite any exceptions and defend them?

SELECTED REFERENCES

Baer, Walter E., *Practice and Precedent in Labor Relations*, Lexington, Mass.: D.C. Heath & Company, 1972.

Bernstein, Merton C., *Private Dispute Settlement*, New York: The Free Press, 1968.

Brodie, Donald W., "Antidiscrimination Clauses and Grievance Processes." *Labor Law Journal*, (June 1974), pp. 352–379.

Coulson, Robert, "Labor Arbitration: The Insecure Profession?" *Labor Law Journal*, (June 1967), **18(6)**: 336–343.

Elkouri, Frank, and Edna Elkouri, *How Arbitration Works*, Washington, D.C.: Bureau of National Affairs, Inc., 1973.

Fisher, Ben, "The Steel Industry's Expedited Arbitration: The Judgment After Two Years." *Arbitration Journal*, (September 1971), **11(9)**.

Fairweather, Owen, *Practice and Procedure in Labor Arbitration*, Washington, D.C.: Bureau of National Affairs, Inc., 1973.

Fleming, R.W., *The Labor Arbitration Process*, Urbana, Ill.: University of Illinois Press, 1965.

Harrison, Allan J., *Preparing and Presenting Your Arbitration Case: A Manual for Union and Management Representatives*, Washington, D.C.: Bureau of National Affairs, Inc., 1979.

Kagel, Sam, *Anatomy of a Labor Arbitration*, Washington, D.C.: Bureau of National Affairs, Inc., 1961.

McDermott, Thomas J., "Arbitrability: The Courts versus the Arbitrator," *Arbitration Journal*, 1968, **23(1)**: 18–38.

McLaughlin, Richard P., "Custom and Past Practice in Labor Arbitration," *Arbitration Journal*, (1963), **18(4)**: 205–228.

Nolan, Dennis R., *Labor Arbitration Law and Practice*, St. Paul, MN: West Publishing Company, 1979.

Prasow, Paul and Edward Peters, *Arbitration and Collective Bargaining*, New York: McGraw-Hill Book Company, 1970.

Slichter, S.H., J.J. Healy, and E.R. Livernash, *The Impact of Collective Bargaining on Management*, Washington, D.C.: The Brooking Institution, 1960.

Smith, R.A., L.S. Merrifield, and D.P. Rothschild, *Collective Bargaining and Labor Arbitration*, Indianapolis: The Bobbs-Merrill Co., Inc., 1970.

Teple, E.R. and Moberly, R.B., *Arbitration and Conflict Resolution*, Washington, D.C.: Bureau of National Affairs, Inc. 1970.

Updegraff, C.M., *Arbitration and Labor Relations*, Washington, D.C.: Bureau of National Affairs, Inc. 1970.

Wiggins, R.L., *The Arbitration of Industrial Engineering Disputes*, Washington, D.C.: Bureau of National Affairs, Inc. 1970.

Witte, Edwin E., *Historical Survey of Labor Arbitration*, Philadelphia: University of Pennsylvania Press, 1952.

Yagoda, Louis, "The Discipline Issue in Arbitration: Employer Rules," *Labor Law Journal*, (1964), **15(10)**: 571–576.

Chapter 14

Other Methods of Dispute Settlement

The most important difference between civilization and savagery is the habitual willingness of civilized men and nations to submit their differences of opinion to a factual test...it is a mark of civilization to present reasons rather than arms.[1]

Labor disputes, which inconvenience the consuming public as well as result in the loss of output, profits, and wages, invariably prompt interest in alternative methods of impasse resolution in collective bargaining. The interest in and need for a dispute settlement technique other than economic warfare is particularly acute in the public sector where, confronted by employees armed with the strike weapon, public employers are expediency prone to accede to union demands because "voters will tend to choose political leaders who avoid inconveniencing strikes over those who work to minimize the costs of settlements at the price of a strike,"[2] and where, denied the ability to impose costs upon an employer (i.e., the right to strike), employees are denied the right to substantively bargain.[3] The purpose of this chapter is to examine alternatives to the strike as methods for resolving bargaining impasses and for guaranteeing joint employer–employee decision making. Specifically, the chapter explores the advantages and disadvantages of mediation, fact finding, arbitration, and variants thereof as alternative impasse resolution techniques. While such techniques may be "the marks of civilization" and do away with the "fang and claw"[4] (i.e., strike and lockout), do they achieve

---

[1] Boland, "Labor Disputes: The Preventive and Cure," *Arbitration in Action* (December 1943), 6, quoted by Frank Elkouri and Edna Elkouri in *How Arbitration Works*, Washington, D.C.: Bureau of National Affairs, Inc., 1973, p. 5.

[2] Jay F. Atwood, "Collective Bargaining's Challenge: Five Imperatives for Public Managers," *Public Personnel Management*, (January-February 1976), **5**: 25.

[3] The unique nature of collective bargaining in the public sector is treated in detail in Chapter 15.

[4] Edward F. McGrady "Industrial Peace: A Joint Enterprise," *Arbitration Journal* (October 1938), 2, pp. 339–343, p. 343.

these benefits at a prohibitive cost, namely, the elimination of bilateral decision making?

Dispute Settlement in Perspective

As noted elsewhere,[5] bargaining impasses can be the result of deliberate provocation or accident. Included within the former category are strikes (i.e., impasses) intentionally provoked by union leadership to enhance the credibility of the strike threat in future negotiations, to quell political factionalism within the union and increase organizational solidarity, and to provide a cathartic outlet for membership discontent, frustration, and emotions, which may be a necessary step for eventual membership ratification of the agreement. Similarly, an employer may provoke a strike (i.e., impasse) in order to reduce excess inventories or, in the case of a public employer, to keep within an allotted budget. Non-deliberate (i.e., accidental) impasses, on the other hand, can be traced to imbalances in bargaining power, the lack of binding decision-making authority, genuine position differences, and bargaining inexperience. The latter encompasses strategic, tactical, and human relations errors that preclude opportunities for concession, compromise, and, therefore, settlement.

Impasse resolution techniques fall into one of two broad categories: (1) techniques internal to the negotiation process, and (2) techniques external to the negotiation process. Internal impasse resolution techniques include thorough preparation for bargaining, the setting of procedural ground rules for negotiation, adoption of package bargaining as opposed to item-by-item bargaining, use of compromise and concession, and adherence to proven methods of conflict avoidance (e.g., bargaining book, "yes habit", forced choice, "ten commandments" of human relations, subcommittees, etc.). Work stoppages (i.e., strikes and lockouts), job actions which stop short of a complete interruption of production (e.g., rolling sickouts, "blue flue", chalkdust influenza, rotation employee parking in areas reserved for management personnel, refusal to perform non-essential duties, work-to-rule, etc.), mobilization of public opinion, lobbying, and third-party intervention comprise the external category of impasse resolution techniques. Third-party intervention as a substitute for the strike and modified forms of the strike is the subject matter of the following discussion. It should be noted at the outset, however, that third-party intervention is only effective as an external dispute settlement mechanism for those impasses that are non-deliberate in nature; it is useless where one or both bargaining parties intentionally seek an impasse—the only exception being compulsory arbitration of unresolved disputes (See below).

Third Party Assistance in Dispute Resolution

Commonly used third-party dispute settlement techniques can be distinguished according to the impact the third party exercises on the substantive

[5] See Chapter 7.

terms of the labor agreement. Accordingly, mediation is the technique of least substantive impact and arbitration the most, with fact finding occupying middle ground.

Mediation

The heart of mediation is compromise. The role of the mediator is to assist the parties in reaching a workable voluntary agreement. According to Professors Bent and Reeves: "The mediator's objective is to progressively narrow the differences between the parties, relying on his abilities to persuade and cajole both parties to compromise."[6] Similarly, Staudohar sees mediation standing or falling as a dispute resolution technique on the basis of the mediator's personality traits: "The mediator's stock-in-trade is persuasion applied through the use of pressure in order to modify attitudes and behavior."[7] Carl M. Stevens, on the other hand, believes that concentration upon the personality traits of mediators as an explanation for the success or failure of mediation is likely to be misleading:

> While these qualities may be a necessary condition for successful performance, they are not also a sufficient condition, a successful mediator must have the specialized skills of conflict resolution.[8]

In other words, the mediator must have some understanding of the negotiation process—why agreement takes place or an impasse develops. According to Stevens, "The choice of effective mediation tactics in a particular dispute will depend upon the kind of tactical situation in which the failure to agree is manifest."[9]

A distinction currently in vogue is that between "crisis mediation" (i.e., the traditional mediation concept) and "preventive mediation." William E. Simkin defines the former as "assistance in dispute settlement when a stalemate develops just prior to a strike deadline or after a strike starts" and the latter as "assistance in the development of ways and means to avoid a crisis or make productive the crisis elements that must remain."[10] Preventive mediation techniques run the gamut from the "more activist" (i.e., earlier intervention during negotiations) mediator approach advocated by W. J. Usery, Jr.[11] to

---

[6] Alan Edward Bent and T. Zane Reeves, *Collective Bargaining in the Public Sector*, Menlo Park, California: the Benjamin/Cummings Publishing Company, Inc., 1978, p. 244.

[7] Paul D. Staudohar, "Some Implications of Mediation for Resolution of Bargaining Impasses in Public Employment," *Public Personnel Management*, (July/August 1973), **2**: 300.

[8] Carl M. Stevens, "Mediation and the Role of the Neutral," in *Frontiers of Collective Bargaining*, John Dunlop and Neil W. Chamberlain, Editors, New York: Harper & Row Publishers, 1967, p. 272.

[9] *Ibid.*

[10] William E. Simkin, quoted in E. Wright Bakke, Clark Kerr, and Charles Anrod, Editors, *Unions, Management, and the Public*, Chicago, Illinois: Harcourt, Brace, Jovanovich, Inc., 1967, p. 320.

[11] W.J. Usery, "A More Activist Approach by Mediators," *Monthly Labor Review*, (September 1973), **96**: 59.

mediator (i.e., agency) administration and direction of joint steward-foreman training, relations by objectives (RBO's), and labor-management study programs discussed under the heading "Minimization of Grievances" in Chapter 11. While the contribution of prenegotiation problem solving to industrial peace as well as the salutary role of neutrals therein are recognized,[12] this is not mediation. "Some term other than 'mediation' should be applied to such assistance".[13] Perhaps the term "conciliation", which is currently used interchangeably with the term mediation, could be reserved to describe these prenegotiation activities of neutrals.

Semantic problems aside, a more substantive criticism of active mediator involvement during the early stages of negotiation as advocated by the proponents of preventive mediation is that such involvement may undermine the basis for traditional mediation's widespread acceptance by labor and management as an impasse resolution technique; early involvement may prostitute the mediator's neutrality. As noted by Stevens:

> if the mediator enters the early stages of negotiation, he will be involved primarily with grandstanding and with the initial giving and seeking of information. If he enters in the middle stages, he will find himself in the most active tactical phase and may well be actively involved with the tactical operations of the parties themselves..[14]

In either case, there lurks the constant danger that the mediator will sacrifice neutrality on the altar of expediency in order to achieve industrial peace. For example, if the mediator can achieve settlement by bringing the parties to a realistic appraisal of the costs of agreement and disagreement during the early stages of some negotiations (a legitimate aspect of mediator activity), might not a party:

> be brought to agreement if he were persuaded to overestimate the cost of a strike, to underestimate the gains of a strike, to underestimate the gains to be had thereby, and to underestimate the cost of agreement. Here the mediator would be abetting the agreement process by deception.[15]

Similarly, if the mediator can achieve industrial peace by truthfully advising a party that an opponent is not bluffing during the middle stages of some negotiations (again a legitimate aspect of mediator activity), might not another party in a different set of negotiations be brought to agreement by deceitfully advising him that his opponent was not bluffing when, indeed, he was?[16] Here, as before, agreement is achieved through mediator deception—through prostitution of neutrality. A few instances of the aforementioned mediator

[12]"The Ontario Experiment with Preventive Mediation," *Proceedings of the Eighth Annual Meeting of the Society of Professionals in Dispute Resolution*, Washington, D.C.: SPIDR, 1981, pp. 64–67.

[13]Carl M. Stevens, "Mediation and the Role of the Neutral," p. 289.

[14]*Ibid.*, p. 276.

[15]*Ibid.*, p. 278.

[16]*Ibid.*

behavior can seriously damage, if not destroy, mediation as an impasse resolution technique.

The danger posed to neutrality and therefore to the mediation process itself does not exhaust the rationale for late mediator intervention. The basic nature of the mediator's expertise also points in this direction. According to Stevens:

> A case for late, rather than early, intervention might be constructed on the grounds that the mediator's special professional competence lies precisely in dealing with those special agreement problems that are likely to arise in the later pre-deadline stages of negotiation. A striking characteristic of these problems is that each is an instance of the technical failure of the parties' unaided direct negotiations. There may be a kind of special legitimacy in bringing the mediator into such situations: given the technical failure, it makes sense to change the structure of the negotiations by adding a third person.[17]

Skills and techniques within the professional competence of the mediator and particularly appropriate for dealing with pre-deadline, special agreement problems are discussed in Box 14–1.[18]

The effectiveness of mediation as a dispute settlement technique is difficult to determine. Sulzner explains the problem in the following fashion:

> Mediation is inherently a private activity. When employed successfully, it remains hidden from view. Only when mediation falters and fact finding is initiated is there an opportunity, and then only indirectly, to assess the mediation process.[19]

Mediation's contribution to peaceful labor relations can, nevertheless, be gauged in an indirect fashion from its widespread acceptance and use by labor relations practitioners in both private and public sectors. The findings of Jennings, Smith, and Traynham concerning the use of mediation in the mass transit industry typify the general attitude of the labor relations community nationwide toward mediation.

> Only five of the labor agreements analyzed in our study explicitly recognized mediation in the resolution of negotiation impasses. However, this is one clear instance where contractual silence must be interpreted cautiously, as our interviews revealed mediation is the most commonly used (70 percent of the interviewed properties) impasse resolution technique. Only one management and four union representatives expressed neutral-to-negative reactions over this form of impasse resolution. Additionally, management representatives at six locations and a union representative at one location qualify the mediator's success on the basis of his personal capabilities. These respondents have experienced both good and bad mediators and suggest no inherent benefits rest with mediation; instead, the potential success of this technique rests solely on the performance of the

---

[17] Carl M. Stevens, "Mediation and the Role of the Neutral," p. 288.

[18] *Ibid.*, pp. 283–87.

[19] George T. Sulzner, "The Impact of Impasse Procedures in Public Sector Labor: An Overview," *Journal of Collective Negotiations in the Public sector*, Vol. 4 (1); 1975, pp. 3–21, p. 6.

BOX 14–1. Mediator Skills and Techniques

Face Saving:

Mediator serves as a scapegoat permitting one or both parties to abandon an untenable position without loss of face either from the perspective of the constituency or the other party.

Rationalization:

Mediator convinces one or both parties that a specific demand (e.g., COLA clause) is not essential to achievement of a high priority goal (e.g., real wage increases) during negotiations.

Alternate Solution:

Mediator recognizes that parties are in latent agreement and suggests a specific contract (i.e., alternate) provision that simultaneously meets the parties' needs and brings the parties to the realization that they are in agreement. For example, a maintenance-of-membership clause may meet a union's requirement for security and at the same time be consistent with an employer's principled opposition to a union shop.

Separation of Parties:

Mediator wins the trust of parties and utilizes separate caucuses as forums for eliciting the confidential information critical to successful implementation of the other mediation techniques noted herein. If the mediator's neutrality is suspect, caucuses become pointless, and mediation breaks down.

Prominent Solution:

Mediator recognizes that any one of many potential solutions is preferred by both parties to a strike and brings both parties to converge on one of the potential outcomes by highlighting it as the natural (i.e., prominent) solution.

Real Solution:

Mediator recognizes that, although the final-offer positions of the parties diverge, their real positions, ascertained during the caucusing process, coincide and simply advises the parties that they are in agreement.

individual mediator. . . . the remainder of the respondents indicated mediation has been very effective for at least two reasons: it has helped keep negotiations going on, or in some cases, helped break the stalemate between the parties; and mediators have educated the parties, particularly those new to the complexities of collective bargaining.[20]

Mediation, however, should not be viewed as a dispute settlement panacea. Its effectiveness as a dispute settlement technique is directly related to the costs of disagreement; all other factors constant, the greater the costs of disagreement the more effective mediation becomes. Mediation is virtually useless where disagreement costs are nonexistent. This is quite frequently the case in the public sector where strikes are prohibited and interest arbitration (see following discussion) banned. In short, mediation works best within a framework where, if mediation fails, there exists subsequent costs of disagreement (i.e., strike costs, arbitration costs, and the like).

Fact Finding

Unlike mediation, the essence of fact finding is adjudication, not compromise. The fact finder is called upon to investigate an impasse, assemble relevant information and data, and submit a report containing recommendations for settlement of disputed issues including detailed supporting arguments for all recommendations tendered. In terms of substantive impact upon contract provisions, fact finding occupies a middle ground between mediation and arbitration—middle ground because the fact finder's recommendations transcend the voluntary compromise of mediation yet do not possess the compelling force of arbitration; the disputants are free to reject the fact finder's recommendations. The theory behind fact finding is that the fact finder's report, rendered by an individual chosen because of his expertise, objectivity, and fairness, coupled with the disputant's knowledge (i.e, fear) that the report may be made public will prompt the parties to renew negotiations and resolve their differences.

The fact finding process has been criticized on three grounds. First, labor relations experts have been quick to point out that the prospect of recourse to fact finding as an impasse resolution technique in any given set of negotiations may thwart collective bargaining by making negotiators intransigent—this unwillingness to bargain and compromise being the result of the negotiator's belief that a more favorable outcome can be won through fact finding.[21] The "narcotic effect" of fact finding upon collective bargaining can be minimized to some extent through the use of what has been termed "final-offer fact finding." Here the fact finder is limited to a choice between the final offers (issue-by-issue or the entire package) of union and management; the fact finder is not free to fashion a compromise settlement. Purportedly, the "all or nothing" feature of

[20] Kenneth M. Jennings, Jay A. Smith, Jr., and Earle C. Traynham, Jr., *Labor Relations in a Public Service Industry: Unions, Management, and the Public Interest in Mass Transit*, New York: Praeger Publishers, Inc., 1978, p. 112.

[21] Arnold M. Zack, "Improving Mediation and Fact-Finding in the Public Sector," *Labor Law Journal*, Vol. 21 (5), pp. 259–273.

final-offer fact finding forces negotiation due to a party's fear that the opponent's final offer will be selected by the fact finder.

The second criticism of fact finding stems from the criteria frequently specified to guide the fact finder in decision making, namely, that the criteria lead to decisions which are unrealistic, artificial, at variance with market realities, and consequently unduly burdensome and oftentimes unworkable. This is particularly true in public employment where fact finding criteria are established by statute or administrative fiat. A case in point are the criteria specified in the Indiana Teacher Bargaining Law, the relevant provisions of which are reproduced in Box 14–2.

BOX 14–2. Fact Finding Provisions of the Indiana Teacher Bargaining Law (Public Law #217, IC 1971, Title 20, Article 7.5)

Sec. 13. Impasse Procedures

(a) ....

(b) Fact-Finding

The purpose of fact-finding is to give a neutral advisory opinion where the parties are unable by themselves, or through a mediator, to resolve a dispute. The board shall establish and hire a permanent staff of fact-finders and a panel of part-time fact-finders. Such persons may also be mediators. When a fact-finder is requested as required under Section 12 of this chapter, the board shall appoint a fact-finder from such staff or panel. The fact-finder shall make such investigation and hold such hearings as he deems necessary in connection with any dispute, may restrict his findings to those issues which he determines significant, may use evidence furnished him by the parties, by the board, its staff, or any other state agency. The fact-finder shall make a recommendation as to the settlement of the disputes over which he has jurisdiction. In conducting such hearings and investigations, he shall not be bound by the provisions of IC 1971, 4-22-1; he shall, however, take into consideration the following factors:

1. past memoranda of agreements and/or contracts between the parties;
2. comparisons of wages and hours of the employees involved, with wages of other employees working for other public agencies and private concerns doing comparable work, giving consideration to factors peculiar to the school corporation;
3. the public interest;
4. the financial impact upon the school corporation and whether any settlement will cause such school corporation to engage in deficit financing.

Although Sec. 13 (b) 2 of the Indiana Law appears, at first glance, to be reasonable, closer scrutiny indicates otherwise. From the wording of the provision, it is unclear as to whether the fact finder is required to compare the wages and hours of school teachers with those "of other employees working for other public agencies" or those "of other employees working for other public agencies doing comparable work." Both comparisons are, economically speaking, untenable. With regard to the former, what inherent relationship is there (or should there be) between the wages and hours of teachers and those of policemen or firemen? As regards the second, the yardstick most often used by fact finders in Indiana and the one advocated by the Indiana Education Employment Relations Board (the agency charged with enforcement and administration of the Indiana Law), what inherent relationship is there (or should there be) between the wages and hours of teachers located in geographically and economically disparate school districts? Without satisfactory answers to the foregoing questions and without adequate attention being paid "to factors peculiar to the school corporation," fact finders have applied the criteria specified by law. The result has been the development of pattern bargaining with negotiators and fact finders alike keying upon early contract settlements as the norm for subsequent agreements. Some school corporations have consequently been saddled with agreements which are inappropriate when viewed in light of the totality of circumstances under which these corporations must operate.

The final criticism of fact finding as a dispute settlement technique is that the procedure only works if the negotiating parties are subject to the pressure of disagreement costs or the pressure of public opinion. Insulated from both types of pressure, as is often the case in public employment, the negotiator is under no compulsion either to accept the fact finder's recommendations or to use them as a basis for further voluntary negotiation. It was this drawback of fact finding, among others, that led Word to conclude that "fact finding will, perhaps, be only a temporary solution in the resolution of public disputes."[22]

Interest Arbitration

As in the case of fact finding, adjudication constitutes the essence of arbitration, with one major difference—the arbitrator's decisions are final and binding upon both parties. Specifically, arbitration may be defined as a procedure wherein disputants submit an impasse for resolution to an impartial umpire whose decision, based upon the merits of the case, is final and binding upon the parties concerned. Arbitration which is voluntarily entered into by the disputing parties is termed "voluntary" arbitration, whereas arbitration mandated by law is referred to as "compulsory" arbitration. Arbitration can also be classified according to the type of dispute adjudicated: the term "rights" arbitration being used to describe the resolution of disputes involving the

[22]William R. Word, "Fact-finding in Public Employee Negotiations," *Monthly Labor Review*, (February 1972), **95**: 64.

interpretation and application of existing contract language,[23] and the term "interest" arbitration being applied to the resolution of disputes involving the creation of new contract language. It is "interest" arbitration as an impasse resolution technique which is the focus of the following discussion.

Interest arbitration represents the final "peaceful" step of the negotiation phase of the labor-management relationship. As such, it is a substitute for the law of "fang and claw" in dispute resolution. When employed by negotiating parties, interest arbitration "usually occurs after the techniques of conciliation or mediation (and possibly fact-finding) have failed to produce agreement."[24] Interest arbitration permits "each side to demonstrate to its constituents a steadfast attitude regarding labor issues"[25] while simultaneously providing an avenue of escape from untenable positions through the decisions of the arbitrator. In this sense, it resembles mediation as a face-saving technique. More importantly, however, interest arbitration provides both parties a voice in decision making without the costs imposed by a strike.

As is true for all things in life, the advantages of interest arbitration are not achieved without cost. Arbitration substitutes the judgment of an outsider, who is, more often than not, unfamiliar with the industry and the specialized issues unique thereto, for the judgment of those closest to the situation, namely, labor and management. Although the theoretical function of the neutral in interest arbitration is "to determine what the parties, as reasonable men, should themselves have agreed to at the bargaining table,"[26] ". . . it can be expected that something new will come from the neutral and that there will be some substitution of the neutral judgment for that of the respective parties."[27] Because of this substitution and consequent loss of control of substantive contract matters, both labor and management have generally opposed the use of interest arbitration to resolve private-sector labor disputes; less than 3 percent of all private-sector labor agreements specifically provide for arbitration of disputes stemming from the creation (i.e., bargaining) of new contract language. Typical of the general attitude of private-sector labor relations practitioners toward interest arbitration is the following statement made by a management representative:

> Arbitration is an abdication on the part of the union and management of any control over their situation. If the company is private, going to arbitration means giving away your responsibilities to the stockholders. If the company is public, going to arbitration means giving away your responsibilities to the taxpayers.[28]

[23]"Rights" arbitration (i.e., grievance arbitration) as well as the general aspects of the arbitration process (e.g., arbitrator selection) are treated in detail in Chapter 13.

[24]Elkouri and Elkouri, *How Arbitration Works*, p. 5.

[25]Jennings et al., *Labor Relations in a Public Service Industry: Unions, Management, and the Public Interest in Mass Transit*, p. 108.

[26]Whitley, P. McCoy, Arbitrator, *Twin City Rapid Transit Co.*, 7 L.A. 848 (1974).

[27]A.J. Lindemann, "Critical Aspects of Interest Arbitration," *Proceedings of the Eighth Annual Meeting of the Society of Professionals in Dispute Resolution*, Washington, D.C.: SPIDR, 1981, pp. 192–98, p. 197.

[28]Jennings et al., *Labor Relations in a Public Service Industry, Unions, Management, and the Public Interest in Mass Transit*, p. 110.

Various National Labor Relations Board (NLRB) and court decisions have reinforced this negative practitioner attitude and further discouraged the use of interest arbitration as a method for establishing new contract terms and resolving bargaining disputes in the private sector:

> According to the NLRB, interest arbitration is not a mandatory subject under section 8 (d) of the National Labor Relations Act. In *Columbus Printing Pressmen* in 1975, the Board determined that interest arbitration is not favored under the national labor policy. Established case precedent imposes no duty to bargain to impasse on the issue of inclusion of an interest arbitration clause. Either the union or the employer will be in violation of the NLRA when demanding arbitration to the point of impasse. The NLRB determined that such activity is a violation of sections 8 (a) 5 and 8 (b) 3, the duty to bargain in good faith. A number of federal courts of appeals have adopted and approved the decisions and rationale of the NLRB.[29]

An equally serious criticism (i.e., cost) of interest arbitration is "that the process would 'chill' interparty bargaining and/or serve as a habit-forming 'narcotic' which would take its place".[30] Critics are quick to point out, for example, that union/management negotiators, aware that contract disputes will go to arbitration and that arbitrators have a propensity to use pre-arbitration final offers as starting points for compromise, will not present (i.e., reveal) their true offers prior to arbitration. Instead of developing and utilizing traditional interparty negotiating skills to mold a private agreement, the negotiating parties develop the skills and talents requisite for influencing the arbitrator and thus achieving a favorable third-party agreement. Recent research tends to confirm the existence of this problem where interest arbitration has been adopted.[31]

Final Offer Arbitration

A number of variants of interest arbitration have been proposed which purportedly minimize the costs associated with "pure" arbitration. The most notable of these are final offer arbitration and mediation-arbitration (med-arb). Under final offer arbitration (sometimes referred to as "either-or" or "best offer" arbitration), the neutral is restricted to selecting, either on a "package" or "issue-by-issue" basis,[32] the last offer of one of the parties; the neutral cannot

---

[29] Clifford Scharman, "Interest Arbitration in the Private Sector," *The Arbitration Journal*, (September 1981), **36**: 16.

[30] Margaret K. Chandler, "Interest Arbitration: The Duty to Rectify Unequal Bargaining Skills," *Proceedings of the Eighth Annual Meeting of the Society of Professionals in Dispute Resolution*, Washington, D.C.: SPIDR, 1981, pp. 199–203, p. 199; also see: Benjamin Rubenstein, "The Bugaboo of Compulsory Arbitration," *Labor Law Journal* (March 1972) 23, pp. 167–186.

[31] Jennings et al., *Labor Relations in a Public Service Industry: Unions, Management, and Public Interest in Mass Transit*, p. 120; Thomas A. Kochan, "Dynamics of Dispute Resolution in the Public Sector," in *Public-Sector Bargaining*, Benjamin Carson, et al., Editors, Madison, WI: Industrial Relations Research Assoc. 1979, pp. 176–77.

[32] Final offer, "package" arbitration describes the arrangement where the neutral is forced to choose between the contract settlement, in its entirety, as proposed by labor or as proposed by management. Final offer, "issue-by-issue" arbitration, on the other hand, permits the neutral to select the proposal of labor or the proposal of management on each issue.

fashion a compromise agreement from the negotiation proposals of labor and management. Presumably, the negotiating parties are motivated to bargain in good–faith out of fear that, if their proposals appear unreasonable, the neutral will select the proposals of the other party—at significant cost to the party whose proposals the neutral did not select.

Evidence is mixed concerning the success of final offer arbitration in overcoming the disadvantages of "pure" arbitration. Long and Feuille, for example, found it to be "relatively successful" in Eugene, Oregon,[33] while Chandler concludes that "the new clout and centrality of the third party has a strong effect on interparty negotiating even when the procedure is designed to soften this result.[34] As for the impact upon substantive contract content, recent research studies seem to indicate that final offer arbitration changes the outcome from what would have occurred without arbitration—initially giving weak unions a "leg up" in achieving what could not be achieved because of deficiencies in bargaining power and/or skills.[35] These results are consistent with the earlier findings of Witney that arbitrators' decisions tend to be artificial, unduly rigid, and generally inferior to privately negotiated outcomes.[36]

Mediation-Arbitration (Med-Arb)

Mediation-arbitration combines the dispute settlement techniques of mediation and arbitration. Under med-arb, the mediator becomes the arbitrator with binding authority to resolve any issue not settled through private negotiations efforts. The parties agree in advance that all decisions, whether achieved through mediated–assisted private negotiation or through arbitration, "become a part of the mediator–arbitrator's award and are final and binding."[37] The essence of med-arb is that the specter of arbitration provides the parties additional incentive to resolve their differences through mediated–assisted private negotiation efforts. As noted by Kagel:

The parties for the first time really have to bare their souls, because if they are dishonest in the sense of holding back on a particular issue, they know the med-

[33] Gary Long and Peter Feuille, "Final-Offer Arbitration: 'Sudden Death' in Eugene," *Industrial and Labor Relations Review*, (January 1974), **27**: 186–203.

[34] Margaret K. Chandler, "Interest Arbitration: The Duty to Rectify Unequal Bargaining Skills," p. 202.

[35] Mary McCormick, "A Functional Analysis of Interest Arbitration in New York City Municipal Government, 1968-1975," in Marvin Levine and Eugene Hagbury, *Labor Relations in the Public Sector*, Salt Lake City, Utah: Brighton Publishing Co., 1979; David A. Bloom, "The Effect of Final Offer Arbitration on the Salaries of Municipal Police Officers in New Jersey," Princeton University, Department of Economics, Unpublished paper, October 1979; Barbara Kemmerer, "Interest Arbitration in New Jersey: The First Two Years," *New Jersey Public Employer-Employee Relations* New Brunswick, New Jersey: Rutgers University Institute of Management and Labor Relations, February 1980.

[36] Fred Witney, "Final-Offer Arbitration: The Indianapolis Experience," *Monthly Labor Review*, (May 1973), **96**: 20–25.

[37] Sam Kagel, "Combining Mediation and Arbitration," *Monthly Labor Review* (September 1973), **96**: 62.

arbitrator is going to make the decision. It really does keep them honest, and that's the whole point in med-arb.[38]

Early entrance by the neutral as a mediator also permits the neutral to become thoroughly familiar with the intricacies of the bargaining relationship and environment, thereby lessening the chance that any decision the arbitrator is called upon to render will be unrealistic and unworkable.

Mixed Impasse Resolution Techniques

Experiments combining two or more of the previously described impasse settlement techniques have been proposed and/or undertaken from time to time. These experiments can be classified according to the nature of their origin as either spontaneous or externally imposed.

Basic Steel's Experimental Negotiating Agreement

The most notable of the spontaneous experiments is the bargaining procedure initiated in 1974 by the United Steelworkers of America and the 10 companies that bargain together as the Coordinating Committee Steel Companies (i.e., Basic Steel). Adoption of this unprecedented approach to industrial peace was prompted by prevailing economic conditions in the steel industry, described by I. W. Abel, president of the United Steelworkers of America, in 1973 as follows:

> In the late 1950's, foreign steel producers started to make inroads on the U.S. Domestic market. The 116-day strike in 1959-the last one, incidentally—provided foreign steelmakers an initial opportunity to acquire and cultivate American customers. That was when our problems started to build up each time we went to the bargaining table. During our negotiating periods, the market was being glutted with more and more imported steel, while the industry kept stepping up production to satisfy the stockpiling steel customers undertook as a hedge against a possible strike.
>
> The stockpiling had its impact not only on our bargaining and on our successes at the bargaining table, but it also had a tremendous impact on the ups and downs of production and employment.
>
> This resulted in a "feast and famine" or "boom-bust" treadmill for our members in the Basic Steel Industry. Most Steelworkers enjoyed steady work and many worked overtime just prior to the negotiating periods and during the negotiating period. But then came the peaceful settlements, the working off of stockpiles, partial plant shut downs, and prolonged layoffs.[39]

In short, the experimental negotiating procedure was the product of economic necessity and survival; economic warfare simply became too costly.

The basic features of the Experimental Negotiating Agreement[40] as well as their underlying rational are listed in Box 14–3.

---

[38] Sam Kagel, "Combining Mediation and Arbitration," p. 62.

[39] I.W. Abel, "Basic Steel's Experimental Negotiating Agreement," *Monthly Labor Review*, (September, 1973) **96**: 39–42, 39–40.

[40] *Ibid.*

BOX 14–3. Experimental Negotiating Agreement: Features and Underlying Rationale

Benefit Guarantees:

Provision of minimum guaranteed union benefits (e.g., wage increases of 3 percent in each year of the 3-year contract, $150 bonus, retention of cost-of-living clause won in 1971, etc.) and protection of certain management rights.

Rationale:

Demonstrate to union rank-and-file the good-faith intent of management. Necessary for union acceptance of arbitration to resolve national issues (See below) and retention of managerial prerogatives critical to industry efficiency.

Arbitration of Unresolved National Issues:

Free negotiation of almost all economic and fringe-benefit issues on the national level with arbitration of unresolved issues.

Rationale:

Motivates private settlement of issues because both sides prefer an agreement tailored by themselves to solve the problems they know best while eliminating the possibility of an economically debilitating national strike.

Resolution of Local Impasses by Strike:

Local unions granted the right to strike over local issues for the first time.

Rationale:

Promotes more rapid resolution of local issues, a long-time sore spot of labor-management relations in the Basic Steel Industry, by increasing the costs of disagreement. Permits local agreements to be shaped by local conditions to a greater extent than ever before without increasing the likelihood of a nationwide disruption of steel output.

The success of Basic Steel's Experimental Negotiating Agreement can be measured by the fact that it was utilized during both the 1977 and the 1980 contract negotiations. Thus, the course of events in the Basic Steel Industry during the past eight years apparently confirms I.W. Abel's optimism voiced shortly prior to the implementation of the Experimental Negotiating Agreement in 1974, namely:

We believe this unprecedented experiment will prove there is a better way for labor and management to negotiate contracts. The new procedure will not only relieve both sides of the pressures of a potential shutdown, but also offers us a genuine opportunity to achieve results equal to those obtainable when the threat of a strike exists. We have carefully preserved the nature and role of our bargaining relationship. What we have done is to extend and refine the tools of collective bargaining to solve a special and highly vexing problem afflicting our industry. . .[41]

Mutual Anxiety System

One of the most innovative of the externally imposed, mixed, impasse resolution procedures is the Mutual Anxiety System proposed to the California State Assembly in 1973. This system seeks to motivate public-sector parties (particularly employers) to bargain in good–faith without exclusive reliance upon the strike.

Basic steps and elements of the Mutual Anxiety System[42] are given in Box 14–4. It goes without saying that the procedure would cease at that step where agreement is reached. The steps, themselves, reflect an attempt to simultaneously protect the public interest and motivate good-faith bargaining—an attempt to strike a balance between public interest and special interest.[43] The motivation for good-faith bargaining stems from the "uncertainty, the fear on both sides of the bargaining table of possible consequences if agreement is not reached"[44] that is, that the fact finder's report will become binding upon both parties. In the words of one of the creators of the Mutual Anxiety System: "What we tried to do was create a structural risk, so that rather than run the risk arising from nonagreement, the parties would prefer to settle."[45]

Summary and Conclusion

The most widely used method of resolving impasses arising during collective bargaining is economic warfare—the strike or lock out. The costs associated with work stoppages, particularly those occurring in public employment, have prompted labor relations experts and practitioners alike to search for alternative means of dispute resolution. The problem reduces to one of identifying techniques which provide incentives for negotiating parties to bargain in good–faith and to fashion their own solutions to problems of mutual concern, but which do not impose the high costs of economic warfare. Various third-party techniques, such as mediation, fact finding, arbitration, and variations/combinations thereof, hold promise as cost-minimizing impasse resolution measures. Each, however, has its own limitations and disadvantages.

[41] I.W. Abel, "Basic Steel's Experimental Negotiating Agreement," p 42.

[42] Donald H. Wollett, "Mutual Anxiety: A California Proposal," *Monthly Labor Review*, (September 1973), **96:** 51–52.

[43] See Chapter 15.

[44] Donald H. Wollett, "Mutual Anxiety: A California Proposal," p. 51.

[45] *Ibid.* p. 52.

BOX 14–4. Mutual Anxiety Impasse Resolution Steps

Mediation

If unsuccessful, then—

Fact Finding with Recommendations

Parties required to negotiate and consider fact-finding proposals for some specified period of time.

Vote on Fact-Finding Report

At the end of the period of time specified in the previous step, both sides are required to submit the fact-finding report to their respective constituencies for acceptance or rejection—prerequisite for right to strike or lock out. If either side rejects the fact-finding report, negotiation continues or—

Strike/Lock Out Notice

Any party wishing to strike or lock out is required to give 5 days' notice to the other side and to the public.

Consumer/Taxpayer–Initiated Court Action

At any time following the strike/lock out notice, judicial relief may be sought by any consumer or taxpayer. The court would then determine (1) whether there exists an imminent threat to public health and safety and, if so, (2) whether there are alternative safeguards (other than the injunction) against the threat to public health and safety. Where there is no threat, court relief is not forthcoming and the work stoppage continues.

Injunctive Relief and Conversion of the Fact-Finding Report to a Binding Arbitration Award

Where the court determines a threat to public health and safety to exist and that there is no alternative method of insulating the public therefrom, it will enjoin the work stoppage and convert the fact-finding report to a binding arbitration award.

Mediation, for example, works best where the parties are motivated by the pressure of a strike deadline. Arbitration, on the other hand, substitutes the judgment of an outsider for that of the parties closest to the problem and may also discourage collective bargaining. The ultimate choice of a dispute resolution technique, therefore, should be based on careful evaluation of the benefits and costs of each proposed technique.

COMMENTARY: Mr. Robert Coulson Speaking on the Role of Arbitration in Labor-Management Relations

Robert Coulson is President of the American Arbitration Association. He is a member of the New York and Massachusetts Bar and a Certified Association Executive (CAE) of the American Society of Association Executives. He is a Director of the Institute for Mediation and Conflict Resolution, Center for Community Justice, Federation of Protestant Welfare Agencies, Fund for Modern Courts and the Edwin Gould Foundation for Children; a Fellow of The New York Bar Foundation; formerly Secretary of the Association of the Bar of the City of New York, 1961–1963. He is a  *member of the International Council for Commercial Arbitration, the London Panel of International Arbitrators, an Honorary Fellow, Arbitrators' Institute of Canada; and Honorary Member, American Society of Appraisers. He is the author of* The Termination Handbook, Business Arbitration-What You Need to Know, Labor Arbitration-What You Need to Know *and* How to Stay Out of Court. *Mr. Coulson has written and lectured extensively on the settlement of disputes. A graduate of Yale University and Harvard Law School, he lives in Connecticut with his family.*

Contractual grievance arbitration plays a vital role in labor-management relations in the United States. Tens of thousands of collective bargaining contracts provide for grievance procedures ending in impartial arbitration: the decisions of neutral labor-relations experts serving as arbitrators interpret and define collective bargaining contracts in many industries where workers are organized. The reported case opinions of labor arbitrators constitute a common law of the shop, respected by representatives of labor and management. To a large degree, these cases shape the rights of all American workers.

For example, the definition of "just cause," defined in thousands of labor arbitration opinions, has established a standard of fair treatment in employment relationships, both in the private and public sectors. Such criteria are not only reflected in collective bargaining contracts and in the work rules of corporate employers: they are to be found in the day-to-day perceptions of American workers and supervisors. The award of a labor arbitrator may be binding only upon the parties to a particular collective bargaining contract: but the accumulated decision of arbitrators, published and collected in various services, have stabilized employment relationships in America and created a climate of industrial justice in the workplace.

Labor arbitrators who render awards involving many different industries and working situations, provide a wealth of experience and understanding of the labor-management relationship. Labor arbitrators are mature, highly educated and responsible professionals. They have achieved broad acceptability with labor and management because they provide a pattern of decisions which has made it possible for parties to maintain a mature, productive relationship. It is fitting that the national labor laws encourage parties to create systems of voluntary grievance resolution and that the courts enforce arbitrators' awards. This system of voluntary industrial justice is crucial to the preservation of a viable collective-bargaining system. In the United States, we accept the concept that labor unions should be authorized under the law to engage in collective bargaining for their members. Our national commitment to voluntary grievance arbitration should be equally steadfast. Students of the labor-relations process should recognize how arbitration supports and reinforces the individual worker's legal right to be represented by a professional organization. Without impartial arbitration, unions and employers would have to settle such matters in court, a forum not calculated to encourage pragmatic problem solving, so necessary in the practical world of labor relations.

DISCUSSION QUESTIONS

1. All impasses share the same thing in common: the failure of the two sides to agree. Consequently, a given impasse resolution technique is equally effective in resolving all types of labor disputes. Discuss.

2. Why are "internal" dispute resolution techniques preferable to "external" dispute resolution techniques? Explain.

3. All "external" dispute resolution techniques are peaceful in nature. Comment.

4. While a persuasive personality on the part of a mediator is a necessary condition for successful dispute settlement, it is not a sufficient condition. Explain.

5. Discuss the dangers associated with active mediator involvement during the early stages of the negotiation process.

6. When does mediation work best, and why is its effectiveness so difficult to determine?

7. "Bargaining parties don't give a damn about public opinion." If this statement is true, what implication does it hold for fact finding as a dispute settlement technique? Explain.

8. "The fact finder shall make a recommendation as to the settlement" taking "into consideration. . .comparisons of wages and hours of the employees involved, with wages of other employees working for other public agencies and private concerns doing comparable work. . ." Critique the foregoing, decision-making criteria established to guide fact finders in public-sector, teacher bargaining disputes.

9. What is the basis of union-management opposition to interest arbitration as a method of the dispute settlement in the private sector? Has this negative attitude been reinforced by the NLRB and/or the courts? Discuss.

10. What is the so-called "narcotic" effect of arbitration. Are there any "costs" that can be built into the arbitration process which might reduce or eliminate this effect? Explain.

11. Based on statements made in the chapter concerning the disadvantages (i.e, costs) of interest arbitration, what factor would recommend final-offer, "issue-by-issue," interest arbitration over final-offer, "package," interest arbitration?

12. Mediation-arbitration (med-arb) as an impasse resolution technique is preferable to simple interest arbitration. Comment.

13. Generally, the greater the costs of disagreement in collective bargaining the more effective are private negotiation efforts in producing a peaceful settlement. Yet, the costs of disagreement may become so great that negotiating parties abandon purely private negotiation efforts. Explain this paradox in context of Basic Steel's Experimental Negotiating Agreement.

14. The "Mutual Anxiety System" of impasse resolution apparently strikes a balance between public interest and special interest. Explain.

SELECTED REFERENCES

Bent, Alan Edward and T. Zane Reeves, *Collective Bargaining in the Public Sector,* Menlo Park, California: The Benjamin/Cummings Publishing Company, Inc., 1978.

Clune, William H. *Parties' and Negotiator's Attitudes Toward the Fairness of Final Offer Arbitration in Wisconsin,* Disputes Processing Research Program, University of Wisconsin Law School, 1980.

"Exploring Alternatives to the Strike" (A Collection of Short Articles Dealing with Alternative Methods of Dispute Resolution) *Monthly Labor Review,* (September 1973), **96:** 35–66.

Grodin, Joseph R., "Either-Or Arbitration for Public Employee Disputes," *Industrial Relations,* (May 1972), **11:** 260–66.

Jennings, Kenneth M. et al., *Labor Relations in a Public Service Industry: Unions, Management, and the Public Interest in Mass Transit,* New York: Praeger Publishers, Inc., 1978.

Kochan, Thomas A. "Dynamics of Dispute to Resolution in the Public Sector," in *Public Sector Bargaining,* Benjamin Aaron et al., Editors, Madison, Wisconsin: Industrial Relations Research Association, 1979.

Luberman, Myron, *Public Sector Bargaining: A Policy Reappraisal,* Lexington, Mass.: Lexington Books, 1980.

Nelson, Nels, "Final-Offer Arbitration: Some Problems," *The Arbitration Journal,* (September 1981), **36:** 24–33.

Sharman, Clifford, "Interest Arbitration in the Private Sector," *The Arbitration Journal*, (September 1981), **36**: 14–23.

Simkin, William E., *Mediation and the Dynamics of Collective Bargaining*, Washington, D.C.: The Bureau of National Affairs, Inc., 1971.

Stevens, Carl M., "Mediation and the Role of the Neutral," in *Frontiers of Collective Bargaining*, John T. Dunlop and Neil W. Chamberlain, Editors, New York: Harper and Row, Publishers, 1967.

Straus, Donald B., "Kissinger and the Management of Complexity: An Attempt that Failed," in *Dynamics of Third-Party Intervention: Kissinger in the Middle East*, Jeffrey Z. Rubin, Editor, New York: Praeger Publishers, Inc., 1981.

Sulzner, George T., "The Impact of Impasse Procedures in Public Sector Labor: An Overview," *Journal of Collective Negotiations in the Public Sector*, (1975), **4**(1): 3–21

Witney, Fred, "Final-Offer Arbitration: The Indianapolis Experience," *Monthly Labor Review*, (May 1973), **96**: 20–5

Zack, Arnold M., "Improving Mediation and Fact-Finding in the Public Sector," *Labor Law Journal*, 1970, **21**(5): 259–73.

Zirkel, Perry A. and J. Gary Lutz, "Characteristics and Functions of Mediators: A Pilot Study," *The Arbitration Journal*, (June 1981), **36**: 15–20.

New Frontiers in Collective Bargaining

Part IV

New Frontiers in
Collective
Bargaining

Chapter 15

Collective Bargaining in the Public Sector:
A Square Peg in a Round Hole?

Collective bargaining has never been sold as an answer to anything, but it is the lesser of a number of evils that exist in the private sector and, in a somewhat modified form, in the public sector. Management and labor have to go through some sort of messy process to find a way of agreeing with each other for a period of time, and the only alternatives are unilateral determination by management—which leads to exploitation...[1]

The marketplace, not union demands, should set pay levels for men and women in comparable jobs, Detroit Mayor Coleman Young said during the strike. Anything else, he said, "flies in the face of reality of the fiscal crises in local government throughout this country."[2]

The laws outlawing strikes in public employment do more to provoke strikes than to prevent them, and they emasculate the collective bargaining process. Petty tyrants, whose arrogance is matched only by their incompetence in labor relations, seem to flourish in public management. They create little dynasties for themselves and use anti-strike legislation as a shield in denying fair treatment to the employees under them.[3]

[1] Albert L. Shanker, "Why Teachers Need the Right to Strike," *Monthly Labor Review*, (September 1973), **96**: 48. Albert Shanker is President of the United Federation of Teachers, AFL-CIO.

[2] Philip J. Trounstine, "Unions Unlid 'Pandora's Box' With Sex Discrimination Suits," *Muncie Star*, (September 20, 1981), p. 16.

[3] Matthew Guinan, "The Unreal Distinction Between Public and Private Sectors," *Monthly Labor Review*, (September 1973), **96**: 47. Matthew Guinan is International President of the Transport Workers' Union of America, AFL-CIO.

Lewis said that Reagan felt "much more deeply about the moral issue" involved. Convening an early-morning briefing beneath a portrait of Calvin Coolidge, whose iron-fisted handling of the 1919 Boston police strike helped propel him to the Presidency, Reagan growled, "Dammit, the law is the law, and the law says they cannot strike. If they strike, they quit their jobs."[4]

The public sector has grown at a more rapid pace than any other sector of the economy over the last twenty-five years. At a time when union penetration of the total civilian labor force was declining, union organization of public employees proceeded at a rate rivaling union private-sector gains made during the 1930's. The growth of the public sector and public-sector unionism has recently encountered stiff opposition from a disenchanted and angry tax-paying public. Begun at the state level in 1978 when California voters overwhelmingly accepted Proposition 13 slashing state property taxes by $7 billion, the backlash against "big government" spending and taxes carried Ronald Reagan to the White House in 1980. The above quotes by principal actors on the public stage not only mirror the complexity of the problems and controversies existent in the public arena but also the deep-seated emotionalism which must be overcome if the issues are to be satisfactorily resolved. The purpose of this chapter is to examine the growth of the public sector and the attendant phenomenon of public-sector unionism, the factors responsible therefore, and the unique characteristics thereof and their impact on the bargaining process, including the controversial right-to-strike issue. The chapter concludes with a discussion of the current public-sector crisis, its underlying causes, the manner in which public-sector unionism has contributed to the crisis, and the right of public employees to meaningful input concerning items directly affecting their economic welfare.

Growth of the Public Sector

The fastest growing employment sector in the nation since the early 1960's has been the public sector. One out of every five employed members of the labor force is either a federal, state, or local government employee. "With about three million civilian employees, the federal government is the largest single employer in the United States; its work force is larger than that of the ten largest industrial corporations combined."[5]

The Classical View of the Public Sector

The influence wielded by all levels of government in today's economy presents a stark contrast to the very limited role for government envisioned by

---

[4]"Who Controls the Air," *Newsweek,* (August 17, 1981), p. 19.

[5]Alan Edward Bent and T. Zane Reeves, *Collective Bargaining in the Public Sector,* Menlo Park, California: The Benjamin/Cummings Publishing Company, Inc., 1978, p. 3.

Adam Smith two hundred years ago. Writing in 1776, the "Father of Modern Economics" stated that the state has but three legitimate functions, namely:

> that of protecting the society from the violence and invasion of other independent societies..[6]
>
> that of protecting, as far as possible, every member of the society from the injustice of oppression of every other member of it, or the duty of establishing an exact administration of justice..[7]
>
> that of erecting and maintaining those public institutions and those public works, which, though they may be in the highest degree advantageous to a great society, are, however, of such a nature, that the profit could never repay the expense of any individual or small number of individuals, and which it therefore cannot be expected that any individual or small number of individuals should erect or maintain.[8]

The first two duties are self-explanatory. By the third, Adam Smith meant provision of institutions "facilitating the commerce of the society and those promoting the instruction of the people"[9]—roads, bridges, canals, harbors, and schools.

Funding of government services was of particular concern to Smith. While national defense "should be defrayed by the general contribution of the whole society..,"[10] general tax revenue should not be the primary source of support for other government services. With regard to the administration of justice:

> The whole expense of justice too might easily be defrayed by the *fees* of court; and, without exposing the administration of justice to any real hazard of corruption, the public revenue might thus be entirely discharged from a certain, though perhaps, but a small incumbrance. [Emphasis added][11]

Likewise:

> it does not seem necessary that the expense of those public works should be defrayed from that public revenue, as it is commonly called...The greater part of such public works may easily be so managed, as to afford a *particular revenue* sufficient for defraying their own expense, without bringing any burden upon the general revenue of society. [Emphasis added][12]

And, finally:

> The institutions for education of the youth may, in the same manner, furnish a revenue sufficient for defraying their own expense. The *fee* or *honorary* which the

[6] Adam Smith, *The Wealth of Nations*, Cannan Edition, New York: The Modern Library, Inc., 1937, p. 653.

[7] *Ibid.*, p. 669.

[8] *Ibid.*, p. 681.

[9] *Ibid.*

[10] *Ibid.*, p. 787.

[11] *Ibid.*, pp. 677–78.

[12] *Ibid.*, p. 682.

scholar pays to the master naturally constitutes a revenue of this kind. [Emphasis added][13]

Smith's preoccupation with user fees and taxes to finance non-defense-related state expenditures stemmed from his concern for equity (e.g., "It is unjust that the whole society should contribute toward an expense of which the benefit is confined to a part of society"[14]) and efficiency. According to Smith, the use of general revenue to support specific government services increased the likelihood of waste. Without a user fee, consumers (i.e., citizens) lack an effective leverage mechanism to guarantee the types and quality of services desired; services are dependent upon general tax revenue and not upon consumer approval.

The Nature of Government Services

Despite changes in the magnitude of the public sector as well as in the relative importance of different revenue sources, one thing that has not changed since the time of Adam Smith is the basic nature of government services. All government services can be classified into one of two categories. First, there are those services which would not be provided at all if not provided by the state. Here, either capital requirements for the service far exceed the financial resources of private individuals to provide the service or, if within the financial wherewithall of private providers, the inability to exclude non-paying individuals from benefits (i.e., the existence of what economists call external economies) renders provision of the service unprofitable. The impact of external economies upon private provision can be illustrated by means of a simple private–sector example. Two homeowners with a common property line desire to enclose their backyards with chain-link fence. Aware that the homeowner who postpones fencing the yard until the other homeowner's fence is in place can realize substantial savings by "tying" into the fence along the common property line, both homeowners delay the installation of fence. Thus, the fence is constructed only after great delay or not constructed at all. In either case, the existence of external economies (i.e., the inability to exclude non-paying individuals from the benefits of a good or service financed by another) has hampered private production of the good. The classic example of a service which falls into this category of government services is national defense. Both resource requirements and external economies preclude its provision by the private sector.

The second category of government services includes all services which would not be provided in sufficient volume if left exclusively to production by the private sector. Quite simply, the market system would price such services beyond the reach of many citizens. To guarantee provision of the socially optimum volume of these essential services, society has seen fit to subsidize their production through taxation. Examples most often cited are education, police protection, and fire protection. Also included within this category are

---

[13] Adam Smith, *The Wealth of Nations*, p. 716.
[14] *Ibid.*, p. 767.

services intended to remedy the failure of the private sector to fully account for all costs of private production. Here, the price of the product does not reflect total production cost; part of the cost of production has been shifted to society as a whole by way of air, water, and land pollution. Societal concern for diseconomies, as these costs are commonly called, has led to a complex system of government standards, rules, and regulations designed to internalize the costs, thereby protecting the environment for all citizens.[15]

Factors Responsible for the Growth of the Public Sector

Having touched upon the magnitude of the present-day public sector, the limited role for government envisioned by Adam Smith, and the basic nature of government services, an important topic has yet to be addressed—the factors responsible for the phenomenal growth of the public sector. Three factors share responsibility for this growth. First, the external diseconomies associated with economic growth have expanded government's role by exacerbating long-standing public problems (e.g., crime, congestion, etc.) and by creating new problems (e.g., pollution). Thus, economic growth has increased the intensity as well as the number of problems within the public domain.

Second, as real income levels have risen during the course of economic growth, services have become a proportionately more important component of aggregate demand. In the jargon of economics, the demand for services is said to be "income elastic". As an intergral part of the service sector of the economy, government has shared in this income-driven growth. In addition, rising levels of affluence have prompted individuals to delegate greater responsibility for services traditionally provided, for the most part, by the private sector (e.g., health care, retirement security, welfare, etc.) to various levels of government. In a real sense, it could be said that social consciousness and generosity are also income elastic.

Finally, and most importantly, society's propensity to accord the state a broader role in the economy has not been checked, until recently, by that factor which limits demand in the private sector, namely, price (i.e., cost). Reliance upon general revenues instead of user fees to finance government services, the consequent diffusion of cost over a large tax-paying public, the temporal separation between provision of a public service and payment for that service by way of general taxes, and the seemingly limitless ability of government to defray cost through borrowing, have all combined to create the erroneous impression that government services are bargain, if not "free", services—thus stimulating overconsumption and overproduction. In short, widely–used methods of funding have masked the real costs of government services and have thereby pushed society in the direction of an expanded role for government. In light of the foregoing discussion, Adam Smith's earlier

---

[15]The rationale for including such services under the second category is that a significant proportion of the population could escape the impact of external diseconomies by moving to non-polluted areas. The critical issue is not whether a clean environment is available to some (it will be at least in the short run) but rather guaranteeing its availability to the broadest possible segment of society. Hence, the inclusion of these services in the second category of government services.

noted preoccupation with user taxes and fees becomes eminently more understandable.

Union Organization of the Public Sector

At the time organized labor was enjoying great success organizing private–sector employees during the 1930's and 1940's, public-sector employees remained notably resistant to the beck-and-call of union organizers. The fact that public employees are, for the most part, white-collar workers, by itself, does not suffice as an explanation for the strength of their resistance to organization. The key to public-sector resistance was the singular nature of public-sector employment conditions. Public employment bestowed benefits not found in the private sector; "merit hiring, broad fringe benefits, almost absolute job security, and an assured income (not dependent on vagaries of weather, availability of risk capital, or the ebb and flow of fads and fashion)"[16] more than offset any of the claimed benefits from unionization. "In truth these were the tradeoffs for private-sector unionism."[17]

The fortunes of organized labor in the public sector changed abruptly at the outset of the 1960's. Where union organizers had earlier been rebuffed in their organizational efforts, they now enjoyed a good measure of success. This success stemmed from the same set of factors responsible for earlier union successes in the goods-producing sector of the economy. First and foremost of these factors was the "proletarianization"[18] of the public employee. As noted in the discussion of private-sector unions in Chapter 2, union growth is predicated upon the development of a working-class consciousness. As long as a worker's basic needs for food, shelter, security, participation, recognition (i.e., status) and self-actualization are realized on the job, there exists no motive for union membership[19]—no working-class consciousness. Indeed, fulfillment of these basic human needs by virtue of employment position tends to breed a prejudice against individuals forced to seek realization of these needs through union membership.[20] Until quite recently, public-sector, white-collar employment was able to satisfy, to a large extent, the full spectrum of worker needs. Just as nineteenth century workers in the goods-producing sector of the economy were proletarianized by the economic changes wrought by the Industrial Revolution, so too have twentieth-century workers in the public sector been proletarianized by recent economic events. Technological innovation in the form of automated production techniques (e.g., data processing) has undercut the ability of public-sector employment to meet basic employee needs. The emphasis upon

---

[16] Sam Zagoria, Editor, *Public Workers and Public Unions*, Englewood Cliffs, N.J.: Prentice-Hall, Inc., Spectrum Books, 1972, p. 1.

[17] *Ibid.*

[18] Stanely Aronowitz, *False Promises: The Shaping of American Working Class Consciousness*, New York: McGraw-Hill Book Company, 1973, Chapter 6.

[19] A.H. Maslow, *Motivation and Personality*, New York: Harper & Row, Publishers, 1954.

[20] This forms the basis of white-collar workers' long-standing antipathy toward blue-collar unionism.

efficiency and labor-saving techniques has methodically reduced job content, skill, challenge, initiative, upward mobility, and security,[21] thereby blurring the basic distinction between private-sector, blue-collar and public–sector, white-collar employment and thus eroding a formidable barrier to union organization. In short, public employees have seen their jobs become blue–collar in nature.

Coincident with the blue-collar metamorphosis of many public-sector jobs were union blue-collar contract gains, particularly in the area of fringe benefits, which worsened the relative economic standing of non-union public employees.[22] Thus, to turn a well known phrase, injury (economic) was added to insult (lost prestige, status, self-fulfillment), providing a positive incentive for union membership. As a result, the identification that public employees previously had with management (i.e., the elitist attitude noted earlier) melted away and was replaced by a growing working-class consciousness which organized labor has successfully capitalized upon.

Increased white-collar receptivity to unionism notwithstanding, organization of the public sector did not come easily for labor. The concerns and needs of public employees were not the same in all respects as those of private-sector, blue-collar workers. For example, of greater concern to public employees than to blue-collar employees are the twin issues of working conditions and product (service) quality. As professionals, many public employees (e.g., teachers, firefighters, healthcare employees, etc.) are convinced that it is their right, indeed, their duty to determine the type of work environment that will guarantee the tax-paying public the quality service it deserves. Viewed from the perspective of professionalism, many "job actions", which at first glance appear capricious or unreasonable, take on greater meaning—for example, the 1976 Los Angeles County hospital strike by interns and residents, the 1981 Professional Air Traffic Controllers' strike, and reoccurring teachers' strikes throughout the country, where the critical issues were (are), respectively, patient care, air safety, and quality instruction. Another issue closely related to professionalism and of deep concern to many public employees is that of image—white–collar, public employees have historically shown a strong reluctance to join traditional labor unions out of the fear that such affiliation would compromise their professionalism and diminish their status in the public eye. Although slow and prompted in part by the competitive challenge presented by the formation and growth of professional employee associations[23], e.g., National Education Association (NEA), American Association of University Professors (AAUP), Fraternal Order of Police (FOP), etc., organized labor has acclimated itself to the needs and concerns of the public employee. As was the case following accommodation of skilled tradesmen in the late nineteenth century and unskilled/semi-skilled industrial workers in the twentieth century, union membership increased dramatically. Organized labor once again demon-

[21] Albert A. Blum, Editor, *White Collar Workers*, New York: Random House, Inc. 1971, p. 17.

[22] Bent and Reeves, *Collective Bargaining in the Public Sector*, pp. 10–11.

[23] Other than in name, professional associations differ little from public-sector unions. Thus, for purposes of this chapter, they will be considered one and the same.

strated that characteristic, adaptability, responsible for its long-term growth and vitality, this time in the public sector.

The final factor responsible for organized labor's successful penetration of the public sector was the highly favorable political/legal environment. Society's militant concern for minority-group rights during the 1960's and 1970's, as evidenced by the passage of one "rights" statute after another, quite naturally spilled over into the public-sector, labor relations arena. President John F. Kennedy's Executive Order 10988 of 1962, authorizing collective bargaining in the federal services, loosed a virtual flood of state legislation protecting the rights of public employees to organize and bargain collectively. This enabling legislation has had the same salutary impact upon public-sector, trade union growth that the 1935 National Labor Relations Act had upon private-sector, trade union growth.

Unique Characteristics of the Public Employer

Critical to any analysis of public-sector collective bargaining and the problems attendant thereto is an understanding of the similarities and differences between public and private employers. All employers execute contracts with their employees whereby the employees agree to accept direction and to render specified labor services toward achievement of employer-set goals in exchange for wages and salaries. Beyond this basic exchange function, however, private and public employers share very little in common. The environment within which goals are determined and employees are directed differs significantly for public and private employers. Differences in the source of decision-making authority, in the distribution of decision-making authority, and in the service-delivery mechanism are primarily responsible for the environmental dichotomy between private and public employers.

Public Employer Sovereignty

Property rights constitute the source of decision-making authority in the private sector. The right to direct a business in an unencumbered fashion as the owners deem appropriate has long been accepted as a fundamental tenet of laissez-faire capitalism. So revered was this ownership principle that it became the cornerstone of early labor relations law, prohibiting collective employee influence upon the terms and conditions of employment. All authority, benefits, and privileges flowed downward, employees enjoying only what the owners of property unilaterally bestowed upon them. It wasn't until the 1930's that the political and legal departments of government recognized the personal rights of private employees to organize and to bargain collectively and placed them on an equal footing with rights stemming from property ownership.[24] The high regard in which society still holds property rights and the decision-making

[24] See Chapter 4.

authority emanating therefrom is evidenced by the widely accepted "residual rights" theory of management. According to this theory, management retains all rights not wrested from its grasp by the union during collective bargaining. Put somewhat differently, employees must look to the collective bargaining agreement for specific enumeration of rights whereas the employer must look to the agreement for specific limitation of rights.

People constitute the source of supreme decision-making authority in the public sector. Sovereignty, "the supreme, absolute, and uncontrolled power by which any independent state is governed"[25], rests with the people. Decision–making authority flows in an upward direction from the people to various levels of government which, in turn, exercise this sovereign power on behalf of the people. The traditional "position on sovereignty maintains that government", as designated caretaker of sovereignty, "has sole authority which cannot be given to, taken by, or shared with anyone"[26] because "the supremacy of its authority in mass society provides the society with its sole rationality"[27]— provides society with the *raison d'être* for the existence of government. Translated and applied to labor relations, the orthodox position on sovereignty mandates unilateral government determination of the terms and conditions of employment, thus serving as the main philosophical argument against collective bargaining in the public sector. As such, it is more than vaguely reminiscent of the property rights argument used by employers to thwart joint employee-employer (bilateral) decision-making in the private sector prior to the 1930's.

The sovereignty doctrine no longer enjoys the popularity it once did as an argument against collective bargaining in the public sector. In the first place, given the execution of government contracts with various business groups wherein terms and conditions are bilaterally determined, the argument is, at best, convoluted, and, at worst, given the government's active encouragement to employees in the private sector to challenge managerial authority, smacks of duplicity. Second, the force of the argument has been reduced to the extent that various governmental units have voluntarily recognized and bargained with public employee representatives. Finally, the sovereign power of government has been limited by legislation and court decision in non-labor relations matters (e.g., the 1948 Tucker Act permitting contract suits against the federal government).[28] Logic would seem to warrant a similar limitation of sovereignty in the labor relations arena when justified by the public interest— as indeed has occurred at the federal and state levels where executive orders and statutes permit organization and bargaining. Despite its decreased overall popularity, the sovereignty concept nonetheless remains a convenient, albeit not very convincing, philosophical argument advanced by government officials and others who fear "that collective bargaining would infringe on management

[25] Michael H. Moscow et al., *Collective Bargaining in Public Employment*, New York: Random House, Inc., 1970, pp. 16–17.

[26] *Ibid.*, p. 17.

[27] Bent and Reeves, *Collective Bargaining in the Public Sector*, p. 58

[28] Michael H. Moscow et al., *Collective Bargaining in Public Employment*, p. 17.

prerogatives, weaken authority, and affect adversely the efficiency of government operations."[29]

The Diffused Nature of Public Employer Decision-Making Authority

Where final decision-making authority is concentrated in the hands of the chief executive in the private sector and delegated to the negotiator for purposes of collective bargaining, the public sector is characterized by a separation and diffusion of decision-making authority within and among levels of government. Separation of power is the product of a system of checks and balances, built into specific political jurisdictions (i.e., levels of government) to prevent abuse of power, and the doctrine of federal (state) preemption by implication, developed to maintain a consistent scheme of control regarding matters over which the federal (state) government has exercised jurisdiction.

Whatever its rationale, horizontal and vertical distribution of decision-making authority is a constant source of irritation and frustration for employee representatives during negotiations. The nominal employer often is not the "real" employer, that is, the agency, unit, or level of government with final, binding, decision-making authority. This bifurcation of authority is nowhere more clearly evident than in the negotiation of union demands which have monetary implications that require legislative approval. As if the existence of dual employers was not a sufficient burden upon the collective bargaining process, the identity of the "real" employer changes in shell-game fashion as employee demands change. Thus, the nominal employer:

> may be able to bargain with employee representatives but not have final authority to accept labor's proposals. Instead, he may have to present the results of negotiations to a legislature or a council for ratification. If the union's demands concern the civil service system, another level of authority is drawn into the decision-making process. If final proposals require a change in existing law of the political unit, the entire electorate may be a part of the ratification system.[30]

The deleterious impact upon meaningful bargaining of a "now-I-do-now-I–don't" posture regarding final, binding, decision-making authority has long been recognized in the private sector. Its adverse effects are such that the National Labor Relations Board (NLRB) has determined that evidence of its existence constitutes proof of an employer's failure to bargain in good–faith. Due to the institutionalized nature of diffused authority in the public sector, the problem is more widespread and, consequently, more severe.

Separation of power and its harmful effects upon bargaining have been advanced as arguments against collective bargaining by public employees. To argue that a process should not be implemented simply because implementation is difficult, is equivalent to "throwing the baby out with the bath water"; it is simply not convincing. Granted, diffusion of authority imposes certain costs,

---

[29] Michael H. Moscow et al., *Collective Bargaining in Public Employment*, p. 18.
[30] Ibid., p. 211.

but these as well as other costs should be evaluated in context of the benefits associated with joint employee-employer decision-making before any decision is made. One benefit often overlooked in regard to the relationship between collective bargaining and separation of power is the increased accountability (efficiency?) on the part of public-sector managers that results from bargaining-induced clarification of the lines of management authority. Also not to be forgotten is the fact that unions encountered a similarly frustrating problem when bargaining in the private sector commenced on a wide scale in the 1930's. The question "Who is management within the framework of a complicated corporate structure?" has since been satisfactorily resolved.

The Public Employer Service Delivery System

In many respects, the private employer is like a juggler who must call upon a variety of skills and talents (e.g., concentration, eye-hand coordination, physical strength) to perform successfully. Long-term survival requires the private employer to ascertain consumer tastes and wants, to organize and combine factor inputs to produce the types of goods and services consumers desire, and to set a price that consumers are willing to pay and which will cover the costs of production including a normal profit. Efficiency is guaranteed by the existence of other sources of supply of the good or service (i.e., domestic and/or foreign competition). Like the case of the juggler, failure in any one of the areas will spell disaster for the private employer.

The precarious position in which the employer finds himself in a laissez–faire capitalistic economy[31] operates as a constraint upon union demands during bargaining, roughly limiting such gains to the long-run increase in worker productivity. More specifically, since increased labor costs must be offset by increased productivity, reduced profits, or increased product price, the private employer's need to remain competitive and earn a normal profit limits collective bargaining gains to productivity increases. The financially ailing automobile industry stands as a stark reminder of what happens to private employers who ignore this economic fact (principle) of life.

By contrast, the public employer operates within a relatively risk-free, secure environment. The needs of consumers are identified through the established political process (i.e., by political, not dollar, votes) and serviced through the government's ability to tax. Operating in such an environment, the public employer is not subject to the same constraints that the private employer is subject to during bargaining. Neither the need to earn a normal profit nor the need to maintain market position (i.e., remain competitive) inhibits the public employer's generosity during bargaining. For, by nature and definition, the public employer is nonprofit and the sole provider of the service.

At first glance, it might appear that taxes play the same role in the public sector that competition (price) plays in the private sector—that of guaranteeing efficiency and restraining labor demands. Presumably, increased taxes to finance additional services and/or higher public–employee wages would be

[31] See the remarks of George W. Taylor contained in Box 6–1 of Chapter 6.

resisted by way of the ballot box whenever taxpayers perceived these costs (i.e., taxes) as exceeding the value of services provided, in much the same way that consumers register opposition to increased prices in the private sector by shifting purchases to alternative sources of supply. Closer examination indicates otherwise. As noted earlier in this chapter, current methods of financing public expenditures create the erroneous impression on the part of taxpayers that government services are bargain–priced—that the value of the services far exceed their cost. With true costs seriously underestimated in the benefit-cost decision rule, anticipated taxpayer resistance (i.e., the guarantor of efficiency and the restrainor of labor demands) never materializes until a critical threshold is reached which spawns a tax revolt, causing dislocations of crisis proportions in the public sector.[32] This absence of an even-handed regulatory mechanism in the public sector constitutes the most cogent argument against public employee bargaining. It is also the factor primarily responsible for the differences between private and public-sector bargaining—where public-sector bargaining does take place.

The Impact of Public-Employer Characteristics Upon Public-Sector Bargaining

The previously-noted characteristics of the public employer have left their imprint upon collective bargaining in the public sector. Virtually all aspects of the joint decision-making process have felt their influence. Of particular importance is the impact these characteristics have had on unit determination, the scope of negotiations, the basic nature of bargaining, and the role of the strike in the bargaining process.

Bargaining Unit Determination

Before bargaining can begin, a decision must be made concerning the proper grouping of public employees for purposes of collective bargaining—an appropriate unit must be determined. Public employers typically favor large bargaining units for several reasons. First, the larger the unit, the more difficult it becomes for the union to win a majority vote of the employees within the unit, particularly if the employees have diverse interests and backgrounds. Second, large units covering a number of nominal employers reduce the possibility of "playing one employer against another to escalate union gains"[33]—whipsawing. Finally, large units increase administrative and bargaining efficiency.

Fragmentation of units and union competition for representation makes constructive bargaining difficult at best. Excessive units cause administrative breakdowns,

---

[32] Achievement of this threshold was the factor apparently responsible for Ronald Reagan's election as President in 1980.

[33] Michael H. Moscow et al., *Collective Bargaining in Public Employment*, p. 212.

employee jealousy, interunion rivalry, and irrational multiple negotiations. Bargaining unit fragmentation leads to a crazy quilt of wage and benefit packages that diverts negotiators from other problems.[34]

Public employers have opted for larger units despite the increased political power (i.e., bargaining power) that accrues to employee representatives from a broader organizational base. Increased political power (i.e., bargaining power) "to influence decisions outside as well as within negotiations"[35] has evidently been considered a worthwhile tradeoff for the employer benefits noted above.

Although a broad-based bargaining unit increases its political influence (i.e., bargaining power) the union's first consideration is survival. A large bargaining unit is meaningless if the union cannot win employee support within the broad confines of that unit. Thus, unions will only "ask for as large a unit as they believe they can win"[36] Since it takes time to build broad-based support, units are likely to be small when bargaining is first undertaken.

Where enabling legislation directly addresses the question of unit determination or where determination is left to the discretion of administrative agencies or management, the criterion most often mentioned is community of interest of employees. As in the private sector, other frequently cited criteria include:

(1) the history, extent, and type of organization of employees in a plant; (2) the history of their collective bargaining; (3) the history, extent, and type of organization and the collective bargaining of employees in other plants of the same employer, or of other employers in the same industry; (4) . . . . . (5) the desires of employees; (6) the eligibility of employees for membership in the union or unions involved in the election proceedings and in other labor organizations; and (7) the relationship between the unit or units proposed and the employer's organization, management, and operation of the plant.[37]

The practical application of these criteria, however, has been dominated by a disproportionate concern for number 7—the locus of management authority. Separation of power with final decision-making authority ultimately resting, in most cases, with the legislative body has acted to reduce the number of bargaining units in the public sector below the number that exist in the private sector for an equivalent number of skills and occupations. In the field of public higher education, for example, disciplines (e.g., business and humanities) which have little in common, particularly in the area of market conditions, are often lumped together in the same bargaining unit. The difficulties that such broadly defined bargaining units encounter in meeting the diverse needs of their constituencies are therefore understandable.

---

[34] Bent and Reeves, *Collective Bargaining in the Public Sector*, p. 66.

[35] Michael H. Moscow et al., *Collective Bargaining in Public Employment*, p. 235.

[36] *Ibid.*, p. 234.

[37] Benjamin Taylor and Fred Witney, *Labor Relations Law*, 3rd Edition, Englewood Cliffs, N.J.: Prentice-Hall, Inc., p. 310.

Bargaining Scope

Bargaining scope is defined as the range of topics negotiated during collective bargaining. For collective bargaining to function as a viable method of worker participation in those decisions affecting total worker welfare, its scope must cover a relatively broad range of issues:

> if the scope of bargaining becomes too narrow, or if important issues, such as wages, are eliminated from bargaining, employees will move away from collective bargaining to other means of participation in decision-making.[38]

Consequently, unions have worked to expand the scope of bargaining to include all items which directly and indirectly affect worker welfare. Their success in achieving this goal in the private sector is mirrored by the long list of topics currently negotiated.

In the public sector, on the other hand, unions have enjoyed only limited success in expanding the scope of bargaining; the concept of sovereignty has proved to be a formidable obstacle. Quite simply, the public employer views joint determination of any issue as an improper abdication of authority not in the public interest and a violation of the public trust. Accordingly, public employers have assumed one of two basic postures toward bargaining scope, namely, "breadth without depth" or "depth without breadth".[39] "Breadth without depth", which provides for open-ended discussion but not negotiation of any issue, preserves the concept of sovereignty in its entirety. Under such "meet and confer" arrangements, the public employer retains unilateral decision-making authority. "Depth without breadth", which provides for joint determination of a limited range of issues, minimizes damage to the sovereignty concept. Here, negotiation is restricted to (i.e., the scope of bargaining is limited to) "only those issues that have a direct, practical impact on an employee"[40]; all topics which affect policy and quality of service remain the prerogative of management.

Legislation or executive orders addressing public employee organization typically attempt to strike a balance between the needs of collective bargaining and public-employer sovereignty with regard to bargaining scope. A thumbnail sketch of the impact of this compromise upon traditional bargaining topics is presented below. Its impact will be highlighted by reference to the Indiana Teacher Bargaining Law, the relevant provisions of which are presented in Box 15–1.

Union Security

While there has been a general trend toward granting employee representatives the right to exclusive recognition and the right to automatic dues deduction, other union security provisions, such as the union shop, have met strong public–employer opposition and, consequently, are rare in the public

---

[38] Michael H. Moscow et al., *Collective Bargaining in Public Employment*, p. 250.
[39] Bent and Reeves, *Collective Bargaining in the Public Sector*, p. 62.
[40] *Ibid.*, p. 61.

sector. The reasons most often cited by public employers for proscribing strong union security provisions are conflicts with (1) civil service/merit systems (i.e., discharge for any reason—nonmembership in a labor organization—other than merit principles is illegal) and (2) the public employee's right to work without becoming a union member (i.e., compulsory unionism). Another reason, not as widely publicized as the preceeding two but of equal, if not more, importance, is the public employer's recognition that the union's bargaining power is enhanced by strong security clauses. Since "for all practical purposes, it has become clear that the relative power of the negotiating parties will determine the scope of bargaining."[41], public-employer prohibition of union security provisions is perceived as one way of limiting union bargaining power and bargaining scope, thereby maintaining management prerogatives (i.e., sovereignty).

Wages and Fringe Benefits

Wage and fringe benefits have long been considered the focal issues of collective bargaining. Indeed, it was employer wage cutting and/or real wage erosion through inflation during the eighteenth century that prompted formation of the first trade unions in the private sector. Yet, for many public employees, wages and fringe benefits are not bargainable. Wherever final decision-making authority in financial matters rests with the legislative body (i.e., wherever there exists separation of powers), wages and fringe benefits are typically excluded from the scope of bargaining, being left instead to unilateral determination by the public employer. Thus, the wages and salaries of most federal employees are determined by congressional action rather than through the collective bargaining process, the notable exception being postal workers who fall within the jurisdiction of the NLRB. Similarly, state and local government employees most typically are solely dependent upon the benevolence of state and/or local legislative bodies as far as wages and fringe benefits are concerned. Even where wages and fringe benefits are not excluded from the scope of bargaining, the negotiated, total wage package must oftentimes conform to broad, legislatively predetermined standards. For example, Section 3 of the Indiana Teacher Bargaining Law makes it "unlawful for a school employer to enter into any agreement that would place such employer in a position of deficit financing as defined in this chapter. . ."

Hours

The total number of hours of work including distribution during the workday and workweek are mandatory items for bargaining in the private sector. Because of the close relationship between hours of work and service quality, however, public employees generally do not enjoy the bargaining latitude that private employees enjoy with regard to this bargaining topic. Bargaining is limited to allocation of hours of employment wherever shorter workweeks and/or shorter workdays are perceived as a threat or challenge to the public employer's unilateral right to set policy and determine service

---

[41] Bent and Reeves, *Collective Bargaining in the Public Sector*, p. 60.

BOX 15–1. Selected Provisions of the Indiana Teacher Bargaining Law

(Public Law #217, IC 1971, Title 20, Article 7.5)

Sec. 3. Duty to Bargain Collectively and Discuss

On and after January 1, 1974, school employers and school employees shall have the obligation and the right to bargain collectively the items set forth in Section 4, and the right and obligation to discuss any item set forth in Section 5, and shall enter into a contract embodying any of the matters on which they have bargained collectively. No contract may include provisions in conflict with (a) any right or benefit established by federal or state law, (b) school employee rights as defined in Section 6 (a) of this chapter, or (c) school employer rights as defined in section 6(b) of this chapter. It shall be unlawful for a school employer to enter into any agreement that would place such employer in a position of deficit financing as defined in this chapter, and any contract which provides for deficit financing shall be void to that extent and any individual teacher's contract executed in accordance with such contract shall be void to such extent.

Sec. 4. Subjects of Bargaining

A school employer shall bargain collectively with the exclusive representative on the following: salary, wages, hours, and salary and wage related fringe benefits. A contract may also contain a grievance procedure culminating in final and binding arbitration of unresolved grievances, but such binding arbitration shall have no power to amend, add to, subtract from or supplement provisions of the contract.

Sec. 5. Subjects of Discussion

(a) A school employer shall discuss with the exclusive representative of certificated employees, and may but shall not be required to bargain collectively, negotiate or enter into a written contract concerning or be subject to or enter into impasse procedures on the following matters: working conditions, other than those provided in Section 4; curriculum development and revision; textbook selection; teaching methods; selection, assignment of promotion of personnel; student discipline; expulsion or supervision of students; pupil-teacher ratio; class size or budget appropriations: Provided, however, that any items included in the 1972–1973 agreements between any employer school corporation and the employee organization shall continue to be bargainable.

(b) Nothing shall prevent a superintendent or his designee from making recommendations to the school employer.

Box 15–1. (continued)

Sec. 6. Rights of School Employees and School Employers

(a) School employees shall have the right to form, join or assist employee organizations, to participate in collective bargaining with school employers through representatives of their own choosing and to engage in other activities, individually or in concert for the purpose of establishing, maintaining, or improving salaries, wages, hours, salary and wage related fringe benefits and other matters as defined in Sections 4 and 5.

(b) School employers shall have the responsibility and authority to manage and direct in behalf of the public the operations and activities of the school corporation to the full extent authorized by law. Such responsibility and activity shall include but not be limited to the right of the school employer to:

1. direct the work of its employees;
2. establish policy;
3. hire, promote, demote, transfer, assign and retain employees;
4. suspend or discharge its employees in accordance with applicable law;
5. maintain the efficiency of school operations;
6. relieve its employees from duties because of lack of work or other legitimate reason;
7. take actions necessary to carry out the mission of the public schools as provided by law.

---

quality (i.e., to public employer sovereignty). This perception is the rule rather than the exception in the federal service. Thus, while federal employees can negotiate the allocation of hours of employment, they are not permitted to bargain total hours. Public employers on the federal level have strongly resisted any usurpation of what is perceived to be a basic policy function. Thus, when the Professional Air Traffic Controllers (PATCO) went out on strike in August of 1981 for, among other things, a shortened work week, they were summarily discharged. A similar nexus between total hours and policy exists at the state and local level in the case of public education. Here, departments of public instruction typically determine the minimum number of school sessions that public schools must hold per year to qualify for state aid. Hence, teacher bargaining is limited to the distribution of hours of employment within the school day.

Working Conditions

Negotiation of hiring, promotion, discipline, transfer, personnel assignment, and layoff criteria, standards and procedures as well as workload are commonplace in the private sector. This contrasts sharply with the public sector where working conditions have generally been excluded from the scope of bargaining due to their unavoidable relationship to service quality and the implication that their joint determination would hold for public policy formulation—abdication of the public employer's sovereign authority and responsibility to formulate policy. Thus, the sovereignty concept precludes joint determination of working conditions by those very employees who, by virtue of education and training, not only are eminently qualified to, but desperately want to be heard on matters of work environment, service quality, and policy formulation—policemen, firemen, teachers, nurses, etc. Ironically, for many of these professionals, it was their inability to be heard on matters of working conditions that prompted their organization in the first place.

> Among faculties in higher education, these matters are considered professional prerogatives. However, as austerity budgets have necessarily had an impact upon what is taught, on size of classes, teaching loads, and so on, the control over teaching and research has shifted from faculty to college administrators. Thus, collective bargaining has taken hold among college faculties.... Nurses have been moved to collective bargaining because of frustration in the absence of a voice on standards and procedures for patient care and other related issues. Social workers are unhappy with their case loads and general administrative indifference to a professional servicing of their clientele.[42]

The growing militancy of professional employees becomes quite understandable in context of the importance accorded working conditions by professionals and the limited scope for bargaining accorded working conditions by public employers. Illustrative of legislative provisions limiting the scope of bargaining in the area of working conditions is Section 5(a) of the Indiana Teacher Bargaining Law, which prohibits the bargaining of:

> working conditions...curriculum development and revision; textbook selection; teaching methods; selection, assignment or promotion of personnel; student discipline; expulsion or supervision of students; pupil-teacher ratio; class size or budget appropriations...

except when voluntarily agreed to by the public employer.

Grievance Procedure

Without a method for resolving disputes concerning the application and interpretation of contract provisions that inevitably arise during the life of the contract, the contract itself becomes meaningless as does the process which led to its creation—collective bargaining. In deference to this labor relations fact of life, the overwhelming majority of contracts negotiated in the private sector provide for the resolution of disputes arising under the contract through grievance procedures capped by binding arbitration. Albeit somewhat reluctantly, the public sector has followed suit; grievance/arbitration procedures are becoming increasingly common in public employment. As was true where other traditional subjects have been excluded from or only reluctantly included within the scope of bargaining in the public sector, the major stumbling block

---

[42] Bent and Reeves, *Collective Bargaining in the Public Sector*, p. 77.

has been the concept of sovereignty. In the case of grievance arbitration, the issue has been whether a public employer can "legally delegate his decision-making authority to a person not responsible to the electorate."[43] That this issue has yet to be completely resolved is evidenced by (1) the continued exclusion of grievance/arbitration from bargaining scope within some jurisdictions, (2) the tentative nature of statutory language where grievance/arbitration falls within the scope of bargaining (See Section 4 of the Indiana Teacher Bargaining Law), and (3) court challenge of grievance/arbitration where mandated by contract or statute.[44]

Management–Rights

Management-rights clauses are common to private and public collective bargaining contracts alike. Such management-rights provisions are intended to protect what are considered to be basic managerial prerogatives which, in the case of the private employer, stem from ownership of property and, in the case of the public employer, from the concept of sovereignty. Management–rights clauses in the public sector, however, are typically stronger and more detailed than those in the private sector, reflecting the public employers' overweening concern for sovereignty. So great is the public-sector's concern for sovereignty that strong management-rights provisions are commonly built into the enabling legislation itself. For example, the Indiana Teacher Bargaining Law devotes more language to what cannot be bargained (i.e., what remains the sole prerogative of the employer) than to what can be bargained (See Section 6 of the Indiana Teacher Bargaining Law).

The Bargaining Process

Collective bargaining in the private sector is essentially a bilateral process wherein decisions are made on the basis of economic criteria. A party's decision to agree or disagree is based on the perceived and/or actual economic costs of each alternative.[45] For example, an employer will agree to a union's proposal only when the perceived costs of disagreement (i.e., strike-induced lost sales, customers, and profits) exceed the perceived costs of agreement (i.e., higher labor costs resulting in lower profits and a declining share of the market). Third-party involvement is, for the most part,[46] limited to whatever market influence consumers have upon those economic variables critical to the decision-making process of the bargaining participants.

Collective bargaining in the public sector, on the other hand, is a multilateral process wherein decisions are made on the basis of political criteria. The multilateral, political nature of public-sector bargaining is the result of three factors. First, the fact that public services are necessary services

---

[43] Michael H. Moscow et al., *Collective Bargaining in Public Employment*, p. 248.

[44] Clarence R. Deitsch and David A. Dilts, "Arbitration Challenged: The Case of Indiana," *Journal of Collective Negotiations in the Public Sector*, 1981, **10**(2): 173–79.

[45] See Chapter 7.

[46] Involvement of third parties in the resolution of impasses, non-emergency and emergency alike, is the most notable exception to the bilateral nature of private sector, collective bargaining.

for which there are no ready substitutes in the private sector (at least from the perspective of some segment of the population) guarantees that the public will take an active interest in employer-employee negotiations which affect service quality and/or, in the event of a job action, service availability. Second, the delivery mechanism for public services also generates public interest in negotiations, the cost of which will ultimately be borne by the taxpayer. Finally, as an elected (appointed) official subject to political defeat, the public manager cannot ignore the wishes of constituents; political survival critically depends on satisfying the majority of constituents. Translated and applied to bargaining decisions, this means that the public manager will agree to a union's proposal whenever perceived costs of disagreement (i.e., a constituency deprived of essential services by an employee job action) exceed the perceived costs of agreement (i.e., a constituency burdened either by lower quality services or a greater tax burden) and will reject the proposal when the reverse is true. Hence, public-sector bargaining decisions are politically motivated whereas private-sector bargaining decisions are economically motivated. Being political, public-sector bargaining automatically involves a third-party—the public.

Purportedly, in the public sector political pressures substitute for market pressures as regulators of the bargaining process. According to this scenario, political pressure brought by a public deprived of essential services replaces lost profits as the factor prompting the employer to settle, while political pressure brought by a public saddled with high taxes replaces the specter of lost sales and market position resulting from higher labor costs as the factor prompting the employer not to settle. Political pressures, however, are at best, a poor substitute for market pressures. Quite simply, political pressure to settle typically dominates political pressure to resist—until a crisis develops. In other words, special interest groups deprived of essential services can rather easily and rapidly mobilize political pressure whereas taxpayer resistance, because of the factors discussed earlier in this chapter, is generally nonexistent or only slow to develop—until a critical threshold is reached. It is precisely because of this built-in propensity to accede to workers' demands that public employers have historically opposed collective bargaining in public employment and continue to oppose the right to strike for public employees.

The Strike Issue

As indicated by the quoted material at the outset of this chapter, probably no other issue in public-sector labor relations evokes as much emotional controversy as does the strike issue. Opposition to the right to strike for public employees is based on the unique characteristics of the public employer (i.e., sovereignty, separation of powers, and service delivery mechanism) and the resultant politicalization of the public-sector bargaining process. More specifically, antistrike proponents are concerned with respect for authority, the need for uninterrupted provision of essential services, efficient use of public resources, the natural proclivity of government to be a "soft bargainer", and the built-in propensity for tax growth. In short, antistrike proponents are concerned with protecting the public interest.

Equally cogent are the arguments tendered by those who support the right of public employees to strike. These include the arguments that:

1. The strike is necessary to make "collective bargaining work by inducing decisions on differences that might otherwise drag on interminably."[47] As Professors Moscow, Loewenberg, and Koziara noted:

   > Without the right to strike to back up their demands, public employees are merely able to make suggestions and recommendations, which the employer is free to reject without fear of reprisal. The strike or the threat of a strike thus resolves impasses in public employee negotiations in the same way it operates in private employment.[48]

2. The strike serves as an outlet for job and non-job-related frustration and hostility, thereby paving the way for increased productivity when work resumes. Professor Kerr noted the cathartic benefits or strike activity when he wrote:

   > In modern industrial society the sources of unrest and hostility are enormous. The strike provides an outlet for them when they are so severe as to require forceful expression. . . reconciliation follows more easily if retribution has preceded. In a sense, thus, strikes are constructive when they result in the greater appreciation of the job by the worker and of the worker by the management.[49]

3. The distinction between public services as essential (i.e., necessary) and private services as nonessential is artificial and cannot in good conscience be used as justification for universally denying public employees the right to strike. The shallow nature of the "essential services" argument for banning public-sector strike activity was best illustrated by Matthew Guinan, International President of the Transport Workers' Union, when he wrote:

   > Here in San Francisco, the city maintains a zoo to care for a lot of interesting animals. Its employees are in the public sector. The city has also some distinguished private hospitals. Their employees are in the private sector. If we are to develop more potent alternatives to the strike in areas where a strike would threaten the greater harm to the public welfare, would we be more concerned over a strike in the zoo than in a hospital? Should we be concerned more about animals than about human beings?
   >
   > In Philadelphia the retail liquor stores are state-owned and operated. The gas and electric utilities are private corporations. I know I am risking some facetious

---

[47] Theodore W. Kheel, "Is the Strike Outmoded?" *Monthly Labor Review*, (September 1973), pp. 35–37, p. 35.

[48] Michael H. Moscow et al., *Collective Bargaining in Public Employment* pp. 283–84.

[49] E. Wright Bakke et al., Editors, *Unions, Management and the Public*, Chicago, Ill: Harcourt Brace Jovanovich, Inc., 1967, p. 295.

replies, but I ask you, would Philadelphians be better off without electricity and gas or without Scotch and gin?[50]

4. Strikes do occur in the public sector despite their legal prohibition. Indeed, there is some evidence that strike activity actually increases under strong anti-strike legislation and penalties.[51] In light of these facts, continued prohibition of strikes merely serves to breed contempt and diminish public respect for legislative and judicial processes. Further,

> if government employees were allowed to strike, attention could be redirected toward substantive issues. Management time and energy would not be spent attempting to enforce untenable no-strike, or slowdown measures.[52]

Underlying these arguments in support of the public employees' right to strike is the concern for protecting the public employees' right to meaningful participation in those decisions which impact the immediate work environment.

The strike issue reduces to one of balancing the public interest against special interest. Strange as it may seem, granting public employees the unqualified right to strike does not always guarantee that they will be heard. Given the direct relationship between the essentiality of the service provided and bargaining power, those public employees providing essential services will be heard while those public employees providing nonessential services can still be ignored. In this light, granting the right to strike only to "nonessential" service employees makes even less sense. Hence, the unqualified right to say no (i.e., to strike) does not necessarily protect the rights of public employees. Nor is the right to strike necessarily the only, or for that matter, the best method of guaranteeing the public employees' right to meaningful participation in those decisions which impact the immediate work environment. As noted by Professors Moscow, Loewenberg, and Koziara, "The key ingredient to joint determination is the ability of each party to impose a cost on the other."[53] The problem then becomes one of finding a method of imposing costs which simultaneously adequately safeguards the public interest while protecting the right of public employees to bargain collectively—a method that strikes a balance between public interest and special interest. Alternative methods of dispute resolution—alternatives to the strike as methods of imposing costs and guaranteeing joint decision-making—are examined in Chapter 14.

Summary and Conclusion

The rapid growth of the public sector has been a byproduct of overall economic growth and development. Specifically, an income-elastic demand for

---

[50] Matthew Guinan, "The Unreal Distinction Between Public and Private Sectors," p. 46.

[51] Alan Balfour and Alexander B. Holmes, "The Effectiveness of No Strike Laws for Public Teachers," *Journal of Collective Negotiation in the Public Sector*, (1981), **10(2)**: 133–43.

[52] Bent and Reeves, *Collective Bargaining in the Public Sector*, p. 223.

[53] Michael H. Moscow et al., *Collective Bargaining in Public Employment*, p. 284.

the type of services that the public sector provides and a system of public finance that perpetrates the false impression that public services are underpriced have been the engines of growth. Coincident with this growth was the "proletarianization" of public-sector jobs which induced public employees to form labor organizations and demand collective bargaining. The characteristics of the public employer (i.e., sovereignty, separation of powers, service delivery mechanism) have operated to fashion a unique process of bargaining in public employment—unique in that bargaining scope is quite limited and that the process itself is multilateral and political in nature. The multilateral, political nature of public-sector bargaining and the characteristics of the public employer responsible have led to a widespread ban on public-employee strike activity, which has, in turn, prompted a search for a strike alternative that will simultaneously safeguard the public interest and protect the right of public employees to bargain collectively.

Given the recent problems of the public sector, it is tempting to point an accusing finger at organized labor and collective bargaining as the group and factor responsible for the difficulties. This temptation, however, should be strongly resisted; organized labor is no more to blame than any other special interest group (e.g., farmers, consumer advocates, etc.) which pleads its case before politically motivated government officials. Indeed, blame cannot be laid at the doorstep of any individual special interest group. Instead, ultimate responsibility for public-sector problems can be traced to the lack of any equivalent to the market mechanism of the private sector. The challenge is to seek ways of increasing efficient resource utilization while at the same time protecting the rights of special interest groups.

DISCUSSION QUESTIONS

1. Why was Adam Smith preoccupied with user taxes as the preferred method of financing government services?

2. Given the reputed efficiency of the private sector in producing goods and services, why has American society accorded government a role in providing services?

3. Why has government's role in providing services expanded during the last thirty years?

4. Public-sector employees remained resistant to the overtures of union organizers until the late 1950's. Why? What factors were responsible for the rapid growth in public-employee, union membership after 1960?

5. Sovereignty has been identified as a unique characteristic of the public employer and used as an argument against public-employee collective bargaining. In similar fashion, construct an argument that the private employer is sovereign and thus should not be burdened by collective bargaining.

6. Explain the separation and diffusion of public decision-making authority, its rationale, and its impact upon public employee bargaining. Is it unprecedented in the annals of bargaining history?

7. Compare and contrast private and public service delivery mechanisms, paying particular attention to the mechanism that restrains employer generosity at the bargaining table in each.

8. Taxes play the same role in the public sector that price (competition) plays in the private sector—that of guaranteeing efficiency and restraining labor demands. Discuss.

9. Why is there a natural tendency toward fewer but larger bargaining units in the public sector? Explain.

10. A relatively broad bargaining scope is essential for the viability of collective bargaining. Explain. Why then is the scope of public-sector bargaining typically narrow?

11. Public employers have strongly opposed the negotiation of union security clauses. Why?

12. What characteristics of the public employer have, in some political jurisdictions, led to the exclusion of wages and fringe benefits from the scope of bargaining? Explain.

13. There appears to be no one more qualified to determine curriculum, choose textbooks, and select appropriate teaching methods than a teacher. Yet, these items are typically excluded from the scope of bargaining. Explain this paradox.

14. Given the political as opposed to economic environment of public-sector bargaining, why is the public employer prone to be a "soft bargainer"? Explain.

15. Public employee bargaining and protection of the public interest are incompatible. Discuss.

SELECTED REFERENCES

Aronowitz, Stanley, *False Promises: The Shaping of American Working Class Consciousness*, New York: McGraw-Hill Book Company, 1973.

Bent, Alan Edward and T. Zene Reeves, *Collective Bargaining in the Public Sector*, Menlo Park, California: The Benjamin/Cummings Publishing Company, Inc., 1978.

Blum, Albert A., Editor, *White Collar Workers*, New York: Random House, Inc. 1971.

Deitsch, Clarence R. and David A. Dilts, "Arbitration Challenged: The Case of Indiana," *Journal of Collective Negotiations in the Public Sector*, (1981), **10(2)**: 173–79.

Duryea, Edwin D. et al., Editor, *Faculty Unions and Collective Bargaining*, San Francisco, California: Jossey-Bass Publisher, 1973.

"Exploring Alternatives to the Strike," (A Collection of Short Articles Dealing with Alternative Methods of Dispute Resolution) *Monthly Labor Review*, (September 1973), **96**: 35–66.

Godine, Morton R., *The Labor Problem in the Public Service*, New York: Russell and Russell Publishers, 1967.

Hildebrand, George H., "The Public Sector" in *Frontiers of Collective Bargaining*, John Dunlop and Neil W. Chamberlain, Editors, New York: Harper and Row, Publishers, 1967.

Jennings, Kenneth M. et al., *Labor Relations in a Public Service Industry: Unions, Management, and the Public Interest in Mass Transit*, New York: Praeger Publishers, Inc., 1978.

Loewenberg, J. Joseph and Michael H. Moscow, Editors, *Collective Bargaining in Government*, Englewood Cliffs, N.J.: Prentice-Hall, Inc., 1972.

Moscow, Michael H. et al., *Collective Bargaining in Public Employment*, New York: Random House, Inc., 1970.

Zagoria, Sam, Editor, *Public Workers and Public Unions*, Englewood Cliffs, N.J.: Prentice-Hall, Inc., Spectrum Books, 1972.

Chapter 16

Collective Bargaining in the Health Care Industry

As manufacturing declined in its relative importance in the American economic system during the previous two decades, unions have turned their attention toward the service industries. The health care industry is among the largest and most critical of all the service industries. Since collective bargaining rights have been protected by the Taft-Hartley Act rather recently, the labor relations of the health care industry have been subject to intensive investigation by scholars in this field. Several interesting observations have been made concerning bargaining in this industry which is the topic of discussion in the present chapter.

This chapter is divided into four major sections; these are: (1) legal developments governing health care institutions; (2) the conduct of collective bargaining; (3) special bargaining problems of health care institutions; and (4) union organization of health care workers.

The health care industry is comprised of a large number of diverse organizations. Hospitals, nursing homes, physicians, dentists, health maintenance organizations (HMO), and various types of clinics are all included under the broad title of health care industry. The characteristics and functions performed by each component of the industry differ substantially even though the basic objective (to relieve human suffering as well as maintain and restore health) is the same. There is also a variety of corporate forms represented in the health care industry such as governmental, private-nonprofit, and proprietary facilities. The result of this wide variety of characteristics in health care facilities has been to produce collective bargaining which is, in large measure, unique to this industry.

Collective bargaining in the health care industry has been a controversial topic for many years primarily because the central importance of this industry is maintaining its customer's good health. The simple fact of the matter is consumers of this industry's services have no substitute supplier of health care services. While it may be perceived as inconvenient for your local grocery store to be shut down due to a labor dispute, it may be frightening for your local hospital to experience the same problem. It is rare that the closing of a grocery would result in a life or death situation while the public may perceive that a strike in a hospital could preclude the availability of life saving services. In other words collective bargaining which is often an emotional issue is especially so in industries which provide the necessities of life and this is particularly true of health care delivery.

The Health Care Industry and Labor Law

Probably more than most industries, the development of the labor law governing the health care industry has guided and shaped collective bargaining within this industry. This statement may be defended on the grounds that because of the diverse sources of corporate control, the industry is actually three highly interrelated groups of firms, and each group is covered by an entirely separate set of collective bargaining statutes.

There are three levels of government which own and operate hospitals: local, state, and federal. Additionally, in the private sector there are two types of hospitals—nonproprietary and proprietary (nonprofit and profit making, respectively). Each category of control of health care facility has had its own unique development of labor law. The development of this body of law will be discussed in the sections which follow.

Health Care Facilities and the Taft-Hartley Act

One important feature of Taft-Hartley has a direct bearing on the development of collective bargaining in the health care industry. All private sector hospitals were covered under the Wagner Act. Under the original Wagner Act, there was only one case reported concerning the coverage of nonprofit hospitals. The National Labor Relations Board, the Circuit Court of Appeals and the U.S. Supreme Court upheld the Act's coverage of nonprofit

**TABLE 16–1. Hospitals—Type of Control,
Percentage of Total 1960–1980**

Type	1960	1970	1980*
Private Nonprofit	52.1%	50.5	49.0
Proprietary	14.2	12.1	12.0
Local Government	19.3	23.6	25.5
State Government	8.1	8.1	7.5
Federal Government	6.3	5.7	6.0

*1980 estimated

Source: American Hospital Association, Hospitals Guide Issue, *Hospital Statistics*, 1972–1979.

hospitals.[1] Taft-Hartley, however, exempted nonprofit hospitals. Section 2 (2) of Taft-Hartley specifically excluded "any corporation or association operating a hospital, if no part of the net earnings inures to the benefit of any private shareholder or individual,..."[2] Nonprofit nursing homes, for-profit nursing homes, and proprietary hospitals remained subject to the jurisdiction of the National Labor Relations Board if the Board chose to assert its jurisdiction. The primary reason that nonprofit hospitals were exempted from the Taft-Hartley Act was Congress' belief that these hospitals were primarily local in character and since they were operated on a nonprofit basis they could not significantly influence interstate commerce.

BOX 16–1. Senator Tydings and Senator Taft Discussing Amendment to Taft-Hartley Exempting Nonprofit Health Care Facilities on May 12, 1947

Mr. Tydings

...this amendment is designed merely to help a great number of hospitals which are having very difficult times. They are eleemosynary institutions; no profit is involved in their operations, and I understand from the Hospital Association that this amendment would be very helpful in their efforts to serve those who have not the means to pay for hospital service, enable them to keep the doors open and operate the hospitals. I do not believe the committee is opposed to it,...

Mr. Taft

The committee considered this amendment, but did not act on it, because it was felt it was unnecessary. The committee felt that hospitals were not engaged in interstate commerce, and that their business should not be so construed. We rather felt it would open up questions of making other exemptions. That is why the committee did not act upon the amendment as it was proposed....

Mr. Tydings

...They (hospitals) are not in interstate commerce. A hospital is a local institution, quite often kept open by the donations of benevolent persons.... Employees of such a hospital should not have to come to the National Labor Relations Board.
A charitable institution is way beyond the scope of labor-management relations in which a profit is involved.

Source: Congressional Record, Vol. 93, part 4, 80th Congress, 1st session. Washington: Government Printing Office, May 12, 1947, pp. 4996–4998.

---

[1] *Central Dispensary and Emergency Hospital,* 44 NLRB 533 (1942), 145 F. 2d 852 (1944), Cert. den. 655 Sup. Ct. 684.

[2] The Taft-Hartley Act, Section 2 (2).

The National Labor Relations Board enjoys rather wide latitude in determining which firms within interstate commerce are subject to its jurisdiction. Prior to 1960, the Board used dollar gross revenue of the firm as a guideline for this determination. In 1960, the National Labor Relations Board completely refused to assert its jurisdiction in proprietary hospital cases. The reasoning of the Board was:

> the operation of proprietary hospitals in general and the Employer in particular have insufficient impact on commerce to warrant assertion of the Board's discretionary jurisdiction over such operations.[3]

In November of 1967 the Board changed its policy and asserted jurisdiction over nursing homes[4] and proprietary hospitals.[5] The Board reasoned that there was sufficient evidence that hospitals and nursing homes did exert substantial influence on interstate commerce and therefore it was appropriate to assert jurisdiction. The reasoning of the NLRB in this policy change is presented in Box 16–2.

In *Butte Medical Properties*,[6] proprietary hospitals with gross revenues of $250,000 per year were brought under the jurisdiction of the Taft-Hartley Act.[7] On the same day, November 16, 1967, the National Labor Relations Board extended jurisdiction to nursing homes with gross revenues of $100,000 or more per year in *University Nursing Home*.[8] The Board used essentially the same reasoning in asserting jurisdiction over nursing homes as it did over proprietary hospitals. The Board stated, in part:

> [The] parties do not contend that the employer's operation is not involved in interstate commerce or that its out-of-State purchases are not of a sufficient magnitude to substantially affect commerce under standards we have applied in cases involving other industries where we have asserted jurisdiction. . . .[9]

The National Labor Relations Board thus changed its mind and decided that hospitals were indeed involved in interstate commerce. In the decisions the Board published on November 16, 1967, the unions established the fact that health care facilities were actively engaged in interstate commerce. In light of

---

[3] *Flatbush General Hospital*, 168 NLRB 144 (1969).

[4] *University Nursing Home*, 168 NLRB 53 (1967).

[5] *Butte Medical Properties, d/b/a Medical Center Hospital*, 168 NLRB, 52 (1967).

[6] The National Labor Relations Board was not prohibited from asserting jurisdiction but had ruled six years earlier that hospitals were not engaged in interstate commerce. The apparent reason for the Board changing its policy was a well documented argument that hospitals do have an impact on interstate commerce. It is also possible that a change in one member of the Board may have had an effect.

[7] Transit systems and public utilities have the same dollar standards applied for jurisdictional purposes. The National Labor Relations Board stated that it could see no reason why hospitals should not be treated as other firms in general industry. The same sort of reasoning was used in the cases affecting the two above-mentioned industries.

[8] Includes both proprietary and nonproprietary nursing homes.

[9] *University Nursing Home*, op cit.

BOX 16–2. NLRB's reasoning in the *Butte Medical Properties* Case

There is no dispute that while all hospitals are primarily humanitarian facilities, some aspects of their operations are essentially business in character. Operationally, they are a multi-billion dollar complex and, as such, comprise one of the largest industries in the United States....

Apart from the impact on commerce occasioned by the purchases of supplies and materials, there is also financial interstate impact of billions of consumer dollars expended by millions of Americans for health protection and care, which dollars travel to and from national insurance companies and the Federal government which, in turn, make payments directly or indirectly to proprietary and other hospitals. The extent of national participation in health insurance benefits is indicated by a Department of Health, Education, and Welfare report showing that as of December 31, 1964, 79.2 percent of the United States civilian population were enrolled for health care benefits by private health insurance companies, viz., 62,429,000 in Blue Cross and Blue Shield, 104,230,000 in various insurance companies, and 6,960,000 in independent programs....

Moreover, the material effect on commerce resulting from the nationwide individual expenditures for health care in which proprietary hospitals participate is further multiplied and augmented by the numerous public health and welfare enactments of Congress which are financed by the expenditure of public funds in which these facilities also participate, directly or indirectly.

---

these NLRB decisions it was only a matter of time before Taft-Hartley was amended to extend coverage of the Act to nonprofit hospitals.

Nonprofit Health Care Institutions: The 1974 Taft-Hartley Amendments

In 1974 Congress amended the Taft-Hartley Act by removing the exemption of nonprofit health care institutions from the Act thus authorizing the National Labor Relations Board to assert jurisdiction over these facilities. Political pressure was brought to bear on Congress by unions, public interest groups, and even groups representing the interests of the profit making sector of the health care industry. The need for legislative action, even without political pressure, was clear:

the exemption of nonprofit hospitals from the Act had resulted in numerous instances of recognition strikes and picketing. Coverage under the Act should

---

BOX 16–3. Hardship Due to Recognitional Strikes in New York City Reported in the Legislative History of the Coverage of Nonprofit Hospitals (p. 85)

Struck hospitals in the metropolitan area (New York) discharged thousands of patients and closed entire floors, and three nursing homes, whose resources were being exhausted by the three-day-old strike, announced they would be sending home all 1,347 patients within the next week.

At the same time, the 48 hospitals and homes affected by the strike sought to cope with mounting, food, fuel, and medicine shortages. The Jewish Institute for Geriatric Care had a helicopter deliver linen....

---

completely eliminate the need for any such activity, since the procedures of the Act will be available to resolve organizational and recognition disputes.[10]

There was also the question of equitable treatment of employees within the health care industry.

> The bill removes the existing exemption in section 2 (2) of the NLRA for employees of non-profit hospitals and extends the protection of the Act to such employees to the same extent as currently applicable to employees of nursing homes and proprietary hospitals.
>
> The committee could find no acceptable reason why 1,427,012 employees of these non-profit, non-public hospitals, representing 56% of all hospital employees, should continue to be excluded from the coverage and protections of the ACT....[11]

The tone of the testimony reported in the *Legislative History of the Coverage of Nonprofit Hospitals Under the National Labor Relations Act, 1974,* and the absence of proprietary hospital associations' opposition testimony is indicative that proprietary hospitals were not disappointed by the coverage of nonproprietary hospitals by the National Labor Relations Act. This is clearly understandable since proprietary hospitals could easily find themselves at a competitive disadvantage if wage differentials between unionized and nonunionized hospital labor became large; evidence suggested this to be the case.

---

[10] *Legislative History of the Coverage of Nonprofit Hospitals Under the National Labor Relations Act, 1974; Public Law 93-360,* Subcommittee on Labor of the Committee on Labor and Public Welfare, United States Senate, Washington: Government Printing Office, 1974, p. 3.

[11] *Ibid.,* pp. 2–3.

Administrative Procedures and Problems under the 1974 Taft-Hartley Amendments

As a result of the 1974 amendments to Taft-Hartley, all hospitals and nursing homes which are privately controlled are included in the definition of employer for the purposes of the National Labor Relations Act. The dollar standards established in *Butte Medical Properties* and *University Nursing Home* of $250,000 and $100,000 respectively remain in force for proprietary hospitals and nursing homes. In 1975 the National Labor Relations Board ruled that the same jurisdictional dollar standards would apply to nonproprietary hospitals. For the first time since 1947, the private sector of the health care industry was covered equally under the same body of labor law.

Certification of a bargaining agent results from elections conducted by the National Labor Relations Board. Determination of the appropriate bargaining units for certification is also the responsibility of the National Labor Relations Board. Congress instructed the NLRB, however, to avoid the proliferation of bargaining units within the hospital portion of this new area of jurisdiction. The instructions Congress issued the National Labor Relations Board in this regard were:

> Due consideration should be given by the Board to preventing proliferation of bargaining units in the health care industry.[12]

Congress was of the opinion that the proliferation of bargaining units within each hospital would not be conducive to industrial peace. Congress believed that it was in the public interest to have as few bargaining units as possible and still assure adequate and fair representation to employees. With many small bargaining units, problems would arise which would be intolerable in the operation of a hospital. For example, a contract negotiation every few months would impair the efficient operation of the hospital by increasing the probability of workstoppages which might threaten to shut down the hospital.

In the hearings prior to the original Taft-Hartley Act and the 1974 amendments, the American Nurses' Association expressed a desire that registered nurses be considered professional employees and be placed in separate units. These professional organizations, such as the American Nurses' Association, had good reason for desiring separate bargaining units:

> The various technical and professional organizations present (i.e., ANA, NFLPAN, and ASHP) stressed the appropriateness of separate bargaining units for their particular technical or professional groups. Unlike the larger service unions, most of these smaller technical or professional organizations, notably the ANA and its local affiliates, are authorized under their respective charters and by laws to represent only one group of technical or professional employees (e.g., only RNs in the case of the ANA). Consequently, since the two- and three-unit proposals suggested by the hospitals and the Service Employees International Union would have meant the inclusion of several different technical or professional groups in a

---

[12] *Legislative History of the Coverage of Nonprofit Hospitals Under the National Labor Relations Act, 1974: Public Law 93–360*, p. 4.

single bargaining unit, the technical or professional organizations either had to persuade the NLRB to reject the hospital proposals or face the prospect of going out of business.[13]

Other professional and technical groups had urged craft separation for their employees, while larger industrial type unions were content with hospital bargaining units being limited to two or three units. Even though registered nurses and other technical and professional workers were not successful in obtaining craft separation for their groups either in Taft-Hartley or the 1974 amendments, the National Labor Relations Board did establish a policy amenable to the Nurses' position. In a series of cases, the National Labor Relations Board ruled that it would follow a policy of allowing four general categories of bargaining units: (1) registered and head nurses; (2) technical and other professional health care employees as well as licensed practical nurses; (3) business office clerical employees; and (4) general service and maintenance employees. Hospital interns and residents are not classified as employees for purposes of the Act and have no protected bargaining rights under the Taft-Hartley Act.

Taft-Hartley and Industrial Conflict in Health Care Institutions

Health care institutions are concerned with the public interest since they provide a service essential to the public health and welfare. As a result, Section 213 was added to the Taft-Hartley Act by the 1974 Amendments. This section requires unions to give thirty days' notice in addition to the sixty days required for general industry prior to the modification or termination of their contract with a health care facility. This section also extends the required notice given the Federal Mediation and Conciliation Service from thirty days for general industry to sixty days in health care facilities. The union must also give ten days' notice prior to taking a job action such as a strike. The reason behind this section of the amendment is:

> The 10-day notice is intended to give health care institutions sufficient advance notice of a strike or picketing to permit them to make arrangements for the continuity of patient care....[14]

Health care institutions were instructed by the Committee on Labor and Public Welfare of the Senate not to take unfair advantage of the extended notices required of labor unions. In part the Committee stated:

> Moreover, it is the sense of the Committee that during the ten-day notice period the employer should remain free to take whatever action is necessary to maintain health care, but not to use the ten-day period to undermine the bargaining relationship that would otherwise exist. For example, the employer would not be free to bring in large numbers of supervisory help, nurses, staff and other

[13]T.P. Pepe and R.L. Murphy, "The NLRB Decisions on Appropriate Bargaining Units," *Hospital Progress*, (October, 1975), **56**: 43–44.

[14]*Legislative History of the Coverage of Nonprofit Hospitals*, p. 4.

personnel from other facilities for replacement purposes. It would clearly be free to take extraordinary steps to stock up on ordinary supplies for an unduly extended period. While not necessarily a violation of the Act, violation of these principles would serve to release the labor organization from its obligation not to engage in economic action during the course of the ten-day notice period.[15]

The Federal Mediation and Conciliation Service is empowered, in the case of a labor dispute in a hospital, to automatically institute mediation of the dispute. The Federal Mediation and Conciliation Service is further required to appoint a fact-finding board for the purpose of assisting in the settlement of the dispute.

Picketing is covered by the same ten-day notice required of a union before striking. Sympathy picketing is subject to the same ten-day notice as is direct pressure by the union actually engaged in the dispute. Employees who engage in either form of job action, strike or picketing, without providing ten days' notice may be discharged for just cause.[16] However, the General Counsel of the National Labor Relations Board will not find a union in violation of the ten-day notice if the employer commits an unfair labor practice which precipitated the union's actions.[17]

Organization of Health Care Employees and Special Union Security Agreements

The National Labor Relations Board has established a special set of standards for union solicitation of employees in this industry. The most notable of these is that hospitals may ban union solicitation of employees and/or distribution of literature on hospital property even during non-working time if patients have access to the area.[18]

Employees with religious convictions which do not allow them to join or support a labor organization are given special exemption under the definition of employees for the purpose of the 1974 amendments:

in recognition of the special humanitarian character of health care institutions, an employee may make payments to a nonreligious charitable fund in lieu of periodic dues and initiation fees....[19]

All other provisions of the National Labor Relations Act as amended by Taft-Hartley and Landrum-Griffin apply to the health care industry as well as general industry. It should be obvious that Congress tailored the 1974 amendments to serve the specific needs of this industry while protecting the

---

[15] *Legislative History of the Coverage of Nonprofit Hospitals Under the Natiounal Labor Relations Act, 1974: Public Law 93–360*, p. 5.

[16] Office of the General Counsel, "NLRB General Counsel's Monthly Report on Health Care Institution Cases," Release 1385, March 27, 1975, p. 2.

[17] *Ibid.*, p. 6.

[18] *Tri-County Medical Center*, 222 NLRB 174 (1976).

[19] Joint Explanatory Statement of the Committee of Conference, Conference Report No. 93–988, U.S. Code, *Congressional and Administrative News*: 93rd Congress, 2d session p. 3959

collective bargaining rights of its employees. Experience to date indicates that Congress was successful in formulating a law which serves the needs of the public, management and organized labor.

Labor Law in the Federal Government's Health Care Institutions

While a full review of the Civil Service collective bargaining laws is not possible here, a few remarks are in order before proceeding. Employees of the federal government were originally extended collective bargaining rights in 1962 when President John F. Kennedy issued Executive Order 10988. The

---

BOX 16-4. Bargaining Items in the Federal Sector

Mandatory (Section 11 (a))

Management must negotiate with respect to personnel policies, practices and matters affecting working conditions so far as appropriate under applicable laws and regulations, including policies set forth in the federal personnel manual, published agency policies and regulations for which a compelling need exists and which are issued at the agency or primary national subdivision level, a national or other controlling agreement at a higher agency level, and the order itself.

Permissible (Section 11 (b))

Management may, but is not required to, negotiate matters with respect to agency mission, budget and organization; number of employees; numbers, types and grades of positions or employees assigned to an organizational unit, work project, or tour of duty; technology of performing its work; or its internal security practices—provided it does not preclude negotiation or appropriate arrangements for employees adversely affected by the impact of realignment of work forces or technological change.

Prohibited (Section 12 (b))

Management may not negotiate away its retained rights to direct employees of the agency and to hire, promote, transfer, assign and retain employees in positions within the agency and to suspend, demote, discharge or take other disciplinary action against employees; to relieve employees from duties for lack of work or other legitimate reasons; to maintain the efficiency of government operations; to determine the methods, means, and personnel by which such operations are to be conducted; and to take whatever actions may be necessary to carry out the mission of the agency in emergencies.

bargaining rights granted these employees differ substantially from their counterparts in the private sector. For example, civil service employees are prohibited from striking and many of the issues which are typically mandatory issues of bargaining in the private sector are prohibited issues under the laws governing federal employees. In addition, applicable law has been changed frequently, further confusing matters for all parties concerned. In 1978, however, Congress passed the Civil Service Reform Act which may serve to eliminate much of this confusion.

Box 16–4 contains the description of bargaining issue classifications for federal employee labor relations.

State Labor Laws Governing Health Care Institutions

Two types of collective bargaining exist on the state and local levels: de facto bargaining and bargaining protected by state law. De facto bargaining occurs when employees organize and attempt to enforce demands or present grievances to their employers where no legal authority exists for such activities. De facto collective bargaining has even occurred when the law prohibits collective action or contractual agreements.[20] The second type of bargaining occurs when the state has established its own labor law. Under the Taft-Hartley Act "any state or political subdivision thereof, . . ." is specifically exempted from the definition of employer for the purposes of the Act. As a result some states have enacted their own state labor laws.

There are 29 states which enacted legislation requiring bargaining for their public employees. There is substantial variation in the rights and procedures established by these state laws. In the previous chapter some attention was focused on various state laws which confirmed the variability of these laws. The impact of these differing state laws has been to create different bargaining environments across states. Few generalizations are possible concerning collective bargaining under these laws.

Even though state experiences under their respective labor laws vary, a few comments concerning bargaining under the state laws may help the student understand the impact of these laws. Indiana allows local government employees to bargain but under this policy there have not been any hospitals organized to date. Nine hospitals have been organized in Indiana under federal laws, only one of which was a public institution. The New York experience differs substantially from Indiana's. Many hospitals, both private and public, have been organized under the New York law. The hostile and turbulent nature of labor relations in New York's health care industry prompted passage of the statute.

In 1972 almost 14 percent of state and local hospital employees in the United States were organized. This percentage represents almost a 25 percent increase in unionization from 1966 levels. Work stoppages, nationwide, at state

[20] Sara Gamm. *Toward Collective Bargaining in Non-Profit Hospitals: Impact of New York Law*. Ithaca, New York: New York State School of Industrial and Labor Relations at Cornell, Bulletin 60, 1968, pp. 2–11.

and local hospitals were almost nonexistent; only 16 were reported for fiscal year 1972 with less than 1 percent lost time due to strikes in the same year.

Conduct of Collective Bargaining

It appears that collective bargaining is more peaceful in the private-sector, health care industry than in other industries. The majority of time lost to strikes in the early 1970's was the result of impasses caused by hospital administrators refusing to recognize labor unions. The passage of the 1974 amendments has protected employees' rights to organize and bargain collectively in the private nonprofit sector of the health care industry. The FMCS reported that during the first full year under the 1974 Taft-Hartley amendments the strike rate (calculated on all closed cases) was approximately 4% in private nonprofit health care institutions, 11% below the strike rate for all FMCS cases.[21]

Contracts negotiated in the private sector of the health care industry appear to be much the same as in other sectors of the American economy. As one researcher has noted:

> the data we do have suggest that with the exception of some small accommodations to peculiar occupational needs in this industry (seniority in promotion, seniority as a sole factor, paid sick leave, joint study committees, and educational leave), the contracts in this industry are developing in a way indistinguishable from steel, auto, meatpacking, police, or fire. To this observer, at least, this is additional evidence to support the thesis that it is the nature of the employment relationship which leads to unionization, that the grievances of workers with respect to that environment appear to be generic, and that they become manifest in similar contractual provisions and language.[22]

Little difference exists between collective bargaining in health care facilities and that observed in general industry. One explanation for the similarity may be the inexperience of health care labor relations personnel in collective bargaining. Faced with the rapid growth of bargaining, health care labor relations personnel have copied solutions and contract provisions useful in general industry rather than develop solutions and provisions addressing their specific needs.

The Economic Package

As noted earlier, fringe benefits such as life insurance, medical insurance, paid vacations, pensions, and sick leave are normally negotiated with wage rates. Referred to as "the economic package", a dollar figure is determined

[21] J.F. Scearce, and L.D. Tanner, "Health Care Bargaining: The FMCS Experience," *Labor Law Journal*, (July 1976), pp. 393–94.

[22] H.A. Juris, "Collective Bargaining in Hospitals: Labor Agreements in the Hospital Industry: A Study of Collective Bargaining Outputs," *Labor Law Journal*, (August 1977), p. 511.

through negotiations and then distributed among various fringe benefits and wages for different groups of employees. Most hospitals covered by the Bureau of Labor Statistics Wage Survey[23] granted fringe benefits prior to unionization.

> Virtually all hospitals visited provided paid holidays and paid vacations, after specified periods of service. Life, hospitalization, surgical, and medical insurance benefits, for which employers paid at least part of the cost, were also widespread among the hospitals studied.[24]

This survey shows that practically no change has occurred in fringe benefits over the period of 1969 to 1975, despite a significant increase in the number of facilities unionized. Facilities with at least one labor contract constituted 12.5 percent of the total in 1969; this figure increased to 21.9 by 1975. The number of employees unionized increased from 11.3 percent of the total to 18.6 percent during the same period.

Many studies exist that trace increased wage levels in hospitals to unionization. The most recent and comprehensive study (Fottler, 1977) indicates initial increases of 10–15 percent where unionization has occurred and very little differential increase between union and nonunion facilities thereafter.[25]

Increases in hospital costs do not appear to be caused directly by unionization. In 1974 all hospital payrolls accounted for only 57.5 percent of variable costs of hospital operation—a decline of 8.8 percent from 1960 and 4.1 percent from 1970.[26] Multiplying Fottler's high estimate for wage increases due to unionization by the percentage of variable costs accounted for by all payrolls and then multiplying this product by the percentage of unionized employees yields the percentage increase in variable costs directly attributable to unionization. The percentage of variable costs attributable to increased wages resulting from unionization in 1974 was less than 2 percent (1 percent of total cost). Even this small percentage may be an overestimate since Fottler's upper estimate was used and the percentage of variable costs accounted for by all payrolls includes the payrolls of supervisory personnel, residents, interns, and staff physicians who are not subject to collective bargaining. It would appear, then, that wage increases due to unionization were not a significant portion of variable or total hospital costs. Variable costs are declining as a percentage of total hospital costs, even though unionization is increasing. There is no evidence unionization and subsequent bargaining have increased hospital costs significantly.

Hospital employees have typically made much less than other employees in virtually every category of service industry.[27] Hospital employees in 1968

---

[23] *Industry Wage Survey: Hospitals*, Bulletin 1940, U.S. Dept. of Labor, Bureau of Labor Statistics, 1976, pp. 112–130.

[24] Ibid., p. 5.

[25] M.D. Fottler, "Union Impact on Hospital Wages." *Industrial and Labor Relations Review*, (April 1977), **30(3)**: 343.

[26] U.S. National Center for Health Statistics, *Health Resources Statistics*, 1975.

[27] See U.S. Department of Labor, Bureau of Labor Statistics, *Employment and Earnings*, various issues 1960–1978.

earned, on the average, 11¢ per hour less than service employees in general and 73¢ per hour less than the total private average hourly wage rate.[28] By 1977 hospital employees earned 3¢ less per hour than the average for service employees and 57¢ less per hour than the average for all private industry's employees.[29] Weekly earnings differentials between private-sector employees and hospital workers increased from $27.34 in 1968 to $30.41 in 1977 indicating that the almost doubling of the rate of unionization among hospital employees from 1968 to 1977 had little impact on reducing earnings differentials.

Special Bargaining Problems of Health Care Institutions

As noted above very little difference exists between health care industry labor contracts and those found in other service industries. What differences do exist are the result of accommodating the special needs of specific professional and technical employees. Three major provisions are typically included in contracts covering professional employees. These three provisions concern: (1) management prerogatives; (2) training and educational leaves; and (3) exclusion of specific categories of employees.

Management prerogatives are always difficult issues in all labor-management negotiations. Management rights clauses in nonprofessional employee contracts generally contain certain language similar to the following:

> The union recognizes the prerogatives of the Employer to operate and manage its affairs in all respects in accordance with its responsibility, and the powers of authority which the Employer has not specifically abridged, delegated or modified by other provisions of this agreement are retained exclusively by the Employer....[30]

Thus, health care industry contracts, for the most part, adhere to the residual theory of management rights. Most of these contracts are silent in regard to the role past practices are to play in contract administration.[31] Hence, unskilled or semiskilled employees do not have the leverage which professional and technical employees have demonstrated in controlling their own job duties.

Professional and technical employee labor contracts generally do not contain strong language retaining authority in management not specifically delegated elsewhere by the contract. Many of these contracts contain no management rights provisions; however, all contain either a Patient Care Committee provision or a Job Duties paragraph. Job Duties clauses are typically worded as follows:

> *Job Duties.* The employer may determine and change job duties for jobs in all

---

[28] *Employment and Earnings*, various issues 1960–1978.

[29] *Ibid.*

[30] Article II, paragraph 2.01, Labor Agreement Between Jefferson County, Wisconsin, Countryside Home and Jefferson County Employees Union Local 2418, AFSCME, AFL-CIO, 1976, p. 1.

[31] D.A. Dilts, "Unions and Health Care Cost Inflation," *Hospital Progress*, (December 1978), pp. 61–78.

departments and determine the qualifications and duties of all jobs after consultation and negotiation with the Association.[32]

This type of Job Duties provision does not differ substantially from Patient Care Committee or Study Committee paragraphs. Both types of contractual language limit employer prerogatives to unilaterally establish work standards for their professional and technical employees. The Patient Care Committee clauses (see Box 16–5) contain more explicit language concerning work standards procedures and for this reason, may present fewer administrative problems. Unlike the case of nonprofessional employees, job duties are an area of joint determination between the employer and union. This may reflect two basic notions: union-management cooperation is a necessary prerequisite for the best possible service to patients or professional employees believe it is a

---

BOX 16–5. Article XVIII Patient Care Committee—Employment Agreement between Southwest Washington Hospital Council and the Washington State Nurses Association, Effective 1975, p. 16

1. Establishment of Patient Care Committee

A Patient Care Committee shall be established consistent with standards as set forth by JCAH.

2. Intent

The hospital recognizes the responsibility of the Patient Care Committee to recommend measures objectively to improve patient care and will duly consider such recommendations and will advise the committee of action taken.

3. Objectives

The objectives of the Patient Care Committee shall be:

1. To consider constructively the professional practices of nurses and nurses' assistants.
2. To work constructively for the improvement of patient care and nursing practice.
3. To recommend to the hospital ways and means to improve patient care.

---

[32] Paragraph 4.06, Agreement between Liberty Division, Monticello Division and Callicoon Division of Community General Hospital of Sullivan County and New York Nurses' Association, 1973, p. 6.

BOX 16–6. Paragraph 2 Educational Leave and Reimbursement—1976–78 Contract between Twin City Hospitals and Minnesota Nurses Association, p. 6

It is the mutual purpose of Minnesota Nurses Association and the Hospital to encourage each nurse to continue and pursue her professional interest and education in nursing. To this end, salary increments for educational advancement are provided for in Section 4, paragraph (b) of this agreement. Provision has also been made in Section II for appropriate leaves of absence for educational purposes.

The hospital shall pay the nurse minimum reimbursement in the amount of seventy-five percent (75%) of tuition and required fees and books up to two hundred and fifty dollars ($250.00) per year for educational course work at an accredited institution under the following circumstances:

(a) The Director of Nursing must approve the proposed course or sequence of studies as having a reasonable relation to the nurse's professional employment.

(b) The nurse must sign a certificate that she will continue to or return to work at the Hospital for at least one (1) year after completion of the course or sequence of studies.

(c) Payment shall be made upon satisfactory completion of each course for which reimbursement has been requested. Provided, nevertheless, that the nurse shall repay the Hospital the reimbursement she has been paid hereunder to the extent that she does not continue to or make herself available to return to work at the hospital for at least one (1) year after the completion of the courses or sequence of studies.

---

necessary prerequisite for maintaining professional prerogatives within their job classifications. Such joint determinations, however, may also result from administrative personnel lacking the professional expertise in every profession and technical classification to make an adequate determination of professional responsibilities. Subjective analysis, however, offers little explanation of the motives for the inclusion of Patient Care Committee provisions.

The second major type of provision contained in professional and technical employees' contracts concerns training. Contract language facilitating continued education to keep professional and technical employees abreast of rapidly changing medical technology reflects the basic need of the health care industry for such investment in human capital. The majority of contracts which cover professional and technical employees contain an educational expense reimbursement and/or an educational leave provision (see Box 16–6).

These types of contractual provisions would make less sense for nonprofessional employees. For professional and technical employees, however, these contractual provisions clearly meet the need of both the employer and the employee in the health care industry to keep abreast of latest developments in the profession.

The final major contractual provision difference between the health care industry and other service industries concerns the exclusion of specific categories of employees. Most health care contracts contain provisions excluding specific employees such as residents, interns, student nurses, and supervisors. The National Labor Relations Board has determined that students as well as management personnel are not within their jurisdiction. Since the National Labor Relations Board's policies have changed in the past, it is not surprising to find such exclusionary contractual language designed to prevent organizational problems if the NLRB should again change its policy.

Contractual provisions excluding students from the scope of organization are clearly unnecessary outside the professional and technical classifications of the health care industry. Many hospitals operate schools of nursing and cooperate with medical schools and therefore have many workers who are both students and employees; such as residents, interns, and student nurses. Organization and collecive bargaining by students would work undue hardship upon, if not destroy, the educational process. Hospitals do not wish to be placed in a position where bargaining must take place between themselves and their students. The problem is one of separating the student function from the employee function. The National Labor Relations Board may yet reach a solution but hospital administrations have not been willing to take a chance and have, therefore, bargained for specific exclusion of students.

Exclusionary contractual language of this type is not found in general industry. Most skilled employee training in general industry is done in apprentice programs controlled either jointly or by the labor union. These students are not treated specifically as students but as employees who are gaining a needed skill on the job. Since the primary function outside the health care industry is not the training of skilled labor, exclusionary language is rarely observed. On the other hand, since a hospital serves in the dual capacity of a school and a hospital, particularly university medical centers, exclusionary language is more common.

Supervisory personnel are excluded from the protections of the National Labor Relations Act, and hospital administrations have also bargained for their specific exclusion.[33] The reason for these negotiated exclusions are not perfectly clear. Two opinions have emerged concerning the rationale for these clauses. There are those authorities who claim that management in this industry has a basic mistrust of NLRB procedures while others claim that this is a sign of management's inexperience with collective bargaining. The true reasoning behind these clauses is not known and it is pure speculation as to why these contract provisions have appeared in so many collective bargaining agreements.

Finally, some health care institutions and their unions have taken creative approaches to collective bargaining in an attempt to both improve the worker's compensation levels and help control hospital costs. One such approach Schultz and McKersie have labeled PAR (Participation-Achievement Reward Sys-

[33] *Bell Aerospace Co. (NLRB v.)*, U.S. Sup. Ct. Case No. 72-1598, April 23, 1974.

tems).[34] The basic idea behind these programs is that traditional work rules and standards be negotiated out of the contract and replaced with worker and union participation in reducing labor costs. The motivation for such participation is that the workers will share in any savings which accrue to the hospital thereby increasing their earnings. While this is not a new idea and is somewhat reminiscent of the old Scanlon plans, the application of these programs to negotiated work rules in the hospital industry is relatively new. The adoption of such plans does point up two interesting points. First, a PAR system requires a great deal of bargaining maturity by the parties to the contract. The fact that such programs have been adopted indicates significant progress toward mature and sophisticated bargaining relationships in the health care industry after less than a decade of negotiations. Secondly, there is evidence that unions as well as management are concerned about escalating health care costs. So much so, in fact, that unions in this industry are willing to participate in relatively innovative approaches to collective bargaining regarding cost issues.

Extent of Organization

Unionization has been occurring in the health care industry since before the Second World War. The private sector was the first to be organized with state and municipal facilities and federal hospitals organized soon thereafter. Although nonproprietary hospitals were not covered by the National Labor Relations Act between 1947 and 1974, unions remained active in the private sector.[35] According to the Bureau of Labor Statistics, by January of 1976:

Collective bargaining agreements generally applied to greater proportions of workers in state and local government hospitals than in private hospitals,....[36]

Contrary to established practice in general industry of focusing efforts upon large facilities believed to be easier to organize and leaving the more challenging (i.e., smaller) facilities until later, existing evidence in the health care industry suggests that smaller hospitals were organized first. Table 16-2 shows that since 1961 a greater percentage of facilities than employees have been unionized, thereby indicating that the facilities organized were less than average size. This phenomenon may have been the result of larger facilities having the financial economies of scale necessary to defeat union organization efforts, and hence, making smaller sized facilities relatively more attractive targets for organization efforts.

---

[34] See M.D. Fottler and W.F. Maloney "Guidelines to Productivity Bargaining in the Health Care Industry" *Health Care Management Review* (Winter 1979), pp. 59–70.

[35] See U.S. Civil Service Commission, *Union Recognition in the Federal Government*, U.S. Commerce Department, *Census of Governments*, Public Employment; Management–Labor Relations in State and Local Governments; and American Hospital Association, *Hospitals*, Guide Issue, *Hospital Statistics*.

[36] *Industry Wage Survey: Hospitals*, p. 2.

TABLE 16–2.   Percentage of Health Care Employees and
Facilities Unionized, 1961–1977

Year	Percentage of Workers Organized	Percentage of Facilities with at Least One Contract
1961	3.0	3.2
1965	5.7	6.2
1970	13.2	14.7
1973	17.2	19.7
1977	10.0	24.1

Source: Derived from data provided by the Bureau of Labor Statistics and the
American Hospital Association.

Many unions are active in organizing private-sector, proprietary and
nonproprietary health care institutions. In nursing, the American Nurses
Association is the most active with independent nursing associations and other
general unions also active.[37] Employees other than nurses have been extensively organized by a number of different types of unions, such as: Service
Employees' International Union, National Union of Hospital and Health Care
Employees (District 1199 of RWDSU/AFL-CIO), and a large number of
independent associations.[38]

In state and municipal health care facilities, the most active union appears
to be The American Federation of State, County and Municipal Employees.
Many of the same unions active in the private sector have also organized state
and local government health care facilities.[39]

Other unions such as the International Union of Operating Engineers,
United Brotherhood of Carpenters and Joiners of America, International
Brotherhood of Painters and Allied Trades, International Association of
Machinists and Aerospace Workers, Graphic Arts International Union, and the
Teamsters have organized employees in health care facilities in both private
and state and local hospitals. The targets of their organizational efforts are those
types of workers which they have traditionally represented in general
industry.[40]

In the federal health care facilities the American Federation of Government Employees, Civil Service Employees Association, and many of the same
independent and AFL-CIO unions active in other health care sectors have
been actively organizing federal employees.[41]

In addition to the aforementioned unions, Local 73 Service Employee
International Union and Local 743 of the Teamsters formed an association in

[37] Dilts, op cit.
[38] Ibid.
[39] Ibid.
[40] Ibid.
[41] Ibid.

the mid-1960s for the purpose of organizing hospital employees in the Chicago area. This organization, entitled HELP, has been quite successful in its organizational efforts.[42]

In summary, organization of health care employees has been accomplished by professional associations, craft unions, and industrial unions of virtually every type. Unlike most other industries no single union has yet emerged as the primary force in collective bargaining in the health care industry.

Summary and Conclusion

Labor law governing collective bargaining in the health care industry has developed independently in three areas: the private sector (both proprietary and nonprofit), federal government, and state and local government. The major characteristic of the development of the labor law governing health care facilities is a lack of uniformity in these laws. The private sector was intially covered by the 1935 National Labor Relations Act. In 1947, Taft-Hartley exempted nonproprietary hospitals from the definition of employer for purposes of the Act. In 1967 the NLRB asserted its jurisdiction over nursing homes and proprietary hospitals but left private nonprofit hospitals uncovered until Taft-Hartley was amended in 1974.

State labor laws are not consistent with federal law. Few if any general trends can be observed in the provisions of these state labor laws. The federal executive orders governing federal employees evolved in two distinct phases. The initial phase was a 1962 executive order issued by John F. Kennedy. Since this date, several other Executive Orders have been issued and the Civil Service Reform Act adopted. All three bodies of law have promoted growth in unionization and fostered industrial peace.

The conduct of collective bargaining in the health care industry has developed in much the same way as it has in most other industries. With some minor concessions granted to professional and technical employees, bargaining has emerged in a manner indistinguishable from that in the steel, auto, or service industries in general. Wage rates and earnings differentials do not appear to have been significantly affected by unionization and collective bargaining. Data gathered by the Bureau of Labor Statistics also indicate that unionization and collective bargaining have not had any appreciable impact upon fringe benefits.

Many unions have been active in the organization of health care employees. These unions are a very heterogenous group. Although some unions have established leadership roles in certain classifications of employees in specific health care sectors, no union has yet emerged as the leader in organizing health care employees.

---

[42]Steven Spirn, "Negotiating and Coexisting with a Union." *Hospital Progress.* (Feb. 1976), pp. 54–55.

DISCUSSION QUESTIONS

1. What special problems may be evident for health care industry unions and employers due to the diversity in the labor laws which govern this industry?

2. What similarities and differences have emerged between collective bargaining in the health care industry and other industries in the service and manufacturing sectors?

3. Does denial of the right to strike in the governmental sectors of the health care industry have any implications for collective bargaining in those facilities?

4. It has been suggested that the strike be prohibited in the private sector of the health care industry. Analyze this suggestion in detail.

5. What may be the reason(s) that no union has assumed a dominant role in the health care industry?

SELECTED REFERENCES

Becker, B. "Hospital Unionism and Employment Stability," *Industrial Relations*, (February 1978), **17** (1).

Boyer, J.M., Westerhouse, C.L., and Coggeshall, J.H. *Employee Relations and Collective Bargaining in Health Care Facilities*, St. Louis,: The C.V. Mosby Company, 1975.

Elkin, R.D., "Recognition and Negotiation Under Taft-Hartley," *Hospital Progress*, (December 1974), **55**.

Fottler, M.C. "The Union Impact on Hospital Wages," *Industrial and Labor Relations Review*, (April 1977), **30** (3).

Miller, J.D. and Shortell, S.M. "Hospital Unionization: A Study of Trends," *Hospitals*, (August 1969), **63**, (16).

Newhouse, J.P. "Toward a Theory of Nonprofit Institutions: An Economic Model of a Hospital," *American Economic Review*, (May 1970), **60**, (1)

Pepe, S.P. and Murphy, R.L., "The NLRB Decisions on Appropriate Bargaining Units," *Hospital Progress*, (October 1975), **56**.

Pointer, D.D., *Unionization, Collective Bargaining, and the Nonprofit Hospital*, Iowa City, IA: Center for Labor and Management, The University of Iowa, Monograph No. 13, 1969.

Rafferty, J. *Health Care and Productivity*, Lexington, MA: Lexington Books, 1974.

Schramm, C.J. "The Role of Hospital Cost-Regulating Agencies in Collective Bargaining," *Labor Law Journal*, (August 1977) **28**, (8).

Sorkin, A.L., *Health Manpower*, Lexington, MA: Lexington Books, 1977.

Stewart, C.T., "Allocation of Resources to Health," *The Journal of Human Resources*, (Winter 1971), **6**, (1).

Strickland, S.P., *U.S. Health Care*, New York: Universe Books, 1972.

Ward, R.A. *The Economics of Health Resources*, Reading, MA: Addison Wesley Publishing Co., Inc., 1975.

Yett, D.E. "Causes and Consequences of Salary Differentials in Nursing," *Inquiry*, (March 1970), 2.

Chapter 17

The Future of Labor Relations and Some Concluding Remarks

The authors have presented a basic introduction to the field of labor relations. The introductory course is by necessity a brief survey of the topic. There are, as should be obvious, many topics which were not given detailed examination and even more which were not discussed at all. The primary reason for this was to keep the present work to one manageable volume. There are, however, several areas of discussion which require attention before putting this work aside. First, a discussion of what has come to be called the "New Industrial Relations" will be offered. Second, and of particular interest to the student, is the role of the labor relations specialist in business, labor, and government. Third, what the student might expect in the way of future developments in this field deserves attention. Finally, a few brief remarks will be made concerning the choice of labor relations as a career.

The New Industrial Relations

As is the case with any discipline where human beings are the primary focus of study, labor relations is a field which is still in the process of evolving. As used here, evolution means that, as more practical knowledge is acquired and applied to labor-management relations, the field advances toward a more paradigmatic study of relevant problems. The labor law, the economic system and the educational system are all dynamic entities which help to shape the field we call labor relations. At present, we are witnessing considerable change and growth in this field. Possibly one of the more interesting developments is the rapid adoption of new modes of management. Managers over the past couple of decades have re-examined why workers turn toward organization and unions. To a large degree, managers have come to believe that workers form,

---

BOX 17-1. "Special Report: The New Industrial Relations"
***Business Week* May 11, 1981, pp. 84-98**

A more enlightened view of worker psychology has taken hold today. It stresses that most people want to be productive and will—given the proper incentives and a climate of labor-management trust—eagerly involve themselves in their jobs. This calls for a participatory process in which workers gain a voice in decision-making on the shop floor. Many companies, some in collaboration with once-hostile unions, are creating new mechanisms to gain worker involvement. Among these mechanisms are "self-managed" work teams, labor-management steering committees in union shops, problem-solving groups—such as "core groups" or the quality circles that are widely used in Japan—and redesign committees that wed social and technical ideas in designing or rearranging plants.

The concepts behind these innovations are not new; social cooperation at work surely predates recorded history. But organized labor's growth as a deeply adversarial institution in the U.S. coupled with management's retention of obsolete methods of controlling workers—Frederick Taylor's "Scientific Management" approach, for example—have blinded both sides to their mutual interests. Only a few days ago, work innovations were looked upon as slightly bizarre, if interesting, projects that "couldn't produce any bottom-line results," as Jerome M. Rosow, president of Work in America Institute Inc., puts it.

But evidence is growing that quality-of-work-life (QWL) programs, as some companies and unions call them, can meet their twin goals of increasing job satisfaction and improving quality and productivity.

---

join and support labor unions because management has failed in some way to be effective and just in its responsibility to operate the firm. In a recent article in *Business Week* a description of the "New Industrial Relations" was presented which incorporates this view of managerial failure as the "cause" of unions. While in the opinion of the authors this article dramatically overstates the case for this view of the development of unions and contains several technical errors, it does describe what a select few managements have put into practice in the last three or four years. An excerpt from this article is contained in Box 17-1.

Whether such programs will meet with enthusiastic success is open to speculation, but this "New Industrial Relations" is a marked departure from the accepted norms of today.

Role of the Labor Relations Specialist

The day of the generalist in business, labor and government as well as academics, for that matter, has passed. The rapid advance of technology, complications stemming from the legal and social environment as well as the overwhelming increase in available information and knowledge has made it difficult if not impossible for the businessperson, the union leader, the government official, and the college professor to be a generalist. In virtually every endeavor, white and blue collar workers are specialists. The neighborhood handyman has given way to the plumber, carpenter, and TV repairman. The small business operator, who has been historically a noteworthy generalist, now typically employs accountants, attorneys, engineers, and the like. Probably the age of the specialist is nowhere more evident than within the professions. For example, in medicine the generalist is no longer even entitled a general practitioner but is given the label specialist in family medicine. Economists now specialize in one specific area of the discipline such as labor economics, public finance, or international trade. The list of examples could be extended for several pages, but the message is clear; speciality is the order of the day.

Today's labor relations practitioner also usually specializes in some particular aspect of labor-management relations or some closely related area. The term labor relations specialist covers a broad category of professionals with different backgrounds and areas of expertise. There are those individuals who have sole responsibility for administering the organization's affirmative action program and ensuring compliance with various antidiscrimination laws and regulations. There are experts in grievance administration who may or may not become involved with the arbitration process. Many firms and unions have individuals or retain attorneys who specialize solely in arbitration advocacy. As you know, there are neutral third parties whose sole function in labor relations is to serve as the impartial arbitrator. There are experts who specialize in other related areas such as human relations, recruiting, compensation, work design and methods analysis, training and development, and rehabilitation. These persons all have two things in common: they fall under the broad category of labor relations specialist and they are concerned with one specific aspect of the total picture.

As used here, the term specialist has an additional meaning. In large organizations employing dozens of specialists working in several labor fields, there must be a manager sufficiently familiar with and competent in each field so as to effectively manage the organization's various labor relations functions. At the other extreme, one labor relations specialist may be responsible for all labor relations functions in a small firm. Contrary to natural inclination, these labor relations specialists cannot be classified as generalists; a more accurate label would be *polyspecialist*. A generalist simply does not possess the expertise or specialized knowledge necessary to effectively function in the aforementioned roles. In practice, both the manager of the large labor relations department and the labor relations specialist in the small firm must have specialized knowledge across most if not all of the various functional fields in labor relations—thus, the label polyspecialist.

Unions also need polyspecialists as well as specialists in specific labor relations areas. Organizers, human relations experts, grievance officials, arbitration advocates, and attorneys specialized in such fields as NLRB practice are all essential to the overall success of the local and international union. Often the technical assistance of a specialist in a narrowly focused area is prohibitively expensive for the local union. The local must therefore rely on the international union or its regional office for much of its technical assistance. Thus, union organizational structure, not to mention democratic election procedures, create a need (i.e., demand) for labor relations specialists either as paid members on the union payroll or as outside consultants. Among other functions, these specialists provide the continuity required for an effective labor organization. Many local unions have opted to hire a business manager to perform these varied tasks including personnel and labor relations functions.

There are a substantial number of local, state, and federal governmental agencies that require labor relations experts to perform management functions in much the same manner as private enterprises. There is, however, another role for labor relations specialists in governments. Such agencies as the NLRB, the FMCS, the EEOC, and the Wage and Hour Division of the U.S. Department of Labor require the services of specialists in several labor areas as well as polyspecialists in the role of regulators and administrators of the various laws governing labor markets. Most state and many local governments also need labor personnel to operate their own organizations and to discharge their regulatory functions.

The requirements for these careers vary substantially from function to function, from employer to employer, and from location to location. A BS or BA in labor relations or a closely related field will suffice for many entry level jobs. In general, the more technical the job requirements the more education and/or relevant job experience required. Some types of functions, such as representing a union or company before the NLRB or courts, require a law degree. Substantial experience and a solid academic background are prerequisites for becoming a labor relations manager with an intermediate size or larger firm.

Finally, most managers spend a substantial amount of their time and effort engaged in labor relations activities. In fact it has been estimated that labor and employee relations consume the single largest share of managerial time. Students who wish to work in some business capacity such as a factory foreman, hospital administrator, or even an accountant may find that their duties will sooner or later be heavily involved with grievance and disciplinary procedure administration as well as other labor relations matters. It is therefore important that college students have at least some background in labor law, collective bargaining and dispute settlement even if they do not choose this area as their career.

Future Developments in Labor Relations

There are a number of topics that may become "hot" issues in the field of labor relations in the future. Labor law reform, the transformation of the nation from a manufacturing to a service-based economy with the consequent growth of traditionally difficult to organize white collar occupations, the continued growth of multinational firms and the problems their growth creates for organized labor, and agricultural organization are but a few of the topics that may occupy center stage in labor relations discussions of the future.

BOX 17-2. New Labor Legislation: Doesn't Labor Deserve An Even Break? by Sol "Chick" Chaikin, President of the (ILGWU) International Ladies Garment Workers Union—an Address Delivered at Columbia University, June 14, 1979

A chill has spread over the U.S. workplace; a climate has been created in which the labor movement is finding it difficult, even dangerous, to grow. We seem to be returning to the mean stormy days of earlier times.

This must be reversed. New national labor legislation is required. The Right to Work laws, which fairly should be renamed "Right to Work for Less Laws," are state statutes. Bad as they are, they handicap unions most only after a union succeeds in signing an agreement with an employer. Something still remains to be done about the delaying tactics and illegal actions of corporations designed to prevent organizing. Laws must give remedy to workers who have been unfairly treated in their workplaces.

For example, an employer who discharges a worker for trying to organize a union is acting illegally. Nevertheless, it will routinely take two to three years for the wrong to be remedied and for back pay to be received. On occasion, it has taken longer than 25 years! New legislation is needed so the worker can be speedily returned to the job. A law with teeth would bar guilty employers from government contract for a stated time and would give abused workers double back pay for time out of work.

For its part, labor must organize more of the unorganized. Historically, skilled tradespeople formed unions, then miners, longshoremen, and workers in manufacturing industries. But almost imperceptibly, except for agriculture, the United States has changed from having a majority of its workers engaged in manufacture to an economy in which more than two-thirds of our workers make a living not producing food or commodities but rather waiting on tables, selling stocks, driving busses—in the service sector.

The United States must re-industrialize. Besides, unions must seek out the more than 50 millions who now have nothing to say about their wages and nothing to say about their working conditions. They work at the whim and fancy of their bosses with no job protection and probably a grim future: Fewer than 1 in 10 will ever collect a full, private pension and so will live out their old age in the poverty of a Social Security income.

When workers reach out to each other to join hands and hearts in union, all of society benefits. Teachers, who bargain collectively for small classroom sizes so they can teach better, improve the schools for everyone. Nuclear workers, who fight for safer work stations, bring us all cleaner air and water. Workers with decent pay checks are the backbone of our consumer economy.

Improved labor legislation, giving workers a better opportunity to decide about joining a union, won the majority of Congress but lost by only one vote in the filibuster mounted to defeat it. Labor did not get beat; it was the democratic process that got kicked in the face. We must fight for new law again. No other free, democratic, industrialized nation places such obstacles in the path of its labor.

Labor Law Reform

Labor law reform has been the subject of much controversy and debate in this country for the past couple of decades. Organized labor has been particularly unhappy with several provisions of the Labor Management Relations Act of 1947 (Taft-Hartley) as amended. First, Section 14(b), probably more than any other provision, has caused organized labor substantial grief. Section 14(b) permits states to pass so-called "right-to-work laws" which prohibit and otherwise regulate the negotiation of union shop and lesser forms of union security clauses. Unions find these laws unacceptable since unions must represent all members of the bargaining unit regardless of whether they choose to join the union or not. Unions argue that these nonunion members of the bargaining unit receive the benefits of unionization without contributing to the organization—that these employees, commonly called "free riders," impose an undue and unreasonable burden on union members. Unions, therefore, wish to see Section 14(b) of Taft-Hartley repealed. Right-to-work proponents, on the other hand, would prefer federal prohibition to the present practice of state regulation of contractual union security clauses. They argue that any form of compulsory union support, financial and/or otherwise, constitutes an unreasonable interference with employees' right of free association. Thus, both sides are dissatisfied with portions of the present law.

Unions would also like to see the Taft-Hartley definition of employee broadened to encompass a wider variety and larger number of workers. Presently, employees of small firms deemed by the NLRB not to significantly affect interstate commerce are excluded from coverage of the Taft-Hartley Act. Agricultural employees, government employees, employees of horse and dog tracks as well as those of law firms are also excluded from the protective features of Taft-Hartley. Supervisors, who had been accorded the status of employees shortly after World War II, were stripped of that status by Taft-Hartley — the argument being that their classification as employees unduly burdened and interfered with the management function. In addition to granting the aforementioned groups of workers the protection afforded other employees under Taft-Hartley, the suggestion has even been made to scrap the Railway Labor Act and bring its employees under the jurisdiction of the Taft-Hartley Act.

There has also been substantial interest in improving, speeding up and streamlining NLRB procedures. Unions have bitterly complained that NLRB procedures suffer from a number of shortcomings that need correction. Foremost of these deficiencies is NLRB procedural time delays. Even without court appeals, the process may take as long as a year; with court appeals, the process may stretch out to five, six, seven, or more years. In the meantime, the wrongfully discharged employee may remain unemployed, or worse, unemployable because of a blemished employment record. Unions therefore contend that "justice delayed is justice denied." As an alternative, they argue that the employee should be reinstated upon NLRB acceptance of the case and discharged only upon employer demonstration of cause. Unions have also been critical of the remedies that the NLRB has utilized in dealing with unfair labor practices. Unions argue that these remedies do not provide employers the incentive necessary to obey the law and, therefore, require substantial strengthening.

Other subjects targeted as possible labor law reform issues include: (1) providing greater freedom for picketing at construction sites; (2) reforming the national emergency impasse procedures; (3) imposing restrictions on multinational firms that violate U.S. labor laws; and (4) making wildcat strikes an unfair labor practice. Whether labor law reform will materialize is purely speculative. Past attempts at labor law reform, however, indicate that many of the proposed changes have wide general support. In the view of the authors, labor law reform is inevitable; the more appropriate question is: When? In all probability, many of the most pressing issues will become the subject of legislative action during the present decade—but probably not until shortcomings in these areas precipitate some sort of crisis such as a crippling public-sector strike or a blatant and deliberate attempt to undermine employee rights by financially bankrupting unions through the use of right-to-work laws.

The Service Sector

Unions have historically had their greatest success in the manufacturing, mining, transportation, and construction sectors of the economy. As the fortunes of these industries have gone, so-to-speak, so have the fortunes of organized labor—up to a point (See Chapter 3). With the relative decline in importance of these sectors and the relative growth in importance of service industries, many authorities predicted that unions would also decline. At the base of this prediction was labor's historical inability to penetrate the service-sector of the economy and the added expense of organizing an industry essentially local in character (i.e., characterized by small firms). Another factor that prompted this dire prediction was the southern migration of firms to "right-to-work" states. Although these factors have created problems for organized labor, "reports of its demise have been greatly exaggerated." Organized labor has demonstrated a remarkable vitality over the years. If labor history mirrors nothing else, it does mirror the pragmatic nature of the American labor movement. Unions are not static organizations wedded to a single industry or set of organizational strategies. Thus, recent years have witnessed concerted efforts by labor unions to organize service workers and firms located in right-to-work law states—many of which have been quite successful.

Organized labor's continued viability can also be attributed to the generic nature of the employment relationship. The organization and formation of unions represents one type of worker response to unmet employee needs in the workplace. These needs and problems of employees are not unique to the manufacturing sector of the economy. The need for an effective method of employee input into decision making affecting wages, hours, and other terms and conditions of employment is therefore present in the service sector of the economy (See Chapter 3). Consequently, it should not come as a surprise that unions are focusing their organizational efforts on service employees as the service sector of the economy grows in relative importance.

A number of interesting developments have recently taken place in the service sector. Retailing and restaurants, once believed to be immune to unionization because of the largely unskilled nature of the work and relatively good working conditions, have yielded large numbers of new union members. Although the banking industry has not yet experienced any significant union penetration, it has recently become the target of limited union organizational efforts.

Professional athletes have been associated with unions since the latter part of the nineteenth century.[1] Today most major league team athletics are organized, including baseball, basketball, football, and hockey. Collective bargaining in major league athletics has drawn considerable attention from the media as well as sports fans since the 1981 baseball strike. The publicity surrounding collective bargaining and work stoppages by professional sports figures may have an impact upon service-sector labor relations far in excess of the relative importance of sports to that sector. Although baseball fans were aware that the 1981 baseball season was severely shortened by the strike, few understood the issues involved. Many fans could identify "free-agency" as the major unresolved issue but few could describe the players and the owners positions or why this issue resulted in a work stoppage. The one thing that baseball fans could, with certainty, relate to was that they missed the televised Saturday "Game of the Week" or that they couldn't take in a Royals or Reds game at the ballpark. In some sense, this is a commentary on labor relations in this country. When vital (or what are perceived to be vital) services are cut off as a result of a labor-management dispute, the consumer often does not care why this interruption occurred, but only that it has occurred and has created an inconvenience. Most goods producing industries rarely experience a work stoppage that prevents consumers from obtaining a demanded commodity. In the service sector, however, the likelihood of a work stoppage that completely deprives the public of a needed service is perceived to be greater than in other sectors. The baseball strike did produce considerable fan alienation and bad press for the union and the owners. This was short lived as consumers forgot these matters when the impasse was resolved. A crucial question, however, was left unanswered: What will the public's response to unions be as the service sector grows and union as well as work stoppage activity spreads throughout the sector? Only the future can satisfactorily answer this question. It is worth noting, however, that as convenience-centered as the American people may appear, they demonstrate the ability, in aggregate, to adapt and become issue oriented when necessary. There are bound to be controversies and injustices but as long as there are responsible and capable leaders in organized labor and management, these transitional difficulties will be of insignificant consequence.

Multinational Corporations and Collective Bargaining

Labor leaders have been particularly critical of multinational corporations. Unions point to multinationals as an important cause of American economic

---

[1] In baseball, the first union was the Brotherhood of Professional Baseball Players which was formed in 1885 and conducted collective bargaining with National League ball clubs.

problems, particularly with respect to unemployment.[2] There are several interesting problems associated with collective bargaining and multinational corporations. Many companies have located part or all of their operations overseas to take advantage of favorable tax structures, lower material, labor, and transportation costs. In many cases, substantial amounts of investment have been diverted from U.S. expansion to foreign operations, undoubtedly costing the American economy jobs.[3] It is quite natural that these activities would draw the wrath of organized labor. On the other hand, there has also been substantial investment by Western European and Japanese firms in the U.S. in the marketing, service, and manufacturing areas—creating new jobs. These firms are also termed multinational corporations and provide some interesting complications for collective bargaining in the U.S.

U.S. corporations operating subsidiaries abroad find that labor relations often become quite complicated. Not only does the firm now have several bodies of labor law with which to deal (that are often quite different and guided by conflicting principles), but frequently the economic, sociological, and political environments are significantly different and even totally alien. If the U.S. firm is located solely within the United States, centralized technical experts in the field of labor relations may be capable of servicing large segments of the firm's operations. Locating abroad may require experts in the law, culture, and government of the host nation. The same is true for many of the foreign companies which have located in this country. For example, a Japanese automaker opened a manufacturing facility in the United States recently. As had been the unquestioned practice in Japan, management provided the American worker with uniform work clothes, including baseball caps bearing the company's name. After several months of operation, a number of employees exchanged their yellow Honda baseball caps for blue ones with the UAW's logo. Put out by this blatant display of disloyalty, the Japanese managers took disciplinary action against the UAW members; in Japan it would be unthinkable for a worker to do such a thing. In the U.S., on the other hand, not only are union caps and jackets common, but an employee's refusal to comply with a directive banning said dress *does not* constitute just cause for discipline.

Unions, faced with having to collectively bargain with multinational corporations, have adopted two basic strategies. These strategies involve: (1) collective bargaining especially designed to offset the bargaining power of the multinational and (2) legislative efforts designed to protect union jobs and bargaining power. Coalition bargaining with unions located abroad, work preservation clauses, and public relations campaigns have been typical union responses. Unions have, however, devised even more creative responses in collective bargaining for application to multinational corporations. One of the most creative responses to multinational corporations have been attempts at

[2] A.C. McLellan and M.D. Baggs, "Multinationals: How Quick They Jump," *American Federationist*, (September 1973), pp. 22–24.

[3] W.K. Chung and G.G. Fouch, "Foreign Direct Investment in the United States, 1977," *Survey of Business*, (August 1978), pp. 35–42.

developing multinational unions.[4] With notable exceptions of some limited success in a few industries such as chemicals[5] and flat glass[6] these unions have not been very effective in transnational collective bargaining. The future may hold some potential for union success in this area if the trend toward the development of multinational corporations continues.

Unions have also applied considerable pressure on the Congress to pass legislation designed to protect domestic jobs and to make locating abroad less attractive to American firms. Pressure for higher tariffs, tax incentives and trade quotas are specifically aimed at discouraging American investment abroad. The Trade Adjustment Assistance Program was developed by Congress to provide income support and retraining assistance to workers adversely affected by foreign trade. It is quite possible that labor unions will expend greater efforts on obtaining such legislation in the future.

Agricultural Labor Organizations

Agriculture has, on a number of occasions, been the focus of union organizational efforts. Farm owners first attempted collective action under the banner of the Grange and more recently under the banner of the National Farmers Organization (NFO). The goals of these *employer* organizations were improving commodity prices, legislative relief, and the sharing of information. As regards the more traditional type of labor organization, the United Farm Workers of America (UFWA), led by Cesar Chavez, has been at the forefront of attempts to organize the farm worker *employee*. Farm workers have historically had great difficulty in organizing for purposes of collective bargaining, primarily because of the highly competitive nature of agricultural product markets and the agricultural workers' exemption from the Taft-Hartley Act. In the absence of federal labor law reform bringing farm workers within the jurisdiction of Taft-Hartley, the UFWA must rely on individual states for legislation protecting collective bargaining rights. To date, the UFWA has met with only limited success in its efforts to obtain such legislation. In 1975, however, California enacted the Agricultural Relations Act. California was the first major agricultural state to pass legislation favorable to agricultural unionization. Since 1975, the UFWA has encountered another problem in organizing farm workers in California—effective competition from other labor organizations, primarily the Teamsters.

White Collar Unionization

Several significant issues fall under the broad category of white collar unionization. Professional employees such as physicians, lawyers, and en-

---

[4]B.C. Roberts and J. May, "The Response of Multinational Enterprises to International Trade Union Pressures," *British Journal of Industrial Relations*, (November 1974), pp. 403–416.

[5]Herbert Northup and R.L. Rowan, "Multinational Union Activities and Plant Closings: The Case of Akzo," *Industrial Relations Journal*, (Spring 1978), pp. 27–36.

[6]Herbert Northup and R.L. Rowan, "Multinational Bargaining Approaches in the Western European Flat Glass Industry," *Industrial and Labor Relations Review*, (October 1976), pp. 32–46.

gineers may be classified under the white-collar category as well as university professors and other professinals. Managerial personnel in manufacturing were among the first white-collar workers to attempt organization and were, for a time, quite successful. As noted earlier, foremen were classified as employees under the National Labor Relations Act until 1947. As such, foremen were afforded the same protection that all other employees were afforded under national labor law. The passage of the Taft-Hartley Act removed the protections of labor law from foremen's unions. The union which had been responsible for most of this pre-1947 organizational activity, the Foreman's Association of America, soon vanished from the ranks of organized labor. In 1974, the United States Supreme Court struck another blow against white collar unions in the *Bell Aerospace*[7] decision. In this case, the court extended the Taft-Hartley exclusion of foremen to all managerial personnel. The Court reasoned that if a person was in a decision making position with a firm, union membership might create a conflict of interest, and, therefore, managerial employees ought not be extended the protections of Taft-Hartley.

Professional employees, on the other hand, are covered by the Taft-Hartley Act and are afforded its protections. A professional employee is defined by Section 1 (12) of the Act as:

(a) any employee engaged in work (i) predominantly intellectual and varied in character as opposed to routine mental, manual, mechanical, or physical work; (ii) involving the consistent exercise of discretion and judgment in its performance, (iii) of such a character that the output produced or the result accomplished cannot be standardized in relation to a given period of time; (iv) requiring knowledge of an advanced type in a field of science or learning customarily acquired by a prolonged course of specialized intellectual instruction and study in an institution of higher learning or a hospital, as distinguished from a general academic education or from an apprenticeship or from training in the performance of routine mental, manual, or physical processes; or (b) any employee, who (i) has completed the courses of specialized intellectual instruction and study described in clause (iv) of paragraph (a) and (ii) is performing related work under the supervision of a professional person to qualify himself to become a professional employee as defined in paragraph (a).

Many different types of professional employees have been organized—actors, engineers, professors, research scientists, laboratory technicians—to name but a few.

Although the employment relation is generic in nature, the unionized professional will pose interesting challenges for management and organized labor. The professional employee has several needs not common to other workers. The need for professional development and to remain current with developments in the employee's field will result in differing union demands as well as the services that the membership will expect from the union. In addition, professional employees may generate higher expectations concerning the terms and conditions of employment as well as the conduct of the bargaining relation. The future of labor-management relations involving professionals should be challenging. Many innovative developments can be

[7]*NLRB v. Bell Aerospace Co.*, 416 U.S. 267 (1974).

expected from management and organized labor concerning the organization and bargaining associated with professional and white collar employees.

As it now stands, *white-collar* unionization on the national level will be primarily limited to the aforementioned professional nonmanagerial category —unless labor law reform occurs.

Managerial Aggression—A Threat to Peaceful Labor Relations

The authors of this text have, to this point, emphasized labor-management cooperation in labor relations. This orientation is based on the belief that the majority of unions and employers are responsible, law abiding and rational. Yet no text concerning collective bargaining would be complete without an examination of the recent return to 1930s ideology on the part of several firms and the rise of the *professional* "union buster."

BOX 17–3. "Return to the Rhetoric of the 1930s?" in *A Labor Viewpoint: Another Opinion* **by Sol Chick Chaikin, President of the International Ladies Garment Workers Union**

I would leave you on a cautionary note. I think the 1980s will be a challenging time. We in the labor movement will have to beat back the challenge of many employers who seem to want a return of the class struggle. This country has not suffered from this attitude for 40 years. In the 1930s when many industries were being organized, forming a union was stark; the struggle was bitter. Workers had to join together to fight against the employer who exploited and oppressed them and against the community which the employer controlled.

We thought that kind of confrontation had been done away with, put to rest. We thought we no longer needed to expend a great deal of energy in that direction. We thought the rhetoric of the 1930s and 1940s was a dead language. Yet that rhetoric has been resurrected by some employers, by the National Association of Manufacturers, by something called the "Committee for Union-Free Environment.

Very few Union leaders are being fooled. If we are to be challenged on the job, in the mines, mills and factories, then we too shall revert to the old rhetoric. . . .

"Union-free environment" is a new slogan that sets a certain tone. It establishes a standard to which some Stone Age employers may wish to. repair. If employers do gather round this slogan, there will be many difficult days ahead for both workers and management. I would not suggest using a renewed class struggle as the basis for contemplating the future. I would hope we do not come to that. But, if we do, then all bets are off as far as rational, equitable collective bargaining is concerned.

The AFL-CIO as well as most other labor organizations have pointed with great distress to the rise of multi-million dollar industry in this country— antiunion consulting services. In the AFL-CIO's publication the *American Federationist* several articles have appeared which denounced these consulting firms as nothing more than thugs who have exchanged their blackjacks for briefcases.[8]

The tactics employed by these antiunion consulting firms vary substantially from extended NLRB and court litigation designed to thwart union organizing, to advising the firm on how to eliminate managerial short-comings associated with the rise of unionization, to outright coersion. The modus operandi of such "union busting" firms also varies substantially. Seminars on maintaining "union free" status, direct management consulting, and legal services are all commonly employed methods.

Regardless of the method employed, the aim is to deny employees union representation. The result of the rise of this activity has been to mire many bargaining relations in legal complications and foster mutual hostility. This regression from mature collective bargaining has luckily not gained widespread acceptance among responsible managers; yet the potential for renewed class struggle and labor unrest is real and must be carefully watched if economic disruption and political instability are to be avoided.

A Career in Labor Relations

The student who goes to work today will undoubtedly be involved with labor relations, in a broad sense, whatever his or her selected occupation. The manufacturing supervisor, hotel or restaurant manager, school teacher and accountant will all have to deal with labor markets, labor laws, and workers, which places them in the firm's or union's labor relations system. Therefore, whether your major is engineering or history, time spent studying labor relations is time well spent. Many students tend to view labor relations as an exciting, people-oriented field. Although this is true, for the most part, a significant amount of time must be allocated to routine and mundane tasks. To select labor relations as a career because you "like" people is definitely the wrong approach. Work of this nature requires, as does almost any career, motivation and dedication. Technical aspects of economics, law, and many other fields must be mastered while in school. Personal characteristics such as good judgment, honesty, and self motivation are also prerequisites to success in this field. Labor relations is challenging and very rewarding but there will be times when people and legalities will frustrate those who enter the area.

The demand for those specializing in the field of labor relations is much greater than the supply. Although many specialist positions in labor relations require job experience, a sound academic background in labor relations will qualify the student for many entry level positions. For those selecting labor

[8] Phillis Payne, "The Consultants Who Coach the Violators," *American Federationist*, (September 1977), pp. 22–29.

relations as a career, the years ahead will be both challenging and rewarding. For those taking only one or two courses in labor relations, it is hoped that these courses provide the insight necessary to understand current labor-management relations issues.

Summary and Conclusions

The day of the generalist has been rapidly disappearing. Specialists in the field of labor relations are more properly referred to as polyspecialists since they must deal with several areas of expertise. There are many developments presently unfolding which may result in significant changes in organized labor and labor-management relations. The continued debate and attempts at labor law reform in the Congress could result in significant changes in labor law. There are significant changes in the American economy and demographics of the labor force which present labor and management with substantial challenges. The multinational corporation and the increasing service orientation of the U.S. economy will result in differing union strategies and tactics which in turn will affect management's goals, strategies and tactics.

It is hoped that many capable students will choose the labor relations field as a career. Labor relations is a challenging and rewarding field in need of more trained professionals. Those students not selecting labor relations as a career will still deal with various aspects of labor-management relations. An effective introduction to labor relations for these students is particularly important so that they may avoid the pitfalls that so often entrap the uninformed.

COMMENTARY: Mr. Harold Scott Speaks on What Advice to Give a College Student Who Might be Preparing for a Career in Labor Relations.*

An individual considering Labor Relations as a career should consider the following:

The ability to communicate to a variety of people from different socio-economic, academic, and professional levels is critical. Generally the bargaining unit is less educated, and the difference in education can inhibit open communications about mutual problems.

Credibility with union officials is more important than a complete knowledge and understanding of the collective bargaining agreement. The intent of the latter statement is not to minimize the importance of knowing and understanding the labor agreement, because the ability to interpret contract language is of paramount importance for anyone in the labor relations field. On the other hand, credibility and trust between the union and corresponding labor relations personnel can overcome most differences.

The adversarial relationship should be minimized and cooperation emphasized. Unions have come to understand that the success of the company is the

*For Mr. Scott's Biography, See Chapter 10, Page 214.

basis for their success; and management, for the most part, has come to understand that they cannot function efficiently in a unionized environment without the cooperation of union representatives and the rank and file.

It is desirable to get a perspective of labor relations from the union point of view. A course in labor history would be helpful. Regardless of the means by which the perspective is achieved, empathy for the union's point of view is the desired by-product.

Tenacious protection of certain basic management prerogatives (rights) is imperative and a principal responsibility of anyone who desires to succeed in labor relations.

Analytical ability is an asset for anyone entering the labor relations field, as is the ability to communicate well in writing.

Finally, academic training in labor relations is also a valuable asset; but since so much of labor relations involves dealing with the idiosyncrasies of individuals, much of what it is important to know cannot be learned in the classroom.

COMMENTARY: Suggestions for the Student Interested in a Career in Labor Relations by Mr. Douglas Fraser.*

If you want a career in labor relations from the union's side of the fence, you must go to work as an hourly worker in a union shop, become active in your local union and get yourself elected as a steward or committeeperson. And even if you are looking for a career in corporate labor relations, I still recommend spending time in a plant as an hourly production worker so you will better understand the problems of working people.

DISCUSSION QUESTIONS

1. Labor law reform has been at controversy in this country for most of the past three decades. Critically evaluate the concept of reformulating the labor law to better serve (i) unions; (ii) management; and (iii) the general public.

2. Why does the service sector orientation of the U.S. economy pose significant problems for labor organizations? How might unions overcome these problems?

3. What is a multinational corporation? Why would a multinational corporation pose any different problems for organized labor than any other major conglomerate? What strategies might unions employ in dealing with multinationals?

4. Outline the three most significant developments for labor-management relations which are likely to be observed in the near future. Defend your selections.

*For Mr. Fraser's Biography, See Chapter 8, Page 174.

SELECTED REFERENCES

Banks, R.F. and Jack Stieber, *Multinationals, Unions and Labor Relations in Industrial Countries*, Ithaca, N.Y.: New York State School of Industrial and Labor Relations, 1977.

Bowen, W.G. and Orley Ashenfelter, eds. *Labor and the National Economy* (revised edition), New York: W.W. Norton & Company, Inc., 1975.

Chaikin, Sol. *A Labor Viewpoint: Another Opinion*. Monroe, N.Y.: Library Research Associates, Inc., 1980.

Craypo, Charles, "Collective Bargaining in the Conglomerate, Multinational Firm," *Industrial and Labor Relations Review*, (October 1975), pp. 3–25.

Gilroy, T.P. and P.J. Madden, "Labor Relations in Professional Sports," *Labor Law Journal*, (December 1977).

Hershfield, D.C., *The Multinational Union Challenges the Multinational Company*. New York: Conference Board, 1975.

Moore, W.J. and R.J. Newman, "On the Prospects for American Trade Union Growth: A Cross-Section Analysis," *The Review of Economics and Statistics*, (1975), **57**: 435–445.

Somers, Gerald G. Ed., *The Next 25 Years of Industrial Relations*, Madison, Wis: Industrial Relations Research Assn., 1973.

Taylor, Benjamin J. and Fred Witney, *Labor Relations Law*, (3rd edition), Englewood Cliffs, N.J.: Prentice-Hall, Inc., 1979, Chapters 10 and 13.

Ulman, Lloyd, *The Rise of the National Trade Union*, Cambridge, MA: Harvard University Press, 1955.

Cases

Case 1

The Case of the Cafeteria and Vending Machines Prices

This is an actual NLRB unfair labor practice case which involved Ford Motor Company and the UAW (230 NLRB 101) in 1977. This case involves the classification of the issues of collective bargaining. The student is to write a one page analysis of the case and determine whether the company violated its obligation to bargain collectively. The student is then to look up the NLRB decision and write a one page analysis of where and how her/his decision differed from the NLRB's.

Ford Motor Company, since 1967 has collectively bargained concerning the quality of food services provided by an independent contractor (ARA Services) in its Chicago Stamping Plant. The company has provided its employees with two air-conditioned cafeterias and numerous air-conditioned vending areas for use during lunch periods.

In 1972 Ford and ARA Services entered into an agreement whereby ARA Services furnishes food, machines and services the vending areas. In return, ARA was guaranteed a cost plus 9% return by Ford Motor Company. In recent years Ford has found that ARA has not been able to cover cost and make its 9% margin. As a result Ford has been subsidizing ARA.

For the past several years the UAW has requested that Ford negotiate concerning the vending and cafeteria services provided for employees' use. The company has refused to negotiate concerning the prices that ARA charges in the cafeteria or the vending areas. Ford has however negotiated contractual provisions concerning quality and quantity of services provided by ARA. The contract further specifies that employees are entitled to a thirty minute lunch period and two twenty minute breaks. The employees are prohibited from leaving the plant during their twenty minute breaks. It is not feasible for employees to leave the plant for lunch since few restaurants are located in the area and the service at these establishments is typically too slow to guarantee that the employee could return to work in the allotted time.

The company provides employees with lockers and they are permitted to bring their lunch to work and use the cafeteria facilities. Few employees leave the plant for lunch and some do bring their lunch to work.

Because of the ARA agreement Ford decided to allow prices to be increased by up to ten percent in the cafeteria and vending areas. The union protested the company's action and about half the bargaining unit participated in a boycott of the cafeteria and vending machine areas. The union, in preparation for upcoming contract negotiations, asked for information from Ford concerning the company's role in providing the cafeteria and vending services. Ford refused to provide any such information and again refused to negotiate concerning cafeteria and vending machine prices. The union then filed charges with the Office of the General Council of the NLRB alleging that the cafeteria and vending machine prices were terms and conditions of employment and that Ford's refusal to bargain constituted an unfair labor practice.

QUESTIONS

1. Do cafeteria and vending machine prices constitute "wages, hours or other terms and conditions of employment?"

2. Does the subcontracting of the subject services to ARA have any bearing on this case?

3. If the union loses this case what actions might be appropriate?

4. If Ford loses this case what actions might be appropriate?

Case 2

The "But For" Rule Case

The purpose of this case is to demonstrate to students some of the problems associated with discipline and union organizing campaigns. The application of the "but for" rule developed by the NLRB and the Courts (NLRB v. Fibers International Corp. 1st Cir. 1971 and NLRB v. Whitfield Pickle Company 5th Cir. 1967) illustrates the difficulty in disciplining employees during an organizing campaign. Stated simply, the "but for" rule states that the employee must be discharged or disciplined for just cause and not for union activity. If the motive for issuing discipline to an employee is at least in part to "chill unionism" then the action probably violates the Taft-Hartley Act. The student is to review the two cases cited above and Sections 7, 8(a) (1), and 8(a) (3) of the Taft-Hartley Act. Upon reviewing this material and the facts in this case the student is to prepare answers to the questions at the end of the case.

Facts and Background

NLM Company is currently in the midst of a union organizing campaign. The company is a small manufacturing concern employing 18 skilled tool makers, electricians and plumbers as well as 85 semiskilled and unskilled workers. The company makes pipe fittings, valves, and water meters and has been in this business since 1941. The company is a family owned business but none of the family members are involved in the actual operation of the business.

Three months ago the NLRB asserted jurisdiction in this case and certified the 103 production nonclerical, nonsales, and nonsupervisory employees as the bargaining unit. One of the skilled plumbers in the bargaining unit, Mr. George Myers, had been obtaining signatures on bargaining authorization cards on behalf of the Plumbers and Pipefitters International Union (PPIU). Over the period from July 24 to October 8, Mr. Myers had gotten all of the skilled employees to sign authorization cards as well as 58 of the semiskilled or unskilled employees. All of the bargaining unit employees knew that George was the motivating force behind the union movement at NLM. George was known to management and his fellow employees as a hard working, honest man but several of the unskilled employees disliked George and disapproved of his stand on unionization. On several occasions these employees baited Mr. Myers and told him that if a union was voted in they would "get" him personally.

On October 14 George was called into the plant manager's office and told there was a complaint concerning George's union activities. Three employees (from among the group George had problems with) stated that they had seen George using the maintenance foreman's telephone several times during the last week. They alleged that they heard him make references to the PPIU in these long distance phone conversations and wondered if he had been given permission by management to make long distance phone calls for union business. If so they thought this was highly unfair. The plant manager then showed George a telephone bill listing six telephone calls to PPIU headquarters in Washington, D.C. totaling $37.50 in charges. George denied that he made any of those calls and stated that these three employees were from the group that had threatened him. The plant manager then warned George that if any other instances arose of this nature he would have to let him go.

Two days later as George was entering the plant, five of the anti–union employees were grouped together at the entrance. As George started to pass them one jumped out in front of him and another tripped him. When George fell forward on the employee who jumped out in front of him the employee grabbed him and fell to the ground while the other four yelled "fight, fight." Several of George's friends arrived on the scene and a fist fight did subsequently occur.

On reviewing the circumstances, the plant manager decided to give everyone involved a one-day disciplinary layoff and fired George. George then complained to the NLRB which conducted a thorough investigation and found that George's story was true. The NLRB field examiner presented the evidence he had gathered to the plant manager and asked if he would like to settle this issue. The plant manager stated he had settled the matter; George was fired for just cause and not union activity. Further, these NLRB allegations were just that, allegations and not fact. The plant manager said he was glad George was gone and the union defeated because it made his operations at NLM much simpler.

QUESTIONS

1. Do the actions of the anti–union employees violate the provisions of Taft-Hartley? Explain. Would your answer change if these employees were acting on the order of management? Explain.

2. What if George were a spokesman for remaining nonunion and the thugs were union organizers, would these employee's actions violate Taft-Hartley? Explain. Do you see a double standard here?

3. Was George Myers unlawfully discharged? How does the "but for" rule apply here?

4. Does the plant manager's actions in firing or refusing to rehire George Myers violate Taft-Hartley? Explain.

5. Have George Myers' Section 7 rights under Taft-Hartley been violated? Explain in detail.

6. If you were the plant manager in this case would you have handled this affair differently? Explain.

Case 3

Arbitrator Selection

Arbitrator selection is typically done by the alternate striking of names from a list of arbitrators containing an odd number of names. This case exercise is designed with two purposes in mind. First, to fully understand the arbitration process and how it works the students must familiarize themselves with how arbitrators reason and the rules and principles they apply. It is therefore important for students to read arbitration awards not only for substance but for form. Secondly, the selection of a specific arbitrator may in part determine how the parties present their cases. Arbitrators differ on how they view certain activities and what principles should be given the greatest weight.

In this case the instructor will divide the class into management and labor teams consisting of three persons each. Given the details of the case and the hypothetical backgrounds of the arbitrators, the parties are to select the arbitrator to hear their cases. After the selection is made each team is to prepare a four or five page report outlining each arbitrator's strengths and weaknesses (as they perceive them and as they relate to this case) and a statement as to why each is either acceptable or unacceptable. Finally, the group should briefly explain how it would proceed in this case and what in the selected arbitrator's background leads them to believe that they will either be successful or unsuccessful.

Facts in This Case

Joe Miller has been discharged for chronic absenteeism. Management took this action after Joe compiled the attendance record shown on page 378.

The suspension pending discharge for chronic absenteeism was made a formal discharge on December 27, 1981. The disciplinary notice is shown in the accompanying box.

Notice of Disciplinary Action Manhattan Municipal Hospital

Date: December 27, 1981   *Employee Name:* Joe Miller
Department: Maintenance   *Clock Number:*   A–137
Cause   Chronic and excessive absenteeism in violation of hospital rule 10–2(a).

Description of Offense: Joe Miller for the fourth quarter of calendar year 1981 either was tardy or absent from work on 16 separate occasions. Two of these occasions were authorized by the hospital's sick leave policy. On eleven occasions, the employee received a disciplinary penalty for missing work. Joe Miller since November 11, 1981 has been issued progressive discipline consistent with the hospital's policy on absenteeism up to the three day disciplinary layoff issued on December 14, 1981. Mr. Miller was suspended pending discharge on December 22, 1981 and is hereby discharged.

Employee: Joe Miller   Supervisor: Susan Gribbs
Union Representative: Hospital Administrator:
           Frank Klein   Roy Clasky

Attendance Record

Manhattan Municipal Hospital

Name: Miller, Joseph T.
Date of Hire: October 7, 1966
Department: Maintenance

Employee Clock Number: A–137
Social Security Number: 333–33–0000
Date of Birth: January 22, 1942

Quarter Ending: December 31, 1981

	Incident	Reason Offered	Action
1. TARDY	October 10, 1981	1 hour 10 minutes	car trouble	supervisory counseling
2. ABSENT	October 12, 1981	without calling in	illness	charged to sick days—2 remaining
3. ABSENT	October 13–14, 1981	called in	illness	charged to sick days—0 remaining
4. TARDY	October 17, 1981	20 minutes	overslept	none
5. TARDY	October 24, 1981	2 hours	car trouble	supervisory counseling
6. ABSENT	October 25, 1981	without calling in	personal business	verbal warning
7. TARDY	October 26, 1981	7 minutes	overslept	verbal warning
8. ABSENT	November 3, 1981	without calling in	illness	verbal warning
9. TARDY	November 4, 1981	22 minutes	overslept	written warning
10. ABSENT	November 11, 1981	without calling in	car trouble	written warning
11. ABSENT	November 13, 1981	called in	illness	verbal warning
12. ABSENT	November 20, 1981	without calling in	illness	1 day disciplinary layoff
13. ABSENT	November 22, 1981	called in—informed unless he reports to work serious discipline	personal business	3 day disciplinary layoff
14. ABSENT	December 14, 1981	without calling in	illness	3 day disciplinary layoff
15. LEFT WORK EARLY	December 20, 1981	4 hours	no reason offered	1 day disciplinary layoff
16. ABSENT	December 22, 1981	called in	car trouble	suspension pending DISCHARGE

17. Previous work record shows employee counseled twice for ABSENTEEISM, March 22, 1969 and June 4, 1969. No other disciplinary action recorded. Discharge recommended December 23, 1981.

The employee Joe Miller then filed a grievance claiming that the hospital violated his contractural rights and that the discharge was capricious and arbitrary.

Upon appeal to the second step the hospital administrator, Roy Clasky said he was aware of all the circumstances involved with Mr. Miller and these three other employees but absenteeism is becoming such a problem that it was "time for some belt tightening."

The union president then demanded arbitration on January 5, 1982 and the personnel director stated that he would see to the matter. The arbitration clause states that management must submit a request to the AAA for an arbitration panel within ten days of the unions demand for arbitration. Present at this January 5th meeting were the union president, the grievant, Mr. Klein, Ms. Gribbs, Mr. Clasky and the personnel director. In addition a transcript was made of this meeting. On January 29, 1981, Mr. Klein asked Mr. Clasky if the American Arbitration Association had sent them a panel yet, Mr. Clasky stated "he did not know but would find out." Upon inquiry Mr. Clasky was informed that no request had been submitted to the AAA since the personnel department had not received a written request from the union. Mr. Clasky so informed Mr. Klein and the union president who demanded Mr. Miller's immediate reinstatement since this was a gross violation of the arbitration clause which makes no requirement of a written demand for arbitration and management had exceeded the prescribed time limits. The parties agreed to proceed to arbitration and to place this issue of the time limits before the arbitrator as well.

Arbitrators

The following arbitrators were placed on the panel for the parties to select from. The cited cases are real arbitration awards rendered by real (not these hypothetical) arbitrators in the *Labor Arbitration Reports-Dispute Settlements* published by the Bureau of National Affairs.

Gary N. Jackson
Private Attorney, J.D. Harvard Law School, MBA Indiana University, B.S. Wayne State University. Member: National Academy of Arbitrators; Cases:
67LA1026
69LA427
69LA77

Barbara T. Smith
Professor of Law, J.D. University of Michigan, MA Eastern Michigan University, B.S. Eastern Michigan University. Member: Society of Professionals in Dispute Resolution; Cases:
61LA125
69LA1123
69LA181

Grievance Claim Local 1283 United Hospital Workers of America

Date: December 17, 1981 *Grievance Number:*   M–81–51
Grievant: Joe Miller   *Union Representative:* Frank Klein
Clock Number: A–137

Claim: That Manhattan Municipal Hospital did capriciously and arbitrarily discharge the grievant, Joe Miller, in violation of established past practice and hospital rule 10–2(a).

Hospital rule 10–2(a) states:

Any employee who chronically absents himself or herself from work without written or contractual authorization will be subject to progressive discipline. The following schedule of penalties is to be applied in all circumstances: (1) an employee must be counseled by supervisor to improve attendance; (2) this failing, a verbal warning issued; (3) this failing, a written warning issued; (4) this failing, a disciplinary layoff of from 3 to 5 days; (6) this failing, suspension pending discharge and discharge.

The grievant's attendance record shows clearly that the discipline immediately preceding his discharge was a one day disciplinary layoff for leaving work early. Discharge cannot be imposed without first another 3 day layoff. Secondly, no effective counseling could have occurred without management being aware that Mr. Miller's wife died on September 20, 1981, before which time Mr. Miller's work and attendance records were unblemished.

Finally, in three separate cases of disciplinary action which have occurred in the present calendar year, employees with worse records have been given lesser penalties. These are:

Jane Miscovy: Eleven tardy incidents, 16 absent days without leave, and two incidents of leaving work early. Ms. Miscovy is being treated for alcoholism and has never received more than a written warning.

Sharon Denton: Twenty-seven tardy incidents, 7 absent days without leave, and 1 incident of leaving work early. Maximum penalty thus far— 1 day disciplinary layoff (d.l.o.).

Susan Giamona: Thirty-nine tardy incidents, 17 days absent without leave, and 5 incidents of leaving work early. Ms. Giamona has received three consecutive 3–5 day disciplinary layoffs. On June 3, 1981 she was issued a 3 d.l.o., on August 17, 1981 she received a 4 d.l.o., and on December 14, 1981 she received a 5 d.l.o.

This discipline issued Mr. Miller is grossly unfair and we ask reinstatement with backpay.

Managements's Answer: Grievance denied.

Supervisor: Susan Gribbs

John C. Davisson
Professor of Economics, Ph.D. Indiana University, MA University of Kansas, B.S. Kansas State University; Cases:
67LA1047
63LA49
70LA630

James G. Robinson
Private Attorney, J.D. Cornell University, MILR, Cornell University, B.S. Syracuse University; Cases:
67LA558
68LA651
69LA102

Jesse H. Caldor
Professor of Economics, Ph.D. University of Illinois, MILR University of Illinois, BS Northern Illinois University. Member: National Academy of Arbitrators; Cases:
62LA209
70LA1099
69LA388

Case 4

The Case of the Denied Merit Increase

This is a public sector arbitration case which actually occurred under a state personnel act in the Midwest. This case illustrates the complications involved in determining merit for purposes of promotions or pay increases. Injury, leaves, seniority and the measurement of merit are all problems which may often complicate the administration of a contract or law.

Given the issue and the positions of the parties, the student is to write an opinion and make an award as though she/he were the arbitrator in the case. Anwering the questions at the end of the case may assist the student with the preparation of her/his opinion and award.

Issue

Arbitrator: Did State Hospital capriciously, arbitrarily, or unreasonably deny the appellant, Darlene V, a merit salary increase on or about October 1, 1979? If Respondent's action was capricious, arbitrary, or unreasonable, the remedy requested is back merit pay for the period from October 1, 1979 to January 1, 1980, the date that the Appellant actually received the disputed merit increase, and movement of Appellant's "anniversary date" back from January to October for purposes of merit pay determination.

Stipulated Evidence

1. All procedural requirements specified by law for the arbitration of this matter were met.
2. Joint Exhibit #1: The Employee Complaint Form containing Darlene V's written complaint and the written responses of her supervisors at Step II and Step III of the Employee Complaint Procedure denying the grievance.
3. Joint Exhibit #2: The written response of the State Personnel Director, Mr. Robert C, denying the grievance of Darlene V.
4. Joint Exhibit #3: The written response of the Chairman of the State Employees' Appeals Commission, Mr. George A, denying Darlene V's request for a hearing in the matter of her grievance against State Hospital.
5. Darlene V was not a poor employee.
6. The reason for the denial of the merit increase for one quarter was the number of days during the course of the year that Darlene V was absent.
7. The absences in question were excused absences; Darlene V was receiving Public Law 35 benefits during the year for a job-related injury sustained in July of 1978.
8. Darlene V was absent approximately 177 of the 236 scheduled work days during the course of the year (i.e., the evaluation period). The Appellant actually worked approximately 59 days.
9. Merit increases for the year in question (i.e., Fiscal Year 1980) were fully funded. The money for merit increases was available.

Position of the Parties

The following positions were taken by the Appellant and the Respondent, respectively, in a hearing before the Arbitrator on Friday, March 28, 1980, in Room 401A of the Statehouse, and by post hearing briefs submitted to the Arbitrator on or before May 6, 1980.

Appellant: Darlene V was first employed by State Hospital as an Institutional Worker in Food Service on August 18, 1975. On July 23, 1978, Darlene V sustained a work-related injury qualifying her for Public Law 35 benefits. Although official authorization was delayed until December of 1978, the Appellant's eligibility period for purposes of Public Law 35 coverage was determined to encompass the period from July of 1978 through July of 1979. She was awarded back pay for job injury-related absences that occurred from July of 1978 until her Public Law 35 eligibility was affirmed in December of 1978.

Darlene V, having exhausted her Public Law 35 benefits in July of 1979, was notified by State Hospital sometime in August of 1979 to return to work. She was informed that the alternative to reporting for work was termination.

The Appellant returned to work on a limited performance basis in the laundry on September 10, 1979. The limited performance classification, resulted from the refusal of Dr. L, Mrs. V's physician, to release the Appellant for any type of work except that which could be termed "light duty." The lateral transfer from Food Service to Laundry was facilitated by Mr. Thomas N of the State Personnel Board upon request from State Hospital. Darlene V had been working in the new position approximately 15 days when, in October of 1979, she was denied a merit increase.

The merit increase denial was based upon the belief of Mrs. A, Darlene V's immediate supervisor in the Laundry, that the Appellant's length of service in Laundry (i.e., 15 days) did not warrant a recommendation for a merit increase. Mr. Francis F, Assistant Superintendent of State Hospital and the Appellant's intermediate supervisor in Food Service and the Laundry, concurred with Mrs. A's recommendation and its underlying rationale.

The denial of the merit increase amounted to approximately $90.00 (i.e., $14.00 per two week pay period) in lost wages to the Appellant during the three–month period from October 1, 1979, to January 11, 1980, January of 1980 being the month in which Darlene V eventually received the merit increase. More importantly, perhaps, is the fact that the delay of the merit increase for one quarter also delays all future merit increases for a like period of time. These delays will result in a constantly growing dollar volume of lost income over time, for however long Appellant remains employed by State Hospital.

Denial of Appellant's merit increase is unreasonable in light of statutory law governing compensation for work-related injuries. Public Law 35 requires that all employees injured on the job be fully compensated for a period of one year following the date of injury. Specifically, Section 4-15-2-5 (b) of the State Personnel Act provides that:

> any pay plan adopted shall include a provision that any employee injured in line of duty shall receive full pay for time lost from his employment because of said injury up to (1) year.

Hence, statutory law mandates full compensation of all benefits to employees for work-related injuries. Full compensation certainly includes credit for satisfactory work service toward merit increases which would have otherwise been earned except for the work-related injury and time-off the job.

Based on the evidence herein set forth and applicable law, Appellant submits that the merit increase denial was improper and requests that the grievance be sustained.

Respondent: State Hospital's denial of Darlene V's merit increase in October of 1979 was correct and proper. The Appellant was absent from her job a total of 177 days out of 236 scheduled work days; Darlene V actually worked only 59 days during the merit increase evaluation period. The administrative staff of State Hospital determined that an adequate and fair basis did not exist for evaluating her job performance for the merit increase. Consequently, Darlene V did not receive a merit increase in the quarter that she was first eligible.

The decision to deny the Appellant the merit increase was made only after serious deliberation; it was not made lightly. The question of performance evaluations for employees absent for long periods of time had simply never arisen at State Hospital prior to the Mrs. V case. Consequently, there existed no hospital policy or past practice concerning performance evaluations in cases of this nature. Further, State policy is that merit evaluation, decisions, recommendations, and policies are the responsibility of each Appointing Authority. Finally, State Hospital contacted other mental hospitals to ascertain what policies and practices were in effect at these institutions regarding merit increases in the case of individuals with extended absences.

Given: (1) the Appointing Authority's responsibility and authority to develop policy in the area of merit evaluation; (2) that at least one other hospital (i.e., City Hospital) had established a policy of denying merit increases in extended absence cases due to lack of sufficient information on which to make performance evaluations; and (3) State Hospital's perception/understanding of the purpose of evaluation and merit increases, State Hospital decided not to recommend a merit increase for the Appellant, Darlene V, in October of 1979. Respondent action constituted a proper and fair discharge of managerial authority. Hence, Respondent requests that Appellant's grievance be denied and that denial of the merit increased be affirmed.

QUESTIONS

1. What specifically constitutes merit in this case?

2. What evidence, if any, was there that the grievant was treated in an arbitrary or capricious manner?

3. How is merit measured? Does this have a bearing upon the merits of the case?

4. Which party bears the initial burden of proof in this case?

Case 5

The Grievance Procedure— The Case of Time Limits

In this case, the student is to report on the specific actions that he/she would take as supervisor.

An employee filed a grievance alleging that management failed to offer him overtime on Saturday in line with his seniority. Such a grievance is required by the contract to be filed within three working days of the incident. The employee met this requirement by filing on the following Monday.

The foreman in this case had been on vacation during the previous week and had no knowledge of the alleged incident and asked for a one-hour recess of the grievance meeting, which the union granted, to check with his immediate supervisor. Upon consulting with his supervisor the foreman was told that the company had received numerous grievances concerning such issues and that he should fully investigate the allegations. If the union's argument had merit he was instructed to grant the grievance but otherwise he should deny the grievance. His supervisor gave him the name of the foreman who was his replacement during the previous week.

The contract requires management to answer grievances within three working days of the date of the first step grievance meeting. The foreman asked the union if a one day recess would be agreeable so as to allow sufficient time to investigate the allegation; this the union granted and a second grievance meeting was scheduled for Tuesday. The foreman then attempted to contact the replacement foreman and was unable to do so before the second grievance meeting on Tuesday. The second meeting was canceled and rescheduled for Wednesday.

The foreman was unable to contact his replacement and was unable to locate any witness or document concerning the alleged incident. The second meeting was again canceled and rescheduled for Thursday (the final day in three day time limit). What might the foreman in this case do?

QUESTIONS

1. Should our foreman simply deny the grievance pushing it into the second step? What benefits or costs are associated with this action?

2. Should our foreman grant the union's grievance and pay the grievant 8 hours at time and one half his normal rate or bargain for a lesser wage bill? What benefits or costs are associated with this action?

3. Should our foreman ask for an extension of the time limit for answering the grievance? Are there dangers associated with this alternative? What benefits or costs are associated with this action?

4. What other alternatives are open to our foreman?

Case 6
The Case of the Christmas Hams

This case is concerned with the role of past practice and compensation issues under a labor agreement. The issue of arbitrability is also placed before the arbitrator, a complication following directly from the nature of the past practice. This case is a composite of two actual cases involving different employers and unions.

Given the issue and the positions of the parties, the student is to write an opinion and make an award as though she/he was the arbitrator in the case. Answering the questions at the end of the case may assist the student in the preparation of her/his opinion and award.

Issue

Arbitrator: The arbitrator is asked to determine whether the employer violated an implicit provision of the contract by unilaterally ceasing to provide hams to each of his employees as a Christmas gift or bonus. The employer further contends that the issue is not arbitrable and asks the present arbitrator to find the issue not properly before him—hence nonarbitrable.

Stipulated Evidence

1. For the past twenty-two years Mr. X, owner of ABC Press Company, gave each worker in his employ a 15 to 18 pound ham at the end of the shift the day before the Christmas vacation.
2. On December 23, 1978, Mr. X announced that this practice would be discontinued because of the expense involved.
3. The grievance has been properly and timely filed with the exception that management contends that the issue is not covered by the contract.

Position of the Parties

Union: The union contends that the stipulated evidence proves the bulk of their case. Management has established a past practice of twenty-two years of providing, as a portion of employees' compensation, a Christmas bonus of a ham of considerable value. Management has admitted that it unilaterally discontinued the practice and claims expense was the basis of this action.

Whether the ham constitutes a gift or a bonus is of no consequence according to the union. As seven witnesses, who have been employed by ABC Press, for the entire 22 year period testified, they had come to rely on the employer providing the Christmas ham and they had no reason to believe that the practice would be discontinued until the end of the shift on December 23, 1978.

The union asks the arbitrator to find that the employer had established a past practice having the weight of contract which the employer violated by failing to provide the Christmas bonus hams on December 23, 1978. The union asks the arbitrator for the appropriate remedy of a 15 to 18 pound ham provided at employer expense and the awarding of a continuation of the practice.

Company: The company contends that this practice of giving employees a Christmas ham began as a gesture of personal kindness at Christmas by Mr. X. For the first ten years of the practice Mr. X slaughtered hogs and cured the hams himself and gave them to his employees as a personal gift. The practice was converted from a personal to a company–paid–for gift on the eleventh year. During the first year of the practice ABC Press had only ten employees testified Mr. X. Largely due to the efforts of those original ten employees and the growth of demand, employment increased to thirty five by the eleventh year. Total employment as of December 23, 1978 was 80. This growth in employment and the increased price of the hams has made this practice prohibitively expensive. The company offered employment records to support the above testimony of Mr. X.

The company also entered into evidence the labor agreement between the union and ABC Press which expires June 15, 1980. The company asked the arbitrator to note that no mention of Christmas hams is made in the agreement. The company asked the arbitrator to take notice of Article II Section 1 which states:

Article II Section 1—Management Rights
Management reserves the right to exercise any prerogative not limited by express provisions of this agreement or by applicable law concerning any issue having to do with, but not limited to the costs incurred by the firm, methods of production, products of company, marketing, hiring of new employees, and any actions normally associated with the efficient, safe and profitable operation of the business.

Further, the arbitrator is asked to take notice of Article XXI Section 6 which states:

Article XXI Section 6—Jurisdiction of the Arbitrator
The arbitrator shall have no power or authority to add to, subtract from, or modify in any form any provision of this agreement. The arbitrator shall have full power and authority to make a final and binding award concerning any dispute arising out of the interpretation or application of any provision of this agreement.

The company contends that since the practice of giving Christmas hams is not included in the express language of the contract and in light of Article II Section 1, this issue is not covered by the contract. Further Article XXI Section 6 clearly places this present issue outside of the arbitrator's jurisdiction. Therefore, the company asks the arbitrator to find the present controversy to be nonarbitrable.

If the arbitrator finds the issue to be arbitrable, the company asks the arbitrator to find that the merits of the case show that no past practice had been established. Since the hams were originally given as personal gifts by Mr. X and employment levels have consistently increased over the twenty-two year period, circumstances have sufficiently changed to warrent the discontinuence of this giving of hams at Christmas.

QUESTIONS

1. Does the arbitration clause limit the arbitrator's jurisdiction in this case?
2. Has a past practice been established which has become a portion of the contract?

3. Had the employer informed the union of his intent to discontinue giving employees Christmas hams prior to December 23, 1978, would this have had a bearing on the case?

4. What role does the management rights clause play in this case?

Case 7

The Case of R—Builders and the Carpenters

This is an actual labor arbitration case involving a real company and a real union. An arbitrator is bound, as are the parties, by the language of the contract. But what happens if the labor dispute involves two contracts and the arbitrator is asked to determine which contract governs? This case illustrates the parol rules of evidence and the role of the labor contract in arbitration.

Given the issue and the positions of the parties, the student is to write an opinion and make an award as though she/he were the arbitrator in the case. Answering the questions at the end of the case may assist the student with the preparation of her/his opinion and award.

Issue

Arbitrator: The issue before this arbitrator is the interpretation of Article IX Section 2 of the residential agreement (Joint exhibit #1)[1] to which R—Builder (a party to the dispute) has acceded. Specifically, the arbitrator is asked to determine whether the construction of the H—Elderly Housing project is residential or qualifies under the exclusionary language of Article IX Section 2 of the residential agreement and is therefore a commercial building and governed by the commercial contract (Joint exhibit #2).[2]

The union grieves for backpay in the amount of the hourly wage differential between the rates established for residential and commercial construction (approximately $1.17 per hour) for work completed and to sustain the union's rights to include the higher hourly wage rate under the commercial contract for work yet to be completed.

[1] Working Agreement: District Council of the United Brotherhood of Carpenters and Joiners of America and R—Builders, Inc. herein called the residential agreement.

[2] Working Agreement: District Council of the United Brotherhood of Carpenters and Joiners of America and the Area Builders Association, Inc. et al (to which R—Builders has acceded) herein called the commercial contract.

Position of the Union

The union bases its claim to rights under the commercial agreement on its interpretation of Article IX Section 2 of the residential agreement. The second sentence of Article IX Section 2 states: "For the purpose of the AGREEMENT residential construction does not include those housing units referred to as 'High Rise', which are in excess of three stories in height and require installation of elevators for use of occupants."

The union contends that the H—Elderly Housing project is in excess of three stories and requires the installation of elevators for use of occupants. In addition, the union alleges that the materials applied on the H—Elderly Housing project are of a commercial variety which lends support to Article IX Section 2 exclusion under the final sentence of that section which states: "This AGREEMENT does not include commercial or retail sales buildings or other structures not permitted on residential zoned ground, but does include allied buildings associated with apartments and housing projects and additions and alterations thereto."

In support of both contentions, the union offers evidence of past practices on the subject and a similar construction project paying the higher commercial wage rate.

Contractual Language—Height and Elevator Requirements for Exclusion

The union established through the testimony of Mr. F and the presentation of the plans for the H—Elderly Housing project that the building consists of three wings of three floors each, contains two centrally located elevators in addition to four stairwells, and has an air space attic under a sloped roof. Mr. F testified that with the addition of gables and windows the air space attic could be converted into useable space. The elevators are located in the junction of the three wings of the building. One elevator is a stretcher elevator, but the other is a general passenger elevator. Elderly or handicapped persons would have their access to the second and third floors of the building severely impaired without the availability of elevators; therefore, the purpose and height of the building require the installation of elevators.

The union, therefore, contends that this building conforms to the standards established by Article IX Section 2 Sentence 2 for exclusion from the residential contract and inclusion under the commercial agreement.

Materials

Mr. F testified that two materials were used in the subject building which are normally used in commercial construction. These two commercial construction materials were flexicore, a precast concrete flooring material, and steel joists. Mr. F stated that these materials are almost never used in single family dwellings, occasionally used in multi-family residences, commonly used in hotels and "High Rise" apartments, and normally applied in commercial construction.

Past Practices

The union established through the testimony of Mr. F that the general contractor paid carpenters the higher commercial hourly wage rate in an elderly housing project built approximately six years ago. In addition, two other carpentry subcontractors having work on the subject building are paying their carpenters the higher commercial rate for the installation of metal studs and partitions in the H—Elderly Housing project. I—Concrete Company, in the same housing project, paid carpenters the commercial wage rate to build cement forms. M—Engineering subcontracted approximately one-half of the total carpentry work on the subject building.

Mr. F indicated that between eight and ten carpenters employed by M—Engineering and I—Concrete were from other Union Districts. Both of these subcontractors, even at the higher commercial wage, found it difficult to obtain the carpenters they required. This shortage of carpenters, in part, may explain the willingness of the other two subcontractors to establish the past practice of paying the higher commercial wage. Mr. F, however, was of the opinion that the basis for M—Engineering and I—Concrete acceding to the commercial agreement was that the building constituted a commercial structure.

The union contends that the language of Article IX Section 2, of the residential agreement, the materials employed, and the established past practices clearly proves this building project falls under the commercial contract and not the residential agreement.

Position of the Company

Height and Elevator Requirements

The company denied the grievance on the basis that the residential contract is clear and unequivocal in its meaning. The exclusionary language of Article IX Section 2 Sentence 2 requires that building must be in excess of three stories (meaning four or more stories) and requires that elevators be installed for the use of occupants before the building may be termed "High Rise" and, therefore, excluded under the residential agreement. The H—Elderly Housing project is exactly three stories in height. A roof is implied in any building and whether sloped or flat does not constitute an appendage making the structure in excess of three stories. The H—Elderly Housing project, therefore, does not meet the height requirement for exclusion as a "High Rise" housing unit for purposes of Article IX Section 2 of the residential contract.

Elevators are required in the subject housing project, however, not because the structure is in excess of three stories but because the Federal Housing Administration requires elevators be installed in elderly housing projects of two or more stories.

Past Practices

The instances of the general contractor and the subcontractors, M—Engineering and I—Concrete, paying the higher commercial wage rate do not establish a past practice binding upon R—Builders. Only two elderly housing projects have been built within the jurisdiction of the District Council of Carpenters in recent years. There is simply not enough experience with these elderly housing projects under Article IX Section 2 of the residential agreement to establish a past practice. R—Builders was not a party to any of the three agreements to interpret Article IX Section 2 so as to exclude elderly housing projects such as the H—Elderly Housing project from the residential contract and include these buidings under the commercial agreement.

Materials

The materials used in the construction of this building are not sufficient grounds to classify the building either residential or commercial. Materials are frequently specified by building codes and these codes often overlap in materials required.

The materials used in the construction of the H—Elderly project, specifically flexicore and steel joists, are not exclusively used in commercial construction. Both materials are commonly applied to many types of structures which are clearly residential for purposes of Article IX Section 2 of the residential contract. Therefore, the use of these materials are not germane to the present issue.

QUESTIONS

1. What roles did the parol rules of evidence and past practice play in your decision?

2. What contract provision(s) governed this case?

3. If there was a surplus rather than a shortage of carpenters how might this have changed your award?

4. Who bears the burden of proof in this case? What evidence controlled your award?

Case 8

The Case of Holiday Pay

This case involves the issue of holiday pay as either a fringe benefit or as a protection of an employee's wages. This case is a composite of two cases involving the same company and union.

Given the issue and the positions of the parties, the student is to write an opinion and make an award as though she/he were the arbitrator in the case. Answering the questions at the end of the case may assist the student with the preparation of his/her opinion and award.

Issue

Arbitrator: The issue before this arbitrator is whether or not the grievant, Ms. J, is entitled to holiday pay for the period December 25, 1980 through January 1, 1981.

Stipulated Evidence

1. Ms. J was granted a leave of absence without pay for the period December 14, 1980 through December 24, 1980 for personal reasons.
2. The grievance of Ms. J was properly and timely filed.
3. Ms. J is a seniority employee with over five years of service to the company.

Positions of the Parties

Union

Ms. J has been improperly denied one week of vacation pay for the period December 25, 1980 through January 1, 1981. Article IX Section 3 of the current labor agreement states:

Article IX Section 3 Qualifications for Holiday Pay
Holiday pay shall be paid to a seniority employee if and only if the employee qualifies under one of the following three requirements:

A. The employee works their full scheduled shift before the day or days for which holiday pay may be paid and their full scheduled shift after the day or days for which holiday pay may be paid.
B. The employee is excused from work on their scheduled shift before and after the holiday pay period. Such excused absence must be requested and granted at least one working day prior to the absence.
C. If the employee is not offered work for the qualifying day prior to and after the holiday pay period because of machinery breakdown, flood, fire, material shortage or other "Acts of God" then the employee will be deemed to have qualified for the applicable holiday pay.

The union contends that Ms. J was excused from work on the 24th of December because of her leave of absence and hence qualifies under Article IX Section 3 (B) of the contract for the work day prior to the Christmas holiday pay period. Ms. J worked her scheduled shift on January 2, 1981, hence, qualifying under Article IX Section 3 (A) of the contract for the work day after the Christmas holiday pay period.

The union further presented three witnesses and supporting documents showing that the company had accepted an excused absence prior to a holiday and regular worked shift after the holiday as sufficient qualification for holiday pay.

The union asks that the grievant be awarded holiday pay for the period December 25, 1980 through January 1, 1981.

Company

The company asks the arbitrator to take notice of the language of Article IX Section 3. The contract specifically states that the employee must qualify under one of sections (A), (B), or (C). The contract says nothing of using two in combination as sufficient holiday pay qualification.

The company called Mr. H who testified that in three separate cases during the past year, since he became personnel manager, he disapproved holiday pay for employees who had an excused absence for one qualifying day and worked the other. Mr. H testified that Article IX Section 3 did not make provision for the use of two of the qualifying standards in combination but rather specified that the employee must qualify under one of the standards. Documents indicated that two employees were denied holiday pay for Thanksgiving and one for Labor Day because of the use of two of the standards in combination rather than one as Article IX Section 3 required. Mr. H further testified that he was aware of the past practices cited by the union but these were before he became personnel manager and he had no intention of continuing a practice which was obviously in violation of the contract.

The company asks the arbitrator to deny Ms. J's grievance on the basis of Article IX Section 3 of the current labor agreement.

QUESTIONS

1. Does the hiring of a new personnel manager have a bearing on this case?

2. What is the intent of Article IX Section 3 of the contract? What evidence of intent is there?

3. Is the subject holiday pay a fringe benefit or protection of earnings potential?

4. Is there an established past practice?

Case 9
The Case of Overtime

This case involves a common problem with the distribution of overtime. The issue is somewhat complicated by the lack of conclusive evidence concerning some aspects of the case.

Given the issue and the positions of the parties, the student is to write an opinion and make an award as though she/he were the arbitrator in the case. Answering the questions at the end of the case may assist the student with the preparation of the opinion and award.

Issue

Arbitrator: The issue before this arbitrator is whether Article XIV Section 2 of the labor agreement between Local 1000 of the Retail Clerks Union and XYZ Grocery Store was violated by management failing to offer the grievant Mrs. A overtime on February 28 and March 1, 1981. If the overtime rights of Mrs. A were violated, the arbitrator is asked to formulate and award an appropriate remedy.

Position of the Parties

Union

The union contends that Mrs. A, a checkout clerk at XYZ Grocery Store #4, was improperly passed over for available overtime on February 28 and March 1, 1981. The applicable contract provision states:

Article XIV Section 2—Overtime
All overtime shall be distributed, when possible, within the occupational group on the shift where the need for overtime has occurred. Seniority shall be the basis for distributing any available overtime. The most senior employee shall be offered the overtime until all employees within the occupation on the shift in question have been offered the overtime. In the event that all employees in the occupation and on the shift in question have been offered overtime and additional workers are required management may require the, in reverse order of seniority, employees in the occupation and on the shift to work the overtime. However, management may not require more than 32 hours of overtime of any employee in any calendar month.

Mrs. A testified that at the end of her regular shift on Friday, February 27, 1981 she was unaware that any overtime was available on Saturday or Sunday of that weekend. She further testified that normally the assistant manager would offer overtime for the weekend by noon on Friday. This testimony was supported by the introduction of a letter of understanding dated March 22, 1977 between Local 1000 of the Retail Clerks and XYZ Grocery Store.

The official seniority list of the first shift checkout clerks at XYZ Grocery Store #4 was entered into evidence indicating that Mrs. A was the second most senior employee on that shift in the checkout clerk occupation. The list indicates that there were fifteen employees in the seniority unit junior to Mrs. A.

Mrs. A further testified that she was able and willing to work any overtime that may have been offered her during the period in question. Mrs. A also testified that she did not leave her home from 5:30 Friday until church at 9:30 Sunday and that her telephone did not ring during the entire period.

The union introduced time cards for two junior employees in Mrs. A's seniority unit indicating that they each worked 8 hours Saturday and Sunday. The union asks the arbitrator to award Mrs. A 16 hours pay at time and one-half her regular hourly wage rate.

Company

The company denies having passed over Mrs. A in offering overtime for the days in question. Mr. S the manager of XYZ Grocery Store #4 testified that at 11:30 a.m. on Friday he went to Mrs. A's checkout lane to offer her the overtime work in question but found that she was on break. He instructed Miss L on the checkout lane next to Mrs. A to have Mrs. A call him when she returned from break. By 3:30 p.m. she had not returned the call and so Mr. S instructed an assistant manager Mrs. T to go ask Mrs. A if she would work the available overtime. At this time one of the two available overtime positions had been filled. At 4:30, one hour before the end of the shift Mrs. T testified that she asked Mrs. A if she wanted to work this weekend and Mrs. A did not respond. At that instant, Mrs. T testified that she was paged over the intercom and did not ask Mrs. A a second time.

Mr. S testified that he attempted to call Mrs. A twice Friday evening and no one answered the telephone. Mr. S then called a junior employee and offered him the overtime and he accepted it.

The company asks the arbitrator to deny the grievance of Mrs. A.

QUESTIONS

1. Was the procedure used to offer the overtime proper and consistent with the contract?

2. Who bears the burden of proof in this case?

3. Was there sufficient evidence to classify this overtime as an emergency?

4. Where is the initial complication in the overtime distribution procedure in this case? Why did it occur?

5. Could additional evidence been obtained which was not presented?

Case 10

The Case of Tom T

This is an actual case that involved a real union, grievant and company. The administration of the grievance and disciplinary procedures presents many problems for both management and the union.

This case illustrates the problems facing management concerning the investigation of a case and the control of a production process.

The student is to review the case, make suggestions where management could improve its disciplinary procedure, and then write an opinion and award as though he/she were the arbitrator in this case. Answering the questions at the end of the case may assist the student in completing this assignment.

Issue

Arbitrator: The issue before this arbitrator is whether management properly and fairly discharged the grievant, Tom T., for sabotage on or about October 3, 1980. The following facts have been stipulated by the parties:

1. Tom T, a utility employee of X Automobile Parts Manufacturers, was assigned to an assembly line position which required him to put distributor caps on distributors during the entire week of August 11, 1980.
2. Tom T, on August 12, 1980, did bring into the plant one bushel of ripe tomatoes.
3. One hundred eighty (180) distributors which had been sabotaged were returned to the firm by Customer D.
4. The nature of the sabotage, complained of by Customer D, was the placement of a tomato under the distributor cap of 180 of its distributors, causing the complete destruction of the internal components of the product.

Position of the Company

Mr. A testified that the company was unaware of the sabotage until reported by Customer D. Therefore, the discipline was timely and procedurally correct. Mr. A further testified that, because of the approximate seven week delay in detecting the sabotage, production records and the foreman's memory were relied on to determine who was assigned to what job during the period in question. The company introduced grievance forms into the hearing record, without union objection, which clearly show that the union and Mr. T admit that he was assigned to the distributor capping job.

The company established through the testimony of Mr. K that, before shipment to Customer D, distributors were handled by only two other employees. Mr. K was to pack the distributors for shipment and Mr. C was to test the distributors to assure that they functioned properly. Mr. C was unable to testify at the hearing due to the fact that he had died of a serious liver ailment shortly after the alleged incident. Mr. K testified that Mr. C could not possibly have properly tested all of the distributors in question because he was drunk the day in question. Management introduced into the hearing record a disciplinary notice for Mr. C dated August 12, 1980 which cited drinking on company property and reporting to work drunk as grounds for the discipline.

In light of the previous argument and testimony the company asks the arbitrator to sustain the discharge.

Position of the Union

Mr. T testified that he brought the fruit in question into the plant and that a large number of employees on the assembly line to which he was assigned ate tomatoes until lunch hour. When he returned from lunch the remainder of the tomatoes (approximately 200) were gone. Mr. T testified that about two hours later Mr. C was disciplined for drinking on the job.

The union introduced into the hearing record Mr. T's work record. The union contends that since Mr. T received only one other disciplinary action, a warning for horseplay over three years ago (throwing tomatoes in the plant), his over twenty years of good and faithful service to the company should serve to mitigate the penalty in this case, should he be found guilty of the allegations.

Finally the union contends that the company failed to prove its case. Mr. T denied placing tomatoes under the distributor caps of the subject distributors. No evidence was produced showing that he indeed committed this alleged offense. The company has produced only hearsay and circumstantial evidence which is insufficient grounds to sustain a discharge in this case.

QUESTIONS

1. What is the proof required to show Mr. T's guilt in this case?

2. Did the company show an adequate investigation of the facts?

3. Does the company need to show a shop rule prohibiting sabotage to justify discharge in this case?

4. Is there a reason upon which to base a doubt as to the guilt of Mr. T? If so, what is that reason?

5. Is there sufficient grounds to mitigate the penalty in this case if Mr. T is found guilty of the allegations?

6. If Mr. C had been available to testify, what evidence might the company have hoped to obtain?

Case 11

The Snake in the Truck Case

Often in the arbitration of disciplinary matters, such issues as the credibility of witnesses and the amount of available evidence pose significant problems. The following case has been constructed from three actual arbitration cases and formulated so as to point out the problems of evidence and credibility. The student is to carefully read the case, answer the questions at the end of the case, and then prepare a written award as though he/she were the arbitrator in this dispute.

Issue

Was Steven M properly discharged for just cause arising out of an incident on August 18, 1981 in which company property (namely, a half-ton pick-up truck) was destroyed? If cause for discipline is determined, is discharge an appropriate penalty?

Stipulated Facts

1. Steven M has been an employee of the ABC Oil Company for sixteen years during which time he has never been disciplined for any reason.
2. Steven M was promoted to the position of oil well inspector effective January 1, 1979.
3. On August 18, 1981 Steven M was involved in a one vehicle accident which totally demolished a half-ton pick-up truck owned by the company and valued at $8,750.
4. The police report shows that the accident occurred on company property at approximately 1:50 p.m. in an area with a 10 mile per hour posted speed limit. Further, there were no skid marks but the investigating officer estimated the speed of the truck at approximately 40 m.p.h. when it left the road, flipped on to its top, and skidded 90 feet to a stop.
5. The procedure utilized by the company in the administration of the discipline was consistent with the contract and Steven M was afforded union representation.
6. Steven M did promptly and properly report the accident.

Position of the Company

The position of the company in this case is that Steven M was properly and fairly discharged for violation of working rule C-17 which states in pertinent part:

> C-17 Violation of any posted traffic regulation on company property which results in damage to or the destruction of company property or the property of any contractor or customer of the company or any employee or in personal injury to any person will result in immediate summary discharge.

The company argues that the stipulated facts in this case establish just cause for discipline and fixes the penalty at discharge. The company also maintains the position that it wishes to be fair and reasonable in its disciplinary policy. To this end, the company has established a policy consistent with working rule F-2 of granting leniency in cases where extraordinary or mitigating circumstances can be shown. In support, working rule F-2 states in pertinent part:

> F-2 The company and its management reserves the right to assign a lesser penalty than prescribed herein or no penalty if such action jeopardizes the efficient

operation of the business, or if circumstances clearly beyond the immediate control of the employee serve to mitigate the offense.

Upon investigation of the accident of August 18, 1981, management was informed by Steven M that the cause of the wreck was that a rattlesnake was present in the cab of the truck and was not discovered by the grievant until after he had proceeded some distance down the gravel road toward well site 20. In his attempt to evict the snake, Steven M claimed that he felt he was losing control of the truck and in his attempt to stop the truck, missed the brake and hit the accelerator resulting in the mishap.

The testimony of the investigating officer indicated that no evidence of the aforementioned snake could be found within a fifty yard radius of the wreck. The officer further testified that he arrived on the scene approximately one hour after the wreck had occurred. The company asked the arbitrator to sustain the discipline and the penalty in this case.

Position of the Union

The union claims that working rule F-2 requires the company to grant leniency in this case. The presence of the dangerous snake in the cab of the truck was clearly beyond the immediate control of Steven M and was the actual cause of the accident which resulted in destruction of company property.

The testimony of Steven M, two of his fellow workers, and his former high school baseball coach was entered into the record which clearly showed that Steven M had an inordinate fear of snakes. Steven M was so fearful of snakes that his fellow workers had made a habit of referring to Steven M's fear in a joking manner. Steven M's former high school baseball coach related an incident which occurred during Steven's senior year in high school. During baseball practice Mr M was playing the position of center field when a fly ball was hit in his direction. On moving into position to catch the ball, Steven sighted a garter snake and froze in his tracks. The ball struck Steven in the face breaking his nose.

The testimony of Steven M was placed in the record. Mr M testified that he had driven about ten miles along the gravel road on which the accident occurred when he noticed movement on the floor in front of the passenger seat. He looked down and saw the rattlesnake crawl out from under the seat. He reached for the tool box on the seat beside him and in so doing knocked it off the seat next to the snake. The snake immediately coiled and began shaking its rattles. Upon witnessing this, Steven said that he attempted to apply the brakes which resulted in his pushing on the accelerator instead. The truck hit some loose gravel, bolted from the road, and turned over. Mr M testified that both he and the snake were thrown onto the ceiling of the cab and the next thing he remembers is running down the gravel road as fast as he could.

Finally, the testimony of Steven's supervisor was placed in the record. The supervisor, Mr. T, testified that Steven was an honest, hard-working employee and that if these were the events claimed by Steven to have occurred then Mr. T was certain that these events did occur. Further, well site 20 was on the

Colorado-Kansas border, an area known to have a considerable rattlesnake population. Mr. T testified that it is not uncommon for snakes of this variety to crawl under or into farm machinery or even cars and trucks. Mr. T, however, states that "a rule is a rule" and disciplinary action was warranted in this case.

QUESTIONS

1. Do the two working rules in this case apply to this incident? Do either of the rules lend insight as to the proper award?

2. Were the circumstances leading to Steven's accident totally within his control? If not, which were not?

3. Is Steven M's testimony credible? If not, why? Does this case rest on the credibility of Steven M's testimony? Explain.

4. Is there any tangible evidence beyond the stipulated facts? If so, what? If not, why?

5. Was the company's action proper? Explain.

6. If you find that working rule F-2 applies and Steven M was given too severe a penalty or that no penalty should be applied, what action might you, as the arbitrator, order to correct the disciplinary action?

Case 12

The Case of the Fist Fight

Often management is placed in the difficult position of determining who did what and what an appropriate penalty is under a given set of circumstances. The union is frequently left in as thorny a position as management in these types of cases. This case is typical of this type of situation even though it is a hypothetical case.

This case is divided into two parts. In the first part of the case, the student is to play the role of management and determine which employee or if both employees should be subject to discipline. If discipline is determined to be warranted by the facts in the case then the student is to assign an appropriate penalty. In the second part, students are to exchange their disciplinary reports and play the role of arbitrator.

Part I—Instructions

Given the following facts in this case, the student, taking the role of management, is to determine if there has been a disciplinary offense committed and if so, what offense and what the appropriate penalty should be. The student should then, in writing, state clearly and simply the nature of the offense of any guilty employee and the penalty assessed. The instructor will inform you when this assignment is to be turned in; (s)he will then distribute your disciplinary reports for the arbitrator's review.

Facts

On Monday, October 12, John Watson reported for work at 8:00 a.m. He was waiting at his foreman's desk for a job assignment when James Parker, another employee in the maintenance department, walked over to Mr. Watson. As Mr. Watson turned and faced Mr. Parker, he said something to Parker who then punched Watson in the face. Watson then backed away from Parker who pursued Watson throwing four or five more punches before Watson defended himself. Watson then threw two punches both landing on Parker's chin who was knocked unconscious. Both men were taken to the plant's first aid room where the union steward was asked to meet with you (management) and these two employees. Two witnesses, both union members, were asked for statements describing the incident. Both described the circumstances but neither said they could hear what Watson had said.

With the steward and another maintenance supervisor present, the employees described the events which lead up to the fist fight. Both men had worked overtime on Saturday and Sunday repairing an automatic lathe in a production department. Mr. Watson who was a union member was upset with Parker who, under the open shop security arrangement, was not a union member. Mr. Parker had worked during a three week strike which ended less than a month prior to this incident. Both men concurred that they had not had difficulty in working together until after lunch on Sunday. Parker apparently called Watson a fool for losing three weeks work because of the strike and Watson then called Parker a "Scab." Parker apparently took greater offense to Watson's statement than Watson had realized. As Parker walked up to Watson Monday morning Watson turned and said "good morning scab." Both men agreed to this description of the morning's events.

The production supervisor where Saturday's and Sunday's overtime had been worked stated he had overheard the Parker-Watson conversation and confirmed their description of the circumstances. The supervisor stated that, especially after a strike, there's a lot of name calling going on and he had always ignored these situations when possible.

Neither employee has a previous disciplinary record. Watson has been employed by the company for twelve years, the last five as machine repairman in the maintenance department. Parker has been employed by the company for five years, the last ten months as an assistant machine repairman in the maintenance department.

Applicable Shop Rules and Contract Language

Article XXV—Disciplinary Offenses
(a) Management is responsible for the safe and orderly operation of the firm. Management shall have the sole and exclusive right to promulgate reasonable shop

rules establishing just cause for disciplinary action. All penalties for violation of these properly promulgated shop rules will be determined in collective bargaining with the union and incorporated into the published statement of the shop rules.

(b) All shop rules and associated penalties will be published at the company's expense and issued to each employee and union official.

Shop Rule 40

Fighting on company property is a serious industrial offense which will result in an appropriate penalty up to and including discharge.

Shop Rule 41

Precipitating a fight on company property may be regarded as actually participating in a fight and will result in an appropriate penalty up to and including discharge.

Shop Rule 66

The use of vulgarity directed at a fellow employee will result in an appropriate penalty. For the first offense, a written reprimand may be issued; the second offense, a disciplinary lay off up to 5 days; the third offense may result in a penalty up to and including discharge.

Part II—Instructions

When your instructor distributes the disciplinary reports, you are to review the reports and write an opinion and award as though you were the arbitrator in this case. The union's position in this case is simply that both men have long spotless work records and the penalties should be mitigated.

In the case of Watson, if he is disciplined, the union will argue that he simply defended himself, which he has a right to do, from a brutal unprovoked attack by Parker. The use of the term *scab*, the union alleges, is a common term for nonunion labor and is not provocation for such an attack as Parker launched against Watson.

Additionally, the union claims and presented several witnesses who testified that members of management have used the term scab and that several instances of union members calling nonunion employees scabs did not result in attacks nor discipline.

Case 13

Fact Finding and Money Problems in Public Schools

Often, in fact finding procedures in the public sector, the neutral is faced with having two independent sources (union and management) of revenue data which are inconsistent with one another. The problem arises in that both sides claim that their data is accurate while the other side's data is inaccurate. Add to this complicating situation that, in general, there is no readily available unbiased source from which all revenue data can be obtained.

In this case, the student is to assume the role of the neutral fact finder in a public school interest arbitration. All issues have been resolved between the parties except for the economic package. The student is to prepare a fact finding report in this case. This is a real fact-finding case decided by one of the authors. The names have been changed and the issues somewhat disguised to protect both guilty parties.

Unified School District Number 31 and the Local Public Teachers Association (LPTA) have settled all noneconomic issues in their collective bargaining agreement but are unable to reach a settlement on the salary schedule and the economic supplements package.

This bargaining relation is governed by a state law that places three requirements on the parties and the fact finder in arriving at an economic settlement; these are:

1. No settlement may require nor fact-finding report recommend a settlement which would require any school district to engage in deficit financing nor the curtailment of necessary academic programs.
2. The fact-finder must consider the following standards when issuing a report concerning economic issues:
   a. the ability of the employer to pay;
   b. the history of settlements in the subject and similar school districts;
   c. the standard of living in the subject and similar school districts; and
   d. the ability of the school district to attract and retain competent faculty.
3. Any fact-finding recommendation should be formulated to provide a guide to the voluntary collective bargaining settlement of impassed issues; the fact-finder should weigh but is not bound by the final offers of the parties, and his or her report is advisory in nature and is neither final nor binding upon the parties.

The Position of the Association

The LPTA asks the fact finder to recommend that an eleven percent increase be granted across the salary schedule as well as that the school district pay the total increase in premiums for health insurance, life insurance, salary continuance, and pension programs. Since the salary schedule is tied to last degree earned and the years of experience, the total cost of the proposed increase, including increments due to increased experience, amounts to a total increase in cost of twelve percent. The total cost per employee of the fringe package amounts to $101.20. There are 150 teaching faculty employed by USD 31 whose average salary is $14,340. The computation of the total cost of the LPTA proposal, $273,000, is presented in Exhibit I.

This, however, overstates the total cost of the LPTA proposal since two

Exhibit I.   Computation of Total Cost of LPTA Economic Proposal

Average present year salary	$ 14,340.00	
Twelve percent increase	× .12	
	1720.8	
Multiplied by 150 faculty members	× 150	
Total salary increase	$258,120.00	
Per faculty increase in fringes	101.20	
Multiplied by 150 faculty members	× 150	
Total fringe increase	$ 15,180.00	
	Salary adjustment	$258,120.00
	Fringe adjustment	15,180.00
	Total Cost	$273,300.00

senior faculty members are retiring before the beginning of the next academic year. The total cost of these faculty members' salaries (with the proposed increase) would have been $43,600.00. One of the faculty members is a high school history teacher, the other a junior high school social studies teacher. These fields are relatively easy to recruit in and both, if replaced with candidates with bachelor's degrees and five years experience, would cost the district $24,100.00. In addition, two faculty members will have completed master's degrees over the summer which will increase their salaries by an average of $260 each. The total savings to the school district from these personnel changes will be $18,980.00. Deducting this sum from the $273,300.00 original cost increase estimate leaves the adjusted total increase in cost of $254,320.

The school district will experience the following increases in revenues according to the state offices of the NEA.

Exhibit II.   USD 31 Revenue Increases (LPTA Estimates)

County Property Tax	$241,153
State Excise Tax	60,340
License Plate Revenues	3,480
County Income Tax	68,050
State Aid	15,870
Federal Aid	− 39,740
	$349,153

Applying the annual inflation rate of 10% to the school district's other accounts and other increased expenditures yields the following increased demands on the district's budgets.

**Exhibit III.   Increased Operating Expenses USD 31.
(LPTA Estimates)**

Utilities, Telephone Service	$ 4,780
Salaries, Fringes-Nonbargaining Personnel	28,400
Classroom Materials	3,280
Building Insurance	260
New Shop Equipment	4,850
Replacement of Front Sidewalks	8,800
Improvement of Library	5,900
New Copying Equipment	14,800
TOTAL	$71,070

Deducting this total increase in the cost of all other programs from the increase in total revenues ($349,153–$71,070) yields $278,083 available for salaries and fringe benefit improvements for bargaining unit personnel. This exceeds the amount necessary to fund the LPTA's proposal by some $23,763.

Further, the salary increases for this school district have averaged roughly 1% below the state average and 3/4% below comparable school districts for the past five years. This fact places the salaries of the teachers in this district below the compensation levels of comparable districts by over 4%. The comparable districts which have settled at this point in the bargaining season have settled for approximately 10.5%. The 12% total increase proposed by the LPTA is therefore believed by the association to be squarely within the comparable range with similar school districts. The LPTA asks the fact finder to recommend adoption of its economic package.

Position of the School District

The School District argues that the annual inflation rate for the present academic year has averaged 10 percent and is forecast to run about 8 percent for the next year. The increases for this district over the previous two years have averaged about 1½% to 2% less than the national inflation rate. The School District proposes to pay the maximum allowed by its limited resources in an attempt to stay within the historical standard of living formula.

The School District proposes a 5% increase in the salary schedules which represents a 6% increase in the district's faculty salary costs. The fringe package proposal is for the district to pay half of the increase in cost of the fringe package or $50.65 per employee. Total cost of this proposed package is presented in Exhibit IV.

Exhibit V presents the School District's estimates of increased revenues for the next academic year.

The USD 31 estimates of increased expenditures for next academic year are presented in Exhibit VI.

In addition to these expenditures the School District proposes to replace three school buses which are becoming maintenance problems. The total cost,

Exhibit IV.   Cost of USD 31's Economic Package

$ 14,480.00	Average salary
× .06	
868.8	
× 150	Number of faculty
130,320.00	Total of salary increase
50.65	Fringe component paid by USD 31
× 150	Number of faculty
$ 7,597.50	Total of fringe increase
$137,917.50	Total increase in economic package cost

Exhibit V.   USD 31 Revenue Increases (USD 31 Estimates)

County Property Tax	$208,530.00
State Excise Tax	53,350.00
License Plate Revenues	–0–
County Income Tax	54,295.00
State Aid	12,030.00
Federal Aid	–42,760.00
	$285,445.00

Exhibit VI.   USD 31 Increased Operating Expenses (USD 31 Estimates)

Utilities	$ 4,380.00
Telephone & Postage	$ 2,970.00
Salaries and Fringes—Nonbargaining Personnel	23,800.00
Classroom Materials	3,510.00
Building Insurance	300.00
New Shop Equipment	6,780.00
Replacement of Front Sidewalks	12,350.00
Improvement of Library	9,400.00
New Copying Equipment	18,200.00
Repaired Fencing	1,050.00
	$82,740.00

less trade for the three buses, is $51,200.00. The total available revenue for bargaining unit economic package improvement is therefore $285,445 minus ($82,740 + $51,200) $133,940 which leaves $151,505. Since several teachers in the district are likely to upgrade their educational levels as well as the possibility of one or more retirements, the District believes the roughly 8.3% working balance between the available revenues and estimated cost of the improved economic package is necessary. The District normally works on an approximately 9% of budget balance.

The District asks the fact finder to recommend the proposed 5% increase in the salary schedule and the payment of 50% of the increase in the cost of the fringe benefits.

Independent Data

The only independent data source was the county tax auditor. The auditor stated that it was certainly too early in the year to accurately estimate county income tax revenues but was reasonably sure that they would run between $60,000 and $65,000 more than last year and probably toward the low end of that range. He did have reasonably accurate estimates for county property tax revenue increases for next year. With over half of the revenue collected, he estimated that property tax receipts would increase for the district by about $230,000 (plus as much as 2 percent or minus as much as 1 percent). No other independent data were available.

Case 14
Baseball Player's Salary Dispute

This case is based on three actual arbitration cases concerning the compensation of major league baseball players. While it is doubtful that many of the students reading this text will ever have the opportunity to become involved with wage determination in major league baseball, the issues involved in this case are common to wage issues in many bargaining relations. The names have been changed in this case to protect the privacy of those concerned.

The student is to answer the questions at the end of the case and then prepare a written award as though (s)he was the arbitrator in this case.

Issue

The issue before the arbitrator is what the just and equitable level of compensation for the services of Mr. David M, second baseman for the Chicago franchise, should be.

The arbitrator may select the final offer of Mr. David M, the Chicago management, or an appropriate sum between the final offers of the parties.

Mr. David M came to Chicago after four years with Cincinnati. Mr. M, after the expiration of his initial four year contract with Cincinnati, was selected in the free agent draft by Chicago and negotiated a three year contract which called for a salary of $100,000 per year as well as $50,000 for signing the contract.

The Chicago franchise has broken even for the last two years. Over the previous 51 years of its existence, this franchise has made money, unlike most major league baseball teams. In fact, over the previous ten years, Chicago has averaged a 7% profit on sales (roughly 3.5 million dollars profit on 50 million dollars worth of sales). At present Chicago has no high priced super-stars on its roster. There are at present only two other Chicago ballplayers which make in excess of $100,000 per year. Both of these players are pitchers who have been named to the league's all-star team for each of the last eight years. Both pitchers are regarded as being the two best Chicago has ever had and among the ten best pitchers in the major leagues. The two pitchers each receive $250,000 per year which makes them the highest paid ballplayers in the history of the Chicago franchise.

All other issues in this dispute have been settled. The contract will be for an effective period of five years. The arbitrator is asked to decide the salary issue for only the first three years of the contract since the last two year's compensation will be negotiated during the third year of the subject contract.

Position of Mr. David M

The final offer of David M was for a progressive salary. For the first year he proposes a salary of $350,000, for the second year $400,000 and $450,000 for the final year which totals $1,200,000 over the three years.

The rationale offered for this salary proposal is that Mr. M has been the best fielding and hitting player, at his position, over the last two years in the major leagues. There are several ball players, at present, who have contributed less to their teams and are paid more.

The following Exhibits I and II were offered into the record by Mr. M.

Exhibit I.   Last Two Years' Statistics—Best Four Major League Second Basemen

Average Salary	Player	Franchise	Fielding Percentage	Average Season Errors	Batting Average	Average Home Runs	Average Runs Batted In
$100,000	Mr. M	Chicago	.999	7	.318	25	97
$175,000	Mr. C	New York	.998	12	.312	20	90
$250,000	Mr. D	Los Angeles	.997	17	.292	14	91
$200,000	Mr. L	Boston	.997	18	.301	10	88

Exhibit II.   Chicago Club Statistics for Past Two Years

Salary	Player	Fielding Percentage	Average Errors	Batting Average	Average Home Runs	Average Runs Batted In
$190,000	Mr. W	.999	8	.320	30	102
$175,000	Mr. L	.999	6	.300	32	117
$100,000	Mr. M	.999	7	.318	25	97
$185,000	Mr. G	.997	20	.321	28	80

As should be obvious from the above statistics, Mr. M has the best record over the past two years of any second baseman in the major leagues. Mr C's contract was negotiated two years ago and will be renegotiated next year. Mr. D negotiated his contract last year. Mr D is 36 years old and was picked up after he was released from Atlanta last year. Mr. D's contract is a two year contract. Mr. L signed a two year contract with Boston last year as a rookie and will renegotiate his contract next year. Mr. M argues that in comparison to his colleagues he is paid an amount totally inconsistent with his contribution to the Chicago ball club.

Furthermore, the Chicago team, alleges Mr. M, is more able to pay than any of the other three ball clubs which each have one of the other four best second basemen. Chicago over the last two years has broken even while New York lost over $500,000 over the same period, Los Angeles $500,000, and Boston $150,000 two years ago but broke even last year.

On the basis of this evidence David M asks the arbitrator to award the salary proposed here.

Position of the Chicago Management

The position of the Chicago franchise rests on three facts: (1) Mr. M has done an excellent job for the team over the past two years and is deserving of a raise but more in line with his overall accomplishments and ability; (2) the Chicago franchise is in the process of expanding and modernizing the oldest and smallest ball park in the league, which limits its ability to pay; and (3) internal equity must be maintained between the ball players on the present roster.

The proposal of the Chicago management is that Mr. M be paid a salary during the first year of the present contract of $200,000, the second year $220,000, and the third year $242,000.00. This amounts to a one-hundred percent increase in the first year and ten percent per year over the final two years, for a total of $662,000 over the period.

While the data presented by Mr. M in support of his proposal is accurate, it presents a distorted picture. Mr. M has the second best fielding percentage of any infielder (committing one more error than our third baseman) on the Chicago team over the past two years. Over the past two years, Mr. M has been fourth in total home runs, third in runs batted in and batting average.

Both Mr. L and Mr. G will renegotiate their contracts next year while Mr. W has two years left on his contract.

Mr. M's lifetime batting average, average of home runs, and runs batted in, are not as good as his performance over the past two years. He has a lifetime batting average of .297, has averaged 17 home runs per year and 81 runs batted in per season. This performance is excellent, but the other three ball players listed in Exhibit II have consistently performed at the level indicated in that exhibit for the past nine, five, and seven years, respectively.

The final issue involves the profitability of the franchise and the expansion and modernization of the stadium. Two years ago management started a program to increase the seating capacity of Chicago Stadium from its present 21,550 to 40,000. The franchise has already spent 4.1 million dollars on this project and has planned or committed another $21,600,000 on the renovation project. If the expansion and modernization of Chicago Stadium is to be accomplished then the line must be held on other costs. To pay excessive player salaries would preclude future ability to pay and the viability of the baseball team.

Management respectfully asks the arbitrator to award the salary proposal put forth herein by management.

QUESTIONS

1. Explain the position of each party on the ability of the ball team to pay.

2. Explain the position of each party on the comparative norm.

3. Why is the standard of living not specifically mentioned? Is this standard implied in any of the parties' arguments?

4. Which group, second basemen or Chicago ball players, are the most appropriate for comparison purposes?

5. Does Chicago have an ability to pay the increased salary demand of David M? Has Chicago denied an ability to pay?

Mock Negotiation

This mock negotiation exercise is designed to give students the opportunity to participate in a form of actual contract bargaining. It has often been said that experience is the best teacher. Lacking the opportunity to participate in or at least to observe labor and management negotiating a labor agreement this mock negotiation problem is a possible second best learning experience. This exercise is strictly hypothetical even though many of the characteristics and facts herein are borrowed from real life negotiations. The students will have the opportunity to utilize the strategies and techniques discussed in Part II of the text. As with any learning experience the students will get as much out of this exercise as they put into it. Honest participation in every phase of the problem and sincere role playing are necessary if the exercise is to be of value. The authors have utilized this and similar problems numerous times over the past years. In virtually every case, this problem has helped the students to better understand the nature and conduct of table bargaining.

Negotiation Rules and Procedure

The following rules have been used by the authors with success. Individual instructors may wish to modify some of the following, but unless otherwise informed, students should consider these to be the rules for their negotiations.

1. The class will be divided into management and union bargaining teams. During its first meeting each negotiating team shall select a chairman. The chairman, with the advice of his team, should delegate responsibilities for the various preparatory tasks among the members of the team.

2. Each team may prepare and present not less than five demands nor more than eight. All demands must be based on the facts and circumstances as outlined in the negotiation exercise. Demands not based on the problem will be disallowed.

3. It is to be assumed that the Taft-Hartley Act and laws of the state and municipality outlined in the problem apply.

4. Each team shall meet in planning sessions so as to be adequately prepared for negotiations. The instructor may or may not allot some class time for this purpose. Each participant must assist in the research and preparation stage.

5. Demands must be consistent with the law governing the topics of collective bargaining. Union demands concerning wages and economic supplements will be considered *one* demand as well as demands concerning union security and dues checkoff. Management demands concerning automation, subcontracting, and management rights clauses may also be considered to be *one* demand.

6. No consultation or collusion with any other team (union or management) will be allowed. The preparation and negotiation of the contract is the responsibility of each individual team.

7. Each team should formulate and negotiate those demands that it believes are the most important, given the information in this exercise.

8. At the beginning of the negotiation session each team should present a written list of their demands to its opponent. While the chairman should coordinate the planning and preparation of the negotiation, each team member should actively participate in the bargaining.

9. Compromises, counterproposals, dropping of demands, and trading of demands are permitted. The result may be that all or only a few issues will be agreed upon and included in the new contract.

10. No extension of the existing contract will be allowed. The bargaining teams must either settle the contract through negotiation or engage in a work stoppage.

11. As issues are settled a member of each team should note the substance of the settlement in writing. It is not necessary to write out in detail specific contract language so long as the intent of the provision is clear.

12. After the negotiation session the chairman of each team will present to the entire class what its team was successful in obtaining, what had to be forgone, and a general impression of their negotiations. Each member of the team should then prepare a two or three page report outlining his/her contribution to the negotiations and why his/her team either settled or instituted a work stoppage. This report will be turned in to the instructor.

The Negotiation Problem

This negotiation problem is divided into four sections: (1) background of the parties and the bargaining relation; (2) financial information; (3) issues in this round of contract negotiations; and (4) the existing labor agreement.

Background

The present three year contract between the Chicago Post Newspaper and Local 14 of the Associated Pressmen and Graphics Workers (APGW) expires at the end of today's negotiation session (the instructor will set the date and exact time for the contract deadline). The union has a long standing policy of "no contract no work;" therefore, at the end of the negotiation session there will either be a negotiated contract or a work stoppage.

The Taft-Hartley Act as amended applies to this particular bargaining relation. The students are also to assume that the present economic environment in the city of Chicago, Illinois also applies to the present negotiation problem.

APGW Local 14 organized the Chicago Post in 1955 after a rather uneventful organizational campaign. The bargaining unit presently contains 1120 employees, many of whom were employees of the Post at the time the union organized the paper. The bargaining unit contains all of the Post's employees except the reporting/writing staff and management. The reporting/writing staff organized in 1960 and their contract expires in approximately 16 months.

During the history of the collective bargaining relation between APGW Local 14 and the Post there has been only one workstoppage. During the last contract negotiation an impasse was reached primarily concerning pension issues. This impasse resulted in a strike which lasted seven calendar days. The strike was rather uneventful and appears to have produced no lasting effects. There has never been an unfair labor practice charge filed by either party. In short, the bargaining relation has been exceptionally peaceful over the years and even cooperative at times.

There have been rumors for the last ten months that a major newspaper conglomerate has an interest in purchasing the Chicago Post. The management of the paper confirmed that they had been contacted by the conglomerate but no details were released. The conglomerate operates eleven newspapers across the country and has a reputation of being extremely antiunion. Of the eleven newspapers operated by the firm none are presently unionized. Management claims that it has no desire to see the Post sold but if the contractual settlement makes it doubtful that current profit levels could be maintained then the owners have indicated it is likely that they would sell the paper.

Financial Status of the Firm

The financial status of the Chicago Post has been relatively stable for the past few years. The paper has shown a profit or broken even each year since 1955. The following income statement is for last fiscal year.

Chicago Post, Inc.
Financial Statement

Net Sales & Subscription Revenue		$29,821,400
Net Advertising Revenue		59,712,020
Total Net Revenue		89,533,420
Cost of Ink, Paper, and Materials		15,102,100
Gross Margin		$74,431,320

OPERATING EXPENSES:

Non Bargaining Unit Wages & Salaries	$28,944,600	
Bargaining Unit Wages & Salaries	24,640,000	
Taxes	310,940	
Insurance	201,400	
Utilities & Postage	504,820	
Uncollectible Accounts	81,150	
Depreciation	11,980,420	
Other Amortization	640,300	
TOTAL OPERATING EXPENSES		$67,303,630
Operating Income		7,138,690
Other Revenue		
Interest	$ 103,400	
Rents	256,210	
	359,610	
Less: Interest Expense	140,310	219,300
Income before Income Taxes		7,357,990
Estimated Income Taxes		3,205,400
Net Income		$ 4,152,590
Earnings per Share of Stock (200,000 Shares)		$ 20.76

The total plant and equipment of the Post presently has a market value of $237,658,900 and the firm's other assets are estimated to be worth $29,945,500. Historically the Post has paid 20 to 25% of its net income in dividends and retained the remainder for capital improvements and diversification.

The Chicago Post is exclusively a morning paper, published from Tuesday through Sunday. The daily circulation of the Chicago Post is about 900,000 copies including Sunday's edition. Circulation of the Chicago Post has varied somewhat since the end of the Second World War. In 1945 the circulation was approximately 700,000; by 1958 circulation topped the one million mark but has been declining by a few hundred copies each year since 1958.

Advertising sales have remained relatively constant since 1960. There has not been an advertising rate increase since 1977 when rates were increased by an average of 10%. The 10% rate increase resulted in an increase in total advertising revenue of almost exactly 10%.

Subscription rates for daily issues of the Post have remained at 15¢ since 1975 while all of the other major Chicago papers have charged 20¢ for the past few years. In the last couple of months one major paper raised its daily rate to 25¢. This particular paper has not suffered any decline in its circulation thus far as a result of the price increase. All Sunday papers are currently priced at 75¢ except for the Post which has remained 60¢ since 1975. At least two of the Post's competitors have announced at 10¢ increase in Sunday paper prices which are effective within thirty days.

The Post does not anticipate any increase in the cost of any of the materials necessary to produce the paper except for newsprint which will increase by 3% at the beginning of next month. Newsprint accounts for less than $4 million per year of the Post's costs of production. The Post estimates that it has an inventory of newsprint sufficient to last the firm for approximately eight months. This is due to the paper shortages of a few years ago and the Post's policy of maintaining large inventories in case of future shortages.

Issues in This Contract Negotiations

The average hourly wage for bargaining unit personnel is $8.94 with another $1.99 in economic supplements. The average hourly wage in the other major Chicago newspapers is approximately $9.40 while economic supplements average about $3.70 per hour. The result of this differential has been that the Post has lost five or six of their best people to other area papers, and the Post has had difficulty in attracting qualified skilled employees over the last four or five years. On the other hand, the Chicago Post is the most profitable of the Chicago papers and has had the least decline in circulation over the past ten years.

Three years ago pensions were the most important issue to the union. The only strike in the firm's history occurred during the last negotiations and was primarily over the issue of pensions. The previous pensions arrangement was that at age 65 with thirty years or more of service the employee would be entitled to a monthly pension of $175.00. For each year of service less than the required 30 years, the employee would lose $5.75 per month, and for each year over 30 years, the employee would receive an additional $5.00 per month up to a maximum of $225.00 per month. The union was successful in increasing all pensions to $180 per month with 30 years service. At age 65, for each year less than the required 30 years, the employee would forgo only $5.00, and for each year over 30, the employee receives $5.50 per year limited to a maximum of $246.00. The new pension arrangement covered presently retired employees as well as those currently working. The union expressed its dissatisfaction with this settlement and vowed to get significant pension improvements in the next contract or go on strike.

No improvements were made in medical and life insurance coverage which were deemed by the union to be inadequate. The increases in the premiums for these economic supplements over the last three years have been paid by the employees. The total monthly bill for these premiums is presently $38.55.

The contract contains a COLA clause. The COLA formula requires that 1¢ per .5 increase in the CPI (U) (1967 base) series for the Chicago area be paid in a lump sum semi-annually. The COLA clause contains a ceiling requiring that no more than 26¢ per hour per year be added to the employee's compensation and that at the end of each fiscal year the COLA will be "rolled in" to the hourly wage. The COLA clause was first negotiated nine years ago and no adjustment to the clause has been made since its original negotiation.

Union security issues have been the subject of negotiations over the last three contracts. There is no dues checkoff provision. The contract contains an agency shop clause which specifies that dues and fees must be paid to the union beginning on the one hundred and twentieth day of employment. The original union security clause allowed employees to wait until the 366th day of employment and exempted all employees with fifteen years of service as of the date the contract was signed (1964). At present, there are only two workers still with the Post who fall under the provisions of this grandfather clause who have not elected to pay union dues nor joined the union.

The contract contains a standard grievance procedure with final and binding arbitration specified as the last step. The arbitration clause may be characterized as a relatively narrow arbitration clause, which in part states:

> The Union may, by written notification to management, require any unsettled grievance arising under the provisions of this contract and not settled to the union's satisfaction in Step III to be submitted to an impartial third party selected from the American Arbitration Association roster of arbitrators for final and binding settlement. Provided that the union's written notification is transmitted to management within thirty working days of management's final answer in Step III, the arbitrator shall have full authority to make an appropriate and equitable award on any dispute submitted for his determination provided that he shall not add to, subtract from or modify this contract.

Management has at times found this language unsatisfactory because many disputes concerning work standards have gone to arbitration which management felt were not subject to collective bargaining or the provisions of this contract. The contract states that management must consult the union before any change in work standards or production methods are instituted. In addition, the contract contains a work preservation clause that states that any work that can be done by bargaining unit employees which was normally assigned to bargaining unit employees will continue to be assigned to the bargaining unit. Last fiscal year, of 503 grievances filed, 14 went to arbitration and 6 of these involved work standards. The union won favorable awards in all six work standards cases.

There are presently 51 unsettled grievances. Twenty-six of these grievances involve issues characterized as speed ups. Management required press room employees to sweep and mop their immediate work areas for which the union grieves for 24 hours pay for each of the 26 employees. The remainder of the grievances concern a variety of issues none of which involves major policy considerations or contract interpretation but do involve a total of $2100 in wage claims.

The contract contains a relatively standard seniority clause. The seniority clause states that the most senior qualified employee is given preference for promotion. For purposes of layoff, recalls, transfers, and shift preference, seniority shall govern. The seniority unit for unskilled employees is the Chicago Post regardless of department.

There are, however, several skilled trades present at the Post and each skill class of labor is its own separate seniority unit. The contract also specifies superseniority for all union officials. All officials are protected from layoffs, shift changes, and transfers.

Union officials are not restricted concerning the use of company time for union business. The contract also specifies that if any employee within a steward's district works overtime the union steward must also be offered overtime, and if refused, the alternate steward must be offered the overtime. The thirty-one union stewards in the facility have averaged about thirty hours per week on grievance work. Management has bitterly complained that the union stewards are abusing their right to utilize company time for grievance work. The union denies that any abuse of this right has occurred. This issue gave rise to an impasse during the last negotiations but management did not press the issue because of the favorable settlement over pensions.

The management has the right to require any employee to work overtime. The union has been bitterly opposed to management retaining this right. During the last contract negotiations management agreed to offer overtime on an hour balance rotation scheme by department and skill class. If an insufficient number of employees accept the overtime then management may require any employee on the balance of hours list to work the overtime. This was included in a letter of understanding, but management retained the contract in the present form. If this arrangement was found to be acceptable over the life of the expiring contract, management agreed to include this provision in the contract. Refusal to work mandatory overtime is subject to discharge for insubordination. Every bargaining unit employee has been required to work overtime during the previous year, and each employee averaged twelve hours of mandatory overtime last year. Complicating this issue is the fact that six weeks ago four employees in the press department (one a thirty-one year veteran who is an alternate shop steward) were given ninety day disciplinary layoffs because they refused to work Saturday and Sunday shifts when they were notified at the end of the shift Friday. The reason given for the refusal was that the employees had made plans to take their wives on a fishing trip to Wisconsin and had paid in advance for the plane tickets and the cabin and could not get a refund at this late date.

Employees are entitled to eight paid holidays; these are: (1) New Year's Day; (2) Memorial Day; (3) Independence Day; (4) Labor Day; (5) Thanksgiving; (6) Christmas Eve; (7) Christmas; and (8) New Year's Eve. Management retains the right to require any employee to work during a holiday. For a holiday an employee has to work, he receives time and one half his regular pay and will receive a paid day off of his choice, consistent with management's needs during the following week.

Vacations are assigned to employees on a seniority basis. Management posts a vacation schedule during January each year and employees in order of their seniority are allowed to select their vacation time but must do so before February 1. Employees with more than one year but less than eleven years seniority are allowed five working days vacation; with eleven or more years the employee is entitled to ten working days vacation. All employees are entitled to three working days paid sick leave annually after their first year of employment, none of which may be accumulated and are forfeited if not utilized. The vacation and sick leave provisions are generally regarded by the membership as inadequate.

Employment has been exceptionally stable at the Chicago Post. Since 1955 there have never been any prolonged layoffs. All layoffs have been for machinery changes or once in 1959 for a fire that closed the paper for three weeks. There is presently no SUB program and last fiscal year there were only fifty-eight employees laid-off for five days while repair work was done on a press and some bundling equipment. There has been some concern among the union membership about a SUB program, but little pressure has been applied to the union leadership to obtain such a program.

Management has expressed concern over the last three years concerning a contractual prohibition of temporarily transferring an employee without the employee's consent. Management has argued that this imposes an unwarranted constraint on management prerogatives. Past practice has developed allowing management, in emergencies and for less than a shift if production is threatened, to temporarily transfer employees within specific skill classifications.

The Chicago Post is the only major paper in the Chicago area that does not utilize automated paper bundling machines and that still sets type by hand. During the past two negotiations, the company has attempted to negotiate the contractual prohibition of automation from the contract. The union has fiercely resisted this management demand. The union charges that the automation of bundling newspapers would cost the bargaining unit 20 jobs. These jobs are held by low seniority unskilled labor. In addition, the union claims that the automation of the type setting jobs would cost the bargaining unit 16 jobs filled by skilled high seniority employees. The company has argued that within the next two years (the time necessary to phase in the new technology) thirty employees would become eligible to retire and this should reduce the burden that the bargaining unit would have to bear. Management in the past has offered to retrain and assist the affected employees in finding other employment.

In an effort to reduce costs last year, the company stopped providing work clothes to employees in the press room and stopped the practice of providing free newspapers to the employees; these actions were unilaterally established by management with the understanding that the practice may be stopped if it proved too costly. When management instituted this change, the case was not taken to arbitration because the union believed its chances of winning a favorable award were small. Dissatisfaction with this management action has been wide-spread within the union, and considerable pressure has been exerted on the union's leadership to get the practice reinstituted.

Management has expressed a desire to change a number of other work rules which it claims are costing a substantial amount of money. Employees are presently given two fifteen and one ten minute break per eight hour shift. Employees are alloted a thirty minute unpaid lunch break and a ten minute clean up time for press room employees per shift. The union has refused to agree to any changes in these rules. The union has complained that lunch and break facilities are absent in the Chicago Post Building and that the nearest restaurant is seven blocks away which is too far for employees to go for a hot lunch or even a cup of coffee. The Union during the last two negotiations asked the Post to install an automat lunch room facility with microwave ovens and adequate seating capacity to serve all employees. The company has refused to do so.

The Chicago Post operates its production shift from 6:00 p.m. through 2:30 a.m. daily. A maintenance and janitorial staff as well as a few production employees work a 9:00 a.m. to 5:30 p.m. shift. No shift premium is paid; over the years this has resulted in some dissatisfaction from some of the night shift employees who would prefer to work the day shift. Several of these employees have complained that it is unfair for employees on the day shift to be paid at the same rate as the night shift workers. Over the years the union has brought the issue of a shift premium up in negotiations but has not pressed the issue.

Employees work staggered shifts to cover the production of the Sunday edition. The (A) shift's workweek begins on Monday at 6:00 p.m. and ends on Saturday at 2:30 a.m. The (B) shift's workweek begins on Tuesday at 6:00 p.m. and ends on Sunday at 2:30 a.m. Again, there is no shift premium, and shift assignments are made on the basis of seniority. Naturally the (B) shift employees are unhappy that their Saturdays are regular workdays for which they do not receive a shift premium. The union has argued during the last two negotiations that the (B) shift is entitled to a shift premium because this shift is less desirable than the (A) shift.

Agreement Between the Chicago Post Newspapers, Inc. and APGW Local 14

Article I—Recognition

The Chicago Post Newspapers, Inc. (herein after referred to as the Company) recognizes APGW Local 14 (herein after referred to as the union) as the exclusive bargaining representative for its press, graphics, circulation, distribution, warehouse, clerical, and maintenance employees. The Company agrees to negotiate with the union for the purposes of determining the terms and conditions of employment and administering this agreement.

Article II—Negotiations

Section 1—For purposes of negotiating and/or renegotiating a labor agreement the parties agree to meet at a reasonable time and place. Renegotiations shall begin no later than ninety days prior to the expiration date of any contract in force.

Section 2—Grievance meetings shall be conducted as necessary and either party can cause such a meeting by giving the other party no less than two working days notice. Minutes, transcripts or other acceptable records of any meeting shall be made upon request of either party at company expense.

Article III—Management Rights

The Company retains the sole right to appoint its management who shall have the right to direct the working forces, discipline, determine the products to be produced, prices of the goods and services provided by the Company, to hire, assign duties, specify rules and regulations necessary to the proper and safe operation of the firm and to do any other thing which is deemed to be at the core of managerial authority.

Article IV—Union Security

Section 1—It is agreed that no employee be required to join the union. An employee who chooses not to join the union must pay the equivalent of union initiation fees on the one-hundred twentieth day of employment and tender the equivalent of union dues on the first pay day of each month thereafter.

Section 2—Employees who fail to tender union dues and fees or the equivalent thereof in accordance with the By-Laws of the union shall be notified on the thirtieth day that such payment is in default and they will be terminated effective on the fifth calendar day after receipt of the notification if payment is not tendered.

Article V—Grievance Procedure

Section 1—(Step I) An employee having a grievance shall present the grievance to his shop steward within five working days of the alleged contract violation or its discovery. The employee, at his option, may discuss the complaint with his supervisor prior to the formal filing of the grievance. If this later option is selected the time limit requirement will be deemed to be satisfied if the employee informs his supervisor of the complaint within five working days. If the grievance is unsettled after discussion with his supervisor the shop steward shall reduce the grievance to writing, date it, and sign it. The supervisor then has two working days in which to answer the grievance.

Section 2—(Step II) If the union is dissatisfied with the supervisor's answer in Step I it has five working days in which to appeal the grievance to Step II. In cases appealed to Step II the grievance becomes the joint property of the company and the union. One copy of the original grievance and the supervisor's answer shall be kept on file by each party. The zone steward and general supervisor shall meet and discuss the grievance in an attempt to reach an equitable settlement consistent with the terms outlined in this labor agreement. If unable to reach a settlement in Step II the general supervisor must answer the grievance in writing within two working days.

Section 3—(Step III) If the union is dissatisfied with the general foreman's answer in Step II it has five working days in which to appeal the grievance to Step III. The chairman of the union bargaining committee and the company's director of labor relations shall meet and discuss the grievance in an attempt to reach an equitable settlement consistent with the terms outlined in this labor agreement. If unable to reach a settlement in Step III the director of labor relations will reduce his final answer to writing, date it, sign it, and deliver it to the union within five working days.

Section 4—(Step IV) The union may, by written notification to management, require any unsettled grievance arising under the provisions of this contract and not settled to the union's satisfaction in Step III to be submitted to an impartial third party selected from the American Arbitration Association's roster of arbitrators for final and binding settlement, provided that the union's written notification is transmitted to management within thirty working days of management's final answer in Step III. The arbitrator shall have full authority to make an appropriate and equitable award on any dispute submitted for his determination, provided that he shall not add to, subtract from, or modify this contract.

Section 5—If either party determines that an extension of the time limits herein specified would result in more effective settlement of the grievance they may request in writing a specified extension of time which must be granted in writing by the other party. If no extension is so requested and granted within the specified time limits the limits shall remain in force.

Section 6—In any case involving discipline, the supervisor is to notify the shop steward of the intent to issue discipline. The employee must then be informed of the cause for discipline and the penalty assessed in the presence of the shop steward. Step I of the grievance procedure shall then be initiated.

Article VI—Seniority

Section 1—Seniority shall be established on a shop-wide basis. Each employee's seniority shall accrue from the date of his hiring, except for those employees who were originally hired in nonbargaining unit jobs whose seniority will accrue from the date of transfer to the bargaining unit.

Section 2—Seniority may be lost only in the event that an employee:

a. Voluntarily quits
b. Retires
c. Is discharged for just cause
d. Dies or becomes totally disabled
e. An employee will be determined to have voluntarily quit if:
   (1) he is on continuous layoff for a period greater than his accumulated seniority or twenty-four (24) months, whichever is the greater period of time.
   (2) he is absent without informing management of his inability to work or fails to obtain an authorization within a period of five working days.
   (3) is convicted of a crime for which he is imprisoned for five or more working days.

Section 3—Union representatives shall remain assigned to the shifts, jobs and departments that they held at the time of their election regardless of seniority. No union representative shall be laid-off during the period of the contract or the term of his office (which ever is the lesser period of time) as long as any of their constituents remain on active duty.

Section 4—For purposes of promotion, the most senior employee qualified to do the subject job shall be promoted. Management shall have the right to determine the minimum qualifications for the subject job so long as the definition of qualification is job specific, reasonable and the minimum necessary to perform the job.

Section 5—The most junior employee shall be the first to be laid-off. Management may lay-off by seniority and skill class within the skilled trades but for all other employees seniority shall be the sole criterion employed for selection of employees to be laid off.

Section 6—The most senior employee shall be the first to be recalled from lay-off. Management may recall skilled trades employees independent of general laborers but must recall by seniority within each skilled class.

Section 7—Seniority units for purposes of this agreement are as follows. Seniority unit (A) consists of all unskilled and semiskilled employees who are not journeymen included specifically in seniority units (B) through (E) inclusive. Seniority unit (B) consists of master mechanics. Seniority unit (C) consists of journeymen typesetters. Unit (D) is all journeymen pressmen. Unit (E) consists of all journeymen electricians and electronics technicians.

Article VII—Transfer and Shift Assignment

An employee may request and be granted a transfer of jobs, departments or shifts if he is senior to an employee holding a job in a department or shift which he is qualified to do. An employee may have no more than three transfer requests on file at any time. The most recent request for transfer will be considered the employee's preference of job, department or shift. An employee may not be voluntarily transferred more than once in any nine month period. No temporary transfer of an employee is permitted except with the expressed consent of the employee.

Article VIII—Holidays

All regular employees are entitled to 8 hours pay at their normal hourly wage rate for the holidays listed below; provided that they either work the full scheduled shift on the day prior and the day after the holiday or have an excused absence for the time not worked: (1) New Year's Day; (2) Memorial Day; (3) Independence Day; (4) Labor Day; (5) Thanksgiving; (6) Christmas Eve; (7) Christmas; and (8) New Year's Eve. If the holiday falls on a Saturday the company will recognize Friday for holiday pay purposes. If the holiday falls on Sunday then Monday will be the effective holiday.

Article IX—Sick Leave

Employees with one year of service to the company are entitled to 24 hours paid sick leave. The 24 hours must be used in blocks of no less than 4 hours and management must be informed in writing that the employee intends to utilize hours under this provision one working day in advance. If prior notification is made the employee need not state the reason for the time off. If prior notification is not made management may require a statement outlining the cause of the absence.

Article X—Vacations

Section 1—Employees with one year of seniority but less than eleven years are entitled to five (5) working days of vacation during the calendar year. Employees with eleven or more years of seniority are entitled to ten (10) working days of vacation.

Section 2—Employees on duly authorized vacation periods are entitled to 8 hours pay at their normal hourly wage for each day of vacation which will be disbursed on the last pay period immediately prior to the beginning of their vacation period.

Section 3—No vacation time may be allowed to carry over from one calendar year to another. Any vacation entitlement not used during the calendar year for which it was earned will be forfeited.

Section 4—Management will post a vacation schedule on the departmental bulletin board on the first working Monday of January. Employees will, by seniority, bid for the desired vacation period on or before February 1. An employee may select up to five choices and management will assign vacation periods on the bases of (in order of priority) seniority, staffing needs of the company, and employee choice. Management will post vacation schedules on the departmental bulletin boards on or before the last payday of February.

Article XI—Relief and Lunch Periods

Section 1—During each eight (8) hour shift employees will be granted a thirty (30) minute unpaid lunch period. The lunch period shall begin at least three (3) hours after the beginning of the shift but no later than four and one half (4½) hours after the beginning of the shift. Management may within these limits assign, at its discretion, the time for the lunch break, provided that in so far as possible, management attempts to maintain consistency in the beginning times assigned for individual lunch breaks.

Section 2—Each employee shall be entitled to two (2) fifteen (15) minute and one (1) ten minute personal relief periods during each eight (8) hour shift. No employee shall be required to take a personal relief period during the first hour of a shift nor the last thirty (30) minutes of a shift.

Section 3—Each employee shall be permitted to cease work ten (10) minutes prior to the end of the shift for purposes of personal clean-up.

Article XII—Subcontracting and Changes in Technology

The company shall submit to the union bargaining committee any proposed subcontracting of bargaining unit work or changes in technology effecting bargaining unit work at least ninety days prior to the date proposed for the change. The union shall have the right to veto any such proposal. Any company proposal which would result in the loss of any bargaining unit job is prohibited.

Article XIII—Union Business

For purposes of administering the terms of this agreement union officials are authorized to conduct union business, to include but not limited to, grievance administration, the collection of dues, the circulation and distribution of union literature, and the conduct of union elections, on company time and property.

Article XIV—No Strike

During the life of this agreement the union shall not engage in any strike or slow-down of production. Any dispute covered by the terms and provisions of this contract shall be resolved by the procedures outlined herein by Article V.

Article XV—Leaves of Absence

The company will approve leaves of absence for reasonable causes such as military service, education, extended illness or rehabilitation, maternity, and personal reasons. Provided, that the employee applies in writing at least sixty (60) days in advance, if possible, and that the period requested is consistent with the reason cited for the leave and the staffing needs of the company. Military leaves are limited to three (3) years or the first enlistment whichever is the lesser period. All other leaves are limited to one year. Seniority shall accrue during all such approved leaves.

Article XVI—Overtime

Section 1—Management retains the right to require employees to work necessary overtime and may discipline employees for refusal of overtime, provided that all overtime is first offered to employees in descending order of the number of hours worked during any month. Such a balance of hours shall be kept by the company, be revised monthly and posted on the departmental bulletin board. All such hour balances shall be for departments and skill classifications.

Section 2—Any employee working overtime shall be granted one ten (10) minute personal relief period for each two (2) hours of work.

Section 3—If any employee within a shop steward's area is assigned overtime, the steward must be offered the opportunity to work the same hours; if he refuses the alternate steward must be offered the hours; if he refuses then a union official shall be designated by the steward to represent the employee(s) during the over time period.

Section 4—Overtime premiums specified by the Fair Labor Standards Act shall apply to overtime hours under this agreement providing that at no time shall an employee be paid less than one and one half times the regular rate for hours in excess of eight during a regularly scheduled shift, or double time during holidays or during Sunday.

Article XVII—Work Standards

Work standards and production rates are left to the discretion of management provided that no change in an existing standard shall be made without at least thirty (30) days notice to the union bargaining committee and that the hourly wage shall be consistent with the effort, knowledge, skill, and risk of the work across all jobs within the company.

Article XVII—Cost of Living Adjustment

Section 1—The basis for Cost of Living Adjustments (COLA) shall be the CPI (U) on the 1967 base year for the Chicago SMSA as reported by the Bureau of Labor Statistics, U.S. Department of Labor.

Section 2—For every .5 increase in the CPI (U) 1¢ per hour shall be added to the compensation of each employee. Provided that during any year of the contract that no more than 26¢ per hour shall be so added.

Section 3—The adjustment in the COLA rate shall be made quarterly. The basis for the adjustment in any current quarter shall be the change in the CPI (U) during the quarter immediately prior to the current quarter.

Section 4—COLA shall be disbursed semi-annually on each multiple of six months from the effective date of the contract.

Section 5—At the end of each fiscal year the COLA shall be added to the base hourly wage and shall be considered a part of the base hourly wage and not COLA.

Article XIX—Hours, Shifts and Workweek

Section 1—Management shall retain the right to establish shifts, hours of work and the standard workweek. Provided that the standard workweek shall be no more than forty (40) hours over no more than five (5) days in any seven (7) day calendar week.

Section 2—A standard shift is defined to be eight (8) working hours uninterrupted except by one thirty (30) minute lunch period. No employee shall be required to work any shift which does not conform to this definition except as provided in Article XVI and/or Article XX.

Article XX—Call-in Pay

An employee who reports to work without being informed at least sixteen (16) hours prior to the beginning of his regularly scheduled shift for whom no work is available shall be entitled to four hours pay at his regular hourly rate.

Article XXI—Economic Package

The economic package including but not limited to wage schedules, pension plan, group insurance policies, and other monetary compensation shall be appended to this agreement and copies provided to each employee at company expense.

Article XXII—Effective Life of Contract

This contract shall be of three (3) years duration.

Appendix 2

Mock Grievance Arbitration

This mock grievance arbitration exercise is designed to give students the opportunity to participate in a form of labor arbitration. A full appreciation of the procedures and practices of arbitration are attained only rarely and generally after years of experience with the process. A working knowledge of the fundamentals of this method of dispute settlement is important to any student who aspires to being a practicing labor relations manager or union official. The student will have the opportunity to participate in the preparation and hearing of the case. This will provide an opportunity to apply many of the concepts learned in the contract administration portions of the text. As with any exercise of this nature, the students will get out of this exercise as much as they put into it. Honest participation in every phase of the problem and sincere role playing are necessary if the exercise is to be of value.

Arbitration Rules and Procedures

The following rules have been used by the authors with success. Individual instructors may wish to modify some of the following, but unless otherwise informed, students should consider these to be the rules for their arbitration.

1. The class will be divided into management and union teams (with no fewer than three members each) and arbitrators.

2. The management and union teams shall select a chairperson during their first meeting. The chairperson, with the advice of his team, should delegate responsibilities for the various preparatory tasks among the members of the team.

3. The various team members are *not* to discuss the case with any arbitrator in the class. They may, however, discuss the case among themselves and with members of other teams.

4. It will be assumed that the Taft-Hartley Act, Fair Labor Standards Act, and the Expedited Rules of the American Arbitration Association apply to these proceedings.

5. All members of each team must participate actively in both the preparation and presentation of the case.

6. The arbitrator must render an oral award within one hour of the parties' closing arguments.

7. The basic content of the testimony of each witness to be called must be provided in brief form to the opposing team at least one-week in advance of the hearing.

8. The day of the arbitration exercise the instructor will assign an arbitrator to hear each case.

The Arbitration Exercise

This case arose out of a dispute concerning the subcontracting of bargaining unit work. Local 444 of the United Manufacturing Employees (UME) represents the 1100 production workers of the Midwest Spring and Screw Company located in Indianapolis, Indiana. This company manufactures a wide variety of wire springs, nuts, bolts, nails and pins. Most of the company's business is conducted with two major hardware retailers and other manufacturing firms in the midwest.

For the past five years, Midwest Spring and Screw has had steadily increasing demand for its products from the hardware retailers, but the firm's business with its manufacturing firm customers has been up and down. The spring winding business has been particularly erratic. As a result, six months ago management decided to approach their customers about the possibility of selling them springs in bulk rather than packaging the springs in the plant. Both the hardware retailers and most of the manufacturing companies agreed to purchase springs in bulk and do their own packaging.

The impact of this decision on the bargaining unit is to reduce total employment by 38 employees. These employees are all unskilled packaging department workers. Several of these employees have in excess of twenty years seniority with the firm; however, most of these workers have less than five years seniority.

Management reasoned that the savings in the direct cost of packaging would be passed on to the customer. The company would reap benefits in three ways: (1) unemployment security taxes could be saved because of fewer layoffs and recalls after the initial 38 layoffs; (2) packaging materials would no longer have to be warehoused and the closing of the packaging departments would create more warehouse capacity which the company is critically short of; and (3) the packaging equipment could be sold to one of the hardware retailers at a significant profit.

When the union was informed of the company's decision, a grievance was immediately filed by the local's president, Frank Gray. The contractual provision cited as the basis of the grievance was the subcontracting paragraph of the work preservation clause, which states:

Article XXV—Work Preservation
1. It is hereby mutually agreed that the union and company will endeavor to assure that the present employment opportunities at Midwest Spring and Screw Company will be maintained.
2. In the event that management determines that automation is necessary it is allowable under the provisions of this agreement if one or more of the following requirements is (are) satisfied:
   A. No reduction in force would result and there are presently no bargaining unit employees on layoff.
   B. No reduction in force would result and there would be no adverse impact on any employees presently on layoff or, laid-off employees would be recalled as a result of the automation.
   C. A reduction in force would result and/or an adverse impact would be suffered by employees on layoff but the management can show that the subject automation is necessary to assure the survival of the business. In such an event management must notify the union of its intent to automate at least sixty calendar days in advance of the change in production methods.
   D. In the event management produces a new product or increases production of existing products management retains the sole right to determine the methods and technology to be used in the new or increased production.
3. Management shall not subcontract any work presently done by bargaining unit personnel unless management complies with all of the following standards:
   A. The union is notified at least ninety days in advance of executing any subcontracting agreement.

B. The subcontracting is the result of the unavailability of skilled employees and/or specialized equipment.

C. Management must show with acceptable evidence that the subject subcontracting will result in substantial cost savings to the firm.

In Step 1 of the grievance procedure, management notified the union that the contract to sell the packaging equipment and to sell springs in bulk had been entered into the day before the union was notified. Management further contended that this action was not necessarily subcontracting but a legitimate exercise of management prerogatives. Mr. Steven Miller, the new plant manager (employed six months prior), stated that:

"This decision was based on the necessity to make more plant space available for inventory purposes. Subcontracting is not an issue, the packaging is going to be done by the customer therefore we're only changing the nature of the product."

Further, management stated that Mr. Jack Davis would provide the union with the data concerning the savings in cost within the next forty-eight hours. Mr. Don Prough, director of marketing, stated that it was his opinion that this action was fully covered by the management rights clause which states:

Article III Management Rights
Except as modified by the expressed provisions of this contract management retains the right to direct the working force and to exercise any prerogative deemed by management to be necessary to maintaining an efficient, safe and profitable operation.

Management then denied the grievance and agreed, in writing, to extend the five working day limit for the union's Step 2 appeal to ten working days after the receipt of the cost savings information from Mr. Jack Davis.

The information provided by Mr. Jack Davis indicated the packaging machinery had been fully depreciated and would be sold for a total 1.2 million dollars. The total cost of removing the equipment and converting the floor space into storage space is estimated at 1.6 million dollars minimum. The alternative warehouse arrangement was to purchase temporary storage buildings for $250,000 but with an estimated life of only fifteen years. The cost of packaging would be deducted from the price of the springs to include a ten percent return to capital and four percent margin.

At the second step meeting, Mr. Frank Gray, the Local's president, and Mr. Mike Clark, chairman of the bargaining committee, stated that they believed the company was acting in direct violation of Article XXV, Section 3. Mr. Mike Clark presented the company with an earlier grievance arbitration award concerning the packaging of nails. The company had agreed to sell roofing nails in bulk to one of the hardware retailers eight years ago and to sell a packaging machine so as to allow the retailer to package one, two, and four pound boxes of nails. The result was the loss of six bargaining unit jobs. In this case, the Company did notify the union ninety days prior to the change; however, no significant cost savings could be shown. The arbitrator awarded this case in favor of the union. In the opinion of the arbitrator in the previous case, it was management's intent to subcontract the packaging work to the customer. Management, in the previous case, had taken bids from two other packaging subcontractors, but the best financial arrangements were available from the customer. The union officials present alleged that this eight year old case was sufficient precedent for management to grant the present grievance.

Mr. Steven Miller stated that he was not plant manager eight years ago and that case did not bind him in the present case. Management denied the union's grievance and the meeting was adjourned.

At the third step meeting, management offered to settle the grievance. Mr. Miller stated that if the union agreed to withdraw its grievance in the present case, the company would allow the 38 affected employees preference in hiring at its plants in Dayton, Ohio, which made cardboard containers, and would agree not to enter into this type of agreement with any customer, nor to subcontract any work for the duration of the contract (approximately 21 months). The union asked for and was granted ten working days to consider management's offer.

After duly considering management's offer, the bargaining committee instructed Mr. Gray to turn management's offer down and demand the case go to arbitration. Mr. Gray scheduled a meeting with Mr. Miller and notified him in writing that the union demanded arbitration in this case. Mr. Miller asked if he could have five working days in which to formulate another offer to settle the grievance. Mr. Gray stated that it was the union's position that the submission to arbitration must be in the mail at the close of business today but that it would be some time before an arbitrator could be selected and if a fair settlement could be negotiated, the union would withdraw its demand for arbitration.

The next day Mr. Miller asked Mr. Gray to come to his office. Mr. Miller stated he was authorized to "sweeten the pot" somewhat. In addition to the other considerations, offered by the company, Mr. Miller stated he was willing to sign a letter of understanding that the selling of products in bulk to customers to package when the packaging had been previously done by bargaining unit personnel constituted subcontracting for purposes of Article XXV, Section 3. However, management must be allowed to proceed in the present case, and the union must withdraw its grievance. Mr. Gray stated that he would relay the offer to the bargaining committee, but he didn't think it would be acceptable.

Two days later Mr. Gray contacted Mr. Miller and stated that management's offer had been rejected by the bargaining committee and that no offer except granting the union's grievance would be acceptable. Mr. Miller then stated that the case should be settled in arbitration and management believed this case to be nonarbitrable and would argue the arbitrability as well as the merits of the case. The arbitration clause addresses procedural matters but also limits the arbitrator's jurisdiction. In part, the arbitration clause states:

Article XXXII Section 7—Jurisdiction of the Arbitrator
The arbitrator may not add to, subtract from or modify in any manner the terms and conditions of this labor agreement. The arbitrator may rule on issues of interpretation and application of this agreement and award remedies consistent with its provisions but has no authority or jurisdiction beyond that authorized herein or by specific submission of the union and management together.

The parties agreed to submit the case to the American Arbitration Association under the expedited rules of that association. Three panels were submitted to the parties by the AAA, but the parties were unable to agree on an arbitrator to hear the case and asked the American Arbitration Association to select an arbitrator for them to hear the case.

The parties were unable to frame the issue in specific language and agreed to frame the language of the issue at the arbitration hearing.

American Arbitration Association Expedited Labor Arbitration Rules

1. Agreement of Parties—These Rules shall apply whenever the parties have agreed to arbitrate under them, in the form obtained at the time the arbitration is initiated.
2. Appointment of Neutral Arbitrator—The AAA shall appoint a single neutral Arbitrator from its Panel of Labor Arbitrators, who shall hear and determine the case promptly.

3. Initiation of Expedited Arbitration Proceeding—Cases may be initiated by joint submission in writing, or in accordance with a collective bargaining agreement.

4. Qualifications of Neutral Arbitrator—No person shall serve as a neutral Arbitrator in any arbitration in which that person has any financial or personal interest in the result of the arbitration. Prior to accepting an appointment, the prospective Arbitrator shall disclose any circumstances likely to prevent a prompt hearing or to create a presumption of bias. Upon receipt of such information, the AAA shall immediately replace that Arbitrator or communicate the information to the parties.

5. Vacancy—The AAA is authorized to substitute another Arbitrator if a vacancy occurs or if an appointed Arbitrator is unable to serve promptly.

6. Time and Place of Hearing—The AAA shall fix a mutually convenient time and place of the hearing, notice of which must be given at least 24 hours in advance. Such notice may be given orally.

7. Representation by Counsel—Any party may be represented at the hearing by counsel or other representative.

8. Attendance at Hearings—Persons having a direct interest in the arbitration are entitled to attend hearings. The Arbitrator may require the retirement of any witness during the testimony of other witnesses. The Arbitrator shall determine whether any other person may attend the hearing.

9. Adjournments—Hearings shall be adjourned by the Arbitrator only for good cause, and an appropriate fee will be charged by the AAA against the party causing the adjournment.

10. Oaths—Before proceeding with the first hearing, the Arbitrator shall take an oath of office. The Arbitrator may require witnesses to testify under oath.

11. No Stenographic Record—There shall be no stenographic record of the proceedings.

12. Proceedings—The hearing shall be conducted by the Arbitrator in whatever manner will most expeditiously permit full presentation of the evidence and the arguments of the parties. The Arbitrator shall make an appropriate minute of the proceedings. Normally, the hearing shall be completed within one day. In unusual circumstances and for good cause shown, the Arbitrator may schedule an additional hearing, within five days.

13. Arbitration in the Absence of a Party—The arbitration may proceed in the absence of any party who, after due notice, fails to be present. An award shall not be made solely on the default of a party. The Arbitrator shall require the attending party to submit supporting evidence.

14. Evidence—The Arbitrator shall be the sole judge of the relevancy and materiality of the evidence offered.

15. Evidence by Affidavit and Filing of Documents—The Arbitrator may receive and consider evidence in the form of an affidavit, but shall give appropriate weight to any objections made. All documents to be considered by the Arbitrator shall be filed at the hearing. There shall be no post hearing briefs.

16. Close of Hearings—The Arbitrator shall ask whether parties have any further proofs to offer or witnesses to be heard. Upon receiving negative replies, the Arbitrator shall declare and note the hearing closed.

17. Waiver of Rules—Any party who proceeds with the arbitration after knowledge that any provision or requirement of these Rules has not been complied with and who fails to state his objections thereto in writing shall be deemed to have waived his right to object.

18. Serving of Notices—Any papers or process necessary or proper for the initiation or continuation of an arbitration under these Rules and for any court action in connection therewith or for the entry of judgment on an Award made thereunder, may be served upon such party (a) by mail addressed to such party or its attorney at its last known address, or (b) by personal service, or (c) as otherwise provided in these Rules.

19. Time of Award—The award shall be rendered promptly by the Arbitrator and, unless otherwise agreed by the parties, not later than five business days from the date of the closing of the hearing.

20. Form of Award—The Award shall be in writing and shall be signed by the Arbitrator. If the Arbitrator determines that an opinion is necessary, it shall be in summary form.

21. Delivery of Award to Parties—Parties shall accept as legal delivery of the award the placing of the award or a true copy thereof in the mail by the AAA, addressed to such

party at its last known address or to its attorney, or personal service of the award, or the filing of the award in any manner which may be prescribed by law.

22. Expenses—The expenses of witnesses for either side shall be paid by the party producing such witnesses.

23. Interpretation and Application of Rules—The Arbitrator shall interpret and apply these Rules insofar as they relate to his powers and duties. All other Rules shall be interpreted and applied by the AAA, as Administrator.

Labor Management Relations Act, 1947

(Taft-Hartley Act)

Act of June 23, 1947, 61 Stat. 136, as Amended by Act of September 14, 1959, 73 Stat. 519. *

Key to Amendments

Portions of the Act which have been eliminated by the Labor-Management Reporting and Disclosure Act of 1959, Public Law 86–257, are enclosed by black brackets; provisions which have been added to the Act are in italics, and unchanged portions are shown in roman type.

[Public Law 101—80th Congress]

An Act

To amend the National Labor Relations Act, to provide additional facilities for the mediation of labor disputes affecting commerce, to equalize legal responsibilities of labor organizations and employers, and for other purposes.

Be it enacted by the Senate and House of Representatives of the United States of America in Congress assembled,

---

*Section 201 (d) and (e) of the Labor-Management Reporting and Disclosure Act of 1959 which repealed Section 9 (f), (g), and (h) of the Labor Management Relations Act, 1947, and Section 505 amending Section 302 (a), (b), and (c) of the Labor Management Relations Act, 1947, took effect upon enactment of Public Law 86–257, September 14, 1959. As to the other amendments of the Labor Management Relations Act, 1947, Section 707 of the Labor-Management Reporting and Disclosure Act provides:

The amendments made by this title shall take effect sixty days after the date of the enactment of this Act and no provision of this title shall be deemed to make an unfair labor practice, any act which is performed prior to such effective date which did not constitute an unfair labor practice prior thereto.

Short Title and Declaration of Policy

Sec. 1. (a) This Act may be cited as the "Labor Management Relations Act, 1947.

(b) Industrial strife which interferes with the normal flow of commerce and with the full production of articles and commodities for commerce, can be avoided or substantially minimized if employers, employees, and labor organizations each recognize under law one another's legitimate rights in their relations with each other, and above all recognize under law that neither party has any right in its relations with any other to engage in acts or practices which jeopardize the public health, safety, or interest.

It is the purpose and policy of this Act, in order to promote the full flow of commerce, to prescribe the legitimate rights of both employees and employers in their relations affecting commerce, to provide orderly and peaceful procedures for preventing the interference by either with the legitimate rights of the other, to protect the rights of individual employees in their relations with labor organizations whose activities affect commerce, to define and proscribe practices on the part of labor and management which affect commerce and are inimical to the general welfare, and to protect the rights of the public in connection with labor disputes affecting commerce.

Title I
Amendment of National Labor Relations Act

Sec. 101. The National Labor Relations Act is hereby amended to read as follows:

Findings and Policies

Sec. 1. The denial by some employers of the right of employees to organize and the refusal by some employers to accept the procedure of collective bargaining lead to strikes and other forms of industrial strife or unrest, which have the intent or the necessary effect of burdening or obstructing commerce by (a) impairing the efficiency, safety, or operation of the instrumentalities of commerce; (b) occurring in the current of commerce; (c) materially affecting, restraining, or controlling the flow of raw materials or manufactured or processed goods in commerce; or (d) causing diminution of employment and wages in such volume as substantially to impair or disrupt the market for goods flowing from or into the channels of commerce.

The inequality of bargaining power between employees who do not possess full freedom of association or actual liberty of contract, and employers who are organized in the corporate or other forms of ownership association substantially burdens and affects the flow of commerce, and tends to aggravate recurrent business depressions, by depressing wage rates and the purchasing power of wage earners in industry and by preventing the stabilization of competitive wage rates and working conditions within and between industries.

Experience has proved that protection by law of the right of employees to organize and bargain collectively safeguards commerce from injury, impairment, or interruption, and promotes the flow of commerce by removing certain recognized sources of industrial strife and unrest, by encouraging practices fundamental to the friendly adjustment of industrial disputes arising out of differences as to wages, hours, or other working conditions, and by restoring equality or bargaining power between employers and employees.

Experience has further demonstrated that certain practices by some labor organizations their officers, and members have the intent or the necessary effect of burdening or obstructing commerce by preventing the free flow of goods in such commerce through strikes and other forms of industrial unrest or through concerted activities which impair the interest of the public in the free flow of such commerce. The elimination of such practices is a necessary condition to the assurance of the rights herein guaranteed.

It is hereby declared to be the policy of the United States to eliminate the causes of certain substantial obstructions to the free flow of commerce and to mitigate and eliminate these obstructions when they have occurred by encouraging the practice and procedure of collective bargaining and by protecting the exercise by workers of full freedom of association, self-organization, and designation of representatives of their own choosing, for the purpose of negotiating the terms and conditions of their employment or other mutual aid or protection.

Definitions. Sec. 2. When used in this Act—

(1) The term "person" includes one or more individuals, labor organizations, partnerships, associations, corporations, legal representatives, trustees, trustees in bankruptcy, or receivers.

(2) The term "employer" includes any person acting as an agent of an employer, directly or indirectly, but shall not include the United States or any wholly owned Government corporation, or any Federal Reserve Bank, or any State or political subdivision thereof, or any corporation or association operating a hospital, if no part of the net earnings inures to the benefit of any private shareholder or individual, or any person subject to the Railway Labor Act, as amended from time to time, or any labor organization (other than when acting as an employer), or anyone acting in the capacity of officer or agent of such labor organization.

(3) The term "employee" shall include any employee, and shall not be limited to the employees of a particular employer, unless the Act explicitly states otherwise, and shall include any individual whose work has ceased as a consequence of, or in connection with, any current labor dispute or because of any unfair labor practice, and who has not obtained any other regular and substantially equivalent employment, but shall not include any individual employed as an agricultural laborer, or in the domestic service of any family or person at his home, or any individual employed by his parent or spouse, or any individual having the status of an independent contractor, or any individual employed as a supervisor, or any individual employed by an employer subject to the Railway Labor Act, as amended from time to time, or by any other person who is not an employer as herein defined.

(4) The term "representative" includes any individual or labor organization.

(5) The term "labor organization" means any organization of any kind, or any agency or employee representation committee or plan, in which employees participate and which exists for the purpose, in whole or in part, of dealing with employers concerning grievances, labor disputes, wages, rates of pay, hours of employment, or conditions of work.

(6) The term "commerce" means trade, traffic, commerce, transportation, or communication among the several States, or between the District of Columbia or any Territory of the United States and any State or other Territory, or between any foreign country and any State, Territory, or the District of Columbia, or within the District of Columbia or any Territory, or between points in the same State but through any other State or any Territory or the District of Columbia or any foreign country.

(7) The term "affecting commerce" means in commerce, or burdening or obstructing commerce or the free flow of commerce, or having led or tending to lead to a labor dispute burdening or obstructing commerce or the free flow of commerce.

(8) The term "unfair labor practice" means any unfair labor practice listed in section 8.

(9) The term "labor dispute" includes any controversy concerning terms, tenure or conditions of employment, or concerning the association or representation of persons in negotiating, fixing, maintaining, changing, or seeking to arrange terms or conditions of employment, regardless of whether the disputants stand in the proximate relation of employer and employee.

(10) The term "National Labor Relations Board" means the National Labor Relations Board provided for in section 3 of this Act.

(11) The term "supervisor" means any individual having authority, in the interest of the employer, to hire, transfer, suspend, lay off, recall, promote, discharge, assign, reward, or discipline other employees, or responsibly to direct them, or to adjust their grievances, or effectively to recommend such action, if in connection with the foregoing the exercise of such authority is not of a merely routine or clerical nature, but requires the use of independent judgment.

(12) The term "professional employee" means—

(a) any employee engaged in work (i) predominantly intellectual and varied in character as opposed to routine mental, manual, mechanical, or physical work; (ii) involving the consistent exercise of discrition and judgment in its performance; (iii) of such a character that the output produced or the result accomplished cannot be standardized in relation to a given period of time; (iv) requiring knowledge of an advanced type in a field of science or learning customarily acquired by a prolonged course of specialized intellectual instruction and study in an institution of higher learning or a hospital, as distinguished from a general academic education or from an apprenticeship or from training in the performance of routine mental, manual, or physical processes; or

(b) any employee, who (i) has completed the courses of specialized intellectual instruction and study described in clause (iv) of paragraph (a), and (ii) is performing related work under the supervision of a professional person to qualify himself to become a professional employee as defined in paragraph (a).

(13) In determining whether any person is acting as an "agent" of another person so as to make such other person responsible for his acts, the question of whether the specific acts performed were actually authorized or subsequently ratified shall not be controlling.

(14) The term "health care institution" shall include any hospital, convalescent hospital, health maintenance organization, health clinic, nursing home, extended care facility, or other institution devoted to the care of sick, infirm, or aged persons.

National Labor Relations Board

Sec. 3. (a) The National Labor Relations Board (hereinafter called the "Board") created by this Act prior to its amendment by the Labor Management Relations Act, 1947, is hereby continued as an agency of the United States, except that the Board shall consist of five instead of three members, appointed by the President by and with the advice and consent of the Senate. Of the two additional members so provided for, one shall be appointed for a term of five years and the other for a term of two years. Their successors, and the successors of the other members, shall be appointed for terms of five years each, excepting that any individual chosen to fill a vacancy shall be appointed only for the unexpired term of the member whom he shall succeed. The President shall designate one member to serve as Chairman of the Board. Any members of the Board may be removed by the President, upon notice and hearing, for neglect of duty or malfeasance in office, but for no other cause.

(b) The Board is authorized to delegate to any group of three or more members any or all of the powers which it may itself exercise. *The Board is also authorized to delegate to its regional directors its powers under section 9 to determine the unit appropriate for the purpose of collective bargaining, to investigate and provide for hearings, and determine whether a question of representation exists, and to direct an election or take a secret ballot under subsection (c) or (e) of section 9 and certify the results thereof, except that upon the filing of a request therefor with the Board by any interested person, the Board may review any action of a regional director delegated to him under this paragraph, but such a review shall not, unless specifically ordered by the Board, operate as a stay of any action taken by the regional director.* A vacancy in the Board shall not impair the right of the remaining members to exercise all of the powers of the Board, and three members of the Board shall, at all times, constitute a quorum of the Board, except that two members shall constitute a quorum of any group designated pursuant to the first sentence hereof. The Board shall have an official seal which shall be judicially noticed.

(c) The Board shall at the close of each fiscal year make a report in writing to Congress and to the President stating in detail the cases it has heard, the decisions it has rendered, the names, salaries, and duties of all employees and officers in the employ or under the supervision of the Board, and an account of all moneys it has disbursed.

(d) There shall be a General Counsel of the Board who shall be appointed by the President, by and with the advice and consent of the Senate, for a term of four years. The General Counsel of the Board shall exercise general supervision over all attorneys employed by the Board (other than trial examiners and legal assistants to Board members) and over the officers and employees in the regional offices. He shall have final authority, on behalf of the Board, in respect of the investigation of charges and issuance of complaints under section 10, and in respect of the prosecution of such complaints before the Board, and shall have such other duties as the Board may prescribe or as may be provided by law. *In case of a vacancy in the office of the General Counsel the President is authorized to designate the officer or employee who shall act as General Counsel during such vacancy, but no person or persons so designated shall so act (1) for more than forty days when the Congress is in session unless a nomination to fill such vacancy shall have been submitted to the Senate, or (2) after the adjournment sine die of the session of the Senate in which such nomination was submitted.*

Sec. 4. (a) Each member of the Board and the General Counsel of the Board shall receive a salary of $12,000 a year, shall be eligible for reappointment, and shall not engage in any other business, vocation, or employment. The Board shall appoint an executive secretary, and such attorneys, examiners, and regional directors, and such other employees as it may from time to time find necessary for the proper performance of its duties. The Board may not employ any attorneys for the purpose of reviewing transcripts of hearings or preparing drafts of opinions except that any attorney employed for assignment as a legal assistant to any Board member may for such Board member review such transcripts and prepare such drafts. No trial examiner's report shall be reviewed, either before or after its publication, by any person other than a member of the Board or his legal assistant, and no trial examiner shall advise or consult with the Board with respect to exceptions taken to his findings, rulings, or recommendations. The Board may establish or utilize such regional, local, or other agencies, and utilize such voluntary and uncompensated services, as may from time to time be needed. Attorneys appointed under this section may, at the direction of the Board, appear for and represent the Board in any case in court. Nothing in this Act shall be construed to authorize the Board to appoint individuals for the purpose of conciliation or mediation, or for economic analysis.

(b) All of the expenses of the Board, including all necessary traveling and subsistence expenses outside the District of Columbia incurred by the members or employees of the Board under its orders, shall be allowed and paid on the presentation of itemized vouchers therefor approved by the Board or by any individual it designates for that purpose.

Sec. 5. The principal office of the Board shall be in the District of Columbia, but it may meet and exercise any or all of its powers at any other place. The board may, by one or more of its members or by such agents or agencies as it may designate, prosecute any inquiry necessary to its functions in any part of the United States. A member who participates in such an inquiry shall not be disqualified from subsequently participating in a decision of the Board in the same case.

Sec. 6. The Board shall have authority from time to time to make, amend, and rescind, in the manner prescribed by the Administrative Procedure Act, such rules and regulations as may be necessary to carry out the provisions of this Act.

Rights of Employees. Sec. 7. Employees shall have the right to self-organization, to form, join, or assist labor organizations, to bargain collectively through representatives of their own choosing, or to engage in other concerted activities for the purpose of collective bargaining or other mutual aid or protection, and shall also have the right to refrain from any or all of such activities except to the extent that such right may be affected by an agreement requiring membership in a labor organization as a condition of employment as authorized in section 8 (a) (3).

Unfair Labor Practices. Sec. 8. (a) It shall be an unfair labor practice for an employer—

(1) to interfere with, restrain, or coerce employees in the exercise of the rights guaranteed in section 7;

(2) to dominate or interfere with the formation or administration of any labor organization or contribute financial or other support to it: Provided, That subject to rules and regulations made and published by the Board pursuant to section 6, an employer shall not be prohibited from permitting employees to confer with him during working hours without loss of time or pay;

(3) by discrimination in regard to hire or tenure of employment or any term or condition of employment to encourage or discourage membership in any labor organization: Provided, That nothing in this Act, or in any other statute of the United States, shall preclude an employer from making an agreement with a labor organization (not established, maintained, or assisted by any action defined in section 8[a] of this Act as an unfair labor practice) to require as a condition of employment membership therein on or after the thirtieth day following the beginning of such employment or the effective date of such agreement, whichever is the later, (i) if such labor organization is the representative of the employees as provided in section 9 (a), in the appropriate collective-bargaining unit covered by such agreement when made [and has at the time the agreement was made or within the preceding twelve months received from the Board a notice of compliance with section 9 (f), (g), (h)], and (ii) unless following an election held as provided in section 9 (c) within one year preceding the effective date of such agreement, the Board shall have certified that at least a majority of the employees eligible to vote in such election have voted to rescind the authority of such labor organization to make such an agreement: Provided further, That no employer shall justify any discrimination against an employee for nonmembership in a labor organization (A) if he has reasonable grounds for believing that such membership was not available to the employee on the same terms and conditions generally applicable to

other members, or (B) if he has reasonable grounds for believing that membership was denied or terminated for reasons other than the failure of the employee to tender the periodic dues and the initiation fees uniformly required as a condition of acquiring or retaining membership;

(4) to discharge or otherwise discriminate against an employee because he has filed charges or given testimony under this Act;

(5) to refuse to bargain collectively with the representatives of his employees, subject to the provisions of section 9 (a).

(b) It shall be an unfair labor practice for a labor organization or its agents—

(1) to restrain or coerce (A) employees in the exercise of the rights guaranteed in section 7: Provided, That this paragraph shall not impair the right of a labor organization to prescribe its own rules with respect to the acquisition or retention of membership therein; or (B) an employer in the selection of his representatives for the purposes of collective bargaining or the adjustment of grievances;

(2) to cause or attempt to cause an employer to discriminate against an employee in violation of subsection (a) (3) or to discriminate against an employee with respect to whom membership in such organization has been denied or terminated on some ground other than his failure to tender the periodic dues and the initiation fees uniformly required as a condition of acquiring or retaining membership;

(3) to refuse to bargain collectively with an employer, provided it is the representative of his employees subject to the provisions of section 9 (a);

(4) (i) to engage in, or to induce or encourage [the employees of any employer] *any individual employed by any person engaged in commerce or in an industry affecting commerce* to engage in, a strike or a [concerted] refusal in the course of [their] *his* employment to use, manufacture, process, transport, or otherwise handle or work on any goods, articles, materials, or commodities or to perform any services [,]; or (ii) *to threaten, coerce, or restrain any person engaged in commerce or in an industry affecting commerce,* where in *either case* an object thereof is:

(A) forcing or requiring any employer or self-employed person to join any labor or employer organization or [any employer or other person to cease using, selling, handling, transporting, or otherwise dealing in the products of any other producer, processor, or manufacturer, or to cease doing business with any other person] *to enter into any agreement which is prohibited by section 8 (e);*

(B) *forcing or requiring any person to cease using, selling, handling, transportng, or otherwise dealing in the products of any other producer, processor, or manufacturer, or to doing business with any other person, or* forcing or requiring any other employer to recognize or bargain with a labor organization as the representative of his employees unless such labor organization has been certified as the representative of such employees under the provisions of section 9 [;]: *Provided, That nothing contained in this clause* (B) *shall be construed to make unlawful, where not otherwise unlawful, any primary strike or primary picketing;*

(C) forcing or requiring any employer to recognize or bargain with a particular labor organization as the representative of his employers if another labor organization has been certified as the representative of such employees under the provisions of section 9;

(D) forcing or requiring any employer to assign particular work to employees in a particular labor organization or in a particular trade, craft, or class rather than to employees in another labor organization or in another trade, craft, or class, unless such employer is failing to conform to an order or certification of the Board determining the bargaining representative for employees performing such work:

Provided, That nothing contained in this subsection (b) shall be construed to make unlawful a refusal by any person to enter upon the premises of any employer (other than his own employer), if the employees of such employer are engaged in a strike ratified or approved by a representative of such employees whom such employer is required to recognize under this Act [;]: *Provided further, That for the purposes of this paragraph (4) only, nothing contained in such paragraph shall be construed to prohibit publicity, other than picketing, for the purpose of truthfully advising the public, including consumers and members of a labor organization, that a product or products are produced by an employer with whom the labor organization has a primary dispute and are distributed by another employer, as long as such publicity does not have an effect of inducing any individual employed by any person other than the primary employer in the course of his employment to refuse to pick up, deliver, or transport any goods, or not to perform any services, at the establishment of the employer engaged in such distribution;*

(5) to require of employees covered by an agreement authorized under subsection (a) (3) the payment, as a condition precedent to becoming a member of such organization, of a fee in an amount which the Board finds excessive or discriminatory under all the circumstances. In making such a finding, the Board shall consider, among other relevant factors, the practices and customs of labor organizations in the particular industry, and the wages currently paid to the employees affected; [and]

(6) to cause or attempt to cause an employer to pay or deliver or agree to pay or deliver any money or other thing of value, in the nature of an exaction, for services which are not performed or not to be performed [.]; *and*

(7) to picket or cause to be picketed, or threaten to picket or cause to be picketed, any employer where an object thereof is forcing or requiring an employer to recognize or bargain with a labor organization as the representative of his employees, or forcing or requiring the employees of an employer to accept or select labor organization as their collective bargaining representative, unless such labor organization is currently certified as the representative of such employees:

(A) where the employer has lawfully recognized in accordance with this Act any other labor organization and a question concerning representation may not appropriately be raised under section 9 (c) of this Act,

(B) where within the preceding twelve months a valid election under section 9 (c) of this Act has been conducted, or

(C) where such picketing has been conducted without a petition under section 9 (c) being filed within a reasonable period of time not to exceed thirty days from the commencement of such picketing: Provided, That when such a petition has been filed the Board shall forthwith, without regard to the provisions of section 9 (c)(1) or the absence of a showing of a substantial interest on the part of the labor organization, direct an election in such unit as the Board finds to be appropriate and shall certify the results thereof: Provided further, That nothing in this sub-paragraph (C) shall be construed to prohibit any picketing or other publicity for the purpose of truthfully advising the public (including consumers) that an employer does not employ members of, or have a contract with, a labor organization, unless an effect of such picketing is to induce any individual employed by any other person in the course of his employment, not to pick up, deliver or transport any goods or not to perform any services.

Nothing in this paragraph (7) shall be construed to permit any act which would otherwise be an unfair labor practice under this section 8 (b).

(c) The expressing of any views, argument, or opinion, or the dissemination thereof, whether in written, printed, graphic, or visual form, shall not constitute or be evidence of an unfair labor practice under any of the provisions of this Act, if such expression contains no threat of reprisal or force or promise of benefit.

(d) For the purposes of this section, to bargain collectively is the performance of the mutual obligation of the employer and the representative of the employees to meet at reasonable times and confer in good faith with respect to wages, hours, and other terms and conditions of employment, or the negotiation of an agreement, or any question arising thereunder, and the execution of a written contract incorporating any agreement reached if requested by either party, but such obligation does not compel either party to agree to a proposal or require the making of a concession: Provided, That where there is in effect a collective-bargaining contract covering employees in an industry affecting commerce, the duty to bargain collectively shall also mean that no party to such contract shall terminate or modify such contract, unless the party desiring such termination or modification—

(1) serves a written notice upon the other party to the contract of the proposed termination or modification sixty days prior to the expiration date thereof, or in the event such contract contains no expiration date, sixty days prior to the time it is proposed to make such termination or modification:

(2) offers to meet and confer with the other party for the purpose of negotiating a new contract or a contract containing the proposed modifications:

(3) notifies the Federal Mediation and Conciliation Service within thirty days after such notice of the existence of dispute, and simultaneously therewith notifies any State or Territorial agency estblished to mediate and conciliate disputes within the State or Territory where the dispute occurred, provided no agreement has been reached by that time; and

(4) continues in full force and effect, without resorting to strike or lockout, all the terms and conditions of the existing contract for a period of sixty days after such notice is given or until the expiration date of such contract, whichever occurs later:

Whenever the collective bargaining involves employees of a health care institution, the provisions of this section 8 (d) shall be modified as follows:

(A) The notice of section 8 (d) (1) shall be ninety days; the notice of section 8 (d) (3) shall be sixty days; and the contract period of section 8 (d) (4) shall be ninety days.

(B) Where the bargaining is for an initial agreement following certification or recognition, at least thirty days' notice of the existence of a dispute shall be given by the labor organization to the agencies set forth in section 8 (d) (3).

(C) After notice is given to the Federal Mediation and Conciliation Service under either clause (A) or (B) of this sentence, the Service shall promptly communicate with the parties and use its best efforts, by mediation and conciliation, to bring them to agreement. The parties shall participate fully and promptly in such meetings as may be undertaken by the Service for the purpose of aiding in a settlement of the dispute.

The duties imposed upon employers, employees, and labor organizations by paragraphs (2), (3), and (4) shall become inapplicable upon an intervening certification of the Board, under which the labor organization or individual, which is a party to the contract, has been superseded as or ceased to be the representative of the employees subject to the provisions of section 9 (a), and the duties so imposed shall not be construed as requiring either party to discuss or agree to any modification of the terms and conditions contained in a contract for a fixed period, if such modification is to become effective before such terms and conditions can be reopened under the provisions of the contract. Any employee who engages in a strike within the sixty-day period specified in this subsection shall lose his status as an employee of the employer engaged in the particular labor dispute, for the purposes of sections 8, 9, and 10 of this Act, as amended, but such loss of status for such employee shall terminate if and when he is reemployed by such employer.

(e) It shall be an unfair labor practice for any labor organization and any employer to enter into any contract or agreement, express or implied, whereby such employer ceases or refrains or agrees to cease or refrain from handling, using, selling, transporting or otherwise dealing in any of the products of any other employer, or to cease doing business with any other person, and any contract or agreement entered into heretofore or hereafter containing such an agreement shall be to such extent unenforceable and void: Provided, That nothing in this subsection (e) shall apply to an agreement between a labor organization and an employer in the construction industry relating to the contracting or subcontracting of work to be done at the site of the construction, alteration, painting, or repair of a building, structure, or other work: Provided further, That for the purposes of this subsection (e) and section 8 (b)(4)(B) the terms "any employer," "any person engaged in commerce or an industry affecting commerce" and "any person" when used in relation to the term "any other producer, processor, or manufacturer," "any other employer," or "any other person" shall not include persons in the relation of a jobber, manufacturer, contractor, or subcontractor working on the goods or premises of the jobber or manufacturer or performing parts of an integrated process of production in the apparel and clothing industry: Provided further, That nothing in this Act shall prohibit the enforcement of any agreement which is within the foregoing exception.

(f) It shall not be an unfair labor practice under subsections (a) and (b) of this section for an employer engaged primarily in the building and construction industry to make an agreement covering employees engaged (or who upon their employment, will be engaged) in the building and construction industry with a labor organization of which building and construction employees are members (not established, maintained, or assisted by any action defined in section 8 [a] of this Act as an unfair labor practice) because (1) the majority status of such labor organization has not been established under the provisions of section 9 of this Act prior to the making of such agreement, or (2) such agreement requires as a condition of employment, membership in such labor organization after the seventh day following the beginning of such employment or the effective date of the agreement, whichever is later, or (3) such agreement requires the employer to notify such labor organization of opportunities for employment with such employer, or gives such labor organization an opportunity to refer qualified applicants for such employment, or (4) such agreement specifies minimum training or experience qualifications for employment or provides for priority in opportunities for employment based upon length of service with such employer, in the industry or in the particular geographical area: Provided, That nothing in this subsection shall set aside the final proviso to section 8 (a) (3) of this Act: Provided further, That any agreement which would be invalid, but for clause (1) of this subsection, shall not be a bar to a petition filed pursuant to section 9 (c) or 9 (e).*

(g) A labor organization before engaging in any strike, picketing, or other concerted refusal to work at any health care institution shall, not less than ten days prior to such action, notify the institution in writing and the Federal Mediation and Conciliation Service of that intention, except that in the case of bargaining for an initial agreement following certification or recognition the notice required by this subsection shall not be

---

*Section 8 (f) is inserted in the Act by subsection (a) of Section 705 of Public Law 86–257. Section 705 (b) provides:

Nothing contained in the amendment made by subsection (a) shall be construed as authorizing the execution or application of agreements requiring membership in a labor organization as a condition of employment in any State or Territory in which such execution or application is prohibited by State or Territorial law.

given until the expiration of the period specified in clause (B) of the last sentence of section 8(d) of this Act. The notice shall state the date and time that such action will commence. The notice, once given, may be extended by the written agreement of both parties.

Representatives and Elections, Sec. 9. (a) Representatives designated or selected for the purposes of collective bargaining by the majority of the employees in a unit appropriate for such purposes, shall be the exclusive representatives of all the employees in such unit for the purposes of collective bargaining in respect to rates of pay, wages, hours of employment, or other conditions of employment: Provided, That any individual employee or a group of employees shall have the right at any time to present grievances to their employer and to have such grievances adjusted, without the intervention of the bargaining representative, as long as the adjustment is not inconsistent with the terms of a collective bargaining contract or agreement then in effect: Provided further, That the bargaining representative has been given opportunity to be present at such adjustment.

(b) The Board shall decide in each case whether, in order to assure to employees the fullest freedom in exercising the rights guaranteed by this Act, the unit appropriate for the purposes of collective bargaining shall be the employer unit, craft unit, plant unit, or subdivision thereof: Provided, That the Board shall not (1) decide that any unit is appropriate for such purposes if such unit includes both professional employees and employees who are not professional employees unless a majority of such professional employees vote for inclusion in such unit: or (2) decide that any craft unit is inappropriate for such purposes on the ground that a different unit has been established by a prior Board determination, unless a majority of the employees in the proposed craft unit vote against separate representation: or (3) decide that any unit is appropriate for such purposes if it includes, together with other employees, any individual employed as a guard to enforce against employees and other persons rules to protect property of the employer or to protect the safety of persons on the employer's premises; but no labor organization shall be certified as the representative of employees in a bargaining unit of guards if such organization admits to membership, or is affiliated directly or indirectly with an organization which admits to membership, employees other than guards.

(c) (1) Whenever a petition shall have been filed, in accordance with such regulations as may be prescribed by the Board—

(A) by an employee or group of employees or any individual or labor organization acting in their behalf alleging that a substantial number of employees (i) wish to be represented for collective bargaining and that their employer declines to recognize their representative as the representative defined in section 9 (a), or (ii) assert that the individual or labor organization, which has been certified or is being currently recognized by their employer as the bargaining representative, is no longer a representative as defined in section 9 (a); or

(B) by an employer, alleging that one or more individuals or labor organizations have presented to him a claim to be recognized as the representative defined in section 9 (a);

the Board shall investigate such petition and if it has reasonable cause to believe that a question or representation affecting commerce exists shall provide for an appropriate hearing upon due notice. Such hearing may be conducted by an officer or employee of the regional office, who shall not make any recommendations with respect thereto. If the Board finds upon the record of such hearing that such a question of representation exists, it shall direct an election by secret ballot and shall certify the results thereof.

(2) In determining whether or not a question of representation affecting commerce exists, the same regulations and rules of decision shall apply irrespective of the identity of the persons filing the petition or the kind of relief sought and in no case shall the Board deny a labor organization a place on the ballot by reason of an order with respect to such labor organization or its predecessor not issued in conformity with section 10 (c).

(3) No election shall be directed in any bargaining unit or any subdivision within which, in the preceding twelve-month period, a valid election shall have been held. Employees [on] *engaged in an economic* strike who are not entitled to reinstatement shall [not] be eligible to vote [.] *under such regulations as the Board shall find are consistent with the purposes and provisions of this Act in any election conducted within twelve months after the commencement of the strike.* In any election where none of the choices on the ballot receives a majority, a run-off shall be conducted, the ballot providing for a selection between the two choices receiving the largest and second largest number of valid votes cast in the election.

(4) Nothing in this section shall be construed to prohibit the waiving of hearings by stipulation for the purpose of a consent election in conformity with regulations and rules of decision of the Board.

(5) In determining whether a unit is appropriate for the purposes specified in subsection (b) the extent to which the employees have organized shall not be controlling.

(d) Whenever an order of the Board made pursuant to section 10 (c) is based in whole or in part upon facts certified following an investigation pursuant to subsection (c) of this section and there is a petition for the enforcement or review of such order, such certification and the record of such investigation shall be included in the transcript of the entire record required to be filed under section 10 (e) or 10 (f), and thereupon the decree of the court enforcing, modifying, or setting aside in whole or in part the order of the Board shall be made and entered upon the pleadings, testimony, and proceedings set forth in such transcript.

(c) (1) Upon the filing with the Board, by 30 per centum or more of the employees in a bargaining unit covered by an agreement between their employer and a labor organization made pursuant to section 8 (a) (3), of a petition alleging they desire that such authority be rescinded, the Board shall take a secret ballot of the employees in such unit and certify the results thereof to such labor organization and to the employer.

(2) No election shall be conducted pursuant to this subsection in any bargaining unit or any subdivision within which, in the preceding twelve-month period, a valid election shall have been held.

[(f) No investigation shall be made by the Board of any question affecting commerce concerning the representation of employees, raised by a labor organization under subsection (c) of this section, and no complaint shall be issued pursuant to a charge made by a labor organization under subsection (b) of section 10, unless such labor organization and any national or international labor organization of which such labor organization is an affiliate or constituent unit (A) shall have prior thereto filed with the Secretary of Labor copies of its constitution and bylaws and a report, in such form as the Secretary may prescribe, showing—

(1) the name of such labor organization and the address of its principal place of business;

(2) the names, titles, and compensation and allowances of its three principal officers and of any of its other officers or agents whose aggregate compensation and allowances for the preceding year exceeded $5,000, and the amount of the compensation and allowances paid to each such officer or agent during such year;

(3) the manner in which the officers and agents referred to in clause (2) were elected, appointed, or otherwise selected;

(4) the initiation fee or fees which new members are required to pay on becoming members of such labor organization;

(5) the regular dues or fees which members are required to pay in order to remain members in good standing of such labor organization;

(6) a detailed statement of, or reference to provisions of its constitution and bylaws showing the procedure followed with respect to, (a) qualification for or restrictions on membership, (b) election of officers and stewards, (c) calling of regular and special meetings, (d) levying of assessments, (e) imposition of fines, (f) authorization for bargaining demands, (g) ratification of contract items, (h) authorization for strikes, (i) authorization for disbursement of union funds, (j) audit of union financial transactions, (k) participation in insurance or other benefit plans, and (l) expulsion of members and the grounds therefor;

and (B) can show that prior thereto it has—

(1) filed with the Secretary of Labor, in such form as the Secretary may prescribe, a report showing all of (a) its receipts of any kind and the sources of such receipts, (b) its total assets and liabilities as of the end of its last fiscal year, (c) the disbursements made by it during such fiscal year, including the purposes for which made; and

(2) furnished to all of the members of such labor organization copies of the financial report required by paragraph (1) hereof to be filed with the Secretary of Labor.]

[(g) It shall be the obligation of all labor organizations to file annually with the Secretary of Labor, in such form as the Secretary of Labor may prescribe, reports bringing up to date the information required to be supplied in the initial filing by subsection (f) (A) of this section, and to file with the Secretary of Labor and furnish to its members annually financial reports in the form and manner prescribed in subsection (f) (B). No labor organization shall be eligible for certification under this section as the representative of any employees, and no complaint shall issue under section 10 with respect to a charge filed by a labor organization unless it can show that it and any national or international labor organization of which it is an affiliate or constituent unit has complied with its obligation under this subsection.]

[(h) No investigation shall be made by the Board of any question affecting commerce concerning the representation of employees, raised by a labor organization under subsection (c) of this section, and no complaint shall be issued pursuant to a charge made by a labor organization under subsection (b) of section 10, unless there is on file with the Board an affidavit executed contemporaneously or within the preceding twelve-month period by each officer of such labor organization and the officers of any national or international labor organization of which it is an affiliate or constituent unit that he is not a member of the Communist Party or affiliated with such party, and that he does not believe in, and is not a member of or supports any organization that believes in or teaches, the overthrow of the United States Government by force or by any illegal or unconstitutional methods. The provisions of section 35 A of the Criminal Code shall be applicable in respect to such affidavits.]

Prevention of Unfair Labor Practices, Sec. 10. (a) The Board is empowered, as hereinafter provided, to prevent any person from engaging in any unfair labor practice (listed in section 8) affecting commerce. This power shall not be affected by any other means of adjustment or prevention that has been or may be established by agreement, law, or otherwise: Provided, That the Board is empowered by agreement with any agency of any State or Territory to cede to such agency jurisdiction over any cases in any industry (other than mining, manufacturing, communications, and transportation except where predominantly local in character) even though such cases may involve labor disputes affecting commerce, unless the provision of the State or Territorial statute applicable to the determination of such cases by such agency is inconsistent with the corresponding provision of this Act or has received a construction inconsistent therewith.

(b) Whenever it is charged that any person has engaged in or is engaging in any such unfair labor practice, the Board, or any agent or agency designated by the Board for such purposes, shall have power to issue and cause to be served upon such person a complaint stating the charges in that respect, and containing a notice of hearing before the Board or a member thereof, or before a designated agent or agency, at a place therein fixed, not less than five days after the serving of said complaint: Provided, That no complaint shall issue based upon any unfair labor practice occurring more than six months prior to the filing of the charge with the Board and the service of a copy thereof upon the person against whom such charge is made, unless the person aggrieved thereby was prevented from filing such charge by reason of service in the armed forces, in which event the six-month period shall be computed from the day of his discharge. Any such complaint may be amended by the member, agent, or agency conducting the hearing or the Board in its discretion at any time prior to the issuance of an order based thereon. The person so complained of shall have the right to file an answer to the original or amended complaint and to appear in person or otherwise and give testimony at the place and time fixed in the complaint. In the discretion of the member, agent, or agency conducting the hearing or the Board, any other person may be allowed to intervene in the said proceeding and to present testimony. Any such proceeding shall, so far as practicable, be conducted in accordance with the rules of evidence applicable in the district courts of the United States under the rules of civil procedure for the district courts of the United States, adopted by the Supreme Court of the United States pursuant to the Act of June 19, 1934 (U.S.C., title 28, sec. 723-B 723-C).

(c) The testimony taken by such member, agent, or agency on the Board shall be reduced to writing and filed with the Board. Thereafter, in its discretion, the Board upon notice may take further testimony or hear argument. If upon the preponderance of the testimony taken the Board shall be of the opinion that any person named in the complaint has engaged in or is engaging in any such unfair labor practice, then the Board shall state its findings of fact and shall issue and cause to be served on such person an order requiring such person to cease and desist from such unfair labor practice, and to take such affirmative action including reinstatement of employees with or without back pay, as will effectuate the policies of this Act: Provided, That where an order directs reinstatement of an employee, back pay may be required of the employer or labor organization, as the case may be, responsible for the discrimination suffered by him: And provided further, That in determining whether a complaint shall issue alleging a violation of section 8 (a) (1) or section 8 (a) (2), and in deciding such cases, the same regulations and rules of decision shall apply irrespective of whether or not the labor organization affected is affiliated with a labor organization national or international in scope. Such order may further require such person to make reports from time to time showing the extent to which it has complied with the order. If upon the preponderance of the testimony taken the Board shall not be of the opinion that the person named in the complaint has engaged in or is engaging in any such unfair labor practice, then the Board shall state its findings of fact and shall issue an order dismissing the said complaint. No order of the Board shall require the reinstatement of any individual as an employee who has been suspended or discharged, or the payment to him of any back pay, if such individual was suspended or discharged for cause. In case the evidence is presented before a member of the Board, or before an examiner or examiners thereof, such member, or such examiner or examiners, as the case may be, shall issue and cause to be served on the parties to the proceeding a proposed report, together with a recommended order, which shall be filed with the Board, and if no exceptions are filed within twenty days after service thereof upon such parties, or within such further period as the Board may authorize, such recommended order shall become the order of the Board and become effective as therein prescribed.

(d) Until the record in a case shall have been filed in a court, as hereinafter provided, the Board may at any time, upon reasonable notice and in such manner as it shall deem proper, modify or set aside, in whole or in part, any funding or order made or issued by it.

(e) The Board shall have power to petition any court of appeals of the United States, or if all the courts of appeals to which application may be made are in vacation, any district court of the United States, within any circuit or district, respectively, wherein the unfair labor practice in question occurred or wherein such person resides or transacts business, for the enforcement of such order and for appropriate temporary relief or restraining order, and shall file in the court the record in the proceedings, as provided in section 2112 of title 28, United States Code. Upon the filing of such petition, the court shall cause notice thereof to be served upon such person, and thereupon shall have jurisdiction of the proceeding and of the question determined therein, and shall have power to grant such temporary relief or restraining order as it deems just and proper, and to make and enter a decree enforcing, modifying, and enforcing as so modified, or setting aside in whole or in part the order of the Board. No objection that has not been urged before the Board, its member agent, or agency, shall be considered by the court, unless the failure or neglect to urge such objection shall be excused because of extraordinary circumstances. The findings of the Board with respect to questions of fact if supported by substantial evidence on the record considered as a whole shall be conclusive. If either party shall apply to the court for leave to adduce additional evidence and shall show to the satisfaction of the court that such additional evidence is material and that there were reasonable grounds for the failure to adduce such evidence in the hearing before the Board, its member, agent, or agency, the court may order such additional evidence to be taken before the Board, its member, agent, or agency, and to be made a part of the record. The Board may modify its findings as to the facts, or make new findings, by reason of additional evidence so taken and filed, and it shall file such modified or new findings, which findings with respect to questions of fact if supported by substantial evidence on the record considered as a whole shall be conclusive, and shall file its recommendations, if any, for the modification or setting aside of its original order. Upon the filing of the record with it the jurisdiction of the court shall be exclusive and its judgment and decree shall be final, except that the same shall be subject to review by the appropriate United States court of appeals if application was made to the district court as hereinabove provided, and by the Supreme Court of the United States upon writ of certiorari or certification as provided in section 1254 of title 28.

(f) Any person aggrieved by a final order of the Board granting or denying in whole or in part the relief sought may obtain a review of such order in any circuit court of appeals of the United States in the circuit wherein the unfair labor practice in question was alleged to have been engaged in or wherein such person resides or transacts business, or in the United States Court of Appeals for the District of Columbia, by filing in such court a written petition praying that the order of the Board be modified or set aside. A copy of such petition shall be forthwith transmitted by the clerk of the court to the Board, and thereupon the aggrieved party shall file in the court the record in the proceeding, certified by the Board, as provided in section 2112 of title 28, United States Code. Upon the filing of such petition, the court shall proceed in the same manner as in the case of an application by the Board under subsection (e) of this section, and shall have the same jurisdiction to grant to the Board such temporary relief or restraining order as it deems just and proper, and in like manner to make and enter a decree enforcing, modifying, and enforcing as so modified, or setting aside in whole or in part the order of the Board; the findings of the Board with respect to questions of fact if supported by substantial evidence on the record considered as a whole shall in like manner be conclusive.

(g) The commencement of proceedings under subsection (e) or (f) of this section shall not, unless specifically ordered by the court, operate as a stay of the Board's order.

(h) When granting appropriate temporary relief or a restraining order, or making and entering a decree enforcing, modifying, and enforcing as so modified, or setting aside in whole or in part an order of the Board, as provided in this section, the jurisdiction of courts sitting in equity shall not be limited by the Act entitled "An Act to amend the Judicial Code and to define and limit the jurisdiction of courts sitting in equity, and for other purposes," approved March 23, 1932 (U.S.C., Supp. VII, title 29, secs. 101–115).

(i) Petitions filed under this Act shall be heard expeditiously, and if possible within ten days after they have been docketed.

(j) The Board shall have power, upon issuance of a complaint as provided in subsection (b) charging that any person has engaged in or is engaging in an unfair labor practice, to petition any district court of the United States (including the District Court of the United States for the District of Columbia), within any district wherein the unfair labor practice in question is alleged to have occurred or wherein such person resides or transacts business, for appropriate temporary relief or restraining order. Upon the filing of any such petition the court shall cause notice thereof to be served upon such person, and thereupon shall have jurisdiction to grant to the Board such temporary relief or restraining order as it deems just and proper.

(k) Whenever it is charged that any person has engaged in an unfair labor practice within the meaning of paragraph (4) (D) of section 8 (b), the Board is empowered and directed to hear and determine the dispute out of which such unfair labor practice shall have arisen, unless, within ten days after notice that such charge has been filed, the parties to such dispute submit to the Board satisfactory evidence that they have adjusted, or agreed upon methods for the voluntary adjustment of the dispute. Upon compliance by the parties to the dispute with the decision of the Board or upon such voluntary adjustment of the dispute, such charge shall be dismissed.

(l) Whenever it is charged that any person has engaged in an unfair labor practice within the meaning of paragraph (4) (A), (B), or (C) of section 8 (b), *or section 8 (e) or section 8 (b) (7),* the preliminary investigation of such charge shall be made forthwith and given priority over all other cases except cases of like character in the office where it is filed or to which it is referred. If, after such investigation, the officer or regional attorney to whom the matter may be referred has reasonable cause to believe such charge is true and that a complaint should issue, he shall, on behalf of the Board, petition any district court of the United States (including the District Court of the United States for the District of Columbia) within any district where the unfair labor practice in question has occurred, is alleged to have occurred, or wherein such person resides or transacts business, for appropriate injunctive relief pending the final adjudication of the Board with respect to such matter. Upon the filing of any such petition the district court shall have jurisdiction to grant such injunctive relief or temporary restraining order as it deems just and proper, notwithstanding any other provision of law: Provided further, That no temporary restraining order shall be issued without notice unless a petition alleges that substantial and irreparable injury to the charging party will be unavoidable and such temporary restraining order shall be effective for no longer than five days and will become void at the expiration of such period [.]: *Provided further, That such officer or regional attorney shall not apply for any restraining order under section 8 (b) (7) if a charge against the employer under section 8 (a) (2) has been filed and after the preliminary investigation, he has reasonable cause to believe that such charge is true and that a complaint should issue.* Upon filing of any such petition the courts shall cause notice thereof to be served upon any person involved in the charge and such person, including the charging party, shall be given an opportunity to appear by counsel and present any relevant testimony: Provided further, That for the purposes of this subsection district courts shall be deemed to have jurisdiction of a labor organization (1) in the district in which such organization maintains its principal office, or (2) in any district in which its duly authorized officers or agents are engaged in promoting or protecting the interests of employee members. The service of legal process upon such officer or agent shall constitute service upon the labor organization and make such organization a party to the suit. In situations where such relief is appropriate the procedure specified herein shall apply to charges with respect to section 8 (b) (4) (D).

(m) *Whenever it is charged that any person has engaged in an unfair labor practice within the meaning of subsection (a) (3) or (b) (2) of section 8, such charge shall be given priority over all other cases except cases of like character in the office where it is filed or to which it is referred and cases given priority under subsection (l).*

Investigatory Powers

Sec. 11. For the purpose of all hearings and investigations, which, in the opinion of the Board, are necessary and proper for the exercise of the powers vested in it by section 9 and section 10—

(1) The Board, or its duly authorized agents or agencies, shall at all reasonable times have access to, for the purposes of examination, and the right to copy any evidence of any person being investigated or proceeded against that relates to any matter under investigation or in question. The Board, or any member thereof, shall upon application of any party to such proceedings, forthwith issue to such party subpenas requiring the attendance and testimony of witnesses or the production of any evidence in such proceeding or investigation requested in such application. Within five days after the service of a subpena on any person requiring the production of any evidence in his possession or under his control, such person may petition the Board to revoke, and the Board shall revoke, such subpena if in its opinion the evidence whose production is required does not relate to any matter under investigation, or any matter in question in such proceedings, or if in its opinion such subpena does not describe with sufficient particularity the evidence whose production is required. Any member of the Board, or any agent or agency designated by the Board for such purposes, may administer oaths and affirmations, examine witnesses, and receive evidence. Such attendance of witnesses and the production of such evidence ay be required from any place in the United States or any Territory or possession thereof, at any designated place of hearing.

(2) In case of contumacy or refusal to obey a subpena issued to any person, any district court of the United States or the United States courts of any Territory or possession, or the District Court of the United States for the District of Columbia, within the jurisdiction of which the inquiry is carried on or within the jurisdiction of which said person guilty of contumacy or refusal to obey is found or resides or transacts business, upon application of the Board shall have jurisdiction to issue to such person an order requiring such person to appear before the Board, its member, agent, or agency, there to produce evidence if so ordered, or there to give testimony touching the matter under investigation or in question; and any failure to obey such order of the court may be punished by said court as a contempt thereof.

(3) [Repealed.]

(4) Complaints, orders, and other process and papers of the Board, its member, agent, or agency, may be served either personally or by registered mail or by telegraph or by leaving a copy thereof at the principal office or place of business of the person required to be served. The verified return by the individual so serving the same setting foth the manner of such service shall be proof of the same, and the return post office receipt or telegraph receipt therefor when registered and mailed or telegraphed as aforesaid shall be proof of service of the same. Witnesses summoned before the Board, its member, agent, or agency, shall be paid the same fees and mileage that are paid witnesses in the courts of the United States, and witnesses whose depositions are taken and the persons taking the same shall severally be entitled to the same fees as are paid for like services in the courts of the United States.

(5) All process of any court to which application may be made under this Act may be served in the judicial district wherein the defendant or other person required to be served resides or may be found.

(6) The several departments and agencies of the Government, when directed by the President, shall furnish the Board, upon its request, all records, papers, and information in their possession relating to any matter before the Board.

Sec. 12. Any person who shall willfully resist, prevent, impede, or interfere with any member of the Board or any of its agents or agencies in the performance of duties pursuant to this Act shall be punished by a fine of not more than $5,000 or by imprisonment for not more than one year, or both.

Limitations

Sec. 13. Nothing in this Act, except as specifically provided for herein, shall be construed so as either to interfere with or impede or diminish in any way the right to strike, or to affect the limitations or qualifications on that right.

Sec. 14. (a) Nothing herein shall prohibit any individual employed as a supervisor from becoming or remaining a member of a labor organization, but no employer subject to this Act shall be compelled to deem individuals defined herein as supervisors as employees for the purpose of any law, either national or local, relating to collective bargaining.

(b) Nothing in this Act shall be construed as authorizing the execution or application of agreements requiring membership in a labor organization as a condition of employment in any State or Territory in which such execution or application is prohibited by State or Territorial law.

(c) (1) The Board, in its discretion, may, by rule of decision or by published rules adopted pursuant to the Administrative Procedure Act, decline to assert jurisdiction over any labor dispute involving any class or category of employers, where, in the opinion of the Board, the effect of such labor dispute on commerce is not sufficiently substantial to warrant the exercise of its jurisdiction: Provided, That the Board shall not decline to assert jurisdiction over any labor dispute over which it would assert jurisdiction under the standards prevailing upon August 1, 1959.

(2) Nothing in this Act shall be deemed to prevent or bar any agency or the courts of any State or Territory (including the Commonwealth of Puerto Rico, Guam, and the Virgin Islands), from assuming and asserting jurisdiction over labor disputes over which the Board declines, pursuant to paragraph (1) of this subsection, to assert jurisdiction.

Sec. 15. Wherever the application of the provisions of section 272 of chapter 10 of the Act entitled "An Act to establish a uniform system of bankruptcy throughout the United States," approved July 1, 1898, and Acts amendatory thereof and supplementary thereto (U.S.C., title 11, sec. 672), conflicts with the application of the provisions of this Act, this Act shall prevail: Provided, That in any situation where the provisions of this Act cannot be validly enforced, the provision of such other Acts shall remain in full force and effect.

Sec. 16. If any provision of this Act, or the application of such provision to any person or circumstances, shall be held invalid, the remainder of this Act, or the application of such provision to persons or circumstances other than those as to which it is held invalid, shall not be affected thereby.

Sec. 17. This Act may be cited as the "National Labor Relations Act."

Sec. 18. No petition entertained, no investigation made, no election held, and no certification issued by the National Labor Relations Board, under any of the provisions of section 9 of the National Labor Relations Act, as amended, shall be invalid by reason of the failure of the Congress of Industrial Organizations to have complied with the requirements of section 9 (f), (g), or (h) of the aforesaid Act prior to December 22, 1949, or by reason of the failure of the American Federation of Labor to have complied with the provisions of section 9 (f), (g), (h) of the aforesaid Act prior to November 7, 1947: Provided, That no liability shall be imposed under any provision of this Act upon any person for failure to honor any election or certificate referred to above, prior to the effective date of this amendment: Provided, however, That this proviso shall not have the effect of setting aside or in any way affecting judgments or decrees heretofore entered under section 10 (e) or (f) and which have become final.

Individuals with Religious Convictions

Sec. 19. Any employee of a health care institution who is a member of and adheres to established traditional tenets or teachings of a bona fide religion, body, or sect which has historically held conscientious objections to joining or financially supporting labor organizations shall not be required to join or financially support any labor organization as a condition of employment; except that such employee may be required, in lieu of periodic dues and initiation fees, to pay sums equal to such dues and initiation fees to a nonreligious charitable fund exempt from taxation under section 501 (c) (3) of the Internal Revenue Code, chosen by such employee from a list of at least three such funds, designated in a contract between such institution and a labor organization, or if the contract fails to designate such funds, then to any such fund chosen by the employee.

Effective Date of Certain Changes

Sec. 102. No provision of this title shall be deemed to make an unfair labor practice any act which was performed prior to the date of the enactment of this Act which did not constitute an unfair labor practice prior thereto, and the provisions of section 8 (a) (3) and section 8 (b) (2) of the National Labor Relations Act as amended by this title shall not make an unfair labor practice the performance of any obligation under a collective bargaining agreement entered into prior to the date of the enactment of this Act, or (in the case of an agreement for a period of not more than one year) entered into on or after such date of enactment, but prior to the effective date of this title, if the performance of such obligation would not have constituted an unfair labor practice under section 8 (3) of the National Labor Relations Act prior to the effective date of this title, unless such agreement was renewed or extended subsequent thereto.

Sec. 103. No provisions of this title shall affect any certification of representatives or any determination as to the appropriate collective bargaining unit, which was made under section 9 of the National Labor Relations Act prior to the effective date of this title until one year after the date of such certification or if, in respect of any such certification, a collective bargaining contract was entered into prior to the effective date of this title, until the end of the contract period or until one year after such date, whichever first occurs.

Sec. 104. The amendments made by this title shall take effect sixty days after the date of the enactment of this Act, except that the authority of the President to appoint certain officers conferred upon him by section 3 of the National Labor Relations Act as amended by this title may be exercised forthwith.

Title II
Conciliation of Labor Disputes in Industries Affecting Commerce: National Emergencies

Sec. 201. That it is the policy of the United States that—

(a) sound and stable industrial peace and the advancement of the general welfare, health, and safety of the Nation and of the best interest of employers and employees can most satisfactorily be secured by the settlement of issues between employers and employees through the processes of conference and collective bargaining between employers and the representation of their employees;

(b) the settlement of issues between employers and employees through collective bargaining may be advanced by making available full and adequate governmental facilities for conciliation, mediation, and voluntary arbitration to aid and encourage employers and the representatives of their employees to reach and maintain agreements concerning rates of pay, hours, and working conditions, and to make all reasonable efforts to settle their differences by mutual agreement reached through conferences and collective bargaining or by such methods as may be provided for in any applicable agreement for the settlement of disputes; and

(c) certain controversies which arise between parties to collective bargaining agreements may be avoided or minimized by making available full and adequate governmental facilities for furnishing assistance to employers and the representatives of their employees in formulating for inclusion within such agreements provision for adequate notice of any proposed changes in the terms of such agreements, for the final adjustment of grievances or questions regarding the application or interpretation of such agreements, and other provisions designed to prevent the subsequent arising of such controversies.

Sec. 202. (a) There is hereby created an independent agency to be known as the Federal Mediation and Conciliation Service (herein referred to as the "Service," except that for sixty days after the date of the enactment of this Act such term shall refer to the Conciliation Service of the Department of Labor). The Service shall be under the direction of a Federal Mediation and Conciliation Director (hereinafter referred to as the "Director"), who shall be appointed by the President by and with the advice and consent of the Senate. The Director shall receive compensation at the rate of $12,000 per annum. The Director shall not engage in any other business, vocation, or employment.

(b) The Director is authorized, subject to the civil-service laws, to appoint such clerical and other personnel as may be necessary for the execution of the functions of the Service, and shall fix their compensation in accordance with the Classification Act of 1923, as amended, and may, without regard to the provisions of the civil service laws and the Classification Act of 1923, as amended, appoint and fix the compensation of such conciliators and mediators as may be necessary to carry out the functions of the Service. The Director is authorized to make such expenditures for supplies, facilities, and services as he deems necessary. Such expenditures shall be allowed and paid upon presentation of itemized vouchers therefor approved by the Director or by any employee designated by him for that purpose.

(c) The principal office of the Service shall be in the District of Columbia, but the Director may establish regional offices convenient to localities in which labor controversies are likely to arise. The Director may by order, subject to revocation at any time, delegate any authority and discretion conferred upon him by this Act to any regional director, or other officer or employee of the Service. The Director may establish suitable procedures for cooperation with State and local mediation agencies. The Director shall make an annual report in writing to Congress at the end of the fiscal year.

(d) All mediation and conciliation functions of the Secretary of Labor or the United States Conciliation Service under section 8 of the Act entitled "An Act to create a Department of Labor," approved March 4, 1913 (U.S.C., title 29, sec. 51), and all functions of the United States Conciliation Service under any other law are hereby transferred to the Federal Mediation and Conciliation Service, together with the personnel and records of the United States Conciliation Service. Such transfer shall take effect upon the sixtieth day after the date of enactment of this Act. Such transfer shall not affect any proceedings pending before the United States Conciliation Service or any certification, order, rule, or regulation theretofore made by it or by the Secretary of Labor. The Director and the Service shall not be subject in any way to the jurisdiction or authority of the Secretary of Labor or any official or division of the Department of Labor.

Functions of the Service

Sec. 203. (a) It shall be the duty of the Service, in order to prevent or minimize interruptions of the free flow of commerce growing out of labor disputes, to assist parties to labor disputes in industries affecting commerce to settle such disputes through conciliation and mediation.

(b) The Service may proffer its services in any labor dispute in any industry affecting commerce, either upon its own motion or upon the request of one or more of the parties to the dispute, whenever in its judgment such dispute threatens to cause a substantial interruption of commerce. The Director and the Service are directed to avoid attempting to mediate disputes which would have only a minor effect on interstate commerce if State or other conciliation services are available to the parties. Whenever the Service does proffer its services in any dispute, it shall be the duty of the Service promptly to put itself in communication with the parties and to use its best efforts, by mediation and conciliation, to bring them to agreement.

(c) If the Director is not able to bring the parties to agreement by conciliation within a reasonable time, he shall seek to induce the parties voluntarily to seek other means of settling the dispute without resort to strike, lockout, or other coercion, including submission to the employees in the bargaining unit of the employer's last offer of settlement for approval or rejection in a secret ballot. The failure or refusal of either party to agree to any procedure suggested by the Director shall not be deemed a violation of any duty or obligation imposed by this Act.

(d) Final adjustment by a method agreed upon by the parties is hereby declared to be the desirable method for settlement of grievance disputes arising over the application or interpretation of an existing collective-bargaining agreement. The Service is directed to make its conciliation and mediation services available in the settlement of such grievance disputes only as a last resort and in exceptional cases.

Sec. 204. (a) In order to prevent or minimize interruptions of the free flow of commerce growing out of labor disputes, employers and employees and their representatives, in any industry affecting commerce, shall—

(1) exert every reasonable effort to make and maintain agreements concerning rates of pay, hours, and working conditions, including provision for adequate notice of any proposed change in the terms of such agreements;

(2) whenever a dispute arises over the terms or application of a collective-bargaining agreement and a conference is requested by a party or prospective party thereto, arrange promptly for such a conference to be held and endeavor in such conference to settle such dispute expeditiously; and

(3) in case such dispute is not settled by conference, participate fully and promptly in such meetings as may be undertaken by the Service under this Act for the purpose of aiding in a settlement of the dispute.

Sec. 205. (a) There is hereby created a National Labor-Management Panel which shall be composed of twelve members appointed by the President, six of whom shall be selected from among persons outstanding in the field of management and six of whom shall be selected from among persons outstanding in the field of labor. Each member shall hold office for a term of three years, except that any member appointed to fill a vacancy occurring prior to the expiration of the term for which his predecessor was appointed shall be appointed for the remainder of such term, and the terms of office of the members first taking office shall expire, as designated by the President at the time of appointment, four at the end of the first year, four at the end of the second year, and four at the end of the third year after the date of appointment. Members of the panel, when serving on business of the panel, shall be paid compensation at the rate of $25 per day, and shall also be entitled to receive an allowance for actual and necessary travel and subsistence expenses while so serving away from their places of residence.

(b) It shall be the duty of the panel, at the request of the Director, to advise in the avoidance of industrial controversies and the manner in which mediation and voluntary adjustment shall be administered, particularly with reference to controversies affecting the general welfare of the country.

National Emergencies

Sec. 206. Whenever in the opinion of the President of the United States, a threatened or actual strike or lockout affecting an entire industry or a substantial part thereof engaged in trade, commerce, transportation, transmission, or communication among the several States or with foreign nations, or engaged in the production of goods for commerce, will, if permitted to occur or to continue, imperil the national health or safety, he may appoint a board of inquiry to inquire into the issues involved in the dispute and to make a written report to him within such time as he shall prescribe. Such report shall include a statement of the facts with respect to the dispute, including each party's statement of its position but shall not contain any recommendations. The President shall file a copy of such report with the Service and shall make its contents available to the public.

Sec. 207. (a) A board of inquiry shall be composed of a chairman and such other members as the President shall determine, and shall have power to sit and act in any place within the United States and to conduct such hearings either in public or in private, as it may deem necessary or proper, to ascertain the facts with respect to the causes and circumstances of the dispute.

(b) Members of a board of inquiry shall receive compensation at the rate of $50 for each day actually spent by them in the work of the board, together with necessary travel and subsistence expenses.

(c) For the purpose of any hearing or inquiry conducted by any board appointed under this title, the provisions of sections 9 and 10 (relating to the attendance of witnesses and the production of books, papers, and documents) of the Federal Trade Commission Act of September 16, 1944, as amended (U.S.C. 19, title 15, secs. 49 and 50, as amended), are hereby made applicable to the powers and duties of such board.

Sec. 208. (a) Upon receiving a report from a board of inquiry the President may direct the Attorney General to petition any district court of the United States having jurisdiction of the parties to enjoin such strike or lockout or the continuing thereof, and if the court finds that such threatened or actual strike or lockout—

(i) affects an entire industry or a substantial part thereof engaged in trade, commerce, transportation, transmission, or communication among the several States or with foreign nations, or engaged in the production of goods for commerce; and

(ii) if permitted to occur or to continue, will imperil the national health or safety, it shall have jurisdiction to enjoin any such strike or lockout, or the continuing thereof, and to make such other orders as may be appropriate.

(b) In any case, the provisions of the Act of March 23, 1932, entitled "An Act to amend the Judicial Code and to define and limit the jurisdiction of courts sitting in equity, and for other purposes," shall not be applicable.

(c) The order or orders of the court shall be subject to review by the appropriate circuit court of appeals and by the Supreme Court upon writ of certiorari of certification as provided in sections 239 and 240 of the Judicial Code, as amended (U.S.C., title 29, secs. 346 and 347).

Sec. 209. (a) Whenever a district court has issued an order under section 208 enjoining acts or practices which imperil or threaten to imperil the national health or safety, it shall be the duty of the parties to the labor dispute giving rise to such order to make every effort to adjust and settle their differences, with the assistance of the Service created by this Act. Neither party shall be under any duty to accept, in whole or in part, any proposal of settlement made by the Service.

(b) Upon the issuance of such order, the President shall reconvene the board of inquiry which has previously reported with respect to the dispute. At the end of a sixty-day period (unless the dispute has been settled by that time), the board of inquiry shall report to the President the current position of the parties and the efforts which has (sic) been made for settlement, and shall include a statement by each party of its position and a statement of the employer's last offer of settlement. The President shall make such report available to the public. The National Labor Relations Board, within the succeeding fifteen days, shall take a secret ballot of the employees of each employer involved in the dispute on the question of whether they wish to accept the final offer of settlement made by their employer as stated by him and shall certify the results thereof to the Attorney General within five days thereafter.

Sec. 210. Upon the certification of the results of such ballot or upon a settlement being reached, whichever happens sooner, the Attorney General shall move the court to discharge the injunction, which motion shall then be granted and the injunction discharged. When such motion is granted, the President shall submit to the Congress a full and comprehensive report of the proceedings, including the findings of the board of inquiry and the ballot taken by the National Labor Relations Board, together with such recommendations as he may see fit to make for consideration and appropriate action.

Compilation of Collective-Bargaining Agreements. Each Sec. 211. (a) For the guidance and information of interested representatives of employers, employees, and the general public, the Bureau of Labor Statistics of the Department of Labor shall maintain a file of copies of all available collective-bargaining agreements and other available agreements and actions thereunder settling or adjusting labor disputes. Such file shall be open to inspection under appropriate conditions prescribed by the Secretary of Labor, except that no specific information submitted in confidence shall be disclosed.

(b) The Bureau of Labor Statistics in the Department of Labor is authorized to furnish upon request of the Service, or employers, employees, or their representatives, all available data and factual information which may aid in the settlement of any labor dispute, except that no specific information submitted to confidence shall be disclosed.

Exemption of Railway Labor Act. Sec. 212. The provisions of this title shall not be applicable with respect to any matter which is subject to the provisions of the Railway Labor Act, as amended from time to time.

Conciliation of Labor Disputes in the Health Care Industry

Sec. 213. (a) If, in the opinion of the Director of the Federal Mediation and Conciliation Service a threatened or actual strike or lockout affecting a health care institution will, if permitted to occur or to continue, substantially interrupt the delivery of health care in the locality concerned, the Director may further assist in the resolution of the impasse by establishing within 30 days after the notice to the Federal Mediation and Conciliation Service under clause (A) of the last sentence of section 8 (d) [which is required by clause (3) of such section 8 (d)], or within 10 days after the notice under clause (B), an impartial Board of Inquiry to investigate the issue involved in the dispute and to make a written report thereon to the parties within fifteen (15) days after the establishment of such a Board. The written report shall contain the findings of fact together with the Board's recommendations for settling the dispute. Each such Board shall be composed of such number of individuals as the Director may deem desirable. No member appointed under this section shall have any interest or involvement in the health care institutions or the employee organizations involved in the dispute.

(b) (1) Members of any board established under this section who are otherwise employed by the Federal Government shall serve without compensation but shall be reimbursed for travel, subsistence, and other necessary expenses incurred by them in carrying out its duties under this section.

(2) Members of any board established under this section who are not subject to paragraph (1) shall receive compensation at a rate prescribed by the Director but not to exceed the daily rate prescribed for GS-18 of the General Schedule under section 5332 of title 5, United States Code, including travel for each day they are engaged in the performance of their duties under this section and shall be entitled to reimbursement for travel, subsistence, and other necessary expenses incurred by them in carrying out their duties under this section.

(c) After the establishment of a board under subsection (a) of this section and for 15 days after any such board has issued its report, no change in the status quo in effect prior to the expiration of the contract in the case of negotiations for a contract renewal, or in effect prior to the time of the impasse in the case of an initial bargaining negotiation, except by agreement, shall be made by the parties to the controversy.

Title III
Suits by and Against Labor Organizations

Sec. 301. (a) Suits for violation of contracts between an employer and a labor organization representing employees in an industry affecting commerce as defined in this Act, or between any such labor organizations, may be brought in any district court of the United States having jurisdiction of the parties, without respect to the amount in controversy or without regard to the citizenship of the parties.

(b) Any labor organization which represents employees in an industry affecting commerce as defined in this Act and any employer whose activities affect commerce as defined in this Act shall be bound by the acts of its agents. Any such labor organization may sue or be sued as an entity and in behalf of the employees whom it represents in the courts of the United States. Any money judgment against a labor organization in a district court of the United States shall be enforceable only against the organization as an entity and against its assets, and shall not be enforceable against any individual member or his assets.

(c) For the purposes of actions and proceedings by or against labor organizations in the district courts of the United States, district courts shall be deemed to have jurisdiction of a labor organization (1) in the district in which such organization maintains its principal office, or (2) in any district in which its duly authorized officers or agents are engaged in representing or actig for employee members.

(d) The service of summons, subpena, or other legal process of any court of the United States upon an officer or agent of a labor organization, in his capacity as such, shall constitute service upon the labor organization.

(e) For the purposes of this section, in determining whether any person is acting as an "agent" of another person so as to make such other person responsible for his acts, the question of whether the specific acts performed were actually authorized or subsequently ratified shall not be controlling.

Restrictions on Payments to Employee Representatives. Sec. 302. (a) It shall be unlawful for any employer *or association of employers or any person who acts as a labor relations expert, adviser, or consultant to an employer or who acts in the interest of an employer* to pay, *lend,* or deliver, or [to] agree to pay, *lend,* or deliver, any money or other thing of value—

(1) to any representative of any of his employees who are employed in an industry affecting commerce [.]:*or*
(2) *to any labor organization, or any officer or employee thereof, which represents,*

seeks to represent, or would admit to membership, any of the employees of such employer who are employed as an industry affecting commerce; or

(3) to any employee or group or committee of employees of such employer employed in an industry affecting commerce in excess of their normal compensation for the purpose of causing such employee or group or committee directly or indirectly to influence any other employees in the exercise of the right to organize and bargain collectively through representatives of their own choosing; or

(4) to any officer or employee of a labor organization engaged in an industry affecting commerce with intent to influence him in respect to any of his actions, decisions, or duties as a representative of employees or as such officer or employee of such labor organization.

(b) (1) It shall be unlawful for any [representative of any employees who are employed in an industry affecting commerce] *person to request, demand,* receive or accept, or [to] agree to receive or accept, [from the employer of such employees] *any payment, loan, or delivery* of any money or other thing of value[.] *prohibited by subsection (a).*

(2) It shall be unlawful for any labor organization, or for any person acting as an officer, agent, representative, or employee of such labor organization, to demand or accept from the operator of any motor vehicle (as defined in part II of the Interstate Commerce Act) employed in the transportation of property in commerce, or the employer of any such operator, any money or other thing of value payable to such organization to an officer, agent, representative or employee thereof as a fee or charge for the unloading, or in connection with the unloading, of the cargo of such vehicle: Provided, That nothing in this paragraph shall be construed to make unlawful any payment by an employer to any of his employees as compensation for their services as employees.

(c) The provisions of this section shall not be applicable (1) [with] in respect to any money or other thing of value payable by an employer *to any of his employees whose established duties include acting openly for such employer in matters of labor relations or personnel administration or* to any representative *of his employees, or to any officer or employee of a labor organization* who is *also* an employee or former employee of such employer, as compensation for, or by reason of, his service[s] as an employee of such employer; (2) with respect to the payment or delivery of any money or other thing of value in satisfaction of a judgment of any court or a decision or award of an arbitrator or impartial chairman or in compromise, adjustment, settlement, or release of any claim, complaint, grievance, or dispute in the absence of fraud or duress; (3) with respect to the sale or purchase of an article or commodity at the prevailing market price in the regular course of business; (4) with respect to money deducted from the wages of employees in payment of membership dues in a labor organization: Provided, That the employer has received from each employee, on whose account such deductions are made, a written assignment which shall not be irrevocable for a period of more than one year, or beyond the termination date of the applicable collective agreement, whichever occurs sooner; [or] (5) with respect to money or other thing of value paid to a trust fund established by such representative, for the sole and exclusive benefit of the employees of such employer, and their families and dependents (or of such employees, families, and dependents jointly with the employees of other employers making similar payments, and their families and dependents): Provided, That (A) such payments are held in trust for the purpose of paying, either from principal or income or both, for the benefit of employees, their families and dependents, for medical or hospital care, pensions on retirement or death of employees, compensation for injuries or illness resulting from occupational activity or insurance to provide any of the foregoing, or unemployment benefits or life insurance, disability and sickness insurance, or accident insurance; (B) the detailed basis on which such payments are to be made is specified in a written agreement with the employer, and employees and employers are equally represented in the administration of such fund, together with such neutral persons as the representatives of the employers and the representatives of [the] employees may agree upon and in the event the employer and employee groups deadlock on the administration of such fund and there are no neutral persons empowered to break such deadlock, such agreement provides that the two groups shall agree on an impartial umpire to decide such dispute or in event of their failure to agree within a reasonable length of time an impartial umpire to decide such dispute shall, on petition of either group, be appointed by the district court of the United States for the district where the trust fund has its principal office, and shall also contain provisions for an annual audit of the trust fund, a statement of the results of which shall be available for inspection by interested persons at the principal office of the trust fund and at such other places as may be designated in such written agreement; and (C) such payments as are intended to be used for the purpose of providing pensions or annuities for employees are made to a separate trust which provides that the funds held therein cannot be used for any purpose other than paying such pensions or annuities [.]; *or (6) with respect to money or other thing of value paid by any employer to a trust fund established by such representative for the purpose of pooled vacation, holiday, severance or similar benefits, or defraying costs of apprenticeship or other training programs: Provided, That the requirements of clause (B) of the proviso to clause (5) of this subsection shall apply to such trust funds.* [; or] (7) With respect to money or other thing of value paid by any employer to a pooled or individual trust fund established by such representative for the purpose of (A) scholarships for the benefit of employees, their families, and dependents for study at educational institutions, or (B) child care centers for preschool and school age dependents of employees: Provided, That no labor organization or employer shall be required to bargain on the establishment of any such trust fund, and refusal to do so shall not constitute an unfair labor practice: Provided further, That the requirements of clause (B) of the proviso to clause (5) of this subsection shall apply to such trust funds; or (8) with respect to money or any other thing of value paid by any employer to a trust fund established by such representative for the purpose of defraying the costs of legal services for employees, their families, and dependents for counsel or plan of their choice: Provided, That the requirements of clause (B) of the proviso to clause (5) of this subsection shall apply to such trust funds: Provided further, That no such legal services shall be furnished: (A) to initiate any proceeding directed (i) against any such employer or its officers or agents except in workman's compensation cases, or (ii) against such labor organizations, or its parent or subordinate bodies, or their officers or agents, or (iii) against any other employer or labor organization, or their officers or agent, in any matter arising under the National Labor Relations Act, as amended, or this Act; and (B) in any proceeding where a labor organization would have been prohibited from defraying the costs of legal services by the provisions of the Labor-Management Reporting and Disclosure Act of 1959.

(d) Any person who willfully violates any of the provisions of this section shall, upon conviction thereof, be guilty of a misdemeanor and be subject to a fine of not more than $10,000 or to imprisonment for not more than one year, or both.

(e) The district courts of the United States and the United States courts of the Territories and possessions shall have jurisdiction, for cause shown, and subject to the provisions of section 17 (relating to notice to opposite party) of the Act entitled "An Act to supplement existing laws against unlawful restraints and monopolies, and for other purposes," approved October 15, 1914, as amended (U.S.C., title 28, sec. 381), to restrain violations of this section, without regard to the provisions of sections 6 and 20 of such Act of October 15, 1914, as amended (U.S.C., title 15, sec. 17, and title 29, sec. 52), and the provisions of the Act entitled "An Act to amend the Judicial Code and to define and limit the jurisdiction of courts sitting in equity, and for other purposes," approved March 23, 1932 (U.S.C., title 29, secs. 101–115).

(f) This section shall not apply to any contract in force on the date of enactment of this Act, until the expiration of such contract, or until July 1, 1948, whichever first occurs.

(g) Compliance with the restrictions contained in subsection (c) (5) (B) upon contributions to trust funds, otherwise lawful, shall not be applicable to contributions to such trust funds established by collective agreement prior to January 1, 1946, nor shall subsection (c) (5) (A) be construed as prohibiting contributions to such trust funds if prior to January 4, 1947, such funds contained provisions for pooled vacation benefits.

Boycotts and Other Unlawful Combinations. Sec. 303. (a) It shall be unlawful, for the purpose [s] of this section only, in an industry or activity affecting commerce, for any labor organization to engage in [, or to induce or encourage the employees of any employer to engage in, a strike or a concerted refusal in the course of their employment to use, manufacture, process, transport, or otherwise handle or work on any goods, articles, materials, or commodities or to perform any services, where an object thereof is—]

[(1) forcing or requiring any employer or self-employed person to join any labor or employer organization or any employer or other person to cease using, selling, handling, transporting, or otherwise dealing in the products of any other producer, processor, or manufacturer, or to cease doing business with any other person;]

[(2) forcing or requiring any other employer to recognize or bargain with a labor organization as the representative of his employees unless such labor organization has been certified as the representative of such employees under the provisions of section 9 of the National Labor Relations Act;]

[(3) forcing or requiring any employer to recognize or bargain with a particular labor organization as the representative of his employees if another labor organization has been certified as the representative of such employees under the provisions of section 9 of the National Labor Relations Act;]

[(4) forcing or requiring any employer to assign particular work to employees in a particular labor organization or in a particular trade, craft, or class rather than to employees in another labor organization or in another trade, craft, or class unless such employer is failing to conform to an order or certification of the National Labor Relations Board determining the bargaining representative for employees performing such work. Nothing contained in this subsection shall be construed to make unlawful a refusal by any person to enter upon the premises of any employer (other than his own employer), if the employees of such employer are engaged in a strike ratified or approved by a representative of such employees whom such employer is required to recognize under the National Labor Relations Act.]

any activity or conduct defined as an unfair labor practice in section 8 (b) (4) of the National Labor Relations Act, as amended.

(b) Whoever shall be injured in his business or property by reason of any violation of subsection (a) may sue therefor in any district court of the United States subject to the limitations and provisions of section 301 hereof without respect to the amount in controversy, or in any other court having jurisdiction of the parties, and shall recover the damages by him sustained and the cost of the suit.

Restriction on Political Contributions

Sec. 304. Section 313 of the Federal Corrupt Practices Act, 1925 (U.S.C., 1940 edition, title 2, sec. 251; Supp. V, title 50, App., sec. 1509), as amended, is amended, to read as follows:

Sec. 313. It is unlawful for any national bank, or any corporation organized by authority of any law of Congress, to make a contribution or expenditure in connection with any election to any political office, or in connection with any primary election or political convention or caucus held to select candidates for any political office, or for any corporation whatever, or any labor organization to make a contribution or expenditure in connection with any election at which Presidential and Vice Presidential electors or a Senator or Representative in, or a Delegate or Resident Commissioner to Congress are to be voted for, or in connection with any primary election or political convention or caucus held to select candidates for any of the foregoing offices, or for any candidate, political committee, or other person to accept or receive any contribution prohibited by this section. Every corporation or labor organization which makes any contribution or expenditure in violation of this section shall be fined not more than $5,000; and every officer or director of any corporation, or officer of any labor organization, who consents to any contribution or expenditure by the corporation or labor organization, as the case may be, in violation of this section shall be fined not more than $1,000 or imprisoned for not more than one year, or both. For the purposes of this section "labor organization" means any organization of any kind, or any agency or employee representation committee or plan, in which employees participate and which exists for the purpose in whole or in part, of dealing with employers concerning grievances, labor disputes, wages, rates of pay, hours of employment, or conditions of work.

Strikes by Government Employees

Sec. 305. It shall be unlawful for any individual employed by the United States or any agency thereof including wholly owned Government corporations to participate in any strike. Any individual employed by the United States or by any such agency who strikes shall be discharged immediately from his employment, and shall forfeit his civil-service status, if any, and shall not be eligible for reemployment for three years by the United States or any such agency.

Title IV
Creation of Joint Committee to Study and Report on Basic Problems Affecting Friendly Labor Relations and Productivity

Sec. 401. There is hereby established a joint congressional committee to be known as the Joint Committee on Labor-Management Relations (hereafter referred to as the committee), and to be composed of seven Members of the Senate Committee on Labor and Public Welfare to be appointed by the President pro tempore of the Senate, and seven Members of the House of Representatives Committee on Education and Labor, to be appointed by the Speaker of the House of Representatives. A vacancy in membership of the committee shall not affect the powers of the remaining members to execute the functions of the committee, and shall be filled in the same manner as the original selection. The committee shall select a chairman and a vice chairman from among its members.

Sec. 402. The committee, acting as a whole or by subcommittee, shall conduct a thorough study and investigation of the entire field of labor-management relations including but not limited to—

(1) the means by which permanent friendly co-operation between employers and employees and stability of labor relations may be secured throughout the United States.

(2) the means by which the individual employee may achieve a greater productivity and higher wages, including plans for guaranteed annual wages, incentive, profit-sharing and bonus systems;

(3) the internal organization and administration of labor unions, with special attention to the impact on individuals of collective agreements requiring membership in unions as a condition of employment;

(4) the labor relations policies and practices of employers and associations of employers;

(5) the desirability of welfare funds for the benefit of employees and their relation to the social-security system;

(6) the methods and procedures for best carrying out the collective-bargaining processes, with special attention to the effects of industry-wide or regional bargaining upon the national economy;

(7) the administration and operation of existing Federal laws relating to labor relations; and

(8) such other problems and subjects in the field of labor-management relations as the committee deems appropriate.

Sec. 403. The committee shall report to the Senate and the House of Representatives not later than March 15, 1948, the results of its study and investigation, together with such recommendations as to necessary legislation and such other recommendations as it may deem advisable and shall make its final report not later than January 2, 1949.

Sec. 404. The committee shall have the power, without regard to the civil-service laws and the Classification Act of 1923, as amended, to employ and fix the compensation of such officers, experts, and employees as it deems necessary for the performance of its duties, including consultants who shall receive compensation at a rate not to exceed $35 for each day actually spent by them in the work of the committee, together with their necessary travel and subsistence expenses. The committee is further authorized, with the consent of the head of the department or agency concerned to utilize the services, information, facilities, and personnel of all agencies in the executive branch of the Government and may request the governments of the several States, representatives of business, industry, finance, and labor, and such other persons, agencies, organizations, and instrumentalities as it deems appropriate to attend its hearings and to give and present information, advice, and recommendations.

Sec. 405. The committee, or any subcommittee thereof, is authorized to hold such hearings; to sit and act at such times and places during the sessions, recesses, and adjourned periods of the Eightieth Congress; to require by subpoena or otherwise the attendance of such witnesses and the production of such books, papers, and documents; to administer oaths; to take such testimony; to have such printing and binding done; and to make such expenditures within the amount appropriated therefor; as it deems advisable. The cost of stenographic services in reporting such hearings shall not be in excess of 25 cents per one hundred words. Subpoenas shall be issued under the signature of the chairman or vice chairman of the committee and shall be served by any person designated by them.

Sec. 406. The members of the committee shall be reimbursed for travel, subsistence, and other necessary expenses incurred by them in the performance of the duties vested in the committee, other than expenses in connection with meetings of the committee held in the District of Columbia during such times as the Congress is in session.

Sec. 407. There is hereby authorized to be appropriated the sum of $150,000, or so much thereof as may be necessary, to carry out the provisions of this title, to be disbursed by the Secretary of the Senate on vouchers signed by the chairman.

Title V
Definitions

Sec. 501. When used in this Act—

(1) The term "industry affecting commerce" means any industry in commerce or in which a labor dispute would burden or obstruct commerce or tend to burden or obstruct commerce or the free flow of commerce.

(2) The term "strike" includes any strike or other concerted stoppage of work by employees (including a stoppage by reason of the expiration of a collective-bargaining agreement) and any concerted slow-down or other concerted interruption of operations by employees.

(3) The terms "commerce," "labor disputes," "employer," "employee," "labor organization," "representative," "person," and "supervisor" shall have the same meaning as when used in the National Labor Relations Act as amended by this Act.

Saving Provision. Sec. 502. Nothing in this Act shall be construed to require an individual employee to render labor or service without his consent, nor shall anything in this Act be construed to make the quitting of his labor by an individual employee an illegal act; nor shall any court issue any process to compel the performance by an individual employee of such labor or service, without his consent; nor shall the quitting of labor by an employee or employees in good faith because of abnormally dangerous conditions for work at this place of employment of such employee or employees by deemed a strike under this Act.

Separability. Sec. 503. If any provision of this Act, or the application of such provision to any person or circumstance, shall be held invalid, the remainder of this Act, or the application of such provision to persons or circumstances other than those as to which it is held invalid, shall not be affected thereby.

Author Index

Subject Index